MASTERING EFFECTIVE ENGLISH

Gilbert Robinson

"As free as gulls upon the wing."

MASTERING
EFFECTIVE ENGLISH

Revised Edition

J. C. Tressler

Claude E. Lewis

THE COPP CLARK PUBLISHING CO. LIMITED

VANCOUVER   TORONTO   MONTREAL

COPYRIGHT, CANADA, 1937, 1950, THE COPP CLARK CO. LIMITED

(1066)

PRINTED IN CANADA

Preface to the Revised Edition

Since the publication of the first edition of *Mastering Effective English*, there has been a considerable shift of emphasis in teaching the various topics in English composition. In preparing the Revised Edition of the book, the authors have kept in mind these changes in emphasis. For example, there have been added to this edition eighty pages of text dealing with the grammatical structure of the language, a chapter on "Improving Your Speech", and another on "Radio Listening, Writing, and Broadcasting".

The whole of the text has been reset, and a new format and type-face used. The authors have taken advantage of this opportunity to rewrite many chapters and to introduce new models which will be more interesting to the student. New illustrations have been used with the hope that they will stimulate the imagination of the students and add incentive to creative expression.

Mastering Effective English is prepared for the use of students in the senior high school grades, including senior matriculation. The name of the text is significant of its purpose. Consistently it sets before the student models of good English, stimulates a thoughtful study of these, and aims at a mastery of their techniques by continuous practice. There is, therefore, a maximum of examples and practice and a minimum of theory and rules. Throughout the book emphasis is placed upon (1) valuing one's experience; (2) observing and investigating; (3) aiming to entertain, instruct, impress, convince, or persuade a definite audience; (4) thinking clearly; (5) planning; (6) speaking and writing correct, vigorous, lively, effective English, and avoiding pretentious, involved, artificial language; and (7) forming the habit of using one's best English.

The book is divided into three parts, intended, roughly speaking, for students in three stages of development. These we have dubbed Apprentices, Journeymen Writers, and Master Craftsmen. Part I is devoted to a study of clear and correct expression in the common uses of English; Part II to a study of the fundamental processes involved, so that the student may develop a knowledge of cause and effect in language; and Part III to a conscious practice of the art of writing and to a mastery of effective English for creative expression. In all three divisions, there is insistence upon apposite choice of word and idiom without which there is no living English, spoken or written.

The three appendices of the first edition have been combined with two units on grammar to form a Handbook for student reference. Throughout the text stress has been laid upon those types of speech and writing most frequently used, such as conversation, letter-writing, story-telling, explaining, making reports, group discussion, public speaking and summarizing, and answering questions. Both in the selections of topics treated and in practice themes suggested there has been always in mind adaptation to the student's life situations.

A book cannot take the place of a teacher in presenting motives, but in the text, motivation has not been overlooked. Without the desire to learn there is no learning, and the authors have tried always to present stimulating examples, to provide for study picturesque, lively, informative sentences, paragraphs, and reports; and to suggest projects which motivate drill and give practice in applying in normal communication what is learned during the drill period.

Models have been graded for student development. In the earlier units there are a number of examples of student work, designed to stimulate effort, but as mastery progresses literary models predominate.

So that students and teachers may measure the degree of progress made, there are frequent mastery tests, the results of which may be entered on individual progress charts. These tests are given in pairs, A and B, of relatively equal difficulty. The teacher who likes to begin with a diagnostic test may give Test A when the pupils start the topic, and Test B when they have completed it, and thus measure achievement and progress.

No student goes far who has not learned to practise self-criticism. He is helped in this valuable educative process by frequent self-criticism charts. It is intended that by the time the student has completed the course presented he will have acquired the ability to learn by his own reading and to measure his progress by self-criticism, weighing his work against his own intention.

The authors wish to acknowledge their indebtedness to the many teachers whose reports have kept them informed of the needs of the classroom, and have been helpful in making this revision. They would particularly thank Mr. C. T. Fyfe, Central Collegiate, Regina, and Miss Muriel K. Steeves, Moncton High School, Moncton, New Brunswick, for their valuable contributions. Acknowledgment is also made to the many students who have permitted us to use their classroom exercises.

—J.C.T.
—C.E.L.

TABLE OF CONTENTS

Part I—Apprentices

Mastering the Fundamentals of Correct English

Part II—Journeymen Writers

Mastering the Processes of Writing

Part III—Master Craftsmen
Mastering the Art of Writing

Handbook of Grammar and Usage

Mastering Effective English
Part I

APPRENTICES

Mastering the Fundamentals of Correct English

UNIT ONE

Conversing

You have doubtless at some time found yourself in a group of silent boys and girls, perhaps at a party, and felt embarrassed and tongue-tied. How you wished you could think of the right topic to set the group talking, or knew something interesting to say!

Good speech has not only social value but also a dollar-and-cent value. Next to personal appearance the world notices one's ability to converse. When a boy applies for a position, an employer notices first his appearance, his manners, and his speech. Even if the applicant's clothes are neat, his shoes polished, and his manners flawless, in normal times he probably won't get the job unless he can talk clearly, correctly, pleasingly, pointedly. The boy who wears a soiled shirt and unshined shoes, who lounges in his chair or leans instead of standing, who speaks in harsh tones, who says "He done," "I seen","He don't," "Wadyetink?" is rated as careless, slipshod, and ignorant.

There's another reason why you'll want to become a good talker. Conversation is fun. By talking with intelligent and congenial people you become acquainted with unusual facts and interesting ideas. You have an opportunity to tell about your experiences, to share with others the amusing and exciting things that happen to you. And, of course, you like to laugh, to hear and to tell jokes and anecdotes, to recite limericks and bits of verse—yes, even to pun. A lively conversation can be just as good sport as a game of tennis or basketball.

HAVING SOMETHING TO TALK ABOUT

If there were no butter, eggs, flour, milk, or sugar in the pantry, you wouldn't think of trying to bake a cake, would you? You can't create a conversation out of thin air, either. You must have something to put into the mixing bowl.

Stock your mental larder with interesting information, worth-while ideas, amusing stories and ancedotes, jokes, bits of verse. When you pick up the evening paper, read more than the comic strips. Dip into magazines and books, too, for information about sports, animals, aviation, famous people, foreign countries, current events. Play games. Find a hobby. Keep your eyes and ears wide open for humorous or unusual scenes.

3

Practice 1. Studying Topics for Conversation

I. Which of these thirty topics can you talk about intelligently?

1. Recent motion pictures
2. Recent scientific experiments
3. Recent inventions
4. Recent books
5. The school football team
6. An exciting sports event
7. Aviation
8. Dogs
9. Hiking
10. Camping
11. How to study
12. Automobiles
13. Tobogganing
14. Hockey
15. Unusual radio programmes
16. Clothes
17. Heroes of science
18. Wild animals
19. My community work
20. My church work
21. Our choir
22. Gardening
23. Raising chickens
24. Rationing
25. Flowers
26. Japan
27. Russia
28. Algonquin National Park
29. Stars
30. Submarines

II. What are five other topics on which you are able to converse?

III. What are five topics on which you are uninformed but about which you would like to be able to talk well? Where would you go for information on these topics?

CHOOSING A TOPIC OF CONVERSATION

Your sense of courtesy will tell you that the topic of conversation should be one to which all can contribute. To chatter about personal matters or people unknown to members of the group is the height of rudeness.

To avoid making enemies, learn to think before you speak. Nobody likes a tactless young blunderer. When Emily is recovering from a severe illness, don't tell her how pale she looks. Your stout friends, by the way, will not appreciate remarks like, "Why, Anne! You look so thin in that blue dress I hardly knew you!"

There are a few topics that are taboo in ordinary conversation. Even with courteous, tolerant people such subjects as race, religion, and politics often act as a call to battle, and in a few minutes a heated argument is in progress.

Practice 2. Suggesting Topics for Conversation

What are three topics of conversation appropriate for each of the following groups?

A family with a guest
Three high school girls
Two girls and a boy

Two boys and the mother of one of them
Three high school boys
A boy, a girl, and their English teacher

TAKING PART IN A CONVERSATION

In your conversation you have an opportunity to show how courteous a young person you are. Don't, like Tennyson's brook, babble on forever. Give others a chance to express their ideas. When someone else is talking, listen pleasantly and attentively to what he has to say. Even if you are fairly bursting with bright remarks, don't interrupt. Your turn will come.

Take the shy member of the group under your wing, figuratively speaking, and ask a friendly question to draw him out: "Marion, what do you think of our forming a Good English Club?" "What did you do during your vacation, Harry?" "Herbert, how did you learn to drive a car?" "What is your favourite game, Ethel?" Questions about personal matters, such as "How much did you pay for that hat?" "What is your father's salary?" "Did you buy that dress or make it?" are, as a rule, to be avoided.

If you are in a group, don't collar a particular friend and drag him off to the corner to hear the latest gossip. Be generous; scatter your attention over the whole group.

In conversation people often make inaccurate statements. To spare them embarrassment, avoid blunt contradictions like "That's not true" and "What a crazy thing to say!" Instead, answer mildly, "That's interesting, because I had always thought—" or "Is that so? It seems to me—"

Be good-natured and cheerful. Bear your troubles on your own broad shoulders. No matter how angry you are, hold fast to your temper.

Practice 3. Drawing Out a Shy Person

What do you think of these attempts to draw a shy person into the conversation? How successful would each one be?

1 Aren't you enjoying the party, Walter? You look so miserable!
2. I saw you and your dad tinkering with the car yesterday, Joe. Were you able to locate the trouble?
3. Do you think the Leafs will win the Stanley Cup this year, Steve?
4. That's such a sweet dress, Louise! It's just like Florence Drew's, isn't it?
5. Do you find our town very different from the city where you used to live, Carol?
6. Is Evelyn always as quiet as she is to-night?
7. What good radio programmes have you heard lately, Leon?
8. Did you have a good time on the hike last Saturday, Jack?
9. Look at Hazel! She's been sitting in that corner all evening without saying a word.
10. Is our school very different from the school you were in last year, Marie?
11. What is your favourite sport? Have you gone out for any school or class team?

DISTINCTNESS

If you were a famous explorer, aviator, statesman, or general, people would listen eagerly to every word you spoke. Since most people do not lend the same flattering attention to the utterances of lesser mortals, you must, if you are just an ordinary person, make it easy for everyone to understand you. When you talk at the dinner table or to the class, open your mouth to let the sound out, speak every word clearly, and cut the words apart. Pronounce distinctly the last sound of each word and the last word of each sentence. Make good speech a habit.

Practice 4.   Producing Correct Sounds

Test yourself on the words and sentences on pages 30–43. Ask your teacher and classmates to help you. Then practise these exercises again and again.

VOICE

Watch the pitch of your voice. Many voices are harsh and grating; others are pitched too high. As you speak, breathe deeply and let the breath out slowly. By holding back the breath instead of letting it rush out, you will always have in your lungs a reserve supply. Keep in mind the comfort of your listeners. They should hear you without strain or effort.

Practice 5.   Checking Improvement in Enunciation

If possible, make a recording of your voice. After practising the exercises on pages 30–43 about two months, make another recording of the selection used in the first recording. Note the improvement in your voice, enunciation, and pronunciation.

If it is not possible to make a recording, let your teacher and classmates decide how much improvement you have made.

OVERWORKED EXPRESSIONS

You're fond of your friends; treat them kindly. Everybody likes variety. Don't submit your friends to a steady conversational diet of *see, say, listen, you know, don't you know, and everything like that, by the way, awfully, great, grand, nice, fine, fierce, lovely, now, well, why, so, and, swell.* These words and expressions have earned a vacation. Listen to your voice and words.

Practice 6. Listening for Overworked Words

1. Listen to your own talk carefully enough to discover which words you overwork. Write them in your notebook.
2. Listen to the conversations and recitations of your classmates for over-worked words. When a pupil overworks a word, write down his name and the word.

Practice 7. Error Box or Contest

Listen for mistakes in pronunciation or grammar in the conversation of high school pupils and educated grownups. When in doubt, consult pages 30–43. Jot down the errors you hear, bring them to class, and be prepared to correct the errors and to give a reason for each change in wording.

Perhaps the class will continue to watch for mistakes and each day place in the Error Box the mistakes seen or heard. Once a week discuss these errors.

Contests between two halves of a class are often exciting. A side scores by reporting an error made by a member of the other side in class or out of class and correcting the error, and is penalized for reporting a correct sentence as an error.

SELF-CRITICISM ON TAKING PART IN A CONVERSATION

After you have taken part in a conversation, answer the following questions. If you can honestly say yes to all the questions, you have one important qualification of a good companion and friend—skill in conversation. By changing *I* to *you*, you can also use the questions to rate your classmates' conversation.

1. *Do I always use my best English and voice?*
2. *Am I a good listener?*
3. *Do I occasionally ask a question to draw out a shy person?*
4. *Do I always have something interesting to contribute?*
5. *Do I speak distinctly?*
6. *Do I avoid overworked expressions?*
7. *Do I find associates who talk well?*
8. *Am I cheerful and good-natured?*
9. *Do I avoid unkind words and malicious gossip?*
10. *Do I avoid interrupting?*
11. *Do I avoid monopolizing the conversation?*
12. *Do I avoid contradicting?*
13. *Do I avoid tactless remarks?*
14. *Do I avoid topics that are likely to cause heated arguments?*
15. *Do I avoid questions about private or personal matters?*
16. *Do I avoid* and-ur, so-ur, *and other* ur's *by turning my voice off when I stop to think?*

Practice 8. Conversing in Class

On the following topics be ready to say something worth listening to. During a class conversation turn about in your seat, if necessary, to face the majority of the class, and speak so distinctly that the pupil farthest from you will easily understand every word (pages 27–43). The leader (a pupil or the teacher) will start the conversation and change the subject when the talk lags. Speak up without the leader's asking you questions. Use correct pronouns (pages 511–520).

For the class conversation perhaps your teacher will sometimes divide you into groups with a leader for each.

1. What famous living person do you admire most? Why?
2. If you had a thousand dollars given to you, what would you do with it?
3. What is your favourite magazine? Why?
4. How important is conversation in our social life? In business? In politics? In a profession?
5. Should we habitually use slang in conversation? Why?
6. What was the most important news of the past week? Why?
7. What good moving picture have you seen recently? Why is it worth seeing?
8. It has been estimated that in normal times seventy men out of a hundred are in the wrong job. How should a pupil decide on a job, business, or profession? When?
9. What school subject do you consider most valuable? Why?
10. How did you spend your vacation? What interesting or educational experiences did you have?
11. Compare your school with other high schools. What can the pupils do to improve it?
12. What kind of radio programme do you like? Why?
13. What do you consider the most interesting (or exciting) experience you have ever had?
14. Are books about animals as interesting as books about people? Give examples.
15. Do animals show intelligence?
16. What is your hobby? Why do you like it? Of what value is it?
17. What benefits are derived from athletics? What is your favourite sport? Why?

Practice 9.   Conversing in Class

Read a number of articles in a magazine. The day before the class conversation hand to the chairman the topics you are prepared to talk about. The pupil chairman will start the discussion on the various subjects, keep it from lagging, and change the topic when advisable. All will speak distinctly enough to be easily heard by those farthest away, do their share to keep the conversational ball moving, and turn about in their seats to see the speakers. For other hints see the self-criticism test on page 7.

CONVERSING WITH STRANGERS OF YOUR OWN AGE

Occasionally you find yourself in a group of young people most of whom are unacquainted with each other. Since someone must take the initiative and break the deadly silence, start the conversational ball rolling by introducing yourself. Some such self-introduction as "I'm William Lorimer, of Fairmont High School," accompanied by a friendly smile, will melt the ice and lead to general introductions.

Agfa-Ansco Film

When young people are getting acquainted, music, books, or the drama are often topics which make conversation easy and pleasant.

The weather, the occasion, or some other broad topic will serve as a jumping-off place for your conversation. For example, discussion of the unusually cold weather will naturally lead the group into the topic of winter sports, in which the average healthy boy or girl has a lively interest.

Practice 10. Conversing with Strangers of Your Own Age

Dramatize each of these scenes. Every member of the class not in a dramatization will write a criticism of each pupil taking part in a conversation and hand it to him at the end. The critics will use the self-criticism test on page 7 as a guide.

1. The editorial board of your school magazine includes one pupil from each class. At the first meeting most of the pupils are unacquainted, and the

faculty adviser has not yet arrived. Introduce yourself to the other pupils and start a conversation.

2. You are representing your school at a city-wide spelling match held in Magee High School. Before the match you find yourself in a group of five young people, all strangers. Introduce yourself and start a conversation.

3. At the first basketball practice of the term most of the candidates are unacquainted with one another. Near you is a group of silent boys. Introduce yourself and start a conversation.

4. You are attending a series of Saturday morning art lectures. The speaker is late in arriving. Introduce yourself to the boy or girl beside you and start a conversation.

5. Your school is planning a performance of Gilbert and Sullivan's *Pinafore*. The candidates for the roles are from many different classrooms, and are, for the most part, unacquainted. Introduce yourself to the pupils nearest you and start a conversation.

CONVERSING WITH YOUR ELDERS

Conversations with parents and older friends play an important part in the life of the average young person. Let the subjects be only those in which both ages are interested. A highly technical discussion of your new motorboat may engross you and Brother Joe, but will, in all probability, bore and confuse Mother and Mrs. Burton, who are also at the dinner table. Books, motion pictures, plays, music, and current events are dependable topics.

Your elders are your superiors in wisdom and experience; show by your manners that you recognize this fact. Remain standing until the older people are seated. Express your opinions; but if Father and Dr. Morsch show an inclination to bear the brunt of the conversation, let them do so. Even if you are sure that Father is wrong, avoid a direct contradiction of his statement.

In your conversation with older people use only your best English. If you must use "swell," "O.K.," "not so hot," "eats," "mutt," "guy," and "peachy," confine your use of slang to your conversations with your classmates.

Grownups like young people who are friendly, who greet them in cultivated tones, who are self-confident but modest, and who have something of interest to say. In the reply to a question or in a greeting, it is courteous to include the person's name, as "Yes, Mrs. Brown," "Good morning, Mrs. Thompson."

Practice 11.   Conversing with Older People

Dramatize these scenes:

1. Prepare an imaginary conversation between you and your father when you want him to sign your report card.

2. A boy dashes into the living room, where his mother is sewing. He drops his books and cap into a chair and begins to talk to her. Reproduce the conversation.
3. At the dinner table are Jerry Burton and his friend Robert Cameron, Jerry's father and mother, and Mr. Ames, the principal of the high school. The five converse.
4. Aunt Mary, Uncle Frank, and Cousin Celia have dropped in for a brief chat with Dr. and Mrs. Richards and their son Henry. The six converse.

THANKS AND APOLOGY

"Thank you, Mr. Jackson" or "Thank you, Mr. Jackson, for the ride" shows more appreciation and courtesy than an abrupt "Thanks." In the expression of regret, "I'm sorry"; "I beg your pardon"; or "I'm sorry to be so clumsy" is preferable to "Beg pardon." When one doesn't hear what his companion says, "I'm sorry, but I didn't understand you"; "I beg your pardon"; "Will you please repeat that remark"; or "I didn't hear that" is more courteous than "What?"

In an apology sincerity of manner and tone is more important than the words used. If you show that you are sorry for a mistake or an accident, a few words of regret are sufficient. It is necessary to explain only when your mistake may appear intentional.

RECEIVING A CALLER

Ting-a-ling! There's the doorbell. Since you're at home alone this afternoon, you run downstairs, open the door, and find on the porch— sure enough, a visitor. What are you to say?

If you recognize the caller, ask him in and make him feel at home. Show unmistakably that you're glad to see him. If the visitor is one of your young friends, you, of course, are mainly responsible for entertaining him. Perhaps, however, the caller has come to see your parents, who are not at home. In that case say courteously, "Mother and Dad have gone to the baseball game, Mr. Blake. They'll probably be home in about fifteen minutes. Won't you sit down and wait for them?" Until your parents return, you, of course, will converse with the visitor

If you do not recognize the caller, say "Good morning" or "Good afternoon" and wait for him to identify himself and to tell you whom he wishes to see.

TABLE CONVERSATION

Not long ago a Russian scientist named Pavlov proved that our emotions have an important influence upon our digestion. Conversation affects our emotions, makes us happy, sad, or angry, embarrasses us, or excites us. For this reason the choice of topics for table conversation is especially important.

Avoid the depressing—ills, operations, automobile accidents, war. Subjects like politics and religion are likely to cause heated arguments and play havoc with digestion. If the day has been thoroughly unlucky for you, save the story of your misfortunes until after dinner.

What are you to talk about? Any fairly light topic is excellent for table conversation—happenings at school, activities of friends or relatives, an amusing story, new books, motion pictures, or radio programmes, for example. If you have a guest, you must, of course, choose a topic on which he can talk.

Incidentally, don't sit staring at your plate with a mentally-I'm-fifty-miles-away expression. Take an active and cheerful part in the conversation. Sit up straight and speak distinctly. Don't try to talk and to chew at the same time.

USING THE TELEPHONE DIRECTORY

In the main part of the telephone directory subscribers are arranged alphabetically by their last names or, in the case of organizations, by the first word in the title. If the first word is *the*, the second word is used. Persons having the same last names are arranged alphabetically according to their first names or initials. In the directory James Beck, for example, precedes Jane, John, and Joseph Beck.

GETTING A CONNECTION

If you are not using a dial telephone, you must tell the operator the number you wish. Speak every word distinctly. Distinguish clearly between *0* and *4*, and *5* and *9*.

Occasionally you will be unable to find a person's telephone number in the directory. In that case call Information and ask for the number. Give plainly the full name and address of the person you wish to call.

Practice 12. Reading Telephone Numbers

Stand in a corner of the room and read to a classmate in the opposite corner each of the following numbers. If you speak distinctly in a natural voice, he will be able to repeat each number after you.

Main 5134	University 4–7640
Oliver 9–4082	Hyland 7–3895
Wickersham 2–0491	Melrose 2–6339
Algonquin 4–5930	Eldorado 5–9660
Riverside 7–8700	Chelsea 3–0459

CONVERSING 13

Practice 13. Studying the Dial Phone

1. If dial phones are used in your city or community, read the instructions in a telephone directory and be ready to explain clearly and completely how to use a dial phone.
2. If your school has a model of a dial telephone, practise dialing each of the numbers in Practice 12.

TELEPHONE CONVERSATION

Points to keep in mind in telephone conversation:

1. Answer the telephone promptly. When somebody wishes to enter your home or place of business through the telephone door, do not keep him waiting.

2. Turn the radio low before going to the phone.

3. Have a pad and pencil at hand for notes.

4. Speak directly into the mouthpiece with your lips about a half inch away from it. If you are asked to repeat what you have said, use a full, natural voice, speak rather slowly, and articulate distinctly. Never place your lips against the transmitter.

5. Don't shout.

6. "Be as courteous voice to voice as you are face to face."

7. If you are asked to repeat a difficult name, spell it out as follows: Sprague—S for Samuel, P for Peter, R for Ralph, A for Andrew, G for George, U for under, E for Edward.

8. Don't ever be guilty of the silly "Guess who this is."

9. When using the telephone for a brief social call, it is considerate to ask if the person is busy: "Hello, Dot. This is Jane. Have you guests or are you busy?"

10. When you call for a person, say, "May I please speak to Jack?"

11. When your telephone rings, lift the receiver and say distinctly but quietly, "Hello," or "This is the Norton residence" or "This is the Norton residence, Marie speaking," or "Harold Norton speaking." The last two answers save time.

12. If the call is for someone who is not at home, say, "I'm sorry, but Father isn't in now. Would you like to leave a message?" Write the message down accurately and deliver it at the first opportunity.

13. When you are called to the phone, say, "This is Jack."

14. Talk naturally. Don't put on an artificial manner for telephone conversation. See in imagination the person with whom you are talking and note his changes of facial expression. Listen courteously and thoughtfully to what he says.

15. Don't tell secrets—military or personal.

16. Don't carry on a long conversation unless the business is important.

17. At the end of the conversation say "Good-bye" and replace the receiver quickly. Don't bang it down. The person making the call usually ends it.

18. If the person has called to inquire about a member of your family who is sick or to give you some information or to do you any favour, say "Thank you for calling" as you replace the receiver.

19. Over the telephone, faces are not seen, but voices are heard. Put into your voice your friendliness, fairness, refinement, and enthusiasm. "The voice with a smile wins."

20. When a person calling neglects to give his name, you can obtain this information by saying, "May I know who is calling, please?" or "I'm sorry, but I didn't hear your name."

Practice 14. Dramatizing Telephone Conversations

Dramatize in class the following telephone conversations. In each case supply a telephone number. Let the person calling and the person who receives the call stand in opposite corners of the room. Speak distinctly; don't shout.

1. Plan with a friend a picnic, a surprise party, or a club programme. Express your ideas clearly. Take notes of decisions reached. Before replacing the receiver rehearse the whole plan.

2. Call your friend Allen. Allen's father, whom you have met several times, will answer the telephone. Tell your name and converse briefly with the father. Then ask for Allen.

3. You are undecided which of two makes of stockings to order. Telephone your local department store and inquire about colours, sizes, quality, and prices. On the basis of this information make your decision and give your order. Repeat the brand, colour, size, and price, or other important details.

4. Telephone to a large department store about a damaged book delivered to you. Ask to be connected with the proper authority; then courteously explain the situation. Tell your story clearly without scolding or complaining.

5. One of your friends is sick. On the telephone inquire about his (her) condition. Be brief. Express your pleasure at the good news or your hope for improvement.

6. Telephone for information about trains, buses, or planes—time, cost, Pullman, berth. Make clear just what you want to know. Jot down the information you receive.

7. Call the captain of a rival basketball or baseball team and arrange a game. Suggest dates and places. Be specific and courteous.

8. By telephone make an appointment with your doctor or your dentist. Be definite about the day and hour.

9. You were scheduled to give a monologue at the weekly meeting of the

Dramatic Club. Because of illness you will be unable to attend the meeting. Call the president of the club and explain.

10. Because of illness you have not attended school for two days. Telephone a classmate for the English assignments.

11. You were to meet your father in his office at five o'clock and then have dinner with him. Because you had to wait for your appointment with the dentist, you will be a half hour late in reaching your father's office. Telephone your explanation.

TRY YOUR SKILL

1. Draw up your own rules for being a good conversationalist and compare them with the rules prepared by your classmates.

2. Report on a conversation you heard at home, in school, on the athletic field, in a store, or somewhere else. In what respects was it a good conversation? How could it have been improved?

3. On Friday night the Science Club, of which you are a member, is giving an exhibit in the school laboratory. With a partner dramatize a scene in which you try to persuade your father to attend the exhibit.

4. Dramatize a conversation in which you try to persuade one of your friends to join a club to which you belong. Give specific reasons why he should join.

5. Find out how to make a long-distance call. With a partner dramatize such a call.

6. With a partner dramatize a scene in which you telephone a telegram to the telegraph office.

UNIT TWO

Interviewing and Talking Business

WHAT are you going to do after you complete your education? To secure a position you will have to be interviewed. An interview is a rather formal type of conversation. The impression you make on an employer or personnel manager will largely determine whether you'll join the ranks of wage earners. If you wish to secure a summer or part-time job while you are still in school, this unit will give you some practical hints for your interview.

ASKING FOR INFORMATION OR ADVICE

One of the best ways to gain information is to interview a person who is an authority on the subject, for his knowledge will be thorough and his point of view fresh and practical. First, make an appointment for the interview, by letter, in person, or by telephone. In this request give your name and your reason for asking for an interview, but let the person to be interviewed name the day and the hour.

Prepare for the interview by learning enough about the subject to ask questions and listen intelligently, and enough about the person to phrase your questions tactfully. Think out in advance several specific questions covering the subject.

Be punctual. Politely introduce yourself. When the person to be interviewed has asked you to be seated, state briefly your purpose in coming and introduce your subject with a good question. It is always courteous to address a person by name—for example, "What qualities must a boy have to become a successful physician, Dr. Saunders?"

If you are well prepared, you will be able to keep the discussion on the topic in which you are interested and secure the information you wish. If you are courteous, earnest, and enthusiastic, the person interviewed will respond with interest, friendliness, and helpfulness. Be as punctual to leave as you were to arrive, and express you appreciation for the interview.

Practice 1. Enacting an Interview

Choose a partner and prepare to present before the class an interview, one pupil acting as interviewer, the other as an authority on

16

some subject: raising chickens, camping, catching trout, teaching a dog tricks, gardening, baking cakes, taking care of an automobile, table manners, kites, radio programmes, motion pictures, stamp collecting, making model airplanes, maintaining a home aquarium, football, photography, or the like. Speak distinctly and pronounce every word correctly.

Practice 2. Reporting an Interview

Interview a person and write a report including (1) the person's name and position, (2) why you interviewed him, (3) where you interviewed him, (4) his personal appearance and (5) your questions and his answers. Do not record every word spoken, but include the main points of the discussion and any especially important remarks. Build clear, concise, varied sentences (pages 220–237). Capitalize and punctuate direct quotations correctly (pages 551–552). Some interesting people to interview are:

1. A teacher of your favourite subject. 2. The football, baseball, track, or swimming coach. 3. The librarian. 4. The oldest resident of your town or neighbourhood. 5. The teller in charge of pupil bank accounts. 6. A public official in your community. 7. The manager of a department store. 8. The editor of a newspaper. 9. The police captain in the school precinct. 10. Any person who does interesting work—farmer, gardener, actor, musician, architect, carpenter, traffic officer, social worker, soldier, sailor, or merchant seaman. 11. A scout troop leader. 12. Director of an employment office. 13. A member of the student council. 14. The faculty adviser of a school club, a publication, dramatics, or another activity. 15. A V.O.N. nurse.

ASKING PERMISSION OR MAKING A SUGGESTION

As a preparation for asking permission or making a suggestion, marshal as many sound reasons as you can. Don't take up a person's time unless you have convincing reasons to support your request or idea. Find out what you can about the person to be interviewed, put yourself in his place, and try to foresee his objections. Your courtesy. sincerity, and correct English will help you to win your case.

After introducing yourself, come to the point immediately and state your purpose clearly and briefly. With his possible objections in mind, state your soundest and most convincing arguments first; then follow up with other reasons. Stress those points which will appeal to him most. If you have carefully studied your subject, you will be able to answer his questions intelligently.

At the end of the interview, even if your request is refused, thank the person courteously for granting you the interview.

Practice 3. Asking Permission

Is Anne's method of making a request good? Why?

ANNE BLAKE. Mr. Nichols, my name is Anne Blake. I should like to make a change on my option card for next term.

MR. NICHOLS. Miss Young, will you please find Miss Blake's option card in the files. What is the trouble, Anne?

ANNE. A month ago I decided to register for a course in typing next term. When I made out my programme, however, I neglected to include typing in my list of subjects desired. If it isn't too late to make a change on my option card, I should like to register for the course now.

MR. NICHOLS. You are an academic student, aren't you, Anne? Why do you want to take typing?

ANNE. I think typing is a skill that is valuable to everyone, Mr. Nichols. At present I plan to go to college after graduating from high school. Ability to type will enable me to prepare my assignments more quickly and to hand in neater reports. Then, too, when I graduate I may find that I can't go to college. In that case I shall probably have a much better chance of finding a job if I know how to type.

MR. NICHOLS. Those are sound reasons, Anne. Let me see— you have four majors for next term. Typing would make your second minor. Yes, we can include typing on your programme.

ANNE. Thank you very much, Mr. Nichols. I won't be so forgetful next term. Good afternoon.

Practice 4. Asking Permission

Choose a partner and act out an interview in which you ask the proper authority for permission to take some action—for example:

1. To visit a printing establishment, a cannery, a creamery, or a factory. 2. To make a change in your programme for next term. 3. To visit a biological experiment station. 4. To use the auditorium for a club entertainment. 5. To use a science laboratory for a meeting of the Science Club. 6. To organize a club or a team. 7. To use the gymnasium for a basketball game. 8. To hold a party or a contest. 9. To use the visual education room one period. 10. To go home for lunch every day. 11. To run a cake sale for the benefit of the Senior Girls' Club. 12. To use your minister's (or another's) name as a reference for a part-time job. 13. To make up the work in English you missed when you were absent.

APPLYING FOR A PART-TIME OR VACATION JOB

Preparing for a Job Interview

How you prepare before you see your prospective employer may determine the success or failure of your interview. Get ready for your interview by following these suggestions:

1. Get a full night's sleep before the interview.

Agfa-Ansco Film

In a job-interview, neatness, good taste in dress, and an air of interest are valuable assets.

2. Bathe and put on fresh, clean, pressed clothes. Polish your shoes. Your outfit need not be expensive but it should be harmonious. Avoid the extremes of sportswear and party clothes. Girls, shun jingling jewelry and bright make-up. Boys, select quiet socks and neckties.

3. Brush your teeth, clean your nails, and comb your hair.

4. Know exactly what job you are applying for. Don't make yourself ridiculous by saying, "I can do anything."

5. Think about your qualifications as a worker. What qualities and skills can you offer an employer? Are you healthy, punctual, trustworthy, industrious, intelligent? Do you get on well with others? Can you type, sell, sew, clean, take care of children, deliver packages, take care of a lawn and garden? What special qualifications have you for the job you want? If the job is to deliver packages, do you know the delivery area thoroughly? If the job is to take care of children, can you say that you haven't had a cold in two years or that you like children and that children like you?

6. Anticipate questions you might be asked, and prepare to answer them clearly and honestly. Some questions for which you should have clear-cut answers are:

What hours can you devote to the part-time job? When do you plan to do your homework for school?
What salary do you expect?
How many days have you been absent from school in the past year?
How many times have you been late?
How good a record have you made in high school?
What extracurricular activities have you engaged in?
Does your family need your financial help?
How do you spend your spare time?
What vocation are you planning to enter?
Why do you want to work here? Who referred you to us?

7. Make a clear, accurate list of the names and addresses of two, three, or four responsible persons who know you well and will answer questions about your character, training, and experience. Avoid, if possible, giving the names of relatives; they are likely to be prejudiced.

8. If you have had experience in the work for which you are applying, take with you the name and address of your former employer and the exact dates of your employment.

9. If you have never had a job, think of the unpaid experience you have had which fits you for the job—for example, a hobby, or service as assistant in the school office, as secretary to a teacher, as junior leader of a church club, or as messenger for the local Red Cross chapter. Prepare to tell the exact dates of service and the name of the person in charge.

10. Be ready to tell what training your school courses have given you for the job, how long you studied each subject, and what your marks were. If the courses were stenography and typewriting, know your speed in taking dictation, typing from straight copy, and transcribing your notes.

11. Your interviewer may ask you whether you have any questions. Think out in advance what you want to know about the work. You may be judged as much by the intelligence of your questions as by the persuasiveness of your answers.

12. Fill your fountain pen. You may need it to make out an application blank.

Your Interview

The qualities your interviewer will look for are courtesy, modest self-confidence, energetic health, alertness, earnestness, straightforwardness, neatness, and clear, natural, correct speech. If you follow these suggestions, you will be more likely to secure the job.

1. Walk in briskly, and introduce yourself with a smile. Say, "Good morning, Mr. Burton. I am Sylvia Wells," not "I am Miss Wells." if you have an appointment for four o'clock, be there when the clock strikes four.

2. State at once your purpose in coming. "Mrs. Norton suggested that I apply for the job of taking care of your son Bobby on Saturday evenings," or "I wish to apply for the job of junior camp counsellor which you advertised in this morning's *Times.*"

3. Don't sit down until invited. Unless Mr. Burton extends his hand, don't offer to shake hands. Don't park your hat on his desk.

4. Sit easily erect. Don't edge up to your hearer while you talk.

5. Park your nervousness and mannerisms outside. Relax. Girls, don't open and close your bag, fuss with your hair or clothes, or fidget. Boys, don't smooth your hair, look at the floor or out the window, play with a pencil, or wriggle.

6. Look your interviewer straight in the eye. Listen sharply. Never interrupt.

7. Answer questions frankly, honestly, fully, but don't talk too much.

8. Never chew gum during an interview.

9. Speak clearly, distinctly, earnestly, and keep your voice pitched low.

10. Use grammatical language. Avoid slang.

11. If you are asked to fill out a written application, fill accurately, neatly, and legibly every blank that applies to you. Be brief. Spell

and punctuate correctly.   Your application will be considered an example of how you work.

12. Avoid, if possible, making negative statements about yourself. Don't volunteer, "I haven't had any experience in office work," even if you intend to follow this immediately with a "but I have had high marks in stenography, typing, and accounting." To the direct question, "Have you ever held a paid selling job, Miss Gardner?" however, answer, "No, Mr. Lewis, but I have sold war stamps, school papers, and baseball tickets in my home room. I like to sell." Tell what your strong points are and express your eagerness to work and learn. Be self-confident but modest—never cocky.

13. At the end of the interview stand up, thank the interviewer, and leave promptly. Walk with firm, rather quick steps.

Practice 5.   Applying for a Job

With a partner acting as interviewer, apply for one of the following jobs or another one.   Put your best foot forward.   The class will decide whether you followed the preceding suggestions and whether you will secure the position in preference to other applicants.   Use natural, pleasing tones.

care of children	garage helper	receptionist
cashier	gardener	salesperson
delivery boy	junior camp counsellor	shipping or stock
dentist's assistant	office boy or page	clerk
farm hand	packer in department	tutor
file clerk	store	typist

Hints on Making a Purchase

1. *If people are ahead of you at the counter, wait your turn patiently.*
2. *Describe clearly the article you wish to see: quality, colour, size, material, manufacturer, or anything else which will help the salesperson to find it quickly. Use vivid, accurate words.*
3. *Be courteous. Say, "Will you please show me" or "I should like to see," not "Show me" or "I want."*
4. *If an article does not meet your requirements, explain why; perhaps the salesman can show you a more satisfactory one. Don't, of course, leave while the salesman is looking for an article you asked about.*
5. *Don't compare unfavourably the article shown you with a competitor's goods. Such criticism is, as a rule, both ill-mannered and useless, for ordinarily the salesman has no control over the price or the type of articles given him to sell.*
6. *Never lose your temper and argue loudly with a salesperson; if you have a legitimate grievance, take it to the proper authority.*
7. *Avoid needless handling and disarrangement of merchandise on a counter.*
8. *Above all, never make a salesperson display his entire stock when you have **no intention** of buying.*

Practice 6. Studying Sales Conversations

Read examples 1 and 2 below. Then, by referring to the preceding hints, explain which customer was the more efficient in making her purchase. What necessary information did one customer omit at the start?

Example 1:

Miss Graham. I'd like to see some gloves.
Clerk. Certainly. What size do you wear?
Miss Graham. Size 6¼.
Clerk. Have you any particular colour in mind?
Miss Graham. Yes, brown.
Clerk. This pair is made of exceptionally soft kid.
Miss Graham. I prefer suède to kidskin.
Clerk. Here's a pair of handsewn, washable, brown suède gloves in your size for $6.50.
Miss Graham. Oh, that's more than I care to spend! Have you a pair for about three dollars in a darker shade of brown?
Clerk. Yes, here's a good value in your size for $3.35.
Miss Graham. They're good-looking, aren't they?

Example 2:

Clerk. May I help you, madam?
Mrs. Kingsley. Yes, please. I should like to see an all-wool, sleeveless pull-over sweater in olive drab, suitable for a soldier, in size 40, for about four dollars.
Clerk. Surely. Here are two of the most popular soldier's pull-overs. This one, priced at $3.60, is 85% new wool and 15% reprocessed wool. This sweater, priced at $4.50, is 95% new wool and 5% new brushed rabbit's hair.
Mrs. Kingsley (*after examining the sweaters*). Are these sweaters washable?
Clerk. We can guarantee our sweaters only if they are dry-cleaned, madam.
Mrs. Kingsley. I'll take the $4.50 sweater.

Practice 7. Dramatizing Purchases

Dramatize purchases suggested by the following list. In each, one pupil will act as the salesperson and another as the customer. Speak distinctly. Use pleasing tones.

baseball or baseball glove
birthday present for a member of your family
butter and eggs, or vegetables
dress, suit, coat, or hat
fountain pen
handbag or wallet
loose-leaf notebook
necktie or scarf

pair of shoes
pair of skates
shoeshine kit for a serviceman
stationery
sweaters for a basketball team
swimming suit
tennis racket
wrist watch
another article

BUSINESS TELEPHONING

When you transact business by telephone, be brief, clear, and definite. Before you pick up the receiver, know exactly what you wish to accomplish. Have clearly in mind names, dates, sizes, and other detailed information. Have handy a pencil and pad, also a catalogue or price list if you will need it.

Many directories have a classified section, in which business and professional subscribers are listed according to the product or service they offer. A few classifications are beauty shops, carpenters, carpet cleaners, florists, laundries, 'painters' supplies, physicians and surgeons, storage. The classes are arranged alphabetically, and under each classification subscribers are listed alphabetically.

When the person or company called answers, say at once who you are and what you want—for example, "This is Frank Evans calling. I should like to make an appointment with Dr. Howard for Tuesday evening." Using your natural tones, speak directly into the mouthpiece with your lips about half an inch from it. Don't mumble, shout, or talk fast. When your call is concluded, replace the receiver gently.

Practice 8. Using the Telephone Directory

1. On your paper arrange alphabetically the following as they would appear in a telephone directory. For help study the arrangement of names in the telephone directory.

Paul Luber
Ludlow Valve Manufacturing Company
Luber Pharmacy, Inc.
The Loyal Dairy
Lucht Dress Company
Loyal Dress House
Mrs. Lucy Lozier
Joseph Luckow
Lucille Beauty Shop

Edwin Lucien
The Lucy Ann Hat Company
John C. Lozier
Claire Ludwin
Ludewig and Deutch, Inc.
R. J. Ludlow, Jr.
The Lucy-Bern Hat Corporation
Dr. Frances Lucton
Ludlow and Minor
Ludlow Studios Inc.

2. Using the classified section of the directory, write on your paper the name, address, and telephone number of a subscriber who offers for sale each of the following products:

brick	flags	shoes	lumber
automobile supplies	pets	storm windows	meat
adding machines	coal	automobile parts	paint

3. In the classified section of the directory find the name, address, and telephone number of each of the following:

a veterinarian	a piano tuner	a church	a hospital
a business school	a nurse	a mover	a hotel
an accountant	an architect	an auctioneer	a doctor

HINTS ON SHOPPING BY TELEPHONE

1. *Think out in advance questions to secure the information you want. Know on what basis you will make your decision—for example, price, quality, brand, style, colour, date of delivery, or a combination of two or more of these.*
2. *Without wasting time tell exactly what type of product you want to purchase. Mention size, colour, style, price, and other details that will help the store to fill your order accurately.*
3. *Before concluding the call, repeat for verification prices, sizes, dates, and other details quoted by the store.*
4. *Don't forget to give your name and address. Spell your name, unless it is Jones, Brown, or the like. Find out when the purchase will be delivered.*

Practice 9. Studying a Telephone Order

Does Mrs. Leeds waste any words in placing her order? How does she know that the clerk has understood her order?

DEPARTMENT STORE. The Rogers Company.

MRS. LEEDS. I wish to place an order.

[*The telephone operator of the Rogers Company connects Mrs. Leeds with the Order Department.*]

ORDER DEPARTMENT. Order Department.

MRS. LEEDS. I should like to order the number three gift package for overseas which you advertised for four dollars in yesterday's *Post.* That is the box containing two pounds of icebox cookies, one pound of fruit-filled hard candies, one pound of mixed dried fruits, one pound of pure strawberry jam, and one pound of grade A peanut butter.

ORDER DEPARTMENT. Yes, madam, that is our number three package. To whom shall we send it?

MRS. LEEDS. To Mr. Raymond J. Dean (D-e-a-n), 341 Lansing Place, Oxford, England. Charge this purchase to my account. I am Mrs. Philip Leeds (L-e-e-d-s), 207 West End Avenue. My account number is 325,784. On the card write, please, "From Marie and Philip Leeds."

ORDER DEPARTMENT. Yes, Mrs. Leeds. We shall enclose a card reading, "From Marie and Philip Leeds" (L-e-e-d-s), in the number three package, to be sent to Mr. Raymond J. Dean (D-e-a-n), 341 Lansing Place, Oxford, England. The gift is to be charged to Mrs. Philip Leeds, account number 325,784. Is that correct?

MRS. LEEDS. Yes, thank you. Good-bye.

Practice 10. Dramatizing a Telephone Order

With a partner dramatize a scene in which you order by telephone one of the following articles or another article. Speak distinctly. Use pleasing tones.

book	vegetables or fruit	flowers
box of candy	gloves	stationery
house dress	chicken, leg of lamb, pork	bread and cookies
stockings	chops, or other meat	canned goods

Making an Appointment

When making an appointment by telephone, mention:

1. Your name.
2. The time for which you desire the appointment.
3. The purpose of the appointment unless it is obvious.

If it is necessary to change an appointment:

1. Give your name.
2. Tell the time of the appointment to be broken.
3. Briefly give your reason for breaking the appointment.
4. Ask courteously for another appointment, suggesting a day and time.

Practice 11.　Making an Appointment by Telephone

With a partner dramatize a scene in which you make an appointment with one of the persons listed below, and later change the appointment. Enunciate distinctly.　Use your best voice.

doctor or dentist	principal of your school
club or scout leader	hairdresser
minister, priest, or rabbi	worker in a field that interests
music teacher	you

Emergency Calls

When an emergency occurs, the first and most important rule to remember is, Keep calm.　Go quickly to the telephone, dial or call the operator, and say, "I want a policeman," "I want to report a fire," "I want an ambulance," or something similar.　Be sure to tell the operator accurately where help is needed.

Improving Your Speech

YOUR speech is an index to your personality. Like most other people, you probably talk a hundred times as much as you write. What do people discover about you when you talk to them?

Do you know George Bernard Shaw's *Pygmalion?* Perhaps you saw the motion picture based on it. The play is about the attempt of Professor Higgins, a speech expert, to train the voice and articulation of an uneducated ditchdigger's daughter so that she might be taken for a lady of breeding.

"If I can teach you how to speak," the professor said to Eliza Doolittle, "I can make you pass for a duchess."

The professor almost succeeded in having her pass for a duchess, too, except that in a moment of forgetful excitement at a fashionable party, Eliza reverted to her old vulgar speech.

Good speech and a pleasing voice are social assets and have also dollar-and-cent value. For rapid advancement on the job an important qualification is speech that is easy to hear and pleasant to listen to.

Have you decided what career you would like to follow? Are you willing to train your speech so that you can be at ease in your chosen social and business fields? You must remember that training implies constant application. You would never want to be embarrassed as Eliza Doolittle was!

SELF-APPRAISAL TEST

Read the following questions and honestly answer yes or no to each.

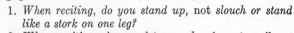

1. *When reciting, do you stand up, not slouch or stand like a stork on one leg?*
2. *When reciting, do you let your hands rest easily at your sides, not fumble with a paper or pencil or fidget with your beads or your necktie?*
3. *Do you recite to all your classmates, not just to the teacher?*
4. *Do you speak and read to your audience, not to the floor, the ceiling, a window, or your book?*
5. *Do you say* riding, going, *and* writing, *not* "ridin," "goin," *and* "writin"; *who is that, not* "whozat"; I want to, *not* "I wanna"?
6. *Do you speak the last words of every sentence distinctly, not die down before the end?*

27

7. *Do your listeners hear you easily?*
8. *Do your listeners understand you easily?*
9. *Do you listen thoughtfully to the speech of others to learn from them both how to speak and how not to speak?*
10. *Are you willing to spend ten minutes a day on improving your speech habits?*

Practice 1.   Discussing Good Speech

1. Mention five motion-picture actors or actresses and five radio announcers or commentators whose speech you might use as models. In what respects is the speech of each person outstanding?
2. In what occupations or professions is good speech essential? In what others is it a definite asset?
3. What will your future occupation or profession probably be? Specifically, how will effective speaking habits aid you on the job and off the job?

HOW DO YOU LOOK

Good posture is important to the speaker for two reasons: first, he must stand well to breathe well, and he must breathe well to be easily heard; secondly, the audience's first impressions of the speaker are created by his bearing. A pupil who in front of the class looks as stiff as a scarecrow or as limp as a rag doll makes an unfavourable first impression. What were your answers to questions 1, 2, 3, and 4 on the Self-appraisal Test? If they were all "yeses," you have a head start in attracting your audience.

GUIDES TO POSTURE

1. *Sit back in your chair or seat and keep your shoulders erect. Don't slouch.*
2. *Stand erect, but not stiffly, with your head up and your weight on both feet.*
3. *Change the position of your body in keeping with changing thoughts. You are not a soldier guarding a post.*
4. *Keep your hands, ordinarily, at your sides. Avoid unnecessary movements which may divert the listeners' attention from what you are saying to what you are doing.*

GETTING ACQUAINTED WITH YOUR VOCAL MECHANISM

Any good mechanic or operator must know the machine he is working with if he is to keep it in good running order and use it with highest efficiency. Like any machine, the voice must have a motor power to set it in action. The motor power in voice is your outgoing breath. That is why it is important to train yourself to breathe properly and to control the air in the lungs. If you breathe in short gasps, your voice will seem breathy and your speech jerky.

Place your index finger over the small protrusion on your neck which you know as the Adam's apple. You are really feeling the voice box, also called the larynx. The larynx contains the vocal cords. Without these two bands of yellow elastic tissue there could be no voice or speech. When they are tightened and brought close together, the outgoing breath passing through them causes them to vibrate. These vibrations produce sound waves or voice.

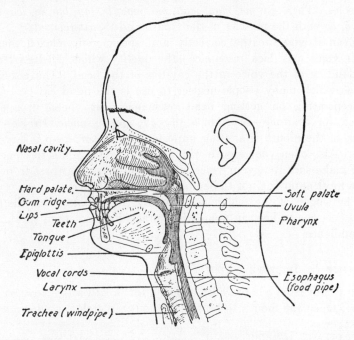

For the enlargement of the tones produced by the vocal cords, the vocal mechanism contains three important resonators or amplifiers: the throat cavity or pharynx, the mouth cavity, and the two nasal cavities. In these places the sounds sent forth by the vibrating vocal cords are greatly amplified. Without these loud-speakers your voice would be hardly more than a peep. Misuse or blocking of your amplifiers will interfere with your best voice use. By sighing aloud or saying *ah*, you can demonstrate the use of the vocal mechanism.

HOW CAN YOU TRAIN YOUR VOICE?

Because voice is made out of breath, a person can't speak well if his lungs are empty. The secret of holding breath, as singers know, is breathing the natural way—principally by the use of the diaphragm. By trying to encircle your waist with your hands, press the air out of your lungs. Then take a deep breath without lifting the shoulders, and you'll notice that your hands are being pushed out. Now take another deep breath and hum as long as you can without taking a breath. Then count from one to twelve on one exhaling breath.

Proper breathing will help a rasping or otherwise unpleasant voice. But tension—that is, tight jaw, throat, or tongue muscles—is often a cause of harsh tones. Take a deep yawn to relax the jaw and throat muscles. Then say *me, may, mah, mo, moo; le, lay, lah, lo, loo; e, ay, ah, o, oo* with the muscles of the mouth and throat relaxed.

Even if you breathe correctly and speak with relaxed muscles, your voice may lack resonance—the quality which results from the resounding of the voice in the cavities of the head. The resonating space which many people neglect to use is the nasal cavity. While concentrating on getting head resonance—with head dropped to chest, for example—say: *bingle, mingle, ringle, single, klingle.* The back of the mouth is another important resonator; keep it large and free. Also open your mouth wide enough for the tones to come out, and make sure that your voice reaches the person farthest from you. It is most annoying not to be able to hear a speaker.

The slogan of the telephone company, "The voice with the smile wins," is one to keep in mind while practising and when speaking to an audience.

Practice 2. Improving Your Voice

1. Count from *one* to *twelve*, pausing for breath after *three, six,* and *nine.* Open the mouth to let the tone out. Watch it go down a long passageway.

2. Practise in a full, round, open-mouth voice such passages as the following. At each pause take a breath.

> Roll on, thou deep and dark blue Ocean, roll!
> Ten thousand fleets sweep over thee in vain;
> Man marks the earth with ruin—his control
> Stops with the shore.—LORD BYRON

> Ring joyous chords!—ring out again!
> A swifter still and a wilder strain!
> And bring fresh wreaths!—we will banish all
> Save the free in heart from our banquet hall.

ENUNCIATING AND PRONOUNCING

When you speak, you do more than produce voice; you make distinct and separate sounds which will be intelligible as words to your listeners. To shape these sounds you must use your articulators: the lips, teeth, upper gum, hard and soft palate, and tongue. In other words, you enunciate sounds and pronounce words.

Enunciation refers to the full, distinct utterance of the sounds in words.

Pronunciation refers to the correct utterance of words.

Two classes of sounds are produced by the speech mechanism: consonants and vowels. In the formation of a consonant the articulators obstruct the voice or breath. In the formation of a vowel the articulators change the sound but do not obstruct it. The passage for the sound is free. The sounds of *a, e, i, o, u,* and sometimes *y* are vowels. The rest of the letters represent consonant sounds

TEST. PRONUNCIATION

Here are twenty common words. Can you pronounce them all correctly? If not, learn to produce the sounds you have difficulty with.

better	fifths	moths	singer
clanging	have to	postage	these
English	huge	progressive	thirty-five
facts	liberty	recognize	whether
fellows	longer	Roosevelt	whining

CONSONANT ERRORS

INTERCHANGING VOICE AND BREATH CONSONANTS

Breath is changed into voice by the vibration of the vocal cords. Look at the following pairs of consonants:

BREATH	VOICE	BREATH	VOICE
p — puppy	b — bubble	k — curl	g — girl
t — tart	d — dart	ch — church	j — judge
f — fan	v — van	th — thin	TH— then
s — hiss	z — his	sh — shun	zh — rouge

Each pair is made by the same action of the articulatory organs. For example, both *p* and *b* are explosions. For both, the lips are pressed together and then released. The sounds differ only in the stuff of which they are made: *p*, breath; *b*, voice.

Place the thumb and a finger on your Adam's apple, or larynx. Sound *s, f,* and *sh,* breath sounds; then *z, v, zh,* voice sounds. Notice the vibration when the voice sounds are produced. A common error in pronunciation is the substitution of a breath sound for a voice sound. Occasionally the opposite mistake is made. Use the following exercises for practice on these sounds.

BREATH VOICE	BREATH VOICE	BREATH VOICE
assure — azure	pitching — pigeon	latter — ladder
luck — lug	breath — breathe	grating — grading
puck — pug	loose — lose	metal — medal
match — Madge	sown — zone	bitten — bidden
batch — badge	half — have	heating — heeding
etching — edging	census — senses	patting — padding

Words for Practice

because	newspaper	vision	baggage
boys	please	judge	pillage
choose	prosaic	mighty	courage
chose	Roosevelt	moths	village
cousin	surprised	mouths	besiege
cruise	usurp	oaths	charge
discern	years	paths	cabbage
favours	yours	wreaths	abusive
figs	acid	thither	decisive
friends	ceases	revive	explosive
houses	was	measure	exclusive
Israel	adhesion	rouge	relative
beauty	fortified	potato	weighty
forty	butter	liberty	adjective
ninety	little	partner	immersion

1. Because the judge fears the pillage of the village, he adopts decisive and progressive measures to avert the disaster.
2. He read *Barnaby Rudge* and *The Red Badge of Courage.*
3. Sitting in the cottage, Madge saw her pigeon foraging for food on the edge of the ridge.
4. When at liberty for ninety minutes, my partner and I rested beneath a little chestnut tree.

ng

Although *ng* has two letters, it represents only one sound. Sometimes *n* is carelessly substituted for *ng*—for example, "runnin" for *running*, "sittin" for *sitting*. People with a foreign background frequently change *ng* to *ngg* or *ngk*. To form the *ng* sound, keep the back of the tongue against the soft palate and send voiced air through the nose. At the end drop the tongue without an explosion or click. An explosion of breath is an added *k*; of voice, an added *g*.

Practise the words in the following list. Produce *ng* correctly. Make sure there is no click (*g* or *k*) after the sound.

anything	evening	morning	something
banquet	going	nothing	strength
clanging	herring	playing	swimming
coming	hoping	pudding	swinging
coughing	leaving	reading	tranquil
doing	length	running	vanquish

In case you are confused about the varied pronunciation of *ng* in different words, practise the following lists. The headings of the columns show you how to pronounce the words.

$n + j$ words	$n + g$ words	ng words	$ng + g$ words	$ng + k$ words
change	engage	Long Island	stronger	anchor
danger	engross	singer	finger	ankle
dungeon	inglorious	hanger	linger	blanket
engine	ingratitude	longing	longer	distinct
fringe	ingredient	speaking	English	donkey
ginger	penguins	during	single	handkerchief
passenger	ungainly	leaving	angle	monkey
stingy	ungodly	cunning	hunger	sink
stranger	ungrateful	hanging	language	thinker
tinge	unguarded	ringing	Congress	uncle

Can you add five words to each list?

Sentences for Practice

1. It was indeed singular, my dear Watson, that he should have been strangled by fingers not human. — A. CONAN DOYLE
2. While bringing the bell to the room, he kept swinging and ringing it and singing.
3. The cataract strong then plunges along,
   Striking and raging as if war waging,
   Rising and leaping, sinking and creeping,
   Showering and springing, flying and flinging,
   Writhing and ringing. — ROBERT SOUTHEY

th

D and t are sometimes substituted for *th*. The error is caused by placing the tongue against the upper gum. Place it against the upper teeth.

Have you heard tough, uneducated, characters in radio or motion-picture plays talk like this: "Dere dey wuz, tin 'n' toisty"? Of course they meant, "There they were, thin and thirsty." Remember the impression such speech conveys and guard against such substitutions in your own speech.

Practise this distinction exercise and the words and sentences following it.

th	*d*	*th*	*d* or *t*	*th*	*d* or *t*
than	Dan	they	day	thirty	dirty
the	Dee	thick	tick	thong	tong
then	den	thin	tin	though	dough
there	dare	thine	dine	thy	die

th Words for Practice

that	the	three	bequeath	moths
this	them	with	breathe	mouths
these	think	width	cloths	oaths
those	thirst	beneath	feathers	truths

1. To thee and thine, while I breathe, there shall be no enmity beneath my roof.

2. Thrice blessed is the man who thrives through his own thrift, strength, and breadth of character.
3. There were thirty thirsty thieves beneath the spreading branches of the three trees.
4. My tough lance thrusteth sure;
My strength is as the strength of ten.
5. Both of them dozed there on the sunny deck of their boat.

The rider said "Whoa!" to his horse.

The rider said, "Woe to this horse!"

wh

$Wh = h + w$. Don't omit the h. Pronounce *when, why, which, wharf, white* as if they were spelled *hwen, hwy, hwich, hwarf, hwite.*

If the sound is difficult for you, hold a piece of paper about six inches from your face and blow the paper with the *wh* sound. Then produce the *wh* in the same way but with less breath.

wh	w	wh	w	wh	w
whacks — wax		what — watt		where — wear	
whale — wail		wheel — weal		whet — wet	
whether — weather		whine — wine		whither — wither	
which — witch		whit — wit		whoa — woe	
while — wile		white — wight		why — y	

wh Words for Practice

wheat	whence	whip	whisky
wheedle	whiff	whir	whisper
wheeze	whim	whirl	whistle
whelp	whimper	whisk	whittle
when	whimsical	whisker	whiz

1. Mr. Watt asked which way Mr. White went.
2. William considered whether it was wise to wear the white wig and whiskers.
3. He whirled about and inquired whether Mr. Whitney whistled when he worked.
4. Whether or not the weather is pleasant, I know where we shall go and which dress I shall wear.

h

At the beginning of a word *h* is frequently carelessly omitted. Take a deep breath before uttering the sound.

Words in Which the Initial *h* Is Pronounced

him	human	humidity	humiliation
her	humid	Hughes	humane
hew	humorous	huge	hospital
hue	humility	humble	hospitality

In some words *h* is silent: *exhaust, exhibit, forehead, vehicle.*

PRONOUNCING FINAL SOUNDS AND DIFFICULT COMBINATIONS

The tongue is naturally lazy. It does no more work than is required of it, and so it often omits the final sound in such words as *lest, last gold* and *cold.* Combinations like *cts, sts dths* are difficult, and the tongue would like to make them easy by omitting one or two of the sounds in each. Practise at first with a slight pause after the first of the three consonants: *ac-ts, fac-ts, objec-ts, lis-ts, fis-ts.*

In the following exercise make each word in the pair clear by careful attention to every sound.

axe — acts	Ann — and	dense — dents
ask — asked	bowl — bold	mince — mints
Bess — best	coal — cold	prince — prints
lass — last	goal — gold	penitence — penitents
less — lest	scale — scaled	sense — cents
pass — past	toll — told	tense — tents
shore — short	use — used	breaths — breadths
worse — worst	confidence — confidants	with — width

Now try these familiar phrases and the following words and sentences. Don't slur any sound. Cut the words apart.

give me that	better than	five cents
let me	length and breadth	could you
want to	don't know	did you ever
What are you doing?	Can't you go?	couple of fellows

Words for Practice

attract	fifths	texts	midst
object	sixths	insects	slightest
perfect	twelfths	kept	must
attacked	widths	except	picture
asks	depths	manuscript	west
facts	strengths	slept	geography
defects	hundredth	attempt	library
rejects	thousandth	second	laboratory
neglects	lists	first	secretary
breadths	next	most	government
eighths	tempts	rest	February

1. My next text may be found in the first, second, third, fifth, seventh, and eighth verses of the second chapter of "Acts."
2. The fact that the adjutant told in the last report of the conflict has had its effect on the coast fight.
3. He leaped to his feet and scanned the cloud-capped mountain; then he crept back and slept peacefully.
4. My little brother always asks to see the attractive pictures in the new geography in the library.

lm and *sm*

Avoid the introduction of a vowel sound between *l* and *m* or *s* and *m* in such words as *elm, helm, overwhelm, film, realm, chasm, enthusiasm, baptism, communism, conservatism.* *M* is produced with the lips closed. Hence close the mouth quickly after the production of *s* or *l*.

w and *v*

Some foreigners interchange *v* and *w*. To produce *w*, round the lips as for $\bar{oo}$. For *v* place the lower lip against the upper teeth.

PRONUNCIATION PRACTICE—Consonants

adjective	blanket	cloths	film
archbishop	blithe	Congress	finger
archipelago	breadths	coughing	friends
architect	butter	decease	fungus (40)
associate	cabbage	decisive	gesture
assure	cavalry	depths (30)	going
athlete	cease	disaster	gradual
auxiliary	chimney (20)	disease	hanging
banging	chore	doing it	has to
banquet (10)	clanging	edge	height
bequeath	clinging	English	his
better	clothes	expressive	hoping

houses	longing	playing	usurp
humour (50)	loose	postage	wheels
immediately	lose	pudding	when (90)
including	mighty	reading	where
Ireland	mileage	revive	whether
journal	morning	running (80)	which
judge	mouths	senses	while
length	niche	singer	why
liberty	ninety (70)	sixths	widths
library	oaths	sphere	with
licorice	partner	sprinkle	worst
little (60)	paths	strength	wrangle
longer	pillage	thither	wreaths (100)

ENGLISH SPELLING AND PRONUNCIATION

Pronounce the following words:

rough   though   hiccough   plough   cough   through

What did you discover about the pronunciation of the *ough* part of the words?

Now pronounce these words:

day   wait   weight   ate   break   veil   they

These are all spelled differently, but what is common to them?

These two illustrations show that we cannot always determine the pronunciation of a word from its spelling, or its spelling from its pronunciation. Because of these inconsistencies it is hard to formulate rules for pronouncing words.

DIACRITICAL MARKS

Every dictionary uses a system of diacritical marks to indicate the pronunciation of words. The key to these marks is found at the bottom of the dictionary page. Learn to consult this key when you are looking up the pronunciation of words. Although each dictionary is likely to have a system of its own, the following eight Webster marks are widely used.

1. A *macron* indicates a long sound: āle, ēve, īce, ōld, cūbe.

2. A *suspended bar* indicates a slight change of a long sound in an unaccented syllable: chȧotic, ȯbey, ēvent, ūnite.

3. A *breve* indicates a short sound: ădd, ĕnd, ĭll, ŏdd, ŭp.

4. A *circumflex* occurs frequently before r in stressed syllables: câre, ôrb, ûrn.

5. Two dots indicate a broad sound: härd.

6. One dot indicates an intermediate sound: ȧ as in *ask* is halfway between ă and ä.

7. The *breve with circumflex* indicates a modification of the short sound: sŏft, mŏss, cŏffee, ŏften.

8. The *tilde* or *wave* occurs frequently before **r** in unstressed syllables: makēr.

WEBSTER'S GUIDE TO PRONUNCIATION

This is part of the guide to pronunciation that is placed at the bottom of the page in a Webster dictionary.

āle	sof*à*	ĭll	cŏnnect	ūnite
chāotic	ēve	charĭty	fōōd	ûrn
câre	ĕvent	ōld	fŏŏt	ŭp
ădd	ĕnd	ŏbey	out	circ*ŭ*s
*ă*ccount	silĕnt	ôrb	oil	then
ärm	makēr	ŏdd	cūbe	thin
àsk	īce	sŏft		

When a letter is printed in italics, the sound is obscure.

ACCENT

Accent is stress. When you pronounce a word, hit the accented syllable harder with your voice. Think of the accented syllable as if it were printed in capitals: CHAM-pi-on, GUAR-di-an, CON-trar-y, dis-CHARGE, mu-NIC-i-pal, su-PER-flu-ous.

In Webster the light (') and the heavy (ˈ) accent marks show you which syllables to stress. Funk and Wagnalls dictionaries have a heavy (ˈ) mark for the principal accent and two light marks (ˈˈ) for the secondary accent.

TEST. Pronunciation

By using the Webster dictionary symbols and markings in parentheses can you pronounce all these words correctly?

absurdity (ăb-sûrd'*ĭ*·tĭ)   malign (m*à*·līn')
albeit (ôl·bē'ĭt)   Navajo (năv'*à*·hŏ)
aviatrix (ā'vĭ·ā'trĭks)   orgy (ôr'jĭ)
bacillus (b*à*·sĭl'*ŭ*s)   positively (poz'*ĭ*·tĭv·lĭ)
chasm (kăz'm)   sanguine (săng'gwĭn)
coagulate (kŏ·ăg'û·lāt)   statistics (st*à*·tĭs'tĭks)
deify (dē'*ĭ*·fī)   suite (swēt)
facile (făs'ĭl)   usurp (û-zûrp')
gnash (năsh)   victuals (vĭt'ˈlz)
harangue (h*à*·răng')   Yosemite (yŏ·sĕm'ĭ·tĕ)

VOWELS AS TONE PRODUCERS

It is through the vowels, which produce tone, that your listener can hear your voice quali*c*y. If you strangle your vowels by not opening y*u*ur mouth, or swallow them by making them too far back in the throat, or denasalize them by shutting off the nasal resonators, your voice quality will be far from pleasant. It is therefore important to keep your resonators free and your jaws relaxed to get full tone value from your vowels and their relatives, the diphthongs.

DIPHTHONGS

A diphthong (pronounced *difthong*) is a blend of two vowel sounds in one syllable. They are so well combined that they seem almost like one sound.

ī = à + ĭ, ice, fly   oi = ô + ĭ, toy, soil
ā = ă + ĭ, play, day   ou = à + ōō, out, owl
ō = ŏ + ŏŏ, home, roam   ū = ĭ or y + ōō, dew, use

VOWEL AND DIPHTHONG ERRORS

ă

Tension in the production of ă will cause a nasal tone. Avoid this by keeping the throat relaxed and the end of the soft palate raised slightly. Don't carelessly substitute ĕ for ă; some people say *kĕtch* instead of *kătch*. On the other hand, don't try to be fancy (and ridiculous as well) by substituting the à sound for ă; as, *händ* for *hănd*.

ă Words for Practice

cat	gather	larynx	land
canning	had	that	tassel
man	hand	barrel	mansion
catch	have	radish	cantaloupe

1. Sam ran to see the catch-as-catch-can wrestling match.
2. Catch the cat and give her some catnip candy.
3. A man who has a vegetable patch back of his cabin can enjoy fresh radishes, carrots, and snap beans.

ĕ

Do not substitute ĭ or ā for ĕ. Say gĕt, kĕttle, and ĕgg, not gĭt, kĭttle, and āg.

ĕ Words for Practice

America	engines	forget	leg	said
any	entire	get	many	ten
berry	error	kerosene	measure	terror
egg	ferry	kettle	merry	very

ŏ

In the production of the ŏ sound the lips are somewhat rounded, the mouth is opened wider than in making the sound of ô as in *or*, and the tongue is slightly raised. Many people mispronounce this

40 MASTERING EFFECTIVE ENGLISH

sound by substituting ô in some words and ä in others. For practice on all three of these sounds try the following exercise.

ŏ	ô	ä	ŏ	ô	ä
cot — caught	— cart		tot	— taught — tart	
dot — daughter	— dart		pod	— pawed — part	
hot — haughty	— heart		stock	— stalk — start	

ŏ Words for Practice

blossom	forest	problem	stock
bottle	John	Scotch	stopped
doctor	possible	sock	what

1. The doctor was shocked to find that his watch had stopped.
2. The jolly Scotchman was watching his clock.
3. John stopped in the forest one October day to see the yellow witch hazel blossoms.

The ǒ sound falls between ŏ in *cot* and the ô in *caught:* dǒg, lǒng, sǒft. Do not open the mouth as wide as you do for *cot*.

ou

The diphthing ou, the sound in *cow*, is made up of a + ōō. Some people incorrectly pronounce it ăōō; some nasalize it. *Cow* is càōō, not căōō; *now*, nàōō, not năōō. Open the mouth for the sound à.

ou Words for Practice

bound	down	gown	how	round
count	drown	hound	mound	sound
crown	found	house	noun	town

1. I found the town surrounded by mountains.
2. Round and round rolls the sound.
3. *Mound, pound, discount, sound, cloud, ground,* and *doubt* may be used as nouns.
4. The hound came down with a bound.
5. The crown and gown were found.

ī

The diphthong ī is composed of the vowel à plus ĭ. A common error is making the first sound too far back in the mouth. The correct sound is à as in *ask*, not ä as in *father*. Stress the first vowel of the diphthong.

ī Words for Practice

aisle	fine	mine	pride	sigh
crime	mind	ninety	shine	time

1. Nine times I tried to climb the side of the lighthouse.
2. The child had a fine time last night on the ride.
3. Side by side the bride and groom came down the aisle as the chimes rang out.

4. Ring out, wild bells, to the wild sky,
   The flying cloud, the frosty light,
   The year is dying in the night.
Ring out, wild bells, and let him die. — ALFRED TENNYSON

$\bar{u}$

The sound $\bar{u}$ is frequently pronounced $\overline{oo}$ by educated and intelligent people. The preferred pronunciation is y + $\overline{oo}$—*dyook*. For a lazy tongue *dook* is easier than *dyook*. The tongue has hard work when *d, t, l, n, s,* or *th* precedes $\bar{u}$. Think of words with $\bar{u}$ as if they were written *dyooty, tyoob, dyook, syoot, tyoon,* and *Nyoo York*. After *r, l* preceded by a consonant, and usually after *j* and the sound of *sh,* the sound is $\overline{oo}$: *bloo (blue), rool (rule), Joon (June), shoor (sure).*

$\bar{u}$	$\overline{oo}$	$\bar{u}$	$\overline{oo}$	$\bar{u}$	$\overline{oo}$
feud — food		tulips — two lips		news — noose	
due — do		tutor — tooter		stew — stool	
duly — Dooley		mute — moot		muse — moose	
lute — loot		studio — stoop		duke — do	

$\bar{u}$ Words for Practice

accurate	enthusiasm	opportunity	suit
avenue	literature	picture	superintendent
constitution	manufacture	produce	superiority
during	new	student	Tuesday
duty	nuisance	stupid	tune

1. The opportunity and duty of the duke was to institute education and manufacture in New York.
2. The wind blew the student from the zoo to the new institution on the avenue.
3. The beauty of June is appreciated only by one in tune with nature's moods.

Adding *r* to Some Vowels

Frequently *r* is incorrectly added to syllables ending in *a, aw, o,* and *ow.* The error results from letting the point of the tongue glide to the front palate and produce an extra sound. To prevent this parasitic *r,* hold the tongue firm; that is, keep the tongue behind the lower teeth on the vowel sound. Use a mirror for this correction.

$\hat{o}$	$\hat{o}r$	No *r*	*r*	
awe — ore		pillow — pillar		
caw — core		raw — roar		
draw — drawer		sawing — soaring		
law — lore		comma —comer		
maw — more		saw I — sore eye — saw rye		
paw — pore		papa — popper		

a, aw, o, and *ow* Words for Practice

drama	veranda	Anna	yellow
extra	Amanda	California	piano
idea	vanilla	Florida	pillow
saw	sarsaparilla	Utica	hollow
sofa	mamma	awning	swallow
soda	Martha	potato	window
straw	China	tomato	fellow
umbrella	America	borrow	innocent

1. Anna and Martha saw that drama in California.
2. On the veranda Amanda drank the vanilla soda and sarsaparilla.
3. Clara's idea was to borrow an extra umbrella at the law office.

ĭ Words Often Mispronounced

captain	hypocrisy	Pilgrim	livelong
city	Italian	pretty	italic
diploma	it is	ridiculous	intestine
dish	liquid	rinse	civil
family	mirror	since	wish
fish	organization	spirit	syrup
genuine	Philip	victim	anti (prefix)

ā Words Often Mispronounced

aviation	gratis	maybe	radiator
aye (*always*)	ignoramus	nape	ultimatum

ŭ Words Often Mispronounced

just	such	umpire	alumnus

PRONUNCIATION PRACTICE—Vowels

abound	champion	gratis	ridiculous
accurate	civil	hearth	said
alms	coupon	Italian	saucy
alumnae	daughter	join	since
alumni	delta	just	sleek
America	describe	kettle	society
anti (prefix)	digestion	khaki	sought
anything	diploma	lurch	spirit
aroma	discretion	many	spurt
aviation (10)	drought (30)	merry (50)	syrup (70)
awning	duty	mischievous	tassel
aye (*yes*)	edge	moist	taught
aye (*always*)	error	nerve	terrible
bade	faucet	oily	thought
barrel	fellows	opaque	toil
bellow	forget	opportunity	Tuesday
berry	gather	penalize	ultimatum
calm	genuine	psalm	umpire
carry	get	radio	vanilla
catch (20)	girl (40)	radish (60)	wish (80)

Vowels and Consonants

abusive	during	hypocrisy	perspiration
altitude	engine	ignoramus	picture
arctic	English	intestine	potatoes
at all	err	introduce	pretty
authority	family	iron	provide
burst	finger	italic	radiator
butter	finis	kerosene	recompense
caucus	formerly	larynx	ridiculous
cello	fraught	laudable	substitute
chalk (10)	fusion (30)	livelong (50)	suite (70)
chef	gaudy	longevity	superintendent
column	gentleman	manufacture	superiority
comfortable	genuine	militia	tremendous
despair	grenade	mingling	twice
dessert	grimy	multiplication	victim
destruction	handkerchief	Nazi	what
diamond	haughty	nothing	whining
discretion	height	parliament	whit
dissolve	human	pathos	wrought
drawer (20)	hundred (40)	peony (60)	zoology (80)

WORDS FREQUENTLY MISPRONOUNCED

abdomen	comely	gist	orgy
acclimated	comparable	governor	poinsettia
address	contemplate	gratis	precedent
adult	contemplative	harass	prelude
alias	conversant	hearth	prestige
alien	cynosure	heinous	pretense
allies	data	hospitable	pumpkin
amenable	decade	hostile	quay
amicable	de luxe	hygiene	quintuplets
applicable	depot	impious	raspberry
appreciative	despicable	implacable	recipe
arctic	desultory	impotent	reparable
artificer	discourse (v.)	inapplicable	reptile
athlete	dishevel	incomparable	research
bade	enervate	inexplicable	reservoir
bouquet	entree	infamous	respite
blasé	exemplary	inquiries	résumé
boudoir	explicable	inveigle	sabotage
bouillon	extraordinary	irrefutable	sinecure
buffet	faucet	lamentable	status
casualty	fiancé	leisure	succinct
centenary	finance	long-lived	trough
chastisement	financier	masseur	trousseau
chauffeur	finis	memorable	vagrant
coadjutor	flaccid	mirage	vaudeville
cognomen	forbade	mischievous	viands
combatant	formidable	museum	zoology
combative	genuine	ordeal	

UNIT FOUR

Listening and Speaking

ĒVERYONE has to listen. Of the four language arts—listening, speaking, reading, and writing—listening is the one you use most frequently.

The radio and the motion picture have made us the most talked-to people in history. Not all the talk that bombards us, of course, is worth listening to or worth remembering.

LISTENING TO LEARN

A person experienced in his own field of work knows when to listen what to listen for, and what is worth remembering. A doctor listening to a patient describing her symptoms listens for meaningful clues to the patient's condition. He will note carefully that the patient has

Royal Canadian Naval Photograph

*There are times when attentive listening is a matter of life and **death.***

44

had a fever and can't sleep but will disregard what has no bearing on his diagnosis: a neighbour's opinion about the illness or gossip about someone else who had the same disease.

Your major job now is learning. In the classroom, listening is not only courteous and helpful to the speaker, but profitable to you. By intelligent, thoughtful listening in class you can reduce substantially the study required to master a subject. The pupil who doesn't listen misses important announcements, assignments, and explanations.

Out of school you are being talked to all the time by the radio, the motion picture, and friends, and have the chance to learn about a variety of subjects. Do you listen discriminatingly? How much do you remember? In conversation do you listen thoughtfully or just wait for your opportunity to jump in and steal the conversational show?

LISTENING FOR POINTS

Listening for points means listening the way the doctor listens to a patient describing his symptoms or the way a jury listens to the testimony of witnesses. When you listen for points you thresh what you hear, blow off the chaff, and keep the meaty kernels for future use.

GOOD MANNERS IN LISTENING

The first courtesy of the listener is to appear interested. The best way, of course, is to *be* interested. Don't fidget or let your eyes wander. A discourtesy as serious as bored silence is the opposite extreme of interrupting the speaker, prompting him when he hesitates, contradicting him rudely, or grimacing at his mistakes. Listen as if you are enjoying what you hear. Don't look as if you are waiting for an opportunity to launch your counterattack. Your facial expression shows that you are following the conversation, so be content to wait for your turn to speak. Good listening is a compliment to the speaker, stimulates him to be more interesting, and is likely to win his friendship.

WHAT IS EFFECTIVE SPEECH?

When it is your turn to speak, be considerate. Make it easy for your audience to listen.

Effective speech is speech that does the job it is intended to do— to entertain, to inform, to convince, or to persuade somebody. Speech is effective if it has: (1) aim; (2) correctness; (3) clarity; (4) force.

Practice 1. Discussing Effective Speech

Discuss the requirements for effective speech. The following suggestions may help you in your thinking.

1. *Aim.* What is the result when the speaker has no aim? Which of the four purposes of speech—to inform, to entertain, to convince, and to persuade—do you think is hardest to achieve? Which aim does a lawyer in court have? Which does a teacher generally have? A hungry boy between meals? A pupil answering a question? A truck driver addressing a motorist in his way? A campaign speaker? An after-dinner speaker?
2. *Correctness.* Why should speech be correct? Should the speech of a farmer be as correct as that of a teacher? How can you make your speech correct? Is it advisable to criticize a person whenever he makes an error? What are the worst errors in your school? Do you agree that the language you speak may indicate the quality of your education and the kind of people with whom you associate?
3. *Clarity.* Is there a difference between correctness and clarity? What is the opposite of clarity? How do you go about making your speech clear? What can you do to improve your enunciating and pronouncing? How will pages 27–43 help you?
4. *Force.* Is loud speech necessarily forceful? How should a speaker emphasize his important ideas? Do you like to listen to generalities or to illustrations? Why? What is repetition? Is it ever desirable? If you have three points in a speech, one extremely important, one important, and one less important, in what order should you place them for greatest force?

PLAN

After deciding what your purpose is and collecting your material, decide what your main points are, arrange them in a natural order, and then fill in the subtopics of the outline.

How to Choose Your Life Work

I. Selecting various vocations you think you will like

II. Testing the vocations
   A. Their advantages
   B. Their disadvantages

III. Testing yourself
   A. Your character
   B. Your ability and strength
   C. Your health
   D. Your interest

IV. Eliminating the work you are not fitted for and selecting a vocation that you like and to which you are adapted.

Practice 2.   Making an Outline

First, select a vocation in which you are interested: accountancy, advertising, agriculture, architecture, army, authorship, aviation, banking, carpentry, civil engineering, dentistry, electrical engineering, forestry, insurance, journalism, law, mechanical engineering, medicine, music, nursing, pharmacy, photography, radio, railroading, secretarial work, salesmanship, social service, teaching, truck gardening, or another occupation. Next, decide whether you wish to inform, convince, or persuade. Collect information from your parents, older brothers and sisters, other relatives, and friends and from such books as Walter B. Pitkin's *New Careers for Youth* and Leverett S. Lyon's *Making a Living.* Then write the outline.

MEMORIZE, READ, OR TALK THE SPEECH?

As a rule, the memorizer sounds like an automaton reciting, not a live boy or girl thinking and speaking. Because of some unexpected happening a written speech may not fit the occasion.

Few people can read a speech and make it sound as if they were conversing with the audience.

The right way is to memorize the main points and then practise the speech a number of times—the more the better—in your own room. If you like, memorize your opening and closing sentences and a few phrases that sound well.

When you have completely prepared a speech, you need no notes unless you wish to quote a fairly long passage or give a set of statistics. Consulting notes, like wriggling, looking at the ceiling, or walking up and down the floor, takes your classmates' attention away from what you are saying to what you are doing.

ENUNCIATION AND PRONUNCIATION

Let us imagine that we are talking into microphones and must make it easy for our radio audience to hear every word we say. Yes, we'll fill our lungs with air, open our mouths, move our lips, speak slowly, enunciate distinctly every sound, especially the endings of words, and cut the words apart. And, of course, we'll not show our ignorance or carelessness by mispronouncing words.

Practice 3. Speaking to the Class

After preparing completely, talk to the class on the vocation you selected. Stand well, look at the class, speak distinctly, and be enthusiastic.

SILENCES BETWEEN SENTENCES

Well, why, and, but, so, and *then* are overworked words. Don't use them unnecessarily. Avoid starting sentences with *well* or *why.* Don't make a speech one long prattling sentence tied together by *and . . .and . . and, so . . . so . . . so,* or *then . . . then . . .then.* End your sentences and begin new ones. Show by a silence where each sentence ends.

Don't fill pauses with *ur's.* When you stop to think, turn your voice off. When you are pondering what to say next, keep your mouth closed until you are ready to say something definite.

GRAMMAR

In speech boys and girls often make grammatical mistakes which they wouldn't be guilty of in written work.

Practice 4. Grammatical Errors

Correct the following mistakes:

This here book; that there book; I ain't going; he don't; they was going; you was; me and Harry went; he don't know nothing; between you and I; it's him; John he went; being I was tired, I went to bed early; these kind; throwed; clumb; drownded; attackted; would of; could of; hisself; them things; we was; wouldn't do nothing; he laid down; he set down; I seen; he come yesterday; he has went.

Practice 5. Personal Experience

Do you own some small object of interest—for example, something you made? If so, bring it to school and tell your classmates about it. If not, tell entertainingly about something you have seen—for example, a picture in a gallery, an object or exhibit in a museum, a place or building of historical or literary interest, a monument, a recent invention, an unusual store window or building, or the funniest sight you ever saw.

An Example of a Pupil's Speech:

AN EGYPTIAN IDOL

Most of you know that the Egyptians worshipped large idols as gods as well as certain animals, but I wonder if you've heard of their personal gods. These gods were strictly private and were not shown even to other members of the household. They were only a few inches tall and were in the form of people or animals. Everyone owned at least a few and the number increased according to rank. Their purpose was to protect only the owner, and at his death the idols were enclosed in the mummy case with the body. This little idol which I have in my hand is one of these gods. It was owned by a daughter of one of the Pharaohs. At her death the idols, which were in her bed for the purpose of curing her, were wrapped right in the mummy case with her. A friend of mine, whose father was a member of the French Embassy, was present at the time the tomb was opened, and this idol was given to her.

It is interesting to note its appearance and construction. The large head, the head-dress, the beads, and the position of the hands probably all have some meaning. What it is, we can only guess, but when we consider that the idol's age is several thousand years and that a princess actually believed in its power, a stranger feeling of wonder is aroused than if we knew the exact facts concerning its origin and meaning. — Pupil's Speech

CLEARNESS AND INTEREST

If we do not understand at first a printed sentence or paragraph, we can re-read it. With a speech it is different. If the hearers do not understand a spoken sentence, they have no other chance to find out what the speaker means. Hence in speech the rule is, Make what you say so clear that nobody can possibly fail to understand you. Von Moltke's final instructions to his officers at the beginning of the Franco-Prussian War were, "Remember, gentlemen, that any order which can be misunderstood will be misunderstood."

Most of the thousands of movie houses in Canada are filled night after night because people like pictures and stories. Here are two suggestions for you. Paint word pictures and introduce occasionally an incident or an anecdote to illustrate a point. Use quotations, blackboard diagrams or sketches, photographs, and models to make your points clear and to hold the interest of your classmates.

ANECDOTE

An anecdote is a brief incident which leads up to a humorous or surprising point or climax. The following six anecdotes will show you what to look for:

1

George H. Doran, American publisher, tells the story of how Charles W. Gordon, D.D., came to be known as Ralph Connor. He says that as a young minister Dr. Gordon was with the Canadian Northwest Missionary Society in Manitoba and wrote, in story form, some sketches of his own parish, which he sent to the "Westminster Magazine" published in Toronto, and edited by Reverend Dr. James A. MacDonald.

For these articles Dr. Gordon used a pseudonym made from the first syllable of the first two names of his society, Cannor. "MacDonald looked at it, misread the name for Connor, and wondered what the man meant by using such an isolated and vagrant name. He thought a moment for some rhythmic first name for Connor and then and there christened him Ralph, and so was born Ralph Connor."

2

John Buchan,—Lord Tweedsmuir, one time Governor-General of Canada—tells two amusing anecdotes showing something of Sir Walter Scott's domestic relations. It seems that Sir Walter did not consider his own poetry of supreme merit and, moreover, had the good sense to see that it would do no good for his children to be too conscious of his reputation.

James Ballantyne, Scott's, publisher, once asked Scott's daughter Sophia what she thought of "The Lady of the Lake." She answered,

"Oh, I have not read it. Papa says there's nothing so bad for young people as reading bad poetry."

At another time young Walter Scott was dubbed "The Lady of the Lake" at the high school he attended, and not having heard of his father's work, thought he had been called a girl and engaged in a violent fist fight.

3

Many stories are current that reveal the unusual wit of Lord Darling. better known as Mr. Justice Darling. On one occasion a salesman pleaded that he be released from jury duty on account of being deaf in one ear:

"You can go," said Judge Darling. "I cannot have anyone in the jury box who cannot hear both sides."

4

During the hearing of another case Judge Darling was disturbed by a young man who kept moving about in the rear of the court.

"Young man," he exclaimed, "you are making a good deal of unnecessary noise. What are you doing?"

"I have lost my overcoat and am trying to find it," the young man replied.

"Well," retorted the Judge, "people often lose whole suits in here without all that fuss."

5

(This anecdote will help you to remember that the past participle of *get* is *got*.)

From his office a New York business man telegraphed to his wife at their home in a remote suburb, "I have gotten tickets for the opera to-night." The telegram delivered was, "I have got ten tickets for the opera to-night."

Delighted, she went to the phone and invited eight friends to the opera that night. All joyously accepted.

When the party of nine reached the opera house, the husband was astonished. As soon as he realized that he had eight guests, he hurried off in search of tickets. He found in front of the box office a "Standing Room Only" sign and on the sidewalk speculators selling tickets at exorbitant prices. His mistake in a verb form proved expensive.

6

There was a discussion in class about the creation. Roger spoke up excitedly: "But my father says we are descended from monkeys."

"Now, that's all right. That's all right, Roger," said the teacher. "But we haven't time to discuss your private family affairs here in class."

Practice 6. Anecdotes

1. What is a pun? Who can give an example?

2. What is meant by the incongruous? The whimsical? Give examples.

3. Who can give examples of humorous exaggeration or understatement? Name humorists who have used these devices.

4. What is satire?

5. What is good and poor taste in telling anecdotes?

Standards for Telling an Anecdote

1. *Begin promptly.*

2. *Travel directly towards the point of the story. Don't waste a word.*

3. *Make your point and stop.*

4. *Enjoy your own story but don't laugh while telling it.*

Practice 7. Telling an Anecdote

Your teacher will announce two or three days in advance "Anecdote Day". Find a good anecdote in a newspaper, magazine, or book—for example, in the writings of Irvin S. Cobb, Ring Lardner, A. A. Milne, Will Rogers, Stephen Leacock, or James M. Barrie—and prepare to tell it. Perhaps you can find an anecdote about Sir Wilfrid Laurier, Sir John A. Macdonald, Abraham Lincoln, Adolph Hitler, Ramsay Macdonald, Charles A. Lindbergh, Amelia Earhart, Richard E. Byrd, or another famous man or woman. Most biographies and autobiographies, such as Chauncey M. Depew's *My Memories of Eighty Years*, W. T. Grenfell's *Adrift on an Icepan*, Helen Keller's *Story of My Life*, Hamlin Garland's *A Son of the Middle Border*, and Jacob A. Riis's *The Making of an American*, include anecdotes.

BEGINNING AND ENDING

First and last impressions are especially important. If the beginning is inviting, your classmates will gladly listen to your speech; if your ending is forceful, they will remember your chief point. If you have two minutes for a speech, time yourself often enough to be sure that you can finish within the two minutes. If the chairman's gavel, bell, or lead pencil stops you, your speech is left hanging in the air and your hearers know that you did not reach your most important point.

Don't utter a word until you have the attention of the entire class. Take a breath. Then speak clearly and firmly.

STANDARDS FOR SPEAKERS

1. *Have a definite purpose and make it clear to your listeners.*
2. *Find adequate, interesting material.*
3. *Plan.*
4. *Practise your speech but don't memorize it.*
5. *Walk to the front of the room as if you had something important to say. Pause a moment and take a breath before beginning to speak. Then speak clearly and firmly. Arouse interest with your first sentence.*
6. *Stand easily, not stiffly. Avoid annoying mannerisms.*
7. *Look at your hearers and talk to them as individuals. Note whether everyone is listening.*
8. *Overcome nervousness by preparing your speech thoroughly and by taking a lively interest in your subject and your audience. If you think about your subject and your audience, you will forget about yourself.*
9. *Speak distinctly and energetically. Don't talk too fast. Take time to end your sentences clearly*
10. *Use a low-pitched, pleasant voice. Speak audibly but don't shout.*
11. *Show by a silence where each sentence ends.*
12. *Avoid* ur *and any unnecessary* well, why, and, but, *or* so.
13. *Avoid errors in grammar, word choice, and pronunciation.*
14. *Make what you say so clear that nobody can possibly fail to understand you.*

15. *Give examples, illustrations, and lively, concrete details.*
16. *End with a forceful sentence. Speak the last sentence slowly and vigorously.*
17. *When you finish your talk, pause for a moment and then turn and walk back to your seat.*

Practice 8. Making a Speech

Prepare to speak to the class entertainingly on one of the following topics. Have a good beginning and a good ending sentence. Every time you practise your speech at home, carry out suggestions 5 to 17 on page 51. This is the way to form good speaking habits.

1. My favourite book. 2. A recent exploration. 3. Making moving pictures. 4. A pet. 5. An interesting experiment. 6. A camping experience. 7. Tramps I have met. 8. A hero. 9. Caught in a storm. 10. My hobby. 11. Why I should like to be a doctor (or something else). 12. My experience as a worker in a store, a bank, an office, a printing shop, or a factory. 13. My Boy Scout work. 14. My Girl Guide work. 15. How I trained my dog. 16. What I saw and heard at the game. 17. How I study English (or another subject). 18. My home duties. 19. My outside interests. 20. What I saw in the woods. 21. My neighbours. 22. The play that won the game. 23. My favourite pictures. 24. The kind of movie I like.

Practice 9. Making a Speech

Health is a corner stone of a happy and successful life and is especially important to a speaker. Prepare to give the class worth-while ideas on one of these topics:

1. Dr. Banting's researches. 2. How to form health habits. 3. A healthy mind. 4. The air in our homes. 5. A healthy mouth. 6. Eating to live. 7. Posture. 8. Healthy feet. 9. Care of the eyes. 10. The benefits of outdoor exercise. 11. Dressing for health and comfort. 12. Alcohol. 13. Tobacco. 14. Madame Curie. 15. Louis Pasteur. 16. Taking care of a sick person. 17. Preventing accidents. 18. First aid. 19. Healthful occupations. 20. How to prevent colds. 21. A sensible school lunch. 22. Sanitary conditions in our town (or school). 23. Why avoid drugs? 24. Why the mosquito and the fly are dangerous. 25. Milk as a food.

ANNOUNCEMENT

An announcement should be explicit. It should leave nothing to one's imagination. In addition to telling attractively what the event is, an announcer should make clear the time, the place, the date, the price of tickets, and the purpose of the event. If necessary, explain how to reach the place.

The Young People's Society of the Westminster United Church, 12th Street and Eastlake Avenue, takes pleasure in announcing its annual play, a side-splitting comedy entitled "Digging Up the Dirt". The cast includes Ruth Rich, Royal Bauser, and many more talented young actors, and the play can't help but be a great success. It will be held at the church on Friday, May 25, at 8:15 sharp. Tickets are fifty cents and may be purchased from any member of the society or at the door. Come, or you'll regret it.

Practice 10. Making an Announcement

Announce either in your English class or in one or more home rooms a game, a club meeting, an entertainment, a lecture, a contest, an exhibit, a social event, or another class or school activity.

INTRODUCTION OF A SPEAKER

For a speech of introduction one needs an outline somewhat like this:
1. The purpose of the meeting.
2. The speaker, his subject, and achievements which qualify him to speak on the subject.
3. The audience's good fortune in having an opportunity to hear him.
4. Words of introduction ["It is my privilege (or a pleasure) to introduce to you ——"].

The speech should be brief and should not embarrass with flattery. It should arouse the attention of the audience and stimulate their interest in the speaker and his subject. The name and the subject should be spoken clearly. If the speaker needs no introduction, one sentence may be enough.

PRESENTATION AND ACCEPTANCE SPEECHES

Sincerity is the keynote of a good presentation or acceptance speech. A smile is always a help; don't act as if you were master of ceremonies at an unveiling. If you are naturally witty, a bright sally will add life to your speech, but forced humour is pathetic.

When presenting a gift—
1. Tell why the gift is presented.
2. Explain why the particular gift was chosen.
3. Make clear that you are representing a group.

When accepting a gift—
1. Without gushing express surprise and pleasure.
2. Thank the givers sincerely and appreciatively and comment on the beauty, usefulness, or value of the gift.
3. Express your best wishes for the success of the club.

Example of presentation speech:

Miss Miller, in the name of the members of the XYZ Club, let me present this writing case to you in the hope that you will remember us and write us about your travels in England. We have enjoyed your considerate and careful supervision of our club, we have enjoyed your presence among us as we grew from four members to twenty-four, and we hope that, upon your return, you will again take up your work with us. May your trip be the real fulfilment of many dreams, and may you return to us with new tales of adventure — PUPIL'S SPEECH.

Practice 11. Introducing a Speaker

1. Let A introduce an assembly speaker, and B, representing the person introduced, speak briefly.

2. Present or accept a gift, a medal, a trophy, or a banner, for example, a baseball championship trophy, a birthday gift, or a gift to the retiring president of a society.

AFTER-DINNER SPEECH

The after-dinner speech offers a special opportunity for the use of the anecdote to drive home an important point and for original treatment of commonplace themes. It should not, however, degenerate into a mere series of anecdotes or a long harangue. The speaker may inform or point a moral; he often reminisces. But since the purpose of his speech is mainly to entertain and to promote a feeling of comradeship and intimacy, a long serious address is ordinarily out of order.

Practice 12. After-Dinner Speech

Prepare a programme of after-dinner speeches for a meeting of the class club or in honour of a championship team or a school celebrity. Select a toastmaster to give a short introductory speech setting the mood of the occasion and to introduce the speakers. Each pupil should prepare a two-minute after-dinner speech appropriate to the occasion. He should have something definite and worth while to say but should enliven his talk with wit or humour.

UNIT FIVE

Sentence Sense

Do you know the difference between a sentence and a sentence fragment? Between one sentence and two sentences?

TEST A (*Diagnostic*). SENTENCE SENSE

Indicate by *0, 1, 2,* or *3* the number of complete sentences in each of the following. On your paper place a period between the number of the example and your answer.

Examples:

a. I left my baby brother and went to work on my homework soon I heard a thump and ran to see what had happened.

b. Hoping that you will visit us during either your Christmas or your spring vacation.

ANSWERS

a. 2
b. 0

The first example is two sentences. The *0* indicates that *b* is not a sentence.

THE TEST

1. Doctor Joachim an eye specialist from New York who had failed in an attempt to restore a man's eyesight and had moved to Labrador.
2. I killed the snake and held the bird in my hands soon it flapped its wings and flew away
3. It is wise to use a small double boiler for this the upper part for cooking the syrup and the lower part filled with boiling water to keep the syrup hot
4. One September when my father mother sister and I arrived in Saint John on our way back to Fredericton after spending our vacation at Rye Beach New Hampshire
5. Jo set the table and Meg started the dinner they were going to have lobster salad bread strawberries and cream
6. A man on second base one down and Jimmy Foxx coming up to bat
7. Twelve members of the Cardinal Audubon Club went on a hike and picnic on Monday May 25 under the supervision of Miss Luciana Snyder, the picnic was held at South Park, before eating supper we saw about ten different kinds of birds in the fields and woods

55

8. What an awful feeling one gets when walking down a dark lonely road at night the trees swaying in the breeze the branches rubbing together making weird noises

9. Have you read *Robinson Crusoe* the story of an English sailor who was shipwrecked on a desert island it was written by Daniel Defoe

10. *The Animal Story Book* by Andrew Lang tells about the life of different animals where they are found how they live and what they eat

PHRASE, SUBORDINATE CLAUSE, AND SENTENCE

A phrase has neither subject nor predicate; a clause has a subject and a predicate. A sentence or a principal clause contains a subject and a predicate and needs no introductory word; a subordinate clause, except a direct quotation, needs an introductory word either expressed or understood. A sentence makes complete sense—really says or asks something—when standing alone; a subordinate clause, as a rule, does not make sense when standing alone.

Relative pronouns and subordinate conjunctions introduce subordinate clauses. The commonly used relative pronouns are *who, which, what,* and *that.* For a list of subordinate conjunctions see page 506.

Practice 1. Phrases, Subordinate Clauses, Sentences

Which of the following are phrases? Subordinate clauses? Sentences? Can you tell why?

1. Every player on the team contributing his share to the victory against the seniors

2. Since every player on the team contributed his share to the victory against the seniors

3. Every player on the team contributed his share to the victory against the seniors

4. As Father Donnelly, the chaplain, gallantly led the men onward in the face of murderous German fire

5. In the face of murderous German fire Father Donnelly, the chaplain, gallantly led the men onward

6. Father Donnelly, the chaplain, gallantly leading the men onward in the face of murderous German fire

7. In Tennyson's "The Charge of the Light Brigade" the thunderous attack of the cavalry on the Russian gun emplacements

8. When the cavalry thunderously attacked the Russian gun emplacements in Tennyson's "The Charge of the Light Brigade"

9. "The Charge of the Light Brigade" by Tennyson paints a vivid picture of the thunderous attack of the cavalry on the Russian gun emplacements

10. The cavalry in Tennyson's "The Charge of the Light Brigade" thunderously attacking the Russian gun emplacements

SENTENCE FRAGMENT

If a period is used after a part of a sentence that does not make complete sense when standing alone, the fraction of a sentence is called a sentence fragment.

An exception is the elliptical sentence in which the subject and verb of the principal clause are sometimes omitted.

How old are you? Thirteen. (I am thirteen years old.)
What high school are you attending? La Grande. (I am attending La Grande High School.)

Pupils sometimes incorrectly use periods and capitals for incomplete sentences or sentence fragments. Make certain that you write real sentences. Do not put a period after a fragment of a sentence. If you are not sure whether you have written a sentence, ask yourself, "Have I made a statement?" or, better yet, find the subject and the verb of the principal clause.

Learn how to avoid the three following kinds of sentence fragments.

1. A group of words without a verb is a sentence fragment.

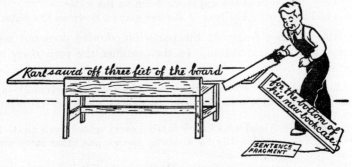

Karl sawed off three feet of the board for the bottom of his new bookcase

(Right) In the White House we saw the different dishes and desks used by former presidents, the large library, and the swimming pool.
(Wrong) In the White House we saw the different dishes and desks used by former presidents. The large library and the swimming pool.
(Right) Howard Pyle has written some good stories—for example, *Men of Iron, Merry Adventures of Robin Hood,* and *Otto of the Silver Hand.*
(Wrong) Howard Pyle has written some good stories. For example, *Men of Iron, Merry Adventures of Robin Hood,* and *Otto of the Silver Hand.*

In each example labelled "wrong" the second so-called "sentence" has no verb. Therefore it cannot be a sentence.

Many authors occasionally use sentence fragments intentionally. Perhaps your teacher will not object to your using now and then a sentence fragment if you place an asterisk (*) before it and write "*Sentence fragment" at the bottom of the page. But first make sure that you always know a sentence fragment when you see it.

Practice 2.   Correcting Sentence Fragments

What is the sentence fragment in each of these? Correct.

1. We first sailed to Bermuda. Then to Cuba and Puerto Rico.
2. Following the band were soldiers carrying flags. Flags of all colours, flags of all nations, but mostly Union Jacks.
3. The well-dressed high school girl is always clean and tidy. Not only on one special day, but every day.
4. The flames were extinguished, but the ship, once an enormous sky bird, was transformed into a charred mass of wood and twisted steel. A sorrowful ending for such a giant.
5. The character of Aunt Polly in *Tom Sawyer* was modelled after Mark Twain's mother. A lovable, charitable, gentle woman.
6. My hobby now is collecting things. Stamps, coins, leaves, and curious stones.

2. Participles, verbal nouns, and infinitives do not make statements or ask questions and therefore never take the place of the verb of the sentence. No word ending with an *ing* suffix is, by itself, a predicate verb.

(Sentence)   The rays of the sun shone down on the water.
(Sentence Fragment)   The rays of the sun shining down on the water.

In the sentence fragment the participle *shining* does not make a statement or ask a question. In the sentence the verb *shone* makes a statement.

(One Sentence)   Good school spirit is what every school needs most—a loyal, hearty backing by the pupils of sports, dances, and other extracurricular activities.
(Two Sentences)   Good school spirit is what every school needs most. Pupils should loyally and heartily back sports, dances, and other extracurricular activities.
(Sentence and Sentence Fragment)   Good school spirit is what every school needs most. A loyal, hearty backing by the pupils of sports, dances, and other extracurricular activities. (In the sentence fragment the verbal noun *backing* does not make a statement or ask a question.)

To get rid of a sentence fragment you may either add it to the preceding sentence or make the fragment a complete sentence.

Practice 3.   Correcting Sentence Fragments

In each of the following get rid of the sentence fragment by writing one or two good sentences. Show that in each of your sentences there is a verb that makes a statement.

1. Lewis and Murray took part in "The Christmas Carol". Lewis taking the part of Scrooge, and Murray of Bob Cratchit.
2. My sister joined the Farm Service Force to do her bit for her country. To free a man for active duty.

3. A sailing ship flying the British flag was becalmed on a placid expanse of water. The mariners lying on the deck with parched lips and throats.
4. Last summer we stayed at Briar Falls Inn. An old hotel famed for its comfort, its excellent food, and its facilities for summer sports.
5. That night we learned of an imminent enemy attack. By intercepting and decoding a message from their headquarters.
6. Canada has many lakes, rivers, and forests. The largest rivers being the St. Lawrence and the Mackenzie.

3. Most sentence fragments have verbs that make statements. These verbs, however, are in subordinate clauses.

(Sentence) Dr. J. W. Gray of Baltimore is spending the summer in Nova Scotia.
(Sentence Fragment) Dr. J. W. Gray of Baltimore, who is spending the summer in Nova Scotia. (The clause beginning with *who* is an adjective clause modifying *Dr. J. W. Gray.*)
(Sentence) After lunch we went through Nature's Trail, where there are all sorts of trees.
(Sentence and Sentence Fragment) After lunch we went through Nature's Trail. Where there are all sorts of trees.

Practice 4. Correcting Sentence Fragments

Correct the following. If necessary, supply a subject and a verb to make a principal clause. Draw one line under the simple subject and two lines under the predicate verb of the principal clause or clauses in each correct sentence you write.

1. I found a good friend in Tom Grogan. One whom I shall never forget.
2. Everyone should come out to see the game between the seniors and the juniors. The date of which will be announced later.
3. Rex proved to be a great pal to all of us, and we were very much attached to him. Till one sad day our happiness was turned to grief.
4. Igor Sikorski, who by years of experimentation conceived a new type of plane, the helicopter.
5. Bill Smith had will power, courage, and grit. All qualities which helped to make him a success in later years.
6. At the civilian defense meetings I learned what to do in case of bombings. That is, how to extinguish an incendiary bomb, how to aid the wounded, and, most important of all, how to conduct myself.
7. Then the pupils sang the school song. After which they went back to their classrooms for the next recitation.
8. In *Guadalcanal Diary*, Richard Tregaskis gives a clear picture of soldiers at the front. How they fought, how they thought, and how some died.

RUN-ON SENTENCE

If a sentence ends with a comma or no punctuation mark and the next one begins with a small letter, the error is called a run-on sentence. The failure to use periods, question marks, and capitals is a serious fault, because it shows inability to recognize a sentence.

A capital starts a sentence and a period stops it. Periods and capitals are signals which help the reader to understand what the writer is saying to him. Reading a paragraph aloud is one way to find where to put capitals and periods.

(Two Sentences)   What do you think of our baseball team?   It hasn't lost a game yet.

(Run-on Sentence)   What do you think of our baseball team, it hasn't lost a game yet.

A question mark should be placed at the end of the sentence "What do you think of our baseball team?" *You* is the subject; *do think*, the verb.

(Two Sentences)   Passengers of all sizes and ages crowded into the bus. The young girls were in gay, summery dresses.

(Run-on Sentences)   Passengers of all sizes and ages crowded into the bus, the young girls were in gay, summery dresses.

A period should be placed after *bus*, because that is the end of the first sentence. *Passengers* is the subject; *crowded*, the verb.

SEMICOLON AND SMALL LETTER

A semicolon is used between the principal clauses of a compound sentence if there is no conjunction between them (read carefully page 549).   When in doubt, use the period and the capital.

Instantly the tumult started; the men yelled and beat upon tom-toms and trees.

I have many friends; among them are Esther, Estelle, and Gladys.

Practice 5.   Correcting Run-on Sentences

Punctuate and capitalize the following. Draw one line under the subject word and two lines under the verb of every simple sentence or principal clause.

1. When Dr. Jekyll changed his form he called himself Mr Hyde as Mr Hyde he was very dangerous
2. Jim hit a low ball over the first baseman's head it struck at least a foot inside the foul line
3. All evening as we drove along the fog had been growing thicker by ten o'clock we couldn't see five feet in front of us
4. I have sixty tropical fish in a tank last year I had only three pairs of them
5. Do not delay send your order to-day
6. It took me a half hour to mend the stocking neatly how I wished that I had taken a minute in the morning to fix that little run
7. Well just wait till we play you again we'll knock you right out of the championship race
8. The Indian called for water it was Deerslayer who got the water for him
9. When the airplane was first invented its maximum speed was about thirty-five miles an hour to-day the Lockheed P-38 fighter can average over four hundred miles an hour

SENTENCE SENSE

10. Concentration has a great deal to do with studying if a person does not concentrate upon the subject he does not learn it
11. While the pirates were looking for the treasure a voice was heard in the trees above this frightened them
12. Dolph Camilli of the Dodgers is at the plate the score is one to nothing in favour of St. Louis it is the last half of the ninth inning and two men are out
13. Robinson Crusoe was on a sailboat which was wrecked he was the sole survivor
14. Zane Grey's style of writing is free and easy he puts a humorous incident in to relieve the tension of a sad part
15. Hit the ball and run to first base if the pitcher catches the ball you are out
16. Agnes what kind of book are you reading is it a mystery story
17. On the top of a decayed branch of the tree I saw a woodpecker feebly struggling coming closer I saw that a bullsnake had wrapped itself around the bird and was slowly squeezing it to death

Practice 6. Punctuating and Capitalizing

Punctuate and capitalize the following paragraph. Be sure to place a period at the end of a sentence and to begin a sentence with a capital. There are eight sentences.

ELECTRONICS—THE NEW SCIENCE

the discovery of electronics is one of the most important contributions science has made to the building of a new world through electronics every home will probably soon enjoy television programmes daily the electron microscope enables scientists to magnify 100,000 times the image of a mosquito larva the X-ray which is electronic in origin locates shell fragments detects tuberculosis and treats skin disorders electronic tubes turn on highway lights as the sky darkens and turn them off when morning comes electronic eyes inspect sheets of metal and spot tiny defects other electronic devices count traffic in tunnels inspect fruit aid ships to dock detect lurking submarines and fill tooth paste tubes only man's imagination limits the possibilities of electronics a new science for a new world — Pupil.

Practice 7. Punctuating and Capitalizing

Punctuate and capitalize this story. Be sure to place a period at the end of a sentence and to begin a sentence with a capital. Insert needed apostrophes and quotation marks.

A BEAR

While at camp last summer I spent a day that I shall never forget my friend Mildred and I were strolling through the woods on a sultry day in August suddenly I looked behind us and saw a strange black animal
Mildred whats that I asked excitedly
She turned around to see the cause of my disturbance and shouted I really dont know what it is but it looks like a bear

Impossible bears dont come around here I snapped striving to appear calm but not succeeding you must be wrong at least I hope so

Suddenly the creature growled my heart jumped without bothering to look again I started to run Mildred was at my heels what fate was to be ours suppose that queer beast overtook us I shuddered at the thought

After what seemed hours we reached camp with that animal peacefully trailing us Mildred and I ran into our tent and collapsed on the cot

The counsellor who had been reading a book glanced up

Whats the matter with you girls she asked you look as if you had seen a ghost

Wild animal we both shouted breathlessly

After looking us over carefully to see whether or not we were crazy she stepped out of the tent in a few minutes she returned giggling

You foolish girls she laughed its a dog with some burs in his hair after saying this she strolled out soon the whole camp knew of our mistake and we were the laughingstock for a few days

Since that day I have learned the difference between a dog and a bear — Pupil.

Does this picture suggest a story?

Practice 8.   Writing a Story

Write a story about a bear, a dog, or another animal. In the introduction answer the questions "Who?" "When?" "Where?" "What?" Make the reader curious when you start the story, and keep him in suspense till you near the end. Make the story move swiftly. Have a point or exciting part, and make it stand out by going into details. Conclude briefly.

After writing the story, look through it carefully for run-on sentences and sentence fragments. If you find any, correct the errors. Read the story aloud as a final check of the wording and sentence structure.

TEST B (*Mastery*). Sentence Sense

Median—8·6

Indicate by *0, 1, 2,* or *3* the number of complete sentences in each of the following. On your paper place a period between the number of the example and your answer.

1. Penrod was a queer sort of child it seems as if the only pleasure he got out of life was in misbehaving
2. If air is removed from the siphon either by filling the tube with water or by sucking the air out
3. Have you ever wanted to read a book that was different from other books a book that does not have a beautiful girl for its heroine and that does not make the heroine the belle of the ball
4. For instance the scene in which Dr Grenfell is the only living object on an expanse of ice
5. The new members of the Press Club are purchasing pins the pins are silver with the word *Journalism* in blue enamel the pupils who were members of the club last year already have their pins
6. The next ball pitched was over the plate and Ott knocked a line drive between Vaughan and Reese both players ran after the ball as fast as they could but neither touched it
7. Thanking you again and hoping I haven't inconvenienced you in any way
8. The waves breaking over the rocks along the coast and the white foam that shot up out of the water from the terrific impact of the waves
9. Have you read *Rebecca of Sunnybrook Farm* the story of a carefree little girl who lived with two aunts it was written by Kate Douglas Wiggin.
10. Three characters of *Tom Sawyer* are Tom a mischievous lad with a lively imagination Huckleberry Finn a homeless boy who is Tom's friend and Aunt Polly

UNIT SIX

Correct and Clear Sentences

MASTERY TEST A—*Grammar*

Select the correct or preferred word or expression to fill each blank:

1, 2. She looks —— she —— tired. (as if, like) (was, were)

3. One of the —— spots in the world is the subway station at Forty-second Street and Broadway, at rush hour. (busiest, most busiest)

4, 5. As we were walking along, we —— to a little sparrow —— on the ground. (came, come) (laying, lying)

6, 7. He is one of those people who always —— to be different —— their associates. (wish, wishes) (from, than)

8. Near the windows —— always seated three men working at the presses. (are, is)

9, 10. Penelope told the wooers that she —— marry one of them as soon as she —— her web. (will, would) (finished, finishes)

11, 12, 13. This is just —— an eye or a hand —— to demand pay for —— services to the body. (as if, like) (was, were) (its, their)

14. I expected to —— you at the game. (see, have seen)

15. At the quarter mile post Bright Star was in the lead, but soon Moonbeam —— him. (passed, passes)

16. When Bill got tired, he —— down. (lay, laid)

17, 18. Was it —— —— you saw yesterday? (she, her) (who, whom)

19. —— do you think threw the snowball? (who, whom)

20. Everyone did —— best. (his their)

21. When Rip Van Winkle awoke, he thought he —— only one night. (slept, had slept)

22. They asked me —— my master was. (who, whom)

23. One of the handkerchiefs that —— given me at Christmas time has an initial on it. (was, were)

24. When —— we start to the basketball game? (shall, will)

25. If it —— stayed warm a week longer, the daffodils would be blooming. (had, would have)

MASTERY TEST B—*Grammar*

Select the correct or preferred word or expression to fill each blank:

1. If she —— told an incident, her report would have been more entertaining. (had, would have)

2. The first important step in a person's life is taken when responsibilities are placed on —— shoulders. (his, their)

3. Pork is —— now than beef. (cheaper, more cheaper)

4. The door was opened by a pleasant young lady ——, I knew, must be Miss Ryan. (who, whom)

5. If anyone had come in, I should have heard ——. (him, them)
6. —— carefully concealed behind the rocks, the boys took turns in guarding the entrance to the cave. (laying, lying)
7. His daughter —— so sad before, and it hurt him to see her grieve. (had never been, was never)
8, 9. "If I —— the king," grumbled Kaji, "I would never ask my subjects to work —— they were slaves." (was, were) (as if, like)
10. Close at my heels trotted Bimbo, ——, I thought, was securely locked in the cellar at home. (who, whom)
11. By to-morrow morning we —— have our first glimpse of the Rockies. (shall, will)
12. He found Westbury very different —— the shabby towns surrounding it. (from, than)
13. Suddenly Clark shook himself free from the rest of the players and —— across the goal line. (plunged, plunges)
14. On the edge of the water —— a battered lifeboat. (laid, lay)
15. Crater Lake is one of those crystal clear lakes which —— like a mirror every cloud and shadow. (reflect, reflects)
16. No one had expected —— the house in such a dilapidated condition. (to find, to have found)
17, 18. "My aunts treat me —— I —— still a chubby boy in rompers," said Big Bill disgustedly. (as if, like) (was, were)
19. The best part of these wild animal stories —— that they are true. (are, is)
20, 21. At first Clive couldn't believe that it was really —— —— the class had elected president. (he, him) (who, whom)
22. One of Mother's best china plates —— broken last evening. (was, were)
23. Just then Peter stumbled into the cabin shouting to us that he —— a ghost. (had just seen, just saw)
24. If the bull —— us, our picnic would have been a huge success. (wouldn't have chased, hadn't chased)
25. All the guests insisted that they —— queer noises in the attic the night before. (had heard, heard)

SYNTACTICAL REDUNDANCE

Syntactical redundance—that is a hard name for a childish mistake. *Redundance* means *excess; syntactical* means *according to the rules of syntax.* Hence syntactical redundance is using two words to do the same grammatical job or using words that do no useful work in the sentence. Sometimes, for example, a pronoun and its antecedent are wrongly used as subject of the same verb.

(Right) The kings at that time usually wore crowns.
(Wrong) The kings at that time they usually wore crowns.
(Right) My father solved the problem for me.
(Wrong) My father he solved the problem for me.

They and *he* are omitted, because these words have no work to do in the sentences. *Kings* is the subject of *wore; father,* of *solved.*

A pronoun and its antecedent are not used as the subject of the same verb.

Occasionally a preposition is carelessly repeated, has no object, has no work to do in the sentence.

(Wrong) Antonio had no money with which to pay Shylock with.

This sentence should look about as queer to you as an automobile with a second engine behind the rear seat.

(Right) Antonio had no money with which to pay Shylock.

Often a preposition is needlessly inserted.

(Right) In the new building the principal will have an office about the size of our present library.

(Awkward) In the new building the principal will have an office of about the size of our present library.

The preposition is understood. Its omission avoids awkwardness.

(Right) Clifford met a young man whose tastes and ambitions were like his own.

(Wrong) Clifford met with a young man whose tastes and ambitions were like his own.

Man is the object of the verb *met; with* is not needed.

(Right) An example of a story having a lesson is Galsworthy's "Quality."

(Wrong) An example of a story having a lesson is in Galsworthy's "Quality."

"Quality" is the predicate nominative of the verb *is; in* is not needed.

Cross out every unnecessary preposition or conjunction.

Practice 1. Sentence Correction

Correct the following sentences. Show that each word which you omit has no work to do in the sentence.

1. Jack one day he fractured his leg.
2. Where have you been at?
3. The trees they make the country gloomy on dark days.
4. Mr. Holmes told about some humorous anecdotes and jokes.
5. The number of classrooms in the new high school will be double over that in the old building.
6. The trustees, having worn themselves out in these quarrels, they had no energy left to make the necessary changes in the building.
7. In through the open window could be seen a boy of about eighteen years of age.
8. From whence did he come?
9. Susie she won't go.
10. He signed to the bond without reading it carefully.
11. We saw two rowboats approach towards us.
12. Leonard W. Wilson crashed to his death at Mitchell Field while he was trying out a gull-like plane on which he had laboured years to perfect.

13. My friend to whom I gave the book to did not return it.
14. The words to which I refer to are those ending in *ing*.
15. Would you like to know with what kind of boys I associated with?
16. A hero is a person to whom we look up to.
17. The great Canadian of whom I am going to write about is Bliss Carman.
18. Sonny selected the faith in which he wanted to be baptized in.
19. Vary your sentences in the ways in which you have studied in class.
20. It was agreed upon that Shylock should have a pound of Antonio's flesh.
21. Mrs. Floyd is a woman of about fifty years of age.
22. The pace set by the leader was killing, but nevertheless Bob stayed with his opponent.
23. They gave chase to the bandits, but, however, they soon gave up hope of catching them.
24. The instructor said that if anyone hadn't finished his composition that he should have it ready on Monday.
25. It is quite natural that when he found an opportunity to defeat his rival that he should take advantage of it.
26. I am trying to find the vocation to which I am best suited for.
27. Mabel was an attractive high school girl of about sixteen years of age.
28. They were looking in the direction from which the cart was to come from.
29. Pirate treasure is a subject about which everyone dreams about at one time or another.
30. The plot is surrounded by a hedge of about four feet high.

ELLIPTICAL SENTENCES

We sometimes omit words which are important grammatically but which are not necessary to make our meaning clear. The sentence from which one or more such words have been omitted is elliptical.

Answers to Questions

Who is there? I [am here].
How long are you going to stay? [I am going to stay] About two weeks.
Whose book is this? [It is] Harry's [book].

Clause Introduced by **Than** or **As**

Our baseball team made a better record this year than [it made] last year.
Jenkins is not so good a pitcher as White [is good].

Conjunctions and Relative Pronouns

I wish [that] I knew the answer.
Had they started [if they had started] an hour earlier, they would have escaped the heavy traffic in the city.
You are the boy [whom] I mean.

Subject, Verb, or Subject and Verb

When [he was] only fifty years old, he retired.
[It is] Twenty-three, to be exact.
[That is] All right, I accept your offer.
[You] Hurry home.
Why [do you] not try harder to form the right kind of friendships?
While [I was] spending a week in Montreal, I enjoyed the tobogganing.

Avoiding Repetition

1. I shall complete Ernest Thompson Seton's *Lives of the Hunted* to-night if I can [complete it].
2. I shall not go to the play unless you wish to [go].

Practice 2. Elliptical Sentences

Insert in brackets the grammatically important words which have been omitted because they are not necessary to make the meaning clear:

1. How old is Arthur? Fourteen.
2. What are you doing? Nothing.
3. Who is there? I.
4. Borup's *A Tenderfoot with Peary* is a more entertaining book than Schurz's *Abraham Lincoln.*
5. Thank you.
6. If necessary, I shall come earlier.
7. Murphy plays right end; Howe, left end.
8. If possible, meet me at nine o'clock to-morrow morning.
9. A tiger is physically stronger than a lion.
10. "Come back, then, and let me know what he says," yelled Harvey. "I certainly will," called Earl.

INCORRECT OMISSIONS

Subjects, verbs, objects, prepositions, and conjunctions needed to make the meaning clear are sometimes omitted.

Subject

(Right)   I hope to receive the suit before December 1.
(Wrong)   Hoping to receive the suit before December 1.

There is no subject. *Hoping* is a participle, not a verb form that makes a statement. To express the idea in a correct sentence we need to insert a subject and use a form of the verb that makes a statement.

(Right)   When George was only four years old, his father died.
(Wrong)   When only four years old, George's father died.

The wrong sentence seems to say that the father died at the age of four.

Verb

(Complete)   I never have understood, and never will understand the mechanism of a radio.
(Wrong)   I never have, and never will, understand the mechanism of a radio.

"I never have understand" is ungrammatical.

Object

(Right)   The blind boy needs someone to educate him and care for him.
(Wrong)   The blind boy needs someone to educate and care for him.

In the wrong sentence the same *him* is used as the object of the infinitive *to educate* and of the preposition *for*. A word may be the object of two verbs or of two prepositions, but not of one verb and one preposition.

Preposition

(Right)   Carl graduated from (or was graduated from) Riverside Collegiate before entering Toronto University.

(Wrong)   Carl graduated Riverside Collegiate before entering Toronto University.

Graduate in this sentence does not take an object; one does not "graduate a school."

Conjunction

(Right)   My English mark is always as high as my French mark, or higher.

(Awkward)   My English mark is always as high or higher than my French mark.

Practice 3.   Incorrect Omissions

Supply the needed word or words. Give a reason for each change.

1. Jane says she has not and will not learn to play golf.
2. Each poem has a separate story to tell but are all linked together because of their relationship to King Arthur.
3. Elizabeth is as tall or taller than her mother.
4. Thanking you for the prompt shipment of the shoes.
5. I have never seen or spoken to him.
6. My brother graduated the University of Alberta last June.
7. When eight years old, my parents moved to Kamsack.
8. Did the boys and girls pity or make fun of the intoxicated man?
9. Is Chicago the chief railroad centre of United States?
10. This is a contest which everyone may compete.
11. The newsboy has a pair of broad shoulders and quite muscular.
12. I hope that your college career will be as successful as your high school.
13. The speed of the new car is almost equal to an airplane.
14. The record of our football team is as good as or better than last year's team.
15. There are two kinds of people who always have and always will exist.
16. He will have to serve a three-year term in jail or a thousand-dollar fine.
17. Geometry is interesting to me and therefore grasp it readily.
18. The town which Mary Antin lived in Russia was a dreary place.

UNITY

Unity means oneness. Every part of a sentence must be subordinate to one governing idea. Don't put into a sentence statements that conspicuously lack connection with each other. A sentence should express a single complete thought. If there are two main ideas in a sentence, they must be related parts of a larger idea.

(Right)   Sergeant Melville is a good leader of men and will make, I believe, an outstanding lieutenant.   (The two main ideas are parts of the large idea that Sergeant Melville has leadership ability.)

(Wrong)   Sergeant Melville is a good leader of men and almost every day he receives mail from home.   (The two ideas are in no way connected.)

Correct a lack of unity (1) by breaking a sentence into shorter sentences or (2) by subordinating one statement.   One main idea may have many modifiers.

(Right)   Punch, a Boston terrier, never chases cats.

(Wrong)   Punch never chases cats, and he is a Boston terrier.

Avoid compound sentences consisting of statements strung together with *and, but,* **and** *so.*   Don't overwork *and.*   The *and* habit is one of the worst English diseases.

(Right)   The call number of W. T. Grenfell's *Adrift on an Ice Pan,* a biography which I am reading, is B41.   (One principal clause.)

(Poor)   The name of my book is *Adrift on an Ice Pan* and the name of the author is W. T. Grenfell and the call number is B41, so the book is a biography.   (Four principal clauses.)

Practice 4.   Building Unified Sentences

Improve the following sentences:

1. Robert Browning married Elizabeth Barrett, and his first poem was published in 1840.
2. My uncle was welcomed by a frail old man who had white hair and a large library.
3. Bob is an excellent swimmer, and last Christmas he visited his cousin in Pittsburgh.
4. Give my regard to your mother, and I hope you are enjoying your work on a farm this summer.

5. Often Oliver Twist and some other boys would have to go away from the table hungry, so one day Oliver went up to the proprietor of the workhouse and asked for more food and when the proprietor heard this he turned him out into the street and poor Oliver was left penniless and homeless.

Avoid unnecessarily tacking an adjective clause to another adjective clause.

(Right) Among his minerals Ted displayed azurite, which is a copper ore.
(Poor) Among his minerals Ted displayed azurite, which is an ore from which copper is obtained.

Do not chop up the thought of one unified sentence into several short sentences. Subordinate the less important ideas.

(Right) Shakespeare is buried in the chancel of the large, venerable Stratford-on-Avon church, which is moldering with age.
(Primer Style) Shakespeare is buried in the Stratford-on-Avon church. He is buried in the chancel. The church is a large, venerable structure. It is moldering with age.

Practice 5. Building Unified Sentences

Improve the following sentences:

A. 1. The sensation is carried to the brain, which in turn sends out a message to your muscles, which do the work.
   2. The lecturer told us about the larch, which is a kind of pine tree which loses its needles in the fall.
   3. The Greek patriots fought long and courageously. They had to face great odds. Their achievement will be remembered.
   4. The museum displayed an astrolabe which is an instrument which was used in early navigation.
   5. Another way in which our school newspaper might be improved is by inserting more advertisements, which would indirectly pay for the pictures which are so badly needed.

B. 1. Friction robs machines of efficiency. Much energy is lost in heat. Ball bearings are used to reduce friction. Lubrication serves the same purpose.
   2. Mathematics stagnated for a long while. Then the zero was introduced. This eliminated the cumbersome system of the Romans. Great strides were made quickly.
   3. With great reluctance Frederick opened the front door to leave the house. He found himself face to face with a stranger. The stranger was a powerfully built man and had ruddy cheeks. The stranger was ascending the steps.
   4. *Ben Hur* tells the story of the young prince who was one of those who tried to free his country from the oppression of Roman tyrants who held the throne.
   5. The story tells about a ship which was caught on a reef near an island which was inhabited by cannibals.
   6. The journalism students who meet in Room 311 the first period under the supervision of Mr. Donnelly, who is chairman of the English Department, are comparing the newspapers of various schools.

Practice 6. Review of Unity

Correct the following sentences. How is unity violated in each?

A. 1. Molly has curly hair and blue eyes, and last week she beat me at tennis four sets out of five.

2. For my second supplementary report I read *Tarawa*. The author is Robert Sherrod. It is the stirring story of a Marine engagement.

3. There was a logical reason why General Nobile allowed himself to be taken first from the ice floe, but the outside world didn't know this, and on his return to civilization he was treated very coldly.

4. Edgar Allan Poe's life was short and tragic, and Poe is usually credited with the invention of the detective story.

B. 1. Petrovitch told the driver to wait. Then Petrovitch got out of the sleigh and entered the church. The church was feebly lit by two or three tapers.

2. Mr. Barclay began to read "Petit, the Poet," but just then the bell rang, so Mr. Barclay stopped reading, and he told the class to study the poem for Monday.

3. "The Spires of Oxford" is a poem honouring the Oxford men who were killed in World War I, in which many young men lost their lives.

4. *Wuthering Heights* is rather long, so I returned it to the library without finishing it, but I kept wondering how it ends, so finally I went back to the library and took the book out again.

COHERENCE

In a coherent sentence the parts are worded and arranged so that they stick together. Coherence includes (1) arrangement, (2) parallel structure, (3) connectives, and (4) clear reference of pronouns.

Arrangement

Put a participle close to the word modified. A participle, an infinitive, a verbal noun, a prepositional phrase, or an elliptical clause at the beginning of a sentence should relate in thought to the subject.

(Wrong) Standing on the ferryboat, many cargo vessels can be seen. (*Standing* seems to modify *vessels*. The vessels are not standing on the ferryboat.)

A participle "dangles" if there is no word in the sentence to which it is firmly attached.

(Right) A person standing on the ferryboat can see many cargo vessels.

(Right) From the ferryboat many cargo vessels can be seen.

(Wrong) Looking out my window, a runaway horse attracted my attention. (*Looking* seems to modify *horse*.)

(Right) Looking out my window, I saw a runaway horse. (*Looking modifies I*.)

If a participle dangles, we may (1) get rid of the participle, (2) place it near the word it modifies, or (3) put into the sentence some word for it to modify.

Practice 7.   Correcting Dangling Modifiers

Correct the following. If you correct a sentence by placing a participle near the word it modifies, tell what word the participle modifies.

Example:

Being a philatelist, most of my allowance is spent on stamps.
Being a philatelist, I spend most of my allowance on stamps.
Being is a participle modifying the pronoun *I*.

A. 1. Glancing through the magazine, the bright-coloured advertisements catch the eye.
   2. Having carefully prepared my lessons, a friend came in.
   3. At the age of fourteen his father died and left five sons.
   4. While speaking to the class, the pupils in the back part of the room could not hear me.
   5. While flying over the target, the antiaircraft fire became intense.
   6. Being one of the earliest spring flowers, people greet the hepatica joyfully.
   7. Entering the English office, a bust of Longfellow caught my eye.
   8. When ill or in need, Florence was always ready to help people.

B. 1. Turning the page, my eye was attracted to a picture of an old open fireplace.
   2. After a night of dreams the rising sun saw us again on the road.
   3. One day while looking out the window, an organ-grinder stopped and played in the street below me.
   4. Without rising from your chair, a book can transport you to foreign lands.
   5. In applying for a position one's manners and English are important.
   6. Having shot a Nazi agent on his trail, two German soldiers captured Jan.
   7. While wet, put the picture on a painting block and pin it down.
   8. Being one of your new pupils, you naturally wonder whether I enjoy writing and speaking.

Place modifiers near the words modified if clearness requires this arrangement.

(Clear)   In the attack the general lost nearly a thousand of his men.
(Not Clear)   In the attack the general nearly lost a thousand of his men.
   (Here *nearly* is placed so as to qualify *lost*, though it was probably intended to modify *thousand*.)

During the next two weeks baseball tickets, will be on sale at

sixty cents. (which will be good for eight home games,)

Do not place between two members of a sentence a modifier applicable to either member.

t
The general who wins battles (*I* in nine cases out of ten) is a

blend of daring and caution in the right proportion.

Practice 8.   Arranging Modifiers Correctly

Correct the following sentences. When you change the position of a modifier, tell what word or words it modifies.

Example:

I missed the three first lessons.
I missed the first three lessons. *First* modifies *three* lessons.

A. 1. I write a letter to my cousin who lives in Florida almost every week.
   2. The blaze was extinguished before any damage was done by the local fire department.
   3. The mortgage company urges owners to pay arrears of taxes and interest by letter, by telephone, and by personal visits.
   4. One pupil was asked to write an account of the book he had read on the blackboard.
   5. *Ivanhoe* and *Treasure Island* were the two first books I read in high school.
   6. Repeat what you have read with your book closed.
   7. A man was walking down the street with long gray hair.
   8. Old Susan places a candle on the window sill, which flickers when the wind blows.

B. 1. The steeds maintained a shambling gait through the sand that was neither a trot nor a lope.
   2. I thought of going to bed several times but decided to complete my work.
   3. Louis XVII, never actually the king of France, died when he was ten years old in prison.
   4. In our club is a young group of boys and girls.
   5. In Cairo bazaars Canadian soldiers pointed at the things they wanted with a stick.
   6. When Private Hargrove entered the Army for the first time he was expected to follow orders promptly and exactly.
   7. What am I offered for this antique child's maple desk?
   8. The journalist has contributed an important chapter through his reporting of battle scenes to war literature.

Parallel Structure

As a rule, *and* **and** *but* **connect like grammatical elements—for example, two nouns, two predicates, two adjectives, two prepositional phrases, two participial phrases, two adjective clauses.**

(Right)   The owner called the dog and at the same time pulled the leash.
   (*And* connects the verbs *called* and *pulled*.)

(Wrong)   The owner called the dog and at the same time pulling the leash.
   (*And* connects the predicate verb *called* and the participle *pulling*.)

There are three ways to correct a sentence in which *and* connects a noun and a clause: (1) change the noun to a clause; (2) change the clause to a noun; (3) get rid of *and*.

(Wrong)   Ernie Pyle told of the bravery of the American doughboys and what victories they won against the enemy. (*And* connects the noun *bravery* and the subordinate clause *what victories they won against the enemy*.)

(Right)

1. Ernie Pyle told how brave the American doughboys were and what victories they won over the enemy. (*And* connects the two noun clauses.)
2. Ernie Pyle reported the bravery of the American doughboys and their victories over the enemy. (*And* connects the nouns *bravery* and *victories*.)
3. Ernie Pyle reported the victories which brave American doughboys won over the enemy. (No *and*.)

Right   Wrong

Practice 9.   Using Parallel Structure

Rewrite the following sentences, making parallel the elements that should be parallel. Separate the parallel elements from the rest of the sentence and number them. Under the sentence show that the numbered elements are parallel.

Examples:

a. Her sister was tall, black hair and eyes, and called by the Indians Wild Rose.
   Her sister
       (1) was tall,
       (2) had black hair and eyes,
   and (3) was called by the Indians Wild Rose.
   Members 1, 2, and 3 are parallel; they are predicates.
b. The treasure, filling two large chests, and which eight men could hardly carry, was seized by the police.
   The treasure,
       (1) which filled two large chests
   and (2) which eight men could hardly carry,
   was seized by the police.
   Members 1 and 2 are parallel; both are adjective clauses.
c. Then I formed the brilliant idea of climbing the sty fence and to hang from the top rail until the bull went away.

Then I formed the brilliant idea of
    (1) climbing the sty fence
and (2) hanging from the top rail
until the bull went away.
Members 1 and 2 are parallel; they are verbal nouns.

A. 1. Jeanne taught Eleanor to read and write, how to draw, and also French.
  2. The experience taught me two lessons: not to disobey Mother and I shall not again eat so much candy between meals.
  3. Hamlin would have enjoyed going to a library and read as many books as he wished.
  4. The book describes the struggles and hardships of Barnum and how he had to fight for fame and fortune.
  5. I have learned this term in speaking always to keep to my subject, and do not discuss two topics in one paragraph.
  6. Ichabod was a tall, thin man with a small head and having large eyes and an upturned nose.
  7. This will teach the student self-control and to be economical.
  8. Three qualities of sailors are quickness, coolness, and they have to be alert.
  9. Miss Simmons teaches the piano, the violin, and vocal.
10. There is more to this hobby than finishing the scrapbook, putting it on a shelf, and forget it.

B. 1. You can improve your posture if you stand erect, correct breathing, and by sitting properly.
  2. The highwayman wears doeskin breeches, a claret coat, a French cocked hat, and around his neck he has a ruffle of lace.
  3. Since I didn't want to eat the food my brother prepared and having convinced my brother that I could cook, I got the job of cook.
  4. Dickens' books are masterpieces because of his sly humour, his ability to weave characters into a mysterious plot, and because each of his characters portrays a certain type of person.
  5. The chief traits of Bottom are overconfidence, and he uses words of which he doesn't know the meaning.
  6. Many associates were unjust to Arrowsmith because they judged him by his outward and visible characteristics and not realizing his true character.
  7. Have a reason for what you do and not because it is custom.
  8. In assembly yesterday Jack Boswell said that just passing is not enough and to work for high marks in all subjects.
  9. I enjoyed reading *To the Ladies* because of its humour and it holds the reader in suspense until the last scene.
10. I can't forgive a person for making an appointment and then leave a friend stranded on some street corner.

Do not join a relative clause to its principal clause or to a phrase by *and*, *but* or *or*.

(Right)   All nations to-day salute Pierre and Marie Curie, brilliant scientists, who succeeded in isolating radium.

(Wrong)   All nations to-day salute Pierre and Marie Curie, brilliant scientists, and who succeeded in isolating radium.

Avoid unnecessary changing of the subject or of the voice, mood, or tense of the verb.

(Right)   I found De Seversky's facts impressive and his arguments forceful.
(Poor)   I found De Seversky's facts impressive and his arguments are forceful.   (Unnecessary changing of the subject.)

Correlative conjunctions join like grammatical elements—for example, two nouns, two predicates, two adjectives, two prepositional phrases—and are placed just before the words or expressions they connect.

We could (neither) reach the survivors by boat nor by plane.
(*Neither* and *nor* connect *by boat* and *by plane*.)

The American ideal (not only) forbids intolerance but also indifference to the fate of others.   (*Not only* and *but also* connect *intolerance* and *indifference*.)

Practice 10.   Parallel Structure

Improve the following sentences.   Give a reason for each change.
A. 1. Ability to speak correctly and fluently is not only an asset in the business but also in the social world.
  2. For the best results a very light rod should be purchased; then go out in your boat and catch the fish.
  3. Instead of looking up the meaning of an unfamiliar word in my reading, I just skip it, and often the idea of the whole sentence is lost.
  4. The long winter evenings were either spent in listening to the radio or reading aloud to the group before the open fireplace.
  5. Mr. C. C. Woodruff, president of the Board of Trade and who is chairman of the Christmas Committee, was the next speaker.
B. 1. George Barry, editor of our school newspaper and who worked last summer in a newspaper office, expects to study journalism.
  2. The president suggested that the club give a party, and each guest should bring an article of food or clothing for the Red Cross.
  3. During the winter months I not only enjoy ice skating but also skiing.
  4. One's shoes should not only be stylish but also comfortable.
  5. Either you must return the book or pay for it.

Practice 11.   Writing Coherent Sentences

Improve the following sentences.   Give a reason for each change.
A. 1. No matter how bright the future may appear, we should not depend on it, but let us act in the present.
  2. Surely the man in overalls was more of a gentleman than the man with gray gloves and who was swinging a cane.
  3. Ralph neither likes to canoe nor to fish.
  4. A pilot not only must be alert but also resourceful.
  5. In building the paragraph I used four connectives, and all the ideas followed one another in order.

B. 1. Make the first sentence tell how far the paragraph will go, and the last sentence should tell how far the paragraph has gone.
   2. During the term I not only read the required books but also eight supplementary books.
   3. Helen Keller was taken to all the local doctors, and finally they took her to an eminent Boston physician.
   4. Not only would the change help the fourth-year students but all other students as well.
   5. Trini, considered one of the most beautiful women of Spain and who made a successful screen debut, will be at the Valencia on Saturday.

Connectives

Use the conjunction that expresses accurately the relation of one clause to another. Think what each conjunction means. *And* equals plus; *but* equals minus. Don't use a plus or a minus word to express condition, time, cause, or concession.

(Right)   Although it snowed for two days, the mail came through as usual. (*Although* expresses accurately the relation between the clauses.)
(Wrong)   It snowed for two days, and the mail came through as usual.

Use *when* for time and *where* for place. After *is* in a definition, use a noun, not *when* or *where* introducing a clause.

a sound in which
A consonant is ~~where~~ the voice or breath is obstructed.

Avoid the *and-so* habit. By substituting adverb or noun clauses for some of the independent clauses and by beginning new sentences, get rid of *and* and *so* joining clauses.

(Poor)   You have done superior work in physics this year, so you may go directly into aeronautics.
(Better)   Since you have done superior work in physics this year, you may go directly into aeronautics.

As, *since*, and *then* are other useful but overworked connectives.

Being is a participle—never a conjunction or part of it.

Because
~~Being that~~ plum trees must be cross-pollinated, we have planted two of them.

Practice 12.   Using Correct Conjunctions

Improve the following sentences. Show that the conjunctions you use express accurately the relation between the ideas.

A. 1. A warrant officer is when an officer holds rank between that of commissioned officer and enlisted man.
   2. A compound sentence is when there are two principal clauses.
   3. Elizabeth's relatives at home wanted her to return, so she came back to Canada.
   4. A first-class lever is where the fulcrum is between the weight and the effort.

5. Well-forested areas hold precious water in reserve, so it is wise to maintain these areas as potential reservoirs.
6. Being my room was the warmest in the house, I always went there to read.
7. Being that this was Angela's first ride in an airplane, she was excited.
8. In conversation one should neither whisper or shout.

B. 1. I saw in the paper where Marjorie Stanton has just entered the University of Manitoba.
2. My uncle does not know where we live and is coming to visit us.
3. Being that Pluto was discovered only recently, many scientists believe there may be other solar planets in outer space.
4. There was always a disagreement as to who would do the work, so they decided that Captain Jerry should marry to secure a housekeeper for them.
5. Democracy is where the people rule themselves through their elected representatives.
6. The most desirable vocations are those requiring much preparation, so it is wise to plan a vocation early.
7. I had an umbrella and the rain came right through it.
8. So far I have seen but one hockey game, and I hope to see another soon.

Practice 13. Writing Complex Sentences

Change the following compound sentences to complex sentences.

1. Irving Langmuir became interested in science at an early age, and he won the Nobel prize in chemistry in 1932. 2. At the age of nine he was given a small workshop of his own, and there he worked happily in his spare time. 3. At the age of eleven he moved with his family from New York to Paris, and there Irving spent most of his time in the school laboratory.
4. On his return to America the boy already had an astounding knowledge of chemistry and physics, so he was excused from science classes in the Manual Training High School of Pratt Institute. 5. The School of Mines of Columbia University offered excellent courses in mathematics and sciences, so in 1899 Langmuir enrolled there for further study. 6. His professor of mechanics recognized the young man's ability, so he allowed Langmuir to do independent research in the field.
7. The three years after graduation from Columbia were passed pleasantly and profitably under Professor Nernst in Europe, but the end of this period of study found Langmuir eager to return to the United States. 8. For a while he taught chemistry at Stevens Institute of Technology, but his desire to devote his life to chemical research prevented him from being happy in his work. 9. In 1909 he joined the staff of the General Electric Laboratories, and there he experimented with vacuum bulbs.
10. Langmuir is noted chiefly for his work in chemical research, but he also made significant contributions to the field of physics.

Practice 14. Review of Clear, Correct Sentences

Correct or improve the faulty sentences. Give a reason for each change. One *A* sentence and one *B* sentence are clear and correct.

A. 1. Odysseus stopped in Sicily, where he was captured by Polyphemus, who ate some of his men who were not able to escape from the cave, which was the home of the giant.

2. Four weeks ago you sent us twenty dollars, leaving a balance of ten dollars, for which we thank you.

3. Children in ragged clothes and dirty faces were laying on the floor.

4. Uriah had no eyebrows and slight eyelashes, and his eyes were reddish brown, and he looked as if he wouldn't be able to go to sleep because of the scant covering of his eyes.

5. Martha has light hair, blue eyes, and good-natured.

6. Reading on in the story, there is another dog introduced.

7. The collie sat with his parched tongue hanging from his mouth feebly wagging his tail.

8. Jack Weel, famous as a football player at Yale and who was coach at Northwestern for years, talked at our last assembly.

9. I think, if you will follow my directions and by inquiring when you are in doubt, you will reach Somerset.

10. Poetry, according to Trevelyan, is in danger of becoming a dying art, appealing only to the cultured minority.

11. I nearly cried for joy when I read your letter, but as you do not know how to reach my house, I will give you the directions now.

12. Rip found his dog when he reached home, but he did not know him.

13. Use a coloured illustration, and also it is wise to have an attractive heading.

14. A classical high school educates the head only, but in a vocational high school attention is paid to the hands as well as the head.

15. *Ruggles of Red Gap* will keep you in fits of merriment, and please tell me when you are coming to visit us.

B. 1. A person who has to be told to do a thing two or three times will not advance rapidly in business.

2. In his will the dying monarch made Namgay king, because he had no children.

3. Standing on the Brooklyn car line near Chicago Avenue, a brown building is visible.

4. One can enjoy himself by going to the library and read good books.

5. Burrows neither succeeded as a clerk nor as a mechanic.

6. A teacher should not expect a pupil to know what he knows.

7. Going home, the wind blew a gale.

8. The reader is suddenly transported to the banks of the Congo, where ebony natives dance, rhythmically beat their drums, and perform fantastic rites.

9. After eating a hearty dinner, our carriages were brought to the door.

10. The carpenter is of medium height, ordinary looking, gray eyes, rather sallow cheeks, a long, thin, trailing mustache, and rather uncouth in his manner.

11. Eastern High School is overcrowded, and it has a commercial and a general course.

12. He said to his friend that since he ordered the fruit he ought to pay for it.

13. Poe invented the short story, and his home in New York has in it many relics.

14. We proved that air is a real substance because it occupies space and by showing that air has weight.
15. Flying at an altitude of ten thousand feet, the country for 132 miles in all directions can be clearly seen.

MASTERING EFFECTIVE SENTENCE STRUCTURE

Practice 15. Imitating Models

Using each of the following sentences as a model, write two sentences of your own, upon your own topic, in direct imitation of the model. Examine the model closely for its structure and do not neglect to imitate the punctuation.

Examples:

Model:

Her garments shone like the summer sea, and her jewels like the stars of heaven; and over her forehead was a veil, woven of the golden clouds of sunset.

Imitation:

1. The wheat waved like a billowy sea, and the grass like the rippling river; and on the field was a cloud-shadow, broken only by the drifting rack.
2. The castle stood like a mountain fixed, and the village like unmoving foothills; while over the scene broke the storm, driven by the desperate wind.

1. Here I observed, by the help of my perspective glass, that they were no less than thirty in number, that they had a fire kindled, and that they had meat dressed.
2. Here they used to sit on summer afternoons, talking listlessly over village gossip.
3. The spirit of my fathers grows strong in me, and I will no longer endure it.
4. From behind his stockade Jack watched them through his field glass as they landed from the launch and set off for the village.
5. She stopped a moment beneath the gently dripping trees and took off her knitted cap and shook it dry.
6. Martin Luther writes, "I was myself flogged fifteen times one afternoon over the conjugation of a verb."
7. A lingering winter and a tardy spring are what we always should like in this part of the world.
8. The fourth largest olive grove in the world is said to be on the outskirts of Beirut.
9. Do you know that the speaker will not disappoint you?
10. He never bluffs, and he dislikes bluffers.
11. At ten o'clock the crack of the starter's pistol announced that the annual six-mile free-style swim across Lake Henley had started.
12. Night after night, with only a flashlight, Ibram prowled about the Arab quarter, seeking adventure.
13. At dusk a slight flurry of snow heralded the coming storm, but by morning the outbuildings were buried under huge drifts.

14. The heavy fog and the still, damp air oppressed his mind and drained his body of strength and energy.

15. A century ago there had been a cart road across the peninsula, but it had been obliterated by jungle growth and floods.

16. At twilight a panther ventured within a stone's throw of our house, slaughtered a calf, and dragged it into the forest.

17. When Gladys had had a hot drink and had donned dry clothes, she felt better about her ducking.

18. That the rain was coming down in sheets, that the picnic lunch was the pray of ants, and that each of the boys had at least two wasp bites did not kill their enthusiasm for camping.

19. The Greeks and Romans thought that thunder and lightning were the punishment of the gods.

20. He corrected himself, blushing as he did so, though why he should blush was not known to Reuben.

Learning to Tell a Story

ENTERTAINING AND BORING

WHEN at a picnic, on a hike, at the table, or at school boys or girls tell their experiences to each other—a ride on a raft or in an airplane, a first dive, a surprise, a trip to Banff, or the winning touchdown, run, goal, or points—have you noticed that some boys or girls thrill and amuse their hearers, while others who have had just as exciting, unusual, or amusing experiences bore them? Why this difference? Storytelling is an art. Some boys and girls have learned it; others haven't.

"TWICE TOLD TALES"

A good start towards learning the art of storytelling is reading carefully and retelling good stories. A reproduction, like an experience, may be highly entertaining or exceedingly dull.

In preparing to produce a story, first select, if you can, a story that your classmates don't know. Then read, re-read, and study the story until you know it.

A good storyteller is wide-awake and enthusiastic and acts out his experience.

Here are four suggestions that will help you to make your first reproduction entertaining:

1. Use your imagination. See the people and places and know how the people feel and how you would feel if you were in their places.

2. At times quote directly. This is a way to add life to a story and make it seem real.

(*Direct*) "I shall be proud to show you my wife," he said, "and the baby —and Goliath."

"Goliath?"

"That's the dog," answered Watson, with a laugh. "You and Goliath ought to meet—David and Goliath!" — ALDRICH

(*Indirect*) Watson said that he would be glad to show me his wife, the baby, and the dog Goliath.

3. Do you like to listen to a person who joins his sentences with *and-ur, but-ur,* and *so-ur?* If not, use a period between two sentences not *and, but,* or *so.*

4. Talk to your classmates. Look into their eyes, not at the ceiling, the floor, or a window.

Practice 1. Retelling a Story

Reproduce orally one of the following stories. After everyone has told his story, the class will select by vote the best storyteller.
1. Keep the story moving swiftly.
2. Stand easily, not stiffly. Don't slouch or wriggle.
3. Speak distinctly.
4. Use a pleasing voice.

1. A myth. (See Herzberg's *Myths and Their Meaning*, Baker's *In the Light of Myth*, Guerber's *Myths of Greece and Rome*, Gayley's *Classic Myths*, and Bulfinch's *Outline of Mythology*.) 2. A narrative poem. 3. An animal story. 4. An Old Testament story—David and Goliath, David and Jonathan, or Naaman, the Leper, for instance. 5. A movie story. 6. An Indian legend. 7. A ghost story. 8. A historical incident—Wolfe's Capture of Quebec, Laura Secord, Madelaine de Vércheres, Dollard Dulac, the Boston Tea Party, Paul Revere's Ride, or other historical happening. 9. A fable—one of Æsop's Fables, for example. 10. An incident in the life of Alfred the Great, Henry II, Kingsford Smith, Amy Mollison, Thomas Lipton, Lindberg, Malcolm Campbell, Lincoln, Mark Twain, Maude Adams, Seegar Wheeler, Vérendrye, Madame Curie, or Pasteur. 11. An incident in a story, not in the words of the narrator—for example, "The Legend of Sleepy Hollow" as told by Katrina, Ichabod, or Brom Bones; Ben Gunn's account of his life on Treasure Island; Ivanhoe's story of the first day's tournament; Dolly Winthrop's account of Silas Marner and his life.

Practice 2. Reproducing a Story

Is the following reproduction of an old story interesting? Why? Could you suggest any improvement? Would more conversation help? Try it.

A Vizier who had displeased the Sultan, his master, was imprisoned for life in a high tower, escape from which seemed impossible.

One day his faithful wife came to the base of the tower weeping bitterly at the thought of her loss.

"O my husband, my husband!" she cried, "how shall we do?"

When the prisoner heard and recognized her he called out, "Don't weep, but do as I bid you, and I may yet be saved. Go home, bring a live black beetle, a little butter, and three clews: one of fine silk, one of pack-thread, and one of whipcord, and lastly, a coil of stout rope."

The wife, very much astonished, but not doubting her husband's sagacity, went home and quickly returned with the whole of these curious articles.

The Vizier then told her to anoint the beetle's head with butter, tie one end of the silk thread around his body and put him on the wall of the tower.

She did this and the beetle, thinking from the smell of butter on his head that there must be a great store of it above, crawled straight up till he came to the hole where the Vizier stood. The Vizier lost no time in getting hold of the silk thread. His wife tied this to the pack-thread, the pack-thread to the whipcord and the whipcord to the rope. Each was drawn up in turn.

After making fast the rope inside the tower, the prisoner soon reached the ground, and the delighted pair speedily made their escape.

Practice 3. Reproducing a Story

Select an interesting incident—one happening, not the whole story—from a book you are reading. Then tell it orally or write your reproduction. Aim to entertain your classmates, to give them an attractive sample of the book, and to induce them to read the book. Be ready to answer questions about the book.

WRITING CONVERSATION

To write good conversation isn't easy. No, it isn't hard to learn to use a separate paragraph for each speech and the introducing words, to place a comma between the speech and the introducing words, and to set off the whole speech or its parts with quotation marks. But to make the conversation natural, lifelike, and appropriate is work. As we have to learn to see with our eyes, so we have to get into the habit of hearing with our ears—that is, of noticing how people talk. Three suggestions may help you to improve the conversation in your stories:

1. Study the conversation you hear, and practise imitating the talk of a variety of people.

2. Write contracted forms as they are spoken—*who's, they'll, where's, wasn't,* etc.

3. Avoid repetition of *said.* Either use a word that tells how the person spoke—*cried, exclaimed, whispered, growled,* or *argued,* for example—or, if the introducing words are not needed to make clear who the speaker is, omit them.

Some substitutes for *said* are—

added	cried	murmured	roared
admitted	declared	muttered	screamed
announced	exclaimed	pleaded	shouted
answered	explained	remarked	sighed
argued	growled	repeated	whined
begged	inquired	replied	whispered
bellowed	mumbled	returned	yelled

Practice 4. Writing Contractions

Learn to spell the following contractions which are frequently used in conversation. Notice that the apostrophe always takes the place of the omitted letter. *Did+not=didn't; does+not=doesn't; you+have=you've* (two letters omitted).

aren't	hasn't	mustn't	we've
can't	haven't	she's	won't
couldn't	I'll	shouldn't	wouldn't
didn't	I'm	that's	you'd
doesn't	isn't	there's	you'll
don't	it's	wasn't	you're
hadn't	I've	weren't	you've

Ain't, hain't, 'tain't are incorrect forms used by some careless and uneducated people.

REPRODUCING A CONVERSATION

The preparation for writing natural, lifelike conversation includes reproducing conversations overheard, and studying the dialogue in good stories.

Example:

IN AFRICAN FOREST AND JUNGLE

While I was walking along the park towards the library the other day, a voice hailed me with, "Hey there! Got any good books?"

Turning around, I saw my friend Bernard walking toward me. "A few," I answered.

We sat down on a park bench for a little chat. "Is this one any good?" he asked, picking up *In African Forest and Jungle.*

"The best of the four. I've finished it. Would you like to read it?"

"What's it about?"

"It's about an explorer and his adventures in Africa."

"Is there a lot of description in the book?"

"Some—when he describes the dress and customs of the natives."

"They're pretty superstitious, aren't they? I mean the natives."

"Somewhat. One incident is about a native who locks himself in a hut for a week to avoid the 'curse of the new moon'."

"Is that all it tells about?"

"Oh, no, there's plenty of adventure, romance, and even pathos."

"Pathos?"

"Yes, in the jungle Du Chaillu's dog has a fight with some animal and dies of loss of blood after killing it, and his pet monkey dies soon after being bitten by a centipede."

"Well, I guess the book must be pretty good."

"It certainly is—I advise you to read it." — PUPIL

Practice 5. Writing Conversation

1. How is conversation paragraphed?
2. What punctuation marks enclose a direct quotation?
3. What punctuation regularly separates a direct quotation from the rest of the sentence?
4. How has the pupil avoided repeating *said*?
5. Why is this reproduction entertaining?

Practice 6. Reproducing a Conversation

Reproduce a conversation you have overheard or in which you have taken part. Without evesdropping, keep your ears open for talk that is unusual, characteristic, bright, or laughable.

1. At the ticket window. 2. In the theatre. 3. At the movie. 4. At the baseball game. 5. At the bargain counter. 6. At the dinner table. 7. Waiting for the train. 8. In the street car. 9. At the concert. 10. After the school entertainment. 11. On the street corner. 12. In the barber shop. 13. In the grocery store. 14. In the meat market. 15. In class. 16. At the football or the basketball game. 17. A quarrel. 18. An automobile accident. 19. A newsboy and a customer. 20. In the restaurant. 21. An interview with father. 22. On the railroad train. 23. Asking the way. 24. Pupil just home from school and his mother. 25. Generous woman and tramp. 26. About homework. 27. Over the radio. 28. About a book. 29. About a movie. 30. On the way to school.

Miller Services

Captain A. C. Course tells a group of boys a true tale of the sea. Has he caught their interest?

WRITING AN AUTOBIOGRAPHY

Chapter I

How much do you know about your ancestors? Would you like to know more? When you ask your father, mother, grandparents, or other relatives about their lives or the lives of their parents or grandparents, don't be discouraged if they say they have nothing to tell. Be a good interviewer; ask such definite questions as: What hardships did you have when you were young? What fun did you have? What thrilling and exciting experiences? How did you select your vocation and get started in it? How did your food, clothing, school, or work as a boy or girl differ from mine? What do you know about our ancestors who had the pluck to leave their homes in Europe for a new world? How did they get their start in Canada? What war stories of our family do you know?

MY MOTHER'S UNUSUAL EXPERIENCES

My mother had an unusual experience when she was sixteen. In Sweden, June 25 is the longest day, and the daylight lasts through the night. If one goes far enough north, he is able to read by this light. Because "Midsummer Night," as it is called, comes only once a year, the people of the town celebrate by gathering in the village park, where candy, cakes, and drinks of all kinds are sold. In preparation for the great event of staying up all night, everyone takes a nap in the afternoon. After my mother and her family had taken their afternoon rest, they set out for the park, where they entertained themselves by dancing and singing. My mother remembers that the quality of the light at night was like that of the sun just sinking below the horizon, where it seemed to stay all night, except for a short time between two and three o'clock when it disappeared like the effect of a cloud passing across it. In what seemed an incredibly short time, the sun rose again on the other side of the horizon.

Another incident which my mother will never forget was her crossing the North Sea. The trip from Hull, England, to Copenhagen, Denmark, was usually made in twenty-four hours. My mother and her family boarded the steamer *Sea Wings* in the late afternoon, expecting to go to bed early that evening and land the following afternoon. She and her sister watched with interest, but with unconcern, the preparations of the sailors, who were fastening and nailing down everything on deck which was loose, and placing in the hatch such things as could be moved. Having previously crossed the Atlantic, where all sorts of things, such as toys, books, and chairs were left on deck, they wondered at the careful preparations. Before morning, however, they knew the importance of these precautions, for they awoke to a storm-tossed world. The ship rocked and pitched until everyone was sea-sick. A crate of chickens, although it was tied to the deck, was swept overboard. Everyone was kept in his cabin, and some of the people were unconscious most of the way. All despaired of ever landing, but finally after three days and three nights on that storm-tossed ship, they were able to set their feet on land again. — Pupil

Practice 7. Writing an Autobiography

With the title "My Ancestors" or "One of My Ancestors" write the first chapter of your autobiography. Make it a lively, entertaining story if you can, but tell the exact truth. There are good stories in every home. Narratives marked "Please do not read aloud" or "Read without the name" will be treated as you request.

Practice 8. Studying a Story

As you study the story "Lost" get ready to answer these questions:
1. Does the writer at the start answer the questions "Who?" "When?" "Where?" and "What?"
2. Does she plunge right into the story or bore us with unnecessary explanation?
3. Does she arouse our curiosity and keep us in suspense? If so, how?
4. Does she hold our interest to the end? If so, how?
5. Is the ending abrupt or leisurely?
6. What use is made of conversation?
7. What word pictures are there in the story?
8. Does she tell how she felt and how her mother felt? Where?
9. In what order are the events told?
10. Could you improve the story? How?

LOST

On a hot day in summer when I was a child about seven years old, Florence, the girl who took care of me while my mother was away, took me to the woods near home.

"Come, Anna," said Florence. "Let's see who can pick the bigger bunch of flowers."

"All right," I replied and immediately started to work. It seemed that the farther I went the more beautiful the flowers grew. Slowly but surely I moved away from Florence until she was entirely lost to my view. I was unconscious of all this until I heard Florence call to me in a frightened voice, "Anna, Anna, where are you?"

Thinking she was fooling, I hid behind a bush. She continued to call until her voice seemed to be far away. I got up laughing to myself. In fact I was rather proud of myself to think that I had fooled Florence, but no Florence could be seen. I called and called, but my calling was of no avail. Only my echo came back to me to increase my fear. Crouching down behind the bush, I feared every moment the bogeyman would take me, or lions, bears, or tigers would spring on me and gobble me up, as in the stories I had heard from my mother and father.

My heart was in my mouth. I hardly dared to breathe. Every move of the branches startled me. How I wished for my mother, for her comforting words and caresses! The trees were darkly lined against the blue sky, and seemed like great giants ready to fall on top of me.

After a while I felt as if something or somebody was scratching on the back of my neck. I didn't dare to look. All sorts of imaginary giants, dragons, evil spirits came to my mind. I wondered what it was. At last a little courage came to my assistance and made me speak.

"Let me go," I cried in terror. "Let me go. I will give you my dolly. I'll promise not to fight with Pauline any more. I'll do whatever Florence tells me to do if you will only let me go." With that I turned around, expecting to see some awful beast. And guess what it was. Why, a sticker that was lying against my dress and partly against my neck, and every time I moved it would scratch my neck.

If I hadn't been in such a sad plight, I would have laughed, but anyway I felt much relieved and began to have a little more courage to look around. Seeing a path, I got up and followed it. Every step I took, I thought some wild animal or a bandit would jump at me.

At last I came to the end of the path and found I was a few blocks from home. My heart leaped with joy. But it suddenly misgave me when I thought of what my father and mother would do to me. This thought quite vanished when, turning a corner, I met my friend Pauline, looking rather excited. Staring at me as if she had seen a ghost, she exclaimed in astonishment, "Anna, is it really you? Nearly everybody you know is looking for you. Where have you been?"

Just as I began to explain, Florence came running up to me in tears. She picked me up bodily, and held me so tightly I could hardly breathe, as if her life depended on me.

When we reached home, there were about a dozen children and some grown-ups on the porch talking excitedly. As soon as they saw me, a shout arose that would have made a deaf man hear. I was borne in triumph to my mother like some grand princess arriving from a foreign land.

The next moment I was locked in my mother's arms with my head against her breast. How happy I felt to be safe and sound in my mother's arms! I think I shall never again be so happy as I was at that moment.

Seeing my mother's eyes full of tears, I said, "What's the matter, Mother? Are you angry at me?"

"No," she replied. "I cry because I am happy." At that time I didn't understand her, but now I realize what she meant. Those were tears of joy and not of sorrow.

When my mother told my father, he didn't spank me, as I had expected. Instead, he laughed till the tears rolled down his cheeks. I felt rather insulted that he should laugh instead of feeling sorry for me, and immediately after supper I took my doll and went to bed. There I told her my adventure but she looked at me so foolishly that I spanked her and turned her face to the wall. — PUPIL

Practice 9.   Writing an Autobiography

Write another chapter of your autobiography. Picture people and places. Tell how you felt. Select your own subject. One class wrote an entertaining book on the following topics:

1. An adventure. 2. My trip to Italy. 3. The country school I attended. 4. My trip to Germany. 5. A storm at sea. 6. My best vacation. 7. Lost. 8. At the circus. 9. My trip to Europe. 10. Two weeks in the Catskill Mountains. 11. My trip to Algonquin Park. 12. Points of interest in Toronto. 13. A visit. 14. My trip to Waskesiu. 15. In Glacier National Park. 16. My first week in camp. 17. An adventure I had last summer. 18. My first visit to the zoo. 19. A thrilling game. 20. Vacation experiences in France and England. 21. My first acquaintance with a policeman. 22. My first dance. 23. Pranks of my youth.

Another class chose these topics:

1. At Jasper Lodge. 2. A summer on a farm. 3. My first year in school. 4. My earliest recollections. 5. My trip to Vancouver. 6. A vacation at Lake Louise. 7. A snake experience. 8. My trip to Niagara Falls. 9. My vacation at camp. 10. Vacation at my uncle's home. 11. My early childhood. 12. My trip to California. 13. My trip to Yellowstone National Park. 14. A week in Victoria. 15. A vacation in British Columbia. 16. My billy-goat. 17. A naughty little girl. 18. Picking blueberries. 19. My first dive. 20. A bicycle ride I shall not forget. 21. Donald and I go fishing. 22. Our club. 23. A visit to Grand Pré.

CLASS AND INDIVIDUAL BOOKLETS

A project of interest to both classes and individuals is to collect together and copy in uniform typing or writing several stories and bind them into a book for binding, giving it an attractive title. Books of autobiographies in each class may be called "Who's Who in 3B." Collections of short stories may be given titles appropriate to the material, "Short Stories of 1950," "Three Star Stories," "Who Killed Cock Robin." Similarly, essays and other material may be collected and bound together. Sometimes a series of essays are written on a single theme, separate essays covering different phases. This forms a fine project in Geography, in History, in Art, in Literature. One class wrote a complete manual for a play of Shakespeare. It included "Life of Shakespeare," "Historical Background of the Play," "Character Sketches of the Principal Characters," "Questions and Answers on the Themes in the Play," "Problems" which grew out of the play's study. Such an ambitious project as this requires an "editorial" staff and a "publication" staff.

Mastering the Paragraph

WHY PARAGRAPHS?

HAVE you ever, when selecting a novel for leisure reading, glanced through it to see how much conversation there was in it? If so, you know that the short paragraphs of conversation are easier reading than long paragraphs. How would you like to read a book that was just one long paragraph? If division into paragraphs helps you when you are reading, remember this fact when you write.

Test—Paragraphing

Recalling that in conversation each speech is in a separate paragraph, rewrite the following in correct form. Show that you have good eyes by spelling every word correctly and punctuating accurately.

A PATIENT FISHERMAN

About six o'clock on a fine morning in the summer I set out from Philadelphia on a visit to a friend, at the distance of fifteen miles; and passing a brook where a gentleman was angling, I inquired if he had caught anything. "No, sir," said he, "I have not been here long enough—only two hours." I wished him a good morning, and pursued my journey. On my return in the evening I found him fixed to the identical spot where I had left him, and again inquired if he had had any sport. "Very good, sir," said he. "Caught a great many fish?" "None at all." "Had a great many bites though, I suppose?" "Not one, but I had a most glorious nibble." — BENJAMIN FRANKLIN

WHAT A PARAGRAPH IS

In dialogue each speech is a paragraph. Ordinarily, however, a paragraph is a group of sentences developing one topic. In the third paragraph of "A Patient Fisherman," for example, Franklin's topic is the happenings between the morning and the evening conversation with the fisherman.

Paragraphs vary widely in length from the short ones to an occasional long one of 250 or 300 words. A good length for ordinary writing is 100 to 150 words. In newspaper articles and business letters shorter paragraphs are used. The average length of paragraphs in business letters is about 60 words; in newspaper articles, about 75 words. Don't make the mistake of writing, in a composition or a test, a paragraph pages long or of starting a new paragraph for each sentence. We shall soon study when to stop one paragraph and begin a new.

TOPIC SENTENCE

When we travel by train, we first buy a ticket, on which our starting point and destination are shown. When we write or speak a paragraph, it is wise to start with a topic sentence making clear exactly what we are going to talk about. A topic sentence is a brief statement of the subject of a paragraph. Although commonly placed at or near the beginning of the paragraph, it may be kept for the last sentence, and is occasionally omitted. At the beginning of the paragraph it furnishes a destination or goal for the writer or speaker and guides him in travelling towards his goal.

A good topic sentence, like a good guide, gives accurate and complete information. Some topic sentences are about as vague as the directions, "Go straight ahead for about a half mile, then turn right, then turn left, then turn left again."

One can develop a narrow topic sentence in a paragraph but usually needs two or more paragraphs to discuss a broad topic. "A true sportsman has many admirable qualities" and "A true sportsman is honest, courteous, self-controlled, courageous, loyal, and enthusiastic" are broad topic sentences. "A true sportsman must be a good loser" and "A true sportsman will never cheat to win" are narrower topic sentences.

Practice 1. Topic Sentences

In each pair which topic sentence is the more useful guide to a person writing a paragraph?

1

a. Canoe tilting is a good sport.
b. Canoe tilting is a good sport, because it takes nerve, strength, and endurance to play the game.

2

a. Dogs often show great intelligence.
b. Dogs are good pets.

3

a. Last Saturday Jack and I fished all day.
b. Last Saturday Jack and I had great luck fishing for trout.

4

a. Camping is a form of recreation which is pleasingly blended with a form of learning.
b. For two reasons camping should appeal to boys and girls.

5

a. A stamp collector does more than gather coloured bits of paper.
b. Stamp-collecting is a good hobby.

Practice 2. Choosing a Topic Sentence

Think of five topics you know something about. Then make a statement about each that you can "back up." For example, if you have read *Treasure Island*, you can "back up" the statement, "Jim was a quick thinker"; if you like to swim, can you prove the statement, "Swimming is a healthful sport"? Then write these five statements down as topic sentences that you can develop into paragraphs. A narrow topic sentence is ordinarily better than a broad one.

KEYS

If you examine the paragraphs which follow, you will notice that the topic sentence not only gives the name of the topic but suggests the thing which it is going to say about it. This key word or phrase is the most useful part of the topic sentence both to the reader and the writer. It is hard to write an incorrect paragraph if the key word is correct and clear.

1. THE POLICE DOG

The character of the police dog is complex. My best pal is one of these half-wild creatures, and from constant companionship I have discovered that he really has a dual personality. At night he slinks along with the stealthy tread of the world, nostrils quivering as he warily follows an imaginary scent and eyes gleaming like two phosphorus lights through the darkness. The ingrown fear of the unknown shows in the strained poise of his body or the suspicious turn of his head. But with the coming of daylight all the eerie illusions that are the companions of darkness vanish, and the police dog becomes a domesticated animal relying on man for the very substance of life. Gone is the cowardly and suspicious wolf, and in his place stands the dog, loyal-hearted and true. — PUPIL

2. "NEXT"

"Next" has a variety of meanings. To the small child sitting in the waiting room of a dentist's office that word means that his hour of torture has come. How different the customer in a crowded store feel when the "next" is meant for her. Generally she heaves a great sigh of relief. In the classroom that monosyllable always causes the pupil who is unprepared to have inward qualms. When the same pupil, however, is playing a game, "next" carries momentary joy with it. To the boy who is seeking a position, "next" may have either of two meanings. To the fellow who has already been interviewed, the words sounds cruel and unreasonable, for it means that he has failed to "land the job." But if he is the next to be interviewed, his hopes rise and his heart goes pitapat. What pictures are called up by the word "next!" — PUPIL

3. PEGGY

My dog, Peggy, is most unusual. As playthings she uses nails, bolts, and tennis balls. She sleeps in an old clothesbasket, which no one dares to touch.

Peggy will not eat her meals unless they are cut up and served on a plate. When she wants something to eat, she has a way of putting out her tongue, and she begs very prettily to win strangers' hearts and their cake. Peggy is just a common dog but, oh, how temperamental! — Pupil

4. THE LINNET CHORUS

One of the most delightful bird sounds or noises to be heard in England is the concert singing of a flock of several hundreds, and sometimes of a thousand or more linnets in September and October and even later in the year, before these great congregations have been broken up or have migrated. The effect produced by the small field finch of the pampas was quite different. The linnet has a little twittering song with breaks in it and small chirping sounds, and when a great multitude of birds sing together, the sound at a distance of fifty or sixty yards is as of a high wind among trees, but on a nearer approach the mass sound resolves itself into a tangle of thousands of individual sounds resembling that of a great concourse of starlings at roosting time, but more musical in character. It is as if hundreds of fairy minstrels were all playing on stringed and winged instruments of various forms, each one intent on his own performance without regard to the others.

— W. H. Hudson, *Far Away and Long Ago*.
By arrangement with J. M. Dent & Sons, London and Toronto.

Many things might be written about police dogs, but this paragraph deals with the complexity of its character. Similarly, "Next," "My Dog Peggy" and "The Linnet Chorus" may each be variously treated, but in these paragraphs we have respectively, variety of meanings, unusualness, and the delight of the music. Each of these is suggested in the topic sentence.

The topic sentence is not always first, but it should be as near the beginning as possible. Sometimes the clear-headed writer may write a clear and consistent paragraph by keeping the key in his mind only, but beginners are recommended to express it in the topic sentence.

Practice 3.   Selecting a Topic

What is the topic of each of the following paragraphs? What gives the key to each topic?

1

After Hautmont, the sun came forth again and the wind went down; and a little paddling took us beyond the iron works and through a delectable land. The river wound among low hills, so that sometimes the sun was at our backs and sometimes it stood right ahead, and the river before us was one sheet of intolerable glory. On either hand meadows and orchards bordered, with a margin or hedge and water flowers, upon the river. The hedges were of great height, woven about the trunks of hedgerow elms; and the fields, as they were often very small, looked like a series of bowers along the stream. There was never any prospect; sometimes a hill-top with its trees would look over the nearest hedgerow, just to make a middle distance for the sky; but that was all.

The heaven was bare of clouds. The atmosphere, after the rain, was of enchanting purity. The river doubled among the hillocks, a shining strip of mirror glass; and the dip of the paddles set the flowers shaking along the brink.

—ROBERT LOUIS STEVENSON, *An Inland Voyage.*
By permission of the publishers, Charles Scribner's Sons.

2

I remember having my juvenile imagination greatly excited by the appearance of a man on stilts. I would have given anything for a pair and the power to use them. What a thing it would be to go through the old town in such wise that the first-floor window-stools would be as familiar as the doorsteps. I thought I should never tire of them, never take them off. But reflection came later, and I bethought me that there were several highly desirable positions with which stilts were manifestly incompatible. How could I sit at meals; indeed, how sit conveniently at all? Above all, how could I go to bed o'nights? Stilts might be very desirable, but only for occasional use.

—FARRELL, *Lectures.*

3

I found him seated on a bench before the door, smoking his pipe in the soft evening sunshine. His cat was purring soberly on the threshold, and his parrot describing some strange evolutions in an iron ring that swung in the centre of his cage. He had been angling all day, and gave me a history of his sport with as much minuteness as a general would talk over his campaign; being particularly animated in relating the manner in which he had taken a large trout, which had completely tasked all his skill and wariness, and which he had sent as a trophy to mine hostess of the inn.

— WASHINGTON IRVING, *The Angler.*

4

There is nothing so horrible as languid study—when you sit looking at the clock, wishing the time was over, or that somebody would call on you and put you out of your misery. The only way to read with any efficacy is to read so heartily that dinner-time comes two hours before you expected it. To sit with your Livy before you, and hear the geese cackling that saved the Capitol; and to see with your own eyes the Carthaginian sutlers gathering up the rings of the Roman knights after the battle of Cannae, and heaping them into bushels; and to be so intimately present at the actions you are reading of, that when anybody knocks at the door, it will take you two or three seconds to determine whether you are in your own study, or in the plains of Lombardy, looking at Hannibal's weather-beaten face, and admiring the splendour of his single eye—this is the only kind of study which is not tiresome; and almost the only kind which is not useless; this is knowledge which gets into the system, and which a man carries about like his limbs, without perceiving that it is extraneous, weighty, and inconvenient. — SIDNEY SMITH.

Practice 4. Developing a Topic Sentence

Select two of the following topic sentences. Keeping in mind the key of each one, write an effective paragraph.

1. In the train opposite me sat the oddest-looking man I have ever seen.

2. My grandfather is an extraordinary man.
3. The Gordons' living-room (or any other room) is attractive.
4. The lake front by moonlight was a beautiful sight.
5. At a glance I knew I should like the cottage.
6. If you watch children at the age of three playing you can expect to have a good laugh.
7. My dinner last night came from many parts of the world.
8. A traveller must become accustomed to all sorts of inconveniences.
9. Shall I ever forget Victoria (or any other place)!
10. I have not always liked reading (skating, swimming, or any other thing in which you get keen pleasure now.)

HOW A PARAGRAPH IS BUILT

After writing a topic sentence ask yourself questions: "How?" "Why?" "What?" "What of it?" "What is it like or unlike?" "What example or illustration will make my point clear?" "How do I know?" If you know enough about the subject to write a paragraph, these questions will call forth particulars, details, examples, illustrations, instances, comparisons, contrasts, reasons, and results, which are, like the boards, stone, shingles, and beams of a house, the material out of which a paragraph is built.

In building a paragraph or a house, one needs, before beginning the actual construction, materials and also a plan in mind or on paper. When planning, arrange your ideas or points in a natural, sensible order. Sometimes—when you are writing about an experiment, for example—the time order is best. On other occasions you will find it wise to lead your reader from what he knows to facts you wish to make clear to him. Ideas and examples are often arranged in the order of importance—the best last.

Examples of plans and paragraphs:

1

Life with Father is the story of a Victorian boyhood.
　Victorian features of Clarence Day's youth
　　Living in a brownstone house
　　Father's wearing formal clothes to work
　　Looking upon the telephone as an intruder

LIFE WITH FATHER

Life with Father is the story of a boy who grew up in the days of Queen Victoria. When Clarence Day was growing up, it was proper to live in a house with a brownstone front. It was proper for Father to wear formal clothes to work. It was proper to look upon the telephone as a terrible instrument of danger which might (and did) break into the sanctity of a private household at hitherto hallowed hours. — PUPIL

2

Every ball player has his first big game
　This first experience came to me when the regular pitcher was hurt and
　　I was allowed to replace him.
　I was panicky and awkward.
　I threw a fast ball in an attempt to fool the batter.
　The batter hit the ball out of range of our outfielders.
　I was dismissed from the game.

MY FIRST BIG GAME

Every ball player has his first big game—I mean, one game among all others which he can look back upon and feel horrible sensations running up and down his spine. To me, this first experience came at the local field when the regular pitcher was struck by a line drive. There was no one else to put in. I was an outfielder, but, like many outfielders, I thought I was a better pitcher. I was sent in; immediately the demon panic seized me. I felt all arms and legs. I threw a few warm-up pitches, but instead of feeling better I felt worse. The ball seemed as big as a grapefruit. My hat was too tight, my pants too loose, and my arm as stiff and cold as an icicle. "Batter up!" I thought, "A fast ball; I'll fool him!" Well, I didn't fool him. The ball sailed over my head, over the head of the second baseman, and coyly out of range of the picturesque epithets of the outfielders—and out I came! — PUPIL

Practice 5. Arranging Paragraphs Logically

The sentences in each of the following paragraphs are jumbled together. Rewrite each paragraph with the sentences arranged in logical order. Search for such clues as time, order, and connecting words like *at the same time, first, then.* Copy the capitals and punctuation marks accurately. When you have finished, read each paragraph aloud. Does the paragraph make sense?

A TENDERFOOT WITH PEARY

I

Outside is the black Arctic night and a howling wind laden with particles of ice. What a great relief to be warm, thinks the youngest boy among them. Inside an igloo, made especially small to conserve the heat, are a few white people, among them Commander Peary. They lie close together in order to keep warm. Ever since his arrival in the far North the Esquimos have been saying that he will soon be "all same Peary"—that is, his feet will freeze. On a previous expedition Peary's feet were so badly frozen that several toes had to be amputated. In a warm igloo with four stoves going the boy is comfortable. But what will become of him out on the sea of ice without a stove?

II

It is a thrilling story of Peary's successful attempt to reach the North Pole, and it is told by a young man who had never been on such a trip before— a tenderfoot. The account of his experiences are humorous, but his wit cannot disguise the terrible hardships which members of the expedition underwent. This question and many others are answered in *A Tenderfoot With Peary*, by George Borup. Instead, by contrast, it reveals even more vividly the bravery and perseverance of the small band of valiant explorers led by Peary.

SUPPLYING DETAILS

One way of developing a paragraph is by adding details. If you start with the topic sentence "Central Park is a recreational haven for the city dweller," you will, of course, add particular facts about the park—its location, its lakes for rowing and skating, its miles of foot-paths, its zoo, and its facilities for bicycling.

Practice 6. Studying the Use of Details

1. Has the following paragraph a topic sentence? If so, what is it?
2. What details are given?

OUR FAMILY POSSESSIONS

Many of the possessions in our family help me to know more about my ancestors. There is the old oak chest which stands in Mother's room. It was built by my grandfather, who took pride in his workmanship. In the den there are old muskets and rifles which revive the interests of my other grand-father, for not only are there several of them but they are remarkably well preserved. On our mantel there still ticks away a large clock that must be much older than my father. In the china closet there are many pieces of hand-painted china of which my mother is very proud, for they are the work of her mother's sister, and a fine example of the china-painter's art they are, too. I am myself proud of these family heirlooms, and of my ancestors, who must have been fine craftsmen. — PUPIL

Practice 7. Using Details

Select two of the following topic sentences, or write two narrow topic sentences of your own. By adding details develop one into a good oral paragraph and the other into an effective written paragraph. Build clear, concise, varied sentences (pages 220–237).

1. My dog (or other pet) shows in various ways that he recognizes me.
2. Learning how to dance was (or was not) an ordeal for me.
3. He's the sort of fellow that makes a worth-while friend.
4. Our outing was spoiled at the start (or at the very end).
5. The beaver is nature's construction engineer.
6. Collecting scrap iron for our drive was a valuable experience.
7. A pinhole camera is easy to make.
8. Here's how to escape minding the baby (washing the dishes, mowing the lawn, or some other task).
9. I recently learned how an incandescent bulb works.
10. The airplane is constantly being improved.

SUPPLYING EXAMPLES

One of the best ways to build a paragraph is by giving examples which furnish vivid proof of the assertion made in the topic sentence. You may give one example and enlarge upon it, or list several examples.

Practice 8. Studying the Use of Examples

1. Which sentence in the following paragraph is illustrated by examples?
2. What examples are chosen?

MY FAVOURITE PICTURES

For a long time I have been making a collection of pictures that I like. My first picture was Tom Tomson's *West Wind*. It is still one of my favourites. Another favourite is *September Gale*, by Arthur Lismer. I love the feel of wind which seems to blow across the waters. Perhaps it is because it is so different that I chose *Above Lake Superior*, by Lawren Harris. *Northern River* and *Jack Pine*, also by Tom Tomson are in my collection. When I can secure a good print I want a copy of A. Y. Jackson's *October Morning, Algoma*. I have been told that my choices are all from the Group of Seven. — Pupil

Practice 9. Using Examples

Select two of the following topic sentences, or compose two of your own, making sure that they are narrow in scope, clear, and interesting. By giving examples develop one sentence into a good written paragraph. Build clear, concise, varied sentences (pages 220–237).

1. High school students are a mirror of the latest American fads.
2. The subway (or bus) is as entertaining as a motion picture.

3. Workers in various parts of the country help to bring food to our breakfast table.
4. A soldier learns much about the ordinary people in whose country he fights.
5. The human hands are man's most remarkable tools.
6. A practical joker soon gets a dose of his own medicine.
7. Plastics administer to our everyday needs.
8. Much information about a country can be gleaned from its postage stamps.
9. Although friction is a cause of waste in all machines, it is put to good use in many.
10. The radio has programmes to satisfy every taste.

USING COMPARISON AND CONTRAST

If you were describing a tiger to a small child who had never seen one, you would compare it with a cat. If you were describing how a child was educated in a dictatorship you would contrast his education with a child's schooling in a democracy. Comparisons (showing how two things are alike or different) and contrasts showing how two things differ) help to clarify our ideas.

Practice 10. Studying the Use of Comparison and Contrast

1. Has the following paragraph a topic sentence? What is it?
2. With what fruits does the author of the paragraph contrast the apple? In what way does the apple differ from each of these fruits?
3. What comparisons can you find in the paragraph?

THE KING OF FRUITS

I prefer an apple to any other fruit. Unlike the orange, no bitter peel has to be stripped from the exterior. The orange conceals surprises for the unwary; one is liable to be sprayed with sticky juice. The pear, on being bitten into, contrives to make your chin a background for a flood. The disposal of the plum's slippery stone may cause embarrassment. The peach, unless one pays handsomely, is either too ripe or too hard, and only Merlin can detect whether it is fit for eating or not. But an apple takes to being bitten gracefully. The teeth sink into it smoothly, like a dagger into flesh. The juice behaves well, and gliding between the teeth, nectar-like, causes the saliva to flow freely. The greenish-white flesh resists pleasantly the pressure of the jaw. And the apple is no hypocrite. One glimpse at its hearty, flushed, honest surface tells the true story of its interior. One can eat it with confidence, knowing that one's face will not be smeared uncomfortably. Take the apple in the hand, a finger in each end, and when you have stripped the flesh from the core, the disposal problem is simple. The apple is the king of fruits, and the idea that it was the apple which caused Adam's and Eve's downfall is a vile slander circulated by crafty orange, peach, and plum growers. — PUPIL

Practice 11. Using Comparison and Contrast

Select two of the following topic sentences or compose two appropriate ones of your own. By comparing or contrasting develop one into a vivid oral paragraph and the other into a pointed written paragraph. Build efficient sentences (pages 220–237). Punctuate correctly (pages 543–557).

1. My best friend looks different from the way he looked when I first met him.
2. I would rather join the Navy than the Army (or vice versa).
3. I would rather join the Air Cadets than the Navy Cadets (or vice versa).
4. Many games we play are like those our parents played as children.
5. I like old clothes better than new ones (or vice versa).
6. I would rather join the Waves than the Wacs (or vice versa).
7. A dog is a better pet than a cat (or vice versa).
8. I prefer to live in a private house rather than in an apartment (or vice versa).
9. The Diesel engine is similar to the gasoline engine.
10. The metric system is superior to the English system of weights and measures.

USING CAUSE AND EFFECT

A common way of building a paragraph is by starting with an assertion and then defending it by giving reasons or results—that is, causes or effects.

Practice 12. Studying the Use of Cause and Effect

1. What is the topic sentence of the following paragraph?
2. What reasons are given?

Coal Waste

It has been estimated that more coal has been wasted than mined. This is due to several things. Mine owners take only the coal which can be mined easily, and in doing this they sometimes make it impracticable to return and get the rest because of caving in of shafts and tunnels. Much has been left for pillars and roof supports, and much more wasted as coal dust. Poor tools make it difficult to cut the coal economically. Mines have been opened for which there is little need. Factories waste valuable by-products because of inadequate machinery. Coke-making companies do not always obtain all the by-products. We waste coal through careless firing in our homes and in heating plants. Power is the very cornerstone of our industrial prosperity, and with the present wasteful methods of using fuel it will not last many generations[1].

— MAUDE MARTIN AND CLYDE COOPER, *The United States at Work*

[1]*Reprinted by permission of the publisher, D. C. Heath and Company.*

Practice 13. Using Cause and Effect

Select one topic from each of the following groups. If you wish, you may choose a topic on why we should not do something, or why you dislike something. By giving reasons build one convincing oral paragraph and another good written paragraph. Speak and write in sentences.

Why we should
1. have outdoor hobbies
2. cultivate more than one good friend
3. be proud of our city (or state)
4. have a student court in high school
5. have homework
6. have coeducational high schools
7. study the customs of foreign peoples
8. learn to play musical instruments

Why I like
1. green (substitute your favourite colour)
2. to build model airplanes
3. a specific radio programme
4. biology (or another subject)
5. a friend of mine
6. to entertain my friends in my home
7. bicycling (or some other sport)
8. to read travel books
9. to go shopping
10. sport clothes

UNITY

Unity means oneness. A paragraph has unity if it sticks to one subject. While planning the paragraph, ask yourself frequently, "Is this on the subject?" If the answer is "No," cross out the detail or example. Likewise when you revise your paragraph, ask, "Have I held to my subject throughout?" If the completed paragraph is unified, you can sum it up in a sentence. If you do not forget your topic sentence and key word you are not likely to lose the unity of your paragraph.

Practice 14. Paragraph Unity

Show that the following paragraphs lack unity:

1

My favourite sport is baseball. Every fair day about a dozen of us go out to Forest Park after school and have a lively game. We knock the ball all over the lot, field it, run bases, and argue until the sun goes down. Then we race home to dinner. When I am reading or am in school, I wear glasses. I attend Jackson High School and am in the ninth grade. — Pupil

2

Methods of travel and transportation in New York City have greatly improved. In the time of the Dutch the methods of travel and transportation in the city were very poor indeed. The only ways to travel in those days were by horseback, carriage, and foot. Travelling over sea was done in sailing vessels, which depended upon the wind for motion. Therefore a trip was long and tedious. As time passed, the methods became better and better, until the steam engine was invented and put into practical use. A little later the steamship was also invented and used. But these motorized vehicles were yet to be greatly improved. And now we come to the present day with subways and overhead trains that greatly improve the method of travelling. — Pupil

Practice 15. Building a Paragraph

Using one of the following topic sentences as a foundation, build a paragraph. First gather material, searching especially for examples, illustrations, comparisons, pictures, and other concrete support of the topic sentence. Ask, "How?" "Why?" "What?" "What of it?" "What is it like or unlike?" "What example or illustration will make my point clear?" and "How do I know?" Then write the paragraph, revise thoroughly and carefully, and copy neatly.

1. There is one like him in every class.
2. There are some people who think cats aren't intelligent, but I say they are.
3. Everyone should learn how to swim.
4. That was the busiest half hour of my life.
5. Forgetfulness sometimes leads to much embarrassment.
6. A hike through the woods is interesting.
7. Clean-up week is essential for the safety of homes and lives.
8. Theodore Roosevelt had outstanding characteristics.
9. During the month the moon presents different appearances to an observer.
10. All is not gold that glitters.
11. The grounds were liberally fringed with spectators, who had never before witnessed a scene so thrilling.
12. To be successful in any branch of business, one must be interested in one's work.
13. There are many things one can do in case of fire.
14. Prompt and intelligent first aid, deftly tendered, is a life-saving accomplishment when accidents occur on the road.
15. People often make fun of "star gazers," but they would be very badly off if it were not for the star gazers.
16. A hunter needs patience, endurance, and skill.
17. Many poor boys have become great men.
18. *Popular Science Monthly* (or another magazine) is a magazine I enjoy.

BRIDGES FOR COHERENCE

Coherence means "hanging together" and includes the proper arrangement of the ideas and bridging over the gaps between sentences with connectives that show the exact relationship of part to part.

Arrangement

The different sentences that compose a paragraph should follow one another in natural and logical order. If they do not, the attention of the reader is distracted, and he finds it difficult, if not impossible, to keep the thread of the discourse.

Connectives

It is not enough that the sentences of a paragraph follow one another in proper order; the connection of each with the preceding context must be made clear and unmistakable.

A steel, concrete, or wooden bridge joins the two banks of a river; a word bridge joins two sentences or paragraphs and keeps the reader's thought in the path the writer or speaker wishes him to take. Taine, speaking of connective words and phrases, says, "The art of writing is the art of using hooks and eyes."

Useful bridges, or, to change the figure, useful hooks and eyes are *this, that, these, those, such,* and *same,* personal pronouns, repeated nouns, synonyms, adverbs, conjunctions, and connective phrases. Some of these expressions carry the idea forward; most of them look backward.

Example:

(The bridge words or phrases are italicized.)

Every girl should learn how to make her own dresses because of the numerous advantages in knowing how to sew. *In the first place,* there is a great saving in money, which she can invest in more materials for new dresses. Every *girl* likes to have an extensive wardrobe. *Moreover* nobody likes to have a dress that is duplicated by almost everyone she meets. In making one's own clothes, *this* danger is lessened. *Indeed,* if a girl is clever, she can design her frocks herself, and so have exclusive models with an individual touch. *Another* advantage of sewing is that it teaches patience, an admirable virtue. *Therefore* the girl who has learned to sew well has a substantial handicap over her helpless sister. — PUPIL

The repeated word is called an "echo word."

To add ideas use: *and, moreover, further, furthermore, also, likewise, similarly, too, in like manner, again, in the same way, besides.* These words are plus signs.

To introduce statements opposing, negativing, or limiting in some way the preceding statements use: *but, nevertheless, otherwise, on the other hand, conversely, on the contrary, however, yet, still.* These words are minus signs.

To show time relation use: *then, now, somewhat later, presently, thereupon, thereafter, eventually, at the same time, meanwhile.*

To indicate order use: *next, in the second place, to begin with, finally, secondly, in conclusion, first.*

To show space relation use: *to the right, in the distance, straight ahead, at the left.*

To introduce illustrations use: *for instance, for example.*

To indicate a consequence or conclusion use: *hence, consequently, thus, so, for this reason, accordingly, therefore, as a result, it follows that.*

To indicate a repetition of the idea use: *briefly, that is to say, in fact, indeed, in other words.*

To compare use: *similarly, likewise.*

When the thoughts are very closely related, no connective is required.

Practice 16. Using Word Bridges

On two of the following topic sentences plan and write paragraphs. Stick to your subjects. Make your development full and complete. Use as many word bridges as are needed. Underscore all conjunctions and connective phrases used to bridge the gaps between sentences.

1. Just then I heard a strange noise outside my window.
2. I fished a long time before I caught anything.
3. He showed great courage that time.
4. You can't get something for nothing.
5. Covering a book is a simple operation if it is done correctly.
6. One night while I was staying at Lake George (or another place) I had a strange experience.
7. There are books and plays that should have poison labels on them to warn us of their contents.
8. During a summer vacation at Lake Mahopac (or another place) one may enjoy many sports.
9. A place of interest I visited this summer was the Parliamentary Library (or another).
10. A *Son of the Middle Border* (or another book) is worth reading.
11. My favourite movie actor is James Mason (or another).
12. Winter is a very enjoyable season.
13. Although some of us do not think so, Latin helps to prepare us for later years.
14. The Y. M. C. A. benefits every boy that joins.
15. He tramped in, where a surprise awaited him.
16. Eat at your table as you would eat at the table of a king.
17. Practice makes perfect.
18. Everyone really ought to read *The Mutineers* by Hawes (or another book).
19. Owning a dog has its disadvantages.
20. There are several reasons why I have chosen detective work (or another occupation) for my life work.
21. The smoking of cigarettes is harmful.
22. What you know after studying depends on the way you study.

EMPHASIS

Emphasis requires that significant matters stand out and unimportant details keep in the background. The beginning and the ending of a paragraph, story, magazine article, or book are especially important. First impressions are lasting, and the ending is longest remembered.

If you have run a hundred-yard race, you know that it is important to be off with the crack of the pistol and to cross the finish line at top speed. To make a paragraph emphatic place the important ideas near the beginning and the end and give them the most space.

Some workmen when the quitting hour arrives just drop their tools and run. Others—bank clerks, for example—complete the work of the day before going home. There are likewise two ways of ending a paragraph—just stopping, and finishing it. A good way to end a paragraph is to close it with the most important sentence.

Practice 17. Studying Paragraphs

Examine each of the following paragraphs and answer these questions about it:

1. Has it a topic sentence? What?
2. Does it show evidence of planning? What?
3. Does the paragraph stick to its subject? Prove.
4. Are word bridges used? What?
5. Are the most important ideas placed near the beginning and the end and given most space?
6. How is the paragraph developed?

1

With the crowding of people into the cities has come a greater appreciation of nature and increased interest in the *Nature Magazine*. Although we city dwellers are deprived of the joys of the fields and woods, we may turn the pages of the *Nature Magazine* and see the same sights, hear the same sounds, and smell the same fragrances as we could in the wide open spaces. Reading the *Nature Magazine* is like spending a holiday in the great outdoors; watching the wild ducks in their flight through the clear, blue sky; drinking in the pure air of the forests while sitting motionless on a rock; and watching and waiting, scarcely breathing, while the timid wild creatures carry on their daily life. What finer sentiment could be inspired in children than the love of living and growing things? — PUPIL

2

How much of our language do dogs understand? Perhaps a good deal more than we generally imagine. In learning a foreign language a person arrives at a stage where most of what the foreign people say is broadly intelligible to him, and yet he cannot express himself. Very young children understand a great deal before they are able to express themselves in words. Even horses—and horses are incomparably less intelligent than dogs—understand a complete vocabulary of orders. May not a dog of ability enter to some extent into the meaning of spoken language, even though he may never be able to use it? — PUPIL

Practice 18. Studying Paragraphs

Find in a magazine article, a newspaper editorial, or a book two unusually good paragraphs and show that they are excellent. Has each paragraph a topic sentence? Unity? A plan? Word bridges? Emphasis?

Studying, Taking Notes, and Answering Questions

IF you want to build a happy high school career, be sure to rest it on a foundation of good study habits. Everyone can learn how to study. No one just naturally knows how. Everyone has to teach himself.

Besides saving time, the boy or girl who knows how to study gets a clearer understanding of a lesson and remembers it longer. As a result he receives higher marks in school and college, and after graduation finds more easily the kind of position he wants. Many vocations demand continual study. The world moves rapidly. Most workers must study to keep up to date. To be efficient and successful the physician, the teacher, the lawyer, the engineer must become acquainted every year with new discoveries or developments in his field.

There is one fundamental rule: **Always study with a purpose.** Think what you are going to learn in each lesson, why you are learning it, and how you can use it.

Practice 1. Examining Study Hints

How many of the following hints do you observe? Rate yourself by counting one point for each habit you have formed. Check your rating every school day to measure your improvement. Aim for a perfect score of 16 and try to maintain it. Have you found any other study hints helpful? Share them with your classmates.

1. Study at a regular time each school day, when neither your body nor your mind is tired. It is better to divide your study time—to study before and after dinner or in the morning and the evening, for example.
2. Study in a quiet, well-ventilated room, where neither radio nor chatter can distract you. Keep the temperature at 68 to 70 degrees.
3. Use a reading light that does not glare and is so placed as to avoid a shadow on your work. Don't read with the sunlight falling directly on the page.
4. Work at a desk or table. Sit in a straight chair. Vary your posture, but never sit on your spine.
5. Before you start to study, have within reach all necessary materials: paper, pencil, eraser, pen, ink, blotter, textbook, notebook, maps, dictionary, ruler.

6. Attack your lessons actively. Don't dawdle or find excuses for doing something else first. Prove to yourself that you are master of the situation by plunging into the job, completing it, and relaxing afterward.

7. Copy your assignments accurately, and do exactly the work expected of you.

8. Learn to read with a purpose. If you are looking in a book for a particular fact, use the table of contents or index to guide you to specific pages. Skim material until your eye catches the fact you are searching for. Develop your judgment about when to skim and when to read thoroughly.

9. Practise remembering what you read. After reading a paragraph or a chapter, close your book and recite aloud what you have learned. Take brief notes (pages 113–114). Help yourself to remember by reading, writing, and saying what you want to retain, but especially by understanding how the idea is important to you.

10. Look for points emphasized. Pay special attention to information in italics or boldface (heavy) type.

11. Notice chapter and paragraph headings and topic sentences. They tell you what to expect.

12. If there is a summary at the end of the chapter, read it with particular care.

13. Use your dictionary freely. Look up the pronunciation and meaning of unfamiliar words.

14. When you have finished, close your book and think over what you have read. Say aloud the important ideas and facts without looking at the text. Talk over with your family and fellow students what you have learned.

15. To rest your eyes and your mind, stop every half hour and exercise for a few minutes.

16. Revise and proofread all your written work. Be watchful of your reputation as a careful, accurate workman.

READING PURPOSEFULLY

To avoid wasting time, know exactly what information you need to secure. If your teacher has assigned questions to be answered in your reading, study them carefully. Know exactly what each one means. Then, as you read the selection, keep your eyes open for the answers. When you find the facts you need, fix them firmly in your memory. Jotting the questions and answers down in your note-book will impress the information on your mind and will help you to review quickly and easily.

Use the table of contents at the front of a book and the index at the back to find material. When you are looking for the answers to specific questions, paragraph headings and topic sentences will help you decide what passages to read.

Practice 2. Reading to Answer Questions

After reading the set of questions, find the answers as quickly as you can in the paragraph following.

1

1. Who established the Pony Express?
2. How old were most of the riders?
3. About how far did a rider travel in a day?
4. About how far did a rider travel in an hour?
5. What was the purpose of the Pony Express?

The life span of the famous Pony Express was only nineteen months. With a capital of $100,000 the firm of Russell, Majors, and Waddell established the system to carry mail from the Mississippi to San Francisco. Every ten to twenty-five miles along the route there were hired or built relay stations, where riders could secure fresh horses. Since the maximum weight of the riders had been set at one hundred twenty pounds, most of them were boys in their teens. Riding from seven to twelve hours a day, a messenger covered from sixty to one hundred miles. Young as the riders were, they showed courage and resourcefulness in their encounters with Indians and bandits.

UNDERSTANDING WHAT IS READ

Reading isn't a lazy man's job. If you want to understand what you read, you've got to keep your mind on it. When you strike a snag in the form of a difficult sentence, stop and dig out the meaning. When an unfamiliar word baffles you, turn for help to your faithful dictionary.

Always concentrate on understanding facts, not on memorizing words. When you have finished a passage, try to repeat the author's ideas in your own words. If the chapter contains questions or problems to test your understanding of what you have read, answer or solve them carefully.

Finding the Main Idea

The first thing to do as you read, of course, is to get the main idea of a passage. Every page of print is divided into paragraphs. Ordinarily in a paragraph one subject is treated. Commonly the paragraph has a topic or key sentence that states briefly what the paragraph is about. In the following paragraph, for instance, the principal clause of the first sentence contains the main idea of the passage: that rivers help man in a variety of ways.

Although rivers sometimes overflow their banks and cause great hardship and suffering, ordinarily they help man in a variety of ways. First of all, they furnish a means of transporting passengers and freight. Some cities obtain their water supply from rivers. Streams irrigate the farmers' lands and carry away sewage and wastes from factories and homes. In time of war a broad, deep river is an excellent defense.

Noting Details

The habit of sharp, discriminating observation makes the world a fascinating place to live in and increases one's fund of usable information. Likewise noting interesting, colourful, important details adds

to the fun and the profit of reading. In the paragraph about the usefulness of rivers, for example, the second, third, fourth, and fifth sentences
add details to support the main idea. Each sentence mentions a
different way in which rivers are helpful to man.

DRAWING CONCLUSIONS

From the way people look and act we can sometimes draw sound
conclusions. If we meet a friend who is normally plump and vigorous
and notice that she is now thin and listless, we conclude that she has
been ill, worried, or overworked. Although nobody actually tells us
in so many words that something unusual has happened to our friend,
we draw our conclusion from the clues presented by her appearance
and her manner.

Frequently, too, we can draw conclusions from the facts given us
by an author. In the preceding paragraph about rivers, for example,
we might conclude after reading the second sentence that it is especially
advantageous for an industrial city like Montreal, which must ship
out large quantities of manufactured goods, to be situated on a river.
From the fourth sentence we might logically draw the conclusion
that the valleys of the Fraser and the Red River are fertile agricultural
areas.

Practice 3.   Drawing Conclusions from What Is Read

Read carefully each of the following. Find all the clues. Then write
on your paper the correct word or number to complete the last sentence.

1

When Achilles was a baby, his mother was warned that her son would die
at an early age. Terrified at the thought of losing the child, she dipped him
in the river Styx. Only his heel, by which she held him, was not submerged
in the water, which, the Greeks believed, rendered the body immune to
wounds. Years later Achilles fought with reckless bravery in the Trojan
War. No one it seemed, could wound him. At last, however, the god Apollo
guided an arrow which killed Achilles by hitting him in the ——.

2

To find the diameter of a circle, divide the circumference by π, which
equals 3.1416. The diameter of a tree nine feet in circumference is approximately —— feet.

3

Arterial blood pressure depends on the force with which the heart propels
the blood through the body. As the blood travels through the arteries away
from the heart, the initial force of the momentum provided by the heart beat
is steadily diminished. Blood pressure in an artery in the foot therefore is
——than blood pressure in an artery in the upper arm.

Practice 4. Reading with Understanding

After reading each of the following paragraphs, answer the questions at the end.

1

With a splash the baby lizard lowered himself into the muddy water of the stream. Near by floated two huge logs; at least, that's what they looked like to the lizard. Suddenly, however, one of the objects came to life; the sharp teeth of a crocodile snapped beneath the lizard's body, and its tail thrashed the water beside him. Desperately the lizard darted toward the bank and scuttled into the forest. On and on he went, not daring to look back lest he see behind him a huge pair of jaws edged with merciless teeth.

1. What word best describes how the lizard felt at the sight of the crocodiles?
   angry   calm   courageous   indifferent   terrified
2. From the facts in the paragraph which of the following statements do you know to be true? Which do you know to be false?
   a. The baby lizard was bathing in a clear, sparkling stream.
   b. The baby lizard was recklessly brave and feared nothing.
   c. A floating crocodile looks like a log.
3. Which of the following conclusions might you draw from the paragraph?
   a. Baby lizards like water.
   b. A baby lizard cannot live out of water.
   c. Crocodiles like to eat baby lizards.

2

As an airplane mechanic you will have full responsibility for the airworthy condition of a plane, checking wings, wires, struts, wheels, and fuel tanks. You must see that every part of the plane is in perfect repair, that all necessary greasing is done, and that the fuel tanks are full. Your work may include assembling new planes. If you are an engine mechanic you will have charge of the servicing, maintaining, repairing, and overhauling of modern aircraft engines. You will give each plane a complete inspection and overhauling after it has spent a given number of hours in the air, and you may be called upon to give quick emergency repairs. The pilot uses navigation instruments in getting information about altitude, direction, temperature, wind velocity, and the speed of his plane. It will be your job as an instrument mechanic to adjust, repair, test, and sometimes install these instruments. As a radio electrician you will install and repair radio and electrical equipment. The law requires the inspection, repair, and repacking of parachutes at stated intervals. This will be your work if you are a parachute rigger. As any other skilled worker, you will perform the work of your group just as you would in any other industry in which you might be employed.[1] — DAVEY, SMITH, AND MYERS, *Everyday Occupations*

1. Which of the following titles tells most accurately and completely what the paragraph is about?
   a. The duties of an airplane mechanic
   b. The duties of skilled workers in an air transport company
   c. The inspection and care of parachutes

[1] *Reprinted by permission of the publisher, D. C. Heath and Company*

2. From the paragraph which of the following statements do you know to
be true? Which do you know to be false? Which may be either true or
false—that is, the paragraph does not include the facts necessary to
determine their accuracy?

a. It is the responsibility of the airplane mechanic to see that fuel tanks
are filled.

b. The instrument which registers the altitude of a plane is called the
altimeter.

c. The engine mechanic tests and repairs radio equipment.

d. After a parachute is packed in a factory, it is never opened except for an
emergency jump.

e. Airplane and engine mechanics are licensed by the Federal government.

3. Which of the following conclusions might you draw from the paragraph?

a. The safety of the pilot and passengers in a plane depends in large measure
on the ground crew.

b. Airplane and engine mechanics must be intelligent, reliable men who
understand planes thoroughly.

c. Every pilot on a transport plane is required to take a parachute jump
at least twice a year to keep in practice.

UNDERSTANDING DIRECTIONS

Before you take a dose of medicine, or use a different kind of shoe
polish, or try a new shampoo, you carefully read the directions on the
container. You know that they will help you get the best results from
the product. Similarly, the directions in your textbook are given to
guide you, to tell you just what to do and how to do it.

When you read instructions, sweep your mind clean of everything
else and concentrate on the printed material. If you don't understand
the directions the first time, read them again—as many times as you
find necessary. A dictionary is probably a student's best friend; use
yours if an unfamiliar word in the directions puzzles you. Finally, ask
yourself, "Do I know just what to do and how to do it?" If—and
that's an important *if*—you can truthfully answer yes, you are ready
to set to work.

TAKING NOTES

For a number of reasons note-taking is a valuable method of studying. A pupil who takes notes as he studies his lessons or listens in
class searches out the main points. Writing down the important ideas
helps him to remember them and makes review easy.

Pupils take notes also in preparation for speeches and reports.
Taking notes helps one to remember what he sees, hears, reads, thinks,
and does.

As you read a selection, search for the main points. Be on the alert
for clues. Read with special care all headings and the first and the
last sentence of each paragraph. After you have selected the main
ideas, notice the subtopics.

EXAMPLE OF NOTE-TAKING WHILE STUDYING A LESSON

Why pupils go to sch.
  Acquire knowledge and develop skills
  Play and make friends
  Fit themselves to make good living
  Enjoy books, art, music, nature, people
  Be intel., responsible citizens
  Develop and maintain health as aid to happiness and success
H. protection in sch.
  Clean floors, corridors, lunchr., washr., and toilets
  Temperature of r.—68°–70°
  Proper adjustment of chairs and desks
  Control of communicable diseases
    Morning inspection
    Insp. after vacation
    Sending home sick pupil
    Staying away from others when danger giving dis.
    Vaccination
  Phys. exam.

How to Take Notes on What You Read

1. Read the lesson through without writing a word.

2. Think over what you have read; or, better yet, close your book and reproduce it aloud.

3. As you read the lesson again, write down the main points briefly in your own words.

4. Group the notes under headings.

5. Abbreviate freely. Omit articles and other unnecessary words.

How to Take Notes in Class

1. As the teacher or a pupil talks, jot down important points.

2. At the earliest opportunity read over your notes. Make sure you will be able to understand them in a month's time.

3. Group the notes under headings.

Practice 5. Taking Notes

1. Take notes this evening as you study one subject. Bring your notes to class to copy on the blackboard. Be ready to reproduce the lesson from your notes.

2. Take notes on a radio speech or a magazine article and reproduce it accurately and entertainingly in class.

3. Take notes on directions your English teacher gives you. Prepare to tell clearly, accurately, completely what you are to do.

HOW SHOULD YOU MAKE A RECITATION?

The first step in making a satisfactory recitation is listening to the assignment. When the teacher is giving the homework for the next day, write down accurately what you are to do. If at the end of the assignment you do not know exactly what is required of you, ask a question to find out.

If you have prepared thoroughly for the day's recitation, you will have at your finger tips the answers to most of the teacher's questions, but be patient and courteous. Volunteer quietly; don't wave your hand wildly in the air or chant happily, "I know, I know!" When you recite, talk to the whole class and speak distinctly so that everyone can hear you. Cut your sentences apart. Avoid a string of *and's* and *ur's*.

When the teacher asks you a question, don't blurt out the first thing that pops into your head. Keep calm; take time to consider what information is called for. Think through your answer before giving it aloud. If possible, include the essential information in your first sentence.

Don't bluff. If you don't know the answer, say, "I'm sorry, Miss White, I can't answer that question," or something similar. If some would-be-helpful soul hisses the answer at you, turn a deaf ear. You're entirely capable of doing your own work.

Be ready to take an active part in the discussion of the lesson. Do not just be on the defensive, waiting to be asked questions. When you go to class, have something to say or some question to ask. In class listen sharply to what the teacher and your classmates say.

HOW SHOULD YOU TAKE AN EXAMINATION?

Skill in taking examinations is valuable in and out of school. To succeed in high school or college, a student must pass tests and examinations. When you apply for a job, you'll probably be given a test. Civil service positions are filled by competitive examinations. In business, civil service, and professions many promotions depend partly on the ability to pass examinations.

HINTS ON TAKING AN EXAMINATION

1. *Keep up with your work from day to day. You can't absorb in three hours' cramming all the information covered in a five months' course.*
2. *Review calmly for the examination. Master the points stressed by your teacher. Reread the summaries in your textbook. With the book closed say aloud the important facts and ideas.*
3. *Ask yourself, "If I were the teacher, what questions would I ask?" Write out or think out your complete answers to the questions that pop into your mind.*
4. *If possible, study previous examination papers to see what type of questions you will probably be called upon to answer.*
5. *To discover your weak points, look over your previous tests in the subject.*

6. *Be physically fit. Get at least eight hours' sleep the night before. Eat a substantial breakfast. Arrive in the examination room early.*
7. *Keep calm. The examination calls for the same kind of work you have done in class.*
8. *Arm yourself with all the equipment you'll need: fountain pen or pens filled with ink, blotter, sharpened pencils, compass. Jot down a list and check off each item before you leave home.*
9. *To relieve your curiosity, look over the entire test. On scrap paper jot down briefly points you might forget.*
10. *Notice how many questions you are required to answer. If you are allowed a choice, select the ones on which you can write from experience or which you understand thoroughly.*
11. *Note the credit assigned to each question and budget your time accordingly. A ten-point question ordinarily deserves only one fourth as much time as a forty-point one.*
12. *Read the directions carefully. Pay special attention to words like and, or, each. Know exactly what the question calls for.*
13. *On practice paper jot down all the facts you know on a topic; then arrange them in order. If you have time, write out each answer first on scrap paper.*
14. *Include in the first sentence the essential point of an answer. Beginning the answer with words of the question will help you to keep to the subject and will show the examiner that you know what you are to do. In answering the question "Why is milk sometimes called the perfect food?" begin, "Milk is sometimes called the perfect food because—." Glance occasionally at the initial sentence to make sure you are keeping to the point.*
15. *After writing each answer, reread the question. Make sure you have included all the information called for.*
16. *Use words that say exactly what you mean.*
17. *Leave a blank line between answers.*
18. *If you write neatly and legibly, your paper will seem clearer and your mark will be higher. Unless otherwise instructed, use ink.*
19. *Use 10 per cent of your time for revision. Correct errors and improve the wording.*
20. *Before handing in your paper, check the questions you have answered and thus make sure you have completed the examination.*

Practice 6.   Analyzing Questions

Analyze each of the following questions. State specifically and completely what information each question calls for. Write in sentences. Spell every word correctly.

Example:

In a single clear-cut sentence for each, present a principal point made in each of five essays. Give titles and authors.

This question calls for the writing of five sentences. Each sentence will include (1) the title of an essay, (2) the name of the author, and (3) an important idea developed in the essay.

1. Are plays, as given over the radio, worthy competitors for our time and attention with plays of the legitimate stage and the screen? Defend your

views in a carefully organized answer. Refer to at least one production of each type.

2. Explain what is meant by the statement: A gas burns but does not support burning. To which gas that you studied does this statement apply? Which gas supports burning but does not burn? Which gases neither support burning nor burn?[1]

3. List four good magazines in the order of their merit. Consider both their educational and entertainment value. In not more than three sentences for each, give the following information for each of the four:
   a. Price
   b. Type of subject matter it contains. Be specific.
   c. Type of reader to whom it appeals
   d. Distinguishing features

Practice 7. Answering Questions

Select one of the preceding questions and answer it thoroughly. Plan before you write. Build clear, concise, varied sentences (pages 220–237). Spell every word correctly.

[1]*Reprinted from Kroeber and Wolff's* Adventures with Living Things *by permission of the publisher* D. C. Heath and Company.

UNIT TEN

Explaining

ALL day long people use their powers of speech to instruct others. The teacher explains to his pupils; the coach, to his team; the foreman, to his men; the manager, to his department heads; the salesman, to his customers; the farmer, to his workmen; the physician, to his patients. You yourself explain every time you answer a question beginning with "Why?" "How?" or "What?"

To succeed in a responsible position a person needs to be able to make good explanations. The engineer who can't explain the advantages of his plans may have a city council, board, or committee reject them for poorer plans the strong points of which are made clear. A salesman who knows his goods and has the best on the market may fail to sell because he can't make clear the superiority of his product. A teacher may know how to solve a problem yet be unable to make the solution clear to the class.

When your teacher calls on you to answer a question, he expects you to explain what you think or have learned, and gives no credit for the answer, "I understand that but can't explain it."

HOW CAN YOU EXPLAIN CLEARLY?

Know Your Subject

The purpose of explanation is to make something plain or clear. No one can explain to another person a subject that is hazy in his own mind. Before you try to explain, therefore, know the subject thoroughly and accurately. If you don't have all the facts necessary for a clear exposition, either find them or don't try to explain the subject.

Practice 1. Knowing the Subject

How many of these subjects do you understand thoroughly? Jot down the numbers of the subjects about which you have accurate, definite, and complete information. You will be called on in class for an oral explanation of one of these subjects. A blackboard diagram may help you to make your explanation clear. Apply what you have learned about verbs.

1. What causes the succession of day and night? 2. What causes the change of seasons? 3. Why the days are shorter in winter. 4. Why an airplane

118

flies. 5. How to pitch a curve. 6. How to salute the flag. 7. How to display a flag either horizontally or vertically against a wall. 8. How one born in another country becomes a citizen of Canada. 9. How to identify a P-38 (or another plane). 10. How a Provincial Premier is elected. 11. What the Junior Red Cross does. 12. How to float on one's back. 13. How to distinguish the tracks of animals. 14. How to kindle a fire in the rain. 15. How to find one's way out of the woods. 16. How to select a camp site. 17. How to care for dairy cattle in the winter. 18. How to stop bleeding from a cut. 19. How to give first aid to a person who has fainted. 20. How to treat a burn. 21. What happens when one lifts the telephone receiver? 22. Why the province maintains public schools. 23. How to remove a foreign body from the eye. 24. How to prevent colds. 25. How to apply artificial respiration. 26. How to tell a Navy officer's rank.

27. The uses of the white cells of the blood. 28. What the signs of approaching rain are. 29. What to do when an electrical appliance fails to work. 30. How to find the positive pole of an unmarked battery. 31. Why the tide comes in and goes out. 32. Why milk turns sour. 33. What the Army uses jeeps for. 34. How to break a colt. 35. Why an iron ship floats. 36. What the carburetor does. 37. How to build a fire without matches. 38. What to do for a snake bite. 39. How to tell an Army officers' branch of service. 40. How to tie a square knot. 41. How to shift gears in an automobile. 42. How a hydraulic press works. 43. How to build a self-feeder for hogs.

Plan and Outline

No boy builds a model plane, a radio set, or a table without first planning. If the construction is very simple, he can, of course, carry the plans in his head. It is usually safer to have them on paper. Likewise you can plan in your head a simple explanation, but you will need pencil and paper for planning a longer or more complicated one.

Three things you must determine in planning are (1) what facts to present, (2) the order in which to present them, and (3) the materials needed to make your explanation clear and entertaining. To explain how to recognize animal tracks, for example, can you show photographs or draw simple diagrams? In deciding what to include, you will have to take into account the general intelligence of your reader or hearer and his knowledge of the subject. Explaining to one of the boys the fake kick that won the football game is quite different from making your grandmother understand.

A good general rule in arranging material is to give first the facts needed in understanding other facts. Plan to lead the reader or hearer, step by step, from what he knows to related facts or ideas you wish to make clear. If you intend, for example, to explain how to do the elementary back stroke, you will first determine whether your pupil can float on his back. Finding that he can, you know that he is ready to learn what to do with his arms and legs. Since the arm movements are relatively simple, you will probably begin with them, using demonstration or a diagram to make the motions clear. Then you will explain to your pupil how to draw up his legs, kick them out, and return them to floating position. Finally you will instruct him to combine the arm and leg movements.

When you explain a process—making a cake, washing dishes, planting seeds, or building a kennel, for example—you will naturally want to arrange the details in time order—that is, the order in which you would do them. Try to carry out in imagination the process you are describing. Say to yourself, "I've just creamed the shortening and sugar, and beaten in the eggs. What do I do next?"

Practice 2.   Arranging Facts Sensibly

If you were explaining each of the following subjects, in what order would you arrange the topics?

How to apply artificial respiration. Applying pressure for two seconds. Placing hands on victim's ribs. Placing the victim in position. Straddling the victim. Continuing process as long as necessary.

How to make a dress. Pinning the pattern on the material. Hemming the skirt. Basting seams. Buying material and a pattern. Cutting out the dress. Sewing seams permanently by hand or on a machine.

OUTLINING

An outline, which is a written plan of what you are going to say, should be definite and meaty. A vague or empty outline, so brief as to give little or no information about the subject, is neither interesting nor valuable. Put important facts into the outline and indicate clearly what you intend to say on every point.

Making an outline will help you to find out whether you really understand your subject, or arrange your ideas in a sensible order, and to discover what additional material you need to secure.

HOW TO TEACH A BABY TO WALK

I. Equipment
    A. Correct shoes
    B. Soft rug, pillows
    C. Rattle or toy

II. Procedure
    A. Placing the baby against a wall
    B. Moving a few feet away
    C. Coaxing the baby to cross the distance by offering a rattle or toy as a reward

III. Things to avoid
    A. Encouraging the baby to walk at too early an age
    B. Tiring the baby
    C. Letting the baby have a bad fall

EXPLAINING

How to Outline

1. Note in the example that the main topics are numbered I, II, III, and the subtopics under each main head, A, B, C. Print these capital letters. Subtopics under capital letters are numbered 1, 2, 3, 4; subtopics under Arabic numerals, a, b, c, d.

2. Subtopics are begun farther to the right than main topics. The second line of a topic begins under the first word of the topic. Keep corresponding letters or numbers in vertical columns: I, II, III, IV; A, B, C, D; 1, 2, 3, 4.

3. Capitalize the first word of each topic and other words that would be capitalized in a sentence.

4. Place a period after each topic number or letter and at the end of each sentence.

5. Never write a single subtopic—that is, an A without a B following it, or a 1 without a 2 following it. Subtopics are subdivisions. When you divide, you have two or more parts. When you would like to write one subtopic, include the main point or fact in the main topic.

6. Express all topics of the same rank in similar form. If I is a sentence, II and III should also be sentences; if A is a noun with or without modifiers, B and C should also be nouns with or without modifiers; if 1 is a phrase, 2 and 3 should also be phrases.

7. Avoid having a large number of main topics. Be sure that each one is an important division of the subject and not merely a subtopic.

Practice 3.   Preparing an Outline

Below are the main topics and subtopics necessary for an outline on how to make peanut brittle. Select the two main topics and on your paper number them I, II. Then arrange the subtopics properly and label them A, B, C, etc.

Melting sugar in frying pan over low heat. Materials. Iron frying pan. Stirring constantly until sugar is melted and is golden brown in colour. Half cup of roasted peanuts. Removing from the heat and adding nuts and salt quickly. Marking in squares when nearly cold. Process. Cake pan. Stirring just enough to mix. Pouring on greased pan in thin sheet. One cup of sugar. Chopping the peanuts. Dash of salt.

Practice 4.   Writing an Outline

Write the outline for an explanation of one of the following. If possible, select something you yourself have done. Arrange your material logically and include every necessary fact. Keep this outline. You will need it later.

1. How to raise roses, tomatoes, or another flower or vegetable. 2. How to teach a dog tricks. 3. How to catch trout (or other fish). 4. How to toast

marshmallows. 5. How to sweep a room. 6. How to pitch a tent. 7. How to put on an automobile tire. 8. How to sharpen a knife. 9. How to patch a bicycle tire. 10. How to mark out a tennis court or a football field. 11. How to drive a team of horses. 12. How to learn to swim. 13. How to read the electric metre. 14. How to build a furnace fire. 15. How to paddle a canoe. 16. How to ride a horse. 17. How to take a picture. 18. How to build a campfire. 19. How to sail a boat.

20. How to make a bed. 21. How to improve the soil of a garden. 22. How to pick cherries or apples. 23. How to use the *Readers' Guide*. 24. How to prepare a campfire dinner. 25. How to remove stains. 26. How to darn socks or stockings. 27. How to do up a package for mailing. 28. How to cover a book. 29. How to make a swan dive. 30. How to set one's hair. 31. How to can peaches, pears, or other fruit. 32. How to entertain a group of boys or girls. 33. How to broil a steak out of doors. 34. How to bandage a sprained ankle. 35. How to make a block print. 36. How to wax an automobile. 37. How to splice a wire or rope. 38. How to distill water. 39. How to patch a garment. 40. How to polish furniture. 41. How to care for one's clothing. 42. How to prepare for an examination.

Explain Completely

If an explanation of handball, raising head lettuce, pitching a tent, catching trout, or diving omits one necessary direction, it is worthless. In raising head lettuce, for example, both fertilizing and cultivating are necessary. If an amateur gardener follows directions that omit either of these essentials, his lettuce will be headless.

Be Clear and Interesting

You may know how to swim, construct a radio set, play tennis, raise beans, or write verse, and yet fail to explain the subject clearly. Explanation is of value only if every important point is made clear to one who does not understand the subject, or perhaps knows nothing about it.

Look into Your Reader's Mind

Think of your reader or hearer as stopping you every ten seconds to ask, "Why?" "What for?" "How?" "What of it?" Answer every question in his mind. When you plan your explanation of how to dive, how to paint a room, how to play handball, or how to prune an apple tree, be an amateur mind reader. Look into the minds of your classmates and find out what some will not understand or what mistakes others will make in carrying out your directions. Then take pains to make these points clear to everyone. Hang a red danger sign on each stumbling block. Spend more time or space on these difficult points and, if necessary, explain them in various ways.

Use Examples and Comparisons

Often a comparison or an example helps a writer or a speaker to make his subject clear. In *Adventures with Living Things*, for instance,

Kroeber and Wolff say, "Scientists have calculated that if all the red corpuscles of a normal person, microscopic as they are in size, were laid out next to one another, they would cover an area larger than that of a baseball diamond. This does not mean much to you unless you appreciate how extremely minute each corpuscle is: 5,000,000 of them would take up only about as much room as a coarse grain of sand." The comparison adds both clarity and force to the explanation.

Use Diagrams, Pictures, and Charts

A diagram or a picture may show at a glance what many words would not make equally clear. A picture, says a Chinese proverb, is worth a thousand words. In explaining how to make or build something, you will almost always need a diagram. When your explanation deals with numbers, often a chart will help you to show the significance of a set of figures. Diagrams, pictures, and charts need not be artistic masterpieces but should be neat, clear, and accurate.

Use Clear, Accurate Language

"When I use a word," says Humpty Dumpty in *Alice in Wonderland*, "it means just what I choose it to mean—neither more nor less." In real life, however, we cannot use words so casually. If your reader or hearer is to understand your explanation, you will need to express yourself in accurate, clear language. When you use a scientific or technical term, define it in simple words for those to whom it is unfamiliar.

Be Concise

Sometimes boys and girls have the idea that the more words they use the clearer will be their explanation. That, however, is not true. When you write or speak, aim to clear a path straight to your goal, not to wander in circles around it. In revision cross out repetitions and useless words. Whenever you can, substitute a simple sentence with a compound predicate for a compound sentence or two simple sentences.

By brevity an explanation gains not only clarity but also vigour. By compact wording a writer or speaker can often in a single sentence explain adequately *how* or *why*.

Examples:

Because people found it inconvenient to carry around gold and silver for use in trading, governments printed paper certificates to represent the metal, which was kept as security in vaults.

Although the jellyfish is not a good swimmer, it can move through the water by waving its tentacles or contracting its body.

Practice 5. Explaining in a Sentence

Using a sentence for each, explain five of the following:
1. How milk is pasteurized. 2. How a motion may be amended. 3. How to fill a fountain pen. 4. How to make lemonade. 5. How to recognize poison ivy. 6. How the government raises money in wartime. 7. How the grasshopper makes a noise. 8. Why milk is often called the perfect food. 9. Why people should wear light-coloured clothes in the summer. 10. Why it is important for the citizens of a democracy to be able to recognize propaganda. 11. Why most reptiles are found in the tropics. 12. Why nature has enabled the chameleon to change the colour of its skin. 13. Why farmers usually favour a low tariff on manufactured goods. 14. Why the friendship of the United States is important to us. 15. How to recognize a Flying Fortress (or another plane).

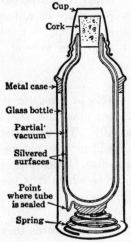

Cup

Cork

Metal case

Glass bottle

Partial vacuum

Silvered surfaces

Point where tube is sealed

Spring

Practice 6. Studying an Explanation

1. Is the following explanation accurate, clear, complete, and concise?
2. Of what use is the diagram?

A VACUUM BOTTLE

A vacuum bottle, used to keep liquids hot or cold, is a double-walled glass container, usually enclosed in a metal case and resting on a spring to prevent its breaking. After most of the air is pumped from the space between the glass walls, the opening is sealed (see diagram). Since the partial vacuum thus created is a poor conductor of heat, the temperature of a liquid in the bottle changes slowly. Both walls of the vacuum are silvered to reflect heat waves and thus retain and keep out heat. Also, heat passes with difficulty through the cork stopper in the mouth of the bottle. — PUPIL

SELF-CRITICISM OF AN EXPLANATION

1. *Do I understand my subject thoroughly?*
2. *Is my explanation accurate?*
3. *Is my explanation complete; that is, have I included all necessary facts and defined technical terms unfamiliar to my classmates?*
4. *Have I arranged my facts in logical order, giving first those that are necessary for an understanding of others?*
5. *Did I plan my explanation before attempting to speak or write it?*
6. *Have I tried to foresee points that will puzzle my classmates and taken pains to make such details crystal clear?*
7. *Have I used comparisons, diagrams, or pictures for greater clarity?*
8. *Is my explanation concise?*
9. *Are my pronouns and verbs correct?*

Practice 7. Explaining the Construction and Operation of a Machine or an Instrument

Explain completely the construction and the operation of one of the following machines or instruments. Make clear how the device does its work. A diagram may help you. Use the self-criticism questions in judging your explanation.

1. ash sifter
2. bicycle pump
3. carpet sweeper
4. coaster brake
5. coffee grinder
6. compass
7. electric toaster
8. water filter
9. fountain pen

10. ice-cream freezer
11. microscope
12. lawn mower
13. mimeograph
14. monkey wrench
15. mousetrap
16. oil lamp
17. phonograph
18. spirit level

19. Stillson wrench
20. thermometer
21. vacuum cleaner
22. windmill
23. wringer
24. soil tester
25. milk tester
26. pencil sharpener
27. recent invention

WHAT KINDS OF EXPLANATIONS ARE CALLED FOR?

Most of the explanations you will be called on to make can be classified in five large groups.

(1) DEFINING

A good way to define something is to tell (1) to what class it belongs and (2) how it differs from others in its class.

Name	Class	Particular Qualities
Ping-pong is	a game	similar to lawn tennis, played on a table with small rackets and hollow celluloid balls.
A submarine is	a boat	armed with torpedoes and capable of operation either on the surface or below.
A triangle is	a figure	bounded by three straight lines.
An infantryman is	a soldier	armed and equipped for service on foot.

The three parts of such a definition are the name, the class, and the particular qualities. In a definition use words familiar to your hearers or readers. A definition more difficult than the word itself is useless.

Avoiding Common Mistakes in Definitions

1. Don't put the term you are defining in a class so big and vague that it means little, or so narrow that your definition becomes inaccurate.

(Class much too broad) A lieutenant is a *person* who . . . (But barbers, painters, and housewives are persons too!)

(Class still too broad) A lieutenant is an *officer* who . . . (Corporals and sergeants are officers too, but they don't rate a salute.)

(Class too narrow) A lieutenant is a *commissioned Army Officer* who . . . (Hold on! The Navy has lieutenants too!)

(Good definition) A lieutenant is a *commissioned officer* who ranks below a captain in the Army and below a lieutenant commander in the Navy. (Ah, now we've got it!)

2. Don't begin your definition with *when* or *where*. The word after *is* should be a noun (the name of the class).

(Wrong) A tourniquet is when something is put on to stop bleeding. (A tourniquet is *when?*)

(Right) A tourniquet is a device to stop bleeding.

3. In defining a term do not use the word itself or a word derived from it.

(Wrong) Courtesy is being courteous to everybody. (We won't get anywhere this way.)

(Right) Courtesy is politeness, plus kindness.

Politeness is a synonym of *courtesy*. The commonest method of defining words is by giving synonyms.

Practice 8. Correcting Definitions

Correct these faulty definitions:

1. Description is describing a person, place, or thing.
2. A hexagon is when a figure is bounded by six straight lines.
3. A democracy is where the people select their own rulers.
4. A journalist is a man who writes or edits material for a periodical.
5. An adjective is when a word modifies a noun or pronoun.
6. Ambition is being ambitious.
7. A paratrooper is a person who jumps out of airplanes.

Practice 9. Defining Words

Define ten of the following names by giving the class and the particular qualities in the form indicated on page 125.

1. adjutant	11. duralumin	21. participle
2. airgraph	12. electromagnet	22. proverb
3. bicycle	13. R.C.M.P.	23. quadrilateral
4. bombardier	14. ferry pilot	24. scissors
5. buffalo	15. furlough	25. secretary
6. carburetor	16. grammar	26. sentry
7. cartoon	17. helicopter	27. square
8. corporal	18. jeep	28. synonym
9. creditor	19. judge	29. tennis
10. dive bomber	20. parachute	30. zebra

(2) GIVING REASONS OR CAUSES

One of the commonest questions in school and out of school is "Why?" An answer to this question should be accurate and specific.

Practice 10. Studying an Explanation

1. In the following explanation does the pupil give specific reasons why the camel has a hump? If so, what are they?
2. Is her explanation clear, concise, and interesting?

WHY THE CAMEL HAS A HUMP

Although the camel is one of our most interesting animals, most of us who live in North America know but little about him, because we have had only a passing acquaintance with him through the menagerie of the circus, the zoo, the museum of natural history, or books. But in some other countries he is as familiar as the dog or cat is to us. Hence it is interesting to know why the camel has his hump.

The hump is the camel's "breadbasket." A camel can go several weeks with hardly any food, and all he is likely to get on a journey across the desert is a few mouthfuls of dry thorns. Even at the end of the day he gets probably only a few dates, and he must live on this diet for several days while travelling forty or fifty miles a day. During this time he secures his nourishment chiefly from his hump. This consists almost entirely of fat and muscle; and as he marches along day after day, this fat passes back into his system and gives him renewed nourishment and energy. By the time he reaches the end of his journey his hump has almost disappeared, and little more is left than an empty bag of skin. The camel is then unfit to work and is set out to graze for a few days until his hump fills out again. — PUPIL

Practice 11. Giving Reasons

Make up a title beginning with *Why I like, Why we should,* or *Why* followed by other words—for example, Why I wish to go to college; Why science (or another subject) is my favorite; Why I'm glad I am a Canadian; Why I like to live in the suburbs (or the country); Why pupils fail in high school; Why I want to be a doctor (nurse, farmer, pilot, or something else); Why trees are valuable to the farmer; Why I wanted to join the orchestra (choir, band). Select pointed reasons and tell them clearly in a speech or written explanation.

(3) EXPLAINING DIFFERENCES

When you are asked to explain the difference between two objects or persons commonly confused, first mention briefly the points of similarity. Then explain exactly how the objects or persons differ. Explain clearly, completely, vividly. Give details. A topic sentence like "There are two important differences between an alligator and a crocodile" will serve as a guide and a reminder of the information you should include.

HOW DOES A STAR DIFFER FROM A PLANET?

Stars and planets are both heavenly bodies which may be seen through a telescope or perhaps even with the naked eye. There are many scientific methods of differentiating stars from planets. Two basic facts, however, will help the layman to distinguish between the two. First, a star keeps the same position in relation to other stars. It always appears in the same group or constellation. A planet, however, is a wanderer, and may appear in different positions. This is due to the fact that planets move about the sun. Second, a planet has a steady, bright light, while a star twinkles on and off. A further difference is that stars generate their own light and heat, but planets reflect the light of the sun. Even through a telescope stars are small and appear as points of light. Planets, on the other hand, have considerable size and are seen as disks of light. — PUPIL

Practice 12. Explaining Differences

Choose one of the following and be ready to explain clearly the difference between the two terms.

1. dive bomber and level bomber
2. profession and job
3. artery and vein
4. volcano and mountain
5. dew and rain
6. telescope and microscope
7. commissioned and noncommissioned officer
8. hurricane and tornado
9. reptile and fish
10. spider and insect
11. humour and wit
12. disinfectant and antiseptic
13. helicopter and ordinary airplane
14. rotation and revolution
15. planet and comet
16. barometer and thermometer
17. mimeograph and multigraph
18. plain omelet and scrambled eggs
19. crosscut saw and ripsaw

(4) EXPLAINING PROCEDURES

How to Make or Build Something

An explanation of how to make or build something should include (1) the materials, and (2) the procedure, arranged step by step in time order. Reasons why the article is useful or enjoyable may be given at the beginning or the end.

HOW TO MAKE A MERCURY BAROMETER

I. Materials
   A. Glass tumbler
   B. Glass tube thirty-four inches long, open at one end and marked off into inches
   C. Mercury

II. Procedure
   A. Filling tumbler and tube with mercury
   B. Inverting tube in tumbler of mercury

III. Possible results
   A. Dropping of mercury to thirty inches if at sea level
   B. Dropping below thirty inches at higher altitudes because of lower pressure

IV. Reading barometer
   A. Falling mercury probably accompanied by rain
   B. Rising mercury probably accompanied by fair weather

The necessary materials for making a mercury barometer are a glass tumbler, a glass tube about thirty-four inches long, open at one end and marked off into inches, and some mercury.

Fill the tumbler and the glass tube with mercury. Holding the thumb over the open end of the tube, carefully invert the tube in the tumbler of mercury. Special care should be taken not to remove the thumb until the tube is under the surface of the mercury in the tumbler.

When the finger is removed, the pressure of the atmosphere on the mercury in the tumbler will force most of the fluid to remain in the tube. If at sea level, the mercury will drop to thirty inches, because the weight of the air over a square inch at sea level is the same as the weight of a column of mercury thirty inches high over a square inch. At higher altitudes, however, the mercury will drop lower, because the higher up one goes, the lighter the air becomes. With the graduated scale on the tube it is possible to measure the variations in the height of the mercury column resulting from increased or decreased air pressure.

If the instructions are properly carried out, the barometer will be accurate. When the mercury in the tube falls, the air pressure is decreasing and rain will probably follow. If the mercury in the tube rises, however, the air pressure is increasing and the weather will usually be fair. — PUPIL

Practice 13.   Judging an Explanation

After reading the preceding explanation, could you make a mercury barometer? Is the explanation complete? Is it clear? Does the diagram help to clarify the directions? Judging the explanation by the standards on page 124, what rating would you give it? Why?

Practice 14.   Explaining How to Make or Build Something

Explain how to make or build one of the following. First write an outline. If you decide to explain how to build a birdhouse, assume that every member of the class is planning to build such a house but knows nothing about birdhouses and little about carpentry. Think what details in your explanation might confuse the class, and give these extra care. Your exposition will be successful if it is a clear and complete guide. A diagram saves words and makes clear. Judge your explanation by the self-criticism guide on page 124.

Agfa-Ansco Film

Makers of models must learn to follow directions with meticulous care.

To test listening, your teacher will ask pupils to retell explanations or important points in them.

1. apple pie
2. apron
3. birdhouse
4. boat
5. bookcase
6. book ends
7. camp bed
8. canoe
9. chicken coop
10. Christmas cards
11. cookies
12. doghouse
13. fireless cooker
14. grape jelly (or another kind)
15. kite
16. lamp shade
17. leather pocketbook
18. mittens
19. model airplane
20. pair of socks
21. picture frame
22. pillow cover
23. pinhole camera
24. popcorn balls
25. raft
26. round table
27. school dress
28. shelter in the woods
29. smock
30. snow fort
31. Spanish omelet
32. willow whistle
33. workbench
34. Yorkshire pudding
35. any article you have made

How to Do Something

When explaining how to do something, you can follow the same general plan you used in telling how to make or build something. Note the steps in the process and ask yourself frequently, "Will this point puzzle my reader? If so, how can I make it clear?"

Practice 15. Studying an Explanation

1. Does Marilyn arrange logically the steps of the process she is explaining? Outline her explanation.

2. After reading her explanation do you think you could give yourself or someone else an attractive manicure?

HOW TO GIVE A MANICURE

Many women and girls think that to have a good manicure they must go to a beautician and pay for it. If you have the necessary equipment at home, however, you can easily take care of your own nails.

Before you start, collect everything you will need—a pan of lukewarm, soapy water, an orange stick, absorbent cotton, an emery board or nail file (preferably the former), polish remover, and nail polish or a buffer, which is a little gadget for polishing the nails. First, remove the old polish, if any, with the cotton saturated with polish remover. Then, preferably with the emery board, file the nails, following the natural shape of the fingertips. Next, soak each hand in the lukewarm water for five minutes, dry, and clean the fingernails. While the cuticle is soft, push it back with an orangewood stick covered with absorbent cotton.

If you use nail polish, apply it with a light stroke. You will get best results by outlining the moon first and then brushing the polish toward the end of the nails. If you don't like polish, you can use a buffer to make your nails smooth and shining.

After you have practised several times, your manicure will look like the work of a professional. — MARILYN B.

Practice 16. Explaining How to Do Something

Prepare to give in class the oral explanation for which you wrote an outline in Practice 4. Explain so clearly that everyone in the class will understand. If your topic is how to can peaches, try to make every boy understand; if you speak about how to patch a bicycle tire, make the process clear to every girl. After practising, test your explanation by the self-criticism guide on page 124.

How to Play a Game

Only a very simple game can be explained in a page or two. A complete explanation of football or basketball is matter for a book, not for a short composition.

Here again you need to arrange steps carefully and to include every point your listener or reader needs to know.

Practice 17.   Explaining How to Play a Game

Select one of the following games or any other game with simple rules and explain it so that every member of the class will be able to play it. As a check on the explanation and the listening, your teacher will ask a pupil to repeat the explanation, or a group to play the game if it is suitable for a classroom.

1. checkers	11. hand wrestle	21. marbles
2. handball	12. fox and geese	22. hare and hounds
3. bowling	13. Indian circle pull	23. volley ball
4. shuffleboard	14. rooster fight	24. treasure hunt
5. dominoes	15. potato race	25. anagrams
6. charades	16. three deep	26. swat to the right
7. deck tennis	17. "O'Grady says"	27. centipede race
8. leapfrog	18. pick-a-back relay	28. the minister's cat
9. cross tag	19. prisoner's base	29. bull in the ring
10. tug of war	20. horseshoes	30. going to Jerusalem

(5) GIVING DIRECTIONS

Before explaining how to reach a place, trace out in your mind the route called for. If there are several ways of reaching the place, choose the simplest and shortest way unless it presents some serious obstacle or other disadvantage. Use freely such terms as *right, left, three blocks north, at the junction of Peach Street and Harley Road.* Mention conspicuous landmarks or buildings—a grove of beech trees a white church with a steeple, the Bank of Commerce—which will enable the stranger to check his course. In directing someone on a route that has many curves and corners, diagram the route; appeal to both eye and ear.

Example of Directions:

To reach the high school, walk to the end of Newbold Place; turn left and walk to the end of Austin Street; then turn right on Lefferts Boulevard, cross the railroad, pass the stores, and continue on Lefferts Boulevard for about three quarters of a mile to an elevated railroad. This is Jamaica Avenue. Turning right on Jamaica Avenue, follow the elevated for four blocks. Turn left on 114th Street and walk a block and a half. The large white brick building on the right is the high school. — PUPIL

Practice 18.   Giving Directions

In pairs dramatize the scene of a stranger asking his way to a railroad station, the post office, a church, a bank, a baseball field, a swimming pool, a theatre, a race track, an airport, a library, a woods, a fish hatchery, a skating pond, a park, a store, a camp, a factory, a gymnasium, a city, or a town, and a courteous, clear-headed resident replying. Select a place that is not easy for the stranger to reach. The inquirer will ask a second question only if the directions aren't clear or complete. Watch your verbs (pages 520–534).

Writing Social Letters

1. The punctuation of the heading may be open or close.
2. The address and date may be placed after the body of the letter.

Form 1 is much more common than *Form 2*.

FORM 1

> 239 Drexel Avenue,
> Yorkton, Saskatchewan,
> January 17, 1950.
>
> Dear Murray,
>
> _____
>
> _____
>
> Cordially yours,
> Harvey Fay

FORM 2

> Dear Murray,
>
> _____
>
> _____
>
> Cordially yours,
> Harvey Fay
>
> 239 Drexel Avenue,
> Yorkton, Saskatchewan,.
> January 17, 1950.

WRITE INTERESTINGLY

We have already learned the manner of the familiar and personal letter, but there is one other thing which very much needs our attention. We have had the experience of reading a letter that was fresh, lively, interesting; as we have also had the experience of reading a letter that was dull and impersonal. Sometimes this is a matter of personality, but usually it is carelessness, inattention, and lack of training. We would all want to write entertainingly if we could. We can if we will.

It is not necessary to have had an unusual experience to write unusually about it. It is, of course, easier if we have had such an experience. It is not necessary to have had an entertaining experience to write entertainingly about it; for by the use of our own wits we may often show amusingly how dull a person, a party, or a speech has been.

If we would write interestingly we should avoid the obvious, court the unexpected, devise unusual approaches, make apt and unusual comparisons.

Practice 1. Studying Social Letters

After reading each of the following letters answer these questions about it:

1. Would you like to receive such a letter? Why?
2. Is it entertaining? Why?
3. What information does it contain?
4. Does it sound like conversation? If so, how does the English differ from that of an ordinary composition?
5. How would you write the heading?
6. What is the salutation? The complimentary close?
7. What does the letter show about the writer?
8. What deliberate devices to maintain the unusual has each writer used?

1.

Lewis Carroll writes to a child friend[1]

Christ Church, Oxford, March 8, 1880.

My dear Ada,—(Isn't that your short name? "Adelaide" is all very well, but you see when one is *dreadfully* busy one hasn't time to write such long words—particularly when it takes one half an hour to remember how to spell it—and even then one has to go and get a dictionary to see if one has spelt it right, and, of course, the dictionary is in another room, at the top of a high bookcase—where it has been for months and months, and has got all covered with dust—so one has to get a duster first of all, and nearly choke oneself in dusting it—and when one *has* made out at last which is dictionary and which is dust, even *then* there's the job of remembering which end of the alphabet "A" comes—for one feels pretty certain it isn't in the *middle*—then one has to go and wash one's hands before turning over the leaves—for they've got so thick with dust one hardly knows them by sight—and, as likely as not, the soap is lost and the jug is empty, and there's no towel, and one has to spend hours and hours in finding things—and perhaps after all

---

[1] *Taken by permission from* The Life and Letters of Lewis Carroll, *published by the Century Company.*

one has to go off to the shop to buy a new cake of soap—so, with all this bother, I hope you won't mind my writing it short and saying, "My dear Ada"). You said in your last letter you would like a likeness of me—I won't forget to call the next time but one I'm in Wallington.

Your very affectionate friend,
Lewis Carroll

2

Lewis Carroll to another child friend:[1]

Christ Church, Oxford,
October 13th, 1875.

My dear Gertrude,

I never give birthday *presents*, but you see I *do* sometimes write a birthday *letter:* so, as I've just arrived here, I am writing this to wish you many and many a happy return of your birthday to-morrow. I will drink your health if only I can remember, and if you don't mind—but perhaps you object?

You see, if I were to sit by you at breakfast, and to drink your tea, you wouldn't like that, would you? You would say, "Boo! hoo! Here's Mr. Dodgson drunk my tea, and I haven't got any left!" So I am very much afraid, next time Sybil looks for you, she'll find you sitting by the sad sea-waves and crying "Boo! hoo! Here's Mr. Dodgson has drunk my health and I haven't got any left!"

And how it will puzzle Mr. Maund, when he is sent for to see you! "My dear madam, I'm sorry to say your little girl has got no health at all! I never saw such a thing in my life!" "You see, she would go and make friends with a strange gentleman, and yesterday he drank her health!" "Well, Mrs. Chataway," he will say, "the only way to cure her is to wait till his next birthday, and then for *her* to drink his health."

And then we shall have changed healths. I wonder how you'll like mine! Oh, Gertrude, I wish you would not talk such nonsense!

Your loving friend,
Lewis Carroll.

3

Thomas Hood to a little friend May Elliot, daughter of his friend Dr. Elliot. (This is a little old-fashioned, but it has some excellent devices.):

Monday, April 1844.

My dear May,—

I promised you a letter, and here it is. I was sure to remember it; for you are as hard to forget as you are soft to roll down hill with. What fun it was! only so prickly, I thought I had a porcupine in one pocket, and a hedgehog in the other. The next time, before we kiss the earth we will have its face well shaved.

Did you ever go to Greenwich Fair? I should like to go there with you,

---

[1] *Taken by permission from* The Life and Letters of Lewis Carroll, *published by The Century Company.*

for I get no rolling at St. John's Wood. Tom and Fanny only like roll and butter, and as for Mrs. Hood, she is for rolling in money.

Tell Dunnie that Tom has set his trap in the balcony and has caught a cold, and tell Jeanie that Fanny has set her foot in the garden, but it has not come up yet. Oh, how I wish it was the season when "March winds and April showers bring forth May flowers!" for then, of course, you would give me another pretty little nosegay. Besides it is frosty and foggy weather, which I do not like. The other night when I came home from Stratford, the cold shrivelled me up so, that when I got home I thought I was my own child!

However, I hope we shall all have a merry Christmas; I mean to come in my ticklesome waistcoat, and to laugh till I grow fat, or at least streaky. Fanny is to be allowed a glass of wine, Tom's mouth is to have a *hole* holiday, and Mrs. Hood is to sit up to supper! There will be doings! And then such good things to eat; but pray, pray, pray, mind they don't boil the baby by mistake for the plum pudding instead of a plum one.

Give my love to everybody, from yourself down to Willy, with which and a kiss, I remain, up hill and down dale,

> Your affectionate lover,
> Thomas Hood.

4

Robert Louis Stevenson to Miss Adelaide Boodle. (Stevenson heard that his friend was teaching a class of children at Kilburn in London, so he wrote this letter to be read to them.)

> Vailima [Samoa],
> January 4th, 1892.

My dear Adelaide,

We were much pleased with your letter and the news of your employment. Admirable, your method. But will you not run dry of fairy stories? Please salute your pupils, and tell them that a long, lean, elderly man who lives right through on the other side of the world, so that down in your cellar you are nearer him than the people in the street, desires his compliments.

This man lives in an island which is not very long, and extremely narrow. The sea beats round it very hard, so that it is difficult to get to shore. There is only one harbour where ships come, even that is very wild and dangerous; four ships of war were broken there a little while ago, and one of them is still lying on its side on a rock clean above water, where the sea threw it, as you might throw your fiddle-bow on the table.

All round the harbour the town is strung out; it is nothing but wooden houses, only there are some churches built of stone, and not very large, but the people have never seen fine buildings. Almost all the houses are of one storey.

Away at one end lives the king of the whole country. His palace has a thatched roof which stands upon posts; it has no walls, but when it blows and rains, they have Venetian blinds which they let down between the posts and make it very snug. There is no furniture, and the king and the queen and the courtiers sit and eat on the floor, which is of gravel; the lamp stands there too, and every now and then it is upset.

These good folk wear nothing but a kilt about their waists, unless to go to church or for a dance, or the New Year, or some great occasion. The children play marbles all along the streets; and though they are generally very jolly, yet they get awfully cross over their marbles, and cry and fight like boys and girls at home.

Another amusement in the country places is to shoot fish with a bow and arrow. All round the beach there is bright, shallow water where fishes can be seen darting or lying in shoals. The child trots round the shore, and whenever he sees a fish, lets fly an arrow and misses, and then wades in after his arrow. It is great fun (I have tried it) for the child, and I have never heard of it doing any harm to the fishes: so what could be more jolly?

The road up to this lean man's house is uphill all the way and through forests; the forests are of great trees, not so much unlike the trees at home, only here and there are some queer ones mixed with them, cocoanut palms, and great forest trees that are covered with blossom like red hawthorn, but not nearly so bright; and from all the trees thick creepers hang down like ropes, and nasty-looking weeds, that they call orchids, grow in the forks of the branches; and on the ground many prickly things are dotted, which they call pine-apples: I suppose every one has eaten pine-apple drops . . .

On the way up to the lean man's house you pass a little village, all of houses like the king's house, so that, as you ride through, you can see everybody sitting at dinner; or if it be night, lying in their beds by lamplight; for all these people are terribly afraid of ghosts, and would not lie in the dark for any favour. After the village there is only one more house and that is the lean man's; for the people are not very many, and live all by the sea, and the whole inside of the island is desert woods and mountains . . .

Here is a tale the lean man heard last year. One of the islanders was sitting in his house, and he had cooked fish. There came along the road two beautiful young women, who came into his house and asked for his fish.

It is the fashion in the islands always to give what is asked, and never to ask folk's names. So the man gave them fish and talked to them in the island jesting way.

Presently he asked one of the women for her red necklace, which is good manners and their way; he had given the fish, and he had a right to ask for something back.

"I will give it you by and by," said the woman, and she and her companion went away; but he thought they were gone very suddenly, and the truth is they had vanished.

The night was nearly come, when the man heard the voice of the woman crying that he should come to her, and she would give the necklace. He looked out, and behold she was standing calling him from the top of the sea. At that, fear came on the man; he fell on his knees and prayed, and the woman disappeared.

It was known afterwards that this was once a woman indeed, but should have died a thousand years ago, and has lived all that while as a devil in the woods beside the spring of the river. Sau-mai-afe (Sow-my-affy) is her name, in case you want to write to her.

Ever your friend Tusitala (tale-writer),

alias Robert Louis Stevenson.

Reprinted from "The Letters of Robert Louis Stevenson, 1868-1894." *Edited by Sir Sidney Colvin.* *By kind permission of Sir Sidney Colvin and Messrs. Methuen & Co., Ltd.*

WRITING SOCIAL LETTERS   139

5

Charles Lamb to a Farmer and His Wife:

Twelfth Day, '23.

The pig was above my feeble praise. It was a dear pigmy. There was some contention as to who should have the ears; but in spite of his obstinacy (deaf as these little creatures are to advice), I contrived to get at one of them.

It came in boots, too, which I took as a favour. Generally these pretty toes (pretty toes!) are missing; but I suppose he wore them to look taller.

He must have been the last of his race. His little feet would have gone into the silver slipper. I take him to have been a Chinese, and a female.

If Evelyn could have seen him, he would never have farrowed two such prodigious volumes; seeing how much good can be obtained in—how small a compass!

He crackled delicately.

I left a blank at the top of my letter, not being determined which to address it to: so farmer and farmer's wife will please to divide our thanks. May your granaries be full, and your rats empty, and your chickens plump, and your envious neighbours lean, and your labourers busy, and you as idle and as happy as the day is long!

VIVE L'AGRICULTURE!

How do you make your pigs so little!
They are vastly engaging at that age:
I was so myself.
Now I am a disagreeable old hog,
A middle-aged gentleman-and-a-half.

My faculties are, thank God, not much impaired! I have my sight, hearing, taste, pretty perfect; and can read the Lord's Prayer in common type, by the help of a candle, without making many mistakes.

Believe me, that, while my faculties last, I shall ever cherish a proper appreciation of your many kindnesses in this way, and that the last lingering relish of past favours upon my dying memory will be the smack of that little ear. It was the left ear, which is lucky. Many happy returns, not of the pig, but of the New Year, to both! Mary, for her share of the pig and the memoirs, desires to send the same.

Yours truly,
C. Lamb.

SOME BEGINNINGS

As with other kinds of writing, the beginning sentence of a letter may prove its making or its unmaking. It should set writer and reader in a common frame of mind, so that communion and communication is ready and pleasing.

Practice 2. Opening Sentences

Consider these openings, and say what kind of relationship of acquaintance or intimacy, what mood or attitude exists between writers and receivers of the letters.

1. Thomas Bailey Aldrich writes to William Dean Howells:

Dear Howells,

We had so charming a visit at your house that I have about made up my mind to reside with you permanently.

2. Robert Louis Stevenson, to his parents, after receiving an offer for *Treasure Island:*

My dearest People,

I have had a great piece of news. There has been offered for *Treasure Island*—how much do you suppose? I believe it would be an excellent jest to keep the answer till my next letter. For two cents I would do so. Shall I? Anyway, I'll turn the page first.

—By arrangement with Charles Scribner's Sons.

3. Leigh Hunt, English essayist and poet, to Shelley and his wife who were resident at Leghorn, Italy:

My dear Friends,—

Whenever I write to you, I seem to be transported to your presence. I dart out of the window like a bird, dash into a southwest current of air, skim over the cool waters, hurry over the basking lands, rise like a lark over the mountains, fling like a swallow into the valleys, skim again, pant for breath, there's Leghorn—how d'ye do?

4. George Bernard Shaw, holidaying in Suffolk, writes to Ellen Terry, the famous actress:

The Rectory, Stratford St. Andrews,
Saxmundham

There are no clocks and no calendars here, but surely it must be September by this time. If not, keep this letter till it *is*, and then read it.

5. Ellen Terry, to George Bernard Shaw, after a long and weary rehearsal of *Cymbeline:*

11 September 1896, Savoy Hotel,
Victoria Embankment, London.

" 'Tis now the witching hour of night." Churchyards yawn and so do I. Oh, the long speeches!

Practice 3.   Writing Social Letters

1. Write to a boy or girl of your age in New Zealand, Japan, Denmark, or Brazil about life in a Canadian high school or in your city or town.
(If you would like to correspond with a student from overseas, write for information to Mrs. R. T. Tanner, Overseas Correspondence Department, United Nations Association in Canada, 678 Huron St., Toronto, Canada.)
2. All boys will write their names on slips of paper and drop them into a hat. Each boy will draw a slip from the hat. From another containing

the names of the girls each girl will draw a name. Then write an entertaining letter to the pupil whose name you draw.

3. Reply to the letter received from your classmate.
4. Write a cheery, sympathetic letter to a sick friend or classmate.
5. Write to a cousin in Florida about Northern winter sports or to a cousin in Australia about Canadian winter sports.

In letter writing, remember that your friends will be interested in the things that interest you.

6. Arrange to meet a friend. Make clear the time and the place.
7. To a friend who has asked, "What is a good book to read?" write entertainingly about a book you have read recently.
8. To a friend who has asked, "What is a good magazine to read?" write entertainingly about your favourite magazine.
9. In a letter to your parents, who are away, tell entertainingly the family news.
10. To a friend write a true travel letter based on a trip you have taken or an imaginative letter based on a travel book you have read. Share the new scenes and acquaintances with your friend.
11. The pupils in rotation have arranged to write a daily letter to an injured classmate and to include the English homework assignment. Write your letter.
12. Write to a friend who has moved to another city. Include school news.
13. As a character in a book you are studying, write a letter about your

experiences. For example, if you are studying *Ivanhoe*, as Cedric write about the rudeness of the Normans at the banquet, or as Rowena tell of your being chosen Queen of Love and Beauty and your discovering that the Disinherited Knight is Ivanhoe.

INFORMAL DISCUSSION

Friendly letters are not limited to personal matters, experiences, descriptions, and reading, but often include discussions on a great variety of subjects. In the following letter Paul tries to persuade Jack to join a club or an athletic team at his high school.

> 49 Eighth Street,
> Govan, Saskatchewan,
> October 14, 1949.

Dear Jack,

You old bookworm! If you were here, I'd take that chem book away from you, drag you out into the open air, and let the wind drive those chemical cobwebs out of your brain.

So you don't think every student should take part in at least one extra-curricular activity! Did you ever stop to think that when you've graduated you'll have to mingle with other people in your business or profession? If you cloister yourself in a chem lab, you'll never learn how to meet people, talk to them, or enjoy the comradeship of those who share your interests. School clubs will help you to make many lasting friendships and prepare you for life outside your high school walls.

Besides, think of the mental stimulation. Do you rise to the bait, my learned friend? It's perfectly all right to formulate your own theories and test them alone, but other people have theories, too. Defending your ideas in club meetings will clear up many hazy points and help you to see the flaws in your own reasoning. You'll learn a lot from the other fellows.

As for athletics—can't you see me beam—a good workout every afternoon would do you good. You can't think clearly or study at your best if you insist on hurrying home to your books immediately after classes every day. You'll never live to a ripe old age if you spend all the best years of your life over a test tube or a dusty tome.

Have I convinced you? Write soon and let me know whether this letter flabbergasted you completely.

> Your friend,
> Paul

Practice 4. Informal Argument

Choose, by drawing names from a hat or in some other way, an opponent who will reply by letter to an informal argument you write him. Suppose, for example, that he, at the end of his third year in high school, has been offered a position with a fair salary and excellent opportunity for advancement. Try to convince him that he should complete his high school course, and then wait for his reply. Instead, you and your opponent may argue about college, poetry, the value of Latin, a candidate for school or public office, the best method of crime prevention, the youth of to-day, the value of athletics, the effects of football, the influence of the movies or the radio, abolishing home work, student government, the use of slang, or any other subject mentioned —or not mentioned—in the unit on discussion, argument, and debate.

INTRODUCTION

Because the purpose of a letter of introduction is to establish a friendship between two people, the letter should make clear what the two people have in common—for example, a love of travel, literature, music, or adventure.   It should also explain why the bearer of the letter happens to be in the city of address.

Near the centre of the envelope write the name of the person addressed; and in the lower left corner, *Introducing Alfred Jordan.* Hand Alfred the letter, unsealed and unstamped.

> 610 West Armstrong Avenue,
> Peoria, Illinois,
> November 26, 1946.

Dear Edward,

Do you remember Alfred Jordan about whose exploits I told you? Well, here he is. He is going to spend his summer at Rocky Hill Camp, right next to your place.

Al played fullback on Excel's team at the same time that you were quarterback at Fulton. And his ideas about life are very similar to yours. He believes that the best life is under the blue sky out in the open spaces. You'll find him a likeable chap, very sociable, and exceedingly clever. You two scouts will, I'm sure, have some good times together.

Write to me soon, and tell me about your various feats.

> Cordially yours,
> Nathaniel Boyle

Practice 5.   Letter of Introduction

When you lived in Halifax (or another city or town), you had one real friend.   Now one of your pals is moving to Halifax.   Write the letter of introduction.

LETTERS OF COURTESY

Thoughtful, sympathetic people write many letters of courtesy; young, selfish, ignorant, and lazy ones frequently neglect these opportunities to make others happy and to increase their circle of friends. Letters of courtesy, which include letters of thanks, congratulation, and condolence, must be written promptly. If a month after a visit you thank your hostess, or months after a death you write a note of sympathy, the letter is of little value.

Letters of courtesy are not lengthy, literary efforts but sincere, direct, genuine expressions of feeling. To express simply what is in one's heart is much better than to search for lofty, meaningless phrases.

Apology and Explanation

A letter of apology in which the writer spends most of his time defending himself is useless—and amusing. Why write at all if you are not ready frankly to admit you're wrong? Of course, one must differentiate between an apology for wrongdoing and an explanation of an unavoidable failure to keep an appointment or a promise.

> 289 Twelfth Street,
> Saint John, New Brunswick,
> December 11, 1949

Dear Paul,

I'm deeply sorry I failed to keep my appointment with you Saturday morning. It was due to my carelessness entirely. When I awoke I had forgotten all about our plans for the day. About ten o'clock I remembered and hurried to the station. Of course, you were no longer upon the platform, but I went to the museum as planned. As you know, I didn't meet you there, and the day was spoiled for both of us.

Please forgive me. I assure you that I'll be less forgetful next time.

> Your friend,
> Walter Arnoldi

Thanks

Every young person understands one must thank a friend for a gift or hospitality, but many people, young and old, neglect to write notes like the following to thank those who help them in a variety of ways.

> 301 West Twentieth Street,
> Wetaskiwin, Alberta,
> October 9, 1949.

Dear Mr. Gleason,

The material that you sent will, I am sure, prove helpful in the coming debate. It was kind of you to give me so much of your time in writing such a full explanation.

I am very grateful for your assistance.

> Sincerely yours,
> Lucille Comstock

> 217 Judge Street,
> Prince Albert, Saskatchewan,
> January 9, 1949.

Dear Alice,

The impassive face of your Buddha smiles at me through the clouds of incense that create an oriental atmosphere in our most prosaic living-room.

I wonder what fairy told you that I am a slave to the mystic East and that the slightest reminder of that far away land will always be dear to me.

Because your attractive gift is so full of this subtle charm, I appreciate it and the kind thought that prompted you.

I hope that the past holiday was a merry one and that this new year will be filled with happiness.

Your loving friend,
Harriet Munro

Congratulations

In congratulating a friend write him an entertaining note showing your joy in his success. When you receive a letter of congratulation, remember that it should be answered.

1643 North Second Street,
Brandon, Manitoba,
May 17, 1950.

Dear Richard,

You cannot imagine how glad I was when I heard of your winning the French medal. It was a wonderful achievement, and we're all proud of you.

I can picture you standing upon the platform on commencement night in front of several thousand people, with your chest thrown out and your head high, receiving the award. I can see you striding across the stage and down the steps like Napoleon himself, while the whole vast auditorium rings with applause. I can see, too, the entire French class gazing with envy at the medal. It must be a fine one, and you must bring it with you the next time you visit us.

Remember me to your parents and write soon.

Your old friend,
Harvey

Condolence

In a letter of condolence show simply and directly that you sympathize with your sorrowing friend.

230 College Avenue,
Toronto, Ontario,
June 6, 1948.

Dear Margaret,

There's a lump in my throat, and no matter how hard I swallow, it won't go down; it just sticks there, because, dear Margaret, I'm sorry, so sorry for you.

Your father's death must have been a great shock; I guess it is only human to suppose that sorrow may come near us, but that it will not touch us. Maybe it is better so.

At such a time words seem idle. I wish there were something that I could do instead of just sending my deepest sympathy.

I hope that you will be a great help to your mother in her grief and find comfort in her love for you.

Affectionately yours,
Isabel Landon

Practice 6. Courtesy Letters

1. Your friend in a distant city wrote a letter of introduction for you to a chum in the town to which you have just moved. Thank your friend for his kindness and write an entertaining account of your first meeting with his chum.
2. Thank a friend or relative for a gift on your birthday, at Christmas or graduation, or on another occasion.
3. Congratulate a friend on an honour or an achievement: winning a medal, a pin, or a prize in an essay, short-story, scholarship, pig-raising, good-citizenship, or athletic contest; election to the captaincy of a team or to a school or other office; a successful piano recital, debate, speech, or radio talk; winning a scholarship; passing his university matriculation examinations; gaining admittance to a first-class college.
4. You have asked for material for an essay or debate, a letter of recommendation or introduction, or advice about the choice of a college or vocation. In a letter thank the person who helped you.
5. Thank a hostess for a delightful week-end visit.
6. Imagine that sorrow has come to one of your friends. Write him (or her) a letter of condolence.
7. You have been mean, cranky, unreasonable, rude, untruthful, or disagreeable. Apologize to a friend who has been a victim.
8. In a letter explain why you were unable to keep an appointment or a promise.
9. Send birthday or anniversary greetings to a friend or relative.
10. To a friend who is recovering from a serious illness write a cheery, entertaining letter.
11. Congratulate a man who is soon to be married, or send best wishes to a girl who has just announced her engagement.
12. Seize the next opportunity to write an actual letter of courtesy. Show it to your English teacher before mailing it.

FORMAL NOTES

Formal notes are sent as invitations to weddings, receptions, and dinner parties. The answer, written on letter paper or a correspondence card, should be similar in wording to the original note.

INVITATION

Mr. and Mrs. James Hamilton
request the pleasure of
Mr. and Mrs. Timothy Gamble's
company at dinner
on Wednesday, the twelfth of December,
at eight o'clock.

ACCEPTANCE

Mr. and Mrs. Timothy Gamble
accept with pleasure
Mr. and Mrs. Hamilton's
kind invitation for dinner
on Wednesday, the twelfth of December,
at eight o'clock.

REGRET

Mr. and Mrs. Timothy Gamble
regret extremely that a previous engagement
prevents their accepting
Mr. and Mrs. Hamilton's
kind invitation for dinner
on Wednesday, the twelfth of December.

Notice that—

1. The note and the replies are in the third person.
2. Formal notes lack heading, salutation, complimentary close, and signature.
3. The present tense is used in the answer.
4. No abbreviations except *Mr., Mrs., Jr.,* and *o'clock* are used.
5. Numbers are written words.
6. The acceptance mentions the day and the hour of the dinner.
7. In a regret the hour may be omitted.

A formal invitation need not be engraved but may be written by hand on the first page of a sheet of good note paper. Follow the arrangement and the spacing of the model on page 146. Also arrange your pen-written reply like the acceptance or the regret shown. **Above** everything else, answer an invitation promptly.

VISITING-CARD INVITATIONS

The hostess' card with the time and kind of entertainment on it is commonly used in inviting to an informal dance, musicale, picnic, or a tea to meet a guest, or for bridge.

The answer to an invitation on a calling card is exactly the same as the reply to a formal penned or engraved invitation. To a close friend a calling card with "With pleasure! Friday at 4" written on it is also correct.

To meet
Miss Mildred Drew

Mrs. Arnold S. Proudfoot

Thursday, May 4
Dancing at 10 o'clock
275 Park Lane

Practice 7. Formal Notes

1. Write both an acceptance of Mrs. Proudfoot's invitation and a regret.
2. Write a correct formal note to Dr. and Mrs. Stokes requesting the pleasure of their company at dinner on Friday, October 22, at eight o'clock. Write an acceptance and a regret from Dr. and Mrs. Stokes.
3. Mr. and Mrs. James Howland Wilson have invited you to be present at the marriage of their daughter Hester to Mr. James Ferguson at four o'clock on June 6 at their home, 4 West 187th Street. Write both an acceptance and a regret.

UNIT TWELVE

Writing Business Letters

WHY LEARN TO WRITE BUSINESS LETTERS?

THE business letter is the backbone of business. Because time, distance, and expense often prevent men's doing business with each other face to face, a business man needs to know how to write a letter which will have a personal touch and will somehow appeal to the particular man written to. To know what he wants to say is not enough. "The vehicle of expression," says a publisher, "even from the purely business standpoint, is quite as important as the thing said."

PROMPTNESS

A business letter calls for a prompt reply. Delay often means loss of business or of an opportunity. Most successful executives try to clear their desks each day before leaving their offices.

PARTS OF A BUSINESS LETTER

The six parts of a business letter are heading, address, salutation, body, complimentary close, and signature.

OPEN PUNCTUATION — SLANT FORM

```
                                    Moose Jaw, Saskatchewan
                                    December 2, 1949
        The Radio Electric Company
            Ninth Street and Broadway
                New Westminster, British Columbia

        Gentlemen:
            _____

            _____

                            Yours truly,

                            (Miss) Grace Glidden
```

149

Open Punctuation — Block Form

(The block form is commonly used in typed letters; the slant, in pen-written letters.)

```
                                        1013 Ballantyne Avenue
                                        Lethbridge, Alberta
                                        December 12, 1949
Mr. James Stern, Manager
Canadian Bank of Commerce
62 West Fourteenth Street
Edmonton, Alberta

Dear Sir:

        _____

        _____


                                        Very truly yours,
                                        Jay Electric Company
                                        by   M. J. Williams
```

Close Punctuation — Slant Form

```
                                        536 Marsden Place,
                                        Fort William, Ontario,
                                        December 4, 1949.
Mrs. Samuel Warner,
    1024 Wabash Avenue,
        Chicago, Illinois.
Dear Madam:

        _____

        _____


                                        Yours very truly,
                                             J. G. Phillips
```

Letter Form Model

The following letter is dictated and has one enclosure. The writer addresses it to a particular member of the firm.

Attention of Mr. C. H. Duell is centred two spaces below the salutation or on the same line with it. Usage varies.

Letterhead	**THE CANADIAN PRINTERS** PRINTING AND ENGRAVING ❖ 316 THIRD AVE., SASKATOON, SASK.
Date	January 2, 1950
Address	John Underwood & Co., 90 Richmond Street, Toronto, Ontario.
Salutation	Gentlemen:
Particular Address	Attention of Mr. C. H. Duell.
Body	_____ _____ _____
Complimentary Close	Very truly yours, THE CANADIAN PRINTERS
Signature	*J. E. Dewitt* Manager
Dictator and typist Enclosure	JED/SM Enc.

ADDRESS

1. The name and address of the firm written to are placed regularly at the left margin just below the heading and rarely at the end of the letter. When writing to a firm, write the name exactly as it appears on the company's letterhead: *The J. H. Fidler Co., Dominion Messenger & Signal Co. Ltd., G. & C. Merriam Company, Henry Holt and Company.*

2. The arrangement and punctuation must follow the system of the heading. If the heading has no punctuation after lines and has a sloping margin, don't change the style in the address.

SALUTATION

1. Common business salutations are—

Dear Sir:	*Gentlemen:*
My dear Sir:	*Ladies:* or *Mesdames:*

Dear Mr. Hawkins: *Dear Madam:*
My dear Mr. Page: *My dear Madam:*

In a letter to a person you know use *Dear Dr. Scott* or *Dear Mrs. Leonard,* not *Dear Sir* or *Dear Madam.*

2. Begin the salutation at the margin two spaces below its address in a typed letter and one space below in a script letter.

3. Use a colon after the salutation.

4. Capitalize the first word and all nouns.

BODY

Our letters are written representatives of ourselves.

1. Indent all paragraphs alike. Don't make the first paragraph an exception.

2. Good English is good business English. Vary the sentence length. The short simple sentence is emphatic but usually not so precise as the longer complex sentence.

3. A good business letter is correct, clear, complete, accurate courteous, and concise. Have clearly in mind what you wish to say and express your ideas exactly and fully in simple, direct language. As a rule, confine a letter to one subject. Clearness requires also a separate paragraph for each idea. Because short paragraphs are easier to read than long ones, paragraphs in business correspondence are shorter than in a book chapter or a magazine article. They should not average more than sixty words and should seldom exceed one hundred.

4. The first sentence is especially important. It should arouse interest and create a favourable impression by telling the reader something he wishes to know, and may refer in a definite and original way to the letter to which it is in reply. Notice these beginnings:

We have asked our representative, Mr. S. J. Tucker, to see that your cash register is put in proper working order at once. Thank you very much for reporting this matter on your card of November 10.

A duplicate shipment of the bedroom set, which you won in the Spring Contest, has been ordered.

5. Because the last sentence also occupies an important position, it should be clean-cut and complete. Avoid the participial conclusion beginning with *hoping, trusting, believing, thanking* or *regretting.* And *oblige* is obsolete. Don't insert *We beg to remain, We remain,* or *I am* before the complimentary close.

Aim to clinch your point and bring the reader "over to your side." Add a few friendly words if you can—for example:

We thank you for placing the order with us and hope the shipment will arrive promptly.

As it is necessary for us to have this information, won't you please telephone to us the first thing to-morrow morning.

6. Conciseness requires that the writer courteously make his point in the fewest possible words. "It has always been the habit of greatness to say much in little." Don't, however, omit such necessary words as the subject, the verb, articles, or prepositions. A business letter is not a telegram. Instead of *Received your letter*, say *I received your letter.* Business men now avoid the hackneyed expressions which were correct in the days of our grandfathers.

Old-fashioned:
  a. Your esteemed favour of the 30th ult. is at hand; are sorry that the twenty pounds of Royal Oak coffee have not arrived.
  b. Yours of recent date received and contents carefully noted and in reply to same would say that your order was shipped on December 10th.
  c. Enclosed herewith please find—
  d. Regretting our inability to serve you along these lines, we beg to remain—

Better:
  a. We regret to learn from your letter of November 30 that you have not received the twenty pounds of Royal Oak coffee.
  b. We are glad to find that the order about which you inquired in your letter of December 14 was shipped on December 10.
  c. I enclose—
  d. We regret that our stock of Humphrey Radiantfires is exhausted.

7. The secret of success in letter writing and salesmanship is putting yourself in the other fellow's place. Remember that courtesy is politeness plus kindness. The *Correspondence Manual* of the Stanley Works, New Britain, Connecticut, says, "Then before you sign your name to a letter ask yourself, 'Would this letter suitably answer me if I were in the customer's place?' "

8. It is better to use no abbreviations except *Mr., Mrs., Messrs., Dr., St. (Saint),* f.o.b., A.M., *Y.M.C.A., C.O.D.,* B.C., A.D. Do not use *etc.* if you can avoid it.

9. When preparing to write a reply read thoroughly the letter you are answering, think what kind of man the writer is, decide what you wish to accomplish with the reply, then plan your letter.

10. Write *January 19,* not *January 19th* or *January nineteenth.* Use figures also for house numbers and page numbers.

11. Use freely such courteous expressions as *thank you, please, we are glad, it is a pleasure,* and such positive words as *confidence, success, enjoy, achieve, approve, energetic, substantial, attractive, genuine, happy, trustworthy,* and *straight-forward.* Use sparingly such negative words as *complaint, misunderstanding, grievance, trouble delay, mistake,* and *inconvenience.*

Practice 1. Good Business English

For the following stereotyped or old-fashioned expressions substitute fresh, terse, conversational ones. If necessary, supply information to complete the sentence.

1. *Kindly* deliver the *same at an early date.*
2. *Enclosed please find as per your request* an itemized bill.
3. *Thanking you in advance* for suggestions *along this line* and *awaiting your further favours, we remain.*
4. Your *kind* order has *come to hand*, and *same shall receive attention at the earliest possible moment.*
5. Your *valued favour* is *at hand* and *in reply would say* that *our* Mr. Johnson will call on you next Thursday.
6. *Kindly* send the cheque *by return mail, and oblige.*
7. *Your complaint of recent date rec'd* and *contents carefully noted* and *in reply would state for your information* that the shoes were shipped on January 14.
8. *Trusting this will prove satisfactory, we beg to remain.*

COMPLIMENTARY CLOSE

1. The complimentary close may be—

Yours truly,	*Very truly yours,*
Truly yours,	*Yours very truly,*

Respectfully yours and *Yours respectfully* are sometimes used in letters to superiors—for example, a student to his principal, the Department of Education, or the Mayor. A business letter to an acquaintance may close with *Cordially yours, Sincerely yours, Yours cordially,* or *Yours sincerely.*

2. Place a comma after the complimentary close.
3. Capitalize the first word only of the complimentary close.
4. Begin the complimentary close about halfway across the page.

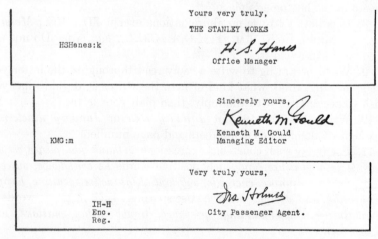

SIGNATURE

1. The signature is placed below the complimentary close and begins farther to the right in slant style and directly underneath the first word of the complimentary close in block style.

2. A period is not necessary after the signature but may be used if the period is used after the address and the heading.

3. Write the signature legibly. Typewritten letters frequently have the signature both typed and pen-written.

4. A woman addressing a stranger should make clear what title he should use in the reply.

UNMARRIED WOMAN: *(Miss) Catherine Thompson*
MARRIED WOMAN: *Catherine Thompson*
(Mrs. James Thompson)

5. In a letter from a firm, if the letterhead does not show the writer's position, the signature should make this clear.

Practice 2. Letter Form

Write the heading, address, salutation, complimentary close, and signature of each letter:

1. Juliet Reiss (wife of John Reiss), 100 Newbury Street, North Battleford, Saskatchewan, writes to Dr. Samuel Pearse, Bethesda Hospital, Oak Street, Weyburn, Saskatchewan.
2. Andrew King, president of Thomson and Company, 297 Washington Street, Dauphin, Manitoba, writes to Hare & Smith, Pittsburgh, Pennsylvania.
3. H. J. Moss, manager of Olney and Warren, 297 Laval Street, Montreal, P.Q., writes to James R. Ross, The Senate, Ottawa, Canada.
4. From your home address write to Miss Jean Royce, registrar of Queen's University, Kingston, Ontario.

LETTER PICTURE

Most typewritten letters are single spaced, except for double spacing between the parts and the paragraphs. In a letter so typed, if the heading and address are in the block form, paragraphs may begin flush with the margin. Most business men, however, think that indention makes the paragraph division clearer and prefer to have all paragraphs indented. Short letters are sometimes double spaced.

A letter makes a more pleasing picture if it is centred on the page. Like the mat of a picture, the margin should extend around the letter and be approximately the same width on the four sides. For a short letter the left and right margins should be two inches wide; for a longer letter, an inch and a half or slightly less. The margin at the bottom of a full-page letter should never be less than the side margins.

PAPER AND FOLDING

Paper, ink, and envelopes of good quality add distinction to correspondence. Use regularly white, heavy paper 8½ by 11 inches in size. For a short letter, paper about 6 by 9½ inches in size may be used. The envelope should match the paper, be strong enough to stand rough handling, and be heavy enough to prevent the writing showing through.

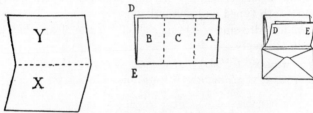

To fold a sheet 8½ by 11 inches, first place the lower half *X* over the upper half *Y* with the lower edge a quarter or a half inch from the upper edge. Then over the centre C fold in turn from the right and the left *A* and *B*, each slightly less than one-third of the folded sheet. Place the letter in the envelope with the loose edges *DE* up and next to the flap. Fold the enclosures with the letter.

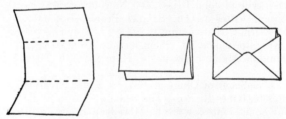

When for a short letter paper 6 by 9½ inches is used, fold the lower third up and the top quarter down. Place the letter in the envelope "with the two flaps next to the back, not the face, of the envelope and with the top edge of the letter at the bottom of the envelope."

REFERENCE DATA AND ENCLOSURES

A business letter should show who dictated it and who typed it. In the model on page 151, *JED* are the initials of the dictator, and *SM*, of the typist. This might be *JED:SM, JED-SM, jed/sm,* or *J.E. Dewitt-SM.*

A notation at the left margin below these initials refers to enclosures, if there are any. The common forms are:

2 Enclosures

Enc.

THE SECOND PAGE

The second page of a long letter is on paper of the same size and quality as the first page but has no letterhead. The name of the recipient is commonly placed in the upper left corner, the page number in the centre, and the date in the upper right corner:

```
Miss Alice French        2          June 30, 1936
```

On the last page there should be at least three lines of the body of the letter.

ENVELOPE ADDRESS AND RETURN CARD

1. The margin, straight or slant, and the punctuation, open or close, should correspond with that of the letter. If close punctuation is used, a period is placed after the last line and a comma after each preceding line.

CLOSE PUNCTUATION, SLANT STYLE

```
J. H. HOLMES,
BROADWAY,
NUTANA, SASKATCHEWAN


          Mr. T. H. Reading,
           734 Business Avenue,
            Fort Hamilton,
             Ontario.
```

OPEN PUNCTUATION, SLANT STYLE

```
JOHN T. WELSH
25 WILMOT AVENUE
LONDON, ONTARIO


          The Scott Enamel Company
           300 Ferry Street
            Winnipeg
             Manitoba
```

OPEN PUNCTUATION, BLOCK STYLE

STEPHEN P. CARR
29 KIRBY AVENUE
ALSASK. SASKATCHEWAN

Dr. P. T. Thomas
608 East Fortieth Street
Prince George
British Columbia

ASKING FOR INFORMATION

1. In your opening sentence explain in general the type of information you desire. If your letter goes to a large business house, the correspondent will be able, without reading the entire contents, immediately to turn it over to the person best fitted to answer your inquiry.

2. Then ask the specific questions you would like to have answered.

3. Make your questions clear, correct, and courteous.

4. Include any information which may be of assistance to your reader in answering your questions fully and accurately. (See the model on page 160.)

5. Explain why you want the information.

6. Enclose a stamped and self-addressed envelope unless you are likely to repay your informant in another way—with an order, for instance.

7. Don't write for information that you can secure in the library or ask questions calling for long answers. If a man's opinion is worth much, he is usually extremely busy.

Suna

The appearance and customs of other people, such as this Mexican charro, are interesting. Before visiting places so far from home, we must write a business letter to arrange for accommodations.

1436 Arlee Boulevard,
Winnipeg, Manitoba,
November 10, 1948.

Brigden's of Winnipeg Limited,
Notre Dame at Langside Street,
Winnipeg, Manitoba.

Gentlemen:

The English 3 B Class of Commercial High School would like to have you estimate the cost of binding in durable dark blue cloth a collection of the best work of the members of the class. On the cover we should like to have stamped in gold the title, "Writer's Cramp".

The classbook consists of two hundred pages of 8½ x 11 inch heavy typewriting paper with an inch and a half margin at the left for binding.

Very truly yours,
Dora McDermott,
Secretary.

Practice 3. Asking for Information

1. Your class is planning to spend Easter week in Hamilton, Ontario. Write to the New Raleigh Hotel for rates. Be specific about the number in the party, the length of time you are to stay, and the accommodations desired.
2. You are preparing to debate the question of moving picture censorship. Write to the National Board of Review of Motion Pictures, 70 Fifth Avenue, New York City, for pamphlets and information. Ask several pointed questions which can be answered briefly.
3. In a letter to the president or the registrar of a college ask what scholarships are open to freshmen, whether an examination is required, when the examination is held. Ask also for any available printed information on the subject.
4. Write to Mr. F. McDowell, Public Relations Department, Canadian National Railways, Toronto, Ontario, and ask whether his department will lend pictures or lantern slides to your club.
5. You are planning a trip down the St. Lawrence from Clayton to Quebec. Write for information to the Canada Steamship Lines Limited, Montreal, Canada.

LETTER OF APPLICATION

The letter of application is really a sales letter because the applicant is trying to sell his services. Like the sales letter, it should arouse interest, create desire, and secure action.

1. As you think what to include in the letter, put yourself in the position of the employer. Don't omit essential information—for example, source of information about vacancy, exact position applied for, age, education, experience, references, request for interview.

2. Make the letter fit the advertisement by touching upon every qualification mentioned. Read the advertisement as if it were an examination question, and don't overlook a point.

3. Use your best English. Avoid hackneyed expressions. John Lyle Harrington says, "Language has large weight in classifying a man—infinitely more than dress. It exhibits his breeding and indicates his social status."

4. By attention to arrangement, neatness, and hand-writing or typing, make the letter picture pleasing.

5. Names and addresses of employers and references should be complete. Notice the tabulation of the references in the following pupil letters.

6. If you have energy, ambition, and initiative and are willing to work hard, in some way let the employer know this. Be modest but self-confident. Don't follow closely any letter of application in a textbook. Think out your letter carefully and by showing individuality, originality, and intelligence create an interest in yourself.

BOY—High school graduate to act as companion for three boys aged 10, 12, and 13
during summer vacation in Northern
Ontario. Salary $15 a week and board.
J. P. 79 Winnipeg Tribune.

413 Onslow Place,
Sault Ste. Marie, Ontario,
May 10, 1950.

J. P. 79 Winnipeg Tribune,
    Tribune Building, Smith Street,
        Winnipeg, Manitoba.

Dear Sir:

In answer to your advertisement in this
morning's Tribune for a companion for your three
sons, I submit my qualifications for the
position.

I am seventeen years old and an honour
graduate of Weston Collegiate Institute, Sault
Ste. Marie, Ontario. At Weston I was captain of
the tennis team and a member of the swimming and
track teams. As an Eagle Scout and assistant
scout master of Troop Number 763, I have had
experience in working with boys ranging in age
from 12 to 15. During the past two summers I
served as junior counsellor at Pine Bluff Camp,
Minaki, Ontario, having under my care boys from
nine to twelve years old.

For further information about my experience,
ability, character, and habits you may
communicate with--

Mr. Charles H. Vosburgh,
  Principal of Weston Collegiate Institute,
  Sault Ste. Marie, Ontario.

Mr. Charles Carlson,
  Director of Pine Bluff Camp,
  Minaki, Ontario.

Dr. Edward W. Cross,
  Pastor, United Church of Canada,
  Sault Ste. Marie, Ontario.

The salary mentioned in the advertisment is
entirely satisfactory.

I hope that these qualifications will meet
your requirements and that you will grant me a
personal interview.

                    Very truly yours,

                      Frank Daly

STENOGRAPHER—Experienced, with
some knowledge of bookkeeping and general
office work: salary $25.   B. W., Box 357,
The Globe and Mail.

171 Bell Avenue,
Toronto, Ontario,
June 26, 1950.

B. W., Box 357 The Globe and Mail,
   Toronto, Ontario.

Dear Sir:

     This letter is in reply to your
advertisement which appeared in yesterday's Globe
and Mail.

My qualifications are as follows:

     Age: Seventeen.

     Education: Graduate of four-year Commercial
Course of Northern Vocational School, Toronto,
Ontario. I have had three years of bookkeeping
and French, two years of stenography and
typewriting, one year of commercial arithmetic,
commercial geography, commercial law, Canadian
history, and business English and correspondence,
and four years of English. I have a knowledge of
single and double entry and corporation
bookkeeping, can operate the standard makes of
typewriters at about sixty words a minute, can
take dictation at the rate of one hundred words
per minute, can use the dictaphone and mimeograph, and understand the filing systems.

Experience: During my last summer vacation
I was employed as stenographer and typist by
J. I. Black, 110 Yonge Street.

References: For further information about my
experience, ability, character, and habits you
may communicate with--

Mr. J. I. Black,
110 Yonge Street,
Toronto, Ontario.

Mr. James McQueen, M.A., B.Paed.,
Principal, Northern Vocational School,
Toronto, Ontario.

Mr. Wm. J. Brown, B.A., B.Com.,
Head of the Commercial Department,
Northern Vocational School,
Toronto, Ontario.

Salary: The salary mentioned in the
advertisement is satisfactory.

I hope you will give me a chance to
demonstrate my ability.

Yours truly,

Fred Joerger

Practice 4. Letter of Application

Answer one of the following advertisements or another clipped from the Help Wanted column of the morning paper:

GIRL — Intelligent, neat high school student with interest in home nursing to care for baby, 20 months, on Saturdays. $4 per day and meals. P.O. Box 49.

BOY — High school graduate who has studied chemistry to do general work in laboratory. Opportunity for experience and advancement. Give age, experience, education, and references. Post Office Box 93.

BOY

An opportunity is offered to a boy who is willing to learn the import and export business; offering many opportunities for advancement; initial salary $20 per week, with bonus twice per annum; high school graduate preferred; applicant must be alert and give full details in first letter. V 773 The Sun.

CLERK — Bright young woman in large departmental store; splendid opportunity; short hours; hot lunch at cost and other benefits; state age, education, experience, if any, and salary expected. V 691 The Free Press.

BANK wants boys and girls just out of school. Only high school graduates considered. Handwriting must be good. Openings in bookkeeping and stenographic departments. State age, references, etc. Leader-Post D 2897.

LETTER TO A LEGISLATOR OR CITY EXECUTIVE

A democracy needs citizens who not only are honest and think straight but also let their legislators and executives know what they are thinking.

Practice 5. Writing to Officials

1. Write to your member of parliament, senator, or member of the legislative assembly to convince or persuade him to support or oppose a bill before parliament or the provincial legislature.

2. Write to the mayor or another city or town official, urging that he exert his influence in favour of better schools, school buildings, police protection, street cleaning, parks, or another improvement.

REPORTING AN ACCIDENT

In case of an automobile accident a person who carries liability and property-damage insurance should promptly write to his insurance company a letter giving as much as possible of the following information:

1. Time and place of accident, speed of both cars at time of accident, and a description of how the accident happened (draw a diagram).

2 Operator of your car at the time of the accident and his license number.

3. License number, owner, driver, and make of other car, and owner's address.

4. Damage to each car.

5. Names and addresses of the occupants of the two cars.

6. Nature of injuries sustained and care of the injured—name of doctor and hospital.

7. Names and addresses of other witnesses.

8. Your policy number.

(For example of letter, see pages 168-9)

Practice 6.   Reporting an Accident

In a letter to the General Insurance Company, Seattle, Washington, in which your car is insured, report an automobile accident. Make your report clear and complete. Include a diagram.

CHANGE OF ADDRESS

In requesting that a magazine be sent to a different address, give the name of the magazine and your old and your new address, and tell how long the magazine is to be sent to the new address if the change is a temporary one. Instead of writing in the body of the letter your new address, you may refer to the address in the heading. Give accurate and complete information. Write legibly.

REPORTING AN ACCIDENT

908 Park Lane South,
Brantford, Ontario,
January 15, 1949.

Motor Insurance Company,
50 Union Square,
New York, New York.

Gentlemen:

    I wish to report an automobile accident that took place in Rockville Centre, Ontario, yesterday, January 14, 1948.

    About one o'clock my brother and I were proceeding westward along Sunrise Highway through Rockville Centre in his 1949 Studebaker at a speed of about twenty-five miles an hour. From our right a car dashed out along Waverly Place into Sunrise Highway. My brother applied his brakes and swerved to the left as quickly as possible but could not avoid a collision. The other car had swerved slightly to the right. Our bumper and right front fender smashed into the left rear wheel of the other car, a 1946 seven-passenger Buick.

    The Buick's left rear wheel was badly damaged; eight of the spokes were bent. Our right front tire was blown out, the steering gear was broken, and the speedometer cable snapped.

    My brother, William Arnoldi, whose driver's license number is 6487, owns the Studebaker and was driving at the time of the accident. The owner and driver of the Buick was Albert Hendrickson of 157 Washington Boulevard, Long Beach, New York. He had no passengers. His driver's license number is 8694N.

    My brother was thrown against the steering wheel by the impact and knocked unconscious, but I was not hurt, as I was in the back seat. He

was taken into the office of Dr. Weber of 23
Waverly Place. His right arm is fractured and
his cheek cut. Later the doctor drove him to our
home. Mr. Hendrickson was uninjured.

   The only witness was Mr. George Hamilton of
37 Elton Place, Rockville Centre, who was
standing on the street corner when the accident
occurred.

   Because my brother is unable to write, I am
reporting the accident for him. His policy
number is M68947.
          Yours truly,

           Walter Arnoldi.

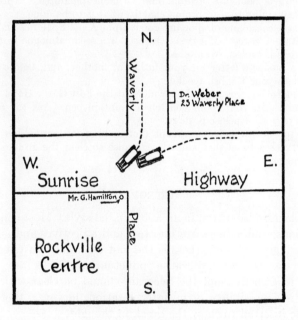

Practice 7. Business Letter

1. *The Reader's Digest* is published by The Reader's Digest Association (Canada) Ltd., 276 St. James St. W., Montreal, P.Q. Assuming that you are a subscriber for this magazine, ask the company to change your address for the summer vacation. Be definite.
2. You have moved to another street, city, or town. Write to *Maclean's*, Maclean-Hunter Publishing Company Limited, 481 University Avenue, Toronto 2, Ont., to change the address of your magazine.
3. You are spending the Christmas vacation with your aunt. Write to the postmaster of your town or city, asking that your mail be forwarded.
4. Write to a farmer to arrange for his supplying your family with eggs, butter, apples, peaches, or potatoes.
5. Your father wishes to have some work done: trees trimmed, lawn improved, car repaired, floors refinished, rooms redecorated, furnace repaired, coal bin enlarged, bookcase or table built, or house repainted. Write for him a letter explaining to a workman exactly what is to be done.
6. Request a catalogue of sporting goods from A. G. Spalding and Brothers, 1410 Stanley Street, Montreal, Quebec, or a seed catalogue from Patmore Nurseries, Brandon, Manitoba.
7. Write a business letter for your father or mother; and, before mailing it, show it to your English teacher.
8. While motoring, you stayed over night at the Fort Garry Hotel, Winnipeg, Manitoba. In your room you left a fountain pen. Ask the manager to mail it to you. Enclose postage.
9. Write to the owner of a vacant plot, asking for permission to use his property as a baseball diamond. Promise to clear the ground and to do no damage.

TELEGRAM

The telegram is written in an abbreviated style. Most conjunctions, prepositions, and articles are omitted, and adjectives and adverbs are used sparingly. Yet clearness is the first essential of a telegram; and brevity, the second. Because punctuation marks are ordinarily omitted in transmission, the telegram should be clear without them. If there is a possibility of misinterpretation, however, the word *stop* should be inserted to show the break in thought.

Notice that the telegram has no salutation or complimentary close, that the numbers are written in words, and that the writer inserts *stop* when he thinks it is needed to make the message absolutely clear.

Counting Words

The minimum charge is for ten words. Each additional word increases the cost. *Four thousand* is counted as two words; *fifty thousand*, as two; *4000*, as four; *50000*, as five. A figure counts as a word. Dictionary words, names of countries, cities, towns, and provinces, and some abbreviations are each counted as one word: *per cent, cannot, New*

York City, North Vancouver, C.O.D., A.M., O.K.   The following are counted as two words each: *Canadian Airways, James Corson.*   The name and address of the sender and receiver are not charged for, but a title like *football manager* after the signature is counted.

Night Letter

The night letter is a telegram sent at night to be delivered the next morning. The rate for a fifty-word night letter is the same as for a ten-word day telegram.

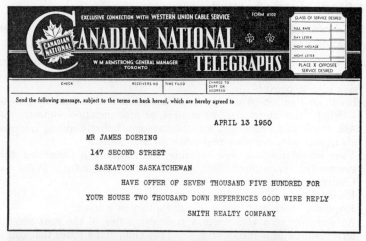

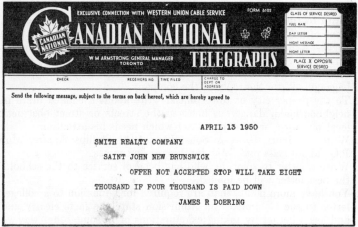

Practice 8. Telegrams

1. On your way home you missed connections. Telegraph your father, who has planned to meet you at the station.

2. As manager of a baseball team cancel a game by telegraph. It is raining, and even if the rain stops, the field will be muddy and soggy.
3. On an automobile trip your expenses are substantially higher than you anticipated. Telegraph home for money.
4. As manager of the school football team telegraph to arrange a game with a neighbouring school. Give full information about dates, officials, field, expenses, and division of the gate receipts.
5. Telegraph your mother on her birthday.

OTHER TYPES OF BUSINESS LETTERS

Practice 9. Business Letters

Jot down points to keep in mind in writing each type of letter. Outline your letter by paragraphs before writing it.

1. As manager of a school team write to another school to arrange a game. Be specific about the place, available dates, expenses, officials, and division of gate receipts.
2. Invite another school or a society of another school to hold a joint contest —debate, algebra contest, art contest, or pronunciation contest.
3. Ask a college to send you a catalogue or a bulletin giving information about expenses, entrance requirements, and courses.
4. Your school needs a new building, an addition, a swimming pool, a gymnasium, an athletic field, or additional equipment. Write to the Chairman, Board of Trustees.
5. Resign from a club or office, giving good reasons.
6. Request a room reservation in a dormitory or a hotel.
7. As secretary of a club write a postcard notice of the next meeting, a letter requesting someone to address the club, and a letter thanking some person for a service to the club.
8. Write to the president of the Alumni Association, urging the establishment of a fund to help needy pupils. Explain why the fund is needed. Suggest a plan for raising the money and administering the fund.
9. Write to a transportation company or express company about discourteous treatment, personal injury, damage to property, or loss of baggage. Write the reply of the company.
10. To the proper city or town official write about a choked drain in your neighbourhood, dangerous holes in the streets or street obstructions, a local nuisance, or another matter which needs his attention.
11. Write to Henry Birks & Sons, Ltd., 1240 Phillips Square, Montreal, P.Q., about class pins. Ask for designs and prices.
12. Write a letter to someone who has been of service to the school. Only the best letter will be mailed.
13. You have more points than are required for admission to a college. In a letter to the Committee on Admission state the facts clearly and fully and ask whether by taking examinations or in some other way you can secure college credit for the courses.
14. Before mailing a business letter you have written at home on your own account, or for your father or mother, show it to your teacher.
15. A month ago you bought from the Oxford University Press, 480 University Avenue, Toronto, Ontario, a copy of the *Concise Oxford Dictionary*

for three dollars. To-day you discovered that pages 641-656 are missing. In a letter to the company present the facts in the case and tell what adjustment you expect.

FORMS OF ADDRESS

PERSON	ADDRESS	SALUTATION	COMPLIMENTARY CLOSE
Prime Minister of Canada	To the Right Honourable Louis Stephen St. Laurent, K.C. Prime Minister of Canada Ottawa, Canada	Honourable and dear Sir: or To the Honourable the Prime Minister of Canada:	Yours respectfully, Yours very truly,
Members of the Dominion Cabinet	(May not always be addressed by name, address the office) The Honourable, The Minister of—	To the Honourable the Minister of—	Yours respectfully, Yours very truly,
The Lieutenant-Governor	The Honourable John M. Uhrich, M.D. Government House Regina, Saskatchewan (Also correct: His Honour the Honourable ....)	To His Honour the Lieutenant-Governor of Saskatchewan	Yours respectfully, Yours very truly,
The Premier of the Province	Honourable D. L. Campbell Parliament Buildings Winnipeg, Manitoba	To the Honourable the Premier of Manitoba: or Honourable and dear Sir:	Yours respectfully, Yours very truly,
The Mayor of a City	Mayor J. S. Mills City Hall Saskatoon	To His Worship the Mayor of Saskatoon: or Your Honour:	Yours respectfully, Very truly yours, Yours very truly,
A Senator	Honourable John Smith Parliament Buildings Ottawa, Canada	Sir: or Dear Sir:	Yours respectfully, Very truly yours, Yours very truly,
Member of Parliament, or Member of Legislative Assembly	C. W. Morrow, M L.A. Parliament Buildings Victoria, British Columbia	Sir: or Dear Sir:	Yours respectfully, Very truly yours, Yours very truly,
Protestant Clergyman	Reverend Nelson Chappel	Dear Sir: or Reverend Sir: or My dear Mr. Chappel	Yours respectfully, Yours sincerely,
Bishop	To the Right Reverend, the Lord Bishop of—	My Lord: or My Lord Bishop:	I remain, my Lord Bishop, Your Lordship's most obedient servant.
Priest	Reverend Francis X. Dolan, D.D.	Reverend and dear Father Dolan:	Yours faithfully, Yours sincerely,
Sisters of Various Orders	Sister M. Jeanette	Reverend and dear Sister Jeanette	Yours respectfully, Yours sincerely,
Canon	The Reverend Canon Armitage	Reverend Sir:	Yours respectfully, Yours sincerely,
Rabbi	Rabbi Jacob W. Stern	Reverend Sir: or Dear Sir: or My dear Rabbi Stern:	Yours respectfully, Yours cordially, Yours sincerely,

Mastering Effective English
Part II

JOURNEYMEN WRITERS

Mastering the Processes of Writing

UNIT THIRTEEN

Public Speaking

I learned to speak as men learn to skate or cycle—by doggedly making a fool of myself until I got used to it. — GEORGE BERNARD SHAW

SPEAKING, like writing, is largely a matter of habit. You can break the bad habit of fidgeting when you speak by (1) determining to break this habit, (2) practising standing still when you converse, answer questions in class, and make a speech, and (3) never allowing an exception, never making purposeless movements when speaking to one person or a group. Think how you learned a dance step or a stroke in tennis or swimming, and learn to speak by the same methods.

To make progress in speech you must practise at every opportunity. A person might make three or four speeches each year for forty years without noticeably improving. To acquire proficiency you need to speak at least two or three times each week. A few weeks of concentrated, purposeful speech work will accomplish more than years of scattered attempts.

PREPARING A SPEECH

Just as the passengers on a ship see only the one ninth of an iceberg which is above water, so the audience is aware of only a small part of the energy expended in preparing and delivering a speech. No matter how talented the speaker, a talk without adequate preparation is usually a failure.

WHAT IS YOUR PURPOSE?

Many speakers are like the man in the old song: "I don't know where I'm going but I'm on my way." To be a successful speaker, however, you must know why you are speaking and what you wish to accomplish by your speech. The five common purposes of speech are to entertain, to inform, to impress, to convince, and to move to action.

Do you, like a radio humorist or an after-dinner speaker, wish to entertain? Or, like a teacher, a manager, or a foreman, to make your ideas clear to beginners? Or, like a patriotic orator, to impress upon your hearers their duties in wartime? Or, like a debater, to convince the judges or the audience? Or, like a speaker selling war bonds or

177

raising funds for the Red Cross or the Community Chest, to collect cash or secure subscriptions? To speak without preparing is to shoot without taking aim. Decide what your aim is; then state it in a complete topic sentence; as, "My purpose is to convince the class that it should vote for the adoption of the honour system in the Long Branch High School." Make sure that your subject is definite and not too broad.

GATHERING MATERIAL

"Blessed is the man," says George Eliot, "who, having nothing to say, abstains from giving us wordy evidence of the fact." If one talks much and says little, he is set down as a bore. But where can you find material? Your school and city libraries, first of all, will furnish you with newspapers, magazines, and reference books. Never base a speech on just one newspaper, magazine, or book. Investigate several sources, select the best, combine the information, and make it your own. Search for facts rather than for opinions; learn to use the facts to draw your own conclusions.

Don't thoughtlessly seize every idea you happen upon. Think whether the idea is sound and, if so, whether it belongs in your speech. Notes on your reading are only raw materials for a speech; to them must be added your own experience, your imagination, your thinking. If you fail to digest and organize your material and deliver it in your own language, your speech will be a serving of "library hash".

Your materials should include not only notes on your reading but also thoughts and scraps of information gathered from other sources. A good speaker keeps his eyes and ears open and with them gathers a variety of firsthand material. Wherever he goes—to the movies, the theatre, on a shopping trip—he is prepared to shape his experience so that it will be useful. He recalls past experiences of his own and of his acquaintances. The result is a speech which can be definitely identified with the speaker himself.

OUTLINING

Outlining is nothing more than the association of ideas, showing the relationship of one part to the other parts and to the whole. Good outlining means good thinking; good thinking means good outlining. If you cannot outline a topic, you need more information on the subject and a better understanding of it. By learning the outline form and subjecting every speech you make to this rigid discipline, you will improve your thinking and make better speeches.

A first step is to find the main props supporting your contention or the big division of the subject and to jot them down in logical order. This statement of main points may be very simple; as,

REASONS FOR VOTING FOR JAMES WILSON FOR PRESIDENT
OF THE ATHLETIC ASSOCIATION

I. His scholarship
II. His executive ability
III. His athletic record

The next job is to arrange appropriate facts and examples under the main points. See pages 120–121 for an example of an outline.

DEVELOPING THE OUTLINE

An outline is only a skeleton. Undeveloped, it is to a speech as a skeleton is to an animal. How would you look walking about in your bones? Just so will your speech appear if you come before your audience with nothing in mind except the backbone and a few ribs of your speech. Somehow you must get some meat on the bones. Do you know how to go about it? Do you know how to transform a topical outline into a fully developed speech? The following methods of development may solve your problem.

1. *Statements of authorities.* The leading men in any field are authorities on their subject. Use statements from them. Always give full credit.

2. *Statistics.* To make your speech more convincing, use statistics, facts, and figures. Choose your statistics carefully, check their accuracy, and they will stand like a stone wall.

3. *Examples.* Well-chosen examples are vital, interesting, and forceful. You can hardly cite too many, but be careful to select those that are strictly appropriate and have punch.

4. *Quotations.* Quotations include not only direct statements from authorities in a specialized field, but also gems of thought and emotion. Literature is rich in truth crystallized in a line or two. A great speaker invariably possesses wide literary knowledge on which he draws as from a treasure house. The Bible, Shakespeare, other poets, philosophers, and essayists can help you. "A dwarf," says Colridge, "can see farther than a giant—if he stands on the giant's shoulders." Hoyt's *New Cyclopedia of Practical Quotations* and H. L. Mencken's *A New Dictionary of Quotations* are arranged alphabetically by subject.

5. *Analogies.* An analogy is an inference that two objects which are alike in some respects are alike in another particular. For example, to show the absurdity of electing magistrates from the Athenian Senate by lot, Socrates asked, "Would it be wise for sailors about to

set out on a long and dangerous journey to cast lots among themselves to see who should be pilot?" The first paragraph on "Developing the Outline" includes an analogy. Analogies are useful in arousing interest and clarifying a subject. Use them sparingly, if at all, as proof of a point. False analogy is evidence of loose or dishonest thinking.

6. *Personal experiences.*

Practice 1. Outlining and Delivering a Speech

Select a subject in which you are especially interested—for example, "A Hero of World War II" or "A Person Who Succeeded in Spite of a Handicap." List haphazardly all the points relating to it that pop into your head. Now organize these items in outline form. Be sure that your main headings are really main headings and include the points you place under them. Using at least three of the methods suggested, develop the outline into a good speech. In the margin of your outline, opposite the proper place, write the method of development used. When you deliver the speech, enunciate distinctly and pronounce every word correctly (pages 27–43).

To test listening and remembering, at the end of your speech ask the class three or four questions which good listeners should be able to answer. After all the speeches the teacher may give a listening test based on them.

BEGINNING AND ENDING

Introduction. Before an audience the first ten seconds are important. A striking, sparkling beginning grips the audience; a pointless, weak beginning induces yawns. Notice the directness with which Franklin D. Roosevelt began one of his wartime broadcasts.

My friends: Yesterday, on June 4, 1944, Rome fell to American and Allied troops. The first of the Axis capitals is now in our hands. One up and two to go.

Besides suggesting the purpose of the speech your introduction may contain a brief history of the subject, a pointed anecdote, a striking illustration, a quotation, or a general statement to be illustrated.

Conclusion. A famous chef once remarked that, no matter how he had to economize on a banquet, he always tried to serve delicious coffee, for that is the taste diners go away with. Similarly your clincher or conclusion is the idea your audience go away with. Sum up forcefully, yet briefly, what you have tried to prove. If your purpose has been to persuade your listeners to act, repeat your appeal in a well-worded sentence. Then sit down.

USING NOTES

After completing the outline, think how the main topics are linked in thought and fix them in your mind so thoroughly that during your speech you will always know what point comes next. When delivering a prepared talk, have no notes unless you wish to use a long quotation, a number of quotations, or a set of statistics.

To memorize or not to memorize is an important question. Because the ordinary memorizer sounds like a reciter, not a speaker, it is better to talk a speech—that is, to speak extemporaneously with the exception perhaps of memorized opening and closing sentences. In later life the ability to speak extemporaneously is much more valuable than skill in reciting memorized speeches. An extemporaneous speech is prepared but the wording is not memorized. Impromptu speaking is offhand, unprepared.

PRACTISING YOUR SPEECH

After preparing the outline, deliver the speech several times to real or imaginary listeners. Parents, brothers, and sisters are a good audience for one or two deliveries and are usually frank and helpful critics. Talk to the cat or canary rather than just into the air. Don't try to fix the exact words. Each time you speak you make a path through your subject and thus become better acquainted with it. Adjust the length to the time assigned you. Listen to your voice, and watch for errors in enunciation and pronunciation (pages 27–43), grammar, sentence structure, and word choice.

Profit by the criticism of anyone who will listen to you. Watch your hearer to see whether he is actually interested in what you are saying. If he isn't, find the reason and try again.

Practice 2. Speaking about Books

Prepare to speak on one of the following topics. For the book named, substitute a book you have recently read. If you like the book, make it so attractive that your classmates will read it. Use examples to prove your points. Hand in your outline. Speak distinctly and pronounce every word correctly.

1. An unusual setting in a book I read recently. 2. A book (or play) I'd like to write. 3. A novel that would make a good motion picture. 4. Comparison of a novel and the motion picture based on it. 5. What I liked in John Buchan's *Prester John*. 6. What I disliked in George Eliot's *Silas Marner*. 7. What I learned from Wendell Willkie's *One World*. 8. Why Ernie Pyle's *Brave Men* is worth reading. 9. A review or criticism of J. F. Hayes' *Treason at York*. 10. Contrast in Charles Rann Kennedy's *The Servant in the House*.

11. The plot of James Hilton's *Lost Horizon*. 12. Why read biography? 13. A book I have recently enjoyed. 14. My favourite book. Why? 15. My favourite character in fiction. Why? 16. The value of novel reading. 17. Why study the drama? 18. A character sketch. 19. The best book of the year. 20. Books I have outgrown.

IMPROVING YOUR POSTURE

Stand easily with chest up, weight well forward, shoulders square, head erect, and chin at right angle to the throat. Relax your arms and hands. Avoid swaying from side to side, twitching the fingers, and other purposeless movements. Usually a speaker stands with the weight on the ball of one foot and with the other foot at a comfortable distance diagonally in front. In this position the weight foot may point straight to the front or be slanted out; the free foot is turned out. Don't jam your hands into your pockets or lean on a desk or a chair. Although it is permissible to put a hand in a pocket or let it rest lightly on a desk at the speaker's side, such a position should be the exception, not the habit. Don't stand regularly with your arms behind your back as if impersonating an armless statute.

Change position occasionally at the beginning of a paragraph. Stand still until you are ready to paragraph in this way. Make the change as you begin to speak the paragraph.

If you find that your hands don't "feel right" when you are talking to the class, or if you think they "look funny" hanging at your sides, stand in front of a large mirror at home and watch the effect of every position you assume and every movement you make while you rehearse a speech. Watch not only your hands but your whole body, including your head, eyes, and facial expression. There are no short cuts to becoming a good speaker, but if you will take this exercise for half an hour two or three times each week, you will soon find yourself freed of the feeling of awkwardness and lack of ease. Look yourself over. That is the quickest, surest road to self-improvement.

COMMUNICATING YOUR IDEAS

To maintain good audience contact, face the audience squarely and look right into the eyes of your listeners, not at the ceiling, the floor, or the windows.

Talk to your hearers, not at them. Use the tone of conversation but speak slowly and especially distinctly if the audience is large. Adopt the style of speech you would use in an earnest and serious dialogue with someone at the other end of the table. Think every idea as you express it. If you think about it, your audience will also. Don't parrotlike recite a memorized speech.

Talk to various parts of the audience. Speak in turn to different individuals—one in the last seat at the right, another in the centre, and a third in the last seat at the left. From the expressions on the faces of these three discover whether they (1) hear you easily and (2) are interested.

SUGGESTIONS FOR OVERCOMING NERVOUSNESS

1. *Remember that nervousness before an audience is normal for beginners and is a good sign. It shows that you have a wholesome respect for your audience.*
2. *The cure for stage fright is repeated practice in speaking.*
3. *Choose a subject in which you are deeply interested.*
4. *Prepare your talk thoroughly. Knowing that you have something worth saying will give you confidence.*
5. *Practise your speech several times before your family and friends.*
6. *Take several deep breaths just as you go to face the audience.*
7. *Think of each member of the audience as a single person and a friend; don't be concerned about the group.*
8. *Speak slowly at first. Take deep breaths. Make sure that everybody hears your opening words but don't begin in a high-pitched voice.*
9. *Avoid such mannerisms as tensing your fingers in awkward positions, rubbing your hands together, playing with a bracelet, a lead pencil, or the buttons on your coat, and clearing your throat, for they advertise your nervousness and distract the attention of your listeners from what you are saying.*
10. *Concentrate on communicating your ideas to your audience. When you think about what you are saying and forget about yourself, you are not nervous.*
11. *Don't exaggerate the importance of the speech or the solemnity of the occasion. In a month's time you and your hearers will have forgotten all about it.*
12. *If your topic and the occasion permit, make your audience laugh at the beginning of your talk. When they laugh, you will relax. You don't have to be screamingly funny; most hearers respond gratifyingly even to mild humour or a witticism.*

USING A CONVERSATIONAL TONE

A good speaker makes each member of the audience feel that he is being talked to as in a private conversation. A conversational tone has the ring of truth and sincerity, and is worth working for. Here are two suggestions:

1. When speaking to a group, keep your mind on the thought you are expressing, rather than on the words.

2. Prepare to speak extemporaneously; don't memorize. The conversational tone and the memorized speech are deadly enemies.

ENUNCIATING DISTINCTLY

Good enunciation is a matter of using the tongue and the lips properly. Lazy lips and tongue produce slovenly sounds. Do you admire the speaker whose words leap from his mouth, each one sharp and clean-cut? It is hard work for us to improve our enunciation, but the will to succeed, with plenty of serious practice, will show results.

Saskatchewan Film Board

The pleasant modulation of volume is constantly watched by the control-room operator in a radio station. In public address, we should be just as careful to modulate our speaking voice.

THE LANGUAGE OF SPEECH

If you do not grasp the ideas in an essay, you can re-read and study it until you understand it. A listener, on the other hand, can't go back.

The language of an effective speech, therefore, is simpler than that of an essay. Short, clipped sentences are easy to listen to and to absorb. More examples and illustrations are necessary. Comparisons and contrasts help to make the speech vivid. Pointed, appropriate, original figures of speech enliven it.

CONCISENESS

To talk much and say little is commonplace. To talk little and say much is genius. At Gettysburg, Edward Everett, the orator of the day, spoke for hours. His speech was soon forgotten. Lincoln spoke only a few minutes, but his *Gettysburg Address* is a masterpiece.

Boil down. Eliminate unnecessary words and repetitions. Avoid long sentences and complicated sentence structure. Gain sentence variety by the use of an occasional question, exclamation, or command.

Omit every unnecessary *well, why, and, but,* or *so.* Don't fill pauses with *ur's.* By pausing before conjunctions and prepositions, not after them, avoid *and-ur, but-ur, that-ur, to-ur.* The *ur* has been described as a whisker on the word and as a grunt. Professor Winans says, "Grunting is no part of thinking." Oliver Wendell Holmes says,

> And when you stick on conversation's burs,
> Don't strew your pathway with those dreadful *ur's.*

USING TRANSITIONAL EXPRESSIONS

Just as the bones of the body are joined by ligaments, so the sentences of a speech are held together by connective words and phrases. To avoid overworking a few connectives, study the list on pages 105–106. Use some of these words and phrases deliberately in your next speech as you prepare it. Don't substitute *well-ur, why, and,* and *so* for genuine transitional expressions. When you pause between ideas, shut off your voice.

Practice 3. Making a Five-Minute Speech

Have you ever thought seriously about your own school, its problems, its good points and its weak spots, its courses of study, its activities? Perhaps there is something you have always wanted to praise or to defend; perhaps there is something you have always wanted to help to improve. Select a phase of your school for consideration in a speech of not more than five minutes. Be specific. Don't deal in generalities. Select an attractive and appropriate title. In a single sentence tell exactly what, in your five minutes, you propose to accomplish. Stick to this thesis throughout the speech. Apply the suggestions for organization and delivery learned so far. You might base your limited subject upon one of these broad topics:

1. Our library
2. Our music department
3. Cliques
4. The honour society
5. Sports
6. Dramatics
7. Recreation facilities
8. Conduct
9. Grades, tests, homework
10. The value of the work done in the classes
11. The school as preparation for earning a living
12. The school as preparation for college
13. The school as preparation for citizenship
14. Our student government
15. Tardiness and absence
16. Habitual failures
17. School parties
18. The cafeteria

HOLDING ATTENTION

A practical problem of the speaker is holding the attention of the audience. Because in every audience there are numerous distractions, the speaker's task is not an easy one. For one the room is too hot; for another it is too cold; one girl's shoes hurt her; another drops her compact or handkerchief; somebody coughs; and a latecomer enters. The wise speaker foresees these distractions and plans to overcome them.

Illustrations and comparisons. Be concrete. Avoid glittering generalities and meaningless abstractions. Keep your hearers wide awake by a free use of *for instance, to illustrate,* and *for example.* Repeat and illustrate your idea until it sinks in but not until your hearers are bored.

If you use statistics, dramatize them. Put them into human terms. In talking about the future of aviation, for example, don't point out

INTEREST, LIKE INATTENTION, IS CONTAGIOUS

that Bombay is only 7875 air-line miles from Toronto. Instead, show that a Torontonian with only a week's vacation will be able to fly to India, visit the Taj Mahal, buy an Indian rug, and return home in time for work the following Monday.

Visual aids. Blackboard talks are popular because they help the audience see as well as hear the main points of the speech. Don't neglect the blackboard or other visual aids when giving an informational talk. Demonstrate if possible.

Variety. "No one," says William James, "can possibly attend continuously to an object that does not change." Because monotony puts an audience to sleep, have a variety of subject matter and vary your rate of speaking and the pitch and volume of your voice.

Enthusiasm. Interest, like inattention, is contagious. If you are enthusiastic about your subject, your classmates are likely to attend to what you say.

ON THE PLATFORM

1. When introduced, walk straight to a position well forward on the platform and pause momentarily to get your bearings.
2. When you rise or when you reach the front of the platform, recognize the chairman with "Mr. Chairman", a bow, or both.
3. Walk on the platform as you walk along the street. Avoid both the stride and the tiny step. When you are walking toward the audience, look at them, not at the floor as if searching for a stray dime.
4. Don't begin to speak at the very edge of the platform. If you do, it will be difficult to change position, and the audience will wonder whether you are likely to step off the edge.
5. Avoid haste in beginning to speak. Take a breath before speaking the first sentence.
6. If you use a salutation, say merely "Fellow students", "Members of the Speech Club", or something similarly brief.
7. Speak slowly and distinctly enough for everyone to hear easily your opening words. Don't begin in a high-pitched, loud voice.
8. If you forget a point, keep looking at the audience and go on without it; don't break the link of sympathy and response established by eye contact.
9. Don't walk the platform as if impersonating a caged lion at feeding time.
10. Take time to impress your last sentence on the minds of your hearers. Don't say, "I thank you."
11. When you finish your talk, pause momentarily and then turn and walk back to your chair.
12. If other speakers follow you on the programme, listen courteously. Don't imply by an inattentive manner that no one else will say anything worth hearing.
13. Practise correct posture and platform behaviour until the correct becomes habitual. Then, when you address an audience, you may forget these details, forget yourself, and centre attention on what you have to say to the audience and their reception of the message. But you can't forget until you have first learned.

MAKING A SPEECH TO INFORM

Have you ever poured water out of a big jug with a small neck? Have yuo ever sympathized with or laughed at a person who blubbered like such a jug when he tried to tell you something? Many persons—

most of us, in fact—are like a big jug with a small neck. Daily our minds are taking in information through all the senses. But what good is all this knowledge if we can't get it out? There is no one of us who does not daily need to give somebody information about something. Every one of us knows more about one thing than does the average person. It is important, therefore, for us to seize every opportunity to bring our ability to speak abreast of what we have to say.

Remember that your speech to inform will be judged, not by how much you tell your classmates, but by how many important facts or ideas they remember. Cold encyclopaedic facts without examples or illustrations arouse little interest and are quickly forgotten.

CHECK SHEETS FOR TALKS

1. Energy and enthusiasm
2. Posture and platform behaviour
3. Communicativeness or audience contact
4. Conversational tones, not recitation of a memorized speech
5. Adequate volume of voice without strain
6. Enunciation and pronunciation
7. Clear, correct, concise sentences
8. Effective timing
9. Variety of rate and force
10. Emphasis of important ideas
11. Beginning
12. Organization
13. Ending
14. Fluency
15. Avoidance of *ur*
16. Avoidance of useless *well, why, and, but,* and *so*
17. Examples and facts
18. Audience reaction—attention and interest

Practice 4.   Making a Speech to Inform

From among the things you know best, select one on which to talk to your class for two or three minutes. It may be something personal —a hobby or a job you have held. Perhaps in school you have carried on an investigation that no other pupil has undertaken. Perhaps you have read an interesting, informative book. Perhaps you have a pet subject you always like to talk on. Choose something you know about, are interested in, and want others to know about. Remember that your single purpose is to inform. Turn in your outline for your teacher's criticism. Speak in sentences. Enunciate distinctly and pronounce every word correctly (pages 27–43). To test listening, at the end of your speech ask the class three or four questions which good listeners ought to be able to answer.

Group programmes may be based on subjects studied in school. On a physics programme, for example, pupils may speak on topics like these:

1. Link trainers
2. What frequency modulation means to radio
3. How a thermostat works
4. History of television
5. How lenses correct nearsightedness
6. Gasoline and Diesel engines
7. Uses of compressed air
8. How a boat sails into the wind
9. Why an airplane flies
10. Centigrade and Fahrenheit thermometers
11. The lie detector
12. Unusual effects of modern photography
13. Electricity on the farm
14. A laboratory experiment
15. The work of a great scientist
16. The use of blood tests with dairy animals
17. Science, the timesaver
18. The contribution to progress made by the electromagnet
19. Noise and musical sounds
20. Making aviation safer
21. How a camera takes a picture
22. Radar, its operation and use
23. Rockets
24. How sounds are made and carried

MAKING A SPEECH TO ENTERTAIN

Do you know what made Will Rogers the most loved comedian for many years? It was his ability to speak and write entertainingly. Certain of his secrets we know—that he was always himself, was never merely silly, drew constantly on his store of personal experience, never said anything mean, and flavoured all he said with his own personality. The ability to make an entertaining speech is like any other highly prized personal skill. If we acquire the ability, one of the roads to success in school and out is paved for us. The entertaining speech is always informal, subject to few rules. Organization is least important here, and what is said is perhaps less important than how it is said. Wit, originality, exaggeration, variety, and wholesome fun are at a premium. An entertaining speech does not, of course, have to be funny; it may be made on a serious subject, but it should be colourful and lively.

Practice 5.   Making a Speech to Entertain

Elect a master of ceremonies for the occasion, and let each one in the class be responsible for an informal talk of not over three minutes. The only purpose is to entertain. The one rule to follow is: Don't be merely silly! In a class discussion, talk over possible subjects. One of the best subjects is "The Funniest Thing I Ever Saw." After a little discussion of this topic you will probably recall an incident that you will be bursting to tell. Rehearse your speech enough to tell it smoothly. The idea is to have a good time yourself and to give others a good time. Make your story funny by telling it seriously.

PERSUADING

Logical reasoning and substantial proof are ordinarily sufficient to convince your audience. Often, however, you may find it necessary to carry your audience one step farther, so that they will take action. Persuasion, by appealing to the emotions (loyalty, pride, fear, admiration, pity), transforms conviction into action.

The *Toronto Daily Star* each Christmas asks for contributions for the neediest cases in Toronto. Instead of giving statistics and generalities about the needy, it prints on successive days word pictures of these poor homes.

Practice 6.   Persuading Other Students

Persuade your class to act on one of these matters. Enunciate distinctly, pronounce every word correctly, and use your best voice (pages 27–43).

1. Your class has been asked to contribute to the Red Cross. The teacher has appointed you to take charge of the collection. Talk to the class.
2. Money is being collected to provide a party for wounded veterans at a near-by hospital. Urge pupils to contribute.
3. Around school you have seen some examples of bad manners. Urge pupils to be courteous and considerate of the rights of others.
4. Persuade your classmates to subscribe for the school publications. Convince them that the school newspaper and magazine are worth what they cost.
5. Prepare a "pep talk" to persuade every classmate to become a member of at least one club or team.
6. Your school has been asked to contribute to the nation-wide collection of books to be sent to Europe. Persuade your classmates to canvass their homes and neighbourhood. Make clear how, when, and where the collection will be made.
7. Your class has decided to study during the term one magazine and before voting will devote a period to discussion. Which magazine do you think best for class study? Why? Be specific and persuasive.

ANNOUNCEMENT

A good announcement is clear, complete, and persuasive. In announcing a game include the place, the opposing team, the day, the hour, and the price of tickets, and, if the game is being played away from home, directions for reaching the field. In an appeal for a large attendance make the game or entertainment so attractive that pupils will not want to miss it; don't overwork the appeal to school spirit.

Practice 7.   Making an Announcement

Announce to your class one of the following. Include an appeal for a large attendance or for a large number of entrants.

a game	an exhibit	an entertainment
a debate	a play	a new club
an open meeting of a club	a concert	a field day
a contest	an excursion	another school event

NOMINATION SPEECH

A speech of nomination commonly includes these points:

1. The kind of boy or girl needed to fill the office
2. The name of the candidate
3. His record, qualities of character, and abilities—to speak and manage, for example
4. His platform or the improvements he can be expected to make

Although the name is often held till the end of the speech, it is better to mention it earlier unless everybody knows who is being nominated.

Practice 8.   Nominating, Presenting, or Accepting

1. Nominate a candidate for a school, a class, a club, a town, or a city offce.
2. Present or accept a gift, a medal, a trophy, or a banner—for example, a baseball championship trophy, a birthday gift, or a gift to the retiring president of a society.

RADIO SPEECH

A radio address differs from other talks in that the audience, invisible to the speaker, consists mostly of family groups seated comfortably in their own homes. A radio speaker therefore has to compete with many possible distractions—the evening paper, family conversation, a visitor. The moment the speaker becomes uninteresting, the relentless hand of Mother or Jimmy will reach out and twirl the dial. Also, because his time is allotted to the fraction of a second, the average radio speaker must write out his talk and read it before the microphone.

To secure the immediate interest of the audience, radio speakers often begin with a question, story, or problem common to many people. Quiet humour helps to hold the attention of the invisible

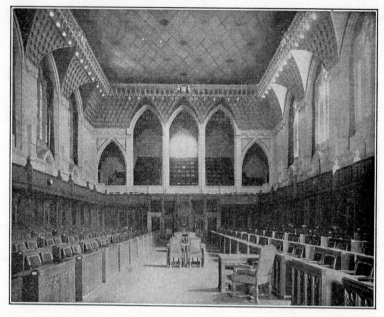

THE HOUSE OF COMMONS CHAMBER—OTTAWA

audience; but flippancy, overfamiliarity, and cheap wisecracks bore or annoy the average listener. Short, crisp sentences, vividly worded, are preferable to long, involved ones that lead the hearer into a mental labyrinth. "The essential rules for radio speaking," says Frank Dunham, "are: (1) have something to say and say it in a few words; (2) speak so as to be understood; (3) create a feeling of being *en rapport* or at ease with your audience."

Think of your audience not as a mass of thousands of people but as a small family group. Then you will achieve the vivid conversational quality so necessary to holding attention. Don't imitate some famous radio personality. Tricks are unnecessary. Simply work hard at achieving good voice quality.

Pitch should be low but natural; don't try to make over your voice for radio. *Volume* should be fairly uniform; it is unnecessary to shout for emphasis. Keep a conversational tone, but be sure to sustain normal volume even on the very last word of every sentence. *Pause, stress,* and *inflection* are your best methods of obtaining variety, emphasis, and interest, of reflecting your mood and personality. Many famous news commentators mark on their manuscripts every pause, every emphasized word, every rise and fall of the voice which they find effective in rehearsal. Naturally, distinct *enunciation* is important.

Don't, however, make your speech overprecise just for radio delivery. Speak distinctly but naturally. And of course check the *pronunciation* of difficult words before you go on the air. One mispronounced word often brings two hundred letters of protest to the broadcasting company.

Although the audience can't see you, good *posture* is important for poise and relaxed breathing. Stand or sit erect about a foot and a half in front of the microphone. Hold your script slightly above eye level and a little to one side of the microphone. That will keep your chin up and direct your voice outward, not down. As you finish reading from each sheet of paper, slip it behind the others. Never rattle papers in front of the microphone. If necessary, mount each sheet on a piece of cardboard.

Practice 10. Rehearsing a Radio Speech

Imagine that you have been asked to broadcast on one of the following topics. Rehearse your speech in class. Enunciate distinctly, pronounce every word correctly, and use your best voice (pages 27–43).

1. Scholarship and the part-time job. 2. The radio (or motion picture) in education. 3. The student court. 4. Why I like the agricultural (or another) course. 5. High school education for rural districts. 6. Project work in vocational agriculture. 7. Health education in the high schools. 8. The importance of vocabulary enrichment. 9. Educational hobbies. 10. Educational vacations. 11. Getting the most out of high school. 12. Why complete the high school course? 13. Working in the vocational agricultural shop. 14. Place of social life in high school. 15. Student government. 16. Why study history (or another subject)?

Practice 11. Comparing Radio Speakers

Compare two speakers you have recently heard over the radio. Which is the better speaker? In what respects is he more effective?

UNIT FOURTEEN

Discussion, Argument, Debate

WHY LEARN TO THINK

In an essay called "Citizenship," James Bryce says that the unwillingness or the inability of people to think is a real danger to democracy. If a person does not know the difference between sound and unsound reasoning, he can't distinguish between the truth and false propaganda and can't vote intelligently. Although thinking is the hardest kind of mental work and hence is heartily disliked by the mentally lazy, it is both an enjoyable and most profitable form of activity.

WHAT THINKING IS

Webster defines *to think* as *to reflect for the purpose of reaching a conclusion; to reason.* When, having a chance to elect either French or physics, you jot down the arguments in favour of each subject, compare them, weigh them, and then decide which would be more advantageous to you, you are thinking. When, having a chance to go to the movies, you compare the pleasure and profit of an evening at a photoplay and an evening of reading, you are thinking. If you play baseball, you probably do some real thinking as you stand at bat. You see the ball leave the pitcher's hand, you watch it, you decide where it is going, and then you decide what you are going to do.

Examples:

1. HOW I DECIDED TO OWN A DOG

When last summer I visited Uncle Will on his big Kansas farm, I played with Punch, his bulldog puppy, and wished I had one just like him. A dog, I knew, is a faithful companion and enjoys playing with boys and girls. But a farm with a barn, sheds, and fields is quite different from a city home with a small yard and a garage. Isn't a dog in the city more bother than fun?

194

When I put this question to two of my friends who have dogs, both said emphatically "No." Then I was ready to ask Father and Mother to buy me a bulldog puppy. They surprised me by saying without a moment's hesitation, "Yes, if you will take care of him." Father also told me what care a dog requires and how much bother he is. After weighing in my mind both the work and the fun, I said, "All right. How soon can we buy him?" — PUPIL

2. FOREST SMELLS BETTER THAN THOSE OF THE SEA

And, surely, of all smells in the world the smell of many trees is the sweetest and most fortifying. The sea has a rude pistolling sort of odour, that takes you in the nostrils like snuff, and carries with it a fine sentiment of open water and tall ships; but the smell of a forest, which comes nearest to this in tonic quality, surpasses it by many degrees in the quality of softness. Again, the smell of the sea has little variety, but the smell of a forest is infinitely changeful; it varies with the hour of the day, not in strength merely, but in character; and the different sorts of trees, as you go from one zone of the wood to another, seem to live among different kinds of atmosphere. Usually the rosin of the fir predominates. But some woods are more coquettish in their habits; and the breath of the forest Mormal, as it came aboard upon us that showery afternoon, was perfumed with nothing less delicate than sweetbrier. — STEVENSON, *An Inland Voyage.*

By arrangement with the publishers, Charles Scribner's Sons.

3. BOTH RICH AND POOR NEED CULTURE

The poor require culture as much as the rich; and at present their education, even when they get it, gives them hardly anything of it. Yet hardly less of it, perhaps, than the education of the rich gives the rich. For when we say that culture is: To know the best that has been thought and said in the world, we imply that, for culture, a system directly tending to this end is necessary in our reading. Now, there is no such system yet present to guide the reading of the rich, any more than of the poor. Such a system is hardly even thought of; a man who wants it must make it for himself. And our reading being so without purpose as it is, nothing can be truer than what Butler says, that really, in general, no part of our time is more idly spent than the time spent in reading. — ARNOLD, *Essays.*

Practice 1. Reaching a Decision

Explain clearly some thinking you have done before reaching a decision. Perhaps these topics will suggest some subject you have thought about.

1. Shall I study Latin? 2. Shall I buy a bicycle? 3. Shall I play football? 4. Shall I smoke cigarettes? 5. Shall I leave school? 6. Shall I work after school? 7. Shall I work during the summer vacation? 8. Shall I join the Boy Scouts, Girl Guides, C.G.I.T., or some other club, organization, or society? 9. Which high school shall I attend? 10. What course shall I take? 11. What subjects shall I elect? 12. Shall I copy my written homework or lend it to a friend to copy? 13. Shall I go out for the track team? 14. What book shall I select for supplementary reading? 15. Shall I buy this suit, dress, or hat, or that one? 16. Shall I subscribe for the school publications? 17. Shall I go to the football game or help Mother? 18. Shall I chew gum? 19. Shall I go to

college? 20. Shall I cheat in an examination if I have a good chance? 21. Shall I work hard for high marks in my school subjects or aim at the lowest passing mark?

FAULTY REASONING

There are many things which contribute to faulty thinking and reasoning, but commonest among them are these two:

1. *Reasoning without Facts*—It is one of the chief faults of children and immature adults to draw hasty conclusions without complete knowledge of the facts. Without sufficient evidence we accept political, social, and religious views as our own. Without sufficient evidence we condemn our leaders, our parents, our friends, our enemies. Reasoning based on wrong facts or too few facts has every chance of being wrong.

2. *Untrustworthy Authorities*—One of the first requisites of the student and the adult is to learn to distinguish between authorities. Always seek the authority in his own field. Sir James Jeans in Astronomy, Marconi in Wireless, Sir Arthur T. Quiller-Couch in Literature, are authorities in their fields; what they think in unrelated fields will depend entirely upon their studies in these other fields. When a distinguished actor talks about acting, he speaks with some authority on the subject; but when he speaks on science, religion, politics, health, beds, and cigarettes, he is no longer an authority, and his opinion is worth no more than that of any other man with equal intelligence and knowledge of the subject. Moreover, if he is receiving thousands of dollars for signing a recommendation of a brand of cigarettes or make of beds, his statement is untrustworthy evidence.

Fallacies in the logic of reasoning will be found on pages 213–215.

DISCUSSION

Whenever a matter of the tactics used in a baseball game, an issue in school politics, or a question of club policy comes up, boys and girls gather in groups to talk over the subject, to consider the different angles of the situation, to exchange facts and opinions bearing on the matter. This is group discussion, in which each member of a group contributes facts and opinions that may help the group as a whole to arrive at a sensible conclusion or plan of action.

Preparing for a Group Discussion

Discussion is a valuable form of mental exercise because it calls for thinking, reading, speaking, and listening. To take an active part in a worth-while discussion, first of all look at the subject with a clear, unbiased view and discover what you know and think about it. Then talk with other people and dip into books and magazines, taking notes when necessary. As you read, distinguish between fact and opinion and between honest opinion and propaganda. Reject material which is not on the topic.

Joining in Group Discussion

1. Contribute your share to the discussion but don't monopolize the time.
2. Speak clearly and audibly.
3. Show self-control and courtesy. Assume that all the members are trying, as you are, to arrive at the truth; don't assume a belligerent attitude.
4. Give facts or the opinions of authorities on the subject to support your statements. Learn to cite your authority gracefully—for example, "In a recent radio address Dr. R. C. Wallace said that—."
5. Stick to the subject.
6. While you are speaking, watch your audience for signs of boredome or inattention. Keep your audience thinking along with you.
7. Listen alertly and open-mindedly to others for the purpose of arriving at the truth, not of having your own way.
8. Relate your remarks to what others have said.
9. Accept good-naturedly the decision of the group.

Discussion Leader

Choose as the leader of a discussion a pupil who (1) speaks clearly and pointedly; (2) listens understandingly; (3) is businesslike and efficient but also courteous, considerate, and fair. The chairman's duties are—

1. To state at the beginning the subject and the main points to be covered.
2. To keep the discussion on the subject. When a pupil wanders away from the subject, the chairman courteously reminds him of the topic under discussion.
3. To give all a chance to contribute. If a pupil talks too long or too often, the chairman reminds him that some pupils have not had a chance to speak.
4. To keep the discussion peaceful.
5. To keep the discussion moving forward until a plan of action is adopted or a resolution formed. The chairman may at any time sum up the points already made to keep them clearly in the minds of the group. He also occasionally asks a question or makes a statement to keep the discussion moving toward a goal. At the close of a discussion he may sum up the conclusions reached and mention points which have not been settled or may call on a member for such a summary.

Example of pupil's contribution to discussion:

ATTITUDE OF YOUNG PEOPLE TOWARD RELIGION

Mister Chairman, the present attitude of many boys and girls of high school and college age toward religion seems to be one of general laxity and indifference. Many declare that religion was all right for their parents to believe in, or for people of a few generations past, but that now things are different; people are more broad-minded—religion is for people with set standards and narrow points of view. As a result of these erroneous beliefs, many of the younger generation have discarded all so-called "old-fashioned" principles of religion, with the argument that we, of to-day, have a free right to express ourselves in word and action as we see fit, and not as others see fit.

In order to have any well-regulated and happy social order, it is, and always has been, necessary to conform to some higher authority—not only political authority, but religious authority as well. The very fact that crime, general lawlessness, and careless moral behaviour have increased these past few years seems to be fairly good evidence that lack of religious belief of some sort has hindered the world from achieving a better social order.

If we are to look for a more idealistic civilization in the future, we must hold on to less worldly ambitions and to more spiritual ambitions. Public laws will never be able to do away entirely with corruption; each individual must regulate his own moral behaviour so as to conform with laws that have been handed down throughout the ages by religions of all kinds—laws made by a higher power than man.

Practice 2. Group Discussion

Choose a discussion leader and prepare to take an active part in the discussion of one of the following topics:

1. Is youth to-day irresponsible?
2. Is all education essentially self-education?
3. Is it desirable to have an international language?
4. Does how a young man spends his time after working hours concern his employer?
5. Being sick is a crime and being well the common duty of every good citizen.
6. The rigours of country life give young people initiative and ambition.
7. The further development of machines gives us more to fear than to hope.
8. The modern evaluation of success is generally with the money yardstick. Give your opinion of this with the purpose of establishing a true standard of success.
9. Emerson said, "There are 850,000 volumes in the Imperial Library at Paris. If a man were to read industriously from dawn to dark for sixty years, he would die in the first alcove." What books should a person read? How select?
10. Henry Ford says, "I believe America's educational system is all wrong. It turns out millions of high school graduates looking for any kind of job and not fitted for any one job in the world, unless it might be lecturing." Would this be true of the Canadian educational system? Why?

11. College. 12. Gambling. 13. Law enforcement. 14. Drinking. 15. The profitable use of leisure. 16. Honesty. 17. Courtesy in school. 18. The attitude of young people toward religion. 19. Modern advertising. 20. Books published this year.

Practice 3. Discussing Moving Pictures

With the following criteria in mind, discuss moving pictures you have recently seen:

1. **Type of motion picture.** Comedy? Tragedy? Melodrama? Farce? Travelogue? Musical drama?
2. **Setting.** Time? Place? Any outstandingly beautiful or unusual scenes? Harmony of setting with mood and theme of the picture?
3. **Main idea or theme running through the story.** Important?
4. **Story.** Is it by a well-known author? Sketch briefly the framework. Is the story original? True to life? What is the conflict inherent in it? What is the climax and in what part of the story is it reached? Is the ending logical? Name the two leading characters. What traits do you admire or dislike in each?
5. **Scene you liked best.** Why? What made it effective?
6. **Acting.** Lifelike interpretation of main character? Any outstanding performances of minor roles? Is the acting exaggerated? Which is more important—the story or the acting?
7. **Direction.** Name the director. Any clever "shots"? Skilful introduction of characters? Of scenes? Use of photographic effects to produce a mood or suspense? Are useless scenes included or necessary ones left out?
8. **Photography.** Smooth transition from scene to scene? How? Fade-outs and close-ups used effectively? Lighting? Describe.
9. **Sound effects.** Subtle or prominent? Does speaking or action predominate? Does the dialogue seem real? Do the actors speak effectively? Are their voices pleasing and suited to the characters? Characteristic noises employed? Is the music suitable?
10. **Critics.** What do the critics say about the picture? Are their opinions sound? Prove your statements.

Practice 4. Discussing Radio Programmes

With the following topics as guides, discuss the most interesting radio programmes you have listened to within a week:

1. **Name** of the programme, time of broadcast, and broadcasting station. Was there a feature artist?
2. **Type** of programme: concert, lecture, drama, news items, interview, forum discussion, sports broadcast.
3. **Highlights** of the programme. Briefly sketch the main features.
4. The **plan** of the programme. If a concert, was there any basis for the selection of compositions? Smooth transition between numbers? Good continuity? If a drama, how were the characters introduced? Scenes? How was the setting implied? Any sound effects?
5. **Speaking.** See pages 51-52.
6. **Advertising.** Inconspicuous? Boresome? Moderately entertaining be-

cause original? Did the advertiser give convincing reasons? Talk as if he believed what he said?
7. **Reason for liking** (or disliking) the programme. Give definite, thoughtful reasons. Prove your points.

FORUM DISCUSSION

As a preliminary to a forum discussion two assigned speakers may present the two major points of view. When both speakers have been heard, the chairman leads the group in an informal discussion. The main purpose of a forum discussion is to present fairly both sides of a question, not to arrive at a plan of action or the adoption of a resolution. In a forum discussion on the subject "Is education by experience as important as education by books?" one speaker will defend the value of education by experience; the other, education by books. In the ensuing general discussion, the members of the group will present their opinions, but a final decision need not be reached.

Practice 5.   Forum Discussion

Select one of the following topics and a speaker for each side. After each speaker has presented his argument, a student chairman will lead a discussion of the question.
1. Should the government own and operate radio stations?
2. Our present-day attitude toward criminals is too sentimental.
3. Debating should be eliminated from the high school English course.
4. The jury system should be abolished.
5. Canada should adopt compulsory military service.
6. Grades and marks should be abandoned in favour of semi-annual letters in which the teachers report to the parents the pupils' progress.

SYMPOSIUM OR PANEL DISCUSSION

Still another form of group discussion is the symposium or panel discussion, in which speakers—often four—present from a number of angles the available material on a subject—for example, "The Future of Air Transportation." In class the students analyze the subject and make a group outline of it, which might look like this:
1. Freight transportation by plane in the future
2. Passenger planes of the future
3. Private pleasure aircraft of the future
4 Future transoceanic air lines
5. Air transportation in urban areas
6. Future legislation for air transportation

The class then divides itself into committees, each taking one phase of the general subject for study and research. When all material has been gathered and organized, each committee elects a speaker, who presents the information, opinions, and ideas on his topic. After the speeches a student chairman leads a general discussion.

Practice 6. Symposium

Choose one of the following topics and outline it in class. Divide the class into committees to study the phases of the subject and present a symposium followed by group discussion. Limit your speech to three minutes.

1. Abyssinia. 2. Opportunities for recreation supplied by our community. 3. Important problems in present-day radio broadcasting. 4. What we know and don't know about electricity. 5. Man's conquest of time and space during the past ten years. 6. Capital and labour. 7. Present-day vocational opportunities. 8. National resources which have not yet been exploited. 9. Living Canadian poets.

ARGUMENT

Value

Concerning the value of argument the English syllabus of the state of California says, "The growing use of free speech in America and the dangers to our ideals and institutions which come from an inability to discriminate between sound and unsound reasoning make definite training in argument a necessity for every student." This is equally true of Canada.

Purpose

The purpose of argument is to change belief or secure desired action. Although the prime purpose of a school debate is to find the truth, an aim of the debaters is to convince the critic judge, the three judges, or the audience. In other aguments the purpose may be to sell tickets for a baseball game, to secure contributions for the Red Cross, to win votes for your candidate for the presidency of the student-body organization, or to sell a book or a pair of shoes. In these cases belief is not enough. In other words such an argument must be both *convincing* and *persuasive*.

Proof and Assertion

The most common fault in argument is assertion, mere "say-so," without proof. Don't say, "I think," "I believe," "It seems to me," "It is my opinion," "Statistics prove," and "Authorities on the subject say," for these expressions suggest easy-going assertion without proof. Unless you are an expert or authority, the audience are not interested in your opinions or beliefs; they want the facts in the case.

Of course, complete, thorough-going, conclusive proof of any debatable proposition is extremely difficult. Although occasionally a schoolboy in discussing a subject about which scholars and legislators are in doubt says, "I have proved my point beyond the shadow of a doubt," one can't demonstrate political, social, or economic propositions with mathematical accuracy and thoroughness. Really to argue at all, however, one must do more than state and restate the proposition and what he thinks about it; he must present facts, figures, quotations, maxims, theories, or comparisons to prove that his assertions are valid. Proof is giving (1) facts, (2) quotations from authorities, and (3) sound reasoning in support of a statement.

Practice 7. Arguing

Speak convincingly on these topics. Assertion without proof is worthless.

1. Perhaps on a crowded street car you have seen a young man who neglected to offer his seat to a shabbily clad old woman suddenly become most polite when a stylishly dressed girl entered. To whom should a person give up his street car seat? Should a girl returning from a matinee expect a tired labourer to offer his seat? Give your opinion on this problem, and try to convince the class of its worth by being logical and definite.
2. "The ordinary vacation," says Walter B. Pitkin, "is a delusion and a snare, in so far as you use it as a rest period." What do you think? Why?
3. What should a high school do with its loafers, who waste their opportunity and the taxpayers' money? For example, would you favour debarring from the privileges of the school any pupil who through lack of work did not in two years complete the work of a year and a half? Prove that your answer is fair to the student and to the taxpayer.
4. Pope says, "A little learning is a dangerous thing." Is this true? Present proof.
5. James Harvey Robinson in *Mind in the Making* says, "Most of our so-called reasoning consists in finding arguments for going on believing as we do." Prove or disprove the statement.

PERSUASION

To persuade is to move someone to action, to cause somebody to do what you would like to have him do. After deciding that you would like to go to camp, you must persuade Mother and Father to let you go and to pay the bills. To move a person to action you need to have good reasons, to be fair and sincere, to paint vivid pictures, and to look at the subject from the other person's point of view. To persuade your teacher, for example, you must try to look at the subject through his eyes.

Example of persuasion:

AN AMAZING SUMMERLAND

Now that summertime is here, don't you long for vacation time, and don't you wish to spend that vacation in Southern California, where you can have a complete change and a continuous outdoor life? There nine nights out of ten you'll sleep under blankets and in the morning be wonderfully rested and refreshed for the thousand and one things to do by day. And just think of the summer sports, bathing in the ocean at the foot of mountain ranges, camping, fishing, hiking, riding horseback up wild mountain trails and over country that you've read about. Then a visit to the great national parks and forests, which are at their best in summer, and to the giant trees, tremendous waterfalls, and sky-blue lakes would be delightful. Don't you agree with me that it would be fascinating to spend a vacation in Southern California? — PUPIL

Practice 8. Persuading

1. By effectively introducing a favourite book to the class, persuade some pupils to read it. You may tell a short, interesting incident, sketch an unusual character, read or reproduce a sparkling bit of conversation, or begin a sketch of the plot and stop at an exciting part.
2. You have twenty tickets for a Magic Evening to be given by the Science Club. In a short speech persuade the pupils in your class to buy them.
3. As campaign manager for a candidate for the secretaryship of your Student Council, make a short speech to persuade your classmates to vote for your candidate.
4. You are president of the Library Helpers' Club, the Book Club, the French Club, or another club. Make a speech to persuade your classmates to join your club.
5. Discuss places and ways to spend the summer. Try to persuade some in the class to spend a summer in a place you recommend or in a way you suggest.
6. With a partner dramatize a scene in which you try to persuade your father to let you go to camp, to teach you to drive the automobile, to permit you to take riding lessons, or to take up any other activity.
7. With a partner dramatize a scene in which you try to persuade a teacher to become a faculty adviser of a school club, to coach a club entertainment, to help you organize a club, or to help in any other school activity.

Practice 9. Persuading

Suppose that the English Department of your school is revising the home reading list and has asked for the opinions of the pupils of the school about books. Discuss a book with the purpose of showing that it should be added to the list, should be removed from the list, or should be retained on the list.

Examples:

Why *A Son of the Middle Border* Should Be
Placed on the Home Reading List

In my judgment Garland's *A Son of the Middle Border* should most decidedly be placed on the home reading list. Considered from the standpoint of literary value, it is a masterpiece. Garland in this book makes one feel as if he were living in the West, playing with little Hamlin and Jessie, and sharing their troubles. From the standpoint of its interest to the reader, it is the best book of its kind that I have ever read, for it made me feel the despair and joy of these helpless farmers struggling to break down impassable barriers. It thrilled me and made me realize how many unknown heroes existed in those Middle Border days. — PUPIL

Why *The Lost World* Should be Added to the Home Reading List

The Lost World by Conan Doyle is a story that should be added to our book list. It is a tale of adventures so vivid and exciting that, nearing the end, one lacks breath. The reader is led to a lost plateau in South America inhabited by prehistoric beasts and wild animals. Cut off from the outside world, four people explore this mysterious land, its wonders and hidden terrors. Tracked by enormous beasts, attacked by huge bird-creatures, half-killed by ape men, the little party finds danger at every step—but no way out. The book is rich in humour, suspense, thrills, chills—all that youth appreciates—then why not put this book on the list? — PUPIL

DEBATE

Debate is formal discussion made into a game with definite rules.

The Question

For a debate choose an interesting two-sided question, and state it clearly, briefly, and definitely. The question should be a timely, vital one that is still unsettled. Avoid a broad or complicated question, a proposition which can never be proved or disproved, and a proposition which has *not* in it. State the question in a sentence having one subject and one predicate unless a modifying clause is needed.

Practice 10.   Questions for Debate

Criticize these questions for debate:
1. The trolley is more useful than the automobile.
2. Cigarette smoking is injurious to boys.
3. The pen is mightier than the sword.
4. Foch was a greater general than Napoleon.
5. Moral requirements for high school graduation should be as high as scholastic requirements.
6. Canada should not belong to the United Nations.
7. Law is a better profession than medicine.

Finding Material

Webster said, "I first examine my own mind searchingly to find out what I know about the subject, and then I read to learn what I don't know about it." The *Readers' Guide*, a debater's best friend, is an index of magazine articles. The card catalogue is a guide to the books in the library. The clipping file is convenient for up-to-the-minute information. In your reading watch for a bibliography or references to other books or magazines. On a local question ask the people who know the facts; on a school question interview the principal, superintendent, teachers, pupils, and parents.

Other publications which contain information valuable in debate are:

Encyclopaedia Britannica
New International Encyclopedia
New International Year Book
Statesman's Year Book
The Canada Year Book
World Almanac
Schlichter's *Modern Economic Society*
Encyclopaedia of Social Science
Hansard
The Canadian Almanac and Directory
The publications of the Canadian Institute of International Affairs.
The publications of the Foreign Policy Association

Main Issues

The main issues map out the work that a debater must do to win. They are the divisions of the proposition, the points which must be proved to prove the case, the points on which there is a clash of opinion. Each is narrower in scope than the main question, but together they cover the whole question. In classroom debate the two sides frequently agree on the issues.

On the question "Examinations in high schools should be abolished," the affirmative will maintain that—

1. Examinations are not fair to the students.
2. Examinations injure the health of pupils.
3. Examinations cause loafing during the term and cramming at the end.
4. Examinations do not prepare for life.
5. Examinations encourage dishonesty.

The negative will maintain that—

1. Examinations aid in the accurate measurement of progress.
2. Examinations motivate study.
3. Examinations prepare for college and later life.
4. The abuses in examinations can be corrected without abolishing the whole system.

Opinions clash on the value of examinations in (1) measuring progress, (2) inducing pupils to study their work thoroughly and intelligently, and (3) preparing for life. The main issues therefore are—

1. Do examinations aid in the accurate measurement of progress?
2. Do examinations motivate study?
3. Do examinations prepare for college and later life?

The health and honesty arguments will be used by the affirmative as proof of the third issue.

Don't select too many issues. Usually two, three, or four are better than six or eight. Combine minor issues. Be sure, however, that the main issues cover the ground, prove the case. In a debate on examinations one team used these issues:

1. Are examinations injurious to the health of pupils?
2. Do examinations help teachers to mark accurately?
3. Do examinations cause cramming?

These issues do not cover the ground, because one of the most important points, the value of examinations as a preparation for later life is omitted.

Avoid also overlapping issues. One debater decided on these issues:

1. Do examinations result in the students' acquiring greater knowledge of the subjects they are studying?
2. Do examinations affect the health of students?
3. Is anything gained by examinations?

These are overlapping issues, because the first is just one part or phrase of the third.

Introduction, Body of Argument, and Conclusion

Every debate includes an introduction, body, and conclusion. The introduction clears the way for the argument; the body of the argument is the proof of the issues; and the conclusion is a summary of the proof.

Introduction

The history of the question is usually given in the introduction but may be omitted if the audience know the origin of the question, its importance, and its relation to them. If any word or expression is not clear to the audience or might be interpreted in two ways, define it. Supplement the dictionary definition by a common-sense analysis of the expression, an appeal to authorities who have defined it, or a study of the history of the question. Exclude irrelevant matter. If points are by agreement omitted from the discussion, state these. Finally, state the main issues.

The introduction should also win the sympathy of the audience. Hence it should be simple, straightforward, modest, and fair. Explain. Do not argue, overstate, or make assertions that need proof.

Practice 11.   Introducing a Debate

Criticize these statements in introductions:

1. Examinations have always been a Waterloo for most students.
2. The question of examinations increasing the mental ability of a student is irrelevant, because there isn't anything gained in this way which could not be gained without examinations

3. Pupils study so hard for an examination that they get nervous in the examination and forget what they know.
4. Moving pictures have degenerated so rapidly that they are now a menace to public morality.
5. The moving picture is admittedly the chief cause of juvenile delinquency.

Body of Argument

The body of an argument should be a logical and emphatic grouping of *facts, authoritative opinion*, and *reasoning* to prove the main issues. Don't advance weak arguments. Hit hard. One good reason is more convincing than several poor ones. An old couplet runs,

> When one's proofs are aptly chosen,
> Four are as valid as a dozen.

What a Brief Is

A brief, as the word indicates, is an argument boiled down. This special kind of sentence outline written by a debater as he organizes his material has three parts: introduction, brief proper (which is the brief of the body of the argument), and conclusion. When completed, it is a storehouse of information so arranged or pigeonholed that the debater can easily find what he needs in his argument on the subject.

How to Construct a Brief

1. The introduction should include (1) the history of the question (origin, immediate cause for discussion, and importance), (2) the definition of terms (if definition is necessary), and (3) points at issue expressed in declarative or interrogative sentences. If there are admitted facts—points on which the two sides have agreed—state them. If your opponents are likely to introduce a point which is off the subject, set it down as irrelevant matter. As every statement requiring proof is excluded, the introduction is the same for the affirmative and the negative.

2. Don't connect the topics of the introduction by *for*.

3. In the brief proper each subtopic is proof of the main topic and is connected with it by *for*. Use a comma before *for* and no punctuation after.

4. Begin the brief proper with a statement of the question for debate. In a negative brief insert *not* in the question.

5. In the brief proper the points at issue are the main topics. In the introduction the points at issue are numbered *A, B, C;* in the brief proper, I, II, III.

6. Use complete sentences. In the brief proper avoid the compound sentence.

7. Number and indent the points or topics as in an outline.

8. Make the conclusion a one-sentence summary of points proved.

9. Use the words *introduction, brief proper, conclusion,* and *refutation,* but don't number them.

For Briefs with Proof of All Assertions

10. In the brief proper distinguish facts or proof from assertion by starring definite, convincing proof.

BRIEF FOR THE NEGATIVE WITHOUT FULL PROOF
OF ASSERTIONS

Resolved, That examinations in high schools should be abolished.

Introduction

I. Because examinations have played an important part in our secondary educational system ever since its inception, and because the abolition of examinations would probably work a radical change in our entire school life, this question concerns everyone interested in secondary education.

II. The question of the abolition of examinations has always been a source of contention.

    A. Students in medieval universities (where examinations originated) questioned the value of examinations.

    B. Many progressive schools have abolished examinations.

    C. In recent years, Johnson, Starch, Elliot, Kelly, Dearborn, and other educators have investigated the accuracy of examinations as measuring instruments and have found wide variations in the marks which different teachers give to the same answer paper.

III. By *examinations* is meant the tests given by the Department of Education and full-period tests at the end of a quarter, third, half term, or term. Short quizzes are excluded.

IV. The points at issue are:

    A. Do examinations aid in the accurate measurement of progress?

    B. Do examinations motivate study?

    C. Do examinations prepare for college and later life?

Brief Proper

Examinations in high school should not be abolished, for

I. Examinations aid in the accurate measurement of progress, for

    A. Examinations gauge for the instructor and student the increase in knowledge made since previous examinations.

    B. Examinations indicate the student's increased ability to apply and adapt to new situations information learned.

    C. Examinations put the entire student body on an equal footing, for,

        1. All students are given the same questions.

        2. All students are given the same length of time.

        3. Shy pupils do not need to talk to the class.

    D. Although teachers vary somewhat in the marking of an essay answer, there is no such variation in the marking of a short-answer test.

II. Examinations motivate study, for

    A. They furnish a goal toward which every student must strive in order to pass his work.

B. They stimulate a spirit of competition.

C. A pupil will study harder and more thoroughly when he knows that a day of reckoning is approaching.

III. Examinations prepare for college and later life, for

  A. Many colleges require entrants to pass the examinations of the College Entrance Examination Board.

  B. To succeed in college a student must be able to pass examinations.

  C. Ability to pass examinations helps young people to enter professions, secure positions, and win promotions, for

    1. To engage in such a profession as medicine, law, or nursing, one must pass a lengthy, difficult examination.

    2. Corporations, as a rule, examine job-seekers.

    3. To enter the civil service one must pass a competitive examination.

    4. In many communities a teacher must pass a competitive examination to secure a position.

    5. In civil service, teaching, banking, and other vocations promotion is often dependent on the passing of competitive examinations.

  D. Every day a worker passes or fails an examination when he is called on to think quickly in an emergency and to use intelligently his knowledge and skill.

  E. Passing examinations gives the student confidence in facing a difficult job.

Conclusion

Since examinations in high school aid in the accurate measurement of progress, since examinations motivate study, and since examinations prepare for college and later life, high school examinations should not be abolished.

BIBLIOGRAPHY

Alilunas, J. L. "What Do Essay Examinations Show?" *Social Education.* Vol. 7, pp. 313–14. November, 1943.

Fowler, B. P. "How Much Do School Marks Matter?" *Parents' Magazine.* Vol. 8, pp. 12–13. January, 1933.

Given, L. I. "Blind Spots in Testing and Grading." *American Journal of Nursing.* Vol. 42, pp. 305–9. March, 1942.

Greene, Harry A., and Jorgensen, Albert N. *Measurement and Evaluation in the Secondary Schools.* Longmans, 1943.

Judd, C. H. "Third Conference of the International Inquiry on School and University Examinations." *School Review.* Vol. 43, pp. 653–63. November, 1935.

MacNeill, D. E. "In Apologia of an Essay Examination." *Social Studies.* Vol. 34, pp. 168–72. April, 1943.

Notice that the four main topics in the introduction of the preceding brief are the importance of the question, the history of the question, the definition of terms, and the points at issue, and that the three main headings (I, II, III) of the brief proper are the points at issue.

Practice 12. Proof

Show that in the preceding brief proper each subtopic is proof of the main topic under which it stands.

Practice 13. Writing a Brief

Write a brief on either side of one of the school questions at the end of the chapter.

Introduction

When in the introduction of the debate you reach the issues, it isn't enough to state them—unless, of course, the two sides have agreed on the issues. Your opponent may in a few minutes show that your issues aren't the main issues. The most important part of the introduction therefore is such an analysis of the question as will make clear to the audience that you have selected the real issues and that if you prove these issues the decision must be in your favour.

Practice 14. Introduction to a Debate

Write or speak the introduction of the argument briefed.

Clearness

The English of debate should be clear as crystal. The audience have no opportunity to return to a statement to search out its meaning. Debaters are prone to forget that matters simple to them after weeks of study on a question may seem complicated or abstruse to the audience, who have never given the question a serious thought.

Accuracy

The debater must say exactly what he means. Exaggeration and inaccuracy destroy the confidence of the audience. One foolish statement is usually enough to lose a debate.

Unity

A debate must be rigidly unified. Sometimes it will be hard for you to eliminate. You may like an argument or an illustration because it is picturesque or because it sounds learned, and yet know that the argument isn't part of your case. Be a hero. Omit everything that doesn't bear directly on a main issue you are proving.

Coherence

Coherence in debate includes (1) logical order, (2) announcement of that order, and (3) attention to transitions. The logical arrangement of a speech or an entire debate is sometimes hard to determine. Often two or more arrangements of the material are possible. A debater should imitate the English dramatist who said he first told the audience what the character was going to do, then showed him doing the act, then told that he had done it. The second speaker, for example, at the beginning of his speech should state briefly what the first speaker proved and what is the task set for the second speaker. When he has proved one point, he should make clear to the audience that he is passing on to another point. He should, however, avoid such hackneyed transitional phrases as "now"; "my next point is"; "I have just proved to you—. I shall now prove to you"; "let us now consider"; "let us now take up." The logical structure of the debate must at all times be kept before the eyes of the audience.

Emphasis

Emphasis includes (1) placing important ideas at the beginning and the end, (2) giving extra time to the chief arguments, and (3) making the entire speech concrete and vigorous. To grip the audience, place at the beginning a strong point vividly phrased and aptly illustrated; to secure a climax put the most convincing argument at the end. The beginning must catch the attention and win the sympathy of the audience, the body of the speech must present convincing proof, and the end must clinch the point. If you and your two colleagues decide on three main issues, don't assume that each debater should prove one issue. Perhaps one issue needs more proof than the other two combined. The concrete, the specific, and the imaginatively picturesque make an argument more forceful. Don't rely on bare statistics. They may be both dull and meaningless. Statistics take hold when comparisons give them significance. For example, the statement that the United States spent during World War I forty-four billion dollars means little to most people. The explanation that this sum exceeded by a half the total government expenditure in the preceding one hundred and twenty-eight years of the republic gives it significance.

Debate Custom

Address the presiding officer as "Mister Chairman" or "Madam Chairman." Do not separately address the judges or other groups in the audience. Do not refer to opponents or colleagues by name. Say "the first speaker on the affirmative," "my colleague," "the preceding speaker," or "the second speaker on the negative." In direct proof, the order of speakers is, first affirmative, first negative, second affirmative, etc. In rebuttal the negative usually speaks first. This plan gives the affirmative the advantage of the last speech—a fair arrangement because the burden of proof rests upon the affirmative. In other words, if neither side advances definite proof or if the negative speakers overthrow the arguments of the affirmative without presenting any of their own, the affirmative have lost the debate, because they have failed to prove the proposition. A warning signal one or two minutes before a speaker's time is up helps him to close before the final gavel instead of leaving his speech hanging in the air. If he is speaking when the final gavel falls, he should conclude the sentence quickly and take his seat.

In refutation use notes freely, but in your direct proof limit your use of notes to sets of statistics and long quotations.

First Speaker Affirmative

The first speaker affirmative clears the way for the argument by presenting the introduction and then proceeds to the proof of his issue or issues. Because a case well explained is half won, the first speaker ordinarily spends about half his time on introductory matter and the rest on proving an issue or beginning the proof of the issue.

First Speaker Negative

The first speaker on the negative side must be prepared to supply any important introductory material omitted by the first speaker affirmative but should not repeat facts already presented. He may either accept the definition of terms and issues or substitute his own and prove to the audience that the affirmative definition is not fair and that the issues they have presented are not the main points to be proved. After this introductory work he proceeds to the proof of his issue.

If the first speaker affirmative explains clearly and argues convincingly and persuasively, he commonly wins the sympathy of the audience of his side. The first speaker negative should by his knowledge of his subject, clearness, earnestness, fairness, sense of humour, and enthusiasm endeavour to win the audience over to the negative side.

Other Main Speeches

A good debate, unlike a series of orations or declamations, is a closely connected series of speeches on a subject. Each debater should listen attentively to what his opponents say, and, by referring to their arguments, changing his speech, if necessary, to meet their case, or refuting thoroughly a point, adapt or adjust his argument to his opponents'.

The last speaker on each side should conclude his speech with a clear, brief, forceful restatement of the main issues and proofs. A good conclusion is neither a bare summary nor a spread-eagle peroration.

Asking Questions

If you insist that your opponents answer a fair question, you may enforce your point and drive them upon the horns of a dilemma. A dozen questions, however, will make the audience think that your arguments are interrogation points rather than facts.

Rebuttal Method and Matter

To be ready for refutation prepare rebuttal cards with facts, statistics, statements of authorities or experts, illustrations, analogies, or reasoning for the attack of every important argument your opponents are likely to advance. During the debate take a few notes. Many a debater makes the mistake of spending his entire time in taking notes instead of using most of it for listening, finding the prepared rebuttal cards, and thinking what arguments are worth answering and how he will meet them.

In preparing to refute an argument, ask these two questions: "How do you know?" and "What of it?" Perhaps you can deny your opponent's facts or statistics or present other facts and figures that put the matter in a different light. Perhaps you can point out that his authorities and experts are prejudiced or unreliable, his reasoning faulty, or his statements inconsistent. An analogy or humorous absurdity may enforce your point. Possibly you can refute his authority with a better authority or produce from one of his authorities a quotation which indicates that the authority's attitude was not fairly presented. Or you may admit what he has said and show that his proofs are inadequate, are beside the point, or really strengthen your case. The last type of refutation is called turning the tables.

Fallacies

A part of the job of refutation is exposing fallacies, which are errors in the reasoning process.

Hasty Generalization

When after observing individual trees, one reaches the conclusion that maple trees shed their leaves in the fall, the generalization is sound. On the contrary, the generalization that the youngest child of a family is always spoiled is unsound. When Cecil Lighthead says, "Howard and Harold White are excellent students; therefore their three brothers will undoubtedly be excellent students," he is jumping at a conclusion. To refute Cecil's statement one might point out that the generalization was based on only two examples and that often the members of a family vary widely as students.

False Analogy

An argument from analogy is an inference that two objects which are alike in some respects are alike in another particular. When we argue that because the squirrel buries nuts for the winter, we should prepare for old age; that because a puppy learns by eating soap and biting the ears of big dogs, a boy should look out for himself; or that because Vancouver Technical Collegiate publishes a weekly newspaper, Weyburn Collegiate should have one, we are using analogies. The argument is valid only if (1) the points of similarity outweigh the points of difference and (2) there is no essential difference. If, for example, Vancouver "Tech" has ten times as many students as Weyburn, this one essential difference destroys the value of the analogy.

Mistaking the Cause

Every happening has both a cause and an effect. An important part of argument is finding causes or effects. When a person testifies, "Your Nervine has cured me. After taking two bottles I can sleep and work again," one wonders what really caused the cure. Perhaps it was nature or freedom from worry. Medicine may be the sole cause of a cure, the major cause, a minor cause, or no cause at all.

Ignoring the Question

Ignoring the question is evading or missing the real point at issue. If on the question "*Resolved*, That pupils should receive credit for participation in athletics" an affirmative speaker spends all his time proving that athletic sports are valuable to boys and girls, he is ignoring the question, for swimming during the summer, cutting the grass, tending the furnace, making a dress, repairing the automobile, and many other activities are valuable but do not receive school credit.

Macaulay attacks this fallacy of arguing beside the point when he says, "The advocates of Charles, like the advocates of other malefactors against whom overwhelming evidence is produced, generally decline all controversy about the facts, and content themselves with calling testimony to character. He had so many private virtues! . . . A good father! A good husband! Ample apologies indeed for fifteen years of persecution, tyranny, and falsehood!" Cracking jokes instead of presenting proof and appealing to tradition and prejudice are common ways of ignoring the question.

Begging the Question

Begging the question is assuming the truth or falsity of what one is trying to prove. When a person argues that Robert Frost is not a great poet because there are no great living American poets, he is assuming the truth of a larger statement which includes the one he started out to prove and hence is begging the question. When a debater states his question "*Resolved*, That the brutal game of football should be abolished," he is assuming that football is brutal instead of proving the game brutal, and therefore is begging the question.

Statistics

"Figures do not lie, but liars do figure" is an old and a true saying. Careless, stupid, and dishonest people often use statistics to prove what the figures do not prove at all, because the units are not comparable, or because the figures cover an abnormal period or do not cover a long enough period of time. If child labourers in one province include boys and girls who do housework and farm work and in another province exclude these classes, the totals are not comparable. In discussing wages, prices, street-car fares, and deposits in savings banks, one must remember that in the past thirty years the dollar has fluctuated widely in purchasing power. The earnings of coal miners illustrate the fact that the figures must cover a sufficiently long period. Because miners are often without work, annual earnings mean more than daily earnings.

Practice 15.   False Reasoning

1. Does the relative number of ships show the comparative strength of the navies of the world? Why?
2. Does the number of arrests for drunkenness show the comparative amount of drunkenness in various cities? Why?
3. Does the average wealth of the people of a community show whether there is need of charity? Why?

Practice 16.   Fallacies in Argument

In most of the following the reasoning is faulty. In each case of unsound or unconvincing reasoning, name the fallacy or defect and show clearly that the argument is not convincing.

1. Sweet peas don't grow well on Long Island. I planted some in my garden in Flushing and they didn't grow.
2. Shelley was a poor speller. Therefore spelling is not important.
3. Going to college doesn't pay. Mr. Williams went to college and has failed in business.
4. The honour system will work in our high school, for it is successful in Blank College.
5. Mrs. Brewer is an excellent housekeeper; therefore she would manage well the provincial housekeeping if elected premier.
6. The B. M. T. is now a paying concern. Lindley A. Garrison, the receiver appointed for the company, made this assertion last week.

7. The left-handed man lacks will power, for, if he did not, he would not be left-handed.

8. I'm not superstitious, but I'll never again start anything on Friday the thirteenth of the month. We started to Cobourg, on Friday the thirteenth and had two blowouts on the way.

9. I won't pay $30 for that suit. I bought just as good a one five years ago for $25.

10. Mr. Brown should never drive an automobile. Last week a runaway horse came down the street while Mr. Brown was driving; and Mr. Brown, being very nervous, drove his car into a telephone pole.

11. Because the Cardinals won the baseball championship of the United States last year, they will win it this year.

12. Earl Christy, who is noted for his portraits of beautiful women, asked me to sit for a portrait; therefore I must be beautiful.

13. I should have been given the job rather than Miss Hersey, for I have been working for the firm much longer than she.

14. Since there is much dishonesty in politics, I shall not vote.

15. In recent football games Hamilton defeated Queen's by a score of 50 to 0, and Sudbury defeated Queen's by a score of 30 to 0. Therefore Hamilton will defeat Sudbury.

16. It is unnecessary for us to include meat among our provisions. Alfred McCann, a food expert, says that many vegetables cheaper than meat possess the same food value.

17. Mrs. Knapp, the first woman elected to an important office in the state of New York, was sent to jail for a misuse of state funds. Therefore women should not be elected to public office.

18. This year we wish to cut down the expenses of our company. Because advertising is a big expense item, we shall start by eliminating it.

19. My father is a Conservative (or a Liberal). Therefore I should regularly vote for Conservative (or Liberal) candidates.

20. There are more than three million people in Chicago. Why should I vote? One vote more or less won't make any difference.

Place of Refutation

If prejudice has been aroused against your side or if some argument blocks your progress, clear the way before presenting your prepared argument. Such rebuttal should be brief and striking. Refuting an argument of an opponent is often a necessary step in proving a point. In the rebuttal speech attack first the strongest argument you can overthrow.

Rebuttal Mistakes

A few common rebuttal mistakes should be guarded against.

1. Don't misrepresent your opponent's argument. If possible, use his exact words in stating the argument to be refuted.

2. Don't begin the refutation of each point with some unvarying formula like "My opponent says—."

3. Don't advance constructive arguments in the rebuttal.

4. Avoid "scrappy rebuttal" by striking at your opponents' main

issues. When you chop down a tree, the branches go with it; when the main arguments fall, the little ones go with them. Don't spend your refutation time clipping off the branches; chop away at the trunk.

5. When your opponent makes a good point, or gives a sound reason or a fact, either admit it or pass it by without comment. Don't attempt to refute arguments which you know you can't overthrow.

6. Refute only the arguments your opponents advance. Memorized refutation answering the arguments the debater thinks his opponents will use is called "canned" rebuttal.

7. Don't be smart or discourteous.

Closing Rebuttal Speeches

In addition to refuting arguments, the speaker who closes the refutation on each side should, by summarizing briefly the arguments of his side which are still standing and pointing out the important arguments of his opponents that have been overthrown, give a bird's-eye view of the debate as it stands at the time. He should, in other words, review quickly and compare the arguments of the two sides.

Practice 17. Refutation

1. Refute a point in the brief in this chapter.

2. Assume that some proof has been advanced by the negative on each of these seven points. Refute number one and two others.

1. Moving pictures do not incite to criminality, for Charles Evans Hughes, Lloyd George, and other famous men read detective stories without emulating the criminals.
2. Masterpieces would be rejected by the censors.
3. The federal censors would be grafters.
4. As the stage, books, magazines, and newspapers are unregulated, the censorship of the moving picture is an unjust discrimination.
5. No board can satisfactorily censor all pictures.
6. Provincial censors have erred in their judgment of pictures.
7. The people themselves are the best censors.

Decision

In intercollegiate debates the no-decision contest, which emphasizes the fact that the purpose of debate is to find the truth, not to win a victory, is growing in favour. Years ago three judges, who either met and discussed the arguments at the close of the debate or voted without such discussion, regularly decided the debate. This system is still used. Sometimes, however, a critic judge, a person who understands argument, takes the place of the three judges, and in some debates the audience vote.

Practice 18. Classroom Debate

Prepare for a series of classroom debates on questions selected from the following list or on other questions. Present proof; don't merely assert.

SCHOOL QUESTIONS FOR DEBATES

1. Our high school should provide greater opportunities for vocational training.
2. Students who do not get a standing of sixty per cent should not be allowed library privileges.
3. Examinations should be abolished in our high school.
4. Pupils should be permitted to read newspapers in the study room.
5. Girls should be permitted to engage in inter-school athletics.
6. Every high school boy should have a course in the elements of carpentry, plumbing, and electric wiring.
7. Every high school girl should be required to take cooking and sewing.
8. Pupils should receive school credit for music taken outside of school.
9. Pupils should receive school credit for gardening, sweeping, washing dishes, tending the furnace, delivering papers, clerking after school, and other work done outside of school hours.
10. The Board of Trustees should furnish (or discontinue furnishing) textbooks for high school pupils.
11. An hour should be added to the school day.
12. Ability to swim twenty-five yards should be a requirement for high school graduation.
13. No girl should be required to study algebra.
14. A pupil should be detained at least a half hour after school for unexcused tardiness, *or* Detention for lateness should be abolished.
15. A pupil, except in case of sickness, should be compelled by law to attend school every day.
16. High school pupils should be charged a tuition fee of five dollars a year.
17. No pupil who is failing in a subject should be permitted to take part in school athletics.
18. Every pupil should be required to take a course in typewriting.
19. There should be a summer session of our high school to provide an opportunity for pupils to make up failures and to take advanced courses.
20. Every high school student should be required to study Latin for at least one year.

CITY, PROVINCIAL, AND DOMINION QUESTIONS

1. Canada should adopt the principle of economic nationalism.
2. Canada should adopt compulsory military service for boys eighteen to twenty years of age.
3. The majority vote of a jury should be substituted for the unanimous vote.
4. The sale of intoxicating liquor should be prohibited (or permitted) in our city.
5. Suffrage in Canada should be restricted by an educational test.
6. A citizen of Canada who neglects to vote should be fined or imprisoned.

7. A Prime Minister should serve but one five year term.
8. The Federal government should establish a system of unemployment insurance.
9. Billboard advertising should be prohibited.
10. The country boy or girl has a better chance to succeed than the city boy or girl.
11. The state should institute more rigid tests for candidates for the license to drive an automobile.
12. War should be declared only by popular vote.
13. Gambling on the races should be prohibited.
14. Sweepstakes should be legalized in Canada.
15. Child labour should be prohibited by constitutional amendment.
16. Our city should adopt the city manager plan.
17. The Canadian government should own and operate all the railroads.
18. In our city (country or province) the manufacture and sale of intoxicating liquors should be prohibited.
19. In this province capital punishment should be abolished (or re-established).
20. Our province should adopt a system of compulsory unemployment insurance.

IN A LIGHTER VEIN

1. The comic strip as at present constituted should be barred from the public press.
2. Unmarried men over the age of thirty should be subject to a bachelor tax.
3. Dagwood Bumstead is a greater benefactor of the human race than Einstein.
4. The emancipation of women is a mistake.
5. The modern girl is superior to her great-great-grandmother.
6. The barbarian is happier than the civilized man.

Building Pleasing, Forceful Sentences

STYLE means *finish* and *polish*. It is the result of carefully choosing the most distinctive way of saying what you mean, of expressing yourself with individuality. It means rejecting the commonplace sentence and insisting on the best. Conciseness, clarity, force, and variety are difficult to achieve, but they are worth striving for. Generalizing is much easier than giving examples, but illustrations clarify and reinforce ideas. The following suggestions will help you.

CONCISE SENTENCES

Coleridge says, "Whatever is translatable in other and simpler words of the same language, without loss of sense or dignity, is bad." The historic radio message, "Sighted sub; sank same," illustrates both calm heroism and terse English. Not a word is wasted. Conciseness and compression lend life and vigour to writing. Learn to cross out in your editing and revision.

Omit unnecessary words. Express each thought as compactly as possible without loss of its meaning. "It's smart to be thrifty," the slogan of the largest store in the world, is a good slogan for a writer or a speaker.

> *W*
> ~~That is most~~ wonderful!
> ~~In my opinion~~ I think *The Haunted Bookshop* should be added to our reading list.

MAX ALLEN IS A ~~MAN WHO IS A VERY~~
SKILLFUL MECHANIC.~~IN HIS FIELD~~

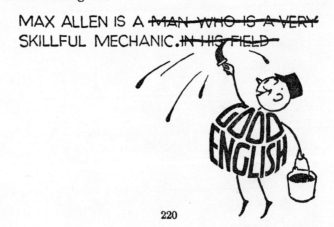

220

(Forceful) Meantime Sculptor Jones went to his Chicago home, learned nothing. — *Time* (10 words)

(Wordy) In the meantime the sculptor, Mr. Jones, made a journey to his home in the city of Chicago but did not learn anything at all. (25 words)

    a. Avoid repetition of ideas.

cheap ~~in price~~	win ~~out~~, lose ~~out~~
the ~~two~~ twins	divide ~~up~~, hurry ~~up~~
the fingers ~~on her hand~~	~~at~~ about one o'clock
the sun rose ~~in the east~~	over ~~with~~
such as . . . ~~and others~~	fell off ~~of~~ the porch
in my opinion / ~~I think~~	remember ~~of~~
refer ~~back~~	inside ~~of~~ the cave

    b. Omit unnecessary preliminaries.

~~I wish to state that~~ I have not ~~yet~~ received the shoes ~~which~~ I ordered on October 16.

    c. When possible, substitute a single word for a phrase or a clause. Strike out every useless *which* and *that.*

      an entertaining
Inside Benchley is ~~the kind of~~ book. ~~that one enjoys reading.~~

Manchukuo, ~~which has~~ fertile, ~~soil and is~~ rich in coal and minerals, and ~~which is~~ as yet thinly populated, is almost twice as large as Texas.

That ash tray was made from a piece of petrified wood ~~which was~~ picked up in Arizona.

    d. Eliminate unnecessary adjectives. Young writers tend to over-use descriptive adjectives.

The ~~magnificent,~~ golden, ~~glorious~~ rays of the setting sun contrasted with the gloomy, ~~deathlike, murky, dismal~~ shadows in the valley.

Practice 1.   Eliminating Useless Words

Strike out the unnecessary words. Express each idea more briefly

A.   1. I have had no business experience at all.
     2. At about half past nine my aunt phoned.
     3. Gordon told the both of us what he wanted to be done.
     4. How can I repay you back for your kindness?
     5. Enclosed you will please find a recommendation from my shop teacher.
     6. In reply to your advertisement in the *Globe and Mail* for artificial flower makers, I beg leave to apply for the position.
     7. In my opinion I consider Lowell Thomas one of the best and finest news reporters and commentators on the air.

8. Another interesting feature of the *American Girl* is the section where they have jokes.
9. Announcements could be made telling of future games that are going to be played.
10. In my estimation, I believe the play has already proved itself a success.

B. 1. The population of Venezuela is 3,492,747 people.
2. Dickens will always be read for the many human and real characters he has created, such as Mr. Micawber, Oliver Twist, Tiny Tim, Little Nell, David Copperfield, and many others.
3. Some of the interesting features of the *New York Times* are: it has very good book reviews; it runs a very interesting sport section; and its editorial page and letters to the editor are very informative.
4. The poets deal with such topics as spring, Indian summer, a brook, the clouds, and similar subjects.
5. In my opinion, I believe that Judge Pyncheon brought about Clifford's imprisonment.
6. There is a brief biography of Walt Whitman's life on page 19.
7. On reaching home I found the door to be locked.
8. Another reason why *Hamlet* is worth studying is due to the fact that there is much comedy in this tragedy.
9. There is no doubt that Raymond deserved the reprimand.
10. The authors feel and believe that a high school education is almost indispensable in order to succeed in the business world.

FORCE

Use simple, specific, suggestive, vigorous, picture-making words.

(Colourful) The turtle's hard legs and yellow-nailed feet threshed slowly through the grass, not really walking, but boosting and dragging his high-domed shell along. — JOHN STEINBECK
(Colourless) The turtle walked over the grass by the roadside.
(Colourful) Uriah's nostrils quivered, he wriggled his body obsequiously, and kept squeezing his palms together. — CHARLES DICKENS
(Colourless) Uriah tried to give the impression of great humility.

Practice 2.   Writing Colourful Sentences

Make eight of the following sentences more forceful by using specific, suggestive, vigorous, picture-bringing words.   Make the sentences graphic by going into particulars.

Example:

He was obviously a rookie.
The private's untanned skin; his uniform, still unlaundered and holding the original folds; and the awkward, self-conscious way he lifted the heavy, bulbous-toed, straight-lasted high Army shoes, not yet scoured with polish, labelled him a rookie.

1. The crowd cheered the touchdown.
2. The storm came suddenly.
3. Japanese beetles attacked our garden in force.

4. The tree outside my window is beautiful.
5. The tuba player was very comical.
6. At the park there was an unusually large crowd of people of all kinds.
7. Jerry is a fine boy.
8. We had an excellent dinner.
—9. Marie was attractively dressed.
—10. We have various kinds of flowers in our garden.
11. In his beautiful summer home he had most of the conveniences of the city.
—12. His speech was poor.

Begin a sentence with important words. Placing key words at the beginning of a sentence connects it with the preceding sentence and challenges the reader's interest.

Liberty is to the collective body what health is to every individual body. *Without health* no pleasure can be tasted by man; without liberty no happiness can be enjoyed by society. — HENRY ST. JOHN BOLINGBROKE

End the sentence with an emphatic word or phrase.

(Emphatic) National injustice is the surest way to *national downfall.* — WILLIAM E. GLADSTONE
(Less Forceful) To national downfall national injustice is the surest road.

Acquire the habit of sandwiching parenthetic expressions between the key words of your sentences. By placing parenthetic expressions in the middle of your sentences you will reserve the emphatic beginning and end positions for key words. Avoid ordinarily beginning with *however, therefore, I think, it seems to me,* or a similar expression.

(Forceful) *Dr. Jekyll and Mr. Hyde* is, *in my opinion,* a masterpiece.
(Weak) *Dr. Jekyll and Mr. Hyde* is a masterpiece in my opinion.

Arrange a series as a climax unless you wish to make an anticlimax for the sake of humour.

(Climax) Quality, will power, geographical advantages, natural and financial resources, the command of the sea, and, above all, a cause which rouses the spontaneous surging of human spirit in millions of hearts—these have proved to be the decisive factors in the human story. — WINSTON CHURCHILL
(Climax) I am in earnest. I will not equivocate; I will not excuse; I will not retreat a single inch; and I will be heard! — W. L. GARRISON
(Anticlimax) Men will confess to treason, murder, arson, false teeth, or a wig. How many of them will own up to a lack of humour? — FRANK M. COLBY

Report conversation directly.

(Forceful) "Youth," commented Bernard Shaw speculatively, "is too precious a thing to waste on children."
(Weak) Bernard Shaw commented speculatively that youth is too precious a thing to waste on children.

Practice 3.   Building Forceful Sentences

Improve the following sentences. Give a reason for each change.

Example:

Al commanded the dog to come to him at once.
"Come here, Peter," snapped Al. (Al's command is reported directly.)

A. 1. Kipling's "Gunga Din" is the best poem I've ever read, I think.
  2. It is time that the world took steps to prevent future wars, wholesale slaughter, and unfair trade discrimination.
  3. In time of crisis men will fight for their country, their rights, and their freedom, invariably.
  4. Alice's father asked whether Alice had put away his briefcase.
  5. Collecting minerals is an educating and fascinating pursuit. However, you must spend a little time studying the properties of minerals, their classification, and ways of distinguishing them.

B. 1. The outstanding characteristic of the Canadian variety of European civilization is our faith in education, according to the best observers.
  2. Cynthia's mother said that whenever Cynthia felt blue it was a good idea to find someone who was bluer than she was.
  3. The invading army murdered, robbed, and annoyed defenseless civilians.
  4. Humanity has had a "sweet tooth" for ages, according to a recent history of sugar.
  5. Shakespeare ranks first among writers as a philosopher, a poet, and a creator of human beings, as I have pointed out.

Place the principal thought of a complex sentence in the principal clause. A *when* clause fixes the time of an event told about in the principal clause.

After
ₐI had driven only ten blocks ~~when~~ the tire blew.

After rowing
~~We rowed~~ on through the storm for an hour ~~when~~ we finally reached our dock.

The active voice is usually clearer, terser, and more forceful than the passive. The passive voice emphasizes the receiver of the act and subordinates the doer.

(Active) Ken carried an armful of fragrant hay and a bucket of water to Flicka.

(Passive) An armful of fragrant hay and a bucket of water were carried to Flicka by Ken.

Practice 4. Building Forceful Sentences

Improve the following sentences by placing the principal thought in the principal clause and by changing a passive voice to an active voice.

Example:

Ted was winding his watch when he heard the brakes squeal outside his door.

When Ted was winding his watch, he heard the brakes squeal outside his door.

1. We hiked about half the distance to the park when we decided to find a place to cook and eat our lunch.
2. We fished for an hour when we were compelled by a storm to seek shelter.
3. The Dodgers had lost all hope of victory when the ball was knocked over the fence and three runs were scored by Walker.
4. The China Clipper was far out over the Pacific when they saw a small fishing vessel.
5. The Vocational Research Bureau was organized by Mr. Taylor, of Carmel, New York, to help boys decide intelligently upon their lifework.
6. Edison was almost in despair when unexpectedly the lamp stayed lit for many breathless hours.
7. General Crerar walked up and down along the runway when suddenly he saw the fliers returning.
8. A fine collection cannot be made by an amateur without assistance.

USING COMPARISONS

Comparisons enable a speaker or writer to say much in little. This important method of gaining vividness and force is used constantly by newspaper columnists and radio commentators, as well as by poets. Many of our common expressions, like "stole second base," "blossomed forth in a new dress," and "swamped with calls," are metaphorical in origin. "A face like a cross pansy" paints a fresher picture than the tarnished comparison "cross as a bear."

Practice 5. Studying Comparisons

Note the condensation and colour in the following. Numbers 1 to 3 are metaphors and 4 to 6 are similes. What are compared in each?
1. Ted waltzed in wearing a rainbow tie.
2. Armed only with a hunting knife, pint-sized, hickory-tough Captain James Kehoe set out on foot through one of the world's densest jungles.
3. The Prime Minister moved to eliminate bottlenecks in production.
4. She barged in with her six children, like a bomber escorted by fighters.
— HAROLD MYNNING
5. Restless as the tip of a cat's tail. — JACK MORRIS
6. Grandfather sat quiet as a stone under the fan-shaped elm.

Practice 6. Writing Similes and Metaphors

Construct similes or metaphors for eight of the following. Avoid worn-out comparisons; make them vivid, not far-fetched.

Example:

anger. When angry, he is hasty as fire.

| an airplane | an old house | a battered hat |
| an old dog | a book | an apple orchard |

the wind	a voice	Vancouver's skyline
a tried friend	silence	hot rolls
a hypocrite	envy	clouds

WRITING OBJECTIVELY

For the most part write objectively, picturing actions rather than describing emotions. Subjective writing depends principally upon the analysis of feeling or the description of emotion. Objective writing does not eliminate feeling but lets the reader draw his own conclusions from a graphic description of what is happening. Because objective writing describes what you could *see* and *hear* if you were present, it can be transferred directly to stage or screen.

(Subjective) When his turn to recite came, little Tom felt so nervous that he thought he would never be able to say the poem.

(Objective) Little Tom walked to the front of the room, tremblingly blurted out the title of his poem, and burst into tears. (The sentence shows how Tom felt by picturing him in action.)

NOTE. There is room for occasional good subjective writing which does not merely tell the emotion a person feels, but pictures it from his point of view. Thus the preceding subjective sentence may be improved: When his turn to recite came, little Tom felt himself go cold, as though someone had poured ice water into his veins.

Practice 7. Writing Objectively

Change the following subjective analyses into objective descriptions. Show what the people do. Make your classmates see the actions and, as a result, know what emotion is felt.

Example:

Cold, bitter anger welled into Joan.

With narrowed eyes, tightly closed lips, and clenched fists, Joan rose and advanced toward her tormentor.

A. 1. Dad welcomed Uncle Jack heartily.
   2. Toby felt deep unrest and uneasiness as the time for his father's arriva passed.
   3. Little Dora felt overwhelming pity for the poor homeless dog.
   4. Ted was badly frightened when he heard an owl for the first time.
   5. The sight of the little black box stirred Marie's curiosity.

B. 1. George had a great affection for his ragged chum.
   2. Harold is a very shy boy.
   3. Mother was enthusiastic about my new hat.
   4. Susie was greatly pleased with her new doll.
   5. The two boys were dead tired when they returned from the hike.

BUILDING VARIED SENTENCES

Vary the length and type of sentence you use. There is no one best kind of sentence. Each kind helps the writer to achieve a particular effect.

a. Short sentences are easier to understand than long ones, and when introduced after a number of long ones, add vim. The short sentence is also used to express strong feeling or create a dramatic effect.

Lafayette, we are here. — CHARLES E. STANTON
I do not choose to run. — CALVIN COOLIDGE

If, however, many short, choppy sentences are used together, the composition sounds like a primer.

b. In a *long sentence* a speaker or writer can express accurately and fully a complicated idea with its details and qualifications.

Thoreau in his generation, and Burroughs in the next, were the poets of Nature who brought us all closest to the purely natural way of thinking, the faith not so much in the ways of the wild as in what is nature in a man's self. — DONALD PEATTIE

c. Long sentences may be either *loose* or *periodic*. A *loose sentence* makes complete sense if brought to a close at one or more points before the end.

The beautiful constellation Scorpius towers high || in the southern sky || in the early summer evenings. ||

d. A *periodic sentence* makes complete sense only at the end.

High in the southern sky in the early summer evenings towers Scorpius.

The loose sentence is simpler, clearer, and more natural than the periodic; but the periodic sentence keeps the hearer in suspense until the last word is reached. Because it holds the attention, impresses the point, and varies the usual subject-verb order, it should be used frequently for effect.

Practice 8.   Writing Periodic Sentences

Change each loose sentence into a periodic sentence.

Example:

We reached home toward dark, after a long ride and some unusual experiences.

Toward dark, after a long ride and some unusual experiences, we reached home.

1. Father Hubbard, the Glacier Priest, enjoyed climbing California's mountains at an early age even though he was not robust.
2. He became interested in geology and paleontology while other boys of his age thought only of sports and frolic.
3. He didn't neglect sports despite his keen interest in natural science.
4. He has made many contributions to science as a result of his years spent in Alaska and the Bering Sea region.

5. His language is colourful, whether he is addressing a large group, writing a book about his explorations, or speaking conversationally to a few people.
6. The Army and the Navy have used his scientific data in the compilation of information on Alaska and the Aleutian Islands.

e. A *balanced sentence* has two parts that are similar in form.

Silence is as deep as eternity; speech is as shallow as time. — THOMAS CARLYLE

Not that I loved Caesar less, but that I loved Rome more. — WILLIAM SHAKESPEARE

A wise son maketh a glad father, but a foolish son is the heaviness of his mother. — BIBLE

From five and a half years of experience we in China are convinced that it is the better part of wisdom not to accept failure ignominiously, but to risk it gloriously. — MADAME CHIANG KAI-SHEK (The infinitive phrases are balanced.)

Practice 9. Writing Balanced Sentences

Construct balanced sentences containing statements about five of the following:

Example:

Youth and age. The young man who has not wept is a savage, and the old man who will not laugh is a fool. — GEORGE SANTAYANA

1. the country and the city
2. winter and summer
3. sleeping and daydreaming
4. wit and wisdom
5. student and teacher
6. hope and despair
7. war and peace
8. Champlain and Sir Wilfrid Laurier
9. poverty and riches
10. subjects of your own choice

f. An occasional interrogation, exclamation, or command adds variety and life to your writing. "Who is equal to him?" is livelier than "He has no equal." "How beautiful!" is stronger than "This is beautiful."

Who will tell us why only in winter do we see that strange chill apple green in the sunset sky? — DONALD PEATTIE

Dost thou love life? Then do not squander time, for that is the stuff life is made of. — BENJAMIN FRANKLIN

How are the mighty fallen! — BIBLE

Frequently place a word or words before the complete subject. Most pupils overuse the simple sentence beginning with the subject. Use both subject-first and subject-not-first sentences.

(Adverb) *Calmly and steadily* the big dirigible proceeded on its way.
(Prepositional Phrase) *On an old street in Honolulu* we came upon a candle factory.
(Introductory Adverb and Verb) *There were* wild strawberries on the other side of Hot Springs Bay. (*There* and *it* are often used to invert sentences.)

(Adverb Clause) *As Grace and her small guide turned the corner,* loud voices could be heard pouring forth from the Judson tenement.

(Participial Phrase) *Calling softly to her lost children,* the mother duck swam around the island.

(Infinitive Phrase) *To tow an ordinary ship through the Panama Canal* four locomotives are required.

(Predicate Adjectives and Verb) *Crisp and white were* the dimity curtains at the cabin windows.

(Noun Clause used as the Direct Object of the Verb) *What we learn by experience* we remember longest.

Practice 10.   Building Subject-not-first Sentences

Revise each sentence by placing a word or words before the complete subject.   Then tell what grammatical event or elements you placed before the subject.

A. 1. Walt Disney is well loved for his contribution to the happiness of the world.
   2. Children and adults everywhere shout their unqualified approval of his work in every conceivable tongue and dialect.
   3. Dale Carnegie says of him, "He made a fortune out of a mouse and three pigs."
   4. Mickey Mouse, the first of Disney's many successes, has become an international figure, achieving a fame equalled by few living persons.
   5. The idea for Mickey Mouse was born when Disney befriended a playful mouse on the floor of an old wooden garage.
   6. He recalled the mouse years later when his cartoon, "Oswald and the Rabbit," failed to arouse interest.

B. 1. Disney, capitalizing on the success of Mickey Mouse, introduced new characters.
   2. He added Minnie Mouse to provide romantic interest for Mickey.
   3. Donald Duck, Pluto Pup, and many other beloved characters soon came from Mr. Disney's studio.
   4. *Three Little Pigs* was the greatest success in the history of animated cartoons up to its time.
   5. His longer pictures, beginning with *Snow White*, stamped cartoons as a striking, original, and beautiful movie art form.
   6. Disney puts whatever profits he makes back into his great love, his pictures.

By writing complex sentences avoid overworking *and* and *so*.

(Grown-up) Vegetation grows so rapidly in the hot, rainy regions of the Amazon basin that they might be the most productive parts of the world if men knew how to cultivate them.

(Childish) Vegetation grows rapidly in the hot, rainy regions of the Amazon basin and they might be the most productive parts of the world but men don't know how to cultivate them.

Practice 11.   Subordinating Ideas

By subordinating one of the ideas change each compound sentence into a complex sentence. Whenever possible, place an adverb clause before the principal clause it modifies. Select conjunctions that show exactly how the clauses are related in thought.

A. 1. Chile stretches along the western coast of South America, and it has emerald lakes, thick forests, giant waterfalls, and snow-mantled volcanoes. 2. The lake region is known as Vacationland, and Chileans call it the best spot in the world for trout fishing. 3. Forests hinder grazing and plowing in the lakeland, so the trees are cut down. 4. The mountain peaks are covered with snow, but inside they smoulder with volcanic fires.

5. Sunny weather is rare in the Chilean lake region, and it rains for about ten months every year.   6. January and February are the summer months, so the weather then is usually fair.

7. Chile has the only workable deposits of natural nitrates in the world, so for a long time the country had a monopoly on the production of these useful compounds.   8. Income from the nitrate fields paid 68 per cent of the cost of government, so it was unnecessary for landowners to pay taxes.

B. 1. A German chemist invented a process for taking nitrogen from air, however, and then the Chilean nitrate industry almost collapsed.   2. Chile manufactures cloth, shoes, chemicals, and paper, but a great many of the people earn their living by agriculture.   3. The principal farming region is the Central Valley, and the soil and climate there are ideal for raising crops. 4. Farther south there are vast forests, and these yield both hard and soft woods suitable for many purposes.

5. Geographically Chile is somewhat isolated, so through the years its people have become self-reliant, aggressive, and sturdy.   6. The Chilean revolution against Spain was led by Bernardo O'Higgins, and his name appears to-day on many streets and hotels.   7. The government has a progressive programme of social welfare and security, and this includes retirement pensions, medical and dental care, vacations, and discharge benefits.

Use appositives to save words and improve sentence structure. Unless you write better than the ordinary pupil in high school, you should use about twice as many appositives as you are in the habit of using.

(Weak) I identified three new wild flowers to-day.   They were the campion, star grass, and the swamp rose.

(Better) I identified three new wild flowers today—the campion, star grass, and the swamp rose.

Practice 12.   Using Appositives

In each of the following, combine the sentences by substituting an appositive for one of them.

1. On his first day in a fashionable school at Ascot, Winston Churchill was whipped twice.   He was a small, red-headed, big-eared boy of seven.
2. At twelve Winston entered Harrow.   It is one of the most famous private schools in England.
3. His mother was an American.   She was a famous beauty of London society.
4. At Harrow, Winston ranked high in two fields.   He was the school champion in fencing and gained a mastery of English.
5. In later life Churchill once said that if he were a teacher he would whip a boy for only one reason.   Any boy deserved a birching, he believed, for not knowing English.
6. At Harrow he prepared to take the examinations for entrance to Sandhurst.   This military school is England's West Point.
7. When he was graduated from Sandhurst at the age of twenty, he was commissioned as a sublieutenant in a famous cavalry regiment.   His regiment was Her Majesty's Fourth Hussars.

8. As an officer of hussars Churchill wore on his head a busby. This is a tall fur hat with a beautiful plume and a bag hanging from the top over the right side.

By building sentences with compound predicates, avoid the overuse of *and I, and we, and he, and she,* **and** *and they* **compound sentences.**

The pirates killed the crew in a bloody fight and then they transferred the cargo to their own ship.

Practice 13. Using Compound Predicates

Improve these sentences by making of each compound sentence a simple sentence with a compound predicate.

1. At an early age Stephen Vincent Benét began writing, and he won prizes offered by *St. Nicholas* magazine.
2. He prepared for college at Summerville Academy, and in 1915 he was admitted to Yale University.
3. As a writer he brought American folklore into the limelight, and he made Americans proud of their heritage.
4. "The Devil and Daniel Webster," his famous short story, was successful as a play and an opera, and it was even more impressive on the screen as *All That Money Can Buy.*
5. He was not satisfied to go on writing short stories, and on a Guggenheim fellowship he spent two years in France writing an epic poem.
6. This long poem, *John Brown's Body,* presents a fresh view of a familiar event, and it won the Pulitzer prize for poetry in 1928.
7. His work is not bulky but it is of high quality.

Most pupils can improve their style by using more participles. An average adult uses twice as many participles as a typical pupil in grades seven to twelve.

(Grown-up) The tall sailing ship, towering above me as I stood on the dock, seemed like a pale ghost in the moonlight.
(Childish) The tall sailing ship towered above me as I stood on the dock. It seemed like a pale ghost in the moonlight.

Practice 14. Using Participles

Improve these sentences by substituting participles for some of the verbs in principal or subordinate clauses.

1. Robert E. Peary, who was brought up on the coast of Maine, acquired at an early age a deep love for outdoor life.
2. Peary completed a course in civil engineering at Bowdoin College, and he first worked as a surveyor for a private company and then entered the service of the United States government.
3. In a Washington bookstore one day he found a paper which described the interior of Greenland.
4. In 1886 Peary, who was fired with enthusiasm for the North, applied for a leave of absence and sailed for Greenland.

5. Five years later the Academy of Natural Sciences supplied him with the money which was needed to lead a second expedition.
6. He explored the frozen country by sledge, and he proved on his second trip that Greenland is an island.
7. On his eighth voyage, which was made in 1909, Peary reached the North Pole and planted there the flag of the United States.
8. Especially happy at his success was his daughter Marie, who was born in the far North and was called by the Eskimos "the snow baby."

Occasionally place adjectives, an adverb, an infinitive, or a parenthetic or adverb clause or phrase between the subject and the verb. Use this arrangement only if the sentence sounds natural.

The royal barge, like an ancient Roman galley, glided along under the rhythmic dip of many oars.

The winters in England, though cold enough to be stimulating, are not so cold as to interfere seriously with most occupations.

Once in a while place adjectives after the nouns modified.

In these regions, hot arid, and barren, most of the rainfall evaporates.

The Camembert, velvety-crusted and creamy-centred, was Dr. Adams' favourite cheese.

PLEASING THE EAR

After writing the first draft of a story, an essay, or a report, read it aloud to see how it sounds.

The round open vowels and the consonants *l, m, n,* **and** *r* **give ease and a liquid quality to the sound:** *momentum, lowly, mole, moonlight, nevermore, rolling.*

When lilacs last in the dooryard bloom'd,
And the great star early droop'd in the western sky in the night,
I mourn'd, and yet shall mourn with ever-returning spring.
— WALT WHITMAN

Avoid the purposeless repetition of sounds or words. Purposeful repetition of a sound may create the proper atmosphere; purposeful repetition of a word may drive home a point.

(Meaningless Repetition of a Sound) Tom tried to tidy up the tent before the two tenderfeet returned.

(Purposeful Repetition of Sound)
> And the silken sad uncertain rustling of each purple curtain
> Thrilled me—filled me with fantastic terrors never felt before.
>
> — Edgar Allan Poe

(Purposeful Repetition of a Word) At a *glance* I didn't like Judy, and during the nine weeks at camp I had more than a *glance* at her.

Practice 15. Improving the Sound of Sentences

Improve the following sentences by eliminating unnecessary repetitions of sounds or words

Example:

> If the furniture cannot be repaired, we shall furnish you with new furniture.
>
> If the furniture cannot be repaired, we shall replace it.

1. Every pupil in our school takes examinations at the termination of each term and is marked according to the marks on these examinations.
2. When you asked me to come, you didn't tell me what time you wanted me to come.
3. In a friendly fashion Frank tried to make friends by speaking gently to the unfortunate foundling.
4. If that time is not convenient for you, write and tell us when it will be convenient for you to have our repairman call to repair your oil burner.
5. The magazine is a monthly magazine coming out on the 25th of every month.
6. That is a country that offers to the oppressed all that they desire.
7. It is not profitable for a company to employ a careless employee whose carelessness results in costly accidents.
8. I fear you were not near enough to hear the weary speaker.

In prose avoid rhyme and a regular rhythm (metre).

(Rhyme and Metre) They tried to win at any cost. They knew not that the game was lost.

(Better) Fighting on with a never-say-die spirit, they failed to realize the game had already been lost.

WAYS OF SAYING THE SAME THING

Isn't he thin!

Here are seven ways of saying the same thing:

> How thin he is!
> He is thin as a rail.

What a thin man!
Did you ever see so thin a man!
There are few men as thin as he.
Isn't he a roly-poly? (Said ironically)
Here comes another Ichabod Crane.

Practice 16. Different Ways of Saying the Same Thing

With these suggestions find at least four ways of saying each of the following:

1. He is exceedingly wise.
2. What a pigmy he is!
3. The building is unusually tall.
4. The sunset was lovely.
5. How quiet the lake is!

Practice 17. Different Sentence Forms

Express the meaning of each of the following questions in the form of an assertion, a command, or a wish.

Example:

"Shall I never hear the end of this?" means "I am weary of having this brought up to me."

1. When shall we be rid of him?
2. Will you please be quiet?
3. When can we have silence?
4. Can you imagine anything more lovely?
5. Am I never to be rid of this pest?
6. Am I my brother's keeper?
7. Will no one rid me of this turbulent priest?
8. What do you expect to gain by this lying?
9. Canst thou not minister to a mind diseased?
10. Of whom then shall I be afraid?

Practice 18. Changing the Subject

Following each of these sentences there is one word or more in parentheses. Give the meaning of the sentence in another sentence, the subject of which is the word or words in parentheses.

Example:

Why do you look at me so reproachfully, as if I were the guilty party? (Your reproachful looks)
Your reproachful looks would imply that I am the guilty party.

1. I have a veneration for the hard hand, although it may be crooked and coarse. (The hard hand)
2. I thank God that my faculties are not much impaired. (My faculties)
3. I have loved Jacob, but I have hated Esau. (Jacob . . . Esau)

4. Actions are better than words for the basis of judgment. (I)
5. Two men and no third are honourable to me. (I)
6. The enthusiastic recognition of certain qualities in others turns most of us into hero-worshippers. (Hero-worship)
7. Is there a person who thinks of turning into ridicule our great and ardent hope of a world to come? (Who)
8. It is said that Solomon's axe spared certain cedars when he was busy with his temple. (There are cedars)
9. A sickening suspicion was inspired within the fortress by the death-like stillness which reigned there. (A death-like stillness)

IMITATION OF MODEL SENTENCES

Practice 19. Imitating Models

Following the rhythm and construction of these models, make sentences of your own as effective as you can devise.

Example:

Model: The more irksome any habit is in its formation, the more pleasantly and satisfactorily it sticks to you when formed. — TOM HUGHES

Imitation: The more pleasant any incident is in our experience, the more lasting and valuable will it be in our memory.

1. Except a living man, there is nothing more wonderful than a book! — CHARLES KINGSLEY.
2. One of the best rules in Conversation is, never to say a thing which any of the Company can reasonably wish we had rather left unsaid. — JONATHAN SWIFT
   (You may omit the old fashioned capitals.)
3. Savoury was the smell of fried pilchard and hake; more savoury still that of roast porpoise; most savoury of all that of fifty huge squab pies. — CHARLES KINGSLEY
4. "Drown me, will you?" said I; "I should like to see you!" — GEORGE BORROW, *Lavengro.*
5. The old gods, worshipped by youth and beauty, are dead; and no immortal power can place a living heart in this stony bosom or lend to these matchless limbs the warm flexibility and rosiness of life. — LAFCADIO HEARN, *Fantastics and Other Fancies.*
6. The stars in their silent courses looked down through the crannies of the tomb and passed on; the birds sang above him and flew to other lands; the lizards ran noiselessly above his bed of stone and as noiselessly departed; the spider at last ceased to renew her web of magical silk; the years came and went as before, but for the dead there was no rest. —LAFCADIO HEARN, *A Dead Love.*
7. Imagine a man in the Sahara regretting that he had no sand for his hourglass. — GILBERT KEITH CHESTERTON, *A Piece of Chalk.*
8. He crossed, snake-like, toward the fire. There that bullying fellow had stood with his back to it—confound his impudence!—as if the place belonged to him. — JOHN GALSWORTHY, *The Stoic.*
9. The night had come, black, inevitable, long. And to those who have no house the night is a wild beast. In every chimney a hollow wind spoke its uncontent. — MARY WEBB, *Over the Hills and Far Away.*

Practice 20. Review of Building Pleasing, Forceful Sentences

In one or more of the ways suggested in this section improve each sentence or change its grammatical structure.

A. 1. General Eisenhower enjoys such activities and sports as fencing, golf, and many others.
   2. General Eisenhower is a leader of men, a reader of character, and a weeder out of defeatism and pessimism.
   3. Her narrow, green, impenetrable eyes smoldered with sullen savagery.
   4. The retina of the eye is sensitive to light, like the film of a camera.
   5. My rubber boots have had many adventures.
   6. Perhaps you have wondered how men are able to foretell the weather.
   7. Captain Larsen said that if I ever happened to be in want of employment, I should remember that as long as he had a ship I had a ship too.
   8. The society again repeated the concert a second time for the benefit of the building fund.
   9. Now these treasures, which are bound in purple and gold, are preserved in the National Library.
   10. It was about eight o'clock on a July evening, and Fred and I were hiking toward camp.

B. 1. The farmer carved the turkey with a sharp knife that didn't require whetting.
   2. The enemy is preparing to slaughter our people, devastate our fields, burn our houses, and devour our poultry.
   3. The new beginner quickly snatched his hat as soon as the bell rang.
   4. It was dastardly of Chilton to dynamite a building in which women and children were hard at work.
   5. That tall building is built beautifully with its massive dome, and it has mighty columns to beautify it.
   6. John Singer Sargent's father was a well-known physician and surgeon, and he taught the boy the value of keen observation and hard work.
   7. Michael Faraday invented the dynamo after years of experimentation, and thus he paved the way for the work of Morse, Field, and Bell.
   8. After escaping from a South American jungle, Lieutenant Harmon said that he certainly was thankful for his years of football.
   9. However, temperatures remained normal yesterday, and little of the snow and ice melted.
   10. In my opinion, Oslo is a comfortable city to live in.

Mastering Effective Words

THE ENGLISH LANGUAGE

We who speak the English language have reason to be proud of it. Fifteen hundred years ago, it was the language of a few thousand people; it had only a couple of thousand words. To-day English is spoken by at least two hundred million people; it has more than three hundred thousand words. It is the language of world trade, and is one of the principal languages of international diplomacy. Of all languages it has proved to be the most adaptable and useful. It is still a living and changing language.

The development of the English language falls roughly into three periods:

(1) **Old English** (from the beginning to 1066)

(2) **Middle English** (1066 to 1485)

(3) **Modern English** (1485 to the present).

OLD ENGLISH

Old English began with the Jutes, Angles and Saxons who invaded Britain about A.D. 450. They came from the Continent, in the region of north-west Germany; conquered the Britons and drove them into the west and north, into what is to-day called Wales and Scotland. The Angles settled north of the Humber; the Saxons, south of the Thames; the Jutes occupied the territory between them.

The oldest extant story in the language is the story of Beowulf. The tale was carried down orally for many centuries and probably dates back to a time before the three tribes moved to Britain. The Angles were the first to record their language, which they called *Englisc* (English). Their land they called *Angle-land* (England). In the eighth century there rose among them two notable writers, Caedmon and the Venerable Bede. In the ninth century the Saxon King, Alfred the Great, established his dialect as the literary language of the country, though it was still called English. This might have remained the language of England had it not been for the Norman Conquest, 1066.

Because of the powerful influence of the court, the language of the Normans (French) superseded all other languages as the *written* language of the country. The rugged individualism of the populace immeasurably influenced the language of the conquerors. To be able to rule and to trade, the Normans learned the spoken dialects of the English. As the years passed the languages fused to develop the Norman-English spoken in London and Oxford. The writings of Wycliffe and of Chaucer helped to establish this dialect as the permanent language of England. This was strongly influenced by the introduction of printing by Caxton (1476); spelling became more fixed, and grew less and less phonetic. It was never so easy afterwards for new dialects to get a wide acceptance.

CHANGES IN THE LANGUAGE

Old English was a highly inflected language. Nouns had **four or** five cases and several declensions.

	CASE	SING.	PLURAL
E.g.	Nominative and Accusative	Stan	Stanas
	Genitive	Stanes	Stana
	Dative and Imperative	Stane	Stanum

It has, however, always been a characteristic of English to strive toward simplicity. Gradually many inflections were dropped and the position or order of the word indicated its use. By the fourteenth century, already, the genitive singular and plural were the same, *stanes, stanes.* To-day the 'e' has been dropped and we indicate the possessive by the apostrophe only. "His lordes werre", of Chaucer has become "His lord's war".

In early English many adjectives agreed with their nouns in number (good, sing., goode, pl.)

His hors weren goode.—His horses were good.

In early English, the verbs, too, had more inflections than we have to-day. These have been largely replaced by auxiliaries. Many past participles were preceded by *ge-* which gave way to *y-*, which was still common in Chaucer's time.

"At mete well *y-taught* was she withalle".

(She was, at the same time, well taught in table manners)

Plural verbs and infinitives sometimes ended in *en.*

And smale fowles *maken* melodye.
That *slepen* al the nyght with open eye.
(And small birds, that sleep all night with open eyes, make melody.)

A manly man to *been* an abbot able.
(A manly man, fit to be an abbot.)

It was natural that the language of the English conquerors should be influenced by that of their neighbours, particularly by borrowing new words used in daily converse, as in trade and commerce. They borrowed from the Celts, whom they conquered, words like *gem, wine,* and *pound;* also *kettle, chest,* and *dish.* From the Romans who occupied Britain from 45 B.C. to 400 A.D. they borrowed such words as *caster, chester, cester* (L. Castra = camp); *wall* (L. vallum); *port* (L. portus = a harbour); *street* (L. strata = a paved road).

With the coming of the Roman missionaries to Britain (597 A.D.) came many new words connected with the church: *altar, priest, apostle, pope, school, candle.*

Similarly, the invasion of Britain by the Scandinavians left imprints upon our language. Our verb *are* is one of the most notable of these. From the Danes also came words like *billow, raft, anger, happy, smile, sky,* and *sister.* One of the interesting Danish words was the word *by,* meaning town. From this we get not only the place names such as Grimsby, Whitby, and Derby, but also our word *by-law.* The Danish court influenced our language toward simplification. The stems of the English and Danish words were similar, and inflections were dropped in order to make communication easier.

MIDDLE ENGLISH

As suggested above, the period between 1066 and 1485 saw the English language established as the written language of Britain. Names, adjectives, and pronouns were used much as they are to-day. It was natural that the Norman invasion should bring with it the polite language of the French court. Sir Walter Scott's story *Ivanhoe* contains an illuminating passage—a conversation between Gurth, the swineherd, and Wamba, the jester—which explains the characteristic changes:

"Gurth," said Wamba, "I advise thee to call off Fangs, and leave the herd to their destiny, which, whether they meet with bands of travelling soldiers, or of outlaws, or of wandering pilgrims, can be little else than to be converted into Normans before morning, to thy no small ease and comfort."

"The swine turned Normans to my comfort," quoth Gurth, "expound that to me, Wamba, for my brain is too dull, and my mind too vexed to read riddles."

"Why, how call you those grunting brutes running about on their four legs?" demanded Wamba.

"Swine, fool, swine," said the herd, "every fool knows that."

"And swine is good Saxon," said the Jester; "but how call you the sow when she is flayed, and drawn and quartered, and hung by the heels, like a traitor?"

"Pork," answered the swineherd.

"I am glad every fool knows that too," said Wamba, "and pork, I think, is good Norman-French; and so when the brute lives, and is in charge of a Saxon slave, she goes by her Saxon name; but becomes a Norman, and is called pork when she is carried to the Castle-hall to feast among the nobles; what doest thou think of this, friend Gurth, ha?"

"It is but too true doctrine, friend Wamba, however it got into thy fool's pate."

"Nay, I can tell you more," said Wamba, in the same tone; "there is old Alderman Ox continues to hold his Saxon epithet, while he is under the charge of serfs and bondsmen such as thou, but becomes Beef, a fiery French gallant, when he arrives before the worshipful jaws that are destined to consume him. Mynheer Calf, too, becomes Monsieur de Veau in like manner; he is Saxon when he requires tendance, and takes a Norman name when he becomes matter of enjoyment."

It was natural that the new words which entered our language at that time should be words dealing with government, feudalism, the church, and the chase—words like *parliament, law, judge, armour, prisoner, homage, fealty, chivalry, tournament, pardoner, penance, forest, archery,* and *falconry.*

MODERN ENGLISH

With the Revival of Learning and the coming of the great scholars to England, new words multiplied with great speed. Many Romance words were introduced, and a large proportion of the Greek words in our language came during that time. Examples of the Greek words are: *oxygen, hydrogen, chemist, narcissus, daffodil, crisis, athlete, fungus, skeleton,* and *elastic.*

World exploration and world trade added new words, as did the coming of machines and the industrial revolution. We have borrowed from all the world as we felt the need.

Yet it is significant that the majority of the words we use every day should be pure English. Words designating concrete objects, words of home and family and country, are largely English. Of the one hundred and seventeen words in the Twenty-third Psalm, one hundred and seven are of English origin.

OTHER EXAMPLES OF BORROWING

ITALIAN: opera, solo, piano, studio, stanza, fresco.
ARABIC: algebra, almanac, alkali, zero, sheik, salaam.
SPANISH: alligator, armada, cargo, cigar, negro, mosquito.
HEBREW: amen, hallelujah, cherub, seraphim, satan.
PORTUGUESE: molasses, veranda, caste, fetish.
DUTCH: sloop, yawl, skipper, yacht, skate, dollar.

Russian: steppe, knout, kopeck.
Persian: bazaar, sofa, shah, caravan, dervish.
Malayan: amuck, gong, sago, bamboo.
Indian: squaw, papoose, wigwam, canoe, potato, tobacco.
Chinese: silk, cash, tea, chop-suey.
India: sugar, cheroot, cheetah, rupee.
Africa: kraal, gorilla, canary.
S. America: quinine, pampas, llama, condor.
Polynesia: taboo, tattoo.
Australia: boomerang, cockatoo.
German: kindergarten, hamburger, hurrah.

WORD BUILDING

Noticing the derivation often helps a student to understand a word and add it to his vocabulary. Behind many an English word there is a good story. The verb *tantalize*, for instance, is derived from the name of King Tantalus, who in the lower world was punished for his wickedness by being placed in water up to his chin. When he stooped to drink, the water receded. Boughs laden with fruit hung over his head but swung out of reach when he tried to seize them. Thus *tantalize* now means *tease*.

Because half the words in the dictionary are Latin derivatives, one needs to know at least the most common Latin prefixes and stems.

LATIN PREFIXES

PREFIX	MEANING	EXAMPLE	DEFINITION
a, ab	from	avert	turn from
ad	to, towards	attract	draw to
ante	before	antecedent	going before
bi	two	biped	a two-footed animal
circum	around	circumnavigate	sail around
contra	against	contradict	speak against
cum (com, con, cor, co)	together, with	convene	come together
de	from, down	depose	put down
dis (di, dif)	apart, from, not	dishonest	not honest
e, ex (ec, ef)	out, out of, from	select	choose from
extra	beyond	extraordinary	beyond ordinary
in (il, im, ir)	in, into, not	insane	not sane
inter	between	interstate	between states
non	not	nondelivery	not delivery
ob (oc, of, op)	against, in front of	object	to throw against
per	through, thoroughly	perfect	thoroughly made

PREFIX	MEANING	EXAMPLE	DEFINITION
post	after	postscript	written after
prae	before	precede	go before
pro	for, forward	pronoun	for a noun
re	back, again	reconsider	consider again
se	apart	secede	go apart
semi	half	semicircle	a half circle
sub (suc, suf, sug, sum)	under	subscribe	write under
super	above	supernatural	above nature
trans	across, beyond	transgress	step beyond

Some of the prefixes are not readily detected because of consonant changes. *Ad* becomes *a(agree)*, *ac(accede)*, *af (affix)*, *ag(aggrieve)*, *al(ally)*, *an (annex)*, *ap(append)*, *ar(arrive)*, *as(assent)*.

Practice 1. Derivations of Words

1. Explain the meaning of the following words:

biweekly	indirect	prepaid	semicircle
coeducation	inhuman	prewar	sublet
disqualify	noninterference	reaction	subtitle
extra-hazardous	postgraduate	rearrange	transcontinental

2. *Irreligious* is the opposite of *religious*. What is the opposite of *polite, direct, legal, perishable, rational, fallible?*

3. Write lists of words in which the following prefixes are used: *sub, super, con (cor, col, com, co), trans.*

Common Latin Verb Roots

VERB ROOT	MEANING	EXAMPLE	DEFINITION
ago, actum	do, act, drive	counteract	act against
audio, auditum	hear	auditor	on who hears
capio, capitum	take, seize, hold	captive	one taken
cedo, cessum	go, yield	precede	go before
credo, creditum	believe	credible	believable
curro, cursum	run	incur	run into
do, datum	give	data	facts given
dico, dictum	say	predict	say before
duco, ductum	lead, draw	induce	draw in
facio, factum	make, do	proficient	making progress
fero, latum	bear, carry, bring	differ	bear apart
flecto, flexum	bend	flexible	bending
fluo, fluxum	flow	fluent	flowing
frango, fractum	break	fracture	a break
gradior, gressus	go, walk, step	progress	go forward
jacio, jectum	throw, cast	eject	cast out
jungo, junctum	join	junction	a joining

VERB ROOT	MEANING	EXAMPLE	DEFINITION
lego, lectum	gather, read, choose	legible	readable
loquor, locutus	speak	elocution	a speaking out
mitto, missum	send, cast	remit	send back
pello, pulsum	drive, urge	expel	drive out
pendeo, pensum	hang, pay	suspend	hang under
pono, positum	place, put	postpone	place after
porto, portatum	carry, bear	import	carry into
rumpo, ruptum	break	rupture	a break
scribo, scriptum	write	scribe	a writer
seco, sectum	cut	section	a cutting
sedeo, sessum	sit, settle	session	a sitting
sequor, secutus	follow	execute	follow out
sto, statum	stand	distant	standing apart
tango, tactum	touch	contagion	touching together
traho, tractum	draw	attract	draw to
venio, ventum	come	convene	come together
verto, versum	turn	avert	turn aside
video, visum	see	vision	sight
voco, vocatum	call	vocation	calling

SUFFIXES WORTH KNOWING

able, ible (capable of being): portable, credible

ance, ence, ity, tude (act, quality, or state of): reliance, independence, inequality, rectitude

ant, ent, er, or ian (one who or pertaining to): servant, president, waiter, navigator, custodian, librarian

ion, tion, ation, ment (action, state of, or result): opinion, direction, conversation, embarrassment

ish (like a): feverish, coltish, mulish, bookish

less (without): lifeless, hopeless, painless, worthless, stainless

ly (forming adverbs from adjectives, participles, or, rarely, nouns): slowly, badly, unexpectedly, timely.

ous, y (full of): precipitous, miscellaneous, bounteous, bushy, husky

ship (skill, state, quality, office): championship, guardianship, partnership, horsemanship, craftsmanship, friendship

Practice 2.   Adding Prefixes and Suffixes

From the preceding lists choose one prefix (except *in, sub, super, cum,* and *trans*), one stem, and one suffix. Write five or more words containing each of the chosen forms. Be ready to explain the meaning of each word and to use it in a sentence.

Practice 3.   Meaning from Derivations

Show from its derivation how each of the following words has acquired its present meaning. When you don't find one part of a word, like *manuscript*, in the prefix and verb lists, look up the word in the dictionary.

Examples:

confer = *con* + *fero* = bring together
anticipate = *ante* + *capio* = take beforehand
capture = *captum* = seizing

1. Agent, actor, transact.
2. Accept, except, capable, deception, inception, precept.
3. Creditor, creditable, credential, creed.
4. Dictionary, dictator, edict, predict, benediction.
5. Aqueduct, educate, conduct, induce, deduct, reduce.
6. Factory, affect, facsimile, imperfect.
7. Conference, fertile, prefer, refer, reference, differ, offer.

LATIN NOUNS AND ADJECTIVES

annus, year
caput, capitis, head
centum, hundred
civis, citizen
cor, cordis, heart
corpus, corporis, body
dignus, worthy
duo, two
mors, mortis, death
nomen, nominis, name
opus, operis, work
pars, partis, part

finis, end, limit
gratus, pleasing, thankful
lex, legis, law
lingua, tongue
littera, letter
magnus, major, maximus, great, greater, greatest
manus, hand
pes, pedis, foot
similis, like
terra, earth
via, way

COMMON GREEK PREFIXES AND ROOTS

anti, against
astron, star
autos, oneself
chronos, time
graphein, write
hyper, over, exceedingly
kratos, rule, government
logos, speech, reason, word, account

metron, measure
monos, sole, alone
onoma, name
pan, all, whole
pathos, suffering
philos, friend, lover
syn (becomes *syl, sym*, or *sy*), with

Practice 4. Derivatives

Make a list of English words derived from the twenty-three **Latin** nouns and adjectives and from the Greek prefixes and roots. Know the meaning of the words listed.

Practice 5. Sources of English Words

From what language are the words in each group derived? Add to as many of the lists as you can. Do the words in each group show anything about the people who use the language? If so, what?

a. bivouac, brunette, chapeau, chauffeur, chiffonier, cretonne, debutante, foyer, garage, matinee, rôle, trousseau

b. alto, andante, canto, gondola, lava, macaroni, opera, piano, regatta, sonata, sonnet, soprano, spaghetti, stanza

c. amen, cherub, jubilee, manna, Sabbath

d. alcohol, algebra, assassin, chemistry, cipher, coffee, cotton, mattress, zero

e. canoe, maize, moccasin, opossum, papoose, potato, squaw, tobacco, tomahawk, tomato, wigwam

f. armada, buffalo, canyon, cargo, cigar, corral, desperado, galleon, mosquito, mulatto, mustang, vanilla

g. ballast, boom, bowsprit, schooner, skates, skipper, sloop, yacht

Test—Writing Vocabulary

By using the words in sentences which show clearly their meaning, prove that twenty of the following words are in your writing vocabulary. Underline in each sentence the word whose use you are illustrating. No credit will be given for any sentence whose context does not clearly set forth the meaning of the word.

Example

(Right) The *genealogy* of Henry Adams reveals there were two presidents and several famous statesmen and writers among his ancestors.

(Wrong) His *genealogy* shows his family is a good one.

   alliteration, annuity, aster, astrology, autobiography, biennial, centipede, conventional, eulogy, graphic, gratutitous, hexameter, hyperbole, ignominy, literal, logical, monotone, nominal, obliterate, panacea, panorama, psychology, subterranean, superannuated, symbolize.

Practice 6. Adding to Your Word List

When you have used a word three times, it is yours. Hand to your teacher a list of new words that you have added to your word hoard by using them three times during the term. If your list now is short, get ready to hand in a longer list at the end of the term.

SYNONYMS

The person who is word poor uses the same word again and again—perhaps a dozen *gets*, *thens*, or *nices* on a page. One who has a synonym ready can avoid this unpleasant repetition.

Some synonyms, like *hard* and *difficult*, have almost the same meaning; others, like *fewer* and *less*, differ widely in either meaning or use. *Fewer* refers to number; and *less*, to quantity, as in the sentence, "I have fewer books and less money than my brother."

Alberta Government Photograph

This picture shows a familiar operation in the Leduc-Woodbend oil field. It is called, "changing the bit". Do you know that workers in the oil fields are called "Roughnecks"?

Practice 7. Synonyms

Examine each group of synonyms. Do the words differ in meaning or in use? How?

1. Reputation, fame, notoriety.
2. Apparent, evident, doubtless.
3. Crowd, audience, spectators.
4. Approve, praise, flatter.
5. Job, vocation, profession.

Practice 8. Choosing Synonyms

Write two or more synonyms of each of the following words. When necessary, consult the dictionary or a book of synonyms.

admit, awkward, big, brave, building, dress, fun, go, hard, interesting, lazy, mistake, needful, odd, poor, promise, reply, sad, say, useful, walk, workman

ANTONYMS

Antonyms are opposites: *good, bad; happy, sad; friend, enemy.*

Practice 9. Choosing Antonyms

What is the antonym of each of the following words?

accept, assemble, assets, cheerful, clumsy, conceal, courageous, deny, develop, doubt, feeble, gaily, healthy, lazy, prose, talkative.

HOMONYMS

Homonyms are pronounced alike but spelled differently: *right, write; scene, seen.*

Practice 10. Using Homonyms

Use each of the following words in a good sentence of at least ten words:

1. aloud, allowed
2. by, buy
3. coarse, course
4. council, counsel
5. forth, fourth
6. its, it's
7. led, lead
8. new, knew
9. piece, peace
10. plain, plane
11. principal, principle
12. right, write
13. seen, scene
14. shone, shown
15. site, cite
16. stayed, staid
17. their, there
18. threw, through
19. to, too
20. ware, wear

OVERWORKED WORDS

We need a Society for the Protection of Overworked Words. Some useful words have been worked so hard that they are worn threadbare and have little meaning left. Among them are: *awful, cute, fierce, fine, funny, gorgeous, get, grand, great, horrid, lovely, nice, pretty, quite, splendid, sure, sweet, swell, terrible, terrific, then, very, wonderful.* One book character, Alverna in Lewis's *Mantrap*, has only four adjectives, *cute, swell, dandy*, and *nice;* and some real people haven't a much longer list. To such people everything is a "thing" and all "things" are "grand," "swell," "awful," "nice," terrible," "great," or "cute."

Practice 11. Word Discrimination

Complete each sentence by selecting the better word or expression:
1. The cover of this magazine is ——. (very nice, artistic)
2. The examination was ——. (exceedingly difficult, just fierce)
3. Marion has —— new dress. (an attractive, a nice)
4. Our neighbours are —— people. (very nice, charming)
5. We had a —— sail up the Hudson and enjoyed the —— scenery while eating our —— lunch (nice, pleasant) (fine, unusual) (delicious, awfully good)
6. We had a —— party. (delightful, grand)
7. Elizabeth's new hat is ——. (nice, becoming)
8. I remained under the tree —— time. (a long, quite some)
9. *A Tale of Two Cities* is —— book. (a lovely, an exciting)
10. For rescuing the boy, John Binns —— a medal. (got, received)
11. By his —— expanations he helped the pupils to understand many difficult problems. (clear, splendid)
12. In the battle he —— in the foot. (was wounded, got a wound)

Practice 12. Effective Word Choice

In the following passage add or substitute specific, fresh, accurate words for the overworked general expressions. Instead of saying, for example, "it is a fine day," "he is at my feet", and "butterflies" tell what was fine about the day, use a more vivid verb, and add a descriptive adjective.

It is a fine day at last, after days and days of perfectly horrid weather! Our big pet named "Tummy" is at my feet on this lovely lawn. He is awfully upset by the doings of two butterflies which are very near his nose. Now everything is all right again. The trees are beautiful against the sky; the insects can be heard; a nice breeze faintly moves the trees' topmost leaves; and, changing all to gold, the sun shines. It's grand to be alive, and young, on such a marvellous day, and to be some part of it all, isn't it?

SLANG

Slang, "inelegant and unauthorized popular language," is the language of a childish or lazy man, inasmuch as a few expressions, such as *okay, real guy, get by, swell, attaboy! tightwad, sponge, cheap skate, cut it out,* and *get his goat,* answer for every occasion. The person who uses slang freely needs few words and hence stunts his vocabulary. Greenough and Kittredge say, "The unchecked and habitual use of slang (even polite slang) is deleterious to the mind."

A few slang words, like *mob,* establish themselves as literary English. *Up to you, put across, chiseller,* and *stand for* are at present useful slang expressions which may earn a permanent place in the language. Most slang words, however, spring up, flourish for a season, and are straightway forgotten. *Skidoo* and *twenty-three,* two of the most popular slang words ever used, are now venerable antiques. *Flat tire, raspberries, cat's meow, baloney, apple sauce, ankle along, cake-eater, the cheese,* and *spiffy* had their day and then gave way to *shoot the works, drugstore cowboy, swanky, boiled shirt, high-hat, oh yeah!* and *how!* and *you're telling me!*

A good rule is, never use slang. If one has in reserve the literary equivalent, an occasional conscious use of slang may add life and spice to conversation, but the habitual use of slang as a substantial part of one's conversation is evidence of lack of intelligence, lack of education, or mental laziness. A person who has a large word hoard is likely to use slang sparingly.

SPECIFIC WORDS

Specific, the opposite of *general,* means *definite* or *particular. Animal* is a general term including whales and mice. *Quadruped,* a more specific word, excludes whales, robins, and snakes. *Bear* is more specific than *quadruped;* and *black bear* and *Japanese black bear* are in turn more specific than *bear. Go* is a general word; *walk* is more specific; *saunter, totter, paddle, stalk, trudge, plod, promenade, march, hobble, stride, toddle, waddle, mince, strut,* and *stroll* are more specific than *walk.* Specific words are more picturesque and accurate than general ones.

GENERAL	SPECIFIC
fly	— swoop, glide, float
food	— chocolate ice cream, bacon and tomato sandwich toasted, lamb chops
reptile	— snapping turtle, copperhead snake, horned toad
say	— yell, whisper, mumble

Practice 13.   Choosing Specific Words

In the manner just shown, write three specific words after each of the following words or expressions:

building	flower	ship	to fasten
colour	insect	tree	to make
dessert	machine	vehicle	to make a sound
dog	music	to change	to take
fish	noise	to cook	to work

Practice 14. Selecting Specific Words

Which words in the following sentences are specific?

1. And I was going to sea myself—to sea in a schooner, with a piping boatswain, and pig-tailed singing seamen! — STEVENSON
2. Except on the crown, which was raggedly bald, he had stiff, black hair, standing jaggedly all over it, and growing down hill almost to his broad, blunt nose. — DICKENS
3. The big blue waves shouldered themselves up from the bosom of the sea, marched toward the beach, and tumbled to pieces in a roaring tumult of white and green. — JOSEPH C. LINCOLN
4. Troopers who have stood charge after charge while victory was possible will fly like sheep, and like sheep allow themselves to be butchered, when they have once turned the back. — WEYMAN
5. Strolling negroes patrolled the sidewalks, thrumming mandolins and guitars, and others came and went, singing, making the night Venetian. — TARKINGTON

Practice 15. Using Specific Words

In the following sentences substitute specific details for the italicized general expressions:

1. For our *meal* we had *soup, meat, vegetables, potatoes, salad,* and *dessert.*
2. In the *building* are two *dogs.*
3. "My *clothing* was torn in a *number of places,*" said the *boy.*
4. *One day some boys* and I *went* to a *lake.*
5. My *friend* read three *books* during *a vacation.*
6. The two *girls* and I *worked awhile* in the *room.*
7. My *friend* and I handed the *man some money* for the *flowers.*
8. The *animals made sounds* when the *man went* into the *building.*

ACCURATE WORDS

People who don't take pains to say precisely what they mean sometimes add to muddled stories or explanations, "Well, you know what I mean." How much better it is for us to say exactly what we mean than to assume that our hearers are mind readers! First, we should think out clearly what we wish to say and then search for accurate words to express our ideas.

The misuse of words is due sometimes to ignorance and sometimes to hurry or carelessness. If in the revision of our written work we ask ourselves often, "Does that word mean exactly what I want to say?" we shall correct many errors in word choice.

Practice 16. Using Accurate Words

Improve each sentence by substituting an accurate word for the italicized one. Make no other change in the sentence.

1. When did you *loose* your ring?
2. I believe this article *answers* these topics.
3. Before the Constitution was *made*, there was but one house in Congress.
4. An essay may *compose* description, explanation, narration, and a little argument.
5. There is need for men and women who can discuss intelligently the great *factors* of the time.
6. Mr. Squeers was arrested for *robbing* the boys' money and clothing.
7. While Puck was *wandering* through the woods, he met a fairy.
8. People do not wish to live in a country in which they have no *say* in the government.
9. We must find out what steps are yet to be *done*.

IDIOMS

An idiom, an expression peculiar to a language, either violates the laws of grammar or has a meaning as a whole entirely different from that obtained by putting together the meanings of its parts. The idiom "How do you do?" for example, doesn't mean exactly what the words say.

Idioms are important because they are the very life of the language. A free use of these homely, terse, vigorous expressions peculiar to the language makes one's English more natural, individual, forceful, sparkling, imaginative, effective. Examples of everyday idioms are *to make good, to fall in love, in the long run, to call in question, to laugh in one's sleeve, to run for office, a red-letter day, had better, side by side,* and *yours truly* (at the close of a letter).

WHAT IS GOOD USE

In speech and writing avoid any use of a word that is not sanctioned by the practice of a large body of educated and intelligent people. A dictionary is not a language law-maker or dictator of usage but a record, on the basis of wide observation and study, of the practice in speech and writing of intelligent people of the present. *A New English Dictionary* is the best authority on good use, because its editors investigated the use by many writers of every word in the language. This dictionary, which was completed in 1928 after seventy years of labour, contains 1,827,306 quotations showing how words are used.

Good use is not determined by logic. For example, "Many a man have crossed this bridge" is logically correct, for *many a man* means more than one. Usage, however, has established the expression, "Many a man has crossed this bridge." In the same way, although "I don't think I shall go" is illogical because the negative is attached to the wrong verb, general usage has made the expression good idiomatic English. On the other hand, *in back of* is patterned after *in front of*, but is not in good use.

LEVELS OF USAGE

Different levels of usage exist, and what is correct on one level may be unacceptable on another. For example, *lots of people* is not good usage in a formal essay but is acceptable in informal conversation. The expression is colloquial. Baldwin defines colloquial language as that "used by good writers or speakers in conversation, but not in public address or writing." Colloquial English is used also in informal letters and essays. Literary English is used in novels, short stories, histories, biographies, magazine articles, and formal letters, essays, and public speeches. A vulgarism is an expression used only by people without culture or education. *Had ought, ain't, h'aint, invite* (as a noun), *kinder* (kind of), *quite some, fix up* (dress elegantly), *busted,* and *critter* are vulgarisms. *Fix* (repair), *back of* (behind), *phone, photo, folks, make* (earn, gain), *mighty* (very), *quite a good deal, anyhow, quite a little,* and *lovely* (dinner) are recognized colloquialisms.

CHOOSE THE BETTER

We use words to get results. If a speaker's language puts him on the defensive or needs explanation, he is not likely to accomplish his purpose. For example, *proven* is defensible in the sentence, "That statement was not proven." *Proven* is used by Tennyson, Bulwer-Lytton, Lowell, Jowett, Thackeray, Spenser, Gladstone, Huxley, and Kipling, and is recognized by *A New English Dictionary* and by Webster. *Proved,* however, needs no defence and is the form used by most careful writers and speakers. Therefore it is better to avoid *proven.*

WORDS OFTEN MISUSED

Above. Sometimes used as an adjective: "the above statement," "the above paragraph." Most careful writers prefer *preceding.*

Accept, except. To *accept* is to *receive; to except, to exclude. Accept* is a verb *except* is commonly a preposition.

(Right) The meeting *accepted* the *report* of the committee.

(Right) All *except me* were called on.

Accept of. Better to omit the *of.*

(Right) I *accept* your *offer.*

Ad. A colloquial abbreviation of advertisement. It has no relation to *add,* and should be written out in full.

Admittance is correct for *allowing one to enter a building or location; admission,* for *admitting to rights or privileges.*

Affect. *Affect* is always a verb; *effect*, commonly a noun. **To *affect* is to** *influence; to effect, to bring about.*

Aggravate. Means *make worse.* Colloquial in the sense of *provoke, vex,* or *annoy.*

(Right) The shock *aggravated* his *misery.*

All of. *Of* is unnecessary.

(Better)) I lost *all my books* (*not* all of my books).

All the farther, as far as. *All the farther* is childish and low colloquial for *as far as.* Avoid it. *All the farther* correctly used means *by that amount, just so much.*

(Right) That was *as far as we could go.*

(Right) Our weariness made home seem *all the farther away.*

Anxious. Colloquial for *eager* or *desirous.*

(Colloquial) I am anxious to begin work at once.

(Literary English) I am *eager to begin* work at once.

Any place, every place, no place, some place. Incorrect. Use *anywhere, everywhere,* etc.

Anywheres, everywheres, etc. Incorrect for *anywhere, everywhere,* etc.

Appreciate means *estimate justly.* Hence we cannot say, "I appreciate your kindness highly."

As. Not to be used too frequently for *because;* substitute *for, because, since.* Not to be used for *that* or *whether.* "I don't know that (not *as*) I blame him."

Athletics. Commonly considered plural.

Audience, spectators. The *audience* hear; the *spectators* see: "the audience at the lecture," "the spectators at the football game."

Avocation, vocation. An *avocation* is a secondary occupation, such as music, fishing or boating.

Awful, awfully. Colloquial as intensive: "awfully cold," "awful toothache," "an awfully nice time."

Back of. Colloquial or low colloquial for *behind;* "The garage stands behind (not *back of*) the house."

Badly. Colloquial for *a great deal* or *very much.* "I want very much (not *badly*) to go."

Balance. A bookkeeping word. Loosely used for *rest* or *remainder.*

Beat. In everyday English correct for *defeat;* "Alberta was badly beaten on the football field."

Beside, besides. *Beside* is a preposition meaning *by the side of.* *Besides* is either an adverb meaning *in addition* or a preposition meaning *in addition to.*

Between. Commonly applies to only two objects. *Among* is used for three or more. *Between,* however, may "express the relation of a thing to many surrounding things severally and individually": "treaty between the three powers," "a railroad between Chicago, Philadelphia, and New York."

Blame . . . on. Crudely used instead of *blame.*

(Right) You needn't *blame me* for it.

(Crude) You needn't blame it on me.

Bound. Colloquial for *determined;* "He was bound to succeed."

Bring, take, fetch. *To bring* requires one motion—toward the speaker; *to take*, one motion—away from the speaker; *to fetch*, two motions—from the speaker and to him again.

(Right) *Take* this message to Captain Morse; *bring* his reply to me; and then *fetch* my horse from the stable.

But what. Incorrect when used instead of *that* or *but that*.

(Right) I had *no doubt that* the dog would bite.

Bye-bye. Colloquial and playful for *good-bye*.

Can, may. Use *can* for ability and *may* for permission, probability, or possibility. Although in conversation *can* is allowable in asking permission, most careful speakers use *may*.

Character, reputation. *Reputation* is what people suppose a person's character to be. *Character* is what the person really is; it is his moral stature or worth.

Claim. Colloquial for *maintain*. The usage is popular, though objected to.

(Better) I *maintain* that Cromwell was not a tyrant.

Consul, council, counsel, councillor, counsellor. A *consul* is a representative of a government; a *council* is a body of men; *counsel* as a noun is advice or a lawyer who gives advice; a *councillor* is a member of a council; a *counsellor* gives advice.

Contemptible, contemptuous. *Contemptible* means *deserving contempt; contemptuous, showing contempt.*

Continual, continuous. *Continuous* means *uninterrupted. Continual* implies frequent repetition.

Could and **might** have the same general distinctions as *can* and *may*.

Credible (*believable*), **credulous** (*inclined to believe*), **creditable** (*deserving praise*).

Cute. Colloquial. Use *vivacious, entertaining, pretty,* or the appropriate designation.

Date. Colloquial for *engagement*.

Deadly, deathly. *Deadly* means *causing death; deathly, looking like death.*

Different than. A common colloquialism for *different from*.

(Wrong) He plays it different than I.

(Right) His playing of it is different from mine. He plays it differently.

(Awkward, but correct) He plays it differently from what I do.

Discover, invent. *To discover* is to find out something that already exists; *to invent* is to produce something entirely new.

Dove. Use *dived*.

Due to. The two words *because of* are used as a preposition. *Due* is an adjective and should modify a noun.

(Right) *Because of the drought* the wheat crop was a failure.

(Right) The failure of the wheat crop *was due to the drought*.

Each other, one another. Used interchangeably.

Either. Loosely used for more than two: "either of the last three syllables." Say *any* or *any one*.

Emigrant, immigrant.

(Right) After *emigrating from Russia*, he became a *Canadian immigrant*.

Expect. Should not be used for *think* or *suppose*.

(Right) I *suppose* the fish are biting this morning.

(Poor) I expect the fish are biting this morning.

Extra. Should not be used to mean *unusually*, as "an extra fine example".

Fewer, less.   *Fewer* refers to number; *less*, to quantity.

(Right)   The farmer had *fewer cows* and *less wheat* than usual.

Fine.   Strictly the word means *refined, delicate, free from impurity, of excellent quality:* "fine flannels," "fine gold," "fine dust," "fine sense of honour." In colloquial use it is a general epithet of approval: "a fine fellow," "a fine ship," "a fine day."

Firstly.   Not thoroughly established for *first.*

Fix.   Colloquial for *repair:* "He fixed the broken door."

Folks.   Colloquial for *people.*

Funny.   Colloquial for *strange* or *odd.*

Gentleman, lady.   Don't use these words for *man* and *woman.*

(Right)   There were only four *women* and five *men* on the eleven o'clock trolley.

Get.   Means *obtain, gain, win, earn, acquire, learn, receive, come to have, catch, contract, meet with, suffer:* "get cholera," "get sick," "get a fall," "get the worst of it," "get ten dollars a week," "get up," "get on," "get off," "get well," "get ready," "get ahead." Do not overwork this useful word. "Have you got a knife with you?" is colloquial.

Gotten.   As a past participle, *gotten* is rarely used by careful speakers or writers. Say *got.*

Graduated.   Correct in active or passive voice.

(Right)   He *graduated from Manitoba.*

Marion expects to *be graduated from Queen's* next June.

Guess.   Colloquial for *think:* "I guess I'll go." In some regions *reckon* is the colloquial equivalent of *think.*

Healthy, healthful, wholesome.   *Healthy* and *healthful* are often used interchangeably. Strictly, *healthy* means *having health* and *healthful* means *promoting health:* "healthy girl," "healthful climate," "wholesome food."

Home.   Sometimes without a preposition expresses result of motion: "He is home from Europe."

Human.   Not in good use as a noun. Say *human being.*

If.   May introduce noun clause after *see, ask, learn, know, doubt:* "He asked if the paper had been found." *Whether* is better.

In, at.

(Right)   We enjoyed ourselves *at* the World's Fair *in* Chicago.

In, into.   Use *into* ordinarily to express motion from one place to another: "He fell *into* the pond."

Kind of, sort of.   Colloquial when used instead of *rather.* Avoid these expressions in speeches and themes.

(Right)   I am *rather* (*not* kind of) glad he was not elected.

Learn, teach.   *To learn* is *to acquire knowledge or skill.* *To teach* is *to give instruction.*

Leave, let.   *To leave* means *to allow to remain* or *to depart from.* *To let* means *to permit.*

(Right)   *Leave* your hat in the hall.

We shall *leave you* for an hour.

Let him have the book.

Let him be.

Leave go.   Vulgarism. Say *let go.*

Likely, liable, apt. *Likely* indicates probability. *Liable* expresses obligation or the possibility of evil. *Apt* means *having a habitual tendency* or *quick to learn.*
  (Right) You are *liable to be hurt.*
  He is an *apt pupil* and is *likely to succeed* as a salesman.
Line. Vulgarism when used for *kind.* What kind (not line) of work. Slang in such expressions as "He has a great line."
Loan. Only occasionally used as a verb. Prefer *lend.*
Locate. Colloquial for *settle* or *find.*
  (Right) He settled in North Bay.
  (Right) Find Saint John on the map.
  (Right) Give the location of Kingston.
Lot of people, **lots** of automobiles. Colloquial.
Lovely. Colloquial in *lovely time, lovely dinner.* Select a more accurate word.
Mad. Colloquial or playful for *angry.* In standard English *mad* means *crazy.*
Majority, plurality. If A, B, and C are candidates in an election at which 500 votes are cast, to have a majority A must have at least 251 votes. To have a plurality he must have more votes than are cast for either B or C. If there are 200 votes for A, 180 for B, and 120 for C, A has a plurality.
Make. Colloquial for *earn* or *gain:* "He makes ten dollars a week."
Manners, morals. *Manners* respect the minor forms of acting with others and toward others; *morals* include the important duties of life. Good manners make us good companions; good morals make us good members of society.
Mathematics. Singular noun.
Mighty. Colloquial for *very:* "I'm mighty glad to see you." If in conversation you use *mighty* in this sense, do not overwork the word.
Most. Dialectal for *almost.*
  (Right) We have *almost completed* the study of emphasis.
Movies. Colloquial for *moving pictures.*
Nice. In literary use *nice* means *minutely accurate, precise, discriminating, refined, finical, subtle:* "nice sense of touch," "nice distinction," "nice eye for distance." In colloquial use it is a general epithet of approval: "a nice fellow," "a nice long letter," "nice to me."
No good. Colloquial when used adjectively. Say "It is worthless."
None. Either singular or plural.
  (Right) None are to blame.
  None of the pupils was prepared.
Off of. Vulgarism for *from* or *off.*
  (Right) I *got* the knife *from* (*not* off of *or* off) Jack.
  I *took* it *off* (*not* off of) the table.
Oral, verbal. *Verbal* means *in words; oral, in spoken words.*
Ought. Do not use with *had.*
  (Bad) He hadn't ought to have done it.
  (Right) He should not have done it.
Party, person. *Party,* except in legal language, means *body of people:* "dinner party," "Liberal party," "foraging party."
Patronize. Colloquial for *trade with.* A *patron* helps, defends, protects, or supports.
  (Right) We *trade with* the oldest *firm* in town.

Per. Use *per* with Latin words, *diem, annum, cent.* Avoid its use with English words. Say, "Five dollars a week."

Plenty. Colloquial if used as an adjective or adverb.
(Bad)   She was plenty tired.
(Right)   She was very tired.
(Better)   She was exhausted.

Politics. Commonly treated as plural.

Posted. Colloquial in sense of *informed:* "Newspapers keep us posted on current events."

Practical, practicable. *Practical* is the opposite of *theoretical.* *Practicable* means *workable.*
(Right)   He is a *practical mechanic.*
The *scheme is* delightful but not *practicable.*

Pretty as an adverb. Colloquial or familiar: "pretty cold," "pretty often," "pretty late."

Principal, principle. Use *a* in the adjective and in the name of the head of a school.
(Right)   The *principal of our school* is a *man of principle.*

Prosecute, persecute.
(Right)   The dishonest *cashier was* dismissed and *prosecuted.*
The early *Christians were persecuted.*

Proven. Has enemies. Better *proved.*

Quick. Correct as adverb.
(Right)   Come quick.   (Right)   Come quickly.

Quite. Precisely used, *quite* means (1) *wholly* or (2) *really, truly, positively:* "quite correct," "quite alone," "quite a scandal," "quite a large party." Loosely or colloquially used, the word means *very* or *rather:* "quite sick," "quite tired."

Quite a few, quite a good deal, quite a little. Low colloquial and dialectal.

Quite some. Vulgar.

Raise. Colloquial for the noun *increase* or the verb *rear.*
(Literary English)   He deserved his *increase in salary.*
(Literary English)   John was *reared by* his *aunt.*

Real. Dialectal and low colloquial for *very* or *really.*

Receipt. Correct for *recipe:* "the receipt for corn bread;" but recipe is in more common use.

Recollect, remember. *Recollect* usually suggests a conscious effort to recall. *Remember* implies only that the impression remains.
(Right)   I *remember* his main *idea* but *can't recollect* his exact *words.*

Remember of. Omit *of.*

Respectfully, respectively. *Respectfully* means *with respect:* "Yours respectfully." *Respectively* means *each to each in order.*
(Right)   Columbus and Boston are the *capitals respectively* of Ohio and Massachusetts.

Right away. Colloquial for *at once.*

Same. Crude and stilted when used instead of a personal pronoun.
(Wrong)   Your letter came to-day, and I shall reply briefly to the same.

Show. Colloquial for *play.*

Show up. Colloquial for *arrive.*

Sit, set. Do clothes *set* or *sit?* Colloquial usage favours *set.* Standard authors prefer *sit.*

Slow. Correct as adverb in some uses, especially when the emphasis is upon the slowness rather than upon the action. Cp. My watch runs *slow*. Go *slow*. They walked *slowly* homeward.

Some. Colloquial for *somewhat*.
   (Literary English) He is *somewhat better*.

State, say. *State* means *set down in detail*.

Stop. Colloquial and dialectal for *stay*.
   (Literary English) In Winnipeg we *stayed at the Fort Garry*.

Sure. Low colloquial or slang for *surely*.

That. Colloquial as an adverb: "I didn't intend to go that far."

Thing. Choose a more specific word.

Truth, veracity. *Truth* belongs to the thing; *veracity*, to the person.
   (Right) Because of the *veracity of the narrator* no one questioned the *truth of the story*.

Very. This word should be given a vacation. It is called upon for too much service by most young writers and speakers. When overworked *very*, instead of strengthening a statement, weakens it.

Would have. Frequently misused for *had*.
   (Wrong) If you *would have played*, we would have won.
   (Right) If you *had played*, we would have won.

Practice 17. The Correct Word

Select the correct or preferred word to fill each blank. Give a reason for each choice.

1. That will —— him a lesson. (learn, teach)
2. The study of English is important because it —— us how to write and speak correctly. (learns, teaches)
3. She —— me the punctuation rules. (learned, taught)
4. Miss Willard —— us how to construct a paragraph. (learned, taught)
5. Kindly —— me know when you are coming. (leave, let)
6. Celia doesn't wish to —— Rosalind go. (leave, let)
7. He —— his brother have the hockey club. (left, let)
8. The lazy ones —— the rest of the class do the reciting. (leave, let)
9. Mary offered to —— me to skate. (learn, teach)
10. Will you —— me hand this in now? (leave, let)
11. —— I have another glass of milk? (can, may)
12. Why don't you —— us go to the exhibit? (leave, let)
13. —— I go to the library? (can, may)
14. —— I go to Room 106 for my fountain pen? (can, may)
15. My brother —— me a new tennis stroke. (learned, taught)
16. You just can't —— it go after you've caught it. (leave, let)
17. I forgot to —— my English book home last night. (bring, take)
18. Yesterday just as I —— Punch loose, he spied a cat. (left, let)
19. Please —— this book to Room 412. (bring, take)
20. The Black Knight gave me money to —— to Isaac. (bring, take)
21. A great —— government positions are held by the intelligent Filipinos. (deal of the, many)
22. —— of the sentences are simple. (a good deal, many)
23. Each sentence contains a great —— descriptive adjectives. (deal of, many)

24. She asked for someone to —— a message to her father. (bring, take)
25. A band of outlaws captured me and —— me to a lonely cabin in the woods. (brought, took)
26. I —— more credits than I need for graduation. (got, have)
27. I —— your knife. (haven't, haven't got)
28. I am sorry I can't —— your invitation. (accept, except)
29. There were —— boys at the scout camp this year than last year. (fewer, less)
30. The people of the town receive —— foolish and harmful publications. (a great deal of, many)
31. My father buys a great —— books. (deal of, many)
32. I'm going to —— this to my English teacher. (bring, take)
33. While I was small, Mother every day —— me to the little school I was attending, and came for me at the close of school. (brought, took)
34. —— accidents occur to children on school days than on holidays. (fewer, less)
35. There have been published this year —— good English historical novels than there were last year. (fewer, less)
36. —— everybody has a group of friends. (almost, most)
37. —— all his poems are about nature. (almost, mostly)
38. When the doorbell rang, he had —— finished sifting the ashes. (almost, most)
39. Are a considerable —— of high school pupils unable to master Latin and algebra? (amount, number)
40. He —— always buys the *Manchester Guardian*. (almost, most)
41. A large —— of pupils go to vacation schools. (amount, number)
42. The —— of deaths in the United States caused by the automobile has increased to 29,000 a year. (amount, number)
43. —— the beans soak for a day. (leave, let)
44. Mrs. Jones wishes —— two eggs. (the lend of, to borrow)
45. Harry —— me *Tales of Courage*. (lent, loaned)
46. The climate —— their health and spirits. (affected, effected)
47. We divided the money —— the ten members. (among, between)
48. The dog jumped —— the water to rescue his master. (in, into)
49. She is the most —— girl I have ever known. (affected, effected)
50. I —— this pen from Frank. (borrowed, loaned)

Practice 18.   Choosing the Correct Word

Select the correct or preferred word in each of the following sentences. Justify each choice.

1. —— my absence from school during the first two weeks all my subjects seem hard. (because of, due to)
2. Meriden was —— we went on Monday. (all the farther, as far as)
3. That our pupils are loyal to the school is shown by the large —— of them at the baseball games. (amount, number)
4. Oscar jumped —— the lake to rescue his little brother. (in, into)
5. Harold —— me to write the ballad stanza. (learned, taught)
6. My father —— me go on the outing. (left, let)
7. His parents —— him do as he pleased. (left, let)
8. Mother, —— I go to the baseball game? (can, may)

9. My aunt didn't wish to be bothered with me and had me —— away to an orphan asylum. (brought, taken)

10. —— the mail from the village immediately. (bring, fetch)

11. I am —— this report to the office for Miss Lockwood. (bringing, taking)

12. Nausicaa promised to —— him to the village. (bring, take)

13. I shall endeavour to prove that in two periods a week a teacher could —— a girl how to make many of her own clothes. (learn, teach)

14. His mother thinks he is —— better. (some, somewhat)

15. I regret that I cannot —— your invitation for May 6. (accept, except)

16. The sign on the factory read: Positively no ——. (admission, admittance).

17. I remained under the tree for —— time. (a long, quite some)

18. Henry and I went swimming —— every day. (almost, most)

19. If children were taught to be more careful, —— lives would be lost. (fewer, less)

20. The suit you received by mistake was made for another ——. (party, person)

21. He is —— to succeed. (liable, likely)

22. What will be the —— of the new tariff law? (affect, effect)

23. —— was one cause of the rapid growth of our population during the decade 1900-1910. (emigration, immigration)

24. The applicant has an excellent —— for honesty. (character, reputation)

25. Every year a certain —— of enlisted men are sent to the Royal Military College. (amount, number)

26. —— interruptions make —— work impossible. (continual, continuous)

27. His address was a highly —— performance, if the newspaper reports are ——. (credible, creditable)

28. The reports of the —— combat made him grow —— pale. (deadly, deathly)

29. ——, May 12 was the date for which the game was scheduled. (first, firstly)

30. For your vacation select a —— spot; eat —— food; and become ——. (healthful, healthy, wholesome)

31. The —— machinist hit upon a —— device for reducing the friction. (practicable, practical)

32. He and his son are —— a lawyer and a journalist. (respectfully, respectively)

33. You —— always choose outdoor books. (almost, most, mostly)

34. The modifiers of the subject do not —— the number of the verb. (affect, effect)

35. Although he —— them well, he was embarrassed by his inability to —— their names. (recollected, remembered) (recollect, remember)

36. The —— applauded the pitcher. (audience, spectators)

37. Two of the party went to Oxford, but the —— spent the day in the Houses of Parliament. (balance, rest)

38. For president, John received 30 votes; Marion, 18; and Jaxon, 10. John had a —— of 2 and a —— of 12. (majority, plurality)

39. His many —— sap his energy and prevent his rapid advancement in his ——. (avocations, vocations) (avocation, vocation)

40. The town —— refused to admit to their meetings the —— for the railroad. (council, counsel)

Practice 19. Reputable English?

Indicate the standing (vulgarism, slang, localism, colloquialism, literary English) of each of the following expressions:

Back out; swell party; auto; a brainy man; brain trust; pep; a square deal; enthuse; exam; hire a hall; phone; raise a family; up against it; toe the mark; hit or miss; by hook or crook; put one over; gent; aboveboard; get away with it; namby-pamby; gabble; deliver the goods; bleachers; grouch; call-down; pell-mell; all in; giggle; bawl out; anyplace; a lot of people; kind of sorry.

Practice 20. Translating into Good English

On what plane does each of the italicized expressions stand? Translate colloquial, slang, and vulgar expressions into literary English. Express the ideas accurately.

1. Open the door *quick*, for it is *awfully* cold out here.
2. Albert was *real mad* when he fell *off of* his horse.
3. It is *kind of funny* that Jerry didn't come.
4. I am *anxious* to verify the *above* statement and shall arrange to meet you *anyplace* you suggest.
5. My *folks claim* that I should enter Toronto when I *graduate* Revelstoke.
6. I am *mighty* glad he is *making* better wages ushering for the *movies*.
7. A *lot* of people *patronize* the new grocer.
8. She is *pretty* well *posted* on *receipts* for making bread.
9. He *sure* started *slow*.
10. We made their *star* pitcher look like *thirty cents*.

Practice 21. Using Good English

Which expressions in the parentheses are colloquial? Write the sentences in literary English.

1. His self-assurance —— her. (aggravated, annoyed)
2. Do you still —— that you know nothing about the accident? (claim, maintain)
3. His impudence made me ——. (angry, mad)
4. Despite his parents' objection he is —— to study law. (bound, determined)
5. It is —— that the cackling of geese saved Rome. (funny, odd)
6. You must choose ——. (immediately, right away)
7. The speaker of the evening didn't ——. (arrive, show up)
8. How soon can you —— my shoes? (fix, repair)
9. I —— the attendance will be small to-day. (guess, think)
10. In Naples we —— at the Continental Hotel. (stayed, stopped)

Practice 22. Using Words in Context

Make clear the differences in meaning. Use each word in a sentence that shows its meaning.

1. Ability, capacity. 2. Adverse, averse. 3. Advise, advice, claim, say, state, maintain. 4. Allusion, illusion. 5. Angle, angel. 6. Apparent, evident. 7. Assent, ascent. 8. Choice, alternative. 9. Compare, contrast. 10. Deceased, diseased. 1. Deprecate, depreciate. 12. Disinterested, uninterested. 13. Distinct, distinctive. 14. Enunciation, pronunciation. 15. Famous, notorious. 16. Formally, formerly. 17. Habit, custom. 18. Last, latest, preceding. 19. Later, latter. 20. Learning, intelligence, wisdom. 21. Loose, lose. 22. Personal, personnel. 23. Prevision, provision. 24. Purpose, propose. 25. Stature, statue, statute.

CHANGES IN MEANING

Words, like people, degenerate in bad company; occasionally they rise to much higher rank in good company. *Soon, by and by, presently,* and *directly* originally meant *instantly* but have changed because people have always liked to put off. *Knave* meant originally *boy* or *boy servant.* Soon it was used for *male servant or man of humble birth.* Another step gave the present use of the word—to indicate a rogue and rascal.

Practice 23. New English Words

What are five new English words recently added to the language? What do they mean? What do they indicate about modern life?

EFFECTIVE WORDS

Effective words are words appropriate for the topic discussed and for the audience. As a rule, direct, simple, clear, brief wording is more effective than a lofty, far-fetched, roundabout style. Homely words like *stark, bleak, sheer, roar, prig, wheedle, boor, dolt, haggle, task, hobnob, job, glum,* and *hodgepodge* are more expressive than lengthy and pretentious ones.

Practice 24. Effective Language

In each group do you consider *a* or *b* more effective? Why?

1

a. The play has not wit enough to keep it sweet. — JOHNSON
b. The play has not vitality enough to preserve it from putrefaction. — JOHNSON

2

a. And sitting on the grass partook
   The fragrant beverage drawn from China's herb. — WORDSWORTH
b. And sitting on the grass had tea. — TENNYSON

3

a. He died poor.
b. He expired in indigent circumstances.

Practice 25. Word Choice

Write after the number of each sentence that follows the single word which would accurately express the thought contained in the italicized words. Be careful as between synonyms. For example, the italicized words in the sentence, "He was *completely done out*," might be accurately expressed by *exhausted*, but not by *tired* or *weary*.

1. Fire-fighters, vigilantly patrolling the area, stamped out the embers before they gained headway and loss *of no consequence* was incurred.
2. Admitting *that he had committed the crime*, he was sentenced to six months' imprisonment.
3. The boys *got* the body *back again* and started their return journey to Aklavik.
4. Plants cannot grow in land without *those elements which plants feed on*.
5. He was dressed *in a very gorgeous manner*.
6. The orator was *not at all hesitant in his choice of words*.
7. His style is *that of a person who wrote long ago*.
8. A student must learn to *do as he is bid*.
9. The man is *continually without money, largely because of his own lack of industry*.
10. The old verb "pill", to rob or to plunder, from which our word "pillage" is derived, is now *entirely out of use* as a verb.
11. He is a *second year student* at the University.
12. Erasmus was a *man of great learning*.
13. The more I looked at him the more I was of the opinion that he was *the suspected person*.
14. There is a *difference* between *the facts of* the two stories.
15. Officials were unable to *come to an opinion about* the amount of money spent on the July road work.
16. British officials admit delays longer than they had *previously thought that they would be*.
17. The amount of our *goods sold outside Canada* has increased in the last two months.
18. We brought back a great many *tokens by which to remember the places we had visited*.
19. Charles Campbell, Canadian sculler, was *knocked out of all further championship chances* in the Olympic finals at Grunau.

Practice 26. Using Idioms

Write sentences making clear the following idiomatic phrases:

1. Fall upon; fall back; fall short of; fall foul; fall on one's feet; fall through; fall to.
2. To turn; to turn a deaf ear; to turn round one's finger; to turn adrift; to turn one's hand to; to turn the scale; not turn a hair; to serve a turn; done to a turn.
3. To be a means of; by all means; by any means; by no means; in the meantime.
4. To take root; to take heart; to take pains; to take the place of; to take counsel; to take by storm.

5. To make much of; to make way; to make head against; to make sail; to make sure; to make up for; to make both ends meet; to make off with; to make a clean sweep of; to make one's mark; to make the most of.

Practice 27. Avoiding Negatives

Without altering the meaning, change the following sentences into sentences which do not contain a negative (no, not, never, nothing, none):

1. I never saw such a boy.
2. She would have nothing to do with it.
3. You must not be late.
4. Nothing is more heartbreaking than ingratitude.
5. Why not say so?

Mastery Test A—Correct Word

Select the correct or preferred word or expression to fill each blank, and place it on your paper after the number of the sentence: (Right— Wrong = Score)

1. Paul —— me to write the composition heading correctly. (learned, taught)
2. He —— his sons drink and disgrace the family. (left, let)
3. —— the car to the nearest garage. (bring, take)
4. —— I go along on the fishing trip? (can, may)
5. Harold jumped —— the water to save the child. (in, into)
6. Shylock would not —— the money. (accept, except)
7. I have —— books than you. (fewer, less)
8. What will be the —— of the new tariff law? (affect, effect)
9. A large —— of qualified voters remained away from the polls. (amount, number)
10. My mother divided the dozen apples equally —— us four boys. (among, between)
11. He tried to —— his dog a new trick. (learn, teach)
12. —— the dough rise in a warm place. (leave, let)
13. I gave him the note and told him to —— it to my father. (bring, take)
14. In my composition I made —— errors in punctuation. (a good deal of, many)
15. I cannot —— that statement without proof. (accept, except)
16. I see him —— every day. (almost, most)
17. He —— a history from his cousin. (borrowed, loaned)
18. They sailed away without —— their purpose. (affecting, effecting)
19. Will you please —— this note to the office. (bring, take)
20. Father —— me go with him to Boston. (left, let)

Mastery Test B—Correct Word

Select the correct or preferred word or expression to fill each blank, and place it on your paper after the number of the sentence: (Right— Wrong=Score.)

1. You —— put your books away now. (can, may)
2. Elwood fell from the dock —— the icy water. (in, into)
3. The farmer —— us sleep in his big red barn. (left, let)
4. There is a keen rivalry —— the six high schools in the city. (among, between)
5. I've decided to —— the hat back to the store. (bring, take)
6. —— boys and girls study music and art. (a great deal of, many)
7. Fear —— a person in many ways. (affects, effects)
8. Peter —— Heidi many interesting things about the mountains and goats. (learns, teaches)
9. Edward —— the baker's offer. (accepted, excepted)
10. We have not —— him walk long distances. (left, let)
11. There were a large —— of booths at the fair. (amount, number)
12. Pete and John —— me horseback riding. (brought, took)
13. In our city there were —— drownings this year than there were last year. (fewer, less)
14. His presence had a quieting —— upon the crowd. (affect, effect)
15. From whom did you —— that book? (borrow, loan)
16. I cannot —— that for an answer. (accept, except)
17. —— everyone likes to write letters. (almost, most)
18. The farmer discovered that we were lost and offered to —— us back to our car. (bring, take)
19. Laura told me she would —— me how to swim. (learn, teach)
20. Why don't you —— the boy ride? (leave, let)

Building Paragraphs

TOPIC SENTENCE

WE have already seen that a topic sentence is a brief statement of the subject of a paragraph. In a paragraph of narration the topic sentence is seldom expressed, in description it is often omitted, and in other writing sometimes omitted. Always, however, it is possible to sum up a good paragraph in a sentence. Commonly the first sentence in a paragraph of explanation or argument is a signpost telling in what direction and how far the speaker or writer expects to travel in the paragraph. The topic sentence may be placed in the middle of the paragraph or at the end. The beginner, however, progresses more rapidly if he forms the habit of expressing the main idea of a paragraph of explanation or argument in the first sentence and using the topic sentence as a foundation on which to build the paragraph. A master of the language writes paragraphs without much thought of topic sentences. In every field the artist has greater freedom than the mechanic.

Sometimes the first sentence of a paragraph links it with the preceding paragraph by taking a backward look, and the second announces the subject of the paragraph.

Example:

These faults perhaps we can overlook. (Transition and introductory sentence.) But his absolute disregard of the rights of others is a more serious matter. (Topic sentence.) During his youth he teased, tormented, bullied, and tortured his younger brother and other boys a size smaller than he, etc.

CLINCHER SENTENCE

After driving home his idea in the paragraph, a writer may clinch it in the last sentence by restating tersely and vigorously the point of the paragraph.

WAR AND HEROISM

Clearly, there is no need of bringing on wars in order to breed heroes. (Topic sentence.) Civilized life affords plenty of opportunities for heroes and for a better kind than war or any other savagery has ever produced. Moreover, none but lunatics would set a city on fire in order to give opportunities for heroism to firemen, or introduce the cholera or yellow fever to give physicians and nurses opportunity for practising disinterested devotion, or condemn thousands of people to extreme poverty in order that some well-to-do persons might practise a beautiful charity. It is equally crazy to advocate war on the ground that it is a school for heroes.[1] (Clincher sentence.)

Practice 1. Examining Paragraphs

1. Has each of the following paragraphs a topic sentence? If so, what is it?
2. Is there a good clincher sentence? If so, what is it?

1

A foolish consistency is the hobgoblin of little minds, adored by little statesmen and philosophers and divines. With consistency a great soul has simply nothing to do. He may as well concern himself with the shadow on the wall. Speak what you think now in hard words, and to-morrow speak what to-morrow thinks in hard words again, though it contradicts everything you said to-day.—"Ah, so you shall be sure to be misunderstood."—"Is it so bad, then, to be misunderstood?" Pythagoras was misunderstood, and Socrates, and Jesus, and Luther, and Copernicus, and Galileo, and Newton, and every pure and wise spirit that ever took flesh. To be great is to be misunderstood. — EMERSON, *Self-Reliance*

2

To most people the attic is just another place to store old furniture and unused household articles, but I have found it an unbelievably good place to study. For several years I have had a hard time doing homework conscientiously, because, you see, I have a brother and a sister, a dog (very lovable), a canary, two radios, a saxophone-playing neighbour, and company at very unexpected times. Imagine trying to study with all those around! Well, I stood it as long as I could and then rebelled and betook myself to the attic, and all my books and my typewriter went with me. There I actually studied in privacy. Now I wouldn't exchange that big old attic "study" for the most magnificent library there is, because no one wants to go up there but me. The whole family would congregate in our splendid library, if we had one, and they'd see that I got no work done. Although it's not much as far as appearance is concerned, the attic serves as a fine place to study—yes, and to dream also. — PUPIL

PLANNING

The paragraph may be spoken or written; it may be part of a long report or may be complete in itself. In any case it should be planned and arranged according to a suitable pattern. Time order, for example, is a good pattern for happenings; space order, for a picture; and order of importance, for ideas or examples.

---

[1]From *Eliot's* Five American Contributions to Civilization *by permission of the publishers, D. Appleton-Century Company.*

Example of plan and paragraph arranged in the order of importance:

ON DOORS

There are many ways of opening a door.

    The waiter carrying a supper-tray
    The housewife before a book agent or pedlar
    The footman in a wealthy home
    The dentist's maid
    The nurse after a baby is born

There are many ways of opening doors. There is the cheery push of the elbow with which the waiter shoves open the kitchen door when he bears in your tray of supper. There is the suspicious and tentative withdrawal of a door before the unhappy book agent or pedlar. There is the genteel and carefully modulated recession with which footmen swing wide the oaken barriers of the great. There is the sympathetic and awful silence of the dentist's maid who opens the door into the operating room and, without speaking, implies that the doctor is ready for you. There is the brisk cataclysmic opening of a door when the nurse comes in, very early in the morning— "It's a boy!" — CHRISTOPHER MORLEY, *On Doors*

PARAGRAPH BUILDING

Paragraph building is the development of the topic (usually the topic sentence) in some logical and natural manner. Five ways are here given in which this may be done.

Details

Specific details which often answer the questions "What?" and "How?" may be used to develop or explain a general statement made in the topic sentence. Details make more vivid a word picture of a person, place, thing, or event. If you make a general statement that Helen is well dressed, you may make the picture clearer by describing her clothing, the colour scheme, the accessories, and the neatness and appropriateness of her outfit.

Practice 2. Developing a Topic by Details

1. Has the following paragraph a topic sentence? A clincher sentence?
2. What details are included?

The Frisby House, for that was the name of the hotel, was a place of fallen fortunes, like the town. It was now given up to labourers and partly ruinous. At dinner there was the ordinary display of what is called in the West a two-bit house: the tablecloth checked red and white, the plague of flies, the wire hencoops over the dishes, the great variety and invariable vileness of the food, and the rough, coatless men devouring it in silence. In our bedroom the stove would not burn, though it would smoke; and while one window would not open, the other would not shut. There was a view on a bit of empty road, a few dark houses, a donkey wandering in its shadow on the slope, and a blink of sea, with a tall ship lying anchored in the moonlight. All about that dreary inn frogs sang their ungainly chorus. — STEVENSON

Practice 3.　Developing a Topic by Details

Choose two of the following topic sentences. Using details, prepare an oral paragraph based on one; develop the other into a written paragraph. Have strong clincher sentences.

1. When I was preparing for school this morning, everything went wrong,
2. Yesterday I decided to dissect my Ingersoll (my alarm clock, the radio. the engine of our car, a lock, my harmonica, or something else).
3. It is not difficult to make a marionette (hat, birdhouse, brass box, dress, model airplane, camp bed, shelter in the woods, apple pie, or something else).
4. If I had fifty dollars, I know exactly how I would spend it.
5. The most interesting room in the school is ———. (Supply the name of the room you like best.)
6. In recent years many advances have been made in ———. (Supply the name of any industry, profession, or science in which you are interested: farming, advertising, raising chickens, protecting trees, irrigation, medicine, chemistry, physics, aviation.)
7. There are several ways in which I could improve my handwriting.
8. The storm did considerable damage in our neighbourhood.
9. The effects of the drought were visible everywhere on the farm.
10. Annabelle was a very superior cat. (You may substitute the name of any other animal.)
11. We found the hotel (tourist cabin, farmhouse) a pleasant home for the night.
12. My first-aid kit saved the day.

Examples

To make an explanation clear or to prove a point, give examples or illustrations. You may discuss fully one example or refer briefly to several. If you say, "The twentieth century has seen great progress in science," you may prove your point by discussing in detail one discovery such as the radio, or by briefly mentioning several—the radio, television, air conditioning, and others.

Practice 4.　Developing a Topic by Examples

1. What is the topic sentence of the following paragraph?
2. Is the example related to the topic? Is it effective?

It is hard to be stern with a baby, yet it so often seems necessary. Let me give you an example from personal experience. Little George refuses to eat his soup. First I try cajolery, but when this fails, patience dies, and I sternly command that George partake of the delicious, life-giving substance or else—! He immediately assumes a wilted air and half-heartedly picks up the spoon. After stirring the soup awhile, he wails, "I can't eat—I—I fink I'm sick." Remembering that he usually likes this kind of soup, I think that he may be ill. After all, a baby is such a delicate bit of humanity. Soon enough my sympathies vanish when he asks if he can't have dessert now, please. I am angry because I have been fooled into feeling sorry for him, and attempt once more to force him to eat the soup. Alas, the end is always the same: he shrinks down into the seat and begins to sob, gradually working up to the most heartbreaking cries. As the tears stream down his face (and roll off into the soup), he looks so utterly woebegone that I haven't the heart to scold any more. Rather, I do everything in my power to placate him. How could anyone be stern after such a demonstration? — PUPIL

Practice 5. Developing a Topic by Examples

Select two of the following topic sentences. Using one or more examples, develop one into an oral paragraph and the other into a written paragraph.

1. A chain is no stronger than its weakest link. (Substitute any other proverb.)
2. Chemistry (or another subject) has many practical applications (or is the most useful subject I have studied).
3. Travel is becoming swifter each day.
4. Successful work requires good equipment.
5. Grown-up people really ought to be more careful.
6. I have found from experience that the world can be seen and appreciated from my own doorstep.
7. "Where there's a will there's a way" is illustrated by the lives of many poor boys who have become famous.
8. We find the most colourful jewels in Woolworth's.
9. There are many disturbers of the peace.
10. There are mind poisons, just as there are body poisons.
11. The endeavour of education to keep pace with the rapidly growing ignorance appears to be quite hopeless, since there are year by year so many new things of which to be ignorant.

Comparison and Contrast

In describing to boys and girls the appearance of the human brain, one doctor compared it to a cauliflower. The doctor was trying to explain the appearance of something unfamiliar by showing that it is like something familiar to his audience. Comparisons (showing how two things are like or different) and contrasts (showing how two things differ) help to clarify our ideas. All the points on one side may be balanced against all the points on the other side, or the two objects may be compared a point at a time.

Practice 6. Studying the Use of Comparison and Contrast

1. What is the topic sentence of the following paragraph?
2. What comparisons are made?
3. What contrasts are pointed out?

FIGHTING FISH

It is surprising how fighting fish differ in their manner of attacking the bait and in the times at which they bite. The bass will bite at any time he pleases. "As moody as a prima donna," says one expert, "as wary as a lynx, and fighting to the last gasp is the true black bass." He has a habit of mumbling the bait—that is running with the bait held in the front of his mouth, so that if you try to set the hook, you'll pull it right out of his mouth. Once this happens to a bass, he rarely bites again. But with the trout it's a different story. The best time to fish for him is in the early morning or at night. He rises lazily to the bait and sucks it down; then the fun begins. When you have seventeen pounds of mad trout at the end of your line, there's no time to think of anything else. One big fellow I hooked had his eye set on a distant mountain and seemed quite determined to reach it, when suddenly he turned about and came racing back for something he had forgotten. You have to work fast with a full-grown muskellunge too. He hits the bait as soon as it strikes the water, and his thirty to sixty pounds hit hard. Once you hook a muskellunge it takes between forty minutes and an hour and forty minutes to end the argument. All three of these fish, but particularly the bass, have a way of shooting out of the water and shaking themselves so that they often rip the hook out of their mouths. — PUPIL

Practice 7. Using Comparison and Contrast

Using comparison, contrast, or both, develop one of these topic sentences into an oral paragraph and another into a written paragraph.

1. It is safer to live in the country than in the city (or vice versa).
2. There is a vast difference between a house and a home.
3. Understanding is better than tolerance.
4. The microscope has contributed more to man's progress than the telescope.
5. A brunette should wear different colours from those worn by a blonde.
6. Boys are better sports than girls (or vice versa).
7. I would rather have a canoe than a rowboat. (Substitute any other possessions—a dog than a cat, for example.)
8. It is more fun to be a guest than a host (or vice versa).
9. I prefer a game of skill to a game of chance.
10. My little brother (or sister) is more grown-up than I was at his age.
11. Hot water heat is preferable to steam heat.
12. Welding is more efficient than riveting.

Cause and Effect

Another plan for paragraph building is to begin with a statement and then give reasons or results—that is, causes or effects.

Practice 8. Developing a Topic by Giving Reasons

1. What is the topic sentence? Clincher sentence?
2. What reason is given?
3. What comparisons make the paragraph more interesting?

Novels certainly should not be illustrated. What is more disappointing than to see a picture of the heroine? The author may have made the lady gloriously beautiful, lithe, and gracefully slender; but you discover that her mouth is too big, that she looks queer and plump in the old-fashioned clothes and is much too stiff and ungainly to be lithe. If you glance too casually at another picture, you will mistake the hero for the villain. Certainly that odd little individual isn't the handsome, broad-shouldered hero! You've all had this experience, I'm sure; so you'll agree with me when I say we should have a new kind of prohibition—of illustrations in novels. — PUPIL

Practice 9. Giving Reasons and Results

Select two of the following sentences. Giving reasons and results, prepare an oral paragraph on one and a written paragraph on the other.

1. Novels should be illustrated.
2. The day was completely spoiled.
3. Advertising controls the very lives of people.
4. I soon discovered that it was wise to do my homework every day.
5. He did not receive his driving license.
6. Crash!
7. There was a sudden grinding of brakes, and then the car stopped dead.
8. The advantage of not being illiterate depends finally on the literature a people produces and reads.
9. The tabloid newspapers are a menace.
10. Liberty ends where law ends.
11. Every boy should learn how to do simple carpentry work.
12. Stamp-collecting (or another hobby) seems to me an ideal hobby.
13. Fear is the greatest enemy of man.
14. If the keynote of a successful life is service, homemaking (or another occupation or profession) is an occupation second to none.
15. Everyone should know how to cook. (You may substitute any other skill or activity.)

Definition

Often, to avoid misunderstanding, it is necessary to define. In explaining a term, one may supplement the dictionary by telling what the term includes and excludes or what it is and is not, by comparing or contrasting it with another term, or by giving an illustration.

Practice 10. Developing a Topic by Definition

1. Has the following paragraph a topic sentence?
2. What example is used in explaining standardized mass production?

The outstanding characteristic of American manufacturing development, distinguishing it from the industrial revolution which went on in other countries, was the utilization of the idea of standardized mass production with the help of automatic machinery. By standardized production is meant the production of innumerable articles or parts of articles exactly alike. Machines were built to do the work of making these articles. This process speeded up and cheapened production, while at the same time it gave a drab sameness to American life. The business genius of Henry Ford was the first to employ this principle on a wide scale in the production of his famous Model T automobile. In the organization of production Ford also adopted the principle of controlling all the various stages of production. He purchased coal and iron mines, railroads, steamships, in an attempt to control all the processes and do all the work involved in turning out an automobile from raw material to a finished product. — HAMM, BOURNE, AND BENTON, *A Unit History of the United States*[1]

Practice 11.   Developing a Topic by Definition

Explain two of the following terms. Include one or more illustrations.

1. A natural monopoly. 2. Complementary colours. 3. The New Deal. 4. Imperialism. 5. Corporation. 6. Patriotism. 7. Snob. 8. Hero. 9. Protective tariff. 10. Labour union. 11. Propaganda. 12. Charity. 13. Radical. 14. Conservative. 15. Liberal. 16. Socialism. 17. Democracy. 18. Dictator. 19. School spirit. 20. Moral courage. 21. Communism. 22. Integrity. 23. Collective bargaining. 24. Reciprocity. 25. Fair wage. 26. Libel. 27. Sissy. 28. Optimism. 29. Superstition. 30. Culture.

Two or More Methods

Commonly two or more methods are combined in the development of a paragraph. Details may be supported by examples; a definition may include details, illustrations, comparison, and contrast.

Practice 12.   Two or More Methods

1. In the following discussion of the causes of war what is the topic of each paragraph?

2. By what method or methods is each paragraph developed?

THE FUNDAMENTAL CAUSES OF WAR

Although there are many conditions which contribute to war, imperialism, militarism, and nationalism are its three fundamental causes. Imperialism is the acquisition of backward areas by an industrially developed country for the purpose of obtaining materials, markets for surplus products, and places for investment of capital. It is true that the conquest of backward areas is more or less essential to the prosperity of the different countries. The nations realize it and are willing to go to any ends to acquire such territory. The nations which have succeeded in increasing their territory are considered the greatest nations. Italy, Germany, and Japan were good examples of imperialistic countries.

To increase its land or to continue to hold land, a country must follow a course of militarism. Militarism is spending large sums of money to build up a powerful army and navy. As long as there is rivalry for land, there will be suspicion and fear. As long as there is fear, there will be militarism. The nation that owns certain desired land says that it must maintain a large fighting force to defend its property. The underdog nation must equal a more powerful rival for fear that the enemy may attempt to add to its possessions. Thus the two nations build. When other countries see what is happening, they become fearful for their own well-being and join the race. Thus the arms-building contest goes on until each nation feels that she is unbeatable and is willing to display her strength at the slightest provocation.

[1]*By permission of the publisher, D. C. Heath and Company.*

Nationalism now plays its part in starting the war. By definition, it is the feeling which binds together people of the same land, history, race, and customs. It is this feeling which diplomats toy with to urge the people to conflict. First, people are shown the battleships, airplane forces, and the army. They are told that their country has the greatest fighting force in the world. Then the government, if it desires war, points out the rank injustices that their nation is being submitted to by some foreign country. Usually this injustice is imagined or, at the least, exaggerated. Feeling throughout the country becomes strong. Nationalism becomes greater and greater. In the other country the same state of affairs exists. Only a match is needed to touch off the explosion. It usually comes in the form of a comparatively minor quarrel, perhaps over some rights in Africa or elsewhere. Each country reasons that it is the stronger. Being anxious to come to blows, they soon do and the war is on. The war could not, of course, have occurred without land greed, or imperialism, or without fighting forces which justify great national pride, or nationalism. — Pupil

Practice 13. Studying Paragraph Development

Clip from the editorial page of a newspaper or from a magazine five well-developed paragraphs. If the topic sentence is expressed, underscore it; otherwise write it out. Explain how each paragraph is developed.

EFFECTIVE PARAGRAPHS

The following paragraphs should be studied carefully for construction, diction, and style, and then used as models for paragraphs of your own construction.

1. STORMING A WASPS' NEST

It is quite a sight to see a party of boys preparing to storm a wasps' nest. They go on an evening when all these fiery creatures are quiet in their holes, with their candle and lantern, their gunpowder made into a paste and fixed on the end of a stick, and with a spade to dig out the nest; and all armed with green boughs, ready if any of the wasps escape to beat them down. They light their gunpowder, and hold it to the hole. It burns hissing away in a stream of fiery sparks like a rocket, which, penetrating down to the nest, fill it with sulphurous fumes, and suffocate the wasps. A sod is clapped in the hole to keep in the fumes for a time; and when they think their purpose is effected, they dig out the nest. Then you may see every boy stand on his guard, with anxious looks and elevated bough, ready to defend himself, if it prove, as it often does, that they have not destroyed but merely irritated the wasps, and the wrathful insects rush out to take vengeance on the assailants. Hark! there is a hum!—the wasps rush out!—the cowards fly—some screaming amain, with a host of angry insects rushing after them, hissing in their ears, tangling in their hair, darting into their bosoms, and stinging them in a dozen places. One brave boy stands at his post, waves his bough gallantly, defends himself stoutly, beats down the insects in clouds, and escapes without a single sting, bearing the nest, finally, away in triumph on the spade. — William Howitt, *The Boy's Country-Book.*

2. THE OLD ANGLER AT HOME

On parting with the old angler, I inquired after his place of abode, and happening to be in the neighbourhood of the village a few evenings afterward, I had the curiosity to seek him out. I found him living in a small cottage containing only one room, but a perfect curiosity in its method and arrangement. It was on the skirts of the village, on a green bank a little back from the road, with a small garden in front stocked with kitchen-herbs and adorned with a few flowers. The whole front on the cottage was overrun with a honeysuckle. On the top was a ship for a weather-cock. The interior was fitted up in a truly nautical style, his ideas of comfort and convenience having been acquired in the berthdeck of a man-of-war.

I found him seated on a bench before the door smoking his pipe in the soft evening sunshine. His cat was purring soberly on the threshold, and his parrot describing some strange evolutions in an iron ring that swung in the centre of his cage. He had been angling all day, and gave me a history of his sport with as much minuteness as a general would talk over a campaign, being particularly animated in relating the manner in which he had taken a large trout, which had completely tasked all his skill and wariness.

How comforting it is to see a cheerful and contented old age and to behold a poor fellow like this, after being tempest-tost through life, safely moored in a snug and quiet harbour in the evening of his days! His happiness, however, sprang from within himself, and was independent of external circumstances, for he had that inexhaustible good-nature which is the most precious gift of Heaven, spreading itself like oil over the troubled sea of thought and keeping the mind smooth and equable in the roughest weather. — WASHINGTON IRVING, "The Angler" from *The Sketch Book*.

3. JACOB'S LADDER

If ever there was a vile, unnerving, and desperate place in the battle zone, it was the Mesnil end of Jacob's Ladder, among the heavy battery positions, and under perfect enemy observation.

Jacob's Ladder was a long trench, good in parts, stretching from Mesnil with many angles down to Hamel on the River Ancre, requiring flights of stairs at one or two steep places. Leafy bushes and great green and yellow weeds looked into it as it dipped sharply into the green valley by Hamel, and hereabouts the aspect of peace and innocence was as yet prevailing. A cow with a crumpled horn, a harvest cart should have been visible here and there. The trenches ahead were curious, and not so pastoral. Ruined houses with rafters sticking out, with half-sloughed plaster and dangling window-frames, perched on a hill-side, bleak and piteous that cloudy morning; half-filled trenches crept along below them by upheaved gardens, telling the story of wild bombardment. Further on was a small chalk cliff, facing the river, with a rambling but remarkable dug-out in it called Kentish Caves. The front line was sculptured over this brow, and descended to the wooded marshes of the Ancre in winding and gluey irregularity. Running across it towards the German line went the narrow Beaucourt road, and the railway to Miraumont and Bapaume; in the railway bank was a lookout post called the Crow's Nest, with a large periscope, but no one seemed very pleased to see the periscope. South of the Ancre was broad-backed high ground, and on that was a black vapour of smoke and naked tree-trunks or charcoal, an apparition which I found was called Thiepval Wood. The Somme indeed! — EDMUND BLUNDEN, *Undertones of War*.

4. SINKING OF THE "LUSITANIA"

In the end my father owed his life to the fact that he chose the port side, for he would never have survived in the water. After looking about for a bit he realized that he had no life-belt and went downstairs to get one. Someone (a steward, I think) gave him a Gieve. He tried to blow it up, but it would not blow, and so he went down to his cabin to get one off his bed, but they had all been taken. Finally he found three "Boddy" belts in his cupboard (the regulation ship's life-belt of that date and a most effective one). He came up on deck again just as the last boat—half empty—was being launched. The *Lusitania* "A" deck was by this time level with the water, and already the boat was about a foot away from the edge of the ship. A woman holding a small child hesitated whether to dare to step over to it. He gave her a shove and sprang after her himself. As the boat drew away, the *Lusitania* slowly sank, and one of her funnels came over to within a few feet of the boat. It seemed as if it must sink with it, but she was sinking by the bow as well as rolling over, and the funnel, passing within a few feet of their heads, sank just beyond them. My father had timed the explosion, and he looked at his watch when the ship disappeared. The whole thing had taken twelve and a half minutes. — VISCOUNTESS RHONDDA, *This Was My World.*
By permission of the publishers, The Macmillan Company of Canada, Limited.

5. THE MUSIC-MAKERS

A stout man with a pink face wears dingy white flannel trousers, a blue coat with a pink handkerchief showing, and a straw hat much too small for him, perched at the back of his head. He plays the guitar. A little chap in white canvas shoes, his face hidden under a felt hat like a broken wing, breathes into a flute and a tall thin fellow, with bursting over-ripe button boots, draws ribbons—long, twisted, streaming ribbons—of tune out of a fiddle. They stand, unsmiling, but not serious, in the broad sunlight opposite the fruit shop; the pink spider of a hand beats the guitar, the little squat hand, with a brass-and-turquoise ring, forces the reluctant flute, and the fiddler's arm tries to saw the fiddle in two. — KATHERINE MANSFIELD, "Bank Holiday" from *The Garden Party.*
By permission of the author's literary agents, Messrs. James B. Pinker & Son.

6.

A number of attempts have been made to provide for individual differences among pupils, two of the most important being classification on the basis of ability (called *homogeneous grouping* by school authorities) and individualized instruction. According to the plan of classifying pupils on the basis of ability, bright pupils are segregated into one class and slower pupils into another. This plan is thought to provide advantages for both groups, and it simplifies, to some extent, the procedure of the teacher. Pupils who learn at a slower rate are not discouraged by unfair contrast with brighter pupils, and the latter will be able to make greater progress. According to the second plan, the teacher tries to adjust assignments to the varying levels of ability. Pupils can read, write, speak, paint, draw, sing, play, construct, and in a variety of ways they give expression to their varying talents. Several methods such as the Dalton, Contract, Block, and Winnetka plans have been worked out in order to allow for these varying abilities. Many schools now use homogeneous grouping and individualized instruction. — WILLIAMSON AND WESLEY, *Principles of Social Science.*
Reprinted by permission of the publisher, D. C. Heath and Company.

UNIT EIGHTEEN

Investigating, Planning, and Writing

"BUT I haven't anything to write about!" boys and girls often complain. "When I sit down at my desk with a blank sheet of paper in front of me, I can't think of a thing to say!" Well, what do other people use for material? A small per cent of the writing we find in books and magazines is entirely imaginative. By far the greater part, however, is based wholly or partly on the author's own experiences, ideas, and investigations.

CHOOSING A TOPIC

When you are permitted to select your own topic, devote time and thought to making a wise choice. These questions will help you to find a suitable subject:

1. *What are you interested in?* How do you spend your leisure time? Have you a hobby? What kind of clubs and other organizations have you joined? What subjects do you like to read about? What sort of motion pictures and radio programmes do you enjoy? What vocation do you wish to enter? What kind of work have you done after school and during vacations?

2. *What are your readers or hearers interested in?* Will your report be read or heard by boys, or girls, or by both sexes? Boys, as a general rule, will understand and enjoy technical and mechanical subjects that bore their sisters. Sometimes, of course, it is possible to present such material so clearly and entertainingly that girls, too, will find it of interest. What other facts do you know about your readers or hearers?

3. *How much time or space is at your disposal?* In a brief report you cannot discuss a broad topic adequately or interestingly. Narrow it down this way:

Much too broad	*Too broad*	*Just right*
1. Contemporary Englishmen I admire	Contemporary English political leaders I admire	Winston Churchill, an Englishman I admire
2. National economy	The fight against inflation	How I can help the government fight inflation
3. Modern medicine	Medical research in the past decade	Penicillin
4. Professions	Scientific professions	Nursing as a profession

Practice 1. Narrowing Topics and Suiting Them to a Specific Audience

Select three of the following broad topics—one from each group—and narrow them in the way shown above. Assume, however, that you will present the subject you choose from the first group to an audience of boys, the subject from the second group to an audience of girls, and the subject from the third group to a mixed audience.

Group I: 1. Aviation. 2. Radio. 3. Electricity. 4. Industrial chemistry. 5. The Navy.

Group II: 1. Clothes. 2. Foods. 3. Care of children. 4. Motion pictures. 5. Dancing.

Group III: 1. Astronomy. 2. Poetry. 3. Agriculture. 4. The Army. 5. Flowers.

WHAT IS YOUR PURPOSE?

Having selected your topic, first set down on paper or say aloud just what you wish to accomplish. The statement should name the person or group at whom you are aiming.

Example:

I wish to tell my classmates pertinent facts about progress made in television, its present status and probable future, and to make clear the unsolved problems on which engineers are still working.

SECURING MATERIAL

Having chosen your topic, you are ready to begin collecting material. If you set to work intelligently, you will find this part of your job interesting and not very hard.

Observation and experience. Interesting things you see or do make excellent material for reports. If you are preparing to speak or write on nursing as a career, for example, you will find it helpful to visit a hospital or public health station. It isn't enough, however, just to look at a person, place, scene, or object; your mind must interpret and record what you see. If you make a habit of jotting down brief notes on interesting observations and experiences, you will accumulate a valuable store of firsthand material for speaking and writing. On a visit to a place of interest you should keep your eyes open, listen closely to the guide if there is one, ask intelligent questions, secure any pamphlets available, and take notes during the trip or immediately after.

Practice 2. Reporting a Visit

Report to the class a visit to a place of interest—for example, a historical landmark, a museum, a factory, an aviation field, a church, a police court, a model farm, a printing establishment, a zoo, a fish hatchery, a library, a college, a motion-picture studio, a botanical garden, a broadcasting station. For help in using connectives to show clearly the relation between ideas, turn to pages 105–106.

Conversation and interview. Your ears as well as your eyes will serve you well in accumulating material. By conversing with parents, teachers, relatives, or intelligent friends, you will clarify your own ideas and gain additional facts and ideas.

In preparation for a report on a topic like nursing as a career, you will probably want to interview a registered nurse, a physician, a supervisor of a hospital, or a similar authority whose knowledge of the subject and good judgment you respect. Because capable people are usually busy, you should make a definite appointment for the interview and plan intelligently for it. Think out five or six key questions that will elicit vital information you need. For a report on nursing, for example, your questions might be these:

1. What qualities does a girl need to be a good nurse?
2. How should a girl choose her training school?
3. How long is the period of training and what does it cost?
4. What are the advantages of nursing as a career?
5. What are the disadvantages of nursing as a career?
6. What fields of service are open to the graduate nurse?

Practice 3.   Presenting a Report

Choose one of the following topics and by interview secure material from a teacher, a librarian, a businessman, a physician, or another authority on the subject. Write a brief report. Build clear, correct sentences.

1. The conservation of clothing. 2. The proper care of the eyes. 3. What a businessman looks for in an employee. 4. An important scientific discovery of the past year. 5. The qualities and training a secretary needs. 6. A serious problem facing our community, city, province, or country. 7. The best kind of education. 8. The relationship between posture and health. 9. The early history of our high school. 10. Differences in the reading tastes of boys and girls. 11. Who should go to college? 12. The kind of boy or girl who succeeds. 13. High school students twenty-five years ago and to-day. 14. A high school education twenty-five years ago and to-day. 15. Opportunities for young chemists. 16. Typing as a steppingstone.

The Library. In the preparation of a report you will usually secure at least part of your material from books, magazines, pamphlets, and newspapers. Naturally the library will be the base of your operations.

Because inaccurate material is worthless, don't waste time on cheap or sensational publications. If you are writing about a current topic, notice the copyright date of books and articles. A publication prepared in 1925 or 1935 will not contain information on opportunities in nursing to-day. For a report on the history of nursing, however, an older book or article may give you the facts you need.

Perhaps you will begin your search with one of the three best-known encyclopaedias: the *Encyclopaedia Britannica*, the *Encyclopedia Americana*, or the *New International Encyclopedia*. If you don't find readily the information you want, look up your topic in the index. Follow up cross references in the articles; and copy, if they look helpful the titles of books listed in the bibliography following the main article.

Next, go to the card catalogue and try to locate the books suggested in the encyclopaedia and other books on your topic. With the call numbers go to the shelves and examine as many books as possible. A quick glance through the table of contents at the front of each book will help you to estimate its value to you. If it looks promising, use the index at the back of the volume to find the material it contains on your topic.

For up-to-the-minute information consult the *Readers' Guide*, an index to magazines, and the pamphlet and clipping file. As you investigate a topic, keep a mental or written record of points on which you still need information and make a special effort to find these facts. Often you will find that your sources do not agree. Writers vary widely, for instance, in their estimates of the average annual earnings of nurses. In such a case further search is necessary.

IDENTIFYING SOURCES

As soon as you find a book, an article, or a pamphlet which you can use in preparing your report, enter on a card or slip of paper information that will completely identify the publication. If you do this accurately and immediately, you will not have to return to the library later to complete your record or correct errors. Here is the form to use:

Book
　　Sutherland, Dorothy G. *Do You Want to Be a Nurse?* Doubleday, 1942.
Part of a book
　　Davey, Mildred; Smith, Elizabeth; and Myers, Theodore. *Everyday Occupations*. D. C. Heath and Company, 1941. pp. 298–314.
Encyclopedia article
　　"Nursing." *Encyclopaedia Britannica*, Fourteenth Edition. 1929. Vol. 16, pp. 643–645.
Magazine article
　　France, Beulah, R.N. "Public Health Jobs." *The American Girl*. May, 1942, pp. 20–22, 41, 45.

Practice 4. Listing Sources of Material

Choose one of the following topics or another on which you will enjoy working, make it narrow enough for a report, and write down the methods—observation, experience, conversation, interview, library research—by which you can obtain material. In the library find at least three reliable sources of information on your topic and list them.

NATURAL SCIENCES

1. The sulfa drugs
2. Fighting tropical diseases
3. A modern hero of science
4. An agricultural problem of my locality or state
5. Rocket guns
6. The production and use of penicillin
7. Modern methods of caring for the wounded
8. Radar, its operation and use
9. Predicting the weather
10. Friendly insects
11. The Diesel engine
12. Effects of chemistry on farming
13. Erosion: its causes and effects
14. Exploring the atom
15. Fighting malaria

SOCIAL STUDIES

1. Inflation: causes, dangers, prevention
2. Juvenile delinquency
3. Socialized medicine
4. Housing conditions in our city
5. Effects of machinery on labour
6. Marketing, the business side of farming
7. The community nurse
8. Social security
9. Educating the consumer
10. Colonization—a benefit or a scourge of civilization?
11. Freedom of the press in Canada
12. Loan sharks
13. Installment buying
14. Preventing labour disputes
15. Military tactics in World War I and World War II

GENERAL TOPICS

1. A vocation I should like to enter
2. Canadian folk songs
3. Learning history through fiction
4. The Trans-Canada highway
5. The motion picture as an educator
6. Summer theatres
7. A great war hero or modern statesman
8. Simon Bolivar and his work
9. Walt Disney and film art
10. The Red Cross in peace time
11. Our national parks
12. Apple raising
13. Educational opportunities in the armed forces

TAKING NOTES

As soon as you have discovered a book or magazine article which seems valuable and have made a record of the title, author, and other identifying information, you are ready to take notes.

1. Use library cards (3 by 5 inches) or small sheets of paper.
2. Write on only one side.
3. Number the cards consecutively in the upper right corner.
4. Place the topic in the upper left corner.
5. Near the top of the card write the author's name and the name and the page of the book or magazine.

6. Read the selection through with your pencil on your desk. Re-read the first paragraph. Don't write while you are reading. Think what the important facts and ideas are. Then begin to take notes.

7. Make free use of contractions, the standard abbreviations, abbreviations of your own invention, and mathematical signs such as $=$, $+$, $-$, $\therefore$, $>$, and $<$. As a rule, omit articles, connectives, and the verb *to be*.

8. Ordinarily jot down only facts and ideas, not the author's words. When you express ideas in your own language and in abbreviated form, you must be careful not to distort a writer's meaning by the omission of qualifying words and phrases.

9. Occasionally you will want to quote directly a particularly vivid passage. Perhaps, too, a sentence or paragraph will be so detailed or so technical that it will be hard to summarize accurately and concisely. In that case take down the author's exact words for inclusion in your report, but enclose the passage in prominent quotation marks, which will remind you the language is not your own.

10. By keeping the subject of your report continually in mind, discard irrelevant material immediately and cut down the quantity of notes you will later be obliged to handle in writing your report. Train yourself to grasp the main points of a selection. In a paragraph from *Occupational Guidance*, for instance, one sentence is particularly important if your topic is "Special Opportunities for Educated Women." Your notes on the passage would look something like this:

Special opportunities for educated women   16

Chapman, Paul W. *Occupational Guidance.* Pp. 477–478.

    West. Reserve U.—"There are at present more positions calling for experienced, successful nurses with a college background than there are women to fill them." Great opport. for college women—prof. leaders seek to int. them in field.

Practice 5. Taking Notes

Take accurate, helpful notes on the three sources you have already located and on other material valuable for your report. Fasten your notes together with a paper clip or a rubber band, or keep them in a small box.

WORKING WITH YOUR NOTES

After securing material you must organize it. Shuffle your cards or small sheets of paper so that those on the same topic are grouped together. If you follow this plan, you will have available on each topic all your notes from various sources.

PLANNING AND OUTLINING

You are now ready to select your main topics. Read over the material you have collected. Into what principal divisions does it fall? On what topics have you gathered the most material?

For a report on nursing as a career these main topics might be selected:

  I. Importance of nursing to society
 II. Qualifications of a good nurse
III. Professional preparation
 IV. Fields open to graduate nurses
  V. The future of nursing

You are now ready to look over the remaining points, which are not of equal importance. Some will serve as subtopics under a main topic, some as subtopics under a subtopic, and a few will have to be dropped entirely.

Arranging Details

The happenings in a story are ordinarily arranged in time order. The details of a picture are arranged in the order of observation, which is usually the space order. In explanation you will often place first the facts necessary for an understanding of later paragraphs. When in doubt, begin with a vital topic and lead up to a climax at the end. These patterns are (1) time order, (2) space order, (3) necessary-facts-first order, and (4) emphasis order.

Simple plans for the arrangement of material are: cause—effect; fact—explanation; easy—difficult; idea—action—consequences; disadvantages—advantages; physical—social—intellectual—moral; profit—duty; interesting happening—the big event; unnecessary—impracticable—injurious.

When time order is possible, it is generally best. In the outline on nursing, for example, preparation for the profession logically precedes the choice of a particular field. Although the importance of nursing to society might be placed later in the outline, a treatment of this topic will make a good introduction to the report.

HOW TO OUTLINE

Review the section on "How to Outline" on page 121. In making your outline, watch for these further points:

1. Avoid overlapping of topics. See that no point disguised in different words is allowed to appear twice.

2. Cover the subject completely. Find subtopics that add up to the topic under which they fall. The outline on "Nursing as a Career" on pages 286–287 is complete if the five main topics cover the subject, if the three subtopics under "Importance to Society" completely cover that subject, and so on.

3. Avoid empty topics. Fill your outline with information. Topics like "Value," "Purposes," "Results," "Economic results," and "Physical benefits" are empty unless subtopics give specific information.

4. If you find any topics that are not on the subject cross them out.

Practice 6. Criticizing Main Topics

Show that the following sets of main topics either overlap or do not cover the subject:

FOREST PROTECTION

  I. Work of the forest rangers
 II. Reforestation
III. Tree surgery
IV. Spraying young trees
 V. Importance of forests

THE SPIDER

   I. Of what use each part of a spider's body is
  II. How he builds his home
 III. How he secures his food
 IV. How he catches flies
  V. How he cares for baby spiders
 VI. Whether on the whole he is a friend or a foe
VII. What harm and what good he does

Practice 7. Making Headings Parallel

Show that in the following examples the phrasing for co-ordinate headings in a set is not grammatically the same. Make the headings parallel in structure.

1

A. The people who attend the story conference
B. The animators sketch out a few principal scenes
C. The musical director suggests appropriate music
D. Breaking down finished scenario into scenes

2

A. Preparing criminals to earn an honest living
B. To deter others from committing crimes

3

A. Government inspection of food
B. Supervision of handling of milk
C. Purify water supply

Practice 8.   Studying an Outline

1. Is the following outline clear, and complete enough to serve as **a** guide and a reminder?
2. Are topics arranged sensibly? Prove.
3. How are main topics numbered? Subtopics?

NURSING AS A CAREER

I. Importance to society
   A. In ordinary peacetime
   B. In war
   C. In time of disaster

II. Qualifications
   A. Physical requisites
      1. Strength and good health
      2. Endurance
      3. Reasonable attractiveness
   B. Mental requisites
      1. Intelligence
      2. Strength of mind
   C. Attitudes and traits
      1. Ability to follow instructions
      2. Ability to take correction
      3. Tact, sympathy, patience
      4. Cheerfulness
      5. Firmness
      6. Liking for people and desire to serve
      7. Willingness to work hard

III. Professional preparation
   A. Academic high school course with emphasis on science
   B. Training schools
      1. Hospital and university schools
      2. Characteristics of a good school

IV. Fields open to graduate nurses
   A. Private duty
      1. Tasks
      2. Income
      3. Advantages and disadvantages
   B. Institutional duty
      1. Tasks
      2. Income
      3. Advantages and disadvantages
   C. Army or Navy service
      1. Tasks
      2. Rank and income
      3. Advantages and disadvantages

    D. Public health work
      1. Jobs in private charities and government service
      2. Income
      3. Advantages
    E. Commercial and industrial jobs

V. The future of nursing
    A. Generally favourable outlook
      1. Increased emphasis on preventive medicine and public health
      2. Rehabilitation of war-torn areas
      3. Care of war wounded
    B. Special opportunities for college women

Practice 9. Arranging an Outline

Below are the topics for a report on X-rays. Select the three main topics and write them on your paper. Then arrange the subtopics logically under the main topics. Capitalize, number, and indent the items correctly.

Invisibility	Powers of penetration
Heinrich Geissler	Discoverers
Professor Wilhelm Roentgen	Similarity to light waves
Characteristics	Sir William Crookes
Discovery of flaws in wood, iron, jewels	Detection of smuggled goods
	Uses
Diagnosing and curing disease	Heinrich Hertz

Practice 10. Outlining a Report

Write the outline of the report for which you have gathered material. Then test it by the questions in the following self-criticism chart and revise.

SELF-CRITICISM OF OUTLINE

1. *Is every main topic and subtopic on the subject?*
2. *Do my main topics cover the subject? Do the subtopics cover the main topics?*
3. *Have I avoided using too many main topics?*
4. *Does every subtopic belong under the main topic to which it is attached?*
5. *Are the main topics and the subtopics sensibly arranged?*
6. *Have I avoided duplications?*
7. *Is the grammatical construction for parallel topics the same—all sentences, for example, or all nouns with modifiers?*
8. *Is there a period after every topic number and letter and after every sentence? Does every topic begin with a capital?*

WRITING THE REPORT

After careful planning, write as freely and rapidly as the thoughts come to your mind, without paying much attention to anything except getting your ideas down on paper. Follow your plan, but put enough flesh on the skeleton to conceal the bones. Write naturally, expressing your ideas simply, pictorially, forcefully. Beware of boring generalities. Concentrate on examples, illustrations, comparisons, and contrasts. It is wise to write on each alternate line and thus leave half the lines for your revision.

Writing the Introduction

The purpose of an introduction is to arouse interest in your topic and to lead the reader or hearer naturally into the body of the report. You may begin, for instance, with one of the following:

1. A startling or relevant fact

In a single year of World War II the government called for fifty thousand girls to enter schools of nursing. What opportunities for present and future service are open to young women who patriotically answer their country's call?

2. A pertinent narrative

At four o'clock the Jerries came over again, and Lieutenant Redmond instinctively fell flat on her face and inched her way toward a foxhole. It took only a small foxhole to accommodate Lieutenant Redmond, for during the past few weeks she had grown painfully thin on quarter rations. But Lieutenant Redmond, like any other good nurse, whether in France or in Montreal, Toronto, or Calgary, was worrying not about herself or her own danger, but about the welfare of her patients.

3. A series of questions which will be answered in the report

How long a period must a student nurse spend in training? What fields are open to her when she graduates? What income can she expect to earn? These are a few of the questions to be considered by young women who are thinking seriously of making nursing their lifework.

4. A simple statement of the purpose of the article

In the immediate future nursing will offer great opportunities for young women who are physically, mentally, and emotionally suited to this exacting profession. It will be helpful, therefore, to consider the qualifications of a nurse, the training she must undergo, and the opportunities open to her on graduation.

5. A relevant comparison or contrast

Less than a hundred years ago nursing was not a profession. It was not even a reputable occupation which a woman of respectable character would consider making her lifework. In those days the care of the sick was left to filthy, illiterate, often drunken women who bore about as much resemblance to the carefully selected and highly trained nurse of today as the Neanderthal man to Albert Einstein.

Practice 11. Writing an Introduction

Write an effective, pertinent introduction for your report. Experiment with several methods until you find the best.

Unity

"The art of writing," says Lowell, "consists in knowing what to leave in the inkpot." Unity requires the rigid exclusion of facts, thoughts, allusions, and statistics that do not directly assist in the accomplishment of your purpose—in other words, that are not clearly subtopics of the main headings chosen. Ask yourself frequently, Is this on my subject? Think of your article as a direct march to a definite point rather than as a ramble at will through woods and fields.

Connectives

Not only should paragraphs be connected in thought, but their relation should be made clear. Paragraph indention serves notice that a new topic is being discussed but does not suggest what the new topic has to do with the old one. Commonly the relation between paragraphs is shown (1) by having a sentence at the end of a paragraph announce the topic of the next paragraph; (2) by having the first sentence of a paragraph refer to the preceding paragraph; (3) by repeating a word used at the end of one paragraph in the beginning of the next: or (4) by using conjunctions and connective phrases.

Practice 12.   Finding Skillful Transitions

Bring to class five examples of skillful transition between paragraphs. Find them in newspaper editorials, magazine articles, or books.

Clearness

To make your speech and writing clear (1) select subjects that are suited to your readers; (2) have clearly in mind what you are going to say; (3) use words which your readers will understand; (4) avoid complicated sentences; (5) use examples, illustrations, comparisons, contrasts, figures of speech, word pictures, anecdotes; and (6) plan before writing or speaking. The most common cause of obscurity is failure to grasp the subject fully and clearly.

Force

In forceful writing the spotlight is on significant facts, and unimportant details occupy the background or are left out. The main idea is put in a prominent place and given more space or time than the minor points. Because final impressions last longest, the end is the most emphatic position. In an article on "Self-consciousness before an Audience" the most important topic, "Remedies," is placed last and given more space than any other topic. Since few people read articles with dull or commonplace introductions, the beginning is second in importance.

Writing the Conclusion

The last paragraph is usually a summary or enforcement of an important idea. It may be used to repeat the chief points, to strengthen conviction, or to emphasize an important idea. The last sentence should be so phrased that it will linger in the hearers' minds. A brief article or report needs no conclusion or just a sentence to enforce the main point. Don't feel that you must say something after you have said everything you have to say.

Giving Credit for Borrowed Material

Your sense of honesty will compel you, of course, to acknowledge your debt to authors from whom you have borrowed material. When you state an accepted fact or idea, you need not give credit to anyone. In other words, anyone has the right to say that Florence Nightingale established nursing as a profession, that Thomas Jefferson wrote the Declaration of Independence, or that a whale is an animal. Such facts are public property. When you include in your report, however, a discussion of an original theory, you should, by the use of such a phrase as "according to Adam Smith," "Mendel's opinion was," "Dr. Banting believed", acknowledge that the idea is borrowed.

Occasionally you will wish to quote directly a pertinent, vivid sentence or paragraph you have jotted down in your notes. Changing a few words doesn't make another writer's sentence or paragraph your property. In your report you can give credit for a quotation in this way: "If one wants to be a nurse and can possibly afford to do so," Beulah France advises in "Public Health Jobs," "the ideal plan is, immediately after graduation from high school, to enter a college where courses are being given which in four to six years prepare one to received a bachelor's degree as well as an R.N."

Place a number after the quotation, and in a footnote at the bottom of the page give the source. If you are referring to a book for the first time, your footnote should include the following information: author, title of book, publisher, date of publication, volume, and page numbers.

Paul W. Chapman, *Occupational Guidance*, Turner E. Smith and Company, 1937, p. 477.

A footnote for a magazine article should mention the author, the title of the article, the magazine, the date, and the page number. A footnote for the quotation from "Public Health Jobs," for example, would appear as follows:

Beulah France, "Public Health Jobs," *The American Girl*, May, 1942, p. 545.

Additional quotations from the same book or article can be acknowledged in this way:

France, *op. cit.*, p. 20.

Op. cit. (*opere citato*) means the book or article by this author previously mentioned.

Ibid. (*ibidem* meaning "in the same place") is used in referring again to the work mentioned in the footnote immediately preceding.

Ibid., pp. 384–386.

You may number your footnotes consecutively throughout your report or begin again with number 1 on each page.

Practice 13.   Studying a Report

Answer these questions about the following report:
1. What method is used to introduce the subject? Is it effective? Why?
2. Does the report follow the outline?
3. Are the facts arranged in sensible order? Prove.
4. Is the transition from topic to topic clear and smooth?
5. Is the report clear? Accurate? Concise? Forceful? Complete? Interesting?
6. Is the conclusion forceful?
7. Are the sentences varied? If so, illustrate.
8. Is borrowed material clearly acknowledged? Give examples.

NURSING AS A CAREER

Have you ever seen someone writhing in pain? Probably in your sympathy you wished ardently that you could relieve his suffering. A nurse, however, need not merely stand by and sympathize with the sick or injured. It is her privilege actively to alleviate suffering and prevent the spread of illness and disease. "With loyalty will I endeavor to aid the physician in his work," she vows at graduation, "and devote myself to the welfare of those committed to my care."

In wartime, as well as in peacetime, the nurse stands ready to fulfil her pledge of service. Soon after the outbreak of hostilities, Canadian nurses saw service in England, Africa, Italy, and France. On every front they established a record for courage, cool efficiency, and selflessness in the face of danger. "To the last, until they were ordered out," Frank Hewlett wrote of American nurses and doctors on Bataan, "the men and the women had remained under fire at the field hospitals, caring for the wounded and the seriously ill, expecting any moment that this enemy would break through upon them."[1]

In time of disaster or epidemic the Red Cross nurse will always be found on the scene. Such nurses, for example, did much to relieve suffering when the Fraser overflowed its banks last year, leaving many people marooned, homeless, and destitute.

Although nursing, offering as it does the opportunity to relieve pain and suffering, appeals emotionally to many young women, not all of them have

[1] Frank Hewlett, *New York Times*, April 12, 1942, p. 37.

the qualifications necessary for success in this profession. Before admitting a candidate, the better schools insist on a personal interview as well as a satisfactory score on intelligence and aptitude tests, as well as a satisfactory recommendation from the educational authorities.

Because a nurse is exposed to disease more than most people are, she must be in perfect health and have plenty of energy. Since her work keeps her on her feet a great deal of the time, she must have endurance and resistance to fatigue. In addition, a nurse should be reasonably attractive so that she will not repel her patients.

Obviously anyone entrusted with the responsibility of giving drugs and treatments must have a good mind. Then, too, a nurse needs intelligence to keep herself in good health and to take proper precautions against infectious diseases. Since a nurse's work brings her in close contact with grief, suffering, and death, she must have the mental and moral strength to face unpleasant realities and to maintain a sane, happy outlook on life.

Perhaps the most important single trait a nurse must have is the ability to follow directions. Unless she can be depended on to carry out accurately the physician's instructions, she is not fit to be entrusted with the care of the sick. In addition, she must, particularly during her student years, be willing to submit to rigorous discipline and to accept criticism and profit from it.

Also essential for the nurse is "a double measure of tact, patience, strength, and poise," John M. Brewer points out, "for she deals with sick people, who often are not altogether responsible for what they say and do. Even with all this, her work will not be effective unless she has also a large supply of cheerfulness and friendliness."[1]

Since a nurse must win the respect and confidence of her patients as well as their obedience to her directions, she needs an air of authority and a pleasant firmness of voice and manner. If she has a genuine liking for people and a desire to aid them—two other essential qualities—she will probably have no difficulty in gaining the co-operation of her patients. The emotional satisfaction obtained from helping others makes a good nurse willing to work hard at unpleasant tasks for long periods of time.

Having decided that she really wants to be a nurse and has the qualities necessary for success and happiness, a girl is ready to begin planning for entrance into the field. The minimum educational requirement of reputable schools of nursing is graduation from the academic course of a recognized high school or other secondary school. "Study all the science you can—general science, biology, chemistry, physics—" Beulah France urges, "and take every available course in civics, economics, and physical education."[2] As soon as a girl has decided what school she wishes to enter, she should send for its calendar to be sure that she has or will have all the subjects required for entrance.

In selecting a school, a prospective nurse must choose between two general types. If her funds are limited and she must earn money as soon as possible, she will probably enter a hospital school—that is, a training school operated within a hospital or near one. To be approved as a training centre in Canada a hospital must meet minimum requirments set out by law in each province. In such a school a student trains for two or three years. During this period she attends classroom lectures and demonstrations part of the time and spends

---

[1]John M. Brewer, *Occupations*, Ginn and Company, 1936, p. 224.
[2]Beulah France, "Public Health Jobs," *The American Girl*, May, 1942, p. 20.

the rest working in the wards. Under ordinary circumstances the tuition in hospital schools ranges from practically nothing to one to two hundred dollars. The majority of these schools pay student nurses a small monthly sum after completion of the first few months of training. In all schools board and lodging are free.

If a prospective nurse can spend a longer period in preparation, she will do well to enter one of the schools affiliated with a university—for example, the School of Nursing at the Universities of Toronto, British Columbia, etc. "If one wants to be a nurse and can possibly afford to do so," Beulah France advises, "the ideal plan is, immediately after graduation from high school, to enter a university where courses are being given which in four to six years prepare one to receive a bachelor's degree as well as an R.N."[1] Since the student is awarded an academic degree on completion of her course, the tuition in university schools is naturally higher than in hospital schools.

Before entering a school, a girl should find out whether its diploma will admit her to the examination for registration in her province. The health programme of the nursing school should include an initial examination with chest X-rays and protective inoculations, adequate medical and nursing care in case of illness, and periodic physical examinations. The school should either have a good library of its own or have access to one. A girl in doubt concerning the status of a particular school can obtain information from the Canadian Nurses' Association, 1411 Crescent Street, Montreal, or the Registered Nurses' Association in her own province.

When a girl has finished her course and won her R.N., she has an opportunity to choose from several kinds of nursing service. The private duty nurse usually cares for a single patient either in a hospital or a private home. Some of her regular duties are taking temperatures, keeping the patient clean and comfortable, reporting progress to the physician, and giving the drugs and treatments ordered. In the past this branch of nursing has been overcrowded and earnings low, averaging in a good year perhaps $1200. However, at the present time nurses are in great demand, and many have entered other fields. The incomes of those still available have naturally risen. Since such a nurse has complete charge of her patients, she has the opportunity to become well acquainted with them and to form interesting friendships. However, "So long as nurses continue to work for themselves," say Myer and Coss, "as private duty nurses do, there is no opportunity for advancement to higher positions."[2]

The institutional nurse works in a hospital. Sometimes she has charge of the general care of patients in a ward. Other nurses work in clinics, and a third group—those with advanced training—assist in the operating room or X-ray laboratory, administer special treatments, or teach students. Institutional nurses usually earn from $1200 to $2000, depending on the hospital and the section of the country in which they work, and receive free maintenance. When a nurse advances to an executive or supervisory position, her earnings naturally increase. Probably the chief advantages of institutional nursing are steady work and pay and opportunity for promotion. Sometimes, however, petty jealousies and friction among various members of the staff make working conditions unpleasant.

When Canada entered World War II, the government appealed to thou-

[1]France, op. cit. 45.
[2]Walter E. Myer and Clay Coss, The Promise of Tomorrow, Civic Education Service, 1938, p. 355.

sands of young nurses to enter military service. In field hospitals here and abroad Army and Navy nurses cared for the wounded and assisted in their physical and mental rehabilitation. A small number of carefully selected nurses served on hospital ships which, equipped with operating rooms and X-ray and pathological laboratories, collected wounded seamen and soldiers and gave them modern, efficent care.

A fourth field open to the graduate nurse with special training is public health. "Without doubt," Myer and Coss assert, "the most promising branch of the entire profession is public health nursing."[1] Employed by a private charity or the local provincial, or Federal government, a public health nurse may be called upon for a variety of tasks. She may, like the famous Victorian Order of Nurses, visit sick patients to provide treatment and advice. Perhaps, instead, she will supervise the health of pupils in a school; instruct mothers in the care of babies and children; or, if she has exceptional educational and professional qualifications, act as a consultant in public health.

A beginner in this field usually earns from $1500 to $2000. Supervisory and executive positions, as might be expected, pay substantially more. "Such positions as these," Beulah France says, "offer travel, good living conditions, permanent employment, promotion as merited, opportunity to carry on studies through library facilities provided, association with a highly qualified group of medical men and professional women, care in case of illness, and retirement with a pension."[2]

Other possible fields of employment are commerce and industry. Most large concerns employ one or more nurses to supervise the health of employees and administer first aid to the ill or injured. Usually such positions pay from $1500 to $2500, the exact figure depending on the firm and the section of the country.

What is the general outlook for nursing as a career? The consensus of opinion is that a girl physically, mentally, and emotionally qualified for the profession will make no mistake in entering it. The years ahead will probably see an increased emphasis on preventive medicine and public health. The rehabilitation of war-torn areas, with their tremendous populations of malnourished and diseased civilians, will provide work for thousands of nurses. In our own country many of the men wounded in service will require treatment over a considerable period of time.

It is probable, however, that in the future, as is now the case, the best opportunities will be open to the woman with a university degree as well as an R.N. "There are at present," Western Reserve University said in peacetime, "more positions calling for experienced, successful nurses with a college background than there are women to fill them."[3] For this reason a girl who expects to make nursing a career should plan to earn a bachelor's degree as well as an R.N. If she cannot afford a four-, five-, or six-year university course, she can take her training in a hospital school and, after she has begun to earn, save the money for her tuition. Such a young nurse will be equipped to earn a good living in a vital and honored profession. — MARY S.

BIBLIOGRAPHY

Brewer, John M. *Occupations*. Ginn and Company, 1936. Pp. 222–224.

[1]Myer and Coss, *op. cit.* p. 357.
[2]France, *op. cit.* p. 45.
[3]Paul W. Chapman, *Occupational Guidance*, Turner E. Smith and Company, 1937, p. 477.

Chapman, Paul W. *Occupational Guidance.* Turner E. Smith and Company, 1937. Pp. 475–479.

Cottler, Joseph, and Brecht, Harold. *Careers Ahead.* Little, Brown, and Company, 1938. Pp. 112–117.

Davey, Mildred; Smith, Elizabeth; and Myers, Theodore. *Everyday Occupations.* D. C. Heath and Company, 1941. Pp. 298–314.

France, Beulah. "Public Health Jobs." *The American Girl,* May 1942, pp. 20–22, 41, 45.

Hewlett, Frank. *New York Times.* April 12, 1942, pp. 1, 37.

Myer, Walter E., and Coss, Clay. *The Promise of Tomorrow.* Civic Education Service, 1938. Pp. 353–360.

Sutherland, Dorothy G. *Do You Want to Be a Nurse?* Doubleday, 1942.

World Almanac. New York *World-Telegram,* 1944. Pp. 115, 121–122.

Practice 14. Writing the First Draft

Write the first draft of the report for which you have been preparing. Give definite facts, examples, and illustrations. Acknowledge borrowed language by the use of quotation marks and footnotes.

Preparing a Bibliography

A research report must include a bibliography—that is, a list of books, encyclopaedias, magazines, pamphlets, and newspapers consulted. A bibliography is valuable in supporting statements which may be questioned and in directing your reader to further information on the subject. A worth-while bibliography has complete and accurate information: author, title, volume, publisher, date, page. For an example of the form see the preceding bibliography.

Revising Your Report

In writing your report you concentrated on getting all your facts down on paper. Now you are ready to polish and perfect this rough copy. Read your report critically several times. Here are the questions to keep in mind as you read:

1. Have I secured abundant interesting material?
2. Are my facts accurate?
3. Have I covered my subject completely?
4. Is my report clear?
5. Have I included only material on my topic?
6. Have I arranged sentences and paragraphs in logical order?
7. Have I used connective words and phrases to show the transition from topic to topic?
8. Are my sentences clear and correct?
9. Is my report concise?
10. Have I avoided repetition?
11. Are my grammar, spelling, sentence structure, punctuation and capitalization correct?

12. Have I indicated by quotation marks and footnotes language that is not my own?

~~I first became interested in~~ Snakes ~~about four~~
Perhaps you find that statement hard to believe. Well,
~~years ago. They~~ are fascinating creatures. ~~In the~~
four years ago I was doubtful too,
~~beginning I was afraid to handle them,~~ but after I
saw   *friend*   *snakes*
~~soon~~ a ~~froind~~ handle ~~them~~ fearlessly, I plucked up
courage
enough ~~heart~~ to hold one. ~~in my hand.~~ From then on
snakes have been my hobby.
~~I became a veritable snake charmer.~~

SAMPLE OF A REVISED REPORT

Practice 15. Completing the Report

After thoroughly revising your report, type it, using double spacing, or copy it accurately and plainly without blots and with a minimum of erasures.

WRITING A SECRETARY'S REPORT

A secretary's report is a record of the business transacted, the motions passed, the committees appointed, and other important happenings. It should be concise, clear, and pointed.

In some English classes the pupils in turn act as secretary, write the minutes, and read them in class or write them on the blackboard. The secretary's report of a meeting of an English class should, as a rule, include the date, the assignment for the next recitation, important announcements or business, a résumé of the work done, and a summary of what the class learned during the period. When you write a report of a meeting of your class, avoid stereotyped expressions. Omit matters of daily class routine which all the pupils understand— for example, "The class met in Room 208"; "The class came to order when the bell rang"; "The teacher then took the attendance"; "When the bell rang, the class was dismissed."

Keep in mind three purposes of the secretary's report: (1) to review at the beginning of a period the work of the preceding period; (2) to let the absent pupil know exactly what he missed and to guide him in the making up of his work; (3) to give the secretary valuable practice in summarizing and in reading aloud. Of course, you know that practice of any sort—summarizing, typing, or playing tennis or the piano, for instance—is of real value only when you take pains and do your best.

Practice 16.   Studying a Secretary's Report

Read the following report carefully.

1. What valuable discussion hints does the report include?
2. Are the sentences efficient and varied? Give examples.

November 3, 19—

Miss Jergens began the work of the period by dictating the assignment for November 4. The class was instructed to read carefully pages 263–89 and 324–49 of *Microbe Hunters* in preparation for a test on the work of David Bruce and Walter Reed.

Miss Jergens then turned the class over to Fred Hamer, the class chairman. After a brief talk on "Modern Science," the topic of the day's panel discussion, Fred introduced Ethel Wolf, the first speaker. In her talk on "Science in the Home" Ethel pointed out that years ago people did not have in their homes such modern conveniences as washing machines, electric lights, vacuum cleaners, telephones, radios, and air-conditioning equipment.

Next Bert Schreiber spoke on "Methods of Microbe Hunters". After describing Koch's discovery of the anthrax bacillus, Bert discussed the four steps of microbe hunting: (1) isolate probable germ; (2) grow germ in artificial culture medium; (3) inoculate animal with suspected germ; (4) if animal dies, dissect it and look for germ. In conclusion Bert told how scientists stain germs to see them more easily under the microscope.

In his discussion of medical science to-day the third speaker, Alfred Deal, pointed out that it is only within the last fifty years that new scientific methods of prevention and cure of disease have been accepted. Because of them the life expectancy of a baby has, within thirty years, been raised fifteen years. To fight pneumonia, one of the chief causes of death, physicians have prepared serums. Although there are thirty-two different types of pneumonia, certain kinds are so rare that five serums cure 95 per cent of all the cases. Within recent years the sulfa drugs have also dramatically reduced pneumonia mortality. In penicillin, a drug obtained from mold, the medical profession has found a new cure for infections and germ-caused diseases.

The last speaker, Charles Stein, sketched the future of aviation as experts envision it. Because of military experience in high altitude flying it is probable that in postwar years planes will cruise at heights well over 20,000 feet without unreasonable consumption of fuel. Bigger, more powerful engines—perhaps of the Diesel type—will be housed in the wings of to-morrow's planes. These planes may have four wheels, a front and a rear on each side of the fuselage. It is probable that the helicopter, a small aircraft which can fly forward, backward, and sideward, rise or descend vertically, and hover motionless in the air, will be as universally owned and operated as the automobile is to-day.

After the speakers had answered several questions, members of the class joined in the discussion. Next Miss Jergens was called on for a criticism. Ethel Wolf was criticized for talking to the floor rather than to the class and for telling the class what everyone knew. Bert Schreiber, on the other hand, had evidently investigated his subject thoroughly and spoke clearly and effectively. Alfred Deal was commended for interesting material. Occasionally, however, he mumbled instead of speaking clearly, and during his talk mispronounced *apparatus, benignant,* and *Becquerel.* Several times Charles

Stein failed to make technical details clear to the class. He lacked vigour and animation and depended too much on his notes.

During the period the class learned many interesting facts about modern science and received valuable pointers about preparing and delivering a speech.

David Schwartz
Secretary

Practice 17.   Writing a Secretary's Report

Write, when your turn comes, a secretary's report of an English recitation. Summarize thoughtfully the work done during the period. Leave out unimportant details of the class routine.

Mastering Effective Story-telling

TELLING EXPERIENCES

Example:

A BEAR STORY[1]

Several years ago I was camping out in Maine one March, in a lumberman's shack. A few days before I came, two boys in a village near by decided to go into the woods hunting, with a muzzle-loading shotgun and a long stick between them. One boy was ten years old, while the other was a patriarch of twelve. On a hillside under a great bush they noticed a small hole which seemed to have melted through the snow, and which had a gamy savour that made them suspect a coon. The boy with the stick poked it in as far as possible until he felt something soft.

"I think there's something here," he remarked, poking with all his might.

He was quite right. The next moment the whole bank of frozen snow suddenly caved out, and there stood a cross and hungry bear, prodded out of his winter sleep by that stick. The boys were up against a bad proposition. The snow was too deep for running, and when it came to climbing—that was Mr. Bear's pet specialty. So they did the only thing left for them to do: they waited. The little one with the stick got behind the big one with the gun, which weapon wavered unsteadily.

"Now, don't you miss," he said, " 'cause this stick ain't very sharp."

Sometimes an attacking bear will run at a man like a biting dog. More often it rises on its haunches and depends on the smashing blows of its mighty arms and steel-shod paws. So it happened in this case. Just before the bear reached the boys, he lifted his head and started to rise. The first boy, not six feet away, aimed at the white spot which most black bears have under their chins, and pulled the trigger. At that close range the heavy charge of number six shot crashed through the animal's throat, making a single round hole like a big bullet, cutting the jugular vein, and piercing the neck vertebrae beyond. The great beast fell forward with hardly a struggle, so close to the boys that its blood splashed on their rubber boots. They got ten dollars for the skin and ten dollars for the bounty, and about one million dollars' worth of glory.

HOW TO NARRATE

What can we learn about storytelling by studying Scoville's "A Bear Story"?

The author at the start answers the questions "Who?" "When?" "Where?" and "What?" by telling us that in Maine one March several

---

[1] From Samuel Scoville's *Everyday Adventures* by permission of the Atlantic Monthly Press, Boston.

years ago a boy of ten and a boy of twelve went hunting with a stick and a shotgun between them.

2. He plunges right into the story. He doesn't tell us how it happened that these two boys went hunting alone, whose shotgun it was, what school the boys attended, or what they ate for breakfast.

3. By introducing the conflict between the boys and the bear, he arouses our curiosity and makes us eager to know whether the boys escaped from the bear.

4. He keeps the climax or the point of the story back till near the end. He doesn't give the story away in the first paragraph by telling us that the older boy shot the bear.

5. The author plunges out of the story. He doesn't take time to tell us what the story teaches us, how large the bear was, how they got him home, or what their parents said.

6. He adds life to the story by having the boy with the stick talk. Notice the separate paragraph for each speech, the quotation marks, and the commas. All boys and girls prefer stories which have a good deal of dialogue or conversation.

7. He pictures the boys and the bear. We can see the cross and hungry black bear rising on his hind legs, the boy of twelve, not six feet from the bear, with his gun pointed unsteadily at the white spot under the bear's chin, and behind him the little boy with the pointed stick.

8. He uses words accurately.

9. By omitting unnecessary words and details he makes the story move swiftly.

10. He tells the events in the order in which they happened.

Practice 1.   Telling an Experience

Using the bear story as a model, narrate an unusual or exciting happening about which a member of your family—Grandfather or Grandmother, for example—or someone else has told you. Perhaps these topics will remind you of a true story you have heard:

World War II, land travel, ocean travel, camping, cooking, exploring, tramping, accident, mistaken identity, surprise, rival, escape, amateur acting, skating, hunting, fishing, baseball, running, swimming, mountain climbing, "roughing it," earlier days in our city or town, learning to fly, a rare chance, everyday heroism.

Leading up to a Climax, Point, or Surprise

Catherine wrote about going fishing with Donald, a six-year-old neighbour. The climax was her falling into the water while Donald was digging worms, and the rescue. This is what Catherine wrote:

Agfa-Ansco Film

Picnics and expeditions make interesting topics for stories and short narratives.

"While tugging at the pole to get the hook loose, I lost my balance and fell into the water. Just then Donald returned and fished me out." The other pupils wondered how deep the water was, why Catherine needed a rescuer, and how Donald, aged six, "fished out" a girl much older than he. Because Catherine skipped important details, her story was uninteresting and sounded "fishy." When you reach the climax, tell every necessary detail.

Practice 2. Studying Narratives

Read carefully the three following true stories:

1. What is the best part of number 1? Why?

2. The author of number 3 wrote first a plan and placed this at the top of his paper. Of what use is such an outline?

3. Which is the best story? Why?

1. MY FIRST VISIT TO THE THEATRE

Of all the things that have happened to me, I think that my first visit to the theatre was the most exciting. Though I was only five years old at the time, I can remember very clearly everything that happened.

As I sat waiting for the curtain to go up, I wondered if the play would be just like the story of the same name, "Jack and the Beanstalk." It was! Most assuredly it was! All the thrilling situations and hairbreadth escapes of the story were in the play. My nerves grew more and more taut. My blood raced; my hands tingled. Finally I could stand it no longer. Just as the brutal giant raised his axe to chop off the head of the pretty little princess, I shrieked. My bored father awoke in annoyance from a sound sleep. My mother looked at me with murder in her eye. If, however, the giant had threatened me with his axe, I could not possibly have restrained myself, for indeed if I were actually beheaded, the sensation could be no worse than the one which my imagination produced. — PUPIL

2. MY BURGLAR

"Crackle, crackle, crackle" in the middle of the night!

"Huh?" I asked myself sleepily.

"Crackle, crackle." I sat up in bed quickly, and as I was lying at one side, I narrowly escaped falling out. Then, making no noise, I listened. More crackles.

"It can't be the fish," I reasoned, "because they can't make any noise. I wonder what it is." Noiselessly getting out of bed, I grabbed my flashlight and crept down to the living-room. The crackles certainly weren't coming from there. I went on, and so did the noise. Next on my route was the dining room. I looked under the table, under the chairs, even in the chandelier, but nowhere could I find the source of those mysterious crackles.

"Maybe it's a burglar!" I thought, and rushed to wake my parents. In doing this I passed through the kitchen and beheld the source of the crackles. It was Pinky, my white mouse, sitting calmly in his cage and philosophically chewing the paper lining.

"You go to sleep," I told him and then, being very tired, I obeyed these instructions myself. — PUPIL

3. AN EXPERIENCE I'LL NEVER FORGET

Situation	1. Uncle Herb's interest in trials
	2. His size and peculiar habit
Events in	3. Our going to hear a robbery trial
time order	4. Examination of the defendant
	5. My uncle's habitual motion
Climax	6. My uncle accused of making signs
Ending	7. Results of the experience

If there's anything Uncle Herb used to love, it was a good stiff trial in the Criminal Court. Whenever he had spare time, he hastened to the building, and always got a seat in the front row.

Whenever my uncle became excited, he had the curious habit of sliding his finger around his mouth in a circular motion. As he is about six feet five inches in height, you can just imagine how conspicuous he is.

One day, with no work before him, he decided to take me to the trial of a dangerous criminal charged with robbery. Uncle Herb made me put on long pants and a felt hat, and I got in safely to one of his "ring-side" seats.

We both enjoyed the tricky questions fired at the defendant by the attorney for the prosecution. After a while the prosecutor asked, "Did you pawn this watch on the morning of October 16?"

The room was tense. So excited was my uncle that he at once resorted to his peculiar habit. "No," said the defendant timidly.

The defense attorney breathed a sigh of relief. "Just one moment!" almost shouted the prosecutor. "That man," pointing an accusing finger at Uncle Herb, "was making signs to the defendant. I demand that he be held!"

You can well imagine what a scare my poor Uncle Herb got. Of course, when everything was over and the criminal put where he belonged, my uncle was let go with many apologies. From that time on, he did his best to conquer his habit and, what was more important, stayed away from courts except when he had a summons. — PUPIL

Practice 3.   Telling an Experience

Using one of the following titles, write entertainingly about an experience of yours. Plan, write, revise thoroughly, copy neatly. Apply what you have learned about narrating. Lead up to a climax or surprise. Tell the truth.

1. A childhood adventure. 2. Our burglar. 3. Lost. 4. A snowball fight. 5. At night alone on a country road. 6. An unexpected bath in January. 7. A narrow escape. 8. An experience with a horse, a mule, or an automobile. 9. A long evening at home alone—noises. 10. My first attempt at learning to swim, skate, fish, snowshoe, or ride a bicycle. 11. An exploration. 12. No gas. 13. Locked out. 14. Caught in a storm in the country. 15. A hasty retreat. 16. The cost of carelessness. 17. Our circus. 18. My part in the game. 19. Just scared. 20. My first airplane ride. 21. A fishing experience. 22. A leaky boat. 23. The raft. 24. Why I hate bees. 25. A fire.

Practice 4. Studying a Narrative

In numbers 1 and 2 following, Virginia and Ted have told the same story.

1. Which telling do you prefer? Give three good reasons for your choice.

2. What words or sentences in Virginia's story make you see pictures?

1. WE DIDN'T GO IN

"Yes," said my mother one morning while we were at Seaside Park, "you may walk down to the beach, but remember you can't go in swimming now."

"Well," said Cousin Ted, as though he had lost his last friend, "we can at least look at the ocean even if we can't go in." And down to the beach we went.

"I can't see why we have to wait for the rest," I remarked gloomily.

"Just look at that water all going to waste while we sit around and wait for some worthless friends to come from the city," Jack said.

"Say," I howled, slapping Ted on the back so that he nearly fell off the jetty where we were sitting, "why couldn't we take off our shoes and socks now and have some fun wading around until they come?" In a second our shoes and socks were off and we were in.

"This isn't as good as swimming, but it's pretty good at that," observed Cousin Ted.

In a short time we had forgotten all about Mother, friends, clothes, and everything else that we should have remembered. Splashing around in the waves, having a wonderful time, we grew careless about getting out of the way of large breakers.

Before long the inevitable happened. My cousin was facing shore. "Look out!" I screamed at him, but he didn't hear me. A huge wave was breaking over him. I can see yet his white blouse and blue tie disappearing beneath the green comber.

Of course, I fell down trying to help him up. Out of the water we came, our light summer clothes soaking wet, and a more unpleasant feeling I cannot describe. Add to that the pricking of a guilty conscience and you see that we were pretty miserable.

My mother met us at the door. "Go in the back way," she said with the air of one who was ready for anything. "You know, I thought you'd do something like that if I didn't watch you."

We weren't scolded. I guess it was because we looked so funny. When the company came we all went for a swim, and my mother mercifully spared us by not telling of our morning's escapade.

2. WE DIDN'T GO IN

Aunt Ellen told Cousin Virginia, Jack, and me not to go in swimming in the morning but to wait and go in after dinner with our friends from the city. We didn't go in but took off our shoes and stockings and waded in the water. After a while a big wave knocked me down, and Virginia fell down trying to help me up. Aunt Ellen didn't scold us and let us go swimming that afternoon.

Practice 5.   Telling a Story

On one of the following topics write entertainingly about one of your experiences. Use words that will make your readers see pictures.

1. The greatest surprise of my life. 2. An incident that taught me a lesson. 3. Something funny in school. 4. The joke was on me. 5. A punishment I deserved. 6. An experience of a bargain hunter. 7. How I earned my first dollar. 8. I was cook. 9. In the nick of time. 10. The trick that failed. 11. A camping experience. 12. The meanest thing I ever did. 13. It never rains but it pours. 14. An experience I shall not forget. 15. A spoiled adventure. 16. The hornets' nest. 17. Why I didn't go swimming. 18. My first visit to the dentist. 19. When Mother was away this summer. 20. The best Christmas I ever had. 21. My bicycle stolen. 22. My birthday party. 23. An embarrassing experience. 24. A dog in school. 25. When I lost my money. 26. My first experience riding alone on a train. 27. What happened when the rising tide turned the streets into canals.

ENTERTAINING WITH AN AMUSING INCIDENT FROM LIFE

MR. PAGE'S PRESENCE OF MIND

(An incident from Mr. Bruce Lockhart's *Retreat from Glory*, being the memoirs of the British observer in Czechoslovakia).

One of the great dangers which zealous diplomats incur in a small capital is loss of perspective. In Prague this danger was averted in our own case by the visits which we received periodically from distinguished and representative British citizens. The most amusing of these visits was a corporate one—a delegation of members of the British intelligentsia, who at the invitation of the Czechoslovak Government descended on us in order to witness with their own eyes the progress of the new Republic. It was a distinguished delegation. It included Mr. H. G. Wells, Lord Dunsany, Sir Henry Wood, Mr. Clifford Sharp, the former editor of the *New Statesman*, the ubiquitous Sir Harry Brittain, Mr. Philip Page, the music critic, and many other celebrities, both male and female, whose fame was at the time unknown to me and whose names have therefore eluded my memory and my diary. This visit, the first of its kind, was organized on the grand scale. The Czechs provided the requisite number of motor-cars and their best English-speaking guides.

When the delegates' train pulled up at the Wilson station, the conductor had forgotten to wake Mr. Page. The platform was crowded with Czech dignitaries—representatives of the Foreign Office, the Army and the City Fathers, who had assembled to welcome the distinguished English visitors. They could not be kept waiting. Mr. Page was equal to the occasion. Unshaven and unwashed, he hastily put on his boots and hat. Then, putting on a huge overcoat over his pyjamas, he stepped down on to the platform and took his place among his brother delegates to a roar of *"Na zdar,"* which is the Czech for *Heil*, from the cheering Czechs. It was midsummer and the heat tropical, and Mr. Page, the heavyweight of the delegation, was at once singled out as the typical "John Bull". I take off my hat to Mr. Page. His dignity never relaxed. He strode down the platform with the slow majesty of the late Sir Herbert Beerbohm Tree. He shook hands with the Lord Mayor. He saluted the generals. He bowed gravely to the beauty chorus in peasant costumes which presented him with a bouquet of carnations. Then, with his striped pyjama trousers fluttering bravely in the sunshine, he took his place in the open carriage and, still saluting, drove through the streets, lined with the tumultuous cheering populace, to his hotel on the famous Square of St. Wenceslaus. It was an epic performance—a supreme example of English presence of mind. The Czechs noticed nothing. Perhaps I do them an injustice. I should have said that they noticed nothing incongruous. Two weeks after the visit a new fashion made its presence felt on the streets of Prague. It took the form of black and white striped flannel trousers.

By arrangement with the publisher, Putnam and Company, Ltd., London.

Practice 6. Telling an Amusing Incident

The above story is from the actual experiences of Mr. R. H. Bruce Lockhart. He has told it with due regard for those things which make the situation amusing. Cull from your experiences an amusing incident, and tell it with as much effect as you can. Try to amuse.

MAKING UP STORIES

Everybody writes best about what he knows thoroughly at first hand—his family, his friends, his home, his own town or city, the grocery store on the next block, his school, a house or place he has visited. If people, places, and happenings are not clear in the mind of the writer, he cannot make his readers see and enjoy them. Many, however, write successfully of people and places they have read and heard a great deal about.

Practice 7. Reproducing a Story

In four minutes reproduce entertainingly a short story—Richard Harding Davis's "Gallegher," Sir Arthur T. Quiller-Couch's "The Two Householders," Mazo de la Roche's "Tiny Tim," Poe's "The Gold Bug," Sir A. Conan Doyle's "The Speckled Band," Kipling's "Wee Willie Winkie," O. Henry's "The Ransom of Red Chief," Hawthorne's "The Great Stone Face," Stockton's "The Lady or the Tiger?" John Fox, Jr.'s "Christmas Night with Satan," or a short story from any one of the following books. Don't hesitate or flounder. Make the story march. Talk to your classmates. Don't overwork *and, but, so,* and *then.*

Aldrich, Thomas B.: *Two Bites at a Cherry; Marjorie Daw, and Other People*
Allen, James Lane: *Kentucky Cardinal*
Andrews, Mary: *Perfect Tribute*
Bayliss, A. E. M. (editor): *Twenty-four Stories*
Davis, Richard Harding: *Van Bibber and Others; Gallegher and Other Stories; Stories for Boys*
de la Ramée, Louise (Ouida): *The Nuremberg Stove; Dog of Flanders*
Dickens, Charles: *Christmas Stories*
Doyle, Arthur Conan: *Adventures of Sherlock Holmes*
Freeman, Mary Wilkins: *A New England Nun; A Humble Romance*

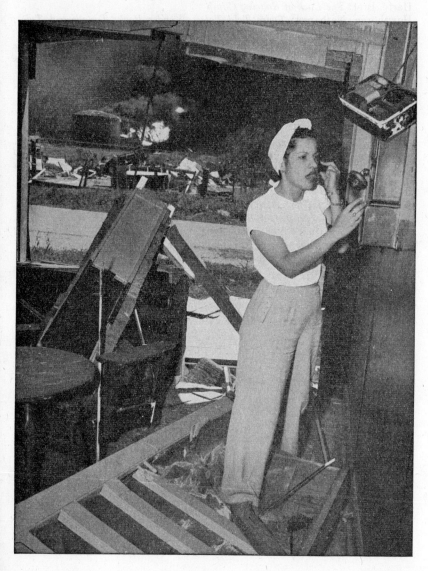

Grahame, Kenneth: *The Golden Age; Dream Days*
Hampden, John (editor): *Ten Modern Stories*
Harte, Bret: *The Luck of Roaring Camp*
Hawthorne, Nathaniel: *Twice Told Tales; Wonder Book; Tanglewood Tales; The Snow Image*
Henry, O. (Sidney Porter): *The Four Million; The Voice of the City; The Trimmed Lamp; The Ransom of Red Chief, and Other O. Henry Stories for Boys*
Kipling, Rudyard: *The Jungle Book; The Second Jungle Book; Actions and Reactions; The Day's Work; Land and Sea Tales for Boys and Girls*
McNally, G. Fred (editor): *A Book of Good Stories*
Poe, Edgar Allan: *Prose Tales*
Pyle, Howard: *The Book of Pirates*
Seton, Ernest Thompson: *Wild Animals I Have Known; Lives of the Hunted*
Stevenson, Robert Louis: *The Bottle Imp; Dr. Jekyll and Mr. Hyde; The Merry Men; New Arabian Nights*
Stockton, Frank: *The Lady or the Tiger?*
Tarbell, Ida M.: *He Knew Lincoln*
Tarkington, Booth: *Monsieur Beaucaire*
Ward, Bertha Evans (editor): *Short Stories of To-day*
Whitfield, Raoul: *Silver Wings*
Williams, Blanche Colton (editor): *New Narratives*

Practice 8.   An Imaginative Story

Make up a story based on the picture on page 307.   Consider the picture an illustration to be printed with the story.   Let your imagination work.

UNIT TWENTY

Mastering Effective Description

SCIENTIFIC VERSUS LITERARY DESCRIPTION

In describing you transmit to others pictures of objects, persons, and places which have interested or pleased you. These pictures can be drawn, however, in two widely different ways. *Scientific description* presents a precise catalogue of details and excludes entirely the writer's personality and impressions; it resembles a diagram. In this type of description are included lost and found advertisements, descriptions in scientific textbooks, and police records. *Artistic description*, which is used in literature of all types, resembles a painting. With a few striking details the literary artist sets the reader's imagination to work at completing the picture and transmits to the reader the emotions and impressions the writer originally experienced.

Scientific Description of Air

Pure air is an invisible gas, colourless, odourless, and tasteless; very compressible and perfectly elastic. It is very mobile and, like all matter, has weight. Though under ordinary conditions gaseous, it may easily be made to assume the liquid state. — AREY, BRYANT, CLENDENIN, AND MORREY, *New Physiography*

Literary Description

Once more the door banged, and a slight, slim-built boy perhaps fifteen years old, a half-smoked cigarette hanging from one corner of his mouth, leaned over the high footway. — KIPLING

Practice 1. Studying Descriptions

1. How many facts about air are given in the brief scientific description?

2. What facts are given in Kipling's description of Harvey Cheyne?

3. "A half-smoked cigarette hanging from one corner of his mouth" arouses the reader's imagination to finish the portrait of Harvey Cheyne and also to tell what kind of boy he was. What is your picture of Harvey?

OBSERVING

To paint word pictures one needs to observe the object, scene, or person, and then to picture what one sees. To observe means to see

309

and note, to examine and note, to watch closely, to look at attentively, not just to look at. When an artist paints a person's picture, he doesn't just glance at his subject or take one look at him and then paint; instead, with the subject "sitting" for his picture, he observes and paints, observes and paints, and continues to observe and paint.

All five senses bring us information about an object. Often, however, our senses, like a knife, become dull and need whetting. This can best be done by using them actively in gathering impressions of our surroundings. Describing is telling what our senses find out for us about the world in which we live—our eyes by seeing, our ears by hearing, our noses by smelling, our tongues by tasting, and our fingers by feeling.

Practice 2. Words That Describe

Pick out the words that describe sounds, tastes, smells, feelings, and sights.

Example:
The next wave crashed and roared over me and filled my mouth with bitter salt water.
Crashed and *roared* describe sounds. *Bitter* and *salt* describe tastes.

1. Even as I looked, there came a red flash and another report that sent the echoes clattering, and once more a round shot whistled through the air. — STEVENSON
2. The unceasing vibration of the engines throbbed through their bodies and numbed their brains.
3. Still tingling from the cold water, we tramped toward camp hungrily sniffing the sharp, pungent odour of frying bacon.
4. Down his throat trickled a thick, tart liquid that made him cough, choke, and gasp for breath.
5. The drummer walloped his drums, a saxophone squawked, and fiddles squeaked. — TARKINGTON
6. Wavelets of creamy-crested green water lapped gently on the mossy rocks.
7. A large oak door creaked dismally as it swung back and forth on its one rusty hinge.
8. Sand gritted between their teeth, seared their eyeballs, and lashed their faces with stinging blows.
9. The monarch is a little, keen, fresh-coloured old man, with protruding eyes, attired in plain, old-fashioned, snuff-coloured clothes and brown stockings.
10. André stood before her, a shadowy figure in the obscurity, pale, unshaven, muddy, smiling a strange, dim, tired, infinitely tender smile. — FISHER

Practice 3. Picture-making Words

In a sentence for each describe a sound, a sight, a taste, a smell, and a feeling suggested by the following. Choose accurate picture-bringing words.

1. A storm. 2. The tea kettle. 3. Olives. 4. A dirigible. 5. Coffee boiling. 6. A plunge in the lake. 7. Birch trees. 8. A wood fire. 9. A hinge that needs oiling. 10. Wild strawberries. 11. Polished wood. 12. Rain on a tin roof. 13. A sunset. 14. Newly ploughed earth. 15. Toasted marshmallows. 16. Satin. 17. Icicles. 18. Salt water. 19. Fog. 20. My kitten's fur. 21. Pop corn. 22. A baby's hand. 23. A gasoline filling station.

Practice 4.   Picture-making Words

Write vivid words appealing to each of these senses: sight, hearing, touch, smell.

Example:

taste—nibble, devour, gulp, gorge, guzzle, crunch, salty, bitter, tangy, spicy, creamy, delicious, sour, sharp, tender, tough, toothsome, flat, nauseating, savoury, tart, sharp, mellow, mild, tasty, gritty, slippery, sugary, peppery

Practice 5.   Picture-making Verbs

For each of the following verbs or word-groups find four or more specific, picture-making equivalents: *be active, speak, sleep, work, hasten, eject, depart, make a noise, smell an odour, feel a fabric, taste a food.*

Example:

Be inactive—lounge, loaf, loiter, loll, lag, dawdle, vegetate, let the grass grow under one's feet, kill time, burn daylight, sleep at one's post, swim with the stream.

WORD PICTURES

"There were clouds in the sky" states a simple fact, but "Feathery clouds scudded across the sky" paints a word picture. The difference lies in two words used: *feathery* and *scudded.* Just as a painting in fresh, vivid colours is more arresting than a drawing in black and white, so the use of vigorous, picture-making adjectives, adverbs, and verbs will produce in your speaking and writing a more telling effect than the colourless verbs and bald nouns so frequently employed. After observing sharply we need to search out vivid, exact words to picture what we see.

Practice 6.   Picture-making Words

Select the picture-making words in each of the following sentences:

Example:

Big Junko sported a wide, ferocious, straggling moustache and low eyebrows, under which gleamed little fierce eyes. — STEWART EDWARD WHITE

The picture words are *wide, ferocious, straggling, moustache, low, eyebrows, gleamed, little, fierce, eyes.*

1. Lou Gehrig has a jolly face with a smile that has won him many friends, broad shoulders, immense hands, powerful forearms, and a pair of sturdy legs, commonly called "bottle" legs because of their appearance.
2. Claude Bowers is a short, slim, dark, studious, scholarly, quiet man in his middle years. — *Time*
3. Donald's apple-like cheeks, ham-like hands, and big, puffy body are accentuated by his tiny round cap, tight-fitting clothes, and choking collar.
4. A silvery moonlight flooded the white beach, and in the inky black lake the stars and moon beheld their reflections.
5. Except on the crown, which was raggedly bald, he had stiff, black hair, standing jaggedly all over it, and growing down hill almost to his broad blunt nose. — DICKENS
6. I remember him as if it were yesterday, as he came plodding to the inn door, his sea chest following behind him in a handbarrow; a tall, strong, heavy, nut-brown man; his tarry pigtail falling over the shoulders of his soiled blue coat; his hands ragged and scarred, with black, broken nails; and the sabre cut across one cheek, a dirty, livid white. — STEVENSON
7. There was Ben Gunn's boat—homemade if ever anything was homemade: a rude, lopsided framework of tough wood, and stretched upon that a covering of goatskin, with the hair inside. — STEVENSON
8. A last tremendous crash, a deep-throated grunt, and a mighty moose, a colossal bull, broke out of the woods and stalked stiff-legged toward them through the berry bushes, staring suspiciously from side to side. — MAC-MILLAN

Practice 7.   Creating a Word Picture

In a good sentence or two for each, describe ten of the following. Observe. Use picture-making words.

1. An old house. 2. A new house. 3. A storm at sea. 4. A sea gull in flight. 5. A canoe. 6. A sailboat. 7. A baseball player sliding to second base. 8. An elm tree in a storm. 9. A tramp. 10. A bald head. 11. A thick head of hair. 12. A skinny boy. 13. A fat girl. 14. A rug. 15. A moving picture actor. 16. A moving picture actress. 17. The Prime Minister of Canada. 18. A face in the crowd. 19. A tennis player returning a hard high ball. 20. Grandfather. 21. A lively street corner. 22. A cat watching a bird. 23. Father landing a fish. 24. A boy scoring a touchdown.

DESCRIBING SOUNDS

How many radio voices can you describe? Have you ever listened to your own voice carefully enough to know how it sounds? To describe sounds listen attentively and thoughtfully and then find words which will cause another to hear what you heard.

Practice 8.   Describing Sounds

In a sentence for each describe six voices or sounds. Listen sharply and then choose words which accurately describe what you hear.

Examples:

1. The booms were *tearing* in the blocks, the rudder was *banging* to and fro, and the whole ship was *creaking, groaning,* and jumping like machinery. — STEVENSON

2. In the park to-day I heard the *barking* of a squirrel, the *chattering* of a bluejay, the *chirping* of a cricket, and the *shrill piping* call of a tree-toad.

1. My voice. 2. Father's voice. 3. Mother's voice. 4. A radio voice. 5. Outside the radio store. 6. At a country fair. 7. The school cafeteria. 8. A touchdown. 9. A mouse in the wall. 10. A robin. 11. An airplane propeller. 12. A dilapidated automobile. 13. A streetcar. 14. A home run. 15. A thunder storm. 16. The riveter. 17. Main Street on election night. 18. Victoria Day. 19. The huckster. 20. In the barn. 21. The baby. 22. Our neighbour's dog. 23. In the kitchen. 24. A cat fight. 25 Any other sound or voice you have heard recently.

COMPARING

Often the quickest and most effective way to picture an object or a scene is by the use of an apt, striking comparison or figure of speech. Three common kinds of figures are simile, metaphor, and personification.

A **simile** is a definitely stated comparison of two unlike objects that have one point in common. Regularly *as* or *like* is used to make the comparison.

The grass rustled like silk.
He talks like a dictonary on its best behaviour. — CONCORDIA MERREL

A **metaphor** is an implied comparison between unlike objects that have one point in common. *As* or *like* is not used.

The road was a narrow ribbon unwinding before us.
Everest, cold and imperious monarch of mountains, has repulsed with death man's latest attempt to conquer her.

Personification, a kind of metaphor, assigns personal attributes to inanimate objects or abstract ideas.

The wind shrieked with fury and rained blows on the house.
The waves danced.

For vividness use figures of speech and comparisons. Avoid, however, hackneyed comparisons: "pearly teeth," "old as the hills," "wise as an owl," "good as gold." If you wish to describe an animal your hearers or readers have never seen, compare it with an animal they have seen. Stevenson calls sea lions "huge slimy monsters—soft snails, as it were, of incredible bigness—two or three score of them together, making the rocks to echo with their barkings."

Practice 9.　Comparisons and Figures of Speech

Pick out the effective descriptive words, comparisons, and figures of speech in the following sentences.

1. He was a scraggly bearded individual in a ragged shirt, which offered glimpses of a hairy chest in need of soap. — HENRY SYDNOR HARRISON
2. His voice was like a buzz saw striking a rusty nail. — FOLWELL
3. Captain Cunningham was a great, florid, burly, drunken brute, not less than sixty years old. — S. WEIR MITCHELL
4. He had a strongly cut face and a soft, purring voice.
5. The moaning and howling of the wind outside served to emphasize the coziness and security of our kitchen.
6. The film moves along with the sweeping speed of an overfed caterpillar. — *New York Evening Post*
7. Love is a breath of fresh air from the highest Heaven brought somehow into the stuffy cellar of our existence. — DE MORGAN
8. They were led up a corkscrew staircase to a squat-ceilinged closet lit by the arched top of a high window, the lower panes of which served for the floor below. — EDITH WHARTON
9. On her mouth is a smug, self-satisfied, conceited smile.
10. His face looked as if it were one freckle, and his pug nose loomed up handsomely between a pair of roguishly blue eyes.

Practice 10.　Adding Vivid Details

Add details to make each of the following pictures more vivid:

Examples:

1. We walked along in the rain.
   With the cold raindrops merrily trickling down our backs, we paddled along, entertained by the steady squish-squosh of our rubbers.
2. He was fat and poorly dressed.
   He was a fat, amiable, seedy, down-at-heels looking man.

1. On the table was a dish containing fruit.
2. There are many flowers in the garden.
3. We had a good dinner.
4. Ted has three dogs.
5. Mr. Norton has two cars.
6. Mr. Jeff's home is very attractive.
7. There are several trees in front of our school.
8. The room was disorderly.
9. In the kitchen the cook was preparing dinner.
10. Two birds were sitting on the fence.
11. The trees last fall were beautifully coloured.
12. Last week we had a bad storm.
13. In the woods I heard a number of interesting sounds.
14. In the tree was a nest full of young birds.
15. A giraffe is a queer-looking animal.

OBSERVATION AND SENSE IMPRESSIONS

Without accurate observation there can be no description. Look carefully at details and fix them well in mind. Learn to employ actively the sense of taste, touch, smell, and hearing as well as that of sight, for these five senses furnish all descriptive material. Be an artist gathering material, not an ordinary unobservant person who can't describe accurately from memory his breakfast table, his home, his living room, the face of his watch, or the faces of the members of his family.

Recording a sense impression is painting for your reader the picture of some memorable sense experience. If your mental picture is clear and your word picture vivid, your reader will himself experience that same sense impression. Take for example, this record of a sense impression: "Weather-beaten walls sagged despondently under the weight of overhanging eaves, and a single remaining shutter swung disconsolately on a rusty hinge, creaking dismally." In a sentence the writer has conjured up a picture of an ancient, dilapidated house.

Practice 11. Sense Impressions

In a sentence or two for each, record five sense impressions, one for each sense, suggested by the following. Have a clear picture in mind and choose vivid descriptive words.

Example:

Each wild strawberry as it touched my lips was a drop of nectar and a crumb of ambrosia, a concentrated essence of all the pungent sweetness of the wildwood, sapid, penetrating, and delicious. — VAN DYKE

1. A clover field. 2. The hoot of an owl. 3. A blanket. 4. A street lamp through a mist. 5. Mint leaves. 6. A waterfall. 7. A wild rose bush. 8. A train whistle. 9. A bakery. 10. The bark of a tree. 11. The ocean. 12. A fog horn. 13. A moss-covered stone. 14. Sand. 15. A sea shell. 16. A ripe tomato. 17. A sty full of small pigs. 18. A fire siren. 19. A lump of sugar. 20. A wheat field. 21. A bass drum. 22. A pebble. 23. Ginger ale. 24. Newly mown hay. 25. Coffee.

BREVITY AND ACCURACY

The best description is short and accurate. No one, Flaubert tells us, can write an effective description more than half a printed page in length. Faguet says, "However considerable M. Valois's nose was, a whole page devoted to its description is, I confess, too much for me."

HOW TO PICTURE

(Suggestions 1 and 7 are discussed earlier in the chapter.)

1. Observe. Flaubert says, "Study an object till its essential difference from every other is perceived and can be rendered in words."

316 MASTERING EFFECTIVE ENGLISH

The "seeing eye" and the "hearing ear" are the foundation of good description.

2. Decide whether your description is to be a scientific or a literary one. Do you wish to take a snapshot or, like most artists, emphasize a central idea or feeling, called an impression? The description of an office, for example, may produce the impression of neatness, untidiness, prosperity, system, or confusion.

3. Describe from a favourable point of view. No one sets up his camera and snaps pictures at random. A word painter commonly makes clear at the outset from what point he is viewing the room, building, or landscape. He may, for example, say, "When we had clambered over the last steep rocks to the summit of Whiteface, we sat down to rest and looked first towards the St. Lawrence River," and then picture what he saw from that point. A snapshot of a home taken at noonday from the middle of the street or road in front of it is quite different from a picture of it at dusk or by moonlight from a point a distance away.

When, as in the description of a town or the exterior of a house or school, the point of view is changed, notify the readers of the shift. In "Westminster Abbey," Irving shows a change of point of view in the following sentence: "From Poet's Corner I continued my stroll towards that part of the abbey which contains the sepulchres of the kings."

4. As a rule, present first such a picture or impression as one would get from a glance at the object. The passenger on an express train, for example, notices the size, shape, and colour of the buildings he passes.

5. Decide how many and what details will make your picture most vivid. Select the most striking, interesting, or significant features. If you present every detail observed, you may weary the reader or hearer and also puzzle him, because he will be unable to hold the parts of the picture in mind long enough to put them together. The picture in his mind will resemble a cut-up picture of which some pieces have been lost. In an impressionistic description select the details that give the idea or feeling desired. If you are describing an untidy schoolroom in which the books on one desk are neatly arranged, either picture this desk as a contrast with the rest of the room, or omit it because it does not change the impression of untidiness produced by the room.

6. Arrange details in the order of observation. The first detail observed is the most striking or unusual one. After especially striking details have been presented, the order of observation is commonly the space order: foreground to background, top to bottom, centre to circumference, or right to left.

7. **For vividness use picture-making nouns, verbs, adjectives, and adverbs, figures of speech, and comparisons.** Avoid overworked general words such as *nice, fine, lovely, wonderful, grand,* and *interesting.* Use *very* and superlatives sparingly. "He is honest" is stronger than "He is very honest" or "He is most honest."

8. **Use "signposts."** Such phrases as *on the right, on the extreme right, just beyond, farther along, somewhat lower, in the distance, farther to the left,* and *just in front of* help the mind to put the parts of the picture together.

9. **End the description with a salient detail or with an effective statement of the central feeling or impression.**

ORDER AND ARRANGEMENT

No fixed rule can be laid down, but as already suggested, the commonest arrangement is

General impression on first view.
Details in any number.
General effect after closer scrutiny.

DOMINANT IMPRESSION

We have already learned that a good paragraph requires a key sentence to lead the mind to anticipate what is to come. This topic sentence is then developed to a more complete understanding. So, too, in description, success depends upon a judicious selection of details to maintain a dominant impression favourable or unfavourable. This must be determined before the first sentence is written, and borne in mind throughout the whole of the writing.

Models:

1. MAY IN IRELAND

That was a pleasant drive. May in Ireland! What does it mean? It means coming out of a dark tunnel into blinding sunshine; it means casting off the slough of winter, and gliding with crest erect and fresh habiliments under leafy trees and by the borders of shining seas, the crab-apple blossoms, pink and white, scenting the air over your head, and primroses and violets dappling the turf under your feet; it means lambs frisking around their tranquil mothers in the meadows, and children returning at evening with hands and pinafores full of the scented cowslips and the voluptuous woodbine; it means the pouring of wineblood into empty veins, and the awakening of torpid faculties, and the deeper, stronger pulsations of the heart, and the fresh buoyancy of drooping and submerged spirits, and the white clouds full of bird-music, as the larks call to their young and shake out the raptures of their full hearts, and the cheery salutations of ploughmen, as the coulter turns over the rich, brown soil, and the rooks follow each furrow for food. — SHEEHAN, *My New Curate.*

By permission of the publishers, The Talbot Press Ltd., Dublin.

2. TINK, TINK, TINK

From the workshop of the Golden Key there issued forth a tinkling sound, so merry and good-humoured that it suggested the idea of some one working blithely, and made a pleasant music. *Tink, tink, tink*—clear as a silver bell, and audible at every pause of the street's harsher noises, as though it said, "I don't care; nothing puts me out; I am resolved to be happy."

Women scolded, children squalled, heavy carts went rumbling by, horrible cries proceeded from the lungs of hawkers. Still it struck in again, no higher, no lower, no louder, no softer; not thrusting itself on people's notice a bit the more for having been outdone by louder sounds—*tink, tink, tink, tink, tink.*

It was a perfect embodiment of the still small voice, free from all cold, harshness, huskiness, or unhealthiness of any kind. Foot-passengers slackened their pace, and were disposed to linger near it. Neighbours who had got up splenetic that morning felt good-humour stealing on them as they heard it, and by degrees became quite sprightly. Mothers danced their babies to its ringing—still the same magical *tink, tink, tink,* came gayly from the workshop of the Golden Key. — DICKENS

Practice 12. Dominant Impression

Write a descriptive composition in which one chief impression is dominant. Determine beforehand what that impression is to be. It may be confusion, peace, silence, tranquillity, grandeur, beauty, mystery, fright, comfort, cosiness, joyousness, oddity, ugliness, dullness.

1. A sunset. 2. A sunrise. 3. A mountain valley. 4. A limestone cave. 5. Mirror Lake. 6. Lake Louise. 7. Midnight Lake. 8. Hot summer afternoon. 9. Noon in a hay field. 10. Under the elms. 11. Three o'clock in the morning. 12. A tropical scene. 13. Sunset Bay. 14. Harvest field. 15. A tramp. 16. A pedlar. 17. Your own choice.

A FIXED POINT OF VIEW

A single point of view may be fixed in place (doorway, hilltop, the road, the boat, the garden gate); or it may be a mental point of view (owner, borrower, traveller, stranger, artist, businessman, woman, hermit). We do not see the same things from different places, nor do people of different interests or temperaments see the same thing from the same local point.

Models:

1. NIGHT SOUND

As I thus lay, between content and longing, a faint noise stole towards me through the pines. I thought, at first, it was the crowing of cocks or the barking of dogs at some very distant farm; but steadily and gradually it took articulate shape in my ears, until I became aware that a passenger was going by upon the high-road in the valley, and singing loudly as he went. There was more of good-will than grace in his performance; but he trolled with ample lungs; and the sound of his voice took hold upon the hillside and set the air shaking in the leafy glens. I have heard people passing by night in sleeping cities; some of them sang; one, I remember, played loudly on the bagpipes. I have heard the rattle of a cart or carriage spring up suddenly after hours of stillness, and pass, for some minutes, within the range of my hearing as I lay abed. There is a romance about all who are abroad in the black hours, and with something of a thrill we try to guess their business. But here the romance was double; first, this glad passenger, lit internally with wine, who sent up his voice in music through the night; and then I, on the other hand, buckled into my sack, and smoking alone in the pine-woods between four and five thousand feet toward the stars. — ROBERT LOUIS STEVENSON, *Travels with a Donkey.*

By permission of Charles Scribner's Sons, New York.

2. THE PASS OF FUENCEBADON

It is impossible to describe this pass or the circumjacent region, which contains some of the most extraordinary scenery in all Spain; a feeble and imperfect outline is all that I can hope to effect. The traveller who ascends it follows for nearly a league the course of the torrent, whose banks are in some places precipitous, and in others slope down to the waters, and are covered with lofty trees, oaks, poplars, and chestnuts. Small villages are at first continually seen, with low walls, and roofs formed of immense slates, the eaves nearly touching the ground; these hamlets, however, gradually become less frequent as the path grows more steep and narrow, until they finally cease at a short distance before the spot is attained where the rivulet is abandoned, and is no more seen, though its tributaries may yet be heard in many a gully, or descried in tiny rills dashing down the steeps. Everything here is wild, strange, and beautiful; the hill up which winds the path towers above on the right, whilst on the farther side of a profound ravine rises an immense mountain, to whose extreme altitudes the eye is scarcely able to attain, but the most singular feature of this pass are the hanging fields or meadows which cover its sides. In these, as I passed, the grass was growing luxuriantly, and in many the mowers were plying their scythes, though it seemed scarcely possible that their feet could find support on ground so precipitous: above and below were driftways, so small as to seem threads along the mountain side. A car, drawn by oxen, is creeping round yon airy eminence; the nearer wheel is actually hanging over the horrid descent; giddiness seizes the brain, and the eye is rapidly withdrawn. A cloud intervenes, and when again you turn to watch their progress, the objects of your anxiety have disappeared. Still more narrow comes the path along which you yourself are toiling, and its turns more frequent. You have already come a distance of two leagues, and still one-third of the ascent remains unsurmounted. — GEORGE BORROW, *The Bible in Spain.*

3. PRAIRIE HUSH

Nature was asleep. Not a breath rustled the drooping leaves or fanned the heated brow; not a chirp relieved the silence which was enhanced by the drowsy hum of the mysterious insect life. From my seat beneath a shady bush I gazed out over a wide, gently-rolling expanse of prairie backed in the distance by a dark line of trees, bluish in the heat haze which spread a delicate, gauzy film of transparent blue over distant objects. Far across the plain a flash of silver proclaimed the thread of a brook winding its glittering way between grassy banks to the river. The wavering heat-waves rising from the overheated prairie distorted and gave fantastic shapes to the solitary cattle that still persisted in grazing after their companions had sought refuge in the shade from the fiery sun. Their red and white hides gave an added note of colour to the scene which was bathed in the golden glory of the sunlight. The scene was devoid of other life save for a hawk which sailed majestically on "wings unweary" high up in the blue vault of heaven. Ever and anon its cry would come sifting faintly down to earth emphasizing the afternoon silence which had enveloped us in its all-embracing folds. And thus nature slept on that drowsy afternoon. — Pupil

4. I STOOD TIP-TOE UPON A LITTLE HILL

I stood tip-toe upon a little hill,
The air was cooling, and so very still
That the sweet buds which with a modest pride
Pull droopingly, in slanting curve aside,
Their scantly leav'd, and finely tapering stems,
Had not yet lost those starry diadems
Caught from the early sobbing of the morn.
The clouds were pure and white as flocks new shorn,
And fresh from the clear brook; sweetly they slept
On the blue fields of heaven, and then there crept
A little noiseless noise among the leaves,
Born of the very sigh that silence heaves:
For not the faintest motion could be seen
Of all the shades that slanted o'er the green.
There was wide wandering for the greediest eye,
To peer about upon variety;
Far round the horizon's crystal air to skim,
And trace the dwindling edgings to its brim;
To picture out the quaint, and curious bending
Of a fresh woodland alley, never ending;
Or by the bowery clefts, and leafy shelves,
Guess where the jaunty streams refresh themselves.
— John Keats

Practice 13.   Point of View

In writing on the following topics, keep in mind the value of picture words, vital observation, and dominant impression. Write three descriptions based on three of the following themes, making the local point of view clear to the reader. Choose the most effective place, or person.

1. Our summer camp. 2. A city park. 3. The old swimming hole. 4. The old mill. 5. Woodland scene. 6. Prairie landscape. 7. January morning. 8. The bridge. 9. The orchard. 10. The sentinel tree. 11. The caravan.

Practice 14. Points of View

Write three paragraphs of description, each one of the same object, seen by three different persons:

1. The valley (hunter, lumberman, artist). 2. The hotel (beggar, architect, guest). 3. The lake (fisherman, discoverer, poet). 4. The school (freshman, teacher, alumnus). 5. The monument (tourist, next of kin, sculptor).

Alberta Travel Bureau

There are almost as many reactions to any scene as there are people who see it. Even a beach may be used for many different activities.

A CHANGING POINT OF VIEW

Description is seldom used in literary writing except as part of the narrative structure. In consequence it is frequently narrative in form, a series of brief pictures at various times, and often in different places. The secret of success in this running description is to keep the reader clear where the scene has shifted in time or place, and to make keen, crisp observations, not so much detailed as etched with deft strokes, a succession of bright miniatures.

Models:
1. THE VALLEY OF THE TARN
The valley below La Vernède pleased me more and more as I went along. Now the hills approached from either hand, naked and crumbling, and walled

in the river between cliffs; and now the valley widened and became green. The road led me past the old castle of Miral on a steep; past a battlemented monastery, long since broken up and turned into a church and parsonage; and past a cluster of black roofs, the village of Cocurès, sitting among vine-lands, and meadows, and orchards thick with red apples, and where, along the highway, they were knocking down walnuts from the roadside trees, and gathering them in sacks and baskets. The hills, however much the vale might open, were still tall and bare, with cliffy battlements and here and there a pointed summit; and the Tarn still rattled through the stones with a mountain noise. I had been led, by bagmen of a picturesque turn of mind, to expect a horrific country after the heart of Byron; but to my Scottish eyes it seemed smiling and plentiful, as the weather still gave an impression of high summer to my Scottish body; although the chestnuts were already picked out by the autumn, and the poplars, that here began to mingle with them, had turned into pale gold against the approach of winter. — ROBERT LOUIS STEVENSON, *Travels with a Donkey.*

By permission of Charles Scribner's Sons, New York.

2. UNDERN HALL

Undern Hall, with its many small-paned windows, faced the north sullenly. It was a place of which the influence and magic were not good. Even in May when the lilacs frothed into purple, paved the lawn with shadows, steeped the air with scent; when soft leaves lipped each other consolingly; when blackbirds sang, fell in their effortless way from the green height to the green depth, and sang again—still, something that haunted the place set the heart fluttering. No place is its own, and that which is most stained with old tumults has the strongest fascination.

So at Undern, whatever had happened there went on still; someone who had been there was there still. The lawns under the trees were mournful with old pain, or with vanished joys more pathetic than pain in their fleeting mimicry of immortality.

It was only at midsummer that the windows were coloured by dawn and sunset; then they had a sanguinary aspect, staring into the delicate skyey dramas like blind, bloodshot eyes. Secretly, under the heavy rhododendron leaves and in the furtive sunlight beneath the yew-trees, gnats danced. Their faint motions made the garden stiller; their smallness made it oppressive; their momentary life made it infinitely old. Then Undern Pool was full of leaf shadows like multitudinous lolling tongues, and the smell of the mud tainted the air—half sickly, half sweet. The clipped bushes and the twisted chimneys made inky shadows like steeples on the grass, and great trees of roses beautiful in desolation, dripped with red and white and elbowed the guelder roses and the elders set with white patens. Cherries fell in the orchard with the same rich monotony, the same fatality, as drops of blood. They lay under the fungus-riven trees till the hens ate them, pecking gingerly and enjoyably at their lustrous beauty as the world does at a poet's heart. In the kitchen-garden also the hens took their ease, banqueting sparely beneath the straggling black boughs of a red-currant grove. In the sandstone walls of this garden hornets built undisturbed, and the thyme and lavender borders had grown into forests and obliterated the path. The cattle drowsed in the meadows, birds in the heavy trees; the golden day-lilies drooped like the daughters of pleasure; the very principle of life seemed to slumber. It was then, when the scent of elder blossom, decaying fruit, mud and hot yew brooded there, that the place attained one of its most individual moods— narcotic, aphrodisiac.

In winter the yews and firs were like waving funeral plumes and mantled, headless goddesses; then the giant beeches would lash themselves to frenzy, and, stooping, would scourge the ice on Undern Pool and the cracked walls of the house, like beings drunken with the passion of cruelty. This was the second mood of Undern—brutality. Then those within were, it seemed, already in the grave, heavily covered with the prison frost and snow, or shouted into silence by the wind. On a January night the house seemed to lie outside time and space; slow, ominous movement began beyond the blind windows, and the inflexible softness of snow, blurred on the vast background of night, buried summer ever deeper with invincible, caressing threats.
— MARY WEBB, *Gone to Earth.*

By arrangement with the publishers, Jonathan Cape, Limited, Toronto.

3. THE SONG MY PADDLE SINGS

August is laughing across the sky,
Laughing while paddle, canoe, and I,
Drift, drift,
Where the hills uplift
On either side of the current swift.

The river rolls in its rocky bed;
My paddle is plying its way ahead;
Dip, dip,
While the waters flip
In foam as over their breast we slip.

And oh, the river runs swifter now,
The eddies circle about my bow!
Swirl, swirl!
How the ripples curl
In many a dangerous pool awhirl!

And forward far the rapids roar,
Fretting their margin for evermore.
Dash, dash,
With a mighty crash,
They seeth, and boil, and bound, and splash.

Be strong, O paddle! be brave, canoe!
The reckless waves you must plunge into.
Reel, reel,
On your trembling keel,—
But never a fear my craft will feel.

We've raced the rapid, we're far ahead!
The river slips through its silent bed.
Sway, sway,
As the bubbles spray
And fall in tinkling tunes away.

— E. PAULINE JOHNSON.

From Flint and Feather, *published and copyrighted by The Musson Book Company Ltd., Toronto.*

Alberta Government Photograph

The burn-off from an oil well produces a dramatic scene. Consider what the scene would be like at night.

Practice 15. Changing Point of View

Describe a scene from two or more points of view, keeping the reader clearly aware of each change.

1. The river drive. 2. The castle (inside and out). 3. The stadium (near and far). 4. A tour of the city (waterfront, lake side, beach). 5. The park. 6. The steamer. 7. The streamlined train. 8. The river-bank (spring, summer, autumn, winter). 9. A masquerader (before and after the unmasking). 10. The church (you saw it building and completed). 11. The duck's nest (bird on; bird off, eggs uncovered; bird off, eggs covered). 12. The oriole's nest (from the ground, at closer view). 13. A swarm of bees (swarming, gathered on a branch). 14. The nursery garden (spring, summer, autumn).

ACTION

When possible, describe in action. For pure description the action should be limited to a moment. Commonly, however, the short story and the novel, like the moving picture, combine story and picture so closely and effectively that it is both difficult and useless to separate the description from the narration.

Practice 16. Studying Action Picture

1. What impression does the following selection from Anthony Gibb's *Peter Vacuum* produce?
2. What words vividly describe sights?
3. What words describe sounds?
4. What action is pictured?

The saxophone reared its brazen head in the air, swayed like some sort of gleaming python intoxicated by the charmer's pipe, sent an excruciating whinny reeling across the room, and squirted a little spout of sucking chuckles to gibber in its wake. A very fat man, with his plump cheeks creased by the thin end of this infernal machine, sent an inspired blast of carbon dioxide roaring through its sweating innards, which, being wrought on by his pudgy fingers, issued forth in the form of weird moans, choking coughs, dyspeptic sighs, and the bleating of lambs.

"It hadda be yew," tittered the violinist through the megaphone.

And the banjos thrummed eternally, and a lean man with india rubber fingers hurled himself at the piano until it squeaked at the violence of his onslaught, or rippled over its placid surface in a rush of twitterings, as if all the sparrows in London had gone suddenly mad, and the saxophone hoicked, and the drum throbbed its insinuating rhythm, and the violin shrieked like a soul in pain, and all the demons in hell swayed to this diabolical syncopation of demented monsters lumbering through fetid swamps; and the pulsing agony became more and more insistent with the last verse, and the music mounted up and up, modulating through penetrating quarter tones that have no place in a printed score, and the time became more and more fantastically distorted, and the cornet lifted up his voice to heaven and let forth a cry of vengeance, until, with a crash of cymbals, and a last howling discord, the band laid down their instruments with every appearance of haste, and disappeared through a small door in the back.[1]

[1]*Reprinted by permission of the Dial Press.*

Models:

BANK HOLIDAY

A crowd collects, eating oranges and bananas, tearing off the skins, dividing, sharing. One young girl has even a basket of strawberries, but she does not eat them. "Aren't they *dear!*" She stares at the tiny pointed fruits as if she were afraid of them. The Australian soldier laughs. "Here, go on, there's not more than a mouthful." But he doesn't want her to eat them, either. He likes to watch her little frightened face, and her puzzled eyes lifted to his: "Aren't they a *price!*" He pushes out his chest and grins. Old fat women in velvet bodices—old dusty pin-cushions—lean old hags like worn umbrellas with a quivering bonnet on top; young women, in muslins, with hats that might have grown on hedges, and high pointed shoes; men in khaki, sailors, shabby clerks, young Jews in fine cloth suits with padded shoulders and wide trousers, "hospital boys" in blue—the sun discovers them—the loud, bold music holds them together in one big knot for a moment. The young ones are larking, pushing each other on and off the pavement, dodging, nudging; the old ones are talking: "So I said to 'im, if you wants the doctor to yourself, fetch 'im, says I."

"An' by the time they was cooked there wasn't so much as you could put in the palm of me 'and!"

The only ones who are quiet are the ragged children. They stand, as close up to the musicians as they can get, their hands behind their backs, their eyes big. Occasionally a leg hops, an arm wags. A tiny staggerer, overcome, turns round twice, sits down solemn, and then gets up again.

"Ain't it lovely?" whispers a small girl behind her hand.

And the music breaks into bright pieces, and joins together again, and again breaks, and is dissolved, and the crowd scatters, moving slowly up the hill.

At the corner of the road the stalls begin.

"Ticklers! Tuppence a tickler! 'Ool 'ave a tickler? Tickle 'em up, boys." Little soft brooms on wire handles. They are eagerly bought by the soldiers.

"Buy a golliwog! Tuppence a golliwog!"

"Buy a jumping donkey! All alive-oh!"

"*Su*-perior chewing gum. Buy something to do, boys."

"Buy a rose. Give 'er a rose, boy. Roses, lady!"

"Fevvers! Fevvers!" They are hard to resist. Lovely, streaming feathers, emerald green, scarlet, bright blue, canary yellow. Even the babies wear feathers threaded through their bonnets.

And an old woman in a three-cornered paper hat cries as if it were her final parting advice, the only way of saving yourself or of bringing him to his senses: "Buy a three-cornered 'at, my dear, an' put it on!"

It is a flying day, half sun, half wind. When the sun goes in, a shadow flies over; when it comes out again it is fiery. The men and women feel it burning their backs, their breasts and their arms; they feel their bodies expanding, coming alive . . . so that they make large embracing gestures, lift up their arms, for nothing, swoop down on a girl, blurt into laughter.

Lemonade! A whole tank of it stands on a table covered with a cloth; and lemons like blunted fishes blob in the yellow water. It looks solid, like a jelly, in the thick glasses. Why can't they drink it without spilling it? Everybody spills it, and before the glass is handed back the last drops are thrown in a ring.

Round the ice-cream cart, with its striped awning and bright brass cover, the children cluster. Little tongues lick, lick round the cream trumpets, round the squares. The cover is lifted, the wooden spoon plunges in; one shuts one's eyes to feel it, silently scrunching. — KATHERINE MANSFIELD, "Bank Holiday" from *The Garden Party and Other Stories*

By permission of the author's literary agents, Messrs. James B. Pinker & Son.

THE PIED PIPER'S MUSIC

Once more he stept into the street
    And to his lips again
    Laid his long pipe of smooth straight cane;
And ere he blew three notes (such sweet,
Soft notes as yet musician's cunning
    Never gave the enraptured air)
There was a rustling that seemed like a bustling
Of merry crowds justling at pitching and hustling,
Small feet were pattering, wooden shoes clattering,
Little hands clapping and little tongues chattering,
And, like fowls in a farm-yard when barley is scattering
Out came the children running.
All the little boys and girls,
With rosy cheeks and flaxen curls,
And sparkling eyes and teeth like pearls,
Tripping and skipping, ran merrily after
The wonderful music with shouting and laughter.

— ROBERT BROWNING, *The Pied Piper of Hamelin*

Practice 17. Action Shots

Describe one or more still scenes or scenes with action in them. Limit the action to a moment. Your purpose is to paint a picture in colours, not to tell a story. If you select a topic like number 1, describe both sights and sounds.

1. An election night scene. 2. At the beach. 3. An exciting moment in a play, a moving picture, or real life. 4. The subway or a streetcar at rush hour. 5. The bargain counter. 6. The bleachers after the home run. 7. A busy office or street corner. 8. Harvesting wheat. 9. The crowd coming from a factory. 10. A wedding. 11. A market scene. 12. The toy department just before Christmas. 13. A fire scene. 14. A storm on the lake, river, or ocean. 15. A street parade. 16. A humorous scene. 17. A country fair. 18. My favourite view. 19. A farmyard. 20. A back yard. 21. The garden. 22. Main Street on Saturday night. 23. Ten minutes before the bell rang. 24. Three minutes after the game ended. 25. The crowd waiting for a parade. 26. When the five o'clock whistle blows. 27. A study in colour. 28. A banquet. 29. A political meeting. 30. A stage spectacle. 31. A fight.

LANDSCAPE—STILL SCENES

In description of scenery you have a fine opportunity to choose dominant effects and to describe sound and colour. Study the models for arrangement, tones, diction. Notice the guide words with which positions are marked.

Models:

1. EVENING ON THE HUDSON

The sun gradually wheeled his broad disk down into the west. The wide bosom of the Tappan Zee lay motionless and glassy, excepting that here and there a gentle undulation waved and prolonged the blue shadow of the distant mountain. A few amber clouds floated in the sky, without a breath of air to move them. The horizon was of a fine golden tint, changing gradually into a pure apple green, and from that into the deep blue of the mid-heaven. A slanting ray lingered on the woody crests of the precipices that overhung some parts of the river, giving greater depth to the dark gray and purple of their rocky sides. A sloop was loitering in the distance, dropping slowly down with the tide, her sail hanging uselessly against the mast; and as the reflection of the sky gleamed along the still water, it seemed as if the vessel was suspended in the air. — IRVING, *Legend of Sleepy Hollow*

2. DEDLOW MARSH

The vocal expression of the Dedlow Marsh was also melancholy and depressing. The sepulchral boom of the bittern, the shriek of the curlew, the scream of passing brant, the wrangling of quarrelsome teal, the sharp, querulous protest of the startled crane, the syllabled complaint of the "killdeer" plover were beyond the power of written expression. Nor was the aspect of these mournful fowls at all cheerful and inspiring. Certainly not the blue heron standing midleg deep in the water, obviously catching cold in a reckless disregard of wet feet and consequences; nor the mournful curlew, the dejected plover, or the low-spirited snipe, who saw fit to join him in his suicidal contemplation; nor the impassive kingfisher, reviewing the desolate expanse; nor the black raven that went to and fro over the face of the marsh continually, but evidently couldn't make up his mind whether the waters had subsided and felt low-spirited in the reflection that, after all this trouble, he wouldn't be able to give a definite answer. On the contrary it was evident at a glance that the dreary expanse of Dedlow Marsh told unpleasantly on the birds, and that the season of migration was looked forward to with a feeling of relief and satisfaction by the full-grown, and of extravagant anticipation by the callow brood.

But if Dedlow Marsh was cheerless at the slack of the low tide, you should have seen it when the tide was strong and full. When the damp air blew chilly over the cold, glittering expanse, and came to the faces of those who looked seaward like another tide; when a steel-like glint marked the low hollows and the sinuous line of slough; when the great shell-encrusted trunks of fallen trees arose again, and went forth on their dreary, purposeless wanderings, drifting hither and thither; when the glossy ducks swung silently, making neither ripple nor furrow on the shimmering surface; when the fog came in with the tide and shut out the blue above, even as the green below had been obliterated; when boatmen, lost in that fog, paddling about in a hopeless way, started at what seemed the brushing of mermen's fingers on the boat's keel, or shrank from the tufts of grass spreading around, and knew by these signs that they were lost upon Dedlow Marsh, and must make a night of it, and a gloomy one at that,—then you might know something of Dedlow Marsh at high water. — BRET HARTE, *High-Water Mark.*

By arrangement with the publishers, Houghton Mifflin Company, Boston.

3. A CALM ON A SCOTCH LOCH

The lake lies stilled in sleep, reflecting every isle and every tree along the shore, its bright plain dimmed here and there by faint breezes, that remain each in its place with singular constancy, as if invisible angels hovered over the waters and breathed upon them here and there. And under the dark mountain what a dark unfathomable calm! What utter repose and peace! It is incredible that ever wind blew there, and though but yesterday this shining liquid plain was covered with ten thousand crested waves, and countless squalls struck it over like swooping eagles flying from every quarter of the heavens, it lies so calmly to-day in its deep bed, that one cannot help believing, in spite of all evidence, that thus it has been from the foundation of the world, and thus it shall be forever and forever!

The hills are clothed with purple, slashed with green. The sky is not cloudless, but the clouds move so languidly that their slowness of movement is more expressive of indolence than the uttermost stony stillness. Like great ships on a rippling sea, with all their white sails spread, they float imperceptibly westwards, as though they had eternity to voyage in. And just under them, in blinding light, behold the shining crests of snow. — HAMERTON, *A Painter's Camp*

4. EVENING

From upland slopes I see the cows file by,
Lowing, great-chested, down the homeward trail,
By dusking fields and meadows shining pale
With moon-tipped dandelions. Flickering high,
A peevish night-hawk in the western sky
Beats up into the lucent solitudes,
Or drops with griding wing. The stilly woods
Grow dark and deep, and gloom mysteriously.
Cool night winds creep, and whisper in mine ear;
The homely cricket gossips at my feet.
From far-off pools and wastes of reeds I hear,
Clear and soft-piped, the chanting frogs break sweet
In full Pandean chorus. One by one
Shine out the stars, and the great night comes on.
— ARCHIBALD LAMPMAN, *Lyrics of Earth.*

Published and copyrighted by The Musson Book Company Ltd., Toronto.

Practice 18.

1. Choose another topic from Practice 12 (page 318) and write upon it.

2. Write upon one of the following. Use clear guide and "echo" words; make sure of the dominant impression.

1. The park after a wet clinging snow. 2. The same on a crisp, biting day in mid-winter. 3. A scene along the river. 4. My favourite view. 5. A landscape you have seen on a holiday excursion. 6. Castle Mountain (or another). 7. Scene from a mountain side. 8. Level prairie. 9. Our favourite hunting marsh. 10. Among the pines. 11. On the silver beach. 12. From the lake. 13. From my bedroom window. 14. The bad lands.

NATURE IN MOVEMENT

With the introduction of movement there is also the introduction of time usually, so that in this kind of description there will probably be—and it is quite proper that there should be—an introduction of narrative. All that is desirable is that we should know whether it has been done, whether we wish to do it.

Model:

1. A THUNDER STORM

Soon the stars are hidden. A light breeze seems rather to tremble and hang poised than to blow. The rolling clouds, the dark wilderness, and the watery waste shine out every moment in the wide gleam of lightnings still hidden by the wood, and are wrapped again in ever-thickening darkness over which thunders roll and jar and answer one another across the sky. Then, like the charge of ten thousand lancers, come the wind and the rain, their onset covered by all the artillery of heaven. The lightnings leap, hiss, and blaze; the thunders crack and roar; the rain lashes; the waters writhe; the wind smites and howls. For five, for ten, for twenty minutes—for an hour, for two hours—the sky and the flood are never for an instant wholly dark, or the thunder for one moment silent; but while the universal roar sinks and swells, and the wide, vibrant illumination shows all things in ghostly half-concealment, fresh floods of lightning every moment rend the dim curtain and leap forth; the glare of day falls upon the swaying wood, the reeling bowing, tossing willows, the seething waters, the whirling rain, and in the midst the small form of the distressed steamer, her revolving paddle-wheels toiling behind to lighten the strain upon her anchor chains; then all are dim ghosts again, while a peal, as if the heavens were rent, rolls off around the sky, comes back in shocks and throbs, and sinks in a long roar that before it can die is swallowed up in the next flash and peal. — GEORGE W. CABLE, *Bonaventure.*

By permission of Charles Scribner's Sons, New York.

2. CANADIAN NIAGARA

But there they change. As they turn to the sheer descent, the white and blue and slate-colour, in the heart of the Canadian Falls at least, blend and deepen to a rich, wonderful, luminous green. On the edge of disaster the river seems to gather herself, to pause, to lift a head noble in ruin, and then, with a slow grandeur, to plunge into the eternal thunder and white chaos below. Where the stream runs shallower it is a kind of violet colour, but both violet and green fray and frill to white as they fall. The mass of water, striking some ever-hidden base of rock, leaps up the whole two hundred feet again in pinnacles and domes of spray. The spray falls back into the lower river once more; all but a little that fines to foam and white mist, which drifts in layers along the air, graining it, and wanders out on the wind over the trees and gardens and houses, and so vanishes. — RUPERT BROOKE, *Niagara Falls*, from *Letters from America.*

By permission of the author's representatives and of the publishers, Sidgwick & Jackson Ltd., London

3. THUNDER AND LIGHTNING

A light flapped over the scene, as if reflected from phosphorescent wings crossing the sky, and a rumble filled the air. It was the first arrow from the approaching storm, and it fell wide.

The second peal was noisy, with comparatively little visible lightning. Gabriel saw a candle shining in Bathsheba's bedroom, and soon a shadow moved to and fro upon the blind.

Then there came a third flash. Manoeuvres of a most extraordinary kind were going on in the vast firmamental hollows overhead. The lightning now was the colour of silver, and gleamed in the heavens like a mailed army. Rumbles became rattles. Gabriel from his elevated position could see over the landscape for at least half a dozen miles in front. Every hedge, bush, and tree was distinct as in a line engraving. In a paddock in the same direction was a herd of heifers, and the forms of these were visible at this moment in the act of galloping about in the wildest and maddest confusion, flinging their heels and tails high into the air, their head to earth. A poplar in the immediate foreground was like an ink-stroke on burnished tin. Then the picture vanished, leaving a darkness so intense that Gabriel worked entirely by feeling with his hands.

He had struck his ricking-rod, or poniard, as it was indifferently called— a long iron lance, sharp at the extremity and polished by handling—into the stack to support the sheaves. A blue light appeared in the zenith, and in some indescribable manner flickered down near the top of the rod. It was the fourth of the larger flashes. A moment later and there was a smack—smart, clear, and short. Gabriel felt his position to be anything but a safe one, and he resolved to descend.

Not a drop of rain had fallen as yet. He wiped his weary brow, and looked again at the black forms of the unprotected stacks. Was his life so valuable to him, after all? What were his prospects that he should be so chary of running risk, when important and urgent labour could not be carried on without such risk? He resolved to stick to the stack. However, he took a precaution. Under the staddles was a long tethering chain, used to prevent the escape of errant horses. This he carried up the ladder, and sticking his rod through the clog at one end, allowed the other end of the chain to trail upon the ground. The spike attached to it he drove in. Under the shadow of this extemporized lightning conductor he felt himself comparatively safe.

Before Oak had laid his hands upon his tools again, out leaped the fifth flash, with the spring of a serpent and the shout of a fiend. It was as green as an emerald, and the reverberation was stunning. What was this the light revealed to him? In the open ground before him, as he looked over the ridge of the rick, was a dark and apparently female form. Could it be that of the only venturesome woman in the parish—Bathsheba? The form moved on a step; then he could see no more.

"Is that you, ma'am?" said Gabriel, to the darkness.

"Who is there?" said the voice of Bathsheba.

"Gabriel. I am on the rick, thatching."

"Oh, Gabriel!—and are you? . . . Can I do anything to help? Liddy is afraid to come out. Fancy finding you here at such an hour! Surely I can do something?"

"You can bring up some reed-sheaves to me, one by one, ma'am, if you are not afraid to come up the ladder in the dark," said Gabriel. "Every moment is precious now, and that would save a good deal of time. It is not very dark when the lightning has been gone a bit."

"I'll do anything," she said resolutely. She instantly took a sheaf upon her shoulder, clambered up close to his heels, placed it behind the rod, and descended for another. At her third ascent the rick suddenly brightened with the brazen glare of shining majolica—every knot in every straw was visible. On the slope in front of him appeared two human shapes, black as jet. The rick lost its sheen—the shapes vanished. Gabriel turned his head. It had been the sixth flash which had come from the east behind him, and the two dark forms on the slope had been the shadows of himself and Bathsheba.

Then came the peal. It hardly was credible that such a heavenly light could be the parent of such a diabolical sound. "How terrible!" she exclaimed and clutched him by the sleeve. Gabriel turned, and steadied her on her aerial perch by holding her arm. At the same moment, while he was still reversed in his attitude, there was more light, and he saw as it were a copy of the tall poplar tree on the hill drawn in black on the wall of the barn. It was the shadow of that tree thrown across by a secondary flash in the west.

The next flare came. Bathsheba was on the ground now, shouldering another sheaf, and she bore its dazzle without flinching—thunder and all—and again ascended with the load. There was then a silence everywhere for four or five minutes, and the crunch of the spars as Gabriel hastily drove them in, could be distinctly heard again. He thought the crisis of the storm had passed. But there came a burst of light. "Hold on!" said Gabriel, taking the sheaf from her shoulder and grasping her arm again.

Heaven opened then, indeed. The flash was almost too novel for its inexpressibly dangerous nature to be at once realized, and Gabriel could only comprehend the magnificence of its beauty. It sprang from east, west, north, south. It was a perfect dance of death. The forms of skeletons appeared in the air, shaped with blue fire for bones—dancing, leaping, striding, racing around and mingling altogether in unparalleled confusion. With these were intertwined undulating snakes of green. Behind these was a broad mass of lesser light. Simultaneously came from every part of the tumbling sky what may be called a shout; since, though no shout ever came near it, it was more of the nature of a shout than of anything else earthly. In the meantime one of the grisly forms had alighted upon the point of Gabriel's rod, to run invisibly down it, down the chain, and into the earth. Gabriel was almost blinded, and he could feel Bathsheba's warm arm tremble in his hand—a sensation novel and thrilling enough: but love, life, everything human seemed small and trifling in such juxtaposition with an infuriated universe. — THOMAS HARDY, *Far From The Madding Crowd.*

By arrangement with the publishers, The Macmillan Company of Canada, Ltd.

Practice 19.   Nature in Movement

Describe vividly one of the following scenes. Strive to achieve the distinction of style of Hardy's writing. Etch every picture with clear, accurate strokes.

1. A thunderstorm on the prairies. 2. A thunderstorm in the mountains. 3. A cyclone. 4. A dust storm. 5. A hail storm. 6. The blizzard. 7. A wind at the lake. 8. A squall on the lake (on the sea). 9. Remarkable cloud effects 10. An unusual whirlwind. 11. A field of waving wheat. 12. Cloud galleons. 13. Birches (elms, maples, poplars, oaks) in the gale. 14. A gentle fall of snow. 15. Landscape in the rain. 16. A Scotch mist. 17. A drizzly day.

Practice 20.

Using the model "A Calm on a Scotch Loch" page 329, write a description on one of the themes in Practice 18 or 19 giving by contrast the same scene in a moment of quiet and again in motion or commotion. Work the contrast in your account as skilfully as Hamerton has done.

OBJECTS OF NATURE, AND OTHERS

Picture-making words, and phrases that live are the main concern in the description of most objects. Apart from scientific description, these have little value unless informed with beauty, grace, sentiment, human association, or reflected human emotions. We should be led to admire, to resent, to condemn, to love, to desire these objects. They must rouse our feelings.

1. THE BULL-FINCH'S NEST

Once I found a bull-finch's nest in a rosebush. It looked like a pink shell holding four blue pearls. Nodding over it hung a rose heavy with dew-drops. The male bull-finch, motionless, stood guard on a neighbouring shrub, like a flower of azure and purple. These objects were mirrored in a glassy pool, with the reflection of a walnut tree for background, behind which was to be seen the light of dawn. God gave me in that little picture an idea of the loveliness with which he has clothed nature. — CHATEAUBRIAND

2. BIRCHES IN THE BREEZE

See the silver birch in a breeze; here it swells, there it scatters, and it is puffed to a round and it streams like a pennon; and now gives the glimpse and shine of the white stem's line within, now hurries over it, denying that it was visible, with a chatter along the sweeping folds, while still the white peeps through. — GEORGE MEREDITH, *The Egoist.*

By permission of the publishers, Constable & Company Limited, London.

3. THE HERON

Pale, shimmering green, and soaked in sun, the miles of sedge-flats lay outspread from the edges of the slow bright water to the foot of the far, dark-wooded, purple hills. Winding through the quiet green levels came a tranquil little stream. Where its sleepy current joined the great parent river, a narrow tongue of bare sand jutted out into the golden-glowing water. At the extreme tip of the sand-pit towered, sentry-like, a long-legged gray-blue bird, as motionless as if he had been transplanted thither from the panel of a Japanese screen.

The flat narrow head of the great heron, with its long, javelin-like, yellow beak and two slender black crest-feathers, was drawn far back by a curious undulation of the immensely long neck, till it rested between the humped blue wing-shoulders. From the lower part of the neck hung a fine fringe of vaporous rusty-gray plumes, which lightly veiled the chestnut-coloured breast. The bird might have seemed asleep, like the drowsy expanses of green sedge, silver-blue water, and opalescent turquoise sky, but for its eyes. Those eyes, round, unwinking, of a hard, glassy gold with intense black pupils, were unmistakable and savagely wide awake. — CHARLES G. D. ROBERTS, *Neighbours Unknown.*

By permission of the publishers, The Macmillan Company of Canada Limited.

4. PORTRAIT OF RAB

I wish you could have seen him. There are no such dogs now. He belonged to a lost tribe. As I have said, he was brindled and gray like Rubislaw granite; his hair short, hard and close, like a lion's; his body thick-set, like a bull—a sort of compressed Hercules of a dog. He must have been ninety pounds' weight, at the least; he had a large, blunt head; his muzzle black as night, his mouth blacker than any night, a tooth or two—being all he had—gleaming out of his jaws of darkness. His head was scarred with the record of old wounds, a sort of series of fields of battle all over it; one eye out, one ear cropped off as close as was Archbishop Leighton's father's; the remaining eye had the power of two; and above it, and in constant communication with it, was the tattered rag of an ear, which was forever unfurling itself like an old flag; and then that bud of a tail, about one inch long, if it could in any sense be said to be long, being as broad as long—the mobility, the instantaneousness of that bud was very funny and surprising, and its expressive twinklings and winkings, the intercommunication between the eye, the ear and it, were of the oddest and swiftest.

Rab had the dignity and simplicity of great size, and having fought his way all along the road to absolute supremacy, he was as mighty in his own line as Julius Caesar or the Duke of Wellington, and had the gravity of all great fighters.

You must have often observed the likeness of certain men to certain animals, and of certain dogs to men. Now I never looked at Rab without thinking of the great Baptist preacher, Andrew Fuller. The same large, heavy, menacing, combative, sombre, honest countenance, the same deep, inevitable eye, the same look—as of thunder asleep, but ready; neither a dog nor a man to be trifled with. — JOHN BROWN, *Rab and His Friends.*

5. GUNPOWDER

The animal he bestrode was a broken-down plough-horse, that had outlived almost everything but his viciousness. He was gaunt and shagged, with a ewe neck and a head like a hammer; his rusty mane and tail were tangled and knotted with burrs; one eye had lost its pupil, and was glaring and spectral; but the other had the gleam of a genuine devil in it. Still he must have had fire and mettle in his day, if we may judge from the name he bore, of Gunpowder. He had, in fact, been a favourite steed of his master's, the choleric Van Ripper, who was a furious rider, and had infused, very probably, some of his own spirit into the animal; for, old and broken-down as he looked, there was more of the lurking devil in him than in any young filly in the country. — WASHINGTON IRVING, *Sketch-Book*.

6. THE COLLAR OF PRESTER JOHN

The priest raised the necklace till it shone above his head like a halo of blood. I have never seen such a jewel, and I think there has never been another such on earth. Later I was to have the handling of it, and could examine it closely, though now I had only a glimpse. There were fifty-five rubies in it, the largest as big as a pigeon's egg, and the least not smaller than my thumb-nail. In shape they were oval, cut on both sides *en cabochon*, and on each certain characters were engraved. No doubt this detracted from their value as gems, yet the characters might have been removed and the stones cut in facets, and these rubies would still have been the noblest in the world. I was no jewel merchant to guess their value, but I knew enough to see that there was wealth beyond human computation. At each end of the string was a great pearl and a golden clasp. The sight absorbed me to the exclusion of all fear. I, David Crawfurd, nineteen years of age, and assistant-storekeeper in a back-veld dorp, was privileged to see a sight to which no Portuguese adventurer had ever attained. There, floating on the smoke-wreaths, was the jewel which may once have burned in Sheba's hair.

As the priest held the collar aloft, the assembly rocked with a strange passion. Foreheads were rubbed in the dust, and then adoring eyes would be raised, while a kind of sobbing shook the worshippers. — JOHN BUCHAN, *Prester John*.

By permission of the copyright holders, Jonathan Cape, Limited, Toronto.

7. THE EAGLE

He clasps the crag with crooked hands;
Close to the sun in lonely lands,
Ringed with the azure world he stands.

The wrinkled sea beneath him crawls;
He watches from his mountain walls,
And like a thunderbolt he falls.

— TENNYSON

8. NIGHTINGALE'S SONG

Thou wast not born for death, immortal Bird!
No hungry generations tread thee down;
The voice I hear this passing night was heard
In ancient days by emperor and clown:
Perhaps the self-same song that found a path
Through the sad heart of Ruth, when, sick for home,
She stood in tears amid the alien corn;
The same that oft-times hath
Charm'd magic casements, opening on the foam
Of perilous seas, in faery lands forlorn.

— JOHN KEATS, *Ode to a Nightingale*

Practice 21. Describing Objects

Describe three of the following. Use a good topic sentence, observe closely, choose an interesting point of view as the writer has in the description of Prester John's collar in your model.

1. An oriole's nest.   2. A gull's nest.   3. A Hungarian partridge's nest. 4. A woodpecker's nest.   5. Silver birches in the moonlight.   6. Weeping birches in a storm (day or night).   7. The bittern.   8. Red-winged blackbird. 9. The pelican.   10. The oriole.   11. White-throated sparrow.   12. The Canada goose in flight.   13. A peacock.   14. *The Queen Mary.*   15. *The Normandie.*   16. A yacht.   17. A young fox.   18. Kittens four months old. 19. A young calf.   20. A fine Percheron.   21. A mastiff.   22. A German police dog.   23. My pet.   24. A curio.   25. A rare coin.   26. An interesting stamp. 27. A well-printed book.   28. A statue (bust, group, memorial).   29. A beaver. 30. A beautiful piece of china.

SEASONS

Perhaps no natural phenomenon has waked such enthusiastic praise and portrayal as the pageant of seasons. As with sunrise and sunset, the seasons are best described by their accompanying changes and effects upon nature. The subject seems to invite poetry and poetic prose.

Models:

1. GARDEN SNOW SCENE

It has snowed all night. I have been to look at our primroses; each of them had its small load of snow, and was bowing its head under its burden. These pretty flowers, with their rich yellow colour, had a charming effect under their white hoods. I saw whole tufts of them roofed over with a single block of snow; all these laughing flowers thus shrouded and leaning one upon another made one think of a group of young girls surprised by a shower and sheltering under a white apron. — MAURICE DE GUERIN, trans. by Matthew Arnold, *Essays in Criticism.*

2. LAKE SEDGES

Taller than the grass and lower than the trees there is another growth that feels the implicit spring. It had been more abandoned in winter than even the short grass shuddering under a wave of east wind, more than the dumb trees. For the multitude of sedges, rushes, canes, and reeds were the appropriate lyre of the cold. On them the keen winds played their dry music. They were parts of the winter. It looked through them and spoke through them. They were spears and javelins in array to the sound of the drums of the north. — ALICE MEYNELL, *Rushes and Reeds.*

By permission of Mr. Wilfred Meynell and the publishers, Burns, Oates and Washbourne Limited, London.

3. THE FALL OF LEAVES

At this season a sky which is of so delicate and faint a blue as to contain something of gentle mockery, and certainly more of tenderness, presides at the fall of leaves. There is no air, no breath at all. The leaves are so light that they sidle on their going downward, hesitating in that which is not void to them, and touching at last so imperceptibly the earth with which they are to mingle, that the gesture is much gentler than a salutation, and even more discreet than a discreet caress.

They make a little sound, less than the least of sounds. No bird at night in the marshes rustles so slightly; no men, though men are the subtlest of living things, put so evanescent a stress upon their sacred whispers or their prayers. The leaves are hardly heard, but they are heard just so much that men also, who are destined at the end to grow glorious and to die, look up and hear them falling. — HILAIRE BELLOC, *Hills and the Sea.*

By permission of the publishers, Methuen & Co. Ltd., London.

4. AUTUMN IN THE SOUTH

The colour of the leaves deepened, and there came a season of beauty singular and sad, like a smile left upon the face of the dead summer. Over all things, near and far, the forest where it met the sky, the nearer woods, the great river, and the streams that empty into it, there hung a blue haze, soft and dream-like. The forest became a painted forest, with an ever-thinning canopy and an ever-thickening carpet of crimson and gold; everywhere there was a low rustling underfoot and a slow rain of colour. It was neither cold nor hot, but very quiet, and the birds went by like shadows—a listless and forgetful weather, in which we began to look, every hour of very day, for the sail which we knew we should not see for weeks to come — MARY JOHNSTON, *To Have and to Hold.*

By permission of the publishers, Houghton Mifflin Company.

5. RICH DAYS

Welcome to you, rich Autumn days,
    Ere comes the cold, leaf-picking wind;
When golden stooks are seen in fields,
    All standing arm-in-arm entwined;
And gallons of sweet cider seen
On trees in apples red and green.

With mellow pears that cheat our teeth,
    Which melt that tongues may suck them in
With cherries red, and blue-black plums,
    Now sweet and soft from stone to skin;
And woodnuts rich, to make us go
Into the loveliest lanes we know.

— W. H. DAVIES.

By permission of the publishers, Jonathan Cape Limited, Toronto.

Practice 22.   Describing the Seasons

An eye to see, an imagination to interpret, and words adequate to your need, are the requisites to good seasonal description. When Davies says that the young leaves of spring have not "outgrown their curly childhood yet," he has combined all these. Use all your skill in writing upon the following topics.

1. Autumn on the prairie. 2. Autumn among the hills (mountains). 3. A forest scene in Autumn. 4. A poplar (maple, oak, elm, plane) tree in colour. 5. Orchards in bloom. 6. Spring comes to the valley (mountain, prairie). 7. Along the waterfront (at any season). 8. In the old muskeg

(any season). 9. The garden after the first soft snow. 10. Winter landscape. 11. A sleet-crusted landscape. 12. Pine trees in the snow. 13. Wrapped in hoar-frost. 14. "Season of mists and mellow fruitfulness." 15. "When the frost is on the pumpkin." 16. "What is so rare as a day in June." 17. "When icicles hang by the wall." 18. "Spring, the sweet spring."

EXTERIOR OF BUILDINGS

In describing the exterior of buildings the general dominant impression is the chief thing. Look at the picture and remember to make an attractive snapshot of it.

Models:

1

At length we stopped before a very old house bulging out over the road; a house with long low lattice-windows bulging out still farther, and beams with carved heads on the ends bulging out too, so that I fancied the whole house was leaning forward, trying to see what was passing on the narrow pavement below. It was quite spotless in its cleanliness. The old-fashioned brass knocker on the low arched door, ornamented with carved garlands of fruit and flowers, twinkled like a star; the two stone steps descending to the door were as white as if they had been covered with fair linen; and all the angles and corners, and carvings and mouldings, and quaint little panes of glass, and quainter little windows, though as old as the hills, were as pure as any snow that ever fell upon the hills. — CHARLES DICKENS

2. MRS. STUBBS'S

Mrs. Stubbs's shop was perched on a little hillock just off the road. It had two big windows for eyes, a broad veranda for a hat, and the sign on the roof, scrawled MRS. STUBBS'S, was like a little card stuck rakishly in the hat crown.

On the veranda there hung a long string of bathing-dresses, clinging together as though they'd just been resued from the sea rather than waiting to go in, and besides them there hung a cluster of sand-shoes so extraordinarily mixed that to get at one pair you had to tear apart and forcibly separate at least fifty. Even then it was the rarest thing to find the left that belonged to the right. So many people had lost patience and gone off with one shoe that fitted and one that was a little too big. . . . Mrs. Stubbs prided herself on keeping something of everything. The two windows arranged in the form of precarious pyramids, were crammed so tight, piled so high, that it seemed only a conjuror could prevent them from toppling over. In the left-hand corner of one window, glued to the pane by four gelatine lozenges, there was—and there had been from time immemorial—a notice.

LOST! HANDSOME GOLD BROOCH
SOLID GOLD
ON OR NEAR BEACH
REWARD OFFERED

— KATHERINE MANSFIELD, "At the Bay" from
The Garden Party and Other Stories.
By permission of the author's literary agents, Messrs. James B. Pinker & Son.

3

As I approached the house, I noticed that the windows were broken out, or shut up with rough boards to exclude the rain and snow; that the doors were supported by wooden props instead of hinges, which hung loosely on the panels; and that long luxuriant clover grew in the eaves, which had been originally designed to conduct the water from the roof, but becoming choked up with dust and decayed leaves, had afforded sufficient food for the nourishment of coarse grasses. The portico, like the house, had been formed of wood, and the flat surface of its top imbibing and retaining moisture, presented a mass of vegetable matter, from which had sprung up a young and vigorous birch tree, whose strength and freshness seemed to mock the helpless weakness that nourished it. I had no desire to enter the apartments; and indeed the aged ranger, whose occupation was to watch over its decay, and to prevent its premature destruction by the plunder of its fixtures and more durable materials, informed me that the floors were unsafe. Altogether the scene was one of a most depressing kind. — HALIBURTON, *The Clockmaker.*

4. MELROSE ABBEY

If thou would'st view fair Melrose aright,
Go visit it by the pale moonlight;
For the gay beams of lightsome day
Guild but to flout the ruins grey.
When the broken arches are black in night,
And each shafted oriel glimmers white;
When the cold light's uncertain shower
Streams on the ruin'd central tower;
When buttress and buttress, alternately,
Seem framed of ebon and ivory;
When silver edges the imagery,
And the scrolls that teach thee to live and die;
When distant Tweed is heard to rave,
And the owlet to hoot o'er the dead man's grave,
Then go—but go alone the while—
Then view St. David's ruin'd pile;
And home returning, soothly swear,
Was never scene so sad and fair!

— SIR WALTER SCOTT, *The Lay of the Last Minstrel*

Practice 23. Exteriors of Buildings

Write a description of the exterior view of some building which has struck you as distinctive for its beauty, architectural design, commodiousness, ruin, picturesqueness, oddity,—or other distinctions.

Suggestions:

1. A hovel. 2. A beautiful residence. 3. A grand hotel. 4. A skyscraper. 5. R. C. A. Building. 6. Empire State Building. 7. Vancouver City Hall. 8. Capitol Building. 9. A cosy cottage. 10. A cabin—"of clay and wattles made." 11. Log cabin. 12. A sod hut. 13. The lodge. 14. The pavilion.

15. Banff Springs Hotel. 16. Chateau at Lake Louise. 17. Jasper Park Lodge. 18. The bridge. 19. The observatory. 20. The Art Gallery. 21. Parliament Buildings.

INTERIORS OF BUILDINGS—ROOMS

As soon as we step inside a building we realize, even more than outside, the reflection of a personality. This must always be made evident—this atmosphere of habitation. Stress the dominant impression—as the domestic cheerfulness of Badger's kitchen.

Models:

1. MR. BADGER'S KITCHEN

The floor was well-worn red brick, and on the wide hearth burnt a fire of logs, between two attractive chimney-corners tucked away in the wall, well out of any suspicion of draught. A couple of high-backed settles, facing each other on either side of the fire, gave further sitting accommodations for the sociably disposed. In the middle of the room stood a long table of plain boards placed on trestles, with benches down each side. At one end of it, where an arm-chair stood pushed back, were spread the remains of the Badger's plain but ample supper. Rows of spotless plates winked from the shelves of the dresser at the far end of the room, and from the rafters overhead hung hams, bundles of dried herbs, nets of onions, and baskets of eggs. It seemed a place where heroes could fitly feast after victory, where weary harvesters could line up in scores along the table and keep their Harvest Home with mirth and song, or where two or three friends of simple tastes could sit about as they pleased and eat and smoke and talk in comfort and contentment. The ruddy brick floor smiled up at the smoky ceiling; the oaken settles, shiny with long wear, exchanged cheerful glances with each other; plates on the dresser grinned at pots on the shelf, and the merry firelight flickered and played over everything without distinction. — KENNETH GRAHAME, *The Wind in the Willows.*

By permission of Charles Scribner's Sons, New York.

2. FAGIN'S ROOM

Oliver, groping his way with one hand, and having the other firmly grasped by his companion, ascended with much difficulty the dark and broken stairs that his conductor mounted with an ease and expedition that showed that he was well acquainted with them. He threw open the door of a back room, and drew Oliver in after him.

The walls and ceiling of the room were perfectly black with age and dirt. There was a deal table before the fire, upon which were a candle stuck in the neck of a ginger-beer bottle, two or three pewter pots, a loaf and butter, and a plate. In a frying-pan, which was on the fire, and which was secured to the mantel-shelf by a string, some sausages were cooking; standing over them with a toasting-fork in his hand, was a very old, shrivelled Jew, whose villainous-looking and repulsive face was obscured by a quantity of matted red hair. He was dressed in a greasy flannel gown, with his throat bare, and seemed to be dividing his attention between the frying-pan and a clothes horse, over which a great number of silk handkerchiefs were hanging. Several rough beds made of old sacks were huddled side by side on the floor. Seated round the table were four or five boys, none older than the Dodger, smoking long clay pipes and drinking spirits, with the air of middle-aged men. These all crowded about their associate as he whispered a few words to the Jew; then they turned and grinned at Oliver. So did the Jew himself, toasting-fork in hand. — CHARLES DICKENS, *Oliver Twist.*

3

The room in which I found myself was very large and lofty. The windows were long, narrow, and pointed, and at so vast a distance from the black, oaken floor as to be altogether inaccessible from within. Feeble gleams of encrimsoned light made their way through the trellised panes, and served to render sufficiently distinct the more prominent objects around. The eye, however, struggled in vain to reach the remoter angles of the chamber, or the recesses of the vaulted and fretted ceiling. Dark draperies hung upon the walls. The general furniture was profuse, comfortless, antique, and tattered. Many books and musical instruments lay scattered about, but failed to give any vitality to the scene. I felt that I breathed an atmosphere of sorrow. An air of stern, deep, and irredeemable gloom hung over and pervaded all. —POE, *The Fall of the House of Usher*

4. DAVID'S BEDROOM

Peggotty opened a little door and showed me my bedroom. It was the completest and most desirable bedroom ever seen—in the stern of the vessel; with a little window which the rudder used to go through; a little looking-glass just the right height for me, nailed against the wall, and framed with oyster shells; a little bed which there was room enough to get into; and a nosegay of seaweed in a blue mug on the table. The walls were whitewashed as white as milk, and the patchwork counterpane made my eyes quite ache with its brightness. — DICKENS, *David Copperfield*

Practice 24. Describing Interior

Describe the interior of a building, or a room, making some one characteristic predominate.

1. A living room (comfort). 2. A living room (luxury). 3. A library (quiet, studiousness). 4. A drawing room (comfort, cheerfulness). 5. A kitchen (bright, cheery, savoury). 6. A den (homely). 7. An attic (disorder, neglect). 8. Theatre (attractiveness). 9. Audience chamber (formal). 10. Dining room (old fashioned spaciousness). 11. A church (solemn, loftly, stately). 12. A church (reverence). 13. A cathedral (beauty, dignity). 14. A restful room. 15. Foyer of a hotel (stir, convenience, comfort). 16. A tea-room. 17. An untidy room. 18. An unkept room. 19. Bedroom after a hurried exit. 20. The living room 'dressed' for vacation. 21. Moving in. 22. After a fire. 23. Marjorie is unpacking. 24. A gymnasium dressing room. 25. The pool at the "Y". 26. An art gallery. 27. A museum. 28. Any other.

TOWNS AND CITIES

In describing towns and cities it is of the utmost importance to form a dominant impression, and not to overload the description with too many details. Watch arrangement of details; but particularly watch selection of details towards a unified impression.

Models:

1. FERRARA

The aspect of this dreary town, half an hour before sunrise one fine morning, when I left it, was as picturesque as it seemed unreal and spectral. It was no matter that the people were not yet out of bed; for if they had all been up and busy, they would have made but little difference in that desert of a place. It was best to see it, without a single figure in the picture; a city of the dead, without one solitary survivor. Pestilence might have ravaged streets, squares, and marketplaces; and sack and siege have ruined the old houses, battered down their doors and windows, and made breaches in their roofs. In one part, a great tower rose into the air; the only landmark in the melancholy view. In another, a prodigious castle, with a moat about it, stood aloof: a sullen city in itself. In the black dungeons of this castle Parisina and her lover were beheaded in the dead of night. The red light, beginning to shine when I looked back upon it, stained its walls without, as they have many a time been stained within in the old days; but for any sign of life they gave, the castle and the city might have been avoided by all human creatures from the moment when the axe went down upon the last of the two lovers. — DICKENS, *Pictures in Italy.*

2. THE ROYAL EXCHANGE

There is a place in front of the Royal Exchange where the wide pavement reaches out like a promontory. It is the shape of a triangle with a rounded apex. A stream of traffic runs on either side, and other streets send their currents down into the open space before it. Like the spokes of a wheel, converging streams of human life flow into this agitated pool. Horses and carriages, carts, vans, omnibuses, cabs, every kind of conveyance cross each other's course in every possible direction. Twisting in and out by the wheels and under the horses' heads, working a devious way, men and women of all conditions wind a path over. They fill the interstices between the carriage and blacken the surface, till the vans almost float on human beings. Now the streams slacken, and now they rush amain, but never cease; dark waves are always rolling down the incline opposite, waves swell out from the side rivers, all London converges into this focus. There is an indistinguishable noise— it is not clatter, hum, or roar, it is not resolvable; made up of a thousand thousand footsteps, from a thousands hoofs, a thousand wheels—of haste, and shuffle, and quick movement, and ponderous loads, no attention can resolve it into a fixed sound.

Blue carts and yellow omnibuses, varnished carriages and brown vans, green omnibuses and red cabs, pale loads of yellow straw, rusty-red iron clanking on paintless carts, high white wool-packs, grey horses, bay horses, black teams; sunlight sparkling on brass harness, gleaming from carriage panels; jingle, jingle, jingle! An intermixed and intertangled, ceaselessly changing jingle, too, of colour; flecks of colour champed, as it were, like bits in the horses' teeth, frothed and strewen about, and a surface always of dark-dressed people winding like the curves on fast-flowing water. — RICHARD JEFFERIES, *The Story of My Heart.*

3. COMPOSED UPON WESTMINSTER BRIDGE

Earth has not anything to show more fair:
Dull would he be of soul who could pass by
A sight so touching in its majesty:
This City now doth, like a garment, wear
The beauty of the morning; silent, bare,
Ships, towers, domes, theatres, and temples lie
Open unto the fields and to the sky;
All bright and glittering in the smokeless air.
Never did sun more beautifully steep
In his first splendour, valley, rock, or hill;
Ne'er saw I, never felt, a calm so deep!
The river glideth at his own sweet will:
Dear God! the very houses seem asleep;
And all that mighty heart is lying still!

— WILLIAM WORDSWORTH

Practice 25.   Describing Towns and Cities

Suggested topics for description of towns and cities:

1. A mountain village seen from a height above.   2. A prairie village.
3. Prairie town in a snow storm.   4. Vancouver (Victoria, Quebec, Saint
John, New York) seen from the water.   5. The city by night (choose advan-
tageous point of view).   6. The city square.   7. Across Burrard Bridge.   8. A
bird's-eye view of Calgary (Regina, Saskatoon, Vancouver, Winnipeg, Toronto,
Halifax, Quebec or another).   9. At the Corner of Portage and Main (Scarth
and Eleventh).   10. Beacon Hill Park.   11. Volunteer Park.   12. Victoria
Park.   13. View of the city from —— (name of vantage point, Fort Garry
Hotel, Chateau Frontenac, Plains of Abraham, Bessborough Hotel, Capitol
Building).   14. Sunset over the city.   15. The city at sunrise.

PEN-PORTRAITS

The pen-portrait is often the beginning of a character portrayal,
and differs from it largely by refraining from much comment upon the
interpretation of the actual picture.   The pen-portrait should bring
before the mind's eye an image of the person described.   It will need,
then, to be vivid, not too detailed, but clear and definite.   These
portraits are frequently merely impressions, but the better ones give
actual pictures.   Examine the following models for order and arrangement, for material included and excluded.   This kind of description is
very important for it is the commonest of all forms in literary writing.
Frequently these are very brief.

Models:

1. THE UNCOMMISSIONED MASTER OF HORSE

The door opened, and the uncommissioned master of horse made his
appearance. His appearance was at once strikingly majestic and prepossessing,
and the natural ease and dignity with which he entered the room might

almost have become a peer of the realm coming to solicit the interest of the family for an electioneering candidate. A broad and sunny forehead, light and wavy hair, a blue cheerful eye, a nose that in Persia might have won him a throne, healthful cheeks, a mouth that was full of character, and a well-knit and almost gigantic person, constituted his external claims to attention, of which his lofty and confident, although most unassuming carriage, showed him to be in some degree conscious. He wore a complete suit of brown frieze, with a gay-coloured cotton handkerchief around his neck, blue worsted stockings, and brogues carefully greased, while he held in his right hand an immaculate felt hat, the purchase of the preceding day's fair. In the left he held a straight-handled whip and a wooden rattle, which he used for the purpose of collecting his ponies when they happened to straggle. An involuntary murmur of admiration ran amongst the guests at his entrance. — GRIFFIN, *The Collegians.*

By permission of the publishers, The Talbot Press Ltd., Dublin.

2. ICHABOD CRANE

The cognomen of Crane was not inapplicable to this person. He was tall but exceedingly lank, with narrow shoulders, long arms and legs, hands that dangled a mile out of his sleeves, feet that might have served for shovels, and his whole frame hung most loosely together. His head was small and flat at the top, with huge ears, large green glassy eyes, and a long snipe nose, so that it looked like a weather-cock perched upon his spindle neck, to tell which way the wind blew. To see him striding along the profile of a hill on a windy day, with his clothes bagging and fluttering about him, one might have mistaken him for the genius of famine, descending upon the earth, or some scarecrow eloped from a cornfield. — WASHINGTON IRVING, *The Legend of Sleepy Hollow.*

3. MARY

She was not more than fifteen. Her form, voice, and manner belonged to the period of transition from girlhood. Her face was perfectly oval, her complexion more pale than fair. The nose was faultless; the lips, slightly parted, were full and ripe, giving to the lines of the mouth warmth, tenderness, and trust; the eyes were blue and large, and shaded by drooping lids and long lashes; and, in harmony with all, a flood of golden hair, in the style permitted to Jewish brides, fell unconfined down her back to the pillion on which she sat. The throat and neck had the downy softness sometimes seen which leaves the artist in doubt whether it is an effect of contour or colour. To these charms of feature and person were added others more indefinable—an air of purity which only the soul can impart, and of abstraction natural to such as think much of things impalpable. Often, with trembling lips, she raised her eyes to heaven, itself not more deeply blue; often she crossed her hands upon her breast, as in adoration and prayer; often she raised her head like one listening eagerly for a calling voice. Now and then, amidst his slow utterances, Joseph turned to look at her, and, catching the expression kindling her face as with light, forgot his theme, and with bowed head, wondering, plodded on. — LEW WALLACE, *Ben Hur*

4. SELINA STONE

Apart from the rest, in deepest black, stood a tall, rather harsh-featured woman, who seemed to have about her something of the atmosphere of the pariah. She leaned against the churchyard wall in the purple shadow of the yew tree, which spread its flat, dark masses over the daisied lawn from the dank enclosure of the churchyard, and she had the look of a creature at bay —sullen, and inexpressive. She was of the age that corresponds to the apple-tree's time of hard, green fruit, half way between maturity and middle age. She had the spare angularity and weathered complexion of all field-workers. Yet, although she had no beauty, she was, in a curious, subtle way, arresting. She had the air of remoteness that some people always take with them, so that their lives seem to move in a different rhythm from the lives around them, and one surprises in their eyes an impassioned secrecy, and feels in their presence the magnetism of great things for ever unrevealed. — MARY WEBB, "The Prize" from *Armour Wherein He Trusted*.

By permission of the publishers, Jonathan Cape Limited, Toronto.

5. OLD SUSAN

When Susan's work was done, she would sit,
With one fat guttering candle lit,
And window opened wide to win
The sweet night air to enter in.
There, with a thumb to keep her place,
She would read, with stern and wrinkled face,
Her mild eyes gliding very slow
Across the letters to and fro,
While wagged the guttering candle flame
In the wind that through the window came.
And sometimes in the silence she
Would mumble a sentence audibly,
Or shake her head as if to say,
"You silly souls, to act this way!"
And never a sound from night I would hear,
Unless some far-off cock crowed clear;
Or her old shuffling thumb should turn
Another page; and rapt and stern,
Through her great glasses bent on me,
She would glance into reality;
And shake her round old silvery head,
With—"You!—I thought you was in bed!"—
Only to tilt her book again,
And rooted in Romance remain.

— WALTER DE LA MARE

By kind permission of the author and Messrs. James B. Pinker & Son

6. SATAN

He, above the rest
In shape and gesture proudly eminent,
Stood like a tower. His form had yet not lost
All his original brightness, nor appeared
Less than Archangel ruined, and the excess
Of glory obscured: as when the sun new-risen
Looks through the horizontal misty air
Shorn of his beams, or, from behind the moon,
In dim eclipse, disastrous twilight sheds

On half the nations, and with fear of change
Perplexes monarchs. Darkened so, yet shone
Above them all the Archangel: but his face
Deep scars of thunder had intrenched, and care
Sat on his faded cheek, but under brows
Of dauntless courage, and considerable pride
Waiting revenge.
— JOHN MILTON, *Paradise Lost*

Practice 26. Creating a Pen-Picture

Withholding the name, write a good pen-picture of some well-known historical figure. The test of your skill will be the ability of the class to recognize the portrait. You may entitle the portrait after the class has had a chance to test it.

Suggestions:

1. Abraham Lincoln. 2. Napoleon. 3. The Duke of Wellington. 4. Socrates. 5. Sir Wilfrid Laurier. 6. King George VI. 7. Queen Victoria. 8. Queen Elizabeth. 9. Elizabeth, Princess of York. 10. Mozart. 11. Mark Twain. 12. Shakespeare. 13. Robert Browning. 14. Oliver Wendell Holmes. 15. Emerson. 16. Longfellow. 17. Tennyson. 18. Ellen Terry as 'Lady Macbeth'.

Practice 27. Another Pen-Picture

Withholding the name write a good pen-picture of some familiar comic figure from the cartoons and comic strips. Make the class recognize the portrait without reference to actions or incidents.

Suggestions:

1. Uncle Bim. 2. Major Hoople. 3. Jiggs. 4. Pop-eye. 5. Dagwood Bumstead. 6. Tillie the Toiler. 7. Mac. 8. The Worry Wart. 9. Caspar Milquetoast. 10. Alley Oop. 11. Any other.

Practice 28. A Pen-Portrait

Still withholding the name, write a pen-portrait of your favourite, or an outstanding, movie actor or actress. You may entitle the portrait when the class has had an opportunity to test it.

1. Ingrid Bergman. 2. Robert Taylor. 3. Clark Gable. 4. Laurence Olivier. 5. Greer Garson. 6. Susan Peters. 7. Olivia de Havilland. 8. Claudette Colbert. 9. Marlene Dietrich. 10. Joan Crawford. 11. Myrna Loy. 12. Hedy Lamarr. 13. Danny Kaye. 14. Alan Ladd. 15. Gary Cooper. 16. Gregory Peck. 17. James Mason. 18. Shirley Temple. 19. Jane Wyman.

Practice 29. Another Pen-Portrait

Write a pen-portrait of some person whom you have known: a member of the class, some striking or unusual person you have met, a prominent member of the community. Remember that unkindness and

discourtesy have no place in class work. Avoid caricature in writing
of real persons.

GROUPS AND ASSEMBLIES

Composite groups are, of necessity, well selected impressions, first of
the whole group, and secondly a few of the outstanding individuals
within the group—a general impression followed by a series of miniatures vividly drawn.

Models:

1. AT THE TRIAL OF WARREN HASTINGS

Neither military nor civil pomp was wanting. The avenues were lined with
grenadiers. The streets were kept clear by cavalry. The peers, robed in gold
and ermine, were marshalled by the heralds under Garter King-at-arms. The
judges in their vestments of state attended to give advice on points of law.
Near a hundred and seventy lords, three fourths of the Upper House as the
Upper House was then, walked in solemn order from their usual place of
assembling to the tribunal. The junior Baron present led the way, George
Eliott, Lord Heathfield, recently ennobled for his memorable defence of
Gibraltar against the fleets and armies of France and Spain. The long pro-
cession was closed by the Duke of Norfolk, Earl Marshal of the realm, by the
great dignitaries, and by the brothers and sons of the King. Last of all came
the Prince of Wales, conspicuous by his fine person and noble bearing. —
MACAULAY, *Essay on Warren Hastings*

2. THE MARKET-PLACE

In the market-place at Goderville was a great crowd, a mingled multitude
of men and beasts. The horns of cattle, the high and long napped hats of
wealthy peasants, the head-dresses of the women, came to the surface of that
sea. And voices clamorous, sharp, shrill, made a continuous and savage din.
Above it a huge burst of laughter from the sturdy lungs of a merry yokel
would sometimes sound, and sometimes a long bellow from a cow tied fast
to the wall of a house.

It all smelled of the stable, of milk, of hay, and of perspiration, giving off
that half-human, half-animal odour which is peculiar to men of the fields.
— GUY DE MAUPASSANT, *The Odd Number.*

3. ELEVEN O'CLOCK, NOVEMBER 11

They stood on the curb while the crowd, noisy, cheerful, exaggerated,
swirled back and forwards around them. Suddenly eleven o'clock boomed
from Big Ben. Before the strokes were completed there was utter silence;
as though a sign had flashed from the sky, the waters of the world were
frozen into ice. The omnibuses in Trafalgar Square stayed where they were;
every man stood, his hat in his hand. The women held their children with a
warning clasp. The pigeons around the Arch rose fluttering and crying into
the air, the only sound in all the world; the two minutes seemed eternal . . .

The moment was over; the world went on again, but there were many there
who would remember. — From *The Young Enchanted* by HUGH WALPOLE.

4. PRESTER'S MEN

The next thing I remember was a movement among the first ranks. The chiefs were swearing fealty. Laputa took off the collar and called God to witness that it should never again encircle his neck till he had led his people to victory. Then one by one the great chiefs and indunas advanced, and swore allegiance with their foreheads on the ivory box. Such a collection of races has never been seen. There were tall Zulus and Swazis with *ringkops* and feather head-dresses. There were men from the north with heavy brass collars and anklets; men with quills in their ears, and ear-rings and nose-rings; shaven heads, and heads with wonderfully twisted hair; bodies naked or all but naked, and bodies adorned with skins and necklets. Some were light in colour, and some were black as coal; some had squat negro features, and some thin, high-boned Arab faces. But in all there was the air of mad enthusiasm. For a day they had forsworn from blood, but their wild eyes and twitching hands told their future purpose. — JOHN BUCHAN, *Prester John.*

By permission of the publishers, Jonathan Cape, Limited, Toronto.

Practice 30. Describing a Crowd

Describe one or more of the following groups of people, and try to avoid mere cataloguing. Pick out the picturesque, the colourful.

1. The Midway at the Fair. 2. A crowd at a football game. 3. A college crowd rooting for a team. 4. The assembly hall or auditorium on a gala occasion. 5. A street scene, such as a Travellers' Day parade. 6. A school (or church, or C.G.I.T. or Boy Scout) bazaar. 7. A departmental store at Christmas shopping time. 8. The concert. 9. A solemn occasion such as the Trooping of Colours, Memorial Day exercises, Armistice Day ceremonies at the Cenotaph. 10. A welcome to the Governor-General. 11. A political rally. 12. A crowd at Market Square. 13. A mob scene. 14. A police court scene.

MOODS AND MENTAL STATES

Success in novel and short story writing often depends upon ability to re-create moods and mental states. This may be only to outward appearance, or it may go very deep, or into the very heart of the characters. It is not so difficult as it first appears, requiring only accurate observation and patient selection of most effective phenomena —with persons, facial and bodily reactions in each mood; with crowds, the more obvious demonstrations. Watch verbs and adverbs closely. The introduction of conversation helps in the portrayal.

Models:

1. VILLON

Suddenly his heart stopped beating; a feeling of cold scales passed up the back of his legs, and a cold blow seemed to fall upon his scalp. He stood petrified for a moment; then he felt again with one feverish movement; and then his loss burst upon him, and he was covered at once with perspiration. — ROBERT LOUIS STEVENSON, *A Lodging for the Night.*

By permission of Charles Scribner's Sons, New York.

2. AFRAID?

I do not know if I was what you call afraid; but my heart beat like a bird's, both quick and little; and there was a dimness came before my eyes which I continually rubbed away, and which continually returned. As for hope, I had none; but only a darkness of despair and a sort of anger against all the world that made me long to sell my life as dear as I was able. I tried to pray, I remember, but that same hurry of my mind, like a man running, would not suffer me to think upon the words; and my chief wish was to have the thing begin and be done with it. — ROBERT LOUIS STEVENSON, *Kidnapped.*

By permission of Charles Scribner's Sons, New York.

3. THE SINKING OF THE "LUSITANIA"

The next thing I can remember was being deep down under the water. It was very dark, nearly black. I fought to come up. I was terrified of being caught on some part of the ship and kept down. That was the worst moment of terror, the only moment of acute terror, that I knew. My wrist did catch on a rope. I was scarcely aware of it at the time, but I have the mark on me to this day. At first I swallowed a lot of water; then I remembered that I had read that one should not swallow water, so I shut my mouth. Something bothered me in my right hand, and prevented me striking out with it: I discovered that it was the life-belt I had been holding for my father. As I reached the surface I grasped a little bit of board quite thin, a few inches wide and perhaps two or three feet long. I thought this was keeping me afloat. I was wrong. My most excellent life-belt was doing that. But everything that happened after I had been submerged was a little misty and vague; I was slightly stupefied from then on. — VISCOUNTESS RHONDDA, *This Was My World.*

By permission of the publishers, The Macmillan Company of Canada Limited.

4. NERVOUSNESS

Father would never forgive them. That was what they felt more than ever when, two mornings later, they went into his room to go through his things. They had discussed it quite calmly. It was even down on Josephine's list of things to be done. *Go through father's things and settle about them.* But that was a very different matter from saying after breakfast:

"Well, are you ready, Con?"

"Yes, Jug—when you are."

"Then I think we'd better get it over."

It was dark in the hall. It had been a rule for years never to disturb father in the morning, whatever happened. And now they were going to open the door without knocking even. . . . Constantia's eyes were enormous at the idea; Josephine felt weak in the knees.

"You—you go first," she gasped, pushing Constantia.

But Constantia said, as she always had said on those occasions, "No, Jug, that's not fair. You're eldest."

Josephine was just going to say—what at other times she wouldn't have owned to for the world—what she kept for her very last weapon, "But you're tallest," when they noticed that the kitchen door was open, and there stood Kate . . .

"Very stiff," said Josephine, grasping the door-handle and doing her best to turn it. As if anything ever deceived Kate!

It couldn't be helped. That girl was. . . . Then the door was shut behind them, but—but they weren't in father's room at all. They might have suddenly walked through the wall by mistake into a different flat altogether. Was the door just behind them? They were too frightened to look. Josephine knew that if it was it was holding itself tight shut; Constantia felt that, like the doors in dreams, it hadn't any handle at all. It was the coldness which made it so awful. Or the whiteness—which? Everything was covered. The blinds were down, a cloth hung over the mirror, a sheet hid the bed; a huge fan of white paper filled the fireplace. Constantia timidly put out her hand; she almost expected a snowflake to fall. Josephine felt a queer tingling in her nose, as if her nose was freezing. Then a cab klop-klopped over the cobbles below, and the quiet seemed to shake into little pieces.

"I had better pull up a blind," said Josephine bravely.

"Yes, it might be a good idea," whispered Constantia.

They only gave the blind a touch, but it flew up and the cord flew after, rolling around the blind-stick, and the little tassel tapped as if trying to get free. That was too much for Constantia.

'Don't you think—don't you think we might put it off for another day?" she whispered.

"Why?" snapped Josephine, feeling, as usual, much better now that she knew for certain that Constantia was terrified. "It's got to be done. But I do wish you wouldn't whisper, Con."

"I didn't know I was whispering," whispered Constantia.

"And why do you keep on staring at the bed?" said Josephine, raising her voice almost defiantly. "There's nothing *on* the bed."

"Oh, Jug, don't say so!" said poor Connie. "At any rate, not so loudly."

Josephine felt herself that she had gone too far. She took a wide swerve over the chest of drawers, put out her hand, but quickly drew it back again.

"Connie!" she gasped, and she wheeled round and leaned with her back against the chest of drawers.

"Oh, Jug—what?"

Josephine could only glare. She had the most extraordinary feeling that she had just escaped something simply awful. But how could she explain to Constantia that father was in the chest of drawers? He was in the top drawer with his handkerchiefs and neckties, or in the next with his shirts and pyjamas, or in the lowest of all with his suits. He was watching there, hidden away—just behind the door-handle—ready to spring.

She pulled a funny old-fashioned face at Constantia, just as she used oↃ in the old days when she was going to cry.

"I can't open," she nearly wailed.

"No, don't, Jug," whispered Constantia earnestly. "It's much better not to. Don't let's open anything. At any rate, not for a long time."

"But—but it seems so weak," said Josephine, breaking down.

"But why not be weak for once, Jug?" argued Constantia, whispering quite fiercely. "If it is weak." And her pale stare flew from the locked writing-table—so safe—to the huge glittering wardrobe, and she began to breathe in a queer, panting way. "Why shouldn't we be weak for once in our lives, Jug? It's quite excusable. Let's be weak—be weak, Jug. It's much nicer to be weak than to be strong."

And then she did one of those amazingly bold things that she'd done about twice before in their lives; she marched over to the wardrobe, turned the key, and took it out of the lock. Took it out of the lock and held it up to Josephine, showing Josephine by her extraordinary smile that she knew what she'd done, risked deliberately father being in there among his overcoats.

If the huge wardrobe had lurched forward, had crashed down on Constantia, Josephine wouldn't have been surprised. On the contrary, she would have thought it the only suitable thing to happen. But nothing happened. Only the room seemed quieter than ever, and bigger flakes of cold air fell on Josephine's shoulders and knees. She began to shiver.

"Come, Jug," said Constantia, still with that awful callous smile, and Josephine followed just as she had that last time, when Constantia had pushed Benny into the round pond. — KATHERINE MANSFIELD, "The Daughters of the Late Colonel" from *The Garden Party and Other Stories.*

By permission of the author's literary agents, Messrs. James B. Pinker & Son.

5. THE SPELL OF THE ROAD

Next moment, hardly knowing how it came about, he found he had hold of the handle and was turning it. As the familiar sound broke forth, the old passion seized on Toad and completely mastered him, body and soul. As if in a dream, he found himself, somehow, seated in the driver's seat; as if in a dream, he pulled the lever and swung the car round the yard and out through the archway; and, as if in a dream, all sense of right and wrong, all fear of obvious consequences, seemed temporarily suspended. He increased his pace, and as the car devoured the street and leapt forth on the high road through the open country, he was only conscious that he was Toad once more, Toad at his best and highest, Toad the terror, the traffic-queller, the Lord of the lone trail, before whom all must give way or be smitten into nothingness and everlasting night. He chanted as he flew, and the car responded with sonorous drone; the miles were eaten up under him as he sped he knew not whither, fulfilling his instincts, living his hour, reckless of what might come to him. — KENNETH GRAHAME, *The Wind in the Willows.*

By arrangement with Charles Scribner's Sons, New York.

6. A GREAT TIME

Sweet Chance, that led my steps abroad,
   Beyond the town, where wild flowers grow—
A rainbow and a cuckoo, Lord,
   How rich and great the times are now!
Know, all ye sheep
   And cows, that keep
On staring that I stand so long
   In grass that's wet from heavy rain—
A rainbow and a cuckoo's song
   May never come together again;
     May never come
     This side the tomb.

                 — W. H. DAVIES.

By permission of the publishers, Jonathan Cape Limited, Toronto.

Practice 31. Presenting a Mood

Write a descriptive composition representing an individual who, in some appropriate circumstance, is in a mood pronounced enough to be easily observable. Represent one of the following:

1. Terror. 2. Awe. 3. Nervousness. 4. Joy. 5. Ecstasy. 6. Cheerfulness. 7 Sadness. 8. Sullenness. 9. Melancholy. 10. Suspicion. 11. Doubt. 12. Enthusiasm. 13. Rapture. 14. Despondency. 15. Bitterness. 16. Cynicism. 17. Contentment. 18. Any other.

Practice 32. Emotional Reaction of a Crowd

Describe an assembly in which conflicting emotional reactions will be represented.

Suggestions:

1. Crowd outside 10 Downing Street at declaration of war, August 14, 1914 (mothers, fathers, generals, young men, young women, profiteers, soldiers, etc.) 2. Crowd waiting at the palace hear of death of George V. 3. The vast body of movie fans hear of the death of Will Rogers. 4. Rain at last! 5. A court room hears the jury deliver its verdict. 6. A school hears announcement of unexpected holiday. 7. The first snow of winter (children, parents, old folk). 8. A room full of people hear a boy on the street shout "Extra!" 9. At the dance. 10. The train is pulling out (newly-weds on honeymoon, business men on business trips, prisoners being escorted to prison, holidayers leaving for holidays, etc., etc.)

WORKS OF ART

With works of art the chief concern is to create an emotional response, which is usually subjective. The writing itself must rise to the level of art—not ornate but sincere and true. The words, for this reason, must be carefully chosen. The models give descriptions of musical compositions, speeches, and painting.

Models:

1. THE MOONLIGHT SONATA

He suffered himself to be led back to the instrument. The moon shone brightly in through the window and lit up his glorious, rugged head and massive figure. "I shall improvise a sonata to the moonlight!" looking up thoughtfully to the sky and stars. Then his hands dropped on the keys, and he began playing a sad and infinitely lovely movement, which crept gently over the instrument like the calm flow of moonlight over the dark earth. This was followed by a wild, elfin passage in triple time—a sort of grotesque interlude, like the dance of sprites upon the sward. Then came a swift, breathless, trembling movement, descriptive of flight and uncertainty, and vague, impulsive terror, which carried us away on its rustling wings, and left us all in emotion and wonder. — Anonymous

2. PRESTER JOHN'S SPEECH

I had heard him on board the liner, and had thought his voice the most wonderful I had ever met with. But now in that great resonant hall the magic of it was doubled. He played upon the souls of his hearers as on a musical instrument. At will he struck the chords of pride, fury, hate, and mad joy. Now they would be hushed in breathless quiet, and now the place would echo with savage assent. I remember noticing that the face of my neighbour 'Mwanga, was running with tears.

He spoke of the great days of Prester John, and a hundred names I had never heard of. He pictured the heroic age of his nation, when every man was a warrior and hunter, and rich kraals stood in the spots now desecrated by the white man, and cattle wandered on a thousand hills. Then he told tales of white infamy, lands snatched from their rightful possessors, unjust laws which forced the Ethiopian to the bondage of a despised caste, the finger of scorn everywhere, and the mocking word. If it be the part of an orator to rouse the passion of his hearers, Laputa was the greatest on earth. "What have ye gained from the white man?" he cried. "A bastard civilization which has sapped your manhood; a false religion which would rivet on you the chains of the slave. Ye, the old masters of the land, are now the servants of the oppressor. And yet the oppressors are few, and the fear of you is in their hearts. They feast in their great cities, but they see the writing on the wall, and their eyes are anxiously turning lest the enemy be at their gates." I cannot hope in my prosaic words to reproduce that amazing discourse. Phrases which the hearers had heard at mission schools now suddenly appeared, not as the white man's learning, but as God's message to His own. Laputa fitted the key to the cipher, and the meaning was clear. He concluded, I remember, with a picture of the overthrow of the alien, and the golden age which would dawn for the oppressed. Another Ethiopian empire would arise, so majestic that the white man everywhere would dread its name, so righteous that all men under it would live in ease and peace.

By rights, I suppose, my blood should have been boiling at this treason. I am ashamed to confess that it did nothing of the sort. My mind was mesmerized by this amazing man. I could not refrain from shouting with the rest. Indeed I was a convert, if there can be conversion when the emotions are dominant and there is no assent from the brain. I had a mad desire to be of Laputa's party. — John Buchan, *Prester John*.

By permission of the publishers, Jonathan Cape Limited, Toronto.

3. THE ANGELUS

Millet was one of the famous group of French painters who founded what is now known as the "Barbizon" School. He was the son of a peasant farmer, and his outlook was coloured by the incidents of peasant life which find such eloquent expression in his pictures. His work is distinguished by an absolute truthfulness to Nature which was the guiding principle of his life. He saw the peasant bent at his work in the fields, and he pictured him in all his gaunt poverty and weariness, while he invested him, by his inspired vision, with the symbolical dignity of labour. Thus, in painting life, Millet reveals the sublime in the commonplace, the promise hidden in the pain, and the mercy that hovers over sorrow.

"The Angelus" completes a series of three pictures by Millet which are considered his masterpieces. "The Sowers" typifies the labourer going forth bearing good seed with him. "The Gleaners" shows the end of the harvest which has supplied the people's wants and left something over for the needy. "The Angelus" depicts the labourers' thanks for the gift of plenty.

The last picture is the most popular of all the works of this artist, and it expresses in full measure the simplicity and devoutness of his nature. His wish was to make the spectator realize the vesper hour, when the soft chimes call the toiler to thankful rest. The man and the woman have worked well, as their full sacks bear witness, and they are bending their heads in gratitude to their Creator for His gifts. On a small canvas, twenty-five inches long and twenty-one inches high, the painter has created a scene that is at once a prayer and an inspiration, which will hold its strong appeal as long as the colours last. — From *Famous Paintings*, Vol. I.

By permission of the publishers, Cassell & Company, Ltd., London

"A PAINTED PRAYER"

4. THE MAN WITH THE HOE

Bowed by the weight of centuries he leans
Upon his hoe and gazes on the ground,
The emptiness of ages in his face,
And on his back the burden of the world.
Who made him dead to rapture and despair,
A thing that grieves not and that never hopes,
Stolid and stunned, a brother to the ox?
Who loosened and let down this brutal jaw?
Whose was the hand that slanted back this brow?
Whose breath blew out the light within this brain?

What gulfs between him and the seraphim!
Slave of the wheel of labour, what to him
Are Plato and the swing of Pleiades?
What the long reaches of the peaks of song,

The rift of dawn, the reddening of the rose?
Through this dread shape the suffering ages look;
Time's tragedy is in that aching stoop;
Through this dread shape humanity betrayed,
Plundered, profaned, and disinherited,
Cries protest to the Judges of the World,
A protest that is also prophecy.

— EDWIN MARKHAM

Copyright by the author and used with his permission.

Practice 33. Describing a Work of Art

Describe some picture, poem, or piece of music which you admire.
Try to justify your admiration by presenting, in words, what is admirable. Do not depend upon apostrophe and emotional ejaculation.
State explicitly and clearly what is beautiful about the object you
describe.

Paraphrase and Précis-writing

WHAT A PRÉCIS IS

A précis (pronounced *pray-see*) is a clear, concise, orderly summary of the contents of a passage and is ordinarily about one-third or one-fourth as long as the original. It is a passage boiled down so that only the essence, pith, or gist is left.

VALUE OF PRÉCIS-WRITING

One purpose of education is to help students to discover what they should not learn. The boy or girl who tries to learn everything in the books he reads and studies wastes his time and masters nothing. The student who is in the habit of searching for main points, understanding them, learning them, and reviewing them is educating himself.

Probably half the failures in school are due directly or indirectly to silent reading deficiency. Teachers of history, mathematics, English, science, accounting, law, and other subjects say that a high percentage of the pupils who fail in their classes fail because they can't read, can't understand the textbook, can't read the examination paper. Training in silent reading is training in the art of studying.

Moreover the ability to get at the gist, pith, or essence of a matter is important professional, business, and social equipment. Précis-writing prepares for getting and explaining tersely the main points of legal papers, laws, rules and regulations, announcements and directions, business letters, speeches, conversations, interviews, and technical, professional, and general books and articles. The higher one goes in a profession or the deeper one goes into any subject the harder the reading one has to do. In conversation the ability to summarize briefly a book or a magazine article pertinent to the subject is valuable. Practise in précis-writing also helps one to establish the habit of clear and concise expression, or putting a maximum of meaning into a minimum of words.

PREPARING TO MAKE A PRÉCIS

The first and most important step in making a précis is reading the passage thoroughly. Thorough reading includes digging out the thought of every difficult sentence and discovering the relationship of the principal and subordinate ideas of each paragraph and of the whole passage.

HOW TO READ A DIFFICULT SENTENCE

1. Know the central idea of the entire poem, article, or chapter, and of the paragraph in which the sentence is imbedded. Each sentence is closely related in meaning to the rest of the paragraph. If a sentence may be interpreted in two or three ways, decide from the rest of the paragraph which interpretation is best.

2. Knowing what the preceding and the following sentences are about will help you to fathom the deepest sentence or unravel the most tangled one.

3. Look up in the dictionary the meaning of any word which is not perfectly clear to you. Don't skip technical terms.

4. Look up allusions which are new to you.

5. In imagination see the pictures suggested by descriptive words and figures of speech.

6. Pick out the key words, think what their relation in thought is, and in this way find the central idea of the sentence. Avoid giving great weight to an unimportant word. Then read the sentence again, being careful to include all details.

PARAPHRASE

Paraphrasing is giving the meaning in other words, sometimes with greater fullness of detail or illustration. All thoughts of the original must appear and must appear exactly, and all compressed expression must be made explicit. No new or different thought should appear.

Example:
Swift to its close ebbs out life's little day.

Paraphrase:
Life is short. It passes away quickly, and its power weakens as it nears its close.

Three significant words give the key to this sentence. *Swift, ebbs,* and *little.* The last clause might have been overlooked had attention not centred on the significant verb *ebbs.*

Example:

WORLDLY PLACE
Even in a palace life may be led well!
So spake the imperial sage, purest of men,
Marcus Aurelius. But the stifling den
Of common life, where, crowded up pell-mell,

Our freedom for a little bread we sell,
And drudge under some foolish master's ken
Who rates us if we peer outside our pen—
Match'd with a palace, is not this a hell?
Even in a palace! On his truth sincere,
Who spake these words, no shadow ever came;
And when my ill-school'd spirit is aflame
Some nobler, ampler stage of life to win,
I'll stop, and say: "There were no succour here!
The aids to noble life are all within."

— MATTHEW ARNOLD.

Paraphrase:

"The compact language may be paraphrased as follows: 'What a strange thing to say, that even in a palace a man can be virtuous! Yet the man who said it was himself an emperor, a philosopher, and the purest of men in his own life. Yet, when we think of our own pain and trouble, how difficult it is for us to believe that the state of an emperor is not happier than the state of a common man. Think of the trouble that we have to earn a living—obliged to work every day in some uncomfortable position, watched by some man not wiser than ourselves, but often even more foolish, who is only watching our work in order to find fault with us. Surely the Emperor, who is the master of all men, and who is not obliged to obey anybody, or even obliged to do anything he does not wish to do, ought to be happier than we. But these are the words of the wisest and noblest of the Roman emperors—'Even in a palace!' Therefore we must understand that it is still harder for an emperor to be good and happy than it is for a common man. To believe this may be difficult, but Marcus Aurelius said it, and in his whole life he never told even the shadow of a lie. I believe him. When I feel myself dissatisfied, when I wish to leave the work that I now do, in order to obtain a higher or a better position, I remember the words of Marcus Aurelius. The secret of happiness and the power of virtue are in our hearts. That is the meaning of life as it was understood by that great teacher and great emperor'." — LAFCADIO HEARN, *Appreciation of Poetry.*

By arrangement with the publishers, Dodd, Mead & Company.

Practice 1. Paraphrasing Sentences

Find the meaning of the following sentences; then paraphrase them.

1. Time wasted is existence, used is life.
2. He is a skilled window-dresser of his own personality — H. H. MUNRO
3. It was a face filled with broken commandments. — JOHN MASEFIELD
4. The conversation fainted again, and again Mr. Lacey leapt forward with restoratives. — ANNE PARRISH
5. No man has a good enough memory to make a successful liar. — ABRAHAM LINCOLN
6. We live on one-third of what we eat and the doctors live on the rest. — ROYAL S. COPELAND
7. The Child is father of the Man.
8. Truth, crushed to earth, shall rise again.

9. One is never so near to another as when he is forced to be separated.

10. When faith is lost, when honour dies, the man is dead.

11. He who would search for pearls must dive below.

12. The applause of listening senates to command,
The threats of pain and ruin to despise,
To scatter plenty o'er a smiling land,
And read their history in a nation's eyes,
Their lot forbade; nor circumscribed alone
Their growing virtues, but their crimes confined. — GRAY

13. The lunatic, the lover, and the poet
Are of imagination all compact:
One sees more devils than vast hell can hold,
That is, the madman: the lover, all as frantic,
Sees Helen's beauty in a brow of Egypt:
The poet's eye, in a fine frenzy rolling,
Doth glance from heaven to earth, from earth to heaven;
And as imagination bodies forth
The forms of things unknown, the poet's pen
Turns them to shapes and gives to airy nothing
A local habitation and a name. — SHAKESPEARE

14. Vice is a monster of so frightful mien
As to be hated needs but to be seen;
Yet seen too oft, familiar with her face,
We first endure, then pity, then embrace. — POPE

HOW TO READ A PARAGRAPH THOROUGHLY

1. Shut out all foreign thoughts.

2. Know the central idea of the entire selection.

3. First, glance through the paragraph to get a bird's-eye view of it.

4. Find or construct a sentence which expresses the central idea of the paragraph.

5. As you read the other sentences thoroughly, think how the ideas are related to the topic of the paragraph and to each other, which are principal, and which subordinate. If the book is your own, underline the words which express the most important ideas.

6. If a paragraph is long and complicated, outline it in your mind or on paper.

WRITING THE PRÉCIS

1. After thoroughly reading the passage write out clearly and tersely in your own words—don't use sentences of the original—the main points of the selection. Subordinate or eliminate minor points. Omit quotations, figures of speech, and most illustrations.

2. Use about one-third or one-fourth as many words as there are in the original.

3. Make the précis a smooth, pointed composition. Show clearly by adequate transition and occasional connectives, such as *then, second, moreover,* the relation of ideas to each other.

4. Read the selection again and criticize and revise your work.

On this page is a diagram of how your mind should work in making a complete and accurate précis. The essential ideas of the paragraph are underscored. Notice that minor details, repetition, and illustrations are omitted. The right-hand column contains the précis with each main idea boiled down to a sentence. Single words or phrases take the place of the clauses and sentences of the original.

ORIGINAL (*175 words*)

Sometimes the grind of the Academy got on High's nerves. He had been accustomed to the varied life of a Texas ranch, and he had come to the Point because the free-roving existence of any army man—the border, the Philippines, other foreign service on isolated posts—appealed to every drop of pioneer blood within him. And he was proud as Lucifer that he had been one of the favoured few who could make the grade. Not so favoured either. He had boned for a solid year to pass the examinations, and ninety-nine days out of a hundred he thought of himself as an embryo officer in his country's army—and was proud and happy.

But often the routine seemed unbearable. Every minute of the day scheduled—even the exact spot in his clothespress where his collars were kept laid out for him. Somehow the yoke lay heavily on him every once in a while, and then the hot independence of spirit which was his heritage leaped into flame. But it usually died as quickly.[1] — THOMSON BURTIS

PRECIS (*50 words*)

High, a Texas man, chose West Point because he liked the wandering life of the army man.

He had worked hard and was proud he had passed.

But often he tired of the grind, the exact timing of every move.

Sometimes his independent spirit rebelled, but he quickly controlled it. — PUPIL

[1]*Reprinted by permission of the* American Boy.

SELF-CRITICISM CHART—PRECIS

Ask yourself these questions:

1. *Have I misunderstood any statement?*
2. *Have I included all important ideas?*
3. *Have I excluded all minor details and crossed out all unnecessary words? Are my sentences compact?*
4. *Is all the language my own?*
5. *Are my words, sentences, and paragraphs correct?*

6. *Will my précis be clear to one who has not read the original selection?*

7. *Are my spelling, punctuation, grammar, and sentence structure correct?*

Finally, copy neatly and legibly the revised précis.

Example:

ORIGINAL (*320 words*)

Within the car there was the usual interior life of the railroad, offering little to the observation of other passengers, but full of novelty for this pair of strangely enfranchised prisoners. It was novelty enough, indeed, that there were fifty human beings in close relation with them, under one long and narrow roof, and drawn onward by the same mighty influence that had taken their two selves into its grasp. It seemed marvellous how all these people could remain so quietly in their seats, while so much noisy strength was at work in their behalf. Some, with tickets in their hats (long travellers these, before whom lay a hundred miles of railroad), had plunged into the English scenery and adventures of pamphlet novels, and were keeping company with dukes and earls. Others, whose briefer span forbade their devoting themselves to studies so abstruse, beguiled the little tedium of the way with penny-papers. A party of girls, and one young man, on opposite sides of the car, found amusement in a game of ball. They tossed it to and fro, with peals of laughter that might be measured by mile-lengths; for, faster than the nimble ball could fly, the merry players fled unconsciously along, leaving the trail of their mirth afar behind, and ending their game under another sky than had witnessed its commencement. Boys, with apples, cakes, candy, and rolls of variously tinctured lozenges—merchandise that reminded Hepzibah of her deserted shop—appeared at each momentary stopping place, doing up their business in a hurry, or breaking it short off, lest the market should ravish them away with it. New people continually entered. Old acquaintances—for such they soon grew to be, in this rapid current of affairs—continually departed. Here and there, amid the rumble and the tumult, sat one asleep. Sleep; sport; business; graver or lighter study; and the common and inevitable movement onward! It was life! — HAWTHORNE, *The House of Seven Gables*

PUPIL PRECIS (*105 words*)

Within the car the pair of emancipated prisoners saw the usual train scene. To them, however, it was something strange and wonderful. They were held in close relationship with fifty other people by a common means of locomotion. Some quietly read English novels; others, not travelling far, glanced over newspapers. A group of young girls and one young man derived huge enjoyment from a game of ball. At each station small boys hurried aboard, sold their tidbits, and dashed off again before the train started. New passengers continually appeared, while others departed. All phases of life were represented here, from quiet sleep to joyous hilarity.

Practice 2. Writing a Précis

Write a précis of each of the following selections. Include every important idea, but omit unimportant details and unnecessary words.

1

On another of these desert journeys Lawrence was captured by a band of Kurd robbers. They took him to their secret refuge, high up on a mountaintop. They put him in a hut and left two of their men to guard him, while the rest of the band went off on another expedition. One afternoon the Kurd sentries were separated, one remaining inside with him and the other sitting outside in the sun. It was a very hot day. The Kurds had had their lunch, and the man on the outside had fallen asleep. The other sentry happened to turn his back, and as he did so Lawrence jumped on his back and overpowered him. He did this without making enough noise to arouse the second man. Then he went out and disposed of the sleeper. The only approach to this rocky mountaintop was up a narrow, winding, precipitous path. Lawrence now had two rifles and plenty of ammunition. Hiding himself at a strategic point, he picked off the rest of the band as they came up that evening. — Lowell Thomas, *The Boys' Life of Colonel Lawrence.*

Reprinted by permission of the Century Company.

2

Billy Bones' stories were what frightened people worst of all. Dreadful stories they were—about hanging, and walking the plank, and storms at sea, and the Dry Tortugas, and wild deeds and places on the Spanish Main. By his own account he must have lived his life among some of the wickedest men that God ever allowed upon the sea; and the language in which he told these stories shocked our plain country people almost as much as the crimes that he described. My father was always saying the inn would be ruined, for people would soon cease coming there to be tyrannized over and put down, and sent shivering to their beds; but I really believe his presence did us good. People were frightened at the time, but on looking back they rather liked it; it was a fine excitement in a quiet country life; and there was even a party of the younger men who pretended to admire him, calling him a "true sea-dog," and a "real old salt," and such like names, and saying there was the sort of man that made England terrible at sea. — Robert Louis Stevenson, *Treasure Island.*

Reprinted by permission of Charles Scribner's Sons.

3

A circumstance which greatly tended to enhance the tyranny of the nobility and the sufferings of the inferior classes in England arose from the consequences of the Conquest of Duke William of Normandy. Four generations had not sufficed to blend the hostile blood of the Normans and Anglo-Saxons, or to unite, by common language and mutual interests, two hostile races, one of which still felt the elation of triumph, while the other groaned under all the consequences of defeat. The power had been completely placed in the hands of the Norman nobility by the event of the Battle of Hastings, and it had been used with no moderate hand. At court and in the castles of the great nobles, where the pomp and the state of a court was emulated, Norman-French was the only language employed; in courts of law, the pleadings and judgments were delivered in the same tongue. In short, French was the language of honour, of chivalry, and even of justice, while the far more manly and expressive Anglo-Saxon was abandoned to the use of rustics and hinds, who knew no other. — Sir Walter Scott, *Ivanhoe*

4

The separate American ideals are all founded on the basic ideal of democracy. Political democracy means government founded on the consent of the governed; but socially, and we might say religiously, democracy means something much deeper. It means the recognition of the dignity of man, of the worthwhileness of every man, woman, and child. Democracy also involves a recognition of the essential dignity of labour—that work is not the hallmark of the slave, but that the doing of a portion of the world's work, no matter how humble, is the rightful task and duty of every man and woman, justifying his claim to share in the bounty of the world. Democracy, then, is a social faith, a faith in the dignity of man, a conviction that it is the duty of men and women to do their daily work conscientiously and to face the tasks and problems of their country as free citizens working together for the common good. — CHADSEY, WEINBERG, AND MILLER, *America in the Making*.[1]

5

If vaccines and antitoxins are injected into a person, he is then immune to the particular disease for which the injection was made. This is acquired immunity. Vaccination results in a seven-year or longer immunity from smallpox. After vaccination, the cowpox, a mild form of smallpox, is the result, and the blood is filled with resisting bodies, called "antibodies," which remain there for years after there is no more trace of cowpox. If one has once had certain diseases, the body is then better able to resist these particular disease germs and will not get the disease again. Well-known examples are whooping cough and measles. This kind of freedom from disease is also called acquired immunity — PULVERMACHER AND VOSBURGH, *The World About Us*.[2]

6

Millions of people, presumably, are going to have in the near future, whether they want it or not, more time off than they ever dreamed of. An entire nation which has never learned to play has been presented with the great gift of leisure. Our playing is now, for the most part, done by proxy. We make paid entertainers rich by our inexperience in amusing ourselves. But vicarious amusements are not going to suffice to fill the spare hours which the future will bring. We must do better than that. We must acquire a new conception of play, one that demands active participation instead of passive acceptance. Radio, movies, athletic spectacles will all have a large place, but they will no longer suffice for a grown-up, healthy population. People must have something to make demands upon them physically and mentally, to develop and express them, and to give exercise to invention and imagination. If these diversions are of the kind that develops the complete man, mentally, socially, and physically, they will profoundly influence the course of human events. Indeed, the wise use of leisure may easily be an important, perhaps the most important, influence on the future course of our civilization. — EARNEST ELMO CALKINS

7

That man, I think, has had a liberal education, who has been so trained in youth that his body is the ready servant of his will, and does with ease and pleasure all the work that, as a mechanism, it is capable of; whose intellect is a clear, cold, logic engine, with all its parts of equal strength, and in smooth

[1], [2]*Reprinted by permission of the publisher, D. C. Heath and Company.*

working order; ready, like a steam engine, to be turned to any kind of work, and spin the gossamers as well as forge the anchors of the mind; whose mind is stored with a knowledge of the great and fundamental truths of Nature and of the laws of her operations; one who, no stunted ascetic, is full of life and fire, but whose passions are trained to come to heel by a vigorous will, the servant of a tender conscience; who has learned to love all beauty, whether of Nature or of art, to hate all vileness, and to respect others as himself.

Such a one, and no other, I conceive, has had a liberal education; for he is, as completely as a man can be, in harmony with Nature. He will make the best of her, and she of him. They will get on together rarely: she as his ever beneficent mother; he as her mouthpiece, her conscious self, her minister and interpreter. — THOMAS HUXLEY

8
WINDOW SHOPPING

She stood before a window, looking in
　At lovely trifles women joy to wear:
Soft silken things—a dainty boutonniere—
A bright-hued scarf—a gleaming jewelled pin;
Here at this shrine the age-old feminine
　Urge comes to womankind, gray embers flare
　Into a blaze again; caught in its snare,
It is a bond that makes them all akin.
Her features glowed—the years slipped away;
　She saw herself transformed in youth's attire,
Forgetful of each stinted yesterday
　When poverty had quenched all bright desire;
Then irony took the stage and closed the play
And raked the ash upon a smouldering fire.

— MARGARET E. BRUNER

Reprinted by permission of the author and Contemporary Verse.

9

The World is too much with us; late and soon,
Getting and spending, we lay waste our powers;
Little we see in Nature that is ours;
We have given our hearts away, a sordid boon!
This Sea that bares her bosom to the moon,
The winds that will be howling at all hours
And are up-gather'd now like sleeping flowers,
For this, for everything, we are out of tune;
It moves us not.—Great God! I'd rather be
A Pagan suckled in a creed outworn,—
So might I, standing on this pleasant lea,
Have glimpses that would make me less forlorn;
Have sight of Proteus rising from the sea;
Or hear old Triton blow his wreathéd horn.

WILLIAM WORDSWORTH

10

I met a traveller from an antique land,
Who said: Two vast and trunkless legs of stone

Stand in the desert. Near them on the sand,
Half sunk, a shatter'd visage lies, whose frown

And wrinkled lip and sneer of cold command
Tell that its sculptor well those passions read
Which yet survive, stamp'd on these lifeless things,
The hand that mock'd them and the heart that fed.

And on the pedestal these words appear:
"My name is Ozymandias, king of kings:
Look on my works, ye Mighty, and despair!"

Nothing beside remains. Round the decay
Of that colossal wreck, boundless and bare,
The lone and level sands stretch far away.
        — PERCY BYSSHE SHELLEY, "Ozymandias of Egypt"

Practice 3. Writing a Précis

From the assignment for to-morrow in history, economics, chemistry, physics, biology, physiography, or any other science, pick one or more paragraphs which seem difficult to you. Make a précis of the passage, applying the rules for reading difficult sentences and paragraphs to help you understand the ideas.

Mastering Effective English
Part III
MASTER CRAFTSMEN

Mastering the Art of Writing

Mastering Creative Expression

WHAT IS CREATIVE WRITING

WITHIN everyone there is a deep power of imagination for which a natural expression is creative writing. Just what is meant by "creative English"? W. Wilbur Hatfield's definition is "writing and speaking to relieve one's own mind and feelings, to share some outward or inward experience that is too good to keep". By no means does it imply far flights of the mind to the lands of the moon and intimate sessions with fantastic, gossamer unreality. In three sentences Joseph Conrad explained what creative writing meant to him: "My task which I am trying to achieve is, by the power of the written word, to make you hear, to make you feel—it is, before all, to make you *see*. That—and no more, and it is everything. If I succeed, you shall find there, according to your deserts, encouragement, consolation, fear, charm—all you demand—and, perhaps, also that glimpse of truth for which you have forgotten to ask."

An imaginative person interprets as well as he observes; he sees not just an untidy boy, down at the heels and raggedly dressed, but a father out of work and a poverty-stricken family, or perhaps a lazy, slovenly, frowzy mother. By observing actions and analyzing motives he "sees into" people, really knows them, and prepares to write about them. On the fact that a thrifty old man was ashamed to be seen picking up a piece of string De Maupassant built one of his masterpieces, "The Piece of String".

WRITERS AT WORK

The way to creative writing is open to all. There is but one password, and that is intelligent work. "Easy writing," remarks Conrad, "is not possible to me. My success seems in proportion to my effort, to my striving." H. G. Wells says, "I write as I walk because I want to get somewhere, and I write as straight as I can, just as I walk as straight as I can, because that is the best way to get there." While it is said that geniuses are born, not made, the average successful writer is made, not born, and even genius rolls up its shirt sleeves.

Practice 1. On Methods of Writing

For an oral report read what you can find about the methods of writing used or recommended by any good author. Read, for example, one or more of the following articles, most of which are reprinted in Rollo Walter Brown's *The Writer's Art* or H. Robinson Shipherd's *The Fine Art of Writing:*

Irvin Cobb: "How to Begin at the Top and Work Down," in the *American Magazine.* August, 1925 (Shipherd. p. 211)
Joseph Conrad: Preface to *The Nigger of the Narcissus* (Brown. p. 251)
Margaret Deland: "To the Girl Who Writes" (Shipherd. p. 220)
Dorothy Canfield Fisher: "How 'Flint and Fire' Started," in *Americans All,* edited by B. A. Heydrick
Benjamin Franklin: *Autobiography*
William Hazlitt: "On Familiar Style" and "On the Difference between Writing and Speaking" (Brown)
Katherine Mansfield: Introduction to "The Doves' Nest" (Shipherd. p. 258)
Somerset Maugham: *The Summing Up*
Christopher Morley: "The English Problem" (Shipherd. p. 262)
Frank Norris: "Simplicity in Art" and "A Problem in Fiction" (Brown)
Robert Louis Stevenson: "A College Magazine" and "On Style in Literature" (Shipherd. pp. 283 and 286)

MATERIAL

If the stars shone only one night in twenty-five years, how people on that happy night would gaze at the heavens and marvel! Because they shine almost every night, many people hardly notice them and don't know one star from another.

Our five senses, like a knife, seem sometimes to grow dull and need whetting by practice in observing attentively and thoughtfully as if we were scientists or story writers gathering material. When a person really sees the appearance and actions of people in classrooms, houses, offices, department stores, and autos, hears the differences in voices, and catches elusive smells and shades of touch and taste, he is assembling the raw materials out of which to build stories, essays, and poems.

Practice 2. Learning to Observe

1. Pass a store window, trying at one glance to see all it contains. Without looking again, note your impressions on a piece of paper. Then return to check the accuracy of your observation.
2. Record everything you see on one street corner on your way to school. On your way home, add details you omitted.
3. Describe the store where you buy your groceries (or another store) so that anyone in your class could recognize it. Include the salesmen and customers.
4. In school or outside of school observe a person's appearance closely and

then watch his actions for five minutes. Then make your reader or hearer see what you saw.

To increase your store of impressions, listen also to the experiences of others and read the best books, magazines, and newspapers. As a storehouse for all impressions, keep a notebook and write in it frequently. "It does not matter," says Christopher Morley, "from whom or what you borrow if you pay it back with earnings of your own."

Notebook

Set aside pages in your notebook for material that might be useful. Include clippings from magazines and newspapers and pictures which tell stories. Put these or similar headings at the tops of pages:

1. Plots—humorous or tragic complications
2. Themes
3. Setting—city, country, local colour
4. Characters—men, women, children
5. Animals
6. Anecdotes
7. Dialogue
8. Descriptions—places, people, things
9. Words
10. Figures of speech
11. Ideas—personal reactions
12. Books read—author, title, quotations, criticism

A YOUNG WRITER AT HIS DESK

All writers have a feeling of blankness before they start. The knitting of the brow and scratching of the head are a common lot; it takes time for the mind to be geared into activity. The thing to do is to have a definite time and place for work, to start work promptly and to keep at it without interruption, no matter if at first only empty phrases come. Stay at your desk, plan, think, and keep your pen moving. You will soon experience the inscrutable "inspiration of the writing table." The ideas will clear up, one idea suggest another, better ideas come, and the subject begin to take shape. On every second line of one side of your paper write out rapidly all that is in your mind. You will need half the lines and the other side of the paper for revision.

On re-reading, you may feel dissatisfied, disappointed with the result. The writing somehow fails to re-create your mood at the time of the experience; you haven't even made the reader see what you saw; the sentences are weak; something is missing. Now for the less thrilling but all-important job of revision! Apply everything you have learned about writing. Vary the beginnings of sentences, subordinate minor details, use sentences of different lengths and kinds.

Cut out flat words and phrases. Condense. With practice you will find it easier to express your ideas tersely and picturesquely.

Much of your time as a beginner will be spent in private, perspiring over the effort to dig your thoughts out of the comfortable recesses of your mind and set them sturdily in the open on paper. The waste-basket will be your chief audience. After much practice, there will be an essay worth having a friend read. Finally, you will be able to re-create in the reader your own original feeling, and you yourself will be satisfied with your work.

WORDS
Pictures

Because the word is the chief tool of expression, we should put ourselves and our feelings into words that will make another chuckle or sigh as we chuckled or sighed while we wrote. As an editorial writer in the *New York Sun* says, "You can put tears into words, as though they were so many little buckets; and you can hang smiles along them, like Monday's clothes on the line; or you can starch them with facts and stand them up like a picket fence; but you won't get the tears out unless you first put them in."

Command of words enables one to convey thought accurately and swiftly. Select concrete, picture-bringing words that exactly fit the meaning. Many words are unemployed, while others are worn to the bone from overwork.

(General) The sound came loudly from a distance.
(Concrete) The shot echoed like thunder from the hills.
(General) The bird sat lightly on my hand.
(Concrete) The sparrow perched gingerly on my index finger.
(General) The wind blew hard against the house.
(Concrete) The blast beat fiercely against the window.
(General) The boat went quickly to the shore.
(Concrete) The canoe shot like an arrow to the wooded shore.

Practice 3. Choosing Words

Using your imagination and the dictionary or Roget's *Thesaurus of English Words and Phrases*, write as many colourful words as you can for each of the following:

Example:

eat—chew, crunch, devour, gnaw, gobble, gulp, munch, peck

ask	do	good	nice	take
answer	fall	help	old	tell
begin	frightful	injury	pleasant	want
big	get	interesting	pretty	walk
break	give	leave	see	work
change	go	like	show	young

Suiting the Sound to the Sense

Words have a definite music of their own, and often suggest their meaning by their sound. Consider the variations of sound in these words, and listen attentively, first to the vowel sounds, and then to the consonant modifications of them: *purl, murmur, babble, chatter, rilling, swish, splash, gush, whirl, eddy.*

Notice the lightness of short vowels: *twinkle, twitter, shimmer, glimmer;* and the emphasis secured by long vowels and monosyllables; *deep, hole, pool, fine.*

From some of these—*babble, chatter, twitter, shimmer, glimmer*—we notice the effect of double consonants. Consider the prolonging effect of *l*, as in *howl, hill, yell*, and contrast with the short crisp *k* sounds in *bark, crag, crack.*

Many words are imitative of the sounds of nature whence they are derived: *buzz, whisper, cuckoo, whip-poor-will.*

Some sounds seem suited to dolorous expressions, as the long *o: woe, moan, alone;* as others are bright, as the long *i: "Arise, shine,* for the *light* of the Lord is upon you."

Poetry has been quicker than prose to make use of this imitative harmony.

1. The lights begin to twinkle from the rocks. — TENNYSON
2. The long day wanes, the slow moon climbs, the deep
   Moans round with many voices. — TENNYSON
3. And ere three shrill notes the piper uttered,
   You heard as if an army muttered;
   And the muttering grew to a grumbling;
   And the grumbling grew to a mighty rumbling;
   And out of the houses the rats came tumbling. — BROWNING

Yet every effective author must write with the sound of the words in his ear.

Practice 4. Suiting the Sound to the Sense

1. Use in effective sentences:

clamour	clatter	hissed	roar	slam
clang	hammer	moan	shriek	squeak

2. List five or more other words the sound of which suggests the sense.

3. List five or more soft, smooth, musical words like *moon, lily, cool, lowly, mole, rill.*

4. Copy into your note-book at least a dozen effective passages where the sound resembles the sense. See that not fewer than three of them are from prose.

The Romance of Words

Besides the exact connotation, the derivation, and the sound, every word carries with it an air of association. Some words have persistently kept bad company and others good; some have a halo of holiness, others an atmosphere of romance, adventure, ecstasy. We must learn to choose our words as we choose our friends for their character and tastes.

WORDS

How I love the mere words, the picturesque and dear words,
    Romany and Patteran and Caravan and Chal—
How they lilt and sing to me; flame-lit, how they bring to me
    Heathered moors and bending skies and gypsy carnival.

The sun-swept and the wild words I dreamed of as a child, words
    Like Lariat and Chaparral, Coyote, Pinto, Sage;
How they flung a dare to me of life without a care to me;
    How the flying hoofbeats rang across the printed page!

The lanthorn-lit, the old words, the scarlet and the gold words,
    Palfrey, Jerkin, Yeoman, Falcon, Glebe, and Glade;
Minstrel, Lance, and Tourney—what an age-long journey
    Through the posterns of the Past, alone and half afraid.

The wind blown and the sea words, the lawless and the free words,
    Spindrift, Doubloon, Cutlass, Jib, Corsair, Yardarm Crew;
Whispering wild tales to me—ah, how each unveils to me
    Palm-fringed islands rising green against the ocean blue!

The balsam-scented North, words that call untamed hearts forth, words
    Like Wanigan, and Mackinaw, Duffel, Tumpline, Trail;
While the languid South to me turns a lover-mouth to me
    Jasmine-scented, passion-flowered, by the Bayou pale,

Some may live their fair dreams, costly, jewelled, rare dreams;
    Some may rove the luring world as free as homing birds;
But still I'll find my all for me, close-waiting at my call for me,
    In my printed palaces, bright-tapestried with words.
        — MARTHA HASKELL CLARKE.

By arrangement with the publishers, The Youth's Companion.

The Exact Word

Discrimination, the ability to make fine distinctions, is essential in conveying exact impressions. Flaubert says, "Whatever may be the thing one wishes to say, there is but one word for expressing it, only one verb to animate it, only one adjective to qualify it. It is essential to search for this word, for this verb, for this adjective, until they are discovered, and to be satisfied with nothing else." In a garden a person who uses his eyes sees asters, roses, larkspurs, zinnias, marigolds, and petunias, not just flowers, and one who is moderately intelligent about flowers also knows the names.

Practice 5. Choosing the Exact Word

1. List fifteen or more colours—for example, lilac-blue, scarlet, crimson, indigo.
2. Prepare a list of as many kinds of each of the following as you know: dogs, animals, birds, trees, bushes, flowers, grasses, vegetables, farm crops, chickens, houses, apples, chairs, carpets or rugs, tools, jewels, cloth.
3. In a sentence for each describe (1) a loud noise, (2) the taste of lemon, (3) the colour of the sunset, (4) the feel of kid gloves, (5) the odour of roses.

Combining Words

Although "adjectivitis"—that is, piling one adjective on top of another—is one of the commonest diseases among young writers, it is possible sometimes to combine two simple words into a vivid expression which causes the reader to hear a sound or see, feel, smell, or taste an object. A boat may be "a wave-tossed canoe," "a flat-bottomed row-boat," "a full-rigged yacht," or "a 30,000-ton battleship."

Practice 6. Two-Word Modifiers

Describe each of the following with a two-word modifier:

Examples:

dog-eared book, thumb-marked page, confetti-strewn streets, carelessly-scrawled message, owl-eyed shoe buttons.

automobile	book	factory	lips	schoolboy
beach	coat	hair	park	street

Suiting the Movement to the Mood

As words have an onomatopoetical sound, suiting the sound to the sense, so sentences and paragraphs may have a movement suitable to the mood. If the mood is dreamy or sentimental, then smooth rhythmic sentences are appropriate; if the mood is vigorous, or hurried, or argumentative, a short, quick or staccato movement is suitable. Sometimes the sentiment requires dignity or grandeur.

Rhythmic style:

1. DEATH OF LITTLE PAUL

Paul had never risen from his little bed. He lay there, listening to the noises in the street, quite tranquilly; not caring much how the time went, but watching it and watching everything about him with observing eyes.

When the sunbeams struck into his room through the rustling blinds, and quivered on the opposite wall like golden water, he knew that evening was coming on, and that the sky was red and beautiful. As the reflection died away, and a gloom went creeping up the wall, he watched it deepen, deepen, deepen into night. Then he thought how the long streets were dotted with lamps, and how the peaceful stars were shining overhead. His fancy had a strange tendency to wander up the river, which he knew was flowing through the great city: and now he thought how black it was, and how deep it would look, reflecting the hosts of stars—and more than all, how steadily it rolled away to meet the sea. — DICKENS, *Dombey and Son*.

2. THE SONG OF THE SIRENS

And all things stayed around and listened; the gulls sat in white lines along the rocks; on the beach great seals lay basking, and kept time with lazy heads; while silver shoals of fish came up to hearken, and whispered as they broke the shining calm. The wind overhead hushed his whistling, as he shepherded his clouds toward the west; and the clouds stood in mid blue, and listened dreaming, like a flock of golden sheep. — KINGSLEY, *The Heroes*

Quick-moving style:

1. THE BARRAGE

The British barrage struck. The air gushed in hot surges along the river valley, and uproar never imagined by me swung from ridge to ridge. The east was scarlet with dawn and the flickering gunflashes; I thanked God I was not in the assault, and joined the subdued carriers nervously lighting cigarettes in one of the cellars, sitting there on the steps, studying my watch. The ruins of Hamel were soon crashing chaotically with German shells, and jags of iron and broken wood and brick whizzed past the cellar mouth. When I gave the word to move, it was obeyed with no pretence of enthusiasm. I was forced to shout and swear, and the carrying party, some with shoulders hunched, as if in a snowstorm, dully picked up their bomb buckets and went ahead. The wreckage around seemed leaping with flame. Never had we smelt high explosive so thick and foul, and there was no distinguishing one shell-burst from another, save by the black or tawny smoke that suddenly shaped in the general miasma. We walked along the river road, passed the sandbag dressing-station that had been rigged up only a night or two earlier where the front line ("Shankill Terrace") crossed the road and had already been battered in; we entered No Man's Land, past the trifling British wire on its knife-rests, but we could make very little sense of ourselves or the battle. —EDMUND BLUNDEN, *Undertones of War*.

By permission of the author and publishers, R. Cobden-Sanderson, Ltd., London.

2. GERARD'S ESCAPE

What followed? Not the men coming out, but the fire rushed in at them like a living death, and the first I thought to fight with was blackened and crumpled on the floor like a leaf. One fearsome yell, and dumb for ever. The feet ran up again, but fewer. I heard them hack with their swords a little way up at the mill's wooden sides; but they had no time to hew their way out: the fire and reek were at their heels, and the smoke burst out at every loophole, and oozed blue in the moonlight through each crevice. I hobbled back, racked with pain and fury. There were white faces up at my window. They saw me. They cursed me. I cursed them back and shook my naked sword: "Come down the road I came," I cried. — CHARLES READE, *The Cloister and the Hearth*.

Dignified style:

SAMUEL JOHNSON TO LORD CHESTERFIELD

Is not a patron, my lord, one who looks with unconcern on a man struggling for life in the water, and, when he has reached ground, encumbers him with help? The notice you have been pleased to take of my labours, had it been early had been kind; but it has been delayed till I am indifferent, and cannot enjoy it; till I am solitary and cannot impart it; till I am known, and do not want it. I hope it is no very cynical asperity not to confess obligations where no benefit has been received, or to be unwilling that the public should consider me as owing that to a patron, which Providence has enabled me to do for myself. — SAMUEL JOHNSON

Practice 7. Writing Rhythmic Prose

Using the *Death of Little Paul* or *The Song of the Sirens* as a model, write a piece of rhythmic prose. Analyze your model, notice the parallel clauses, the repetitions, and the variations. Use the same devices in your own paragraph. These topics may be suggestive:

1. Dr. Manette in prison watches the sunlight on the walls of his cell and recalls his home. 2. An old negro sits beside the river and in reverie recalls his southern home. 3. An old Highlander sits dreaming of his highland home. 4. A young man, stirred by an incident he has witnessed or read about, builds dreams of the future. 5. A description of a field of waving wheat lying between rolling hills.

Practice 8. Writing About Action

With *The Barrage* or *Gerard's Escape* as model, write a paragraph of prose imitative in its movement of action, commotion, haste. Are these suggestions helpful?

1. A frightened child races through the woods. 2. A kingbird chases a hawk. 3. Terror stricken people scramble from a circus tent. 4. A runaway car careens down a street. 5. Hornets chase a boy who has molested the nest.

FIGURES OF SPEECH

What is a Figure of Speech?

Notice the two ways of expressing each of the following ideas:

1. When we are in trouble, we find who our real friends are.
2. The light of friendship is like the light of phosphorus—seen plainest when all around is dark.
3. Everybody has some envy in his make-up.
4. Envy lurks at the bottom of the human heart, like a viper in its hole.
5. He was nervous and excited.
6. He was about as calm and collected as a man with St. Vitus dance walking a tight rope over Niagara Falls in a hurricane. — WITWER
7. She showed in many ways that she liked him.
8. She threw herself at him like a medicine ball.

Numbers 1, 3, 5, and 7 are straightforward, matter-of-fact expressions of the ideas. In 2, 4, 6, and 8 figures of speech, or intentional deviations from the usual forms of expression, are used to make the ideas concrete, vivid, beautiful, forceful, or amusing. Everybody enjoys moving pictures and word pictures, but few can understand lengthy abstractions.

Simile

A simile is a definitely stated comparison of two unlike objects that have one point in common. Regularly *as* or *like* is used to make the comparison.

Her thoughts in the morning are as tangled as her hair.
He burst out of the door like an explosion.
Red as a rose is she.
You have about as much chance as a woodpecker making a nest in a concrete telephone pole.

Likening one man to another, one house to another, or one river to another is not a figure of speech: "He looks like his father."

Metaphor

A metaphor is an implied comparison between unlike objects that have one point in common. *As* or *like* is not used.

Exactitude in small matters is the soul of discipline.
Some books are to be tasted, others to be swallowed, and some few to be chewed and digested. — BACON
The Giants uncorked a devastating six-run rally in the fifth inning.
As runs began to pour over the plate in a torrent, the crowd roared itself purple.

A mixed metaphor results from using in a sentence two or more contradictory metaphors. Occasionally metaphors are effectively mixed for humorous effects. Avoid, however, in serious speech or writing such ridiculous mixtures as the following:

The politicians will keep cutting the wool off the sheep that lays the golden eggs, until they pump it dry.
I smell a rat, I see it floating in the air, but I shall nip it in the bud.

A mixture of a metaphor and a literal expression is often absurd.

Boyle was the father of chemistry and the brother of the Earl of York.

As two of the preceding sentences indicate, metaphors are frequently used in sports stories. Many slang expressions are metaphors: *bats in his belfry, crash the gate, dry up, spill the beans, step on the gas, get his goat, high-hat, hit the hay, peachy, the big cheese, hold your horses, a good egg, also-ran.*

Practice 9.   Metaphors in Slang

To the list just given add five slang expressions that are metaphors.

Metaphors are commonly used in advertising—for example, "a fleet of superb trains"; "a whale of a success"; "weigh the evidence"; "breeze-swept apartments"; "an oasis in the blistering desert of torridity"; "you'll be convinced in the wink of a humming bird's eyelash."

✓ ***Practice 10.***   Metaphors in Advertisements

Find five metaphors in advertisements.

Difference Between a Metaphor and a Simile
Similes
1. His laugh was shrill and high, like the sound of a cock crowing.
2. He had an expression of self-assurance which covered him like a coat of enamel.
3. The long deserts are like flames, burning the camel's foot.
Metaphors
1. He had a shrill, high cock-crow of a laugh.
2. He has an expression of enamelled self-assurance.
3. Long, long deserts scorch the camel's foot.

Note that every metaphor may be changed to a simile and every simile to a metaphor, and that the metaphor is briefer, swifter, and livelier than the simile. The metaphor is a condensed simile. Usually, however, the longer simile, in which the comparison is expressed, is easier to understand or picture than the terse metaphor, in which the comparison is implied.

✓ ***Practice 11.***   Naming Figures of Speech

Name the figure in each of the following.   What are compared? What is the point of likeness?   Which figures seem to you particularly striking or effective?   Why?

Example:
> Life's but a walking shadow, a poor player,
> That struts and frets his hour upon the stage
> And then is heard no more. — SHAKESPEARE

Metaphor.   Life is compared with a shadow and with a poor actor.   Life, like a walking shadow or the performance of a poor actor, doesn't last long. This is an effective figure because in a striking, unusual, and rememberable way Shakespeare reminds us that life is short.

1. He felt like the symptoms on a medicine bottle.
2. Contentment is a pearl of great price.
3. To listen to the advice of a treacherous friend is like drinking poison from a golden cup.

4. Your face, my thane, is as a book where men
May read strange matters. — SHAKESPEARE

5. Good nature, like a bee, collects honey from everywhere. Ill nature, like
a spider, sucks poison from the sweetest flower.

6. Life is an isthmus between two eternities.

7. The woman was a tigress in the defense of her children.

8. Writing is like pulling the trigger of a gun; if you are not loaded, nothing
happens. — CANBY

9. The human mind should be like a good hotel—open the year round. —
PHELPS

10. Spare moments are the gold dust of time.

11. There are many minds that are like a sheet of thin ice. You have to
skate on them pretty rapidly or you'll go through. — MORLEY

12. For joy is the best wine, and Silas's guineas were golden wine of that
sort. — GEORGE ELIOT

13. I had been all this time a very hedgehog, bristling all over with determination. — DICKENS

14. Liddy, like a little brook, though shallow, was always rippling. — HARDY

15. He has the sense of humour of a crocodile.

16. She sings as if mere speech had taken fire. — YEATS

Notebook

Watch for striking similes and metaphors and copy them on the
page of your notebook reserved for figures of speech.

Practice 12.   Changing Figures of Speech

Complete the similes and then change the first ten of them to metaphors:

1. Marie was as quiet as a ——.
2. They were as swift as —— and as strong as ——.
3. Her locks were yellow as ——.
4. Gloom hung like a —— over the land.
5. Fred's shoes look like ——.
6. Father is as wise as ——.
7. He is as sly as ——.
8. Tom is as noisy as ——.
9. Jack was blinking like ——.
10. He was as restless as ——.
11. He is as angry as ——.
12. The answer came clear as ——.
13. When Juliet's father heard of her refusal to marry the prince, he roared
like a ——.
14. Some clever folk are as changeable as ——.
15. She is as sad as ——.
16. Her heart beat quickly like ——.
17. His reasoning was as clear as ——.
18. It was as hard to catch as ——.
19. He was as agile as ——.
20. He is as faithful as ——.

Practice 13. Using Figures of Speech

Express these thoughts in metaphorical language. Then change the first ten metaphors to similes. Do you prefer the similes or metaphors? Why?

1. He is a hard worker.
2. He is stubborn.
3. You are foolish.
4. When he knows what he wants, he tries until he gets it.
5. Everyone in the schoolroom was busy.
6. He is innocent.
7. He was brave in the fight.
8. He swims well.
9. He thought quickly.
10. She had black hair.
11. There were a great many faces in front of me.
12. He was thoroughly indignant.
13. He kept his eyes on the floor.
14. She walks softly.
15. In love he was fickle.
16. She arose quickly.
17. The children ran to him.
18. She spoke quickly.
19. He was eager to go.
20. She had soft skin.

Other Figures

Personification, a kind of metaphor, consists in giving personal attributes to inanimate objects or abstract ideas. Sometimes the names of the things personified are capitalized.

The wind whistled, wailed, sobbed, and whispered.

But I am faint; my gashes cry for help. — SHAKESPEARE

Joy and Temperance and Repose
Slam the door on the doctor's nose.

The gloom slinks up the tenement stairs.

Apostrophe is an address to the absent as if present, or the inanimate as if human.

Shine! shine! shine!
Pour down your warmth, great sun! — WHITMAN

Byron! how sweetly sad thy melody!
Attuning still the soul to tenderness. — KEATS

Metonymy is a figure of speech in which one word is put for another which it suggests. Four common relations that give rise to metonymy are—

1. Container and thing contained
Please address the chair (chairman).

2. Sign and thing signified

The pen (books, newspapers, and magazines) is mightier than the sword (armies and navies).

Have you no respect for gray hairs (age)?

3. An author and his books

We are reading George Eliot (her novels).

4. The part for the whole

She has seen sixteen summers (years).

All hands (men) to the deck!

antithesis is a contrast of words or ideas. As white seems whiter when placed beside black, and a sound seems loudest on a quiet night or in a quiet place, so words or ideas which are contrasted are emphatic. Antithesis is most effective if the phrasing of the contrasted ideas is parallel.

His body is active, but his mind is sluggish.

Easy writing makes hard reading; hard writing, easy reading.

Whoso loveth instruction loveth knowledge, but he that hateth reproof is brutish. — BIBLE

To use too many circumstances ere one come to the matter is wearisome; to use none at all is blunt.

A bird in the hand is worth two in the bush.

Hyperbole is exaggeration not intended to deceive. Some humorists —Mark Twain, for example—use hyperbole freely as a device for making people laugh.

His hands dangled a mile out of his sleeves. — IRVING

Waves mountain-high broke over the reef.

When he told me the joke, I almost died laughing.

The movie bored me to death.

So frowned the mighty combatants that hell grew darker at their frown. — MILTON

His voice could be heard a mile away.

Irony is saying the opposite of what is meant in a tone or manner that shows what the speaker thinks.

After Norman had wasted his evening in nonsense, his father remarked, "Don't you think you have studied too hard this evening?"

It was very kind of you to remind me of my humiliation.

To cry like a baby—that's a fine way for a man to act.

Practice 14. Effective Figures of Speech

Name the figures of speech in the following sentences. If the figure is a comparison, name the objects compared. Which figures do you consider most effective? Why?

1. The greatest art is always as obvious as the sea, and as immense.

2. Thy word is a lamp unto my feet. — BIBLE

3. Our birth is but a sleep and a forgetting. — WORDSWORTH
4. O wild West Wind, thou breath of Autumn's being. — SHELLEY
5. His trousers are a mile too short.
6. Now Rumour the messenger went about the street, telling the tale of the dire death and fate of the wooers. — HOMER
7. All the world's a stage. — SHAKESPEARE
8. Pleasures are like poppies spread. — BURNS
9. The train flew at lightning speed.
10. The Puritan hated bear-baiting, not because it gave pain to the bear but because it gave pleasure to the spectators. — MACAULAY

Agfa-Ansco Film

The rhythmic motion of good skating couples would be easier to express by figures of speech than by literal statement.

11. Sport that wrinkled Care derides,
    And Laughter holding both his sides. — MILTON
12. I have no spur to prick the sides of my intent. — SHAKESPEARE
13. Roll on, thou deep and dark blue Ocean, roll. — BYRON
14. At one stride comes the dark. — COLERIDGE
15. Walter the Doubter was exactly five feet six inches in height and six feet five inches in circumference. — IRVING
16. His bump of humour is a dent. — JOSEPH LINCOLN
17. The express train ran so fast that the mile posts looked like fence rails.
18. He bought a hundred head of cattle.
19. There is a tide in the affairs of men,
    Which, taken at the flood, leads on to fortune. — SHAKESPEARE

20. One occasion trod upon the other's heels. — DICKENS
21. You look about as fat as a stall-fed knitting needle. — WHITE
22. Life is a leaf of paper white,
    Whereon each one of us may write
    His word or two. — LOWELL
23. They work to pass, not to know; and outraged Science takes her revenge.
    They do pass, and they don't know. — HUXLEY
24. Every man would live long, but no man would be old.
25. The tale of his ungentle past was scarred upon his face. — LOCKE
26. When people have wooden heads, you know, it can't be helped. — GEORGE ELIOT
27. To err is human; to forgive, divine. — POPE
28. Character is what we are; reputation is what men think we are.
29. The harbour was crowded with masts.
30. What has the gray-haired prisoner done?
    Has murder stained his hand with gore?
    Not so; his crime is a fouler one—
    God made the old man poor. — WHITTIER

Practice 15. Effective Expressions

Of the two expressions of each idea, which is more effective? Tell why you prefer it. Name the figure of speech if there is one.

1. He wore canoes on his feet.
   He wore very big shoes.
2. There are five hundred houses in the village.
   It is a village of five hundred chimneys.
3. Night's candles are burnt out.
   The stars, which are like candles, are gone since it is morning.
4. His clothes did not fit him.
   His garments fitted him like a shirt on a handspike.
5. He bent with dour determination to pluck a coy snail from its reverie beneath a head of lettuce.
   He leaned over to pick up the snail that was under a head of lettuce.
6. Rain scampers over the shingles.
   The rain falls lightly and quickly on the roof.
7. He had a big snow-white beard which hid his whole face.
   He was lost behind his beard, as behind a snowdrift.
8. The birches stood like frozen feathers.
   The tall thin birches were frozen and looked like feathers.
9. She doesn't like anything that is not what it seems to be.
   She prefers genuine cotton to imitation silk.
10. His vest pocket was crowded with pencils and cigars.
    His vest pocket was so filled with cigars and pencils, he looked like a miniature pipe organ.
11. She had a sudden thought, but it vanished as quickly as it came.
    A little mouse of a thought went scampering across her mind and popped into its hole again.
12. It is disappointing to meet a well-dressed but unintelligent woman.
    A well-dressed but mindless woman is like a silly book in a beautiful binding.

13. Life has for everyone happy experiences and unpleasant ones.
    Life is made up of marble and mud.
14. The short evening flew away on gossamer wings.
    The evening passed quickly.
15. You have put the cart before the horse.
    You have put first what should be last.

TOWARDS A MORE PICTURESQUE SPEECH

The use of metaphor is habitual with some people, and gives to their conversation a vitality which is lacking in most of us. It is not the prerogative of university graduates. Peasants, farmers, and artisans often shame the more literate both by the penetration of their observation and the picturesqueness of their language. The *Reader's Digest* quotes, month by month, some of the most striking of the phrases and sentences which it has gleaned. Let us try to keep our language alive by vigilance and effort, speaking and writing as vividly as we can.

Practice 16. Choosing Picturesque Expressions

Cull from your reading picturesque phrases and sentences and make a note-book collection of them. For a taste:
1. She's learned to say things with her eyes that others waste time putting into words. — CAREY FORD
2. A sleight-of-tongue performance. — MARGARET AYRES BARNES
3. She felt in italics and thought in capitals. — HENRY JAMES
4. The wrinkled half of my life. — THOMAS HARDY
5. The sky had been washed with rain and scrubbed with wind until it shone. — ANNE PARISH
6. The bells and clocks of the town were discussing midnight. — KATE O'BRIEN
7. He lights one question on the stub of the last. — MARGUERITE HENRY
8. Fireflies were lighting matches on black shadows. — CAPTAIN FREDERICK MOORE
9. A smile as contagious as a yawn. — R. H. MACDONALD
10. Sleet wrapped the land in cellophane. — WALTER B. PITKIN

UNIT TWENTY-THREE

Effective Literary Devices

READERS of good prose, admiring the beauty of its language and structure, seldom analyze that structure to learn how the effect has been secured; yet when we have done so, we have an additional source of delight in the recognition of the skill of the artist. It would be impossible to detail all the devices by which authors have enhanced the effectiveness of their writing, but if we can master a few of these and recognize the deliberation with which they have been made, we have a stimulation for personal endeavour in our own inventions to secure whatever effect we desire.

ON THE USE OF MODELS

Creative writing follows the mastery of technique, though there is no reason why the student should not make the occasional essay as he learns. For the learning process there is no more effective method than the study and imitation of good models. Professor Lounsbury says:

"The art of writing, like that of painting and sculpture, is an imitative art. Accordingly the culture and perception of beauty necessary to produce success in it are best and soonest acquired, not by the study of grammatical and rhetorical text-books, but by the imitation, conscious or unconscious, of some one, or some number of those whom the race regard as its great literary representatives. Different minds, or minds in different grades of development, will exhibit preferences for different authors. The choice is not a matter of moment, provided the one chosen is worthy and appeals to the chooser, not because the study of him is a duty, but because it is a delight. To become thoroughly conversant with the work of a great writer, to be influenced by his method of giving utterance to his ideas, to feel profoundly the power and beauty of his style, is worth more for the development of expression than the mastery of all the rhetorical rules that were ever invented. This has been the inspiration and salvation of numberless men, who have never seen the inside of an institute of learning. He who of his own accord has sat reverently at the feet of the great masters of English literature, need have no fear that their spirit will not inform, so far as in him lies, the spirit of their disciple. Connected with it, too, there is incidentally one further benefit. Constant familiarity with the language of authors of the first rank, imparts in time that almost intuitive sense of what is right or wrong in usage which distinguishes the cultivated man of letters from the sciolist who bases his judgment upon what he has found in grammars and manuals."

386

Similar evidence is given by Robert Louis Stevenson, one of the most finished stylists who has written in English.

Whenever I read a book or passage that particularly pleased me, in which a thing was said or an effect rendered with propriety, in which there was either some perspicuous force or some happy distinction in style, I must sit down at once and set myself to ape that quality. . . . That, like it or not, is the way to learn to write; whether I have profited or not, that is the way. It was so Keats learned, and there was never a finer temperament for literature than Keats'; it was so, if we could trace it, that all men have learned.

ON KILLING ORIGINALITY

Perhaps I hear some one cry out, But this is not the way to become original! It is not; nor is there any way but to be born so. Nor yet, if you are born original, is there anything in this training that shall clip the wings of your originality. There can be none more original than Montaigne, neither could any one be more unlike Cicero, yet no craftsman can fail to see how much the one must have tried in his time to imitate the other. Burns is the very type of a prime force in letters; he was of all men the most imitative. Shakespeare himself, the imperial, proceeds directly from a school. It is only from a school that we can expect to have good writers; it is almost invariably from a school that great writers, these lawless exceptions, issue. Nor is there anything here that should astonish the inconsiderate. Before he can tell what cadences he prefers, the student should have tried all that are possible; before he can choose and preserve a fitting key of words, he should long have practised the literary scales; and it is only after years of such gymnastics that he can sit down at last, legions of words swarming to his call, dozens of turns of phrase simultaneously bidding for his choice, and he himself knowing what he wants to do and (within the narrow limits of a man's ability) able to do it." — ROBERT LOUIS STEVENSON, *A College Magazine.*

By permission of the publishers, Charles Scribner's Sons.

From here to the end of our course we shall be studying the devices by which the artist and the artificer have worked their magic—which is often simpler than the uninitiated believe.

The two models and imitative exercises which follow will give you an idea how models may be imitated. It is not always necessary to follow so closely as the first of these, but it is sometimes good judgment to do so.

Model:

THE STRANGER
By LAFCADIO HEARN

The Italian had kept us all spellbound for hours, while a great yellow moon was climbing higher and higher above the leaves of the bananas that nodded weirdly at the windows. Within the great hall a circle of attentive listeners, —composed of that motley mixture of the wanderers of all nations, such as can be found only in New Orleans, and perhaps Marseilles,—sat in silence about the lamplit table, riveted by the speaker's dark eyes and rich voice. There was a natural music in those tones; the stranger changed as he spoke like a wizard weaving a spell. And speaking to each one in the tongue of his own land, he told them of the Orient. For he had been a wanderer in many lands; and afar off, touching the farther horn of the moonlight crescent, lay awaiting him a long, graceful vessel with a Greek name, which would unfurl her white wings for flight with the first ruddiness of morning.

"I see that you are a smoker," observed the stranger to his host as he rose to go. "May I have the pleasure of presenting you with a Turkish pipe? I brought it from Constantinople."

It was moulded of blood-red clay after a fashion of Moresque art, and fretted about its edges with gilded work like the ornamentation girdling the minarets of a mosque. And a faint perfume, as of the gardens of Damascus, clung to its gaudy bowl, whereupon were deeply stamped mysterious words in the Arabian tongue.

The voice had long ceased to utter its musical syllables. The guests had departed; the lamps were extinguished within. A single ray of moonlight breaking through the shrubbery without fell upon a bouquet of flowers, breathing out their perfumed souls into the night. Only the host remained— dreaming of moons larger than ours, and fiercer summers; minarets white and keen, piercing a cloudless sky, and the many-fountained pleasure-places of the East. And the pipe exhaled its strange and mystical perfume, like the scented breath of a summer's night in the rose-gardens of a Sultan. Above in deeps of amethyst, glimmered the everlasting lamps of heaven; and from afar, the voice of muezzin seemed to cry, in tones liquidly sweet as the voice of the stranger—

"All ye who are about to sleep, commend your souls to Him who never sleeps."

By arrangement with the publishers, Houghton, Mifflin Company.

Imitation:

THE LECTURER

(*After* LAFCADIO HEARN)

The lecturer had held our close attention for an hour or more, while the heavens grew dark above the towers of the steeple that crowned the church. In the hall, a circle of fascinated listeners, composed of hero-worshipping school girls in a group typical of a church club, sat in silence about their leader's chair, awed by the speaker's marvellous story and clear, deep voice. There was a witchery in those tones. The lecturer gazed at us as she spoke, like one hypnotized, and speaking to us in the common parlance of the day, she told us of the Arctic. And as she talked, the listeners discovered a strange new land with her. For the first time, they beheld the rough, wild beauty of a Northern springtime, and struggled under the ice-mailed fist of the tyrant winter. They sensed the over-powering vastness of earth and sea and sky, and felt the loneliness of the Barren Lands. For the lecturer had the distinction of being the first white woman to live in the R.C.M.P. post at Chesterfield Inlet; and already the tongueless, voiceless waste was calling her back to her Northern home.

"Now, I would like to leave your leader something from my collection of souvenirs," observed the lecturer, before she left. "May I give you this Eskimo lamp? I brought it from Chesterfield Inlet."

It was cut from rich black soapstone, in the fashion of all primitive races, and smooth about the lid, with an edge like the tapering blade of a knife.

And a faint odour, as of some light oil, clung to its black bowl, whereon was attached a small, crude handle.

The voice had long ceased to utter its bell-toned syllables. The club members had departed, leaving the hall in quiet darkness. A quiet wind, wandering through the belfry, shook a few golden notes from the chimes, winging from their Gothic arches into the night. Only the leader remained, dreaming of a climate colder than ours, and of months-long nights; northern lights, cathedral-arched and rainbow-tinted, shifting through the sky; and the daring courage of the adventurous nomads who dwelt beneath them; the endless blinding snows—nothing but mounds of ice and age-old rock, and hills of rock, and age-old ice, and snow, and snow, and still more snow.

And the lamp exhaled its oily odour, like the warm breath of a fat-fed fire in an icy igloo. Above, through the branches, flickered the eternal candles at the altars of Heaven; and from afar the choir of the Arctic winds seemed to sing, deep as the voice of the lecturer:

"All ye who love to brave the danger of a great adventure, come, try your strength in the romantic North." — Pupil

Model:

THE WINE-SHOP
(*A Tale of Two Cities*, Chapter V)

This wine-shop keeper was a bull-necked, martial-looking man of thirty, and he should have been of a hot temperament, for, although it was a bitter day, he wore no coat, but carried one slung over his shoulder. His shirt-sleeves were rolled up, too, and his brown arms were bare to the elbows. Neither did he wear anything more on his head than his own crisply curling, short dark hair. He was a dark man altogether, with good eyes and a good bold breadth between them. Good-humoured looking on the whole, but implacable-looking, too; evidently a man of a strong resolution and a set purpose; a man not desirable to be met rushing down a narrow pass with a gulf on either side, for nothing would turn the man.

Madame Defarge his wife, sat in the shop behind the counter as he came in. Madame Defarge was a stout woman of about his own age, with a watchful eye that seldom seemed to look at anything, a large hand heavily ringed, a steady face, strong features, and great composure of manner. There was a character about Madame Defarge, from which one might have predicted that she did not often make mistakes against herself in any of the reckonings over which she presided. Madame Defarge, being sensitive to cold, was wrapped in fur, and had a quantity of bright shawl twined about her head, though not to the concealment of her large ear-rings. Her knitting was before her, but she had laid it down to pick her teeth with a tooth-pick. Thus engaged, with her right elbow supported by her left hand, Madame Defarge said nothing when her lord came in, but coughed just one grain of cough. This, in combination with the lifting of her darkly defined eyebrows over her tooth-pick by the breadth of a line, suggested to her husband that he would do well to look round the shop among the customers for any new customer who had dropped in while he stepped over the way.

The wine-shop keeper accordingly rolled his eyes about, until they rested upon an elderly gentleman and a young lady, who were seated in a corner.

Other company was there; two playing cards, two playing dominoes, three standing by the counter lengthening out a short supply of wine. As he passed behind the counter, he took notice that the elderly gentleman said in a look to the young lady, "This is our man."

"What the devil do *you* do in that galley there!" said Monsieur Defarge to himself; "I don't know you."

But he feigned not to notice the two strangers, and fell into discourse with the triumvirate of customers who were drinking at the counter.

"How goes it, Jacques?" said one of the three to Monsieur Defarge. "Is all the spilt wine swallowed?"

"Every drop, Jacques," answered Monsieur Defarge.

When this interchange of Christian names was effected, Madame Defarge, picking her teeth with her toothpick, coughed another grain of cough, and raised her eyebrows by the breadth of another line.

"It is not often," said the second of the three, addressing Monsieur Defarge, "that many of these miserable beasts know the taste of wine, or of anything but black bread and death. Is it not so, Jacques?"

"It is so, Jacques," Monsieur Defarge returned.

At this second interchange of the Christian name, Madame Defarge, still using her toothpick with profound composure, coughed another grain of cough, and raised her eyebrows by the breadth of another line.

The last of the three now said his say, as he put down his empty drinking vessel and smacked his lips.

"Ah! So much the worse! A bitter taste it is that such poor cattle always have in their mouths, and hard lives they live, Jacques. Am I not right, Jacques?"

"You are right, Jacques," was the response of Monsieur Defarge.

This third interchange of the Christian names was completed at the moment when Madame Defarge put her toothpick by, kept her eyebrows up, and slightly rustled in her seat.

"Hold then! True!" muttered her husband. "Gentlemen—my wife!"

The three customers pulled off their hats to Madame Defarge with three flourishes. She acknowledged their homage by bending her head, and giving them a quick look. Then she glanced in a casual manner round the wine-shop, took up her knitting with great apparent calmness and repose of spirit, and became absorbed in it.

"Gentlemen," said her husband, who had kept his bright eye observantly upon her, "good day. The chamber, furnished bachelor-fashion, that you wish to see, and were inquiring for when I stepped out, is on the fifth floor. The doorway of the staircase gives on the little courtyard close to the left here," pointing with his hand, "near to the window of my establishment. But, now that I remember, one of you has already been there, and can show the way. Gentlemen, adieu!"

They paid for their wine and left the place.

Imitation:

THE SIGNALS

The Chinese chop suey house stood alone, unlighted, and sinister-looking. Involuntarily the Englishman shuddered as he gave the rap—three long, two short. He was admitted by a Chinaman, who silently conducted him through a bare hall to a huge room where several people sat eating chop suey. This, the Englishman knew, was not the real business of the place, for behind the wall at the end was a gambling den, and it was the Englishman's duty to see that no one entered who was not to be trusted.

He ordered a drink and sat down at one of the tables. Presently three prosperous-looking business men came in, and strolling up to the bar addressed the man behind it.

"Very nice night," said one.

"Yes, velly nice night," came the response from behind the counter, as the bar-tender glanced up while he ran a damp cloth over the bar. But in the glance there was time enough to notice that round the Englishman there were floating placid rings of tobacco smoke.

"Too bad," spoke up the second of the businessmen, "that there are so few good chop suey houses in this city—really clean, fine places like this of yours," and he let his eyes wander over the comfortable appointments of the hall. Without any sense of wonder he noticed, as did the bar-tender, that the Englishman was still exhaling placid clouds of tobacco smoke round him.

"Likee oll place, ha?" the Chinaman was saying.

The third business man spoke up, "How about a quiet little table, and three juleps, China?"

More quickly, more casually than the most trained observer might have noticed, Chang looked up for his cue, at the Englishman. He was just finishing three luxurious smoke rings. Genially the Chinaman replied,

"Most cellanly, come wit me."

And he led the way to the end of the room. As they approached a curtained wall tapestried with exquisite dragons, the tapestries parted and admitted the men to the most luxurious gambling den in the western city. — Pupil

It will be observed that whereas the student who imitated Lafcadio Hearn's little "fantastic" has imitated the rich rhythmic style with complete appropriateness, the second student, who has borrowed Dickens for a model has not tried to imitate the style of Dickens, but has borrowed the device of the signals for his plot.

PARALLELISM AND BALANCE

1. LICHENS AND MOSSES

Yet as in one sense the humblest, in another they are the most honoured of the earth-children. Unfading as motionless, the warm frets them not, and the autumn wastes not. Strong in lowliness, they neither blanch in heat nor pine in frost. To them, slow-fingered, constant-hearted, is entrusted the weaving of the dark eternal tapestries of the hills; to them, slow-pencilled, iris-dyed, the tender framing of their endless imagery. Sharing the stillness of the unimpassioned rock, they share also its endurance; and while the winds of departing spring scatter the white hawthorn blossom like drifted snow, and summer dims on the parched meadow the drooping of its cowslip-gold,— far above, among the mountains, the silver lichen-spots rest, star-like, on the stone; and the gathering orange-stain upon the edge of yonder western peak reflects the sunsets of a thousand years. — John Ruskin, *Modern Painters, Vol. V. Pt. vi. chap. 10.*

2. THE MASTER'S LOOK

She softly crept toward the door, but as she went the master lifted his gloomy chestnut-coloured eyes under their thatch of grizzled hair, and so transfixed her. She could not move with that brown fire upon her, engulfing her. So he always looked when he was deeply stirred. So he had looked down at his father's coffin years ago, at his mother's last year. So he had looked into the eyes of his favourite dog, dying in his arms. The look was the realization of the infinite within the finite, altering all values. Never once in all the fifteen years during which she had been calling here had he seemed to look at Margaret at all. — MARY WEBB, "Over the Hills and Far Away," from *Armour Wherein He Trusted.*

By arrangement with Jonathan Cape, Limited, Toronto.

Parallelism is one of the most effective of all devices; but it must be used sparingly. It is most effective at points of climax and in emotional passages. The passage from Mary Webb is perhaps the better model because it is more restrained, not so obvious. Notice that always the parallelism is given sufficient variation and change to avoid monotony.

Practice 1. Parallelism

From your own reading, in magazines or books, bring to class five paragraphs where parallelism is effectively used.

Practice 2. Parallelism

On one of the models above, or on one of those you have chosen, write a paragraph using parallelism effectively. Suggested topics:
1. Flowers of the prairie. 2. Stratified rock. 3. Beach combers. 4. Kittens playing. 5. A bear in a zoo (going round and round his cage). 6. A paragraph containing several 'when' clauses. 7. A paragraph containing three sentences beginning 'So' (or 'Thus' or 'Now' or 'Never').

REPETITION

1

Pines and pines and the shadows of pines as far as the eye can see. — ROBERT SERVICE

2. THE DESERT

As long as you are journeying in the interior of the Desert you have no particular point to make for as your resting-place. The endless sands yield nothing but small stunted shrubs—even these fail after the first two or three days, and from that time you pass over broad plains—you pass over newly reared hills—you pass through valleys dug out by the last week's storm, and the hills, and the valleys are sand, sand, sand, still sand, and only sand, and sand, and sand again. — KINGLAKE, *Eothen.*

Before repetition can be effective it must be built up to, as you see in this second passage; and it must be varied again and again. You will find this device used by Dickens many, many times.

Practice 3. Using Repetition

1. Imagine yourself in Captain Bligh's little boat when he was cast adrift. Describe the endless watching for land.
2. Elaborate Robert Service's line into a paragraph of description of the forests of the North seen from a mountain vantage point.
3. Describe one of the following: the Bad Lands of the West, the drought stricken prairies, burnt over forest region, northern Ontario, fruit valleys in bloom, the northern "wastes" in bloom during the short summer, the ice and snow fields of the Arctic or Antarctic, a fruitless search for a rooming house, the dreary grind of daily routine.

ALLITERATION
1. SUNRISE

What a sunrise it was on the morning! Yet I stood with my back to it, looking west; for there I saw, firstly, the foam on the reef—as crimson as blood—falling over the wine-stained waves: then it changed as the sun ascended, like clouds of golden powder, indescribably magnificent, shaken and scattered upon the silver snow-drifts of the coral reef, dazzling to behold, and continually changing. — CHARLES W. STODDARD, *South-Sea Idylls.*

By permission of Charles Scribner's Sons.

2. SPANISH FORCES AT GRANADA

Never had Christian war assumed a more splendid and imposing aspect. Far as the eye could reach, extended the glittering and gorgeous lines of that goodly power, bristling with sunlit spears and blazoned banners; while beside, murmured and glowed and danced the silver and laughing Xenil, careless what lord should possess, for his little day, the banks that bloomed by its everlasting course. — LORD LYTTON

You will notice that alliteration is not confined to nouns and their modifiers, but is even more effectively used with verbs, and even adverbs. We must be warned with alliteration, as with repetition and parallel structure, not to make it too obvious nor to use it too often.

Practice 4. Using Alliteration

Read the models given until the sound of the alliterative phrases becomes familiar and then try a passage of description choosing alliterative phrases wherever you can devise them. You will be struck with the readiness with which you can pick up this device. Suggested topics:

1. A sunset scene which you have particularly enjoyed. 2. The flowers of a valley. 3. The rolling of the tide. 4. A secluded spot in the woods. 5. Moonlight on the mountains. 6. A city street scene. 7. A section of the slums.

WORD SENTENCES

When a writer has become a master of clear and correct sentence structure, he is entitled to attempt effective impression, using verbal devices of any sort that may secure the effect he desires. These need not be grammatically complete so long as they are perfectly clear. Examine the following passage for unusual constructions.

1. POOH GREETS EEYORE

"Good morning, Eeyore," said Pooh.

"Good morning, Pooh Bear," said Eeyore gloomily. "If it *is* a good morning," he said. "Which I doubt," said he.

"Why, what's the matter?"

"Nothing, Pooh Bear, nothing. We can't all, and some of us don't. That's all there is to it."

"Can't all *what?*" said Pooh, rubbing his nose.

"Gaiety. Song-and-dance. Here we go round the mulberry bush."

"Oh!" said Pooh. He thought for a long time, and then asked, "What mulberry bush is that?"

"Bon-hommy," went on Eeyore gloomily. "French word meaning bon-hommy," he explained. "I'm not complaining, but There It Is."

Pooh sat down on a large stone, and tried to think this out. It sounded to him like a riddle, and he was never very much good at riddles, being a Bear of Very Little Brain." — A. A. MILNE, *Winnie-the-Pooh.*

By permission of the publishers, McClelland and Stewart, Limited, Toronto.

Do not try to make too much sense out of this delightful nonsense. About all it says is that Eeyore and Pooh are queer, muddleheaded little animals, and Eeyore is not very happy. But could it be better done!

2

Suddenly he put his foot in a rabbit hole, and fell down flat on his face. B A N G ! ! ! ? ? ? * * * ! ! !

Piglet lay there, wondering what had happened. — A. A. MILNE, *Winnie-the-Pooh.*

By permission of the publishers, McClelland and Stewart, Limited, Toronto.

3. HEYTHORP GROWS REMINISCENT

Lying in that steaming brown fragrant liquid, old Heythorp heaved a stentorous sigh. By losing his temper with that ill-conditioned cur he had cooked his goose. It was done to a turn! and he was a ruined man . . . His tree had come down with a crash! Eighty years—eighty good years! He regretted none of them, regretted nothing. . . . He smiled and stirred a little in the bath till the water reached the white hairs on his lower lip. It smelt nice! And he took a long sniff. He had had a good life, a good life! . . . He closed his eyes. They talked about an after-life—people like that holy woman.

Gammon. You went to sleep—a long sleep; no dreams. A nap after dinner!
Dinner! His tongue sought his palate! Yes, he could eat a good dinner! That
dog hadn't put him off his stroke! — JOHN GALSWORTHY, *The Stoic.*

By permission of the publishers, William Heinemann, Ltd., London.

4. THE WILD DUCK

Twilight. Red in the West.
Dimness. A glow on the wood.
The teams plod home to rest.
The wild duck come to glean.
O souls not understood,
What a wild cry in the pool;
What things have the farm ducks seen
That they cry so—huddle and cry?
Only the soul that goes.
Eager. Eager. Flying.
Over the globe of the moon,
Over the wood that glows.
Wings linked. Necks astrain,
A rush and a wild crying.

. . . .

A cry of the long pain
In the reeds of a steel lagoon,
In a land that no man knows.
— JOHN MASEFIELD, *Ballads and Poems.*

By permission of the publishers, The Macmillan Company of Canada Limited, Toronto.

Practice 5. Using Incomplete Sentences

Reputable writers rarely take liberties, but when the artist is
skilful the devices are extremely effective. Try a piece of descriptive
writing similar to that of Masefield's.

1. A prairie sunset. 2. Moonlight over a lake. 3. Resting time for a thresh-
ing outfit. 4. The city lights over a river or a lake. 5. Shadows under a bridge.
6. A church spire silhouetted against the sky. 7. One of your own topics.

ADDRESSING THE INANIMATE AS IF ANIMATE

This device, like the apostrophe and the ode, gives opportunity for
emotional expressions which otherwise would be impossible. It is
reserved, obviously, for such personal experiences and reflections as
that in the model.

TO MY OLD HIKING SHOES

It is a funeral pyre, not an ordinary rubbish heap, and I cannot give you
to the flame without a backward glance at the days we spent together.

Do you remember the slopes of slippery pine needles that you trod so surely,
the great fallen tree trunks and boulders over which you scrambled? All
your scars are honourable. You never failed me on the roughest trails; on
glistening deck and spray-glazed rocks you were as steady as on the level
beach.

What adventures we have known! There was that perfect June day when we forded the noisy creek, and a great silver bass, mistaking you for a couple of his fellows, edged closer, until he was nuzzling your toes! And then you hung astride the rustic verandah railing of a certain small log cabin, glistening like Cinderella's slippers, until you were dried by the wind that made music in the nearby pines, and teased the water lapping on the rocks below.

Let's not forget the morning we hunted orange lilies. The wild cherry showered its snowy petals on our path, and the flowers we sought, glowing on the green slopes, tempted us on and up. We went home drenched with dew and that peace which fills the wilderness at sunrise.

But, best memory of all is the day when with one other we scaled Lookout Rock. How joyously we climbed, laughing breathlessly as we overcame each obstacle. It was steep and rugged, but surely, without a slip, you brought me to the very peak. But, ah, you brought me down again, alone. Down from the height of Lookout, down from the highlands of the north, down into this southern valley of Reality, so far, so very far from all my dreams!

And you, travel-worn and weary, have come to rest on this bonfire at the foot of an orchard. The eager little flames leap towards you. I see you writhe at first, then settle down contentedly. Now little curls of blue smoke are rising from you. You'll go to make the sunsets that linger vividly behind the pines. At night you'll drift, a luminous veil, across the moon, and your shadow will touch the water of the little lake. Some day, I think, I'll join you there, and we'll wander on again together through the haunts we loved.
— MARION ROWLAND, "The Home Forum," *The Globe.*

By arrangement with the publishers, The Globe, *Toronto.*

Practice 6. Addressing the Inanimate as if Animate

Upon this model, write an address to some object of your own with which you have had interesting experiences. If this seems too personal, (though it need not) try your dramatic power by choosing some other object and, imagining yourself in the place of its supposed owner, and inventing their experiences together, write an address to it. Write sincerely, do not burlesque your topic.

1. To my fountain pen. 2. To my skating jacket. 3. To a pair of moccasins. 4. To an old glove. 5. To a cigarette lighter. 6. To a neck scarf. 7. To a party dress. 8. To a dress suit. 9. To a pair of dancing pumps. 10. To a favourite fireplace. 11. To a finger ring. 12. To some gift (book, crest, brooch, sweater, or any other.) 13. To a school pin.

AUTOBIOGRAPHY

A useful, but somewhat time-worn device for interesting people in objects which otherwise might escape notice is to represent them as telling their own story.

THE ADVENTURES OF A SHILLING

I was born on the side of a mountain, near a little village of Peru, and made a voyage to England in an ingot, under the convoy of Sir Francis Drake. I was, soon after my arrival, taken out of my Indian habit, refined, naturalized, and put into the British mode, with the face of Queen Elizabeth on one side, and the arms of the country on the other. Being thus equipped, I found in me a marvellous inclination to ramble, and visit all parts of the new world into which I was brought. The people very much favoured my natural disposition, and shifted me so fast from hand to hand that before I was five years old I had travelled into almost every corner of the nation. But in my sixth year, to my unspeakable grief, I fell into the hands of a miserable old fellow, who clasped me into an iron chest, where I found five hundred more of my own quality who lay under the same confinement. The only relief we had was to be taken out and counted over in the fresh air every morning and evening. After an imprisonment of several years, we heard somebody knocking at our chest, and breaking it open with a hammer. This, we found, was the old man's heir, who, as his father lay dying, was so good as to come to our release: he separated us that very day. What was the fate of my companions I know not; as for myself, I was sent to the apothecary's shop for a pint of sack. The apothecary gave me to a herb-woman, the herb-woman to a butcher, the butcher to a brewer, and the brewer to his wife, who made a present of me to a non-conformist preacher. After this manner I made my way merrily through the world; for, as I told you before, we shillings loved nothing so much as travelling. I sometimes fetched in a shoulder of mutton, sometimes a play-book, and often had the satisfaction to treat a Templar at a twelve-penny ordinary, or carry him with three friends to Westminster Hall.

After many adventures, which it would be tedious to relate, I was sent to a young spendthrift, in company with the will of his deceased father. The young fellow, who I found was very extravagant, gave great demonstrations of joy at the receiving of the will: but opening it, he found himself disinherited and cut off from possession of a fair estate by virtue of my being made a present to him. This put him in such a passion, that after having taken me with his hand, and cursed me, he squirred[1] me away from him as far as he could fling me. I chanced to light in an unfrequented place under a dead wall, where I lay undiscovered and useless, during the usurpation of Oliver Cromwell.

About a year after the king's return, a poor cavalier that was walking there about dinner-time fortunately cast his eye upon me, to the great joy of us both, carried me to a cook's shop, where he dined on me, and drank the king's health. When I came again into the world, I found that I had been happier in my retirement that I thought, having probably, by that means, escaped wearing a monstrous pair of breeches.

I shall pass over many other accidents of less moment, and hasten to the fatal catastrophe, when I fell into the hands of an artist, who conveyed me underground, and with an unmerciful pair of shears, cut off my titles, clipped my brims, retrenched my shape, rubbed me to my inmost ring, and, in short, so spoiled and pillaged me that he did not leave me worth a groat. You may think what a confusion I was in, to see myself thus curtailed and disfigured. I should have been ashamed to show my head had not all my old acquaintances been reduced to the same shameful figure, except some few that were punched through the belly. In the midst of this general calamity, when everybody thought our misfortune irretrievable, and our case desperate, we were thrown into the furnace together, and (as it often happens with cities rising out of the fire) appeared with greater beauty and lustre than we could ever boast of before.

What has happened to me since this change of sex which you now see, I

[1] squirred—to throw away with a jerk.

shall take some other opportunity to relate. In the meantime I shall only repeat two adventures, as being very extraordinary, and neither of them having happened to me above once in my life. The first was my being in a poet's pocket, who was so taken with the brightness and novelty of my appearance that it gave occasion to the finest burlesque poem in the British language, entitled, from me, "The Splendid Shilling". The second adventure, which I must not omit, happened to me in the year 1703, when I was given away in charity to a blind man, but indeed this was by mistake, the person who gave me having heedlessly thrown me into the hat among a pennyworth of farthings. — JOSEPH ADDISON (abridged)

Practice 7. Autobiography

Write an imaginative autobiography based on one of the following topics. Notice the sidelights which further help Addison's story. What do you learn about English history, about church donations, about counterfeiting and debasement of coins, being "cut off with a shilling," the poverty of poets, and charity to the poor? These are, strictly speaking, additional to his story, but they have helped the story to live for two hundred years. Use your own invention, take your time.

1. The story of a piece of coal. 2. The story of a violin. 3. A good luck piece. 4. A horse-shoe nail ("and all for the loss of a horse-shoe nail"). 5. A rosary. 6. A pocket-knife. 7. A library book. 8. A museum piece. 9. A mummy ("And thou hast walked about, How strange a story!"). 10. Nelson's Monument in Trafalgar Square. 11. Vimy Ridge. 12. The Four Horses in front of St. Mark's (consult Encyclopedia). 13. An adventurous engagement ring (!).

SUSPENSE

The principle of suspense is used in many ways. It consists in creating, by suggestion, a growing sense of climax. Things are reaching a head, but the outcome, however much anticipated, is still unsure. The two models immediately following illustrate this sense of apprehension. Notice the emphatic short paragraphs, the repetitions with change. Notice the pace, faster and faster; the false alarms. Study these models closely for words, for sentences, and for proportion. The third model is included as an example of this device used for the purpose of giving a humorous surprise ending.

1. LOST IN THE WILD WOOD

With great cheerfulness of spirit Mole pushed on toward the Wild Wood, which lay before him low and threatening, like a black reef in some still southern sea.

There was nothing to alarm him at first entry. Twigs crackled under his feet, logs tripped him, funguses on stumps resembled caricatures, and startled him for the moment by their likeness to something familiar and far away; but that was all fun, and exciting. It led him on, and he penetrated to where the light was less, and the trees crouched nearer and nearer, and holes made ugly mouths at him on either side.

Everything was very still now. The dusk advanced on him steadily, rapidly, gathering in behind and before; and the light seemed to be draining away like flood-water.

Then the faces began.

It was over his shoulder, and indistinctly, that he first thought he saw a face; a little, evil, wedge-shaped face, looking out at him from a hole. When he turned and confronted it, the thing had vanished.

He quickened his pace, telling himself cheerfully not to begin imagining things, or there would be simply no end to it. He passed another hole, and another, and another; and then—yes!—no!—yes! certainly a little narrow face, with hard eyes, had flashed up for an instant from a hole, and was gone. He hesitated—braced himself up for an effort and strode on. Then suddenly, and as if it had been so all the time, every hole, far and near, and there were hundreds of them, seemed to possess its face, coming and going rapidly, all fixing on him glances of malice and hatred: all hard-eyed and evil and sharp.

If he could only get away from the holes in the banks, he thought, there would be no more faces. He swung off the path and plunged into the untrodden places of the wood.

Then the whistling began.

Very faint and shrill it was, and far behind him, when he first heard it; but somehow it made him hurry forward. Then, still very faint and shrill, it sounded far ahead of him, and made him hesitate and want to go back. As he halted in indecision it broke out on either side, and seemed to be caught up and passed on throughout the whole length of the wood to its farthest limit. They were up and alert and ready, evidently, whoever they were! And he— he was alone, and unarmed, and far from help; and the night was closing in.

Then the pattering began.

He thought it was only falling leaves at first, so light and delicate was the sound of it. Then as it grew it took a regular rhythm, and he knew it for nothing else but the pat-pat-pat of little feet still a very long way off. Was it in front or behind? It seemed to be first one, and then the other, then both. It grew and it multiplied, till from every quarter as he listened anxiously, leaning this way and that, it seemed to be closing in on him. As he stood still to hearken, a rabbit came running hard toward him through the trees. He waited, expecting it to slacken pace, or to swerve from him into a different course. Instead, the animal almost brushed him as it dashed past, his face set and hard, his eyes staring, "Get out of this you fool, get out!" the Mole heard him mutter as he swung round a stump and disappeared down a friendly burrow.

The pattering increased till it sounded like sudden hail on the dry leaf-carpet spread round him. The whole wood seemed running now, running hard, hunting, chasing, closing in round something or—somebody? In panic, he began to run too, aimlessly, he knew not whither. He ran up against things, he fell over things and into things, he darted under things and dodged round things. At last he took refuge in the deep dark hollow of an old beech tree which offered shelter, concealment—perhaps even safety, but who could tell, Anyhow, he was too tired to run any further, and could only snuggle down into the dry leaves which had drifted into the hollow and hope he was safe for a time. And as he lay there panting and trembling, and listened to the whistling and the pattering outside, he knew it at last, in all its fullness, that dread thing which other little dwellers in field and hedgerow had encountered here, and known as their darkest moment—that thing which the Rat had vainly tried to shield him from—the Terror of the Wild Wood! — KENNETH GRAHAME, *The Wind in the Willows.*

By permission of Charles Scribner's Sons, New York.

2. THE ESCAPE

The same shadows that are falling on the prison are falling, in the same hour of that early afternoon, on the Barrier with the crowd about it, when a coach going out of Paris drives up to be examined.

"Who goes here? Whom have we within? Papers!"

The papers are handed out and read.

"Alexandre Manette. Physician. French. Which is he?"

This is he; this helpless, inarticulately murmuring, wandering old man pointed out.

"Apparently the Citizen-Doctor is not in his right mind? The Revolution-fever will have been too much for him?"

Greatly too much for him.

"Hah! Many suffer with it. Lucie. His daughter. French. Which is she?"

This is she.

"Apparently it must be. Lucie, the wife of Evrémonde; is it not?"

It is.

"Hah! Evrémonde has an assignation elsewhere. Lucie, her child. English. This is she?"

She and no other.

"Kiss me, child of Evrémonde. Now, thou has kissed a good republican; something new in thy family; remember it! Sydney Carton. Advocate. English. Which is he?"

He lies here, in this corner of the carriage. He, too, is pointed out.

"Apparently the English advocate is in a swoon?"

It is hoped he will recover in the fresher air. It is represented that he is not in strong health, and has separated sadly from a friend who is under the displeasure of the Republic.

"Is that all? It is not a great deal, that! Many are under the displeasure of the Republic, and must look out at the little window. Jarvis Lorry. Banker. English. Which is he?"

"I am he. Necessarily, being the last."

It is Jarvis Lorry who has replied to all the previous questions. It is Jarvis Lorry who has alighted and stands with his hand on the coach door, replying to a group of officials. They leisurely walk round the carriage and leisurely mount the box, to look at what little luggage it carries on the roof; the country-people hanging about, press nearer to the coach doors and greedily stare in; a little child, carried by its mother, has its short arm held out for it, that it may touch the wife of an aristocrat who has gone to the Guillotine.

"Behold your papers, Jarvis Lorry, countersigned."

"One can depart, citizen?"

"One can depart. Forward, my postilions! A good journey!"

"I salute you, citizens—and the first danger passed!"

These are again the words of Jarvis Lorry, as he clasps his hands, and looks upward. There is terror in the carriage, there is weeping, there is the heavy breathing of the insensible traveller.

"Are we not going too slowly? Can they not be induced to go faster?" asks Lucie, clinging to the old man.

"It would seem like flight, my darling. I must not urge them too much; it would rouse suspicion."

"Look back, look back, and see if we are pursued!"

"The road is clear, my dearest. So far, we are not pursued."

Houses in twos and threes pass by us, solitary farms, ruinous buildings, dye-works, tanneries, and the like open country, avenues of leafless trees. The hard uneven pavement is under us, the soft deep mud is on either side. Sometimes we strike into the skirting mud, to avoid the stones that clatter us and shake us; sometimes we stick in ruts and sloughs there. The agony of our impatience is then so great, that in our wild alarm and hurry we are for getting out and running—hiding—doing anything but stopping.

Out in the open country, in again among ruinous buildings, solitary farms, dye-works, tanneries, and the like, cottages in twos and threes, avenues of leafless trees. Have these men deceived us, and taken us back by another road? Is not this the same place twice over? Thank Heaven, no. A village. Look back, look back, and see if we are pursued! Hush! the posting-house.

Leisurely, our four horses are taken out; leisurely, the coach stands in the little street, bereft of horses, and with no likelihood upon it of ever moving again; leisurely, the new horses come into visible existence, one by one; leisurely, the new postilions follow, sucking and plaiting the lashes of their whips; leisurely, the old postilions count their money, make wrong additions, and arrive at dissatisfied results. All the time, our overfraught hearts are beating at a rate that would far outstrip the fastest gallop of the fastest horses ever foaled.

At length the new postilions are in their saddles, and the old are left behind. We are through the village, up the hill, and down the hill, and on the low watery grounds. Suddenly, the postilions exchange speech with animated gesticulation, and the horses are pulled up, almost on their haunches. We are pursued!

"Ho! Within the carriage there. Speak, then!"

"What is it?" asks Mr. Lorry, looking out at window.

"How many did they say?"

"I do not understand you."

"—At the last post. How many to the guillotine to-day?"

"Fifty-two."

"I said so! A brave number! My fellow-citizen here would have it forty-two; ten more heads are worth having. The guillotine goes handsomely. I love it. Hi, forward! Whoop!"

The night comes on dark. He moves more; he is beginning to revive, and to speak intelligibly; he thinks they are still together; he asks him, by his name, what he has in his hand. Oh, pity us, kind Heaven, and help us! Look out, look out, and see if we are pursued.

The wind is rushing after us, and the clouds are flying after us, and the moon is plunging after us, and the whole wild night is in pursuit of us; but, so far, we are pursued by nothing else. — DICKENS, *A Tale of Two Cities.*

3

A hush came over the room. A dead silence fell upon the gay crowd. The dancing stopped, the laughing stopped, the shouts of gaiety stopped. Everyone was motionless, staring with wide open eyes at the dark brown object in the corner. What was to happen? Then, a low rumbling which grew louder and louder, a clang, a clash! a beating of drums and a wild savage cry, "Tarzan is on the air!" — Pupil

Practice 8. Creating Suspense

The devices given throughout this section are meant to stimulate your own invention and to draw your attention to the fact that effects may be produced—are produced—by conscious effort and invention. Use "The Terror of the Wild Wood" as a model and write a story using the short paragraph for emphasis, inventing a suitable cause for fear or apprehension.

Suggestions:
1. A small child wanders off into the woods. 2. You have to pass through an underground cave. 3. You are sleeping in a strange house in a strange city. 4. You walk through the narrow streets of Chinatown. 5. You sleep in the woods for the first time. 6. Two boys go exploring an abandoned castle. 7. Some experience you have had, suitably retold for its full effect.

Practice 9. Creating Suspense

Write on one of the topics given below, managing the creation of suspense as in Dickens' story of the escape of Lucy Manette and her party, in *A Tale of Two Cities.* Do not omit the false alarm.
1. Mickey Mouse and Minnie move from the old barn. 2. Mrs. Duck takes Donald and starts to move from the mill pond. 3. Two girls lost in New York come at sundown to the negro section of Harlem. 4. Two boys have been kidnapped and manage to escape. 5. In John Buchan's story *Prester John* Davey escapes with the necklace and is pursued through the forest by the blacks. Retell the story after the Dickens' manner.

Practice 10. Creating Suspense

Read in Dickens' *A Tale of Two Cities,* Book II, Chapter xiv, the story of Jerry Cruncher's Fishing Expedition. Young Jerry follows him, gets scared and is pursued home by the coffin. Notice that because Jerry said he was going fishing, Dickens maintains the language of fishing ("a saw, a crowbar, a rope and chain, and other fishing tackle of that nature" . . . "They fished with a spade first" . . . "The three fishermen" . . .). Make a story of your own where one person,—not necessarily Father—gives another person a put-off answer, and does something else. Translate Dickens' terms to suit your own story.
1. Going fishing. 2. Late at the office. 3. Going to the dentist. 4. Off to see Bert. 5. Out for a walk. 6. To Martha's for a game of Bridge. 7. Going to the hospital to see Aunt Bessie.

REPEATED SENTENCE AND PARAGRAPH

In the model on page 400, "The Escape," we noticed that the feeling of terror was created, or re-created, by the repetition of the sentence "Look back, look back, and see if we are pursued!"; and further by the repetition of the objects of scenery which gave the impression that the fugitives were going again over the same road. This repetition of a sentence, or even of a paragraph, may be very effective. Dickens has used it with fine effect in *Dombey and Son*.

In *A Tale of Two Cities*, Book III, chapter xiv, Madame Defarge sets out to trap Lucie Manette. Lucie has gone, fortunately, and only Miss Pross is in the house. When Dickens tells the story he says, "Thus accoutred, and walking with the confident tread of such a character, and with the supple freedom of a woman who had habitually walked in her girlhood, barefoot and barelegged, on the brown sea-sand, Madame Defarge took her way along the streets." Dickens' story then turns to Miss Pross and Jerry Cruncher who are planning to escape from Paris without attracting attention. The theme is pursued for a thousand words, when this paragraph is inserted "And still Madame Defarge, pursuing her way along the streets, came nearer and nearer." The story of Miss Pross continues, this time for one paragraph; then we find again, "Still Madame Defarge, pursuing her way along the streets, came nearer and nearer." Six lines more about Miss Pross and, "Madame Defarge was drawing very near indeed." Thereafter the two stories merge and the meeting of Miss Pross and Madame Defarge is given.

Practice 11. Repetition

Read the story in *A Tale of Two Cities*; read the student exercise *The Artist* which follows, and then write a story of your own using the same device.

THE ARTIST
(Based on Dickens' *A Tale of Two Cities* Bk III. Ch. XIV)

It was dark—the darkest hour of the night, and the inky blackness lay like some dark spirit over the land. Not a single star shone in the heavens above, for a thick canopy of clouds covered the sky. It was a bitter night. The wind shrieked and moaned and, in its anger, blew down trees and destroyed barns. The stout little house that resisted its terrific strength seemed to incense it more as it thrashed at the building in an effort to raze it.

Inside that stout little house, which so bravely battled against the wind, there was also a storm—not a storm of the elements, but the storm of a human soul. In the awful darkness that filled the one room of the house, a man lay, sick unto death. Writhing with pain, the tortured man tried to calm himself for the coming ordeal; for off in the distance he saw death drawing towards him slowly and silently; and the gaunt figure was pointing a long white finger at him.

The man closed his eyes to shut out the awful vision; but as he listened to the wailing of the wind, it seemed only to be the echo of the tumult of his own soul. Then, as he listened more closely, a voice seemed to arise out of the wind, and whisper to him, "Get up! Get up! It is almost too late. He is coming. Get up!"

The sick man opened his eyes, and still he saw the tall, gaunt figure of death approaching him, and the long white finger seemed more accusing.

With a sob the man arose suddenly. Forgetting his pain and sorrow, he threw his one thin blanket around him, and in the darkness groped for a candle. Finding it, he lit it and looked about the room. Ah! there they were—his paints and easel in the corner. Praying that he would be given the strength to get them, the man stopped to get his breath. But as he stopped, the wind hissed at him, "Hurry! Hurry! It is almost too late. He is coming. Oh, hurry!" And again he saw the figure of death with its accusing finger, drawing very near indeed.

Frantically he grabbed for his brush and paints. Then seating himself, he tried to calm his spirit. He must complete his picture. He would paint the face of Jesus—Jesus whom he had forgotten in his wicked life. The numbness gone from his fingers, he took up his brush and painted. Gradually an outline appeared, then it grew more distinct; and soon, smiling, the painter put down his brush. He had finished his work, for before him was the face of the Christ, and around the picture a bright light shone.

Once more the artist shut his eyes and listened to the wind. But instead of the hissing, he heard soft music and sweet sounds, and when he opened his eyes he beheld in the place of the dark figure of death, a beautiful angel.

A party searching for him came to his lonely hut, and, as they opened the door, the picture caught their eye. Reverently they approached it, and found, lying beside it, the body of the dead artist. Solemnly they buried him, but the picture was shown to the world, which, seeing it, loved him and forgot his sins. — PUPIL

PERSONALITY TO ANIMALS

We omit, because of its length, the allegory proper which you may examine at its best in Bunyan's *Pilgrim's Progress* or any episode from it, such as 'Doubting Castle,' and turn to such allegorical devices as have been so successful in *The Wind in the Willows* by Kenneth Grahame, and in A. A. Milne's *Pooh* books. Here the stories of animals are given in their own habitat but the actions are those of people, and their feelings and emotions are human. For example, *The Wind in the Willows* begins with this delightful paragraph:

The Mole had been working very hard all the morning, spring-cleaning his little home. First with brooms, then with dusters; then on ladders and steps and chairs, with a brush and a pail of whitewash; till he had dust in his throat and eyes, and splashes of whitewash all over his black fur, and an aching back and weary arms. Spring was moving in the air above and in the earth below and around him, penetrating even his dark and lowly little house with its spirit of divine discontent and longing. It was small wonder, then, that he suddenly flung down his brush on the floor and said, "Bother!" and "O blow!" and also "Hang springcleaning!" and bolted out of the house without even waiting to put on his coat. Something up above was calling him imperiously, and he made for the steep little tunnel which answered in his case to the gravelled carriage-drive owned by animals whose residences are nearer to the sun and air. So he scraped and scratched and scrabbled and scrooged, and then he scrooged again and scrabbled and scratched and scraped, working busily with his little paws and muttering to himself, "Up we go! Up we go! 'till at last, pop! his snout came out into the sunlight, and he found himself rolling in the warm grass of a great meadow. — KENNETH GRAHAME, *The Wind in the Willows.*

By permission of Charles Scribner's Sons.

In your stories of animals do not hesitate to introduce dialogue, as in any narrative. Consider the effectiveness of Jerome K. Jeromes' account of Montmorency's experiences:

Montmorency went for the cat at the rate of twenty miles an hour; but the cat did not hurry up—did not seem to have grasped the idea that his life was in danger. It trotted quietly on until its would-be assassin was within a yard of it, and then it turned round and sat down in the middle of the road, and looked at Montmorency with a gentle, inquiring expression, that said:

"Yes, you want me?"

Montmorency does not lack pluck; but there was something about the look of that cat that might have chilled the heart of the boldest dog. He stopped abruptly and looked back at Tom.

Neither spoke; but the conversation that one could imagine was clearly as follows:

THE CAT: "Can I do anything for you?"

MONTMORENCY: "No—no thanks."

THE CAT: "Don't you mind speaking, if you really want anything, you know."

MONTMORENCY (*backing down the High Street*): "Oh, no,—not at all—certainly—don't you trouble. I—I am afraid I've made a mistake. I thought I knew you. Sorry I disturbed you."

THE CAT: "Not at all—quite a pleasure. Sure you don't want anything, now?"

MONTMORENCY (*still backing*): "Not at all, thanks—not at all—very kind of you. Good morning."

THE CAT: "Good morning."

— JEROME K. JEROME, *Three Men in a Boat.*
By permission of the publishers, J. W. Arrowsmith (London) Ltd.

Practice 12. Giving Personality to Animals

Write an imaginative story on one of the following topics. Give personality to each animal; give them human actions and re-actions, feelings, ambitions, emotions. You will feel more in the way of it, if you read two or three chapters from *The House at Pooh Corner*, by A.A. Milne, or Kenneth Grahame's *The Wind in the Willows.*

1. That Monday feeling. 2. Jenny Wren Puts on a Concert. 3. Ground-Hog Looks at the Weather. 4. Jimmy Skunk Attends the Animal Fair. 5. Mickey Serenades Minnie. 6. Toad Takes His Lady for a Drive. (Use as a sub-title Touchstone's sentence "We that are true lovers run into strange capers.") 7. Any other animal's adventures.

HUMOROUS EXAGGERATION

We all enjoy the "tall" story. There are Liars' Clubs where prizes are given for the most imaginative stretcher. These lies are not con--travention of fact so much as exaggeration of it. It is the core of American humour, as under-statement and punning are at the base of much English humour. Both, of course, turn upon the unexpected.

1. MY FINANCIAL CAREER

When I go into a bank I get rattled. The clerks rattle me; the wickets rattle me; the sight of the money rattles me; everything rattles me. The moment I cross the threshold of a bank I am a hesitating jay. If I attempt to transact business there, I become an irresponsible idiot.

I knew this beforehand, but my salary had been raised to fifty dollars a month, and I felt that the bank was the only place for it. So I shambled in and looked timidly round at the clerks. I had an idea that a person about to open an account needed to consult the manager. I went up to a wicket marked "Accountant." The accountant was a tall, cool devil,—the very sight of him rattled me. My voice was sepulchral.

"May I see the manager?" I said, and added solemnly, "alone". I don't know why I said "alone".

"Certainly," said the accountant, and fetched him. The manager was a grave calm man. I held fifty-six dollars clutched in a crumpled ball in my pocket.

"Are you the manager?" I asked. Heaven knows I didn't doubt it.

"Yes," he said.

"May I see you?" I asked. "Alone?" I didn't want to say "alone" again, but without it my question seemed self-evident.

The manager looked at me in some alarm. He felt that I had a terrible secret to reveal.

"Come in here," he said, leading the way to a private room, and turning the key.

"We are safe from interruption here," he said, "sit down."

We both sat down and looked at one another. I found no voice to speak.

"You are one of Pinkerton's men, I presume," he said.

He had gathered from my mysterious manner that I was a detective. I knew what he was thinking and felt all the worse.

"No, not from Pinkerton's," I said, seemingly to imply that I came from a rival agency. "To tell the truth," I went on, as if I *had* been prompted to lie about the matter, "I am not a detective at all. I have come to open an account. I intend to keep all my money in this bank."

The manager looked relieved, but still serious; he concluded now that I was a son of Baron Rothschild, or a young Gould.

"A very large amount, I suppose," he said.

"Fairly large," I whispered. "I propose to deposit fifty-six dollars now, and fifty dollars a month regularly."

The manager got up and opened the door. He called to the accountant.

"Mr. Montgomery," he said, unkindly loud, "this gentleman is opening an account; he will deposit fifty-six dollars. Good morning."

I rose. A big iron door stood open at the side of the room.

"Good morning," I said, and stepped into the safe.

"Come out," said the manager coldly, showing me the other way.

I went up to the accountant's wicket and poked the ball of money at him, with a quick, convulsive movement as if I were doing a trick. My face was ghastly pale.

"Here," I said, "deposit it." The tone of the words seemed to mean, "Let us do this painful business while the fit is on us."

He took the money and gave it to another clerk. He made me write the sum on a slip and sign my name in a book. I no longer knew what I was doing. The bank swam before my eyes.

"Is it deposited?" I asked, in a hollow, vibrating voice.

"It is," said the accountant.

"Then I want to draw a cheque."

My idea was to draw out six dollars for present use. Some one gave me a cheque-book through a wicket, and some one else began telling me how to write the cheque. The people in the bank had the impression that I was an invalid millionaire. I wrote something on the cheque and thrust it in at the clerk. He looked at it.

"What! Are you drawing it all out again?" he asked in surprise. Then I realized that I had written fifty-six instead of six. I was too far gone to reason now. I had a feeling that I could not explain my act. All the clerks had stopped writing to look at me.

Reckless with misery, I made a plunge.

"Yes, the whole thing."

"You withdraw your money from the bank!"

"Every cent of it."

"Are you not going to deposit any more!" said the clerk, astonished.

"Never!"

An idiot hope struck me that he might think some one had insulted me while I was writing the cheque and that I had changed my mind. I made a wretched attempt to look like a man with a fearfully quick temper.

The clerk prepared to pay the money.

"How will you have it?" he said.

"Oh." I caught his meaning and answered without even trying to think, "In fifties."

He gave me a fifty dollar bill.

"And the six?" he asked dryly.

"In sixes," I said.

He gave me the money and I rushed out. As the big doors swung behind me I caught the echo of a roar of laughter that went up to the ceiling of the bank. Since then I bank no more. I keep my money in cash in my trousers pocket, and my savings in silver dollars in a sock. — STEPHEN LEACOCK, *Literary Lapses*.

By permission of the author.

2. PINEAPPLE FOR LUNCH

We are very fond of pineapple, all three of us. We looked at the picture on the tin; we thought of the juice. We smiled at one another, and Harris got a spoon ready.

Then we looked for the knife to open the tin with. We turned out everything in the hamper. We turned out the bags. We pulled up the boards at the bottom of the boat. We took everything out on the bank and shook it. There was no tin-opener to be found.

Then Harris tried to open the tin with a pocket knife, and broke the knife and cut himself badly; and George tried a pair of scissors, and the scissors flew up, and nearly put his eye out. While they were dressing their wounds, I tried to make a hole in the thing with the spiky end of the hitcher, and the hitcher slipped and jerked me out between the boat and the bank into two feet of muddy water, and the tin rolled over, uninjured, and broke a teacup.

Then we all got mad. We took the tin out on the bank, and Harris went up into a field and got a big sharp stone and I went back into the boat and brought out the mast, and George held the tin and Harris held the sharp end of the stone against the top of it, and I took the mast and poised it high up in the air, and gathered up all my strength and brought it down.

It was George's straw hat that saved his life that day. He keeps that hat now (what is left of it), and, of a winter's evening, when the pipes are lit and the boys are telling stretchers about the dangers they have passed through, George brings it down and shows it round, and the stirring tale is told anew, with fresh exaggerations every time.

Harris got off with merely a flesh wound.

After that I took the tin myself, and hammered at it with the mast, till I was worn out and sick at heart. Whereupon Harris took it in hand.

We beat it out flat; we beat it back square; we battered it into every form known to geometry—but we could not make a hole in it. Then George went at it, and knocked it into a shape, so strange, so weird, so unearthly in its wild hideousness, that he got frightened and threw away the mast. Then we all three sat around it on the grass and looked at it.

There was one great dent across the top that had the appearance of a mocking grin, and it drove us furious, so that Harris rushed at the thing, and caught it up, and flung it far into the middle of the river. — JEROME K. JEROME, *Three Men in a Boat.*

By permission of the publishers, J. W. Arrowsmith (London) Ltd.

Practice 13. Humorous Exaggeration

Write a humorous account of one of your own experiences, depending for its effect upon exaggeration and the unexpected. Copy the model as closely as you desire.

Suggestions:

1. A hike. 2. A weiner roast. 3. A picnic. 4. A motoring experience. 5. A fishing expedition. 6. A laboratory experiment. 7. A holiday episode. 8. An unusual incident in church. 9. At a wedding. 10. A rookie tries to harness (hitch, halter, bridle, or ride) a horse. 11. Any other amusing experience.

Practice 14. Humorous Exaggeration

Recall some embarrassing experience and tell it after the manner of *My Financial Career.* The more ordinary the experience and unusual the person's embarrassment, the more amusing the episode.

1. Writing a letter. 2. Learning to skate (remember Sam Weller). 3. Giving a toast at a banquet. 4. The first dance. 5. Invited to supper. 6. A formal presentation. 7. Explaining to mother. 8. A 'bit part' in a play. 9. Entertaining Mother's (sister's, brother's) friend till Mother (sister, brother) appears. 10. An impromtu entry!

Radio Listening, Writing, and Broadcasting

RADIO LISTENING

ALTHOUGH nation-wide surveys indicate that the radio is turned on four to six hours a day in the average Canadian home, many listeners do not know what is on the air. Planned listening—finding out in advance what one wishes to hear and adjusting one's activities accordingly—takes more effort than indiscriminate dial-twisting, but it is effort well repaid.

Practice 1. Finding Out About Future Broadcasts

Have members of the class report what may be learned about future broadcasts from different sources. Reserve a portion of the class radio bulletin board for a "Coming Events on the Radio" feature, and ask the teacher to appoint weekly committees to keep the class posted. Some reliable guides are:

Tune In, a monthly magazine listing programmes a month in advance.

CBC Times, published by the Canadian Broadcasting Corporation, gives details of programmes a week at a time and appears well in advance of the listening time.

Canadian Broadcaster, a semi-monthly bulletin of Canadian programmes, with selections from U.S.A. networks.

Young Canada Listens—School Broadcasts in Canada, published each year by the Canadian Broadcasting Corporation.

Write to the Department of Education, Radio Branch, of your own province for listings of school broadcasts originating in your province.

Some newspapers carry daily a column of radio comment and network listings.

Selecting Programmes

What are the best radio programmes? This question cannot be answered without limiting it. A radio forum on an important national problem would not be "best" for a sixth-grade child, nor would a programme by the liveliest dance band be "best" for a lover of classical music. We must evaluate programmes according to their purpose.

On the other hand, a person is lacking in discrimination if all programmes of one type appeal equally to him. Radio offers such a wide variety of educational and entertainment programmes that one's daily listening should include a sampling of several types.

Practice 2.   Reporting on Programmes

1. Using a week's programmes, list the types of educational information you can get on the radio (nutrition, health, foreign language
instruction, science, history, books).   What types of entertainment
are available (quizzes, comedy, drama, music)? Pool your class findings
and have each week's bulletin board committee note the programme
type, station, and time on the "Best on the Air" list.

Louis M. Harrison

Stuart MacFarlane of Saint John, N.B., broadcasting at a CHSJ studio.

2. Listen to an educational and an entertainment programme new
to you and write a brief review of each for your own class "Radio
Guide." Your review should include: title of programme, type, time,
station, sponsor, announcer, musical director (if any), names of outstanding performers, and your estimate of the programme's worth.
In criticizing, apply the following standards.

GUIDES FOR JUDGING RADIO PROGRAMMES

Tastes differ, but the intelligent person chooses and judges radio
programmes on the basis of certain standards.

1. *Is the advertising neither excessive nor objectionable?*
2. *Does the programme avoid presenting false ideas about life?*
3. *Is the programme free from objectionable propaganda and faulty reasoning?*
4. *Is the speaking clear and entertaining?*
5. *Are the performers outstanding in their field?*
6. *Does the programme assume that the audience has at least average intelligence?*
7. *Is good craftsmanship evident in choice of words, speech, plan, music, acting, timing?*
8. *Is there a worth-while purpose noticeable behind the programme and is it intelligently and appropriately accomplished?*

In addition to the preceding general guides we need specific standards for each type of programme.

JUDGING NEWS REPORTERS AND COMMENTATORS

1. *Is the reporting of the news accurate and impartial? Are all important items in the day's news reported?*
2. *Is comment on the news authoritative—that is, based on personal experience or through knowledge of history, government, and economics?*
3. *Is there a plan evident—a grouping of items or a planned alternation of types of news?*
4. *Is the broadcaster's voice intentionally emotional and sensational?*
5. *Does he spend too much time on trivialities in the news?*
6. *When he gives his opinion, does he make clear that he is commenting, not giving straight news?*
7. *Does he transform unwieldy, hard-to-remember statistics into arresting, familiar terms?*

Practice 3. Comparing Two Broadcasts

Take notes on the topics included by two news reporters or two news commentators broadcasting during one morning, afternoon, or evening.

1. Compare the number of items of local, national, and international news. Did either broadcaster omit anything of importance covered by the other?
   Did they report straight news or include "human interest" items? Was there a difference in the amount of detail given?
2. The first George Foster Peabody Radio Award for Reporting, similar to the Pulitzer Prize for journalism, went to Elmer Davis for his "terse, incisive, and impartial reporting of the news." If you heard reporters, how did they measure up to this standard?
3. If you heard commentators, how much personal opinion was expressed? How much interpretation was given?

Prepare a report of your findings, indicating which you prefer of the two broadcasts analyzed.

Practice 4. Analyzing a Sports Report

Using the standards for news broadcasting, analyze the broadcasts of your favourite sports reporter. In addition you may want to consider these questions:

1. Does he enthusiastically emphasize examples of excellent performance instead of capitalizing on errors and fumbles?
2. Is his vocabulary technical enough to make his reporting accurate, yet understandable to the average listener?
3. Is he able to re-create colourful scenes and personalities for the armchair sports fan?

JUDGING THE RADIO PLAY

1. *Does the action begin immediately and move rapidly toward the climax?*
2. *Is the plot probable, avoiding reliance on coincidence and far-fetched events?*
3. *Are there few characters? Are they clearly differentiated?*
4. *Are the characters individuals rather than types—for example, the sweet young thing, the brawny hero, the fussy old man?*
5. *Is each character consistent throughout the play with the personality presented at first?*
6. *Are the voices suitable for the roles?*
7. *Can you picture the scenes and the characters?*
8. *Are realistic and suitable sound effects used?*
9. *Is music used appropriately to bridge changes in scene and mood?*
10. *Is the play of suitable length and compactness to be presented in the time allotted, or is it so drastically cut as to seem a mere skeleton?*

Practice 5. Reporting on a Radio Play

Listen to a radio play or a programme of dramatized facts Find answers to the preceding questions. What parts were particularly gripping, effective, boring, hackneyed? If the play was adapted from a motion picture, compare the two. In what ways did they differ? Which was more effective? Why?

JUDGING THE RADIO COMEDIAN

Everyone enjoys a laugh but people laugh at different things. A child will laugh at misused words or farcical actions which will not amuse a person overfamiliar with them through repetition. Whatever your preferences in humour, the following questions will help you in judging radio comedians.

1. *Does the comedian offer fresh humour rather than rely chiefly on old gags?*
2. *Is his humour identifiable with himself, or is he obviously an imitator?*
3. *Is his humour without malice? Does he make you laugh at human frailties without ridiculing minority groups? Can he make fun of himself?*
4. *Does he always rely on an assistant to "feed" him his lines, or is he able to work independently?*
5. *Does his routine have variety, yet flow smoothly without awkward breaks?*

Practice 6. Comparing Two Comedians

Listen to two radio comedians and take notes to illustrate the types of humour used: mispronunciation, slang, misuse of words, puns, exaggerated statements, gags, making fun of ignorance or nationality, embarrassment of someone, references to current events, common foibles of human nature, realistic situations. In preparing your report keep in mind the preceding standards.

Practice 7.   Writing Letters to Sponsors

1. To the sponsor write a letter pointing out some details of a programme which you feel are not in keeping with the programme as a whole.   Give suggestions for improvement.   Use correct letter form (pages 149–173).

2. In a letter tell a sponsor in detail what you like about a programme.

Practice 8.   Discussing the Radio

Use the following statements as a basis for group discussion, debate, or report.

1. Radio dramatizations, even when not of the horror type, are too exciting for the imaginative child.
2. Because young people often have the radio turned on without listening to what is being broadcast, they form a non-listening habit, which results in inattentiveness in the classroom.
3. Listening to the radio is destroying interest in reading.
4. To reach all the people, radio programmes in general are directed to minds at the thirteen-year-old level.
5. At the 70th Annual Congress of the American Prison Association it was stated that "certain commercial radio programmes devoted ostensibly to crime prevention have in reality emphasized the lurid details and specific techniques of crime and have had a tendency to contribute to the delinquency of juveniles, rather than to discourage crime."

WRITING AND BROADCASTING RADIO PROGRAMMES

To-day many schools are taking advantage of the opportunity for presentation of regularly scheduled school programmes over local radio stations.   Whether or not your school is able to obtain actual time on a radio broadcast, you will enjoy preparing a programme or series of programmes suitable for public reception.

How to Secure Broadcasting Time for Your School

Many of the radio stations are commercial stations which broadcast chiefly network programmes.   But the large stations are in the minority.   For every "big-time" broadcaster there are many smaller stations which are willing and eager to secure school talent for their schedules.

Your school has a duty to perform in asking for radio time.   You must prove to the operators of the station that you will make good use of their valuable time by:

1. Preparing your copy carefully in advance.
2. Preparing at least three sample "shows."
3. Presenting vital, entertaining programmes.
4. Being fully responsible.
5. Preparing a programme which fully and honestly represents the school and the radio station to the community.

What Kind of Programme Shall We Write?

There are an indefinite number of programmes that you might try, but perhaps the simplest is a straight news programme with musical interludes. Appoint one member of the class the editor, select two more as assistants, have others undertake the duties of sports reporter, book reviewer, play or motion-picture critic, columnists (such as Roving Reporter, Classroom Commentator, Locker-Room Spy, Armchair Editor), announcer of coming events, musical director, and newsgatherers.

After trying this straight newspaper type of broadcast, branch out a trifle with humour skits, five-minute plays, musical monologues, poetry, scenes from history, and novelty tricks and stunts. As a third step feature faculty interviews or serious discussions by faculty members, group guessing games and quizzes, orchestral and vocal numbers, theme songs, a "Who's Who," and a short editorial entitled "The Principal Says."

Thus far the programme has been an "on-paper" production. Writing the "show" has been the main consideration. Revise your copy carefully, correct all errors in English, and then either type it with double spacing or write it plainly in ink, so that it can be easily read. Your next problem is the actual presentation of your programme.

How to Present the Programme

After your copy has been carefully written, edited, and re-written, you will naturally want an audience on which to try out your programme. There are two possibilities.

First, you may schedule a trial broadcast before your class, a study hall group, or an assembly gathering. You have selected the members of your class who are to do the reading—good speaking voices are highly important—and have arranged the various features in an attractive order, with some consideration for increasing interest and climactic effect near the end of the programme. You have timed the various speakers to find out if they conform to the exacting limits of a fifteen-or thirty-minute broadcast; you have prepared an expository paragraph to be given by one of your members at the start of the broadcast, informing the public of your plans, and are ready for the on-the-air signal. At a definite minute you should begin with a snatch of theme song, follow with your expositor, introduce your master of ceremonies—and your programme is under way.

Making a Real Broadcast

But doubtless you would like the real, nerve-tingling sensation of a true broadcast over a live microphone and through the medium of your local station. Because of the exacting nature of radio young broadcasters are careful about such vital matters as:

Scripts. Scripts should be submitted about two weeks in advance (especially if the programme is to be broadcast on regularly scheduled hours). Require your editors to meet the deadline with 100 per cent faithfulness.

Auditions. Ask your faculty supervisor, the script editors, and an audition committee to attend tryouts and select the cast. If possible, a microphone should be used at the auditions.

Rehearsals. Arrange definite times for at least three rehearsals. At the first (without the microphone) the members of the cast will simply read the script to become familiar with it while the director times it and gives individual instructions. The second should be a studio rehearsal with microphone at which final adjustments are made and timing is tested to the second. The third should be a full rehearsal with music and sound effects and special attention to timing.

Production details. Arrange and test all your sound effects in advance. Be sure to "clear" one week in advance all music to be used; that is, notify the studio of the title, composer, and publisher of every bar of music to be broadcast.

Studio deportment. Certain stations insist on absolute quiet. Others permit applause and laughter but insist that it be controlled. Some are generous about allowing students free use of their studios, their time, and their staff. Be sure that you know just what your station demands of you. It may save some embarrassment later.

Broadcasting Do's and Don'ts

For the cast:

1. *Stand quietly before the microphone. Don't back away from it (unless the director signals) or shift from one foot to the other.*
2. *Use a normal conversational tone, as if you were speaking to someone a few feet away.*
3. *Relax. Remember that you are a group merely carrying on a lively conversation.*
4. *Don't hurry. Keep the same speed (tempo) you used in rehearsal, but be alert to pick up your cues promptly.*
5. *Don't rustle your script. As you approach the bottom of a page, shift it quietly downward and to the right. Then as you continue at the top of the next page, slip the discarded sheet behind the rest.*

6. *Don't force your humour, jokes, or effects. Your audience will enjoy them even if you cannot hear their applause.*
7. *Don't move about the studio. Remain seated until your time comes to appear on the programme.*
8. *Never touch any studio equipment, particularly the microphone.*
9. *Watch the signal light. Many a radio amateur's words have gone out over the air when he hadn't planned them for broadcasting.*
10. *Keep one eye on the director. His signals will indicate his wishes.*

For the producers:

1 *Announce yourselves clearly and completely, so that the audience may know the name of the school providing the programme, the title of the selection, and the names of pupils participating.*
2. *Alternate music and speaking for relief effect. Consecutive musical numbers or continuous talking often causes the listener to dial off.*
3. *Plan the programme to the exact minute (with reasonable respect to music at "open" and "close" to lengthen or shorten the programme).*
4. *Change the content, but not necessarily the plan, of your programme at each broadcast. Beware of monotony.*

Glossary of Radio Terms

Every industry has its own language to fit its own needs. Radio is no exception. A few radio terms appear below.

ad lib, speak extemporaneously, without script
audition, studio test of talent before broadcasting, to determine whether a person should broadcast
bit, small part in a cast
biz., sound effects indicating action and the passing of time
clean it up, rehearse until defects are eliminated
cold, starting a programme without musical background or theme
commercial, programme paid for completely by the advertiser; also an advertisement
continuity, text to be read by the announcer—introductions of music, speakers, commercial announcements
cue, signal
cushion, use of theme melody to fill in time when a programme is too short
dead spot, a period of silence during a programme
dress, a programme rehearsed for the last time before broadcasting
drooling, padding a programme with unimportant talk
fade in, increase the volume (of voice, music, or sound effect)
fade out, decrease the volume
gag, joke, bit of comedy
in the mud, dull, uninteresting delivery
light and shade, variations in tenseness and loudness
M.C., Master of Ceremonies
off mike, the position of the actor or sound effect at a distance from the microphone
on the head, a programme concluded on the exact second
on the nose, a programme that appears to be going exactly on schedule
pace, speed of delivery
read-y, speech that sounds like reading rather than talking

script, the text of the programme

signature, the identifying theme (music or sound effect) that regularly introduces a programme

sneak it in, begin the sound effect or music quietly and gradually increase the volume

stand by, a direction to be ready to go on the air within a few seconds

tag line, the line of dialogue that brings a play to its climax

theme, music, sound, or talk used regularly to open a programme

tight, a programme which in rehearsal is a bit too long and must be cut or played rapidly if the material permits

transition, shifting from one scene to another

Sample Programme

The following programme was presented over the radio by high school students:

Open: piano—school theme song

Introduction: Master of Ceremonies

The Strolling Reporter: odds and ends of school life

The Principal Says: short editorial

Musical Interviews: a solo or duet by members of vocal department

News of the Day: three students reading news items. Two read alternately; one read headlines. (Use contrasting voices: two girls and boy or two boys and girl.)

Faculty Interview: A department head explains home economics

Musical Novelty: instrumental trio

Personalities in the News: outstanding students and what they are doing

Dog Days: three-minute student skit

Good Old Central: We point with pride at recent honours

What's Next: calendar of coming events

Close: piano—school theme song

Practice 9. Planning a Radio Programme

Using the activities in your own school as a basis, construct the outline of a programme for broadcasting.

Writing Original Radio Plays

Since the writer for radio can appeal only to the ear of his audience, he depends on sound to convey his ideas (plot, characters, and background). His three main tools, therefore, are (1) dialogue, (2) sound effects, and (3) music. With these three alone he must create in the listener's imagination what the theatre achieves with stage settings, scene shifts, backdrop, props, lighting, costumes, make-up, pantomime, actors' facial expressions, and programme notes.

Writing the Story

It must not be supposed that tricks with sound effects and musical interludes can take the place of a carefully thought-out story. On the contrary, something must be happening every moment you are on the air. That takes patient planning.

The very first minute of the play must have what Max Wylie calls "shock value". In that time the principal characters should be introduced, the conflict between characters or with nature or circumstance should be made clear, and the plot should be well on its way.

Variety is also important. You will want to change tempo occasionally (from a fast scene to a slow and back) and to shift the focus of attention from one group of characters to another.

Despite these changes in scene the play should be building steadily toward a climax or toward the accomplishment of the purpose for which it was written. That is the third reason for careful planning.

Lastly, choose for your play situations with which you have intimate acquaintance. High school students and their problems (mothers and their little boys, as in "Disaster Busters" on pages 419–421) make better script material for the beginning writer than the tribal feuds of Fiji Islanders or the intrigues of enemy agents.

Creating Characters

Some basic rules for choosing and developing characters in the radio drama are:

1. Limit the number of characters to six at the most. More will only confuse the listener.

2. Select characters who will present a sharp contrast to each other. The difference in voice quality and in speaking tempo will help the audience to identify each easily.

3. Avoid the use of speech defects (stuttering, lisping) to distinguish your characters. It may give offence. Broad dialect is also a source of confusion.

4. Choose types with whose actions and speech you are familiar.

Practice 10. Studying a Radio Play

1. Read the selection from "Disaster Busters," a radio play written by a high school class to stimulate contributions to the annual Red Cross drive.

2. What is the value of beginning "cold"? (See Glossary of Radio Terms, pages 417–418.)

3. How much information does the listener get (about time, place, circumstances) in the first minute of performance?

4. What other types of characters could the authors have used in handling the disaster and the scene at headquarters?

DISASTER BUSTERS

ANNOUNCER. Disaster Busters—a story of the Canadian Red Cross and its miraculous work. In Canada every year, even in peacetime, many disasters occur—sometimes fire (*fading out*), sometimes flood, sometimes . . . (*Fade into gusts of wind, heavy rain against windowpane . . . Continue as background for the following.*)

MOTHER (*querulously*). What time is it, Billy? Can you see?

BILLY (*reassuringly*). Now, Ma! Stop worrying. Dad's prob'ly had to help the men further up the river . . . near the dam.

MOTHER (*tensely, more sternly*). Billy, I asked you what time it is.

BILLY. Aw, it's only a little after two.

Biz. Louder gust of wind and rain. Windowpanes rattle.

MOTHER (*despairingly*). Only a little after two! That's nine hours your father's been gone—no supper, no food in his stomach since noontime, most likely.

BILLY. But gee, Mom—

MOTHER (*half to herself*). Doesn't he realize we're in danger, too . . . cooped up here. (*Her voice trails off.*)

BILLY (*stoutly*). Well, I guess I can take care of you, I guess. Now you stay here. I'm just gonna take another look around downstairs. (*Fading out.*) Maybe the water's gone down a little.

Biz. Footsteps and door opening.

MOTHER (*nervously calling after him*). Now you be careful, Billy. You're just like your (*door slams quickly*) father, always barging . . . (*Pauses . . . then more sharply.*) What's the matter? I thought you were going downstairs.

BILLY (*fade in, shakily*). Aw, I guess I'll stay up here . . . save the battery in this flash. These darn things always dim out . . .

Biz. Scrape of chair, quick footsteps under next speech.

MOTHER (*urgently*). Answer me, Billy! What's the matter? (*Fade out.*) Or must I . . . (*Door opens off mike.*) Oh! (*Aghast.*)

BILLY (*gently*). Yeah. (*Pause, then more bravely.*) Don't be scared, Mom. We'd better just move up to the attic, I guess. Wanna take something up with you?

MOTHER (*in panic*). No, no. Just come quickly. Another foot . . .

Biz. Quick footsteps mounting stairs. Use echo chamber for following. Rain and wind should be louder now.

BILLY. Well (*uncertain, then more cheerfully*), it's a sight drier than down there. (*Trying to be funny.*) An' there's always the roof.

Biz. Rumble begins here . . . crescendo till Mother's last speech.

MOTHER (*almost in tears*). My brand new carpet . . . and all those seedlings your father put in. All our work . . .

Biz. Opening of window. Wind and rain up and hold.

BILLY (*speaking above wind, but off mike*). Gee, you can't even see Brace's house from here. (*Breaks off sharply . . . then with rising terror.*) Mom, Mom, c'mere. Look! What's that white out there? (*Rumble grows louder . . . fade in "Fingal's Cave" music a few bars from climax, building with the rumble.*) Just like a wall! Mom, it's water! (*Almost a scream.*) The dam . . .

MOTHER (*rumble almost drowning out her scream*). Billy!

Biz. Up music, crash, splintering of wood, then fade out roar of rushing water, music reverting to quieter opening bars. Continue under announcement and following.

ANNOUNCER. Up and down the river there were many Billys and their mothers. But most of them were saved—through heroic and speedy aid from the Canadian Red Cross. National Headquarters had its finger on the pulse of the entire flood area. And each new demand on its vast resources was quickly satisfied. In the office of the regional director . . . (*Fade out.*)

Biz. Telephone bell.

MISS JORDAN (*crisply*). Miss Jordan speaking.

OPERATOR (*on filter mike for sound of voice over telephone*). Chilliwack calling, Miss Jordan. Can you take it now?

MISS JORDAN. Yes, on this extension, please.

OPERATOR. Go ahead, Chilliwack.

DR. POTTER (*on filter mike*). Miss Jordan?

MISS JORDAN. Speaking.

DR. POTTER. This is Dr. Potter at the Chilliwack field hospital. Another dam broke north of Agassiz at 3 A.M. They're bringing in the survivors now. We'll need fifteen more nurses at least. Can you give them to us?

MISS JORDAN. Just a moment, please. (*Pause.*) Can we fly them in? Is there an airport?

DR. POTTER. Yes, the emergency landing field's only two miles from our base hospital—and on high ground.

MISS JORDAN. Good. You'll need additional supplies, Dr. Potter?

DR. POTTER. Yes, and send us three hundred extra doses of typhoid antitoxin. We're beginning mass inoculations immediately. And toothbrushes . . . and soap. — PUPIL

Writing Dialogue

It has been estimated over 90 per cent of all radio drama consists of dialogue. The action, the characters, the setting, the mood are all developed mainly by dialogue. Don't depend on the announcer to do all that for you. Here are some guides to follow:

1. Write short, pointed sentences. Use contractions freely. Don't be afraid to break off a sentence or leave a question unanswered. Such things occur in real life.

2. Keep sentences and vocabulary simple.

3. Substitute a picturesque action word for a noun bolstered by several adjectives.

4. Avoid the soliloquy. It's artificial. In real life normal people rarely talk to themselves. Develop the action through conversation.

5. To avoid confusion, ordinarily include no more than three characters at a time in a conversation. Then switch the action to another group of characters.

6. Use conversation and exclamation to suggest action that the audience cannot see: passage of time, movement of characters from one spot to another, change in facial expression, change in lighting.

7. Use dialogue to reveal the personality of each character: what he says, how he says it, and what others say about him.

8. Suggest; don't overwrite. Notice that neither Billy nor his mother actually says that the water has almost reached the second floor. How do you know it has?

Practice 11. Studying Dialogue

What does the dialogue of "Disaster Busters" reveal or suggest about: (a) the time, (b) the place, (c) the circumstances, (d) the action preceding the first speech, (e) the characters of Billy and his mother, (f) their mood at the opening, (g) the scene shift to the attic, (h) the reason for the shift?

Using Sound Effects

"Sound effects," says Pauline Gibson, "are the backdrops, props, spotlight, and very often the action of the radio play." The following are six simple sound effects:

Crashes—Break berry boxes. To give the effect of shattered glass, drop a heavy iron bar into a box of broken glass.
Fire—Crinkle cellophane.
Motors—Hold a folded piece of paper against the blades of a fan.
Rain—Roll cellophane between the palms.
Crunching snow—Pinch cornstarch close to the microphone.
Surf—Roll dried peas on a drum head.

Radio sound-effects men can produce over fifty-five thousand different sounds; yet it is possible to write an effective script without a single sound effect. If the effect fulfils no definite purpose, it becomes so much noise—and is resented as such by the audience.

Practice 12. Studying Sound Effects

How do the sound effects in "Disaster Busters" (a) set, then intensify the mood; (b) indicate the movement of characters; (c) indicate the setting (note the use of the filter mike and echo chamber); (d) develop the action; (e) emphasize the climax of the first scene?

Writing Production Notes

Accompanying your script should be a clear indication of the type of actor and voice quality you want for each part.

Be careful also to give in parentheses or in brackets detailed cues for the actor, the sound-effects man, and the musical and dramatic directors: *quietly, fade in, crash, up theme, and back.* The more specific you are, the closer the production of your script will be to your original plan.

Practice 13. Planning a Radio Sketch

Plan a fifteen-minute radio sketch on one of the following or on a topic of your own choosing.

1. Boost contributions to the Community Chest.
2. Stimulate interest in a course in first aid, nutrition or home nursing, the Science Club, a safety campaign, or another cause.

3. Write a biographical sketch of some prominent living person or some famous figure in history. Limit yourself to one or two significant incidents.
4. Dramatize a great moment in scientific discovery or invention for a series entitled "Drama behind the Lab Door."
5. Dramatize an unusual news item or human interest story.
6. Adapt a one-act play, a short story, a narrative poem, or a scene from a novel—for example, "A Night at an Inn," "The Gift of the Magi," "My last Duchess," Jerry Cruncher versus John Barsad from *A Tale of Two Cities*.

As you work, use as a guide the following questions and directions:

1. How much of the action will you reveal in the first minute of broadcast? What will be the conflict?
2. What character contrast will best serve your purpose in developing the plot?
3. Write the dialogue following the suggestions on page 421. Then test by listening to it with closed eyes as someone reads it back to you. Does the conversation sound natural, spontaneous? Does every speech lead to the climax?
4. What sound effects and music will create the mood and atmosphere not obtained by dialogue?
5. Write detailed production notes for your script.
6. Copy your play, using the form of "Disaster Busters."

The Essay

THE student is constantly asked to write essays upon the subjects he is studying—fascism, the development of parliamentary government, the operation of banks, social security, uses of electricity, handy devices in the kitchen, William Shakespeare, character of Julius Caesar, Pakistan. In school the word is used in its true meaning, an interim report or "try", a brief review of the question. It is always by way of an interim study, complete enough for the occasion, or for the space, or at the present state of information. Non-fiction "articles" in magazines are usually essays, and are to be distinguished from the more learned, more complete treatises which may be called monographs and theses. The long formal essays of Carlyle and Macaulay more nearly resemble these than they resemble the true essay such as those of Montaigne, Bacon, Lamb, E. V. Lucas, Robert Lynd, which are to-day called familiar essays. We shall come to the familiar essay later.

Some special types of essays are the Editorial, the Book Review, Literary Criticism, and Literary Appreciation.

WHY PLAN AN ESSAY?

The purpose of an essay plan is to give order, logical arrangement, and impressive form to its matter. It induces all possible brevity and assures proportion. It reduces the risk of confusion, repetition, or omission. Some students try to carry the outlines in mind and refuse to be finally bound by pre-conceived plans committed to writing. They feel that an outline cramps the ready flow of their discourse.

Such students usually labour under a misunderstanding of the use of the plan, which should never be a master but a patient and un-obtrusive slave. No plan should be so rigid as to preclude a desirable alteration, but it should serve as a reminder, a guide, and a check. More good school essays are written with careful planning than without it; and adults always use brief plans or "notes".

HOW TO PLAN AN ESSAY

1. As in other expository writing, the first step toward logical arrangement is to determine the purpose of the essay. This should be written out in a single sentence at the head of the outline.

2. The collected data should then be arranged under a few broad headings, four or five.

3. These general headings should be studied carefully to determine which of them may require to follow others, or which must of necessity come before others so that that which follows will be clear. Another consideration is, what constitutes the most effective final observation to close with? For it is probable that one of the facts is of particular importance. It is almost equally important to make a good beginning—to arrest the attention, to lure the reader into the essay.

4. If one or two headings do not with absolute logic place themselves in the scheme, devise ways of bridging the gaps between these and the ones which are more definitely set, and place them as effectively as possible with this in mind.

5. Prepare your examples, illustrations, proofs, authorities, for all expression of opinion should be substantiated by authority, by experience, or by reasoning.

PURPOSE

An essay on "School Spirit" may have a number of purposes. It may be to congratulate the students on their display of school spirit; it may be to rouse a latent, or create a missing, school spirit; it may be to complain about the abuses which have grown up under the name of school spirit—or it might be others still. Be clear whether the object is instruction, admonition, reproof, commendation, or whatever it may be, for this will materially affect the choice of material, and the arrangement of it.

COLLECTING MATERIAL

Sometimes when we are faced with a topic not of our own choosing we are at a loss to know what to say about it. Under such circumstances—and under more favourable ones—remember Rudyard Kipling's serving men; they will serve you as they served him.

> I keep six honest serving men.
> They taught me all I know.
> Their names are *What*, and *Where*, and *When*,
> And *How*, and *Why*, and *Who*.

Read, talk to friends, think. These are the best ways of getting information. Read again pages 278-298.

SOME TENTATIVE PLANS

1. MY FAVOURITE HOBBY

(Purpose: I shall try to recommend my favourite hobby, stamp collecting, to other students of the class—especially those who are not collectors already.)

1. *What stamp collecting is*—specialization and systematization *versus* accumulation—knowledge of philatelly,—knowledge of stamps, their issues, their variety, their values, their uses, their subjects, their stories.
2. *What recommends stamp collecting*—many famous collections,—an educative hobby,—increasing value of collections,—requires and develops skill,—and, especially, an interesting and pleasurable hobby.
3. *Some famous collectors*—Late King George V, the Duke of Windsor, President Franklin D. Roosevelt, Herbert Hoover, Roger Babson, Ellis Parker Butler, Austrian Count Phillip la Renatiere von Ferrari.
4. *Educational value*—knowledge of geography, knowledge of history and biography—training in accurate observation and recording.
5. *Skills required and developed*—true and fake stamps,—stamps that look alike and are not,—perforations and "imperforates,"—watermarks—stamp papers—varieties and how to find them—deft handling.
6. *Interesting Philatelly*—some famous stamps (British Guiana, 1856, 1 cent, on Magenta paper—Mauretius, 1847, 1 penny orange—Spain, 1851, 2 reales, error in colour, printed in blue instead of red). Some famous subjects (The Winged Horse,—Austrian Archduke Franz Ferdinand,—The Trench of Bayonets,—the Faith Issues). Some interesting stamp stories (The Fiery Throne, St. Martin's Cloak).
7. *Literature and Recommendation*—What has not been treated in this essay: the cost, how to collect, stamp clubs, stamp literature. But if any student does not desire to become a stamp collector, let him dip into this interesting literature at peril of his resolution.

Bibliography

Description of United States Postage Stamps—Post Office Department, Washington.
Canadian Stamps—Armstrong.
The Young Stamp Collector's Own Book—Ellis Parker Butler.
Postage Stamps and their Stories—Stanley Phillips.
Pageant of Civilization—F. B. Warren.
Stamp Collecting—Why and How—Prescott Holden Thorp.
"Canadian Geography and Stamps," in *Canadian Geographical Journal*, September, 1936.

2. ON BUYING BOOKS

(Purpose: To induce students to build a home library.)

Do we buy books?—Evidently not, cite the number of homes without books—those that are there are accidental acquisitions or gifts—exclamations when they see a library even of moderate size.
What does this signify?—A standard of taste—a standard of values—we think meanly of our minds or we would feed them—a reflection upon the cultural development of Canada.
Buying versus borrowing—Book friends—bedside books—having books by us —reading and re-reading—exceptions.
Starting and going—Begin by reading and collecting favourites—standard authors and cheap editions—good reprints—quality versus quantity—"read" books, not shelf books—Buy books we have been specially curious about—special recommendations and book clubs—reviews.

Having a library—Pride of possession—greater pride of knowledge—the satisfaction (apart from pride) of cultural possession—friendly exchange of book knowledge.

Bibliography

"On Buying Books"—A. G. Gardiner, *Alpha of the Plough.*
Literary Taste and How to Form It—Arnold Bennett.

3. RADIO AND EDUCATION

(Purpose: To review the great and growing importance of radio in education.)

I. *The Coverage*—Educational opportunity because it reaches nearly all people, young and old, at work and play—Standard wave and short wave cover the world, both for subjects and for listeners, in homes, hotels, restaurants, clubs, offices, schools, even automobiles.

II. *Subjects*—Anything that can be conveyed by sound: news, special addresses, lectures, music, operas, symphonies, school lessons.

III. *Some Disadvantages*—Listeners cannot choose time of reception, nor the subject,—he often suffers much to learn much—he is misinformed as well as informed—music may be no higher than the listener's tastes, sometimes below it.

IV. *Some Conclusions*—Disadvantages may be overcome in part: you can turn a programme off,—you can make selection beforehand from press reports—you can support proper programmes.—Offers many opportunities not otherwise available, we conclude its advantages outweigh its disadvantages.—We must realize it will go on whether we approve or not, let us mould it to our needs.

Bibliography

Radio in Canadian Schools—R. S. Lambert.

Practice 1. Making Essay Plans

Construct helpful outlines for essays on as many of the following topics as your teacher may choose:

1. Making camp in the snow. 2. Running a trap-line. 3. The pleasures of gardening. 4. Breeding pigeons. 5. Constructing bird-houses. 6. The Canadian Broadcasting Corporation. 7. The B.B.C. 8. Sunday observance. 9. Temperance teaching in our schools. 10. On behalf of the Y.M.C.A. (or Y.W.C.A.) 11. Life-saving. 12. Winter sports. 13. Amateur hockey. 14. Modern poetry. 15. Reading fiction. 16. Reading aloud. 17. Essay writing. 18. The Red River Settlement. 19. Pioneering. 20. The future of aviation. 21. The history of aviation. 22. Boulder Dam. 23. Drought control. 24. Reforestation. 25. Apex (or Thatcher) Wheat. 26. Farm Boys' Camp. 27. Boys' and Girls' clubs. 28. Competition in industry. 29. Co-operation in industry. 30. Consumers' co-operatives. 31. A modern school of music. 32. Travelling libraries. 33. The open-shelf library. 34. The library needs of our school. 35. Kagawa. 36. Gandhi. 37. Macbeth. 38. Our movies. 39. The schools of to-morrow. 40. Government correspondence schools.

EDITORIALS

The editorial columns of the great dailies are powerful instruments in the formation of public opinion, reinforced as they usually are by such selection and display of the news as will direct the attention of the reading public to the matters under consideration. And this is the function of the editorial: to mould public opinion. The news reporters glean the day's news and the editorial writers comment upon it. They may congratulate, criticize, commend, condemn, or crusade, on political or social questions. They usually clarify the interpretation of news; they might be used for the opposite purpose, though this is beneath the ethical code of reputable editors.

"Third Leaders"

The usual editorial "leaders" are not intended for preservation or expected to be of permanent interest. "Like the news of the day," says Professor Mackail, "the daily comment on it is transitory and soon forgotten. One thinks as little of re-reading yesterday's leading article as of re-reading yesterday's news. . . The news of the day and and the daily comment made upon it give necessary information, and help (or are supposed to help) to interpret it to us. Between them, they rouse feeling and suggest action, as well as keep us in touch with the daily movement of the world; but they do not satisfy the intelligence, nor, except incidentally, do they enlarge the mind, or lead it toward the real realities. Those who read nothing but newspapers—how many!—are starving their minds; and the starvation is none the less real for those who gorge themselves with this food."

Metropolitan newspapers try to make up this editorial deficiency by including an editorial of a different, less occasional kind. This editorial, known as the "third leader", resembles the familiar essay, but is less personal and more topical. "They are meant," says Professor Mackail, "to turn the reader from affairs and interests of the moment to a consideration 'of man, of nature, and of human life' in their larger, more permanent aspects. They may still deal not indeed with events, but with fashions or tendencies, theories or experiences, of the immediate present. But even with these they deal in a more detached way, from a wider point of view. Oftener still they are concerned with things that have a more true permanence; with the elements of human nature, the springs of action, the problems of life and conduct; with the effective meaning of art or of science; with the recurrent and perpetual pageant of the visible world."

These headings are chosen from "third leaders": "On Friendship," "Ugliness," "On Being a Gentleman," "Childishness," "Amateur and

Professional," "Castles in the Air," "Philosophy and Poetry," "Grumbling," "Strawberries," "Living in the Past."

Models (Leading Articles):

COURAGE IN CIVIL LIFE

Periodically the world hesitates in its every-day run of work and pleasure to contemplate some act of high courage. Such an incident seems to lift the average man or woman out of the mundane routine of life which they are at times tempted to term "meaningless."

In northern Canada the curtain has just been lowered on the final act in one of these great living dramas by the successful rescue of Flight Lieutenant Sheldon Coleman and Leading Aircraftsman Joseph Fortey by other members of the Royal Canadian Air Force.

For more than a month, the two lost airmen waited for help near a small lake, inadequately sheltered by timber and warmed by their ingenious camp-made stove. They had little to eat and the country afforded less provision than one would expect. There was the continuous pressure of the rapidly approaching Arctic Winter with its prospect of greater suffering and privation.

Thinking of these things, one wonders how many times their fitful sleep must have been broken by the lash of an imaginary propeller and how they stood for hours scanning the horizon hoping against hope for sign of a rescue ship. It is inactive waiting like that which breaks the nerve of most men.

Then there were the men who conducted the search. The leader of this party tended to minimize in his public statement the hazards his men undertook in their rescue work. Yet there will be few who read the story of airmen returning to their base with empty gasoline tanks or of the constant strain of flying in bad weather who do not feel that lift about the heart that comes from the contemplation of shining courage.

After witnessing a rescue like the one just completed, or many others that take place on the frontier or in the mines or on the sea, it seems almost senseless for certain kinds of ardent militarists to continue their arguments that war and slaughter are necessary to bring out the highest virtues of the human race.

SLAUGHTER STILL PREVAILS ON THE HIGHWAYS

Two judges of the High Court of Ontario have this week denounced the increase of motor accidents and the general practice of reckless driving on the highways. A few drivers have been sent to jail on charges of manslaughter when they were responsible for the deaths of others. Chief Justice Rose is quoted as saying: "I am not sure we are following the logical course in prosecuting only when there has been a serious accident or death." There must be punishment to suit the crime, but punishment will not be inflicted until public opinion is sufficiently aroused to demand it. The officers of the law should rigidly enforce existing regulations, and the courts should not hesitate to convict.

One of the causes of accidents on the highways is the persistence of the vast majority of drivers in neither dimming nor dipping their lights in the face of opposing traffic. We doubt if five per cent of the motor users of this part of the country ever think of lessening the glare from their own headlights in consideration for motorists who are travelling the other way. If a motorist driving south has to meet a succession of cars driving north, he is partially blinded so that he cannot discern what is on the road ahead of him. We have printed a series of editorials on the subject of glaring headlights. The Minister of Highways has appealed for courtesy on the road, but very few people appear to pay any attention to these appeals. It is probable that a few examples will have to be made of a few individuals before a very grave abuse is checked or even modified.

By permission of The Globe and Mail, *Toronto.*

Model (Third Leaders)

ON FRIENDSHIP

Friendship is above reason, for, though you find virtues in a friend, he was your friend before you found them. It is a gift that we offer because we must; to give it as the reward of virtues would be to set a price upon it, and those who do that have no friendship to give. If you choose your friends on the ground that you are virtuous and want virtuous company, you are no nearer to true friendship than if you choose them for commercial reasons. Besides, who are you that you should be setting a price upon your friendship? It is enough for any man that he has the divine power of making friends, and he must leave it to that power to determine who his friends shall be. For, though you may choose the virtuous to be your friends, they may not choose you; indeed, friendship cannot grow where there is any calculated choice. It comes, like sleep, when you are not thinking about it; and you should be grateful, without any misgiving, when it comes.

So no man who knows what friendship is ever gave up a friend because he turns out to be disreputable. His only reason for giving up a friend is that he has ceased to care for him; and, when that happens, he should reproach himself for this mortal poverty of affection, not the friend for having proved unworthy. For it is inhuman presumption to say of any man that he is unworthy of your friendship, just as it is to say of any woman, when you have fallen out of love with her, that she is unworthy of your love. In friendship and in love we are always humble, because we see that a free gift has been given to us; and to lose that humility because we have lost friendship or love is to take a pride in what should shame us.

We have our judgments and our penalties as part of the political mechanism that is forced upon us so that we may continue to live; but friendship is not friendship at all unless it teaches us that these are not part of our real life. They have to be; and we pay men, and clothe them in wigs and scarlet, to sit in judgment on other men. So we are tempted to play this game of judgment ourselves, even though no one has paid us to do it. It is only in the warmth of friendship that we see how cold a thing it is to judge and how stupid to take a pleasure in judging; for we recognize this warmth as a positive good, a richness in our natures, while the coldness that sets us judging is a poverty. Just as our criticism of a work of art begins only when we have ceased to experience it, so our criticism of our friends begins only when we have ceased to experience them, when our minds can no longer remain at the height of intimacy. But this criticism is harmless if we know it for what it is, merely the natural reaction, the cold fit that comes after the warm, and if we do not suppose that our coldness is wiser than our warmth.

There are men who cannot be friends except when they are under an illusion that their friends are perfect, and when the illusion passes there is an end of their friendship. But true friendship has no illusions, for it reaches to that part of a man's nature that is beyond his imperfections, and in doing so it takes all of them for granted. It does not even assume that he is better than other men, for there is egotism in assuming that. A man is your friend, not because of his superiorities, but because there is something open from your nature to his, a way that is closed between you and most men. You and he understand each other, as the phrase is; your relation with him is a rare success among a multitude of failures, and if you are proud of the success you should be ashamed of the failure.

There is nothing so fatal to friendship as this egotism of accounting for it by some superiority in the friend. If you do that you will become a member of a set, all, in their assertion of each other's merits, implying their own, and all uneasy lest they are giving more than they get. For if you insist upon the virtues of your friend, you expect him to insist upon your virtues, and there is a competition between you which makes friendship a burden rather than a rest. Criticism then becomes treachery, for it implies that you are beginning to doubt those superiorities upon which your friendship is supposed to be based. But when no superiorities are assumed, criticism is only the exercise of a natural curiosity. It is because a man is your friend, and you like him so much and know him so well, that you are curious about him. You are in fact an expert upon him, and like to show your expert knowledge. And you are an expert because in the warmth of friendship his disguises melt away from him, and he shows himself to you just as he is. Indeed, that is the test of friendship and the delight of it, that because we are no longer afraid of being thought worse than we are we do not try to seem better. We know that it is not our virtues that have won us friendship, and we do not fear to lose it through our vices. We have reached the blessed state of being nearer to heaven than anything else in this life, in which affection does not depend upon judgment; and we are like gods, who have no need even to forgive, because they know. It is a rare state, and never attained to in its perfection. We can approach it only if we know what friendship is and really desire it, and especially if we admire that man who is a friend without ever wondering at his choice of friends or blaming him for his faithfulness to them whatever evil they may do. — From *"Modern Essays from The Times"*

By permission of the publishers, Edward Arnold & Co., London.

Practice 2. Studying Editorials

Cut out and bring to school three editorials which you think are good ones and after pasting them in your exercise book write under each what you think its merits are.

Practice 3. Writing an Editorial

Write an editorial (leading article) on some topic in this week's news.

Practice 4. Writing a "Third Leader"

Write a "third leader" editorial for your school paper.

BOOK REVIEW

Why do magazines and newspapers print pages of reviews of books, moving pictures, plays, operas, art exhibits, concerts, and recitals? Of what use are book reviews? By helping us to decide what books we ought to read and giving us information about the books we have not time to read, reviewers make us more intelligent about books of the day. In the field of contemporary literature reviews are as useful as a history of literature is in the realm of older books: they guide and inform. And well-written book reviews are also entertaining.

Fiction

The job of the critic is to find out what the author was trying to do and whether or not he succeeded and when to express what he thinks and feels about the book. The topics of a review vary with the type of book read. A fiction or drama report may be a discussion of a number of these topics: setting (time, place, atmosphere); plot; scenes that would be effective on the stage; characters; theme or central idea; suspense; beginning; ending; contrast; climaxes; words added to reader's vocabulary; clearness, force, and beauty of style; probability; methods of gaining a semblance of reality; movement of the story; humour; quotations; the best part of the story; reasons for liking or disliking the book; comparisons with other books by the same author or by other authors. That is a long list. Of course, no book review includes a discussion of all these topics. It is better by use of incidents, illustrations, and citations to prove three or four points than to mention and discuss a dozen vaguely. A pointed reason for liking or not liking the book makes an effective ending of a report.

Poetry

Many of the topics given under fiction and drama may be used in a report on poetry. Other topics often discussed are: themes treated, moods reflected, the sound (metre, rhyme, rhythm, onomatopœia, alliteration, assonance, most melodious lines); pictures; feelings expressed by the poet or aroused by the reader; lines worth remembering; word choice. Most good poetry has beauty of theme, imagination, emotion, sound, and diction.

Biography

A report on a biography should tell what the person discussed has done for the world, what he has added to the available hope, goodness, beauty, knowledge, or contentment. Useful topics are: the lasting work done by the subject of the biography; his early experiences as preparation for his life work; his traits; his ideals; his helps in achieving success; his handicaps or hardships; the author's style; the fairness and accuracy of the biographer; a comparison with other biographies; and reasons for liking or disliking the book.

Essays

For a report on a volume of essays, letters, or orations good topics are: the author's purpose; traits of author shown; his style; his mood; humour; main thought of each essay, letter, or oration; ideas worth remembering; sentences worth memorizing; words added to reader's vocabulary; a comparison with other books; reasons for liking or disliking the book.

SEVENTEEN
By Booth Tarkington

A lovelorn youth of seventeen, a beautiful young lady who talks baby talk, a few other youths, and a little sister who has a passion for sugared applesauce on bread—mix these ingredients and add Booth Tarkington. Place on a pedestal Miss Lola, and—oh, yes—Floppit! Underneath the pedestal, with an adoring expression in his eyes, place William Baxter, romantically aged seventeen, who discovers he can write poetry. The result is an extremely humorous and well-written book, for around those characters Booth Tarkington builds a delightful story. *Seventeen* could not be anything but utterly charming and entertaining, for Tarkington is at all times a master at portraying love-sick youth. So to everyone, be he under seventeen, over seventeen, or just at that eventful age, I say, read this book—for it is an antitote for everything depressing—except perhaps seventeen-year-old lovesickness. — PUPIL

Practice 5. Writing a Book Review

After reading the preceding review write a lively, pointed, entertaining one-paragraph report of a book you have recently read.

MEN AGAINST THE SEA
By Charles Nordhoff and James Norman Hall

When Nordhoff and Hall wrote their *Mutiny on the Bounty* a couple of years ago, I felt that I had read a first-class sea book and a piece of writing remarkable for its simplicity, directness, and narrative power. I also felt that I had read the last word on the *Bounty* case; and readers in the present generation, particularly those unacquainted with nautical literature, can hardly realize the wealth of material published during the last century about this most famous and romantic incident of early sea-faring days.

But now the same authors have gone themselves one better in reviving another aspect of the grim old story, and in *Men Against the Sea*, the tale of Captain Bligh's extraordinary trip with nineteen men in an open boat across the Pacific Ocean after they had been set adrift by the *Bounty* mutineers, have produced a book so fine, in my opinion, that I almost hesitate to say all that I think about it. It is not Bligh's history, or the story of any character, or even the story of the trip itself, that makes the book so fine. The book is fine because it is written with true imagination and abundant narrative power, because it makes the scene live vividly in the mind from page to page, because with unfailing instinct for detail every desire of the reader's imagination is quickly supplied, because the psychological aspects of men in the midst of distress are presented with a sure touch, and because from beginning to end the note of extreme directness and simplicity is never departed from. I am frankly lost in admiration of the deftness and art with which the narrative flows on. Stevenson would have delighted in *Men Against the Sea;* it is his sort of book entirely. This, to my mind, is the best boy's book published in English since *Treasure Island;* and what that means as a book for adult boys we all understand.

Much could be said on the score of nautical fidelity. These young authors, living in Tahiti, familiar with small craft on the open Pacific, are admirably equipped to cover Bligh's long and terrible journey. They cannot make a slip because they are telling what they know. The boat, Bligh's launch, is one of the noblest and clearest characters in the book; and the winds and weather of the Pacific are characters, also.

I defy any right-minded man or boy to read *Men Against the Sea* and not come out of it uplifted and exhausted. And if by chance he believes as firmly as I do in the power of titles, here is one strong and suggestive and mouth-filling enough to please the most captious requirement. It is more than the right title; it is an inspiration. So much for an emotional estimate of a brief work that has moved and satisfied me deeply, and given me what I believe books of fiction ought to give. — Lincoln Colcord in New York *Herald-Tribune* "Books"

MARK TWAIN
By Stephen Leacock

Wise, shrewd, vivid, plain-spoken, this vigorous little biography of Mark Twain fills a real need. There have been great detailed books written about Mark, and there have been sombre psychological studies. Here is the voice of one of his own kidney, a fellow humorist, a man peculiarly well fitted to understand him. Mr. Leacock tells again the amazing story of which one never wearies—the country boy, the river pilot, the young printer and then the world-famous author and lecturer; the financial and family tragedies; the old lion with a white mane. It is a familiar story but it has never been told with more sympathy and comprehension. Mr. Leacock is just near enough, and also just far away enough, from Mark Twain, to see his thrilling and savage genius with the keenest edge of understanding. "To many of us" (he says) "who are old enough to remember most of Mark Twain's works from the time of their appearance, there is a certain list which seemed then and seem now the real Mark Twain. The rest doesn't matter. The list includes *Roughing It, Life on the Mississippi, The Innocents Abroad, Tom Sawyer, The Adventures of Huckleberry Finn* and the *Connecticut Yankee.* We don't need to care what the critics say; we can recall the sheer unadulterated joy of that first perusal." A brilliantly forcible and honest little book. We're grateful for it. — CHRISTOPHER MORLEY

By permission of the author

THE MUTINY ON THE BOUNTY

(This review, from *John O'London's Weekly*, was published in July, 1936, after Nordhoff and Hall's book had become widely read, had been filmed and perhaps more widely seen.)

Those who have seen the recent film of this melodrama of the sea will especially welcome *The True Story of the Mutiny on the Bounty* (Newnes, 2s. 6d.) The author of this concise little book, Mr. Owen Rutter, has the best of qualifications to write the story, for he has already edited for publication the journals of Fryer, the *Bounty's* master, and Morrison, the boatswain's mate, as well as the minutes of the courtmartial of the mutineers, and he is soon to publish the log and journal of Captain Bligh, which has lain for a century in manuscript. Previous writers have blamed Bligh's conduct as the cause of the mutiny which followed the gathering of the cargo of breadfruit at Tahiti, but Mr. Rutter shows that Bligh was a wise disciplinarian until he was irritated by the shortcomings of Fletcher Christian, the lieutenant whom he had himself promoted. He analyzes succinctly the incidents at Tahiti which led to the mutiny, and having dealt in one dramatic chapter with the mutiny itself, he relates Bligh's wonderful voyage in the launch of the *Bounty*, the sojourn of the mutineers at Tahiti, and their division into two parties, the one being eventually picked up, conveyed home, and court-martialled, while the other, under Christian, founded the settlement at Pitcairn Island, still inhabited by their descendants. Mr. Rutter has such complete mastery of his subject that he has distilled from documents and law-reports a fascinating and lively narrative, which reads like a novel, but is so faithful to fact that even the conversations are taken from the records.

By permission of the publishers, John O'London's Weekly, *London.*

Practice 6. Book Review

Clip from a magazine or a newspaper a good book review and paste it on a sheet of paper. Then beside the review write a list of the topics the critic discusses and tell why you think the review a good one.

Practice 7. Book Reviews

1. Write a clear, convincing, and entertaining review of a book you have read recently. Base it on a number of the topics given in the discussion of book reviews. Avoid trite phrases by telling directly and pointedly why you like or dislike the book. A mere retelling of the story or the life of the author is not a review.

2. Compare two books you have read this term. Use some such title as "Why I like *A Tale of Two Cities* better than *David Copperfield*" or "A Comparison of *Alice Adams* and *So Big.*"

The Familiar Essay

ALTHOUGH essays are commonly divided into the formal and informal or familiar, no sharp dividing line can be drawn between the two types. The formal essay is usually an orderly, logical, impersonal, instructive treatment of a subject. Carlyle's "Essay on Burns," Emerson's "Self-Reliance," Macaulay's "Life of Johnson," and Palmer's "Self-Cultivation in English" are four formal essays often studied in high school.

Of the familiar essay Mr. A. C. Benson says, "The true essay, then, is a tentative and personal treatment of a subject; it is a kind of improvisation on a delicate theme; a species of soliloquy, as if a man were to speak aloud the slender and whimsical thoughts that come into his mind when he is alone on a winter evening before a warm fire, and, closing his book, abandons himself to the luxury of genial reverie." He adds that the familiar essay is natural, clear, and rambling.

The personal note in the informal essay is one of its attractive features. The successful informal essayist writes as a man talks to his friend, and is so good-natured, fair, frank, reasonable, and entertaining that his readers come to know him. They learn of his whims, foibles, experiences, blunders, visions, likes, dislikes, and prejudices; feel his mood; and sense his personality.

THE IDEA

To write an informal essay one needs to have an interesting or unusual idea and to tell it skilfully. Of the subject matter Charles S. Brooks says, "Pieces of this and that, an odd carrot, as it were, a left-over potato, a pithy bone, discarded trifles, are tossed in from time to time to feed the composition."

The idea must be the cornerstone on which rests the complete structure of the essay. No matter what digressions the writer may make later on, he must at length return to his original thought and make the reader feel that it permeates the entire work. Since the general idea or theme is so important it should be introduced near the beginning of the essay.

STYLE

The style of the essay very often holds the chief interest of the reader. It should be adapted to the subject and mood, and may be gay and sprightly, or full of deep yet controlled feeling. One good test of the effectiveness of an essay's style is to read it aloud. If it has the cordial, intimate, sincere tone of good conversation, it is good essay style.

The essay is perhaps the literary form which needs the most polishing. To express skilfully an interesting or unusual idea takes time. Brooks says, "Essayists, as a rule, chew their pencils." Variety in sentence structure, in paragraph structure and length, and in vocabulary and phrase is the keynote. Use your dictionary freely, and consult Roget's *Thesaurus* and a good dictionary of synonyms when you find that you have fallen into worn-out words or hackneyed phrases.

Models:

1. ON BIG WORDS

I was cutting down the nettles by the hedge with a bill-hook when a small man with spectacles, a straw hat, a white alpaca jacket, and a book under his arm came up, stopped, and looked on. I said "Good evening," and he said "Good evening." Then, pointing to my handiwork, he remarked:

"You find the nettles very difficult to eradicate?"

I said I found them hard to keep down.

"They disseminate themselves most luxuriantly," he said.

I replied that they spread like the dickens.

"But they have their utility in the economy of Nature," he said.

I replied that Nature was welcome to them as far as I was concerned.

He then remarked that it was most salubrious weather, and I agreed that it had been a fine day. But he was afraid, he said, that the aridity of the season was deleterious to the crops, and I replied that my potatoes were doing badly. After that, I think it occurred to him that we did not speak the same language, and with another "Good evening" he passed on and I returned to the attack on the nettles.

It is an excellent thing to have a good vocabulary, but one ought not to lard one's common speech or everyday letters with long words. It is like going out for a walk in the fields with a silk hat, a frock-coat, and patent leather boots. No reasonable person could enjoy the country in such a garb. He would feel like a blot on the landscape. He would be as much out of place as a guest in a smock-frock at a Buckingham Palace garden-party. And familiar conversation that dresses itself up in silk-hatted words is no less an offence against the good taste of things. We do not make a thing more impressive by clothing it in grand words any more than we crack a nut more neatly by using a sledge-hammer. We only distract attention from the thought to the clothes it wears. If we are wise our wisdom will gain from the simplicity of our speech, and if we are foolish our folly will only shout the louder through big words.

Take, for example, that remark of Dr. Johnson's about the swallows. "Swallows certainly sleep all the winter," he said. "A number of them conglobulate together, by flying round and round, and then all in a heap throw themselves under water and lie in the bed of a river." It was a foolish belief, but it would be unfair to scoff at Johnson for not being better informed than his contemporaries. It is that bumptious word "conglobulate" that does for him. It looks so learned and knowing that it calls attention to the absurdity like a college cap on a donkey's ears.

A fine use of words does not necessarily mean the use of fine words. That was the mistake which Humpty-Dumpty made in *Alice in Wonderland*. He thought that "impenetrability" was such a magnificent word that it would leave Alice speechless and amazed. Many writers are like that. When the reporter says that So-and-So "manipulated the ivories" (meaning that he had played the billiard-balls into position), or that So-and-So "propelled the sphere" (meaning that he had kicked the football), he feels that he has got out of the rut of common speech when in fact he has exchanged good words for counterfeit coin. That is not the way of the masters of language. They do not vulgarize fine words. They glorify in simple words, as in Milton's description of the winged host:

> Far off their coming shone.

Quite ordinary words employed with a certain novelty and freshness can wear a distinction that gives them not only significance but a strange and haunting beauty. I once illustrated the point by showing the effects which the poets, and particularly Wordsworth and Keats, extract from the word "quiet." Shakespeare could perform equal miracles with the trivial word "sweet," which he uses with a subtle beauty that makes it sing like a violin in the hands of a master. Who can be abroad in the sunshine and singing of these spring days without that phrase, "the sweet o' the year," carolling like a bird in the mind? It is not a "jewel five words long." It is a dewdrop from the very mint of Nature. But Shakespeare could perform this magic with any old word. Take "flatter." A plain, home-spun word, you would say, useful for the drudgery of speech but nothing more. Then Shakespeare takes it in hand, and it shines bright as Sirius in the midnight sky:

> Full many a glorious morning have I seen
> Flatter the mountain tops with sovran eye.

I once wanted to use for purposes of quotation a familiar stanza of Burns, but one word, the vital word, escaped me. I give the stanza, with the word I lacked missing:

> To make a happy fireside clime
> For weans and wife
> That's the true   and sublime
> Of human life.

You, perhaps, know the missing word; but I could not recall it. I tried all the words that were serviceable, and each seemed banal and commonplace. I dare not, for shame, mention the words I tried to use as patches for Burns. When I turned up the poem and found that poignant word "pathos," I knew the measure of my failure to draw the poet's bow.

We carry big words in our head for the expression of our ideas, and short words in our heart for the expression of our emotions. Whenever we speak the language of true feeling, it is our mother tongue that comes to our lips. It is equal to any burden. Take the familiar last stanza of Wordsworth's: "Three years she grew in sun and shower":

> Thus Nature spake—the work was done—
> How soon my Lucy's race was run!
> She died, and left to me

> This heath, this calm and quiet scene;
> The memory of what has been,
> And never more will be.

It is so simple that a child might have said it, and so charged with emotion that a man might be forgiven if he could not say it. *A Shropshire Lad* is full of this surge of feeling dressed in homespun, as when he says:

> Into my heart an air that kills
> From yon far country blows:
> What are those blue remembered hills,
> What spires, what farms are those?
>
> That is the land of lost content,
> I see it shining plain,
> The happy highways where I went
> And cannot come again.

Even in pictorial description the most thrilling effects, as in the case I have quoted from Milton, are produced not by the pomp of words but by the passion of words. In two rapid, breathless lines:

> The sun's rim dips, the stars rush out,
> With one stride comes the dark,

Coleridge flashes on the mind all the beauty and wonder of the tropic night. And though Shakespeare, like Milton and Wordsworth, could use the grand words when the purpose was rhetorical or decorative, he did not go to them for the expression of the great things of life. Then he speaks with what Raleigh calls the bare intolerable force of King Lear's:

> Do not laugh at me,
> For as I am a man, I think this lady
> To be my child Cordelia.

The higher the theme rises the more simple and austere becomes the speech, until the words seem like nerves bared and quivering to the agony of circumstance:

> *Lear.* And my poor fool is hanged! No, no, no life!
> Why should a dog, a horse, a rat, have life,
> And thou no breath at all? Thou'lt come no more,
> Never, never, never, never, never!
> Pray you, undo this button. Thank you, sir.—
> Do you see this? Look on her, look, her lips,—
> Look there, look there!
> *Edgar.* He faints! My lord, my lord!—
> *Kent.* Break, heart; I prithee, break!
> *Edgar.* Look up, my lord.
> *Kent.* Vex not his ghost: O let him pass! he hates him
> That would upon the rack of this tough world
> Stretch him out longer.

The force of words can no farther go. And my friend in the white alpaca jacket will notice that they are all very little ones. — "ALPHA OF THE PLOUGH" (A. G. GARDINER), from *Many Furrows*.

By arrangement with the publishers, J. M. Dent & Sons, London and Toronto.

2. TRIVIA

STONEHENGE

They sit there for ever on the dim horizon of my mind, that Stonehenge circle of elderly disapproving Faces—Faces of the Uncles and Schoolmasters and Tutors who frowned upon my youth.

In the bright centre and sunlight I leap, I caper, I dance my dance; but when I look up, I see they are not deceived. For nothing ever placates them, nothing ever moves to a look of approval that ring of bleak, old, contemptuous Faces.

THE STARS

Battling my way homeward one dark night against the wind and rain, a sudden gust, stronger than the others, drove me back into the shelter of a tree. But soon the Western sky broke wide open; the illumination of the Stars poured down from behind the dispersing clouds.

I was astonished at their brightness, to see how they filled the night with their soft lustre. So I went my way accompanied by them; Arcturus followed me, and becoming entangled in a leafy tree, shone by glimpses, and then merged triumphant, Lord of the Western Sky. Moving along the road in the silence of my own footsteps, my thoughts were among the Constellations. I was one of the Princes of the starry Universe; in me also there was something that was not insignificant and mean and of no account.

THE KALEIDOSCOPE

I find in my mind, in its miscellany of ideas and musings, a curious collection of little landscapes and pictures, shining and fading for no reason. Sometimes they are views in no way remarkable—the corner of a road, a heap of stones, an old gate. But there are many charming pictures too: as I read, between my eyes and book the Moon sheds down on harvest fields her chill of silver; I see autumnal avenues, with the leaves falling, or swept in heaps; and storms blow among my thoughts, with the rain beating for ever on the fields. Then winter's upward glare of snow appears; or the pink and delicate green of Spring in the winds sunshine; or cornfields and green waters, and youths bathing in Summer's golden heats.

And as I walk about, certain places haunt me; a cathedral rises above a dark blue foreign town, the colour of ivory in the sunset light; now I find myself in a French garden, full of lilacs and bees, and shut-in sunshine, with the Mediterranean lounging and washing outside its walls; now in a little college library, with busts, and the green reflected light of Oxford lawns— and again I hear the bells, reminding me of the familiar Oxford hours. — LOGAN PEARSALL SMITH, *Trivia*.

3. CANDILLI

That there are landscapes whose beauty is intrinsically mournful, I admit; there are summer afternoons in England when the clouds lie low on the horizon, and the shadows of the hedges stretch out over the fields whose loveliness we recognize as sad. But in other lands than England reign endless sunshine and bright colour, and the scene that met my eyes all to-day should make the veriest dullard dance to behold its radiant joy. I have been staring for hours out of my window to-day, letting my thoughts and glances wander down the cobbled and precipitous street of Candilli, where dog and man lie sleeping, past the village minaret, out across the Bosphorus and all the myriad laughter of the tiny waves, to the further shore where rise the chivalrous old towers of Roumeli Hissar, which men called the Castle of Damalis five hundred years ago. If the world holds a fairer prospect, I, who have wandered a little, have not seen it; yet all its brightness and splendour does but fill my mind with sorrow and unrest. I have been watching for three hours the tracts of warm light on those giant-rounded keeps, and the thousand boats that ply the highway of the salt sea-river, sad I know not why. I have waited till evening, idle in my chair, till the brown castle walls turned gold, and the blue sea white and wet, till the sun went down not amid the patches and pageantry of our Northern settings, but gently leaving a sky as softly coloured as the petals of a rose; and the lamps were swung high on to the masts of the great ships steaming out to Russia through the gloom. Sick at heart with so much loveliness was I, and then brief twilight came, netting the world in spectral blue, till I cried out for the darkness like a cave-beast blinded by the glare. And now darkness is here with her fixed and trailing stars, and the whole European shore is ablaze from Therapia to Stamboul; the Muezzin has cried from his little minaret, the Ottoman night has begun.

Is it unmanly or decadent of me to long for a slag-heap or a gaswork, or any strong, bold, ugly thing to break the spell of this terrible and malignant beauty that saps body and soul? Yet there are few who did not feel what they might call a "touch of sadness," in the sweet popular phrase, when first they saw the boundless sea, or mountains capped with snow. The misery I feel lies deep in the nature of man; such thoughts as I am thinking, millions have thought before. For here, it seems, is the very face of Beauty, here one may gaze into her eyes and watch them change. But who am I to enjoy this high gift of the gods? What can I do with it, how make it my own? Why is it there, part of my foolish daily life: can I treat it as a common thing? To deserve, to enjoy its magnificence, a man should have a high work, or at least a noble plan. A poet might sing of it, and find peace; or a painter paint it; glorious would it shine to a man returning from a long journey, if among those countless lights one light meant home. Even to me these scenes were joyful that day I rode over the Anatolian hills, and the weariness of the body banished all sickness from the mind, and my head was void of fancies, and I saw little as we cantered along the sandy tracks save spars of sunlight and flashes of sea. But now, though my limbs are aching to be up and doing, I am fascinated by deadly wonder; and he who sinks before this spell sits in his chair for hours and plays with his dreams. He dreams of a mistress as Thais gentle or as Helen fair, and of the palace one might raise upon the hill in marble symmetry and store with curious broideries of the East; and of all that life might be to a man who conquered it, and why Antony was wise. And he dreams vain private hopes of his own of which he is ashamed. And he ponders on the narrow lane of sea, and of all that Ancient histories have told him; of Sultans and Emperors; he remembers how the proud flags of Venice once flew splendid in the breeze, and how relentless Romans before them built walls and ways, and how once the little *Argo* rounded the point with blue-eyed Jason on her prow, and the merry, toiling crew, bound on the first adventure of the world. And a light fever distracts the dreamer's body, and his mind longs for some coercive chain, and he begins to understand why men of the East will sit by a fountain from noon to night, and let the world roll onward. — JAMES ELROY FLECKER, from *Collected Prose*.

By permission of Mrs. Flecker and the publishers, William Heineman Ltd., London.

Self-Criticism Chart—Familiar Essays

1. *Will my reader share the full flavour and significance of my idea?*
2. *Have I particularized, expanded, illustrated sufficiently?*
3. *Is it easy to see how my ideas are related?*
4. *Have I chosen the most appropriate words?*
5. *Is my style easy and conversational?*
6. *Have I enriched the essay with quotations, allusions, experiences, comparisons, and figures of speech?*
7. *Are my sentences and paragraphs varied?*
8. *Have I revised and polished to make my ideas and expression clear and interesting?*

Practice 1. The Familiar Essay

Write an informal essay on a topic of your own choice, but choose one that gives you a chance to write about your experience, observvation, reading, or reflection. The topics listed below may suggest ideas and experience which are of interest to you and in which you can interest others. In your revision apply the eight standards above.

1. Dreams. 2. Family expectations. 3. Young experimenters. 4. Ho, for camp! 5. Eavesdropping. 6. On erasing boards. 7. A quiet afternoon with baby. 8. Table conversation. 9. Shoes. 10. Movies. 11. On hobbies. 12. Applying for a position. 13. Lightning. 14. Rubbish cans. 15. Stairs. 16. Back-seat driving. 17. On handshakes. 18. On sandwiches. 19. The radio. 20. On keeping a diary. 21. Radio advertising. 22. On wearing new clothes. 23. Overnight cabins. 24. Camping during a storm. 25. Mountain-climbing. 26. The uses of adversity. 27. In defense of rainy days. 28. What price publicity? 29. On mothers. 30. Novice in the kitchen. 31. Just a dog. 32. Shopworn excuses. 33. The "road hog." 34. Practical jokers. 35. On streetcars. 36. Is chivalry dead? 37. Bargain-hunting. 38. It isn't done. 39. Morning exercise. 40. Secondhand textbooks.

LITERARY APPRECIATION AND CRITICISM

One of the commonest forms of the modern essay is that which seeks to appraise literary writing, poetry or prose. Usually if the emphasis is upon the merits of the piece we use the phrase literary appreciation: if upon its demerits we use the phrase literary criticism. The object of such writing is to recommend those works which have given the reader pleasure, and to evaluate others. This writing differs from book reviewing in not being, usually, professional, in not being confined to recent publications, and in not necessarily applying to whole books. It may treat a single poem or even portion of it.

Literary appreciation and criticism usually deal with (1) the author, (2) his personal style, (3) his place in literature, and (4) a review of the work under discussion, covering (a) the spirit of the piece, (b) its character, (c) particular merits, and (d) short excerpts, (e) comparison with other works of same author, or even by another author.

INTRODUCTION TO *GONE TO EARTH*

Gone to Earth was published in the dark days of 1917. It was the first of Mary Webb's novels to come into my hands. I read it at a time when everything that concerned the soil of England seemed precious, and one longed for the old things as a relief from a world too full of urgent novelties.

The scene is laid in the Welsh marches, a haunted country, like all borderlands. There are only a few human characters—a girl in her teens, the daughter of a gipsy and a crazy bee-keeper; a local squireen; a half-educated minister and his mother; a peasant or two. But there are multitudes of others, for winds and seasons, day and night, God's Little Mountains, the Callow, Hunter's Spinney, the house of Undern, are as much persons of the drama as the men and women. The animate and the inanimate combine to work out tragedy.

The book is partly allegory; that is to say, there is a story of mortal passion, and a second story behind it of an immortal conflict, in which human misdeeds have no place. Hazel Woodus suffers because she is involved in the clash of common lusts and petty jealousies, but she is predestined to suffer since she can never adjust herself to the straight orbit of human life. She is a creature of the wilds, with no heritage in the orderly populous world. In the end she is "gone to earth," as she has come from it. She is eternally a stranger.

The chief beauty of the book is the picture of Hazel, which is done with extraordinary tenderness and subtlety. She is at once the offspring of the mysterious landscape, and the interpretation of it. Wild and shy as a wood nymph, she has none of the natural world's callousness to pain. She is the protector of all wounded and persecuted things—a lame cat, a blind bird, bees frozen in winter, a fox-cub saved from the hounds. With the elemental things of hill and shaw she is at home, but when she travels beyond them she is a wild creature in a trap. Mary Webb is curiously insensitive to the cruelties of nature. To her *Natura* is only *benigna*. It is the world of men and their works in which alone dwells evil. "Oh, filthy, heavy-handed, blear-eyed world," she cries, "when will you wash and be clean?"

The progress of the tale is as simple and inevitable as a Greek tragedy. Hazel, in her innocence, becomes the prey of Jack Reddin, the yeoman-squire of Undern; craving for gentleness she finds it in Edward Marston, the minister, whom she marries; but Reddin drags her from her shelter. When she returns to it, broken and soiled, it is to find that the minister has become, through suffering, a man and a lover. But it is too late; destiny has set the game; in her efforts to save her fox-cub from the hounds she is driven over the rocks of the quarry—the victim of both man's cruelty and man's love.

The story marches to its close with a fierce impetus, but there are lovely interludes, like flutes among the trumpets. These are the quiet places which give relief, as when Hazel tries the charms which her mother had taught her, before returning to Reddin, or goes out to the stream side in the summer dawn, or wanders among the old, musty, haunted corridors of Undern. For grave irony I know few scenes in modern literature more effective than her interview with Reddin's discarded mistress. The character-drawing is on the same high level as the drama. Reddin is subtly conceived; his power over Hazel is due in part to the fact that he, too, is near the elemental world. The minister, Edward Marston, tends at first to be too much an embodiment of abstract virtues, but he awakes before the end into vivid life. His mother, the notable housekeeper, is a little masterpiece—the indoors, fireside dweller as a foil to the child of the woods. But apart from Hazel herself, the chief triumphs of portraiture are the gnarled figures of an elder England—the old father, harper and bee-keeper, coarse as a clod but gifted with a poet's fancy; Andrew Vessons, Reddin's servant, clipping his yews and philosophizing like one of Shakespeare's clowns.

The style, as in all Mary Webb's books, is impregnated with poetry, rising sometimes to the tenuous delicacy of music, but never sinking to "poetic prose." There are moments when it seems to me superheated, when her passion for metaphor makes the writing too high-pitched and strained. But no one of our day has a greater power of evoking natural magic. The landscape, the weather, the seasons, are made to crowd in upon us as we follow the doings of the protagonists, and we are perpetually aware of these things as a fateful background. That is right, for they are Hazel's world, and part of her character. Mary Webb need fear no comparison with any writer who has attempted to capture the soul of nature in words, and to "tease us out of thought" by glimpses into our ancient inheritance.

"The echoes are in us of great voices long gone hence; the unknown cries of huge beasts on the mountains; the sullen aims of creatures in the slime; the love-call of the bittern. We know, too, echoes of things outside our ken —the thought that shapes itself in the bee's brain and becomes a waxen box of sweets; the tyranny of youth stirring in the womb; the crazy terror of small slaughtered beasts; the upward push of folded grass, and how the leaf feels in all its veins the cold rain; the ceremonial that passes yearly in the emerald temples of bud and calyx—we have walked those temples; we are the sacrifice on those altars."

In her best moods the style clarifies to a rare beauty and simplicity. Take this of the old bee-keeper:

"Whenever an order for a coffin came, Hazel went to tell the bees who was dead. Her father thought this unnecessary. It was only for folks that died in the house, he said. But he had himself told the bees when his wife died. He had gone out on that vivid June morning to his hives, and had stood watching the lines of bees fetching water, their shadows going and coming on the clean white boards. Then he had stopped and said with a curious confidential indifference, "Maray's jead." He had put his ear to the hive and listed to the deep, solemn murmur within; but was the murmur of the future, and not of the past, the preoccupation with life, not with death, that filled the pale galleries within."

And this of Hazel in the churchyard in the early morning:

"It was as if the dead had arisen in the stark hours between twelve and two, and were waiting unobtrusively, majestically, each by his own bed, to go down and break their long fast with the bee and the grass-snake in refectories too minute and too immortal to be known by the living. The tombstones seemed taller, seemed to have a presence behind them; the lush grass, lying grey and heavy with dew, seemed to have been swept by silent passing crowds."

If that is not the true magic, I do not know where to look for it. — JOHN BUCHAN, Introduction to *Gone to Earth*.

By permission of the publishers, Jonathan Cape Limited, Toronto.

ON FIRST LOOKING INTO CHAPMAN'S HOMER

Much have I travell'd in the realms of gold,
 And many goodly states and kingdoms seen;
 Round many western islands have I been
Which bards in fealty to Apollo hold.
Oft of one wide expanse had I been told
 That deep-brow'd Homer ruled as his demesne;
 Yet did I never breathe its pure serene
Till I heard Chapman speak out loud and bold:
Then felt I like some watcher of the skies
 When a new planet swims into his ken;
Or like stout Cortez when with eagle eyes
 He star'd at the Pacific—and all his men
Look'd at each other with a wild surmise—
 Silent, upon a peak in Darien.

      — JOHN KEATS

Practice 2. Studying the Essay

1. Make a topical analysis of Buchan's essay on *Gone to Earth.*
What subjects are treated.

2. For what has each excerpt been selected?

3. Is the essay itself a complete literary essay?

Practice 3. Writing Literary Criticism

1. Write an appreciative essay of one of your supplementary
reading books (or substitute another).

2. Write a critical estimate of a piece of verse you have found in a
current periodical, magazine, or newspaper.

3. Write an appreciative essay on your favourite poem.

UNIT TWENTY-SEVEN

The Short Story

WHY WRITE SHORT STORIES?

Most of the millions of magazines mailed each month to subscribers or sold on the news stands are filled, half filled, or quarter filled with short stories. People of all ages and classes like occasionally to leave their work, problems, and routine and live for a while in the world of the imagination. Because the short story can be read easily at one sitting, it has an especial appeal to our restless generation.

If you, like most other people, are going to read short stories in school and out of school, it is worth your while to learn to judge and appreciate them. A tennis player gets out of a championship tennis match keener and higher enjoyment than one who has never played the game, because he appreciates fine points of the contest to which the one who has not played tennis is blind. So one who has written stories selects more discriminatingly stories to read and appreciates more thoroughly their artistry and truth.

Most students class story-writing with swimming and football as hard work but the best of fun. After learning the technique of all story-writing many a pupil discovers that he has stories to tell and tries his hand at writing stories to sell. All who study and write short stories learn how to narrate true or imaginary incidents entertainingly.

But perhaps the most important advantage of short story writing is the training and the stimulation which it gives to see life closely and with large imagination. In reading we train ourselves to consider and appraise life as others have seen and recorded it; but to see and record it ourselves is instructive and inspiring.

WHAT IS A SHORT STORY?

Dr. Blanche Colton Williams's terse definition is, "The short story is a narrative artistically presenting characters in a struggle or complication which has a definite outcome." J. Berg Esenwein says that the true short story is marked by seven characteristics: (1) a single predominating incident; (2) a single pre-eminent character; (3) imagination; (4) plot; (5) compression; (6) organization; and (7) unity of impression.

Here is a recent short story you will enjoy reading:

A STUDENT OF LANGUAGES

Mrs. Wagonseller, waking early, heard Victoria above her head. The tapping of her heels was regular, unremitting, masterful. Victoria was a masterful young woman.

Having blinked her eyes open, Mrs. Wagonseller turned them upon her sleeping husband. His name was James but before her marriage she had been too shy to address him familiarly and afterward she called him "Mister," and then when he had a right to the title, "Pop." His round head was an almost perfect sphere against the white pillow and his hands folded and laid under his cheek gave him the look of a cherub. His wife would have made no such comparison, however; to her he was a man of personal distinction, profound wisdom, and wide learning.

He yawned and threw his short arms above his head. At this instant the clock struck five.

"It is early," he said. "Something must a waked me."

"It is Victoria," explained Mrs. Wagonseller, pronouncing the V carefully. "She is already at it. Just listen once!"

"Like a steam hammer," he remarked, grinning. "What has got into her at this hour?"

Mrs. Wagonseller sat up. At the same instant there was a snapping sound which came apparently from outside the window.

"She is shaking her sheets in the air," said Mrs. Wagonseller. "That means she will make her bed right away. Now she's pounding her pillow." Mrs. Wagonseller stepped from bed. "Something is up, Pop."

"She knows her lessons all right," said Wagonseller.

But he too sat up, glancing humorously at his pleasant wife. He knew what worried her; she was always anticipating the day when Victoria would marry and leave them, and lately her fear had been sharpened by the elopement of a young neighbour. It was true that so far as they knew Victoria was unsought and she was only seventeen, but no one had dreamed that Alice Aughinbaugh had a lover and she was only sixteen. It was not because Victoria was unattractive that she lacked attention; it was because she held herself too high.

Wagonseller rose and began to dress. In his heart he, too, feared for Victoria. He had wished to be a preacher but he had not been able to afford an education and he dreamed of Victoria becoming a distinguished scholar. Thanks to his increasing urging and assistance and to Victoria's own ambition and ability she had never stood elsewhere than at the head of her class.

"Ach, it isn't anything serious," he assured his wife. "She is now quiet; it is just a little extra work. Perhaps she forgot something. Mom, have no fear."

At six-thirty Victoria came down to the kitchen. The sun's rays fell upon a half-bushel basket of freshly gathered tomatoes on the table. Breakfast was ready, substantial ham and eggs and molasses cake for Mr. and Mrs. Wagonseller, toast and coffee for Victoria. Mrs. Wagonseller mourned every day because Victoria ate so little but Victoria's red cheeks and her hundred and forty pounds distributed over five feet four inches of height made starvation seem remote.

"Well," said Victoria cheerfully, looking at the tomatoes, "what's up?"

"I will to-day make catsup," explained Mrs. Wagonseller. "It is a long work." She spoke not in the least complainingly but with pleasure in the prospect. Nor did she imply a desire for Victoria's help.

Victoria set the coffee pot on the table, transferred the fried potatoes from the pan to a hot dish and filled the glasses; then she walked to the door and called toward the garden, "Pop. Breakfast." When Wagonseller entered she sat at the table eating her toast with delicate precision. All the Wagonsellers had good manners but Victoria's were of a later generation than her father's and mother's.

"Pop," announced Victoria briskly, "you must hear me a little Latin yet before I go." At school Victoria spoke correct, sometimes painfully correct English, but at home she dropped into the vernacular.

"But you knew it good last night!"

"This is to-morrow's lesson. I studied it this morning."

Mrs. Wagonseller's frightened eyes sought her husband's. Victoria never had engagements which made advance preparation necessary. Wagonseller's eyes twinkled back—did she suppose that if Victoria meant to elope she would continue to study Latin? He finished his breakfast and took up Victoria's Caesar—this was happiness! Sometimes while he waited for customers at the stocking counter in the store where he worked, he wrote down the following words: *English, Pennsylvania German, German, Latin, French;* and in moments like that, and like this, his proud heart swelled almost to bursting.

In Victoria's Caesar he found written two lists of words, one Latin, one English, and he began to pronounce them distinctly.

"*Ducit.*"

"Third person singular, present tense, verb *duco*, to lead," rattled off Victoria. "*Duco, ducere, duxi, ductum.*"

"*Dare.*"

"To give," translated Victoria. "Present infinitive of *do. Do, dare, dedi, datum.*"

Having finished the Latin words, he pronounced the English and Victoria gave their Latin equivalents. He did not correct her; whether he was able to or not, she seemed to need no correcting. She took her book and read two sections first in Latin, then twice in English, once in a literal and then in a free translation. There was no scamping for Victoria.

"Now who were the Sequani?" asked Mr. Wagonseller proudly. "And who was Dumnorix? And how many were in a legion?"

"It is one thing I hope," said Mrs. Wagonseller from her place at the sink, "and this is it, that Victoria will not have to read any more stories like last year, about boiling fathers in hot oil and poisoning people and tearing them up."

"Pelias, you mean?" said Wagonseller, smiling condescendingly. "Those are different times from ours, Mom, and it was one of those sort of goddesses that done it."

"I haven't any use for those goddesses, either," said Mrs. Wagonseller. "And the words were so hard."

"Do you mean Symplegades and Eumenides and Agamemnon and Clytemnestra?" asked Wagonseller. His pronunciation was perfect and the airiness with which he said the words indescribable. "Anything else, Victoria?"

"I have yet a few French verbs, such irregular ones."

Victoria handed her father a third list and took out pencil and pad. Wagonseller had often heard that French was easier than Latin and that, to one who knew Latin, French offered no difficulties, but he had not found this to be the case. These words he spelled.

"*B-o-u-i-l-l-e-r*," said he.

Victoria wrote rapidly.

"*V-o-i-r*," said Wagonseller.

Victoria dashed off the part of "*voir*." There were ten verbs in all. When she had finished she compared her writing with the grammar.

"More yet?" asked Wagonseller.

"No," said Victoria. "I have everything else."

She fetched her hat from the hall and took her books under her arm.

"It is surely a nice day," she said happily. Then, unconscious of their curiosity, she ended their suspense. "There is a lecture this evening on the Value of Science to Mankind. That is why I learned my lessons this morning."

"We will not have so much dinner to-day as sometimes," announced Mrs. Wagonseller. "But this evening I will cook *schnitz und knep*. I will feel by that time for something hearty."

Wagonseller went to the store and Mrs. Wagonseller began to scald and peel tomatoes. She was very happy—who would not be with a good husband and a bright daughter and sufficient income and plenty to do?

But such bliss is almost sure to be a precursor of trouble and at dinner Mrs Wagonseller's castle crashed to earth. As she sat at table her cheeks were flushed, her eyes shone, and there was a smile on her cheerful face—until Victoria spoke. Victoria had finished her dinner and was folding her napkin.

"Mom," said she, "we will have company for supper."

"Who, who?" asked Mrs. Wagonseller astonished.

"A teacher from the high school," said Victoria.

"Then I will not bottle my catsup till to-morrow," said Mrs. Wagonseller, not in the least disturbed but on the contrary very much pleased. "I will make a good supper."

"No," said Victoria, blushing a little. "That isn't the idea. You have what you said. This teacher has never eaten *schnitz und knep;* that is the reason I fixed it for this evening. We will have *schnitz und knep* and good pie and preserves and cake and coffee. If you have too much besides you cannot enjoy *schnitz und knep*."

"*Ach*, Victoria!" This time Mrs. Wagonseller's *v* was a *w*.

"The teacher is coming especially for *schnitz und knep*. Mom," answered Victoria firmly. "Afterwards I go along to the lecture." Rising and putting on her hat, she continued to talk: "Remember, Mom! To those who have never eaten *schnitz und knep* it is a wonderful thing. And I will be home to set the table and fix flowers."

"All right," said Mrs. Wagonseller, somewhat ruefully. "But sometime we have this teacher for a right meal."

Her father saw Victoria blush. He was brighter than his wife and his brow had clouded as hers had cleared.

"And what is this teacher's name?" he asked.

"Mather," said Victoria as she went through the door. "*M-a-t-h-e-r*."

"*Ach*" said Mrs. Wagonseller when she was out of hearing. "This is no way. I have a mind to fry chicken."

Wagonseller went toward a table in the corner of the room and taking up yesterday's newspaper turned to an inner page and pointed to a brief personal. His wife read it over his shoulder.

Mr. Charles Mather, teacher of mathematics in the high school, has returned from a visit to his home.

"Not a man!" gasped Mrs. Wagonseller "Is this teacher then a man?"

"We will see how much of a man he is," said Wagonseller grimly. "I was afraid something was up when I heard her this morning." His wife was too unhappy to remind him that it was she who had scented trouble in advance; besides she was not that kind of person.

According to his custom Wagonseller tried to meet the situation with humour.

"Have I then all my great learning for nothing?" But his voice shook.

"Victoria was always so quick," said Mrs. Wagonseller. "It is no telling what she might do. It cannot be that she would bring him here married! That is what Alice did to her Mom and Pop."

"Now don't be foolish," answered Mr. Wagonseller. But he did not speak with any heartiness.

"A teacher!" said Mrs. Wagonseller.

"You wouldn't expect Victoria to take anyone lower than that," said Wagonseller.

Wagonseller entered the kitchen at a quarter past five o'clock. In four hours he had had ample time to see his home despoiled of its pride. No more would he sit watching Victoria add to her learning by the dining–room lamp, no more would he leave his companions at the barber shop with the excuse that he must hear his daughter's lessons, adding casually and invariably that Victoria always stood first. She might even go elsewhere to live, or her husband (especially one named Mather) might consider her parents beneath him. Wagonseller had had a very unhappy afternoon.

The kitchen was in perfect order except for the few utensils needed in preparing supper. Beyond, in the dining room, the table had been set with a stiff outstanding starched cloth, the best china, and a bowl of asters. The house was deliciously scented with cloves and allspice which had gone into the catsup.

Wagonseller looked round uneasily; then he called "Mom!" and his wife appeared from the dining room. She wore a blue and white striped gingham dress and large stiff white apron.

"Were you then listening to them?" asked Wagonseller, trying to be gay.

Mrs. Wagonseller turned tearful eyes upon him.

"He is a big good-looking young man" she said. "Victoria said I must come in. I think he looks already down on me. But they are sitting on chairs yet and not on the sofa."

"I should hope so!" protested Wagonseller. He tiptoed up the back stairs to change his suit.

"You don't know how far this has gone," Mrs. Wagonseller called after him in a mournful whisper.

Having completed his change of raiment and brushed his brown hair with a wet brush, Wagonseller descended the steps. He felt the same embarrassment as his wife but he was too proud to show it. Mrs. Wagonseller had not ceased to cry and her nose was growing red.

You must brace up," said Wagonseller sternly.

"But he is such a learned one!"

"Well, the preacher is learned and you are not afraid of him, are you?"

"I'm afraid of my manners," wept Mrs. Wagonseller. "I never thought

I would have to have such a one in the family. If I could only stay in the kitchen."

"That you can't do," said Wagonseller firmly. "You won't need to talk; let Victoria do the talking. She brought him here. And I will help along too." For the first time in Victoria's life her father thought of her with irritation. "I'm now going in."

Passing through the narrow hall toward the parlour, Wagonseller heard no sound and remembered with a sinking heart the rapturous silences of his courtship. It might be that already they had reached the point where speech was unnecessary.

Victoria rose when her father entered, not from the young man's side but from a chair across the room. Her cheeks were a little brighter than usual and her motions a little jerky.

"This is Mr. Mather," she said. "Mr. Mather, this is my father." Yesterday Victoria would have said, "Meet my father"; but last evening in an advertisement of a book of etiquette on the back of a magazine she had read that this was an abominable form of introduction. Victoria needed but one hint.

It seemed at first as though the young man did not intend to rise. When finally he made up his mind, he did not quite get to his feet before Wagonseller was directly in front of him holding out his hand.

"I'm pleased to meet you." Wagonseller began in a loud cordial tone but his voice dropped toward the end of the sentence. This was, as Mrs. Wagonseller had said, a very big and good-looking young man and he did seem to look down.

"It is a very nice day," Wagonseller continued pleasantly.

"I thought it hot," said Mr. Mather.

A short response like this was not according to Wagonseller's rule for polite conversation and he backed away.

"I will help Mom a little," he said as he went through the door. "It will soon be everything ready".

In the hall Wagonseller slipped his finger inside his tight collar as though to move it away from his neck. His face was red with shame; he knew that he had not made a good impression.

Then Mrs. Wagonseller announced supper. She had bathed her eyes in cold water and she stood in the doorway and said, "Supper, Victoria," in a fairly steady voice; then she went to her place at the table. The preacher always pulled out her chair for her and she was uncomfortable throughout the meal—would this young man shove her halfway under or leave her too far away?

The young man did neither; he walked to the place indicated to him and sat down and opened his napkin and fixed his eyes upon the covered dish before Mr. Wagonseller.

"I hear this is a wonderful concoction," said he in a deep voice.

Mr. Wagonseller smiled and then unaware of the astonishment of his guest he bowed his head and prayed. At the head of his table with so much good food before him to dispense he lost his uneasiness. *Schnitz und knep* was, as Mr. Mather said, a wonderful concoction. Made of dumplings boiled with pork and dried sweet apples and cooked in Mrs. Wagonseller's fashion, it was a delicious and substantial viand. Wagonseller helped the guest and then Victoria and then his wife, and as the aroma reached him it sent a reviving impulse through his brain.

"It has often wondered me what those old Romans ate," he remarked pleasantly.

The menu of the old Romans was apparently of less interest to the guest than the menu of the modern Wagonsellers. Mrs. Wagonseller had not finished pouring the coffee, Victoria obedient to the laws of good behaviour was still sitting with her hands clasped lightly in her lap as though the food before her were nonexistent, Wagonseller was just beginning to help himself— not too generously the first time, he remembered; but the young man had already begun to eat. He was really a very fine-looking young man but his good looks seemed eclipsed as he bent over his plate.

"Those old Sequani, for instance," continued Mr. Wagonseller after a pause. "And old Caesar and old Dumnorix—what did they eat now? For every day and for a feast?"

The young man made no answer.

"They had grain and meat like we have," said Victoria, making no motion toward beginning her supper. With despair her mother saw her bright colour and remembered her own lack of appetite when Wagonseller had taken his first meal at her father's house. "They made bread and cakes and we hear about their roasting meats and, of course, they had wine." She looked intently at Mr. Mather but his eyes were on his plate.

"Now Mrs., she don't like to hear of those old times," said Wagonseller pleasantly. "She don't like to hear about how Pelias was boiled and killed or how the other chap had the same treatment and come out a young man."

"I never heard of them," said Mather.

Victoria was astonished.

"What Latin did you study?"

"Never studied Latin," said Mr. Mather with his mouth full of dumpling. "Math's my specialty. Went to technical school where they had no use for that stuff."

"Well, well," said Wagonseller. "I thought you all had to study Latin." He refilled Mr. Mather's plate for the second time. What could one talk about? "You studied history, of course, and you know about old Caesar?"

"I know about old George Washington and his cherry tree," answered the young man, laughing in his own wit. "That was enough history for me." He began to talk in his deep voice and continued until he had finished his *schnitz und knep* and until Victoria had removed the main dish and brought on three kinds of pie, a cherry pie, an apple pie, and a delectable raisin pie. At sight of them the young man's eyes glittered, but before they were offered to him he had said a good deal. He had a really beautiful voice and his pronunciation was excellent. It was his voice and his broad *a's* and his elided *r's* which had captivated Victoria.

"We had a gump of a history teacher, an old maid with false hair. She was a perfect fool for history and we wouldn't learn to spite her. She used to say to me, 'Now, Charlie,' in a tone like that. Once she cried. No use anybody teaching unless they can slam the kids round. She had to stop. Now math I liked, and I had a teacher I could respect—he used to swear at us like the dickens. The rest I didn't care for, taught a lot of rot. In the Latin room— ye gods!" Suddenly the young man looked at the cloth beside his plate. "I have a fork here for this pie but no knife."

It is astonishing how large a little room may suddenly become when the silence of a great amazement spreads over it. Wagonseller flushed a little and Mrs. Wagonseller bent her head. To eat pie with a fork was, according to Victoria, the conspicuous and essential hallmark of good manners. Their hearts ached for Victoria. Then her father almost groaned. Victoria did not mind! She rose with the pleasantest face in the world and went to the sideboard drawer. Moreover, Victoria told a lie!

"It's my fault," said she gaily. "I set the table. I forgot your knife."

Then Victoria began to talk. She had eaten almost no *schnitz und knep* and now she did not touch her pie. She talked about everything and nothing, about the weather, about the tricks played in school, speaking rapidly as her father and mother had never heard her speak. She urged more pie on Mr. Mather and he consented to have a second piece of each variety. When he finished he took his watch from his pocket and looked at it and rose.

"Come on, Victoria," said he. "We got to beat it." Then he glanced around. "Got any toothpicks?" he asked.

For this too Victoria fell—thus Wagonseller phrased it in the slang which he heard daily. His colour was now as red as Victoria's. The phrase was exact—it was a fall for Victoria. A toothpick belonged, according to her creed, with a toothbrush and a nail file and a washcloth, in one's bedroom or bathroom. But Victoria opened the sideboard drawer. Back in a corner was a forgotten and long outlived receptacle and this Victoria brought forth and offered. She opened the door into the hall and the young man preceded her through it. He said, "Good-bye," for both him and Victoria.

Still at his place at the table, Mr. Wagonseller sat motionless. The door was shut tight and the voices came faintly to his ears. Victoria was speaking in her positive tones; her voice sounded gay. Wagonseller put his elbows on the table and cradled his head in his hands. He heard a door close with a slam and then there was silence. Mrs. Wagonseller came and stood beside him and put her hand on his shoulder.

"*Ach*, don't take it so hard, Pop! Perhaps he isn't such a bad fellow."

Wagonseller shook his head. He heard Victoria's voice, which had been music to his ears; he saw her capable and strong body, which had been the delight of his eyes. He seemed to hear her quick step on the stairs and so real was his delusion that he lifted his head. To his astonishment the door opened and there stood Victoria, not dressed for the street but with a book under her arm.

"Aren't you going then?" gasped Mrs. Wagonseller.

"No," said Victoria with flaming cheeks. "I certainly am not going with him anywhere. It is all right to give such a person a meal but there it stops."

"Did you have to hurt his feelings?" asked Mrs. Wagonseller.

"No," said Victoria. "He hasn't any. But I told him I had work to do; I made up my mind that I, at least, would show I had manners."

"Have you work to do?" asked Mrs. Wagonseller. Now that Victoria had begun, was she going to keep on lying?

"Yes, I have. Father, listen once."

Wagonseller lifted his head. Above his clasped hands, which hid his mouth, his eyes glittered.

"Well?" he said.

"I have a plan," said Victoria. "There is a Greek class starting in the high school and I'm going to get into it. I can easily do that along with my other studies. They say it is more interesting than Latin."

"And what am I to do?" asked Wagonseller, trying to look grave.

"Well, I thought if you could just learn the letters you could help me. Here is the alphabet."

Wagonseller bent his head over the page. At sight of the strange characters he was both terrified and inexpressibly proud.

"Then I could get into college without an examination," continued Victoria. "You can do it, Pop."

Wagonseller's head bent still lower. There was a college in the town— it would mean years more of Victoria. He lifted his head and blinked at her, his face sober, almost blank. It was the way he looked when he was about to say a good thing.

"All right," he said, pretending a weary patience. "I have already five languages, but I never thought I'd have to learn Greek yet."

He saw a long list: *English, Pennsylvania German, German, Latin, French, Greek.*

Were there, Mr. Wagonseller wondered with ambitious hunger, any more? — ELSIE SINGMASTER.

Reprinted by permission of the author.

RAW MATERIALS

"A Student of Languages" deals with material within the experience of high school boys or girls—the friendly, understanding relationship between a girl and her parents; her methodical performance of daily household duties; her interest in her school lessons, especially Latin and French; and her corresponding interest in the finer points of living as evidenced by good manners.

First we should study ourselves. Arnold Bennett says that all the greatest novels are autobiographical. If a person thoroughly understands the working of his own mind, he knows much about other people. Next we should observe. Every professional writer knows that setting down in a notebook what he sees opens his eyes so that he sees more to jot down. Only by developing a seeing eye can one really know the people, scenes, and characters he wishes to write about. We should also read. The newspaper, histories, biographies, travel books, and magazine articles present characters and incidents that may be used as starting-places for stories.

ELEMENTS OF A SHORT STORY

The four elements of a short story are plot, character, atmosphere, and theme. In a character story the emphasis is on the presentation of a character; in a plot story, on complicated, novel, or surprising plot; in an atmosphere story, upon the setting and subjective colouring. A story of theme illustrates strikingly an idea or a truth of human life. The short story writer may begin with a theme; begin with a plot and fit characters to it; start with a character and fit the action and setting to it; or start by creating an atmosphere to which he fits people and actions. One of the four must dominate.

"A Student of Languages" is primarily a study of character, with the action based on the contrast between the sincere, sensitive, considerate, and courteous Wagonsellers and the self-centred, inconsiderate, crude Mr. Mather.

PLOT

A story is more than a mere sequence of events. It is a sequence which has a logical development through cause and effect, leading from a state or condition which is accepted by the reader as an agreed starting point, through complication and conflict, which is imposed upon or discovered in this *status quo*, and leads to a climax and rearrangement where a new and final condition is accepted. A plot must make provision for these stages of development, and furnishes the vehicle by which they are created and resolved.

The author may be arrested by some striking incident, and ask himself how it came about, and how it will end, for he knows that every event has had a past and will have a future. As soon as his imagination begins to fashion this causal sequence into a coherent story he has begun to plot, and when he has so arranged it, he has created a plot and arranged his observations as a logical part of a piece of fiction.

A common germ-idea or starting-point of a short story is an incident, a situation, or an anecdote. The incident may be an experience of the writer or of one of his friends, a happening recorded in a history, biography, or newspaper, or an imagined happening.

Goethe says that there are only thirty-six tragic situations. Some of these that are useful to the story writer are the pursued, revolt, fatal imprudence, rivalry of kinsmen or friends, unequal rivalry, obstacles to love, an enemy loved, ambition, mistaken identity, the saviour, self-sacrifice for an ideal, self-sacrifice for kindred or friends, discovery of the dishonour of a loved one, and recovery of a lost one.

Examples of incidents or situations that have story value:

1. A man crossing the street is knocked down by an automobile. He crawls to his feet and calls a traffic officer. Much to his amazement, he discovers his wife to be the driver of the machine.
2. A man has just moved into a neighbourhood where the houses are all alike. Coming home late at night, he finds he has no key, climbs through an open window, and discovers he has entered the wrong house.
3. A poor woman loses the diamond necklace she borrowed from a wealthy friend.

4. A man steals to pay for his son's college education.
5. Two young people whose families are enemies secretly become friends.
6. At a masquerade party a young man falls in love with a beautiful and fascinating oriental princess, who proves to be a boy.

Practice 1. Finding Story Material

1. Find in the newspaper, a history, or a biography an incident or a situation that might be used as a story-germ—for example, the headline *Dog Saves Master Who Broke His Leg on Ice.*

2. What experience of your own or of a friend's might be the starting-point of a short story?

3. Find an anecdote that might be expanded into a short story.

4. Find or invent three other incidents, situations, or anecdotes that might be used as starting-points for stories. Do not include hackneyed material such as the weird experiences that prove to be a dream or the athletic hero who wins the game and thus wins the hand of the beautiful girl he loves.

BUILDING A PLOT

A simple plot may be diagrammed in this way:

A is the cause or initial impulse, the incident or force which starts the story. In "A Student of Languages" it is Mrs. Wagonseller's announcement that she will have *schintz und knep* for supper. Without this decision there would have been no story that day. The line AB represents the complication, entanglement, mix-up, or rising action; B is the effect or the climax. In "A Student of Languages" the entanglement includes Victoria's announcement that she has invited a teacher to supper, the discovery that the teacher is a young man, the careful preparations for the meal and the Wagonsellers' concern about the impression they will produce on the guest, the increasing evidence of his bad manners, and Mather's saying good-bye for Victoria and himself.

In this story the climax comes with Victoria's almost immediate return, "not dressed for the street but with a book under her arm." Barrett defines climax as "the apex of interest and emotion, the point of the story." The untangling, consisting of Victoria's explanation of her decision to remain home that evening, is brief. The conclusion, the picture of Victoria continuing her studies with her father, follows swiftly. A good rule for story-writing is to make the untangling and conclusion as brief as possible.

Motivation

An essential difference between the incidents of a plot and the incidents of a fishing trip is that the happenings of a fishing trip are like a string of beads or a train of cars, whereas the incidents of a short story are related by cause and effect or are motivated. In "A Student of Languages," Mrs. Wagonseller's desire to make catsup causes her to plan a supper of *schnitz und knep;* this leads Victoria to invite her teacher to supper; his conduct at the table reveals to the parents and Victoria how ill-bred he is; and scorn of him causes Victoria to decide to remain at home and study Greek with her father that evening, so easing the minds of her parents, who feared she was in love with Mr. Mather.

Complication

The essential difference between an incident and the plot of a short story is complication. When Victoria Wagonseller, a high school girl, wishing to go to a lecture at night and yet be well prepared the next day, gets up at five o'clock to prepare her next day's lessons in advance, her overcoming an obstacle to her going out at night is an incident. When her parents, however, fear it may be the first sign of a secret love affair, the complication gives the incident story value.

"The Gift of the Magi" illustrates a favourite method of O. Henry —complicating by having the characters work at cross-purposes. Della and Jim need money to buy Christmas gifts. Della's love for Jim prompts her to sell her hair to buy him a platinum fob chain for his watch; Jim sells his watch to buy Della pure tortoise shell combs, side and back, with jewelled rims.

Struggle

Conflict is the essence of the short story. Everyone is interested in a race between two men for the quarter-mile championship, the control of a corporation or political party, or the hand of a girl in marriage, or the conflict between the man who wants his son to carry on the family hardware business and the son who is determined to be an actor. The struggle in a man's mind when he has a chance to "get even" with a rival is no less dramatic. All are interested, too, in the mysterious—the strange noise, the secret door, the letter written in code, the haunted house. Everybody also enjoys action, especially unusual or striking action in which the performers arouse our sympathy

—marching soldiers, a hero aviator riding up Main Street, a man rescuing a horse from a burning barn, the freshman substitute fullback winning the game.

The struggle is an important element of plot construction. The struggle may be physical or mental and may be between man and nature, man and animal, man and man, man and supernatural forces, or man and himself. When, for example, Jim Vaughn hesitates between rescuing an enemy and letting him die, the mental struggle has story value. Stevenson's "Markheim" and De Maupassant's "The Coward" are other illustrations of the struggle between a man and himself.

Suspense

Complication and struggle lead to suspense, an important element in a plot. When the action is complicated and the struggle between man and man, man and himself, or man and a supernatural power seems equal, the reader does not like to lay down the magazine or book until he knows how the story ends. If the reader knows early in the story that the substitute will win the game, that the girl will marry her guardian, that Margy will prevent the robbery, that the ghost is a mischievous boy, that the girl has lost all respect for the crude young man, he is not likely to finish the story. Conceal something from the reader; let him have something to look forward to.

In "A Student of Languages" there is suspense at the very beginning. Why does Victoria get up so early? The answer does not come until after breakfast. Likewise, the author leaves us in doubt as to whether or not Victoria will go to the lecture with Mr. Mather, placing this information at the end. The paragraph near the climax which begins "Still at his place at the table Mr. Wagonseller sat motionless" is a good example of suspense.

DEVELOPMENT

In developing the plot, and (as we shall see later) in developing character, the unit of progress is the incident or episode. It is to the management of episode that the student should direct his greatest care, for the story is no more than the logical and natural sequence of episodes, each of which has one, and sometimes more, specific purposes.

Our story "A Student of Languages" has eleven episodes:

1. Victoria is heard bustling about at five in the morning.
2. They have breakfast.
3. Mr. Wagonseller hears Victoria's lessons for the following day.
4. They all go about the day's labours.
5. Victoria announces a visitor for supper.
6. Mr. and Mrs. Wagonseller talk it over.

7. Preparing for supper.
8. Mr. Wagonseller meets Mr. Mather.
9. They have supper.
10. Victoria announces her decision not to go out.
11. They plan to begin the Greek class.

In this sequence of events the emphasis is upon character and most of the episodes are for character portrayal. Strictly speaking, the plot is contained in the announcement of Mrs. Wagonseller that there will be *schnitz und knep*, in the invitation, in the display of rudeness, and in Victoria's decision.

Episode 1 gives a picture of the three Wagonsellers and distinguishes them clearly one from the other. We learn also the family character, devotion, and apprehension. Suspense is roused and we are fully prepared for the action which follows.

Episode 2—Time sequence is maintained; reason is provided for the *schnitz und knep* supper; Victoria is further characterized.

Episode 3—Character development of Victoria and Mr. Wagonseller and the fine family spirit is established, which is to rouse our favourable concern and prepare for the possibility of trouble,—making disaster not unreasonable.

Episode 4—Plot development. Time goes forward, and the important announcement is made.

Episode 5—Plot development. Announcement of visitor.

Episode 6—Rouses apprehension. Visitor is a man. Anything may happen.

Episode 7—Character development. Fears are increased by reason of Mather's appearance.

Episode 8—Character episode. Mr. Mather makes his first mistake.

Episode 9—The plot grows to a head. Mr. Mather is revealed in all his selfish, uncultured person.

Episode 10—The climax is reached. Victoria justified her parents' (and our) fine opinion of her.

Episode 11—The story is resolved into a new and final settlement to our evident satisfaction.

Practice 2. Recognizing Episodes

Select any favourite short story or one-act play and analyze it into episodes and say what purpose each episode serves in the story or the drama.

CREATING CHARACTERS

The recent trend has been toward placing the stress on the characters, rather than on plot, setting, or theme. Commonly in a story there are not more than six persons, one of whom occupies the centre of the stage. "A Student of Languages," which has four characters, Mrs. Wagonseller, Mr. Wagonseller, Victoria, and Mr. Mather, is the record of an important decision which Victoria made.

As a rule, the prominent character is an unusual, striking, or fascinating person who has a dominant, individual trait, characteristic, desire, weakness, power, ambition, or ideal upon which the plot is built—kindness, shrewdness, ability to reason, faithfulness to duty, devotion to a master, desire for revenge, interest in crimes, determination. In "A Student of Languages" the outstanding trait of Victoria is a determination to be a cultured woman.

Sometimes a minor or humorous weakness or striking contradiction is associated with a desirable dominant trait. For example, a benevolent gentleman loves everybody and everything but hates cats; a prosperous, generous man never throws away a string; or a hero in battle is afraid to face an audience.

LEARN TO OBSERVE

To put real people into stories one must first know thoroughly some interesting people. Hence students of life and of story-writing should form the habit of studying and understanding the boys, girls, men, and women they see or meet in the home, the church, the theatre, the classroom, and the streetcar, discovering the distinguishing mark or trait of each, and using in their stories these people, not army officers, industrial leaders, racketeers, farmers, or the "four hundred," unless they really know these people.

Examples:

1. A young man who instead of taking responsibility relies on his widowed mother, a saleswoman, to get him to school on time, to see that he does his homework, to pay his college bills, to find a job for him, and to get him to work on time.
2. A woman who, like a child, builds air castles and then tells her friends again and again about trips abroad, country estates, servants, and expensive cars which she expects soon to enjoy but which never become realities.
3. A mechanical genius who enjoys taking a car apart more than riding in it and thinks out ways to improve his automobile, radio, and other machines. Sometimes the "improved" machines don't work.
4. A girl who is never sincere, who always wears a mask to hide her real self.
5. A boy who attends a private school and spends much of his time telling how popular he is and how much he does for the school, when in reality he plays but a very small part in the school's life.

Practice 3. Character Study

In the manner indicated, describe briefly four people who belong in a book. Start with people you know, have studied on the street or at a meeting, have heard about, or have read about, but change them if you wish.

CHARACTER TRAITS

Traits of character are best portrayed by acts and by speech, but may be suggested in a description of the person or explained in an analysis of his character. In "A Student of Languages," Elsie Singmaster does not tell us Mr. Mather was rude and inconsiderate; she tells us what Mr. Mather said and did, and how he did it and said it, so that we may get acquainted with him as we do with a person we meet. Mr. Mather's failure to rise promptly when his host entered the room, his brief "I thought it hot," his haste to begin eating, his request for a knife and a toothpick, the glitter in his eyes at the sight of the three kinds of pie, his taking "a second piece of each variety," and his "good-bye" unaccompanied by any word of thanks, present dramatically his rudeness and selfishness.

Practice 4. Studying Character Traits

1. What is the outstanding trait of Mrs. Wagonseller? Mr. Wagonseller? Mr. Mather?
2. How does Elsie Singmaster make her people real to us? What significant incidents, habits, or actions are shown?
3. Using the preceding analysis of Mr. Mather as a model, discuss the author's portrayal of the character of Mr. Wagonseller, Mrs. Wagonseller, or Victoria.
4. Analyze briefly the character of the girl or the boy on page 471.

Practice 5. Writing a Biographical Sketch

Write the biography of a person you intend to put into your story. Start with someone you know but change the character as you see fit and use your imagination for details. Include in your biography birth, parentage, childhood, later life, achievement, character, dominant trait, temperament, and appearance.

INDIVIDUALIZING

In character drawing there are two important and distinguishable processes. The first of these is individualization, giving to each character a name and individual traits or differences which will set him off in the mind as a person. Literature is filled with these individuals who would never be mistaken, even in appearance, for any one else: Sir John Falstaff, Long John Silver, Uriah Heep, Captain Cuttle, Mr. Micawber, Prester John. The distinguishing marks differ very much, for we would grow very tired if they were always the same. Sir John has his "tun of flesh"; Silver his wooden leg; Heep his lashless eyes, his writhing, moist, fishy hands; Micawber his pomposity, his love of big words, his pet phrases ("in short," "turn up"); Captain Cuttle, like Silver, his sea language for land purposes; Prester John his superb physique, and his colour. Jerry Cruncher cannot pronounce a *v*,—he calls his wife an "aggerawaiter," he desires to "circumvent ewents"; his hair is like spikes; he has rust always on his fingers.

Practice 6. Individualizing

Either from life or from imagination choose a character well distinguished from others by appearance and so vividly describe him (or her) as to make him stand out unmistakably to the mental eye of the reader as never to be mistaken for anyone else.

Suggestions:

1. A very stout person. 2. A very thin person. 3. A man with misshapen features, prominent nose, ears, lips; a hare-lip, cast in the eye, protruding or receding chin, etc. 4. A dour face. 5. A face wreathed in smiles. 6. One-armed man. 7. A club-footed man. 8. A very tall man. 9. A man with a square jaw. 10. A hunchback.

(*Warning:* Characters that are misshapen or deformed are usually reserved for stories of crime and mystery, or unnatural stories; yet some of the best stories have shown how absurd this natural feeling toward deformity is. It is not necessary to choose such unusual persons for stories, but they are less likely to be confusing at the start.)

Practice 7. Individualizing by Speech

Choose either the same or another character, and invent an episode including conversation in which the character is individualized by his speech.

Suggestions:

1. Oddities of pronunciation, such as: pronouncing 'v' for 'w', or 'w' for 'v' as Germans sometimes do (as Mrs. Wagonseller did under excitement); or pronouncing 'j' like 'y' as Scandinavian peoples often do in learning English; or 't' for 'th'; or 'l' for 'r' such as we attribute to Orientals. 2. Some one who stutters. 3. A man who whistles in his speech. 4. A girl who has some pet word or phrase which is used habitually, *lovely, grand, wow, keen, gosh!, and everything, you know, don't you think.* 5. One who hesitates and repeats without making progress.

Practice 8. Individualizing by Actions

Invent other episodes for the same or other characters who are distinguishable from others by habitual actions.

Suggestions:

1. Walks or handles his legs and arms oddly. 2. Has a peculiar eye affliction which makes him wink frequently (sometimes at embarrassing times). 3. A

nervous, fidgety person. 4. A hacking, habitual cough. 5. A writhing, wriggling person like Uriah Heep. 6. One who habitually uses his hands in talking. 7. One who smacks his lips as he talks. 8. A giggling person.

CHARACTERIZATION

Individualization is already a good step toward revelation of character and often the two things go forward together, but yet two persons may have much the same individual traits and be very different in character. Characterization must reveal the personality, the sincerity, frivolousness, honesty, cupidity, selfishness, thoughtfulness, pride, modesty of the person. These may be shown by description as Chaucer has so well done; by action or speech, or by both, as has been done by nearly all writers.

In this important part of the short story technique, the episode is again the chief instrument. Many story episodes, incidents, and situations are for character drawing almost entirely.

Consider individually the episodes in "A Student of Languages" and in the story analyzed in Practice 2 for what each reveals of character.

Practice 9. Characterizing

Write an episode which will reveal by his speech one of the following characters:

1. A man given to very great exaggeration for personal advertising. 2. A man who likes to tell 'tall' stories, stretchers, merely for the sake of their artistic effect, but with no malice. 3. A girl who is very snobbish. 4. A student who is fond of self-display. 5. An incident in the life of Caspar Milquetoast, or one in the life of Major Hoople. 6. A southerner, fond of saying "Down South," makes unfavourable comparisons between your district and his beloved South. 7. A newly-rich man betrays his lack of culture among cultured folk. 8. A girl of sound good sense keeps up her end in a verbal battle with some haughty rival (You might read Chapter LVI of Jane Austen's *Pride and Prejudice* before starting this one.)

Practice 10. Characterizing by Action

Write an episode which will reveal by action without saying it in so many words one of the following characters:

1. A dishonest rogue. 2. A furtive, sneaking individual. 3. A thoughtful, considerate boy. 4. A motherly woman. 5. A selfish boy. 6. A brave, courageous person. 7. An untrained, unmannerly boy. 8. A girl who would sacrific another girl in an attempt to save herself. 9. A girl who would take undeserved blame to shield a timid, fearful classmate. 10. A bullying boy, man. 11. A self-sacrificing boy, man, teacher. 12. A student with high ideals. 13. An avaricious person. 14. A dreamy, slow, indolent man.

NAMES

The names chosen for your characters should be in keeping with their personality, background, and surroundings. An Italian immigrant would hardly be called "Ruby Kaufman." "Knute Axelbrod" suggests a sturdy pioneering farmer; "Hetty," a practical, reliable person; "Wagonseller," a Pennsylvania "Dutch" family. "Willie" is a soft little boy; "Bill," a sturdy one whom "Percival" thinks rather rough; "William," a dignified, serious young man.

Practice 11. Studying Names in Fiction

1. Choose five names from short stories, novels, or plays you have read. Does each name fit the character? Why do you think so?
2. List five names of people that you think have good story value. Suggestions may be found in the telephone book, "Who's Who," or a catalogue.

THEME

Sometimes the story writer starts with an idea or theme; most novels and short stories illustrate an idea or present in concrete form a truth of human life. James Lane Allen's *The Kentucky Cardinal* instills a love of birds; *Silas Marner* shows the influence of a little child upon a man; Tarkington's *Alice Adams* shows the effects of posing; his *Seventeen* interprets the youth of high school age; Sinclair Lewis's *Main Street* pictures the self-satisfied dullness of small-town life; his *Babbitt* shows the foibles of successful and self-sufficient city people; Dickens' *Nicholas Nickleby* attacks the abuses of charity schools and brutal schoolmasters; his *Oliver Twist* exposes the wretched condition of the poor in the English workhouses. The text of Hawthorne's *House of Seven Gables* is, "The fathers have eaten sour grapes, and the children's teeth are set on edge."

Examples of themes for short stories:
1. Jealousy leads to folly and injustice.
2. A mother's sacrifice, while seeming to benefit her child, in reality causes the girl to lose the most precious thing in life.
3. Judge a person by what he does, not by what he says.
4. Sudden wealth is dangerous.
5. A friend to everybody is a friend to nobody.
6. All is not gold that glitters.

Practice 12. Studying Story Themes

1. What is the theme of "A Student of Languages?"
2. Find or invent three themes which might be used as starting-points for stories.

SETTING

Occasionally an author starts with a setting. Stevenson says, "Some places speak distinctly. Certain dank gardens cry aloud for a murder; certain old houses demand to be haunted; certain coasts are set apart for shipwreck." High school students, however, as a rule write more easily and entertainingly when they begin with an incident, a situation, an anecdote, a character, or a theme than when they use setting as the starting-point for an atmosphere or local-colour story. Setting includes time, place, occupations, and conditions. When the curtain rises, one sees the setting of a scene of a play. Although important features of the background or setting are pictured near the beginning of the story, details are often presented as the story progresses. Long paragraphs of description slow up the story and confuse the reader; brief vivid descriptions help the reader to visualize the action.

LOCAL COLOUR AND ATMOSPHERE

Local colour suggests the London streets of Dickens' stories; the Wessex country-side of Thomas Hardy; the Mississippi river life of *Tom Sawyer;* the Yukon of the *Trail of 98*, the French regime in old Quebec of *Seats of the Mighty*. Each of these presents in details the manners, customs, dress, dialect, and scenery of a particular district. In "A Student of Languages" the references to the pronunciation of *v* and to *schnitz und knep*, Mr. Wagonseller's including Pennsylvania German among his languages, and such expressions as "I will to-day make catsup" and "Pop, you must hear me a little Latin yet before I go" are illustrations of local colour.

The *Winston Simplified Dictionary* defines atmosphere as "the influence effected by a work of art or literature upon the spirit or emotion." Edgar Allen Poe says that there should be no word in a short story which does not help to produce a preconceived effect. His stories illustrate his theory and influence us by their atmosphere of gloom, mystery, weirdness, and horror. An effective ghost story has an atmosphere of uncanniness, spookiness, or creepiness. The snapping of Victoria's sheets, the sunshine in the kitchen, the substantial breakfast, the good manners of the family, the house "deliciously scented with cloves and allspice" from the catsup suggest a busy, wholesome, refined atmosphere.

Practice 13.   The Story's Setting

Picture the setting of your story. Does it have a definite atmosphere? What? How will you make your reader feel it?

POINT OF VIEW

Before writing the first word of a story, one should decide whose story it is or who should tell the story. The common narrators are a major, a minor, or a silent character who tells the story in the first person; the author who tells the story objectively; and the author who looks over the shoulder of the main character and tells the story from that person's point of view. Stockton's "The Lady or the Tiger?" Ellis Parker Butler's "Fleas Is Fleas," Mary Wilkins Freeman's "The Revolt of 'Mother'," and Elsie Singmaster's "A Student of Languages" are examples of stories told objectively in the third person. Poe's "The Cask of Amontillado," "The Pit and the Pendulum," "The Manuscript Found in a Bottle," and "The Gold Bug" are told in the first person.

Barrett Wendell says, "Most people have a strong impulse to preface something in particular by at least a paragraph of nothing in particular, bearing to the real matter in hand a relation not more inherently intimate than that of the tuning of a violin to a symphony." A good beginning catches the reader's interest.

OPENING

The student can find out how to begin his story by studying the openings of successful stories. "A Student of Languages" begins with incident and characterization.

Freeman's "The Revolt of 'Mother' " begins with dialogue:

"Father!"

"What is it?"

"What are them men diggin' over there in the field for?"

Stockton's "The Lady or the Tiger?" begins with characterization:

In the very olden time, there lived a semibarbaric king, whose ideas, though somewhat polished and sharpened by the progressiveness of distant Latin neighbours, were still large, florid, and untrammelled, as became the half of him which was barbaric.

In "The Gold Bug," Poe starts with setting, characterization, and needed explanation:

Many years ago I contracted an intimacy with a Mr. William Légrand. He was of an ancient Huguenot family, and had once been wealthy; but a series of misfortunes had reduced him to want. To avoid the mortification consequent upon his disasters, he left New Orleans, the city of his forefathers, and took up his residence at Sullivan's Island, near Charleston, South Carolina.

Brand Whitlock's "The Gold Brick" begins with incident and characterization:

Ten thousand dollars a year! Neil Kittrell left the office of the *Morning Telegraph* in a daze.

The rule is to begin a character story with character delineation, an atmosphere story with setting, and a plot story with incident or dialogue. When in doubt, begin with action and tuck in a bit at a time the antecedent explanation, characterization, and setting.

Often, as in Poe's "The Cask of Amontillado," the first part of the story is omitted. Poe does not include the incidents which made Montresor desire revenge. This story is represented by the numbers 7, 8, 9, 10, 11, 12; incidents 1, 2, 3, 4, 5, and 6 are omitted. A safe rule for the opening is to start as near to the climax as possible.

The order of the detective story is 12, 11, 10, 9, 8, 7, 6, 5, 4, 3, 2, 1. The author begins with the commission of a crime and gradually unwinds the tangled incidents until he reaches the first one and hence completes the solution of the problem.

Practice 14. The Opening of the Story

1. Study the openings of a dozen stories. How many open with incident? With dialogue? With setting? With characterization? With necessary antecedent explanation? With a general proposition, or theme, which the story will illustrate? With a combination of these?

2. Decide whether in your story you will stress plot, character, theme, or setting. Then write the opening of your short story. Arouse the reader's interest.

DIALOGUE

Although uncritical readers like a story with "lots of conversation in it," a story by a beginner usually contains little dialogue. Conversation is hard to write, and no conversation is preferable to stilted, unnatural talk that does not fit the characters. Likewise conversation which does not serve a purpose—characterize or advance the plot, for example—should be rigidly excluded from the story.

To learn to write dialogue one must get out among people, know them, and also observe carefully the details of their speech—coherence, point, accuracy, length of sentences, type of sentences, fluency, vocabulary, grammar, pronunciation, tone, mannerisms.

Instead of a string of *he saids* and *he replieds*, a story writer can use for variety *grunted, roared, snarled, sneered, maintained, contradicted, explained with icy precision, cried angrily, shouted, corrected, asked, drawled, whispered, volunteered, yelled, mumbled, rejoined, retorted, ventured, muttered, stammered, snickered, boasted, chuckled, dashed in, exclaimed, gasped, growled,* or *hinted darkly.*

The introductory *he said, he mumbled,* or *he shouted* may be placed at the beginning of the speech, in the middle, or at the end. When there is no possibility of confusion, the introductory expression is omitted.

Other ways to make dialogue natural, interesting, and sprightly are by having the speeches short, using freely for most characters contradictions and colloquialisms, having one speaker break in on another before a speech is completed, letting a character ask another question instead of answering the question asked, having a person anticipate a question and answer it before it is asked, and breaking the dialogue with brief passages of description and comment.

Practice 15. Conversation

1. Study the conversation of "A Student of Languages." Show how it is made natural, interesting, and lively. Is there any talk out of character, or wooden or dull talk?

2. Jot down in your notebook words and turns of speech you hear used by special classes of people: a fisherman, a small boy, a gardener, a typist, a ribbon salesgirl, a farmer, a German, an Italian, a Norwegian, an Irishman.

3. Write a conversation that will form a part of the story for which you have already written the opening.

SELF-CRITICISM CHART—CONVERSATION

1. *What variations of* he said *and* he replied *have I used? Is it always clear who the speaker is?*
2. *Is the talk in character?*
3. *Is tone of voice suggested? Manner? Pronunciation?*
4. *If I have used dialect, is it accurate? Easily understood by the reader?*
5. *Are speeches long or short? Broken by questions, description, narration?*

PICTURES AND CONTRAST

One way to make the story seem real is by picturing vividly but tersely the characters and the setting. The writer who does not observe or see in imagination the sparse hair, wrinkled face, faded coat, square jaw, and keen, kindly eyes of the heroic failure in his story will write about phantoms, not about real people.

Another device for making clear and forceful what one has to say is contrast. Elsie Singmaster contrasts the courtesy of the Wagonsellers with the bad manners of Mr. Mather, and the calmness of Victoria with her parents' agitation.

Practice 16. Pictures and Contrasts

1. In "A Student of Languages" find another example of contrast expressed or implied.

2. In "A Student of Languages" what are two illustrations of the fact that Elsie Singmaster is an accurate observer?

3. Find two vivid pictures in "A Student of Languages."

PLAUSIBILITY

Because "truth is stranger than fiction," to say of an incident in a short story that it really happened is not proof that it is plausible. To be plausible an incident must seem true. In other words, in a story every effect has a cause; every act grows out of the character delineated and the preceding action. Although no one probably ever lived on a desert island in the manner depicted in *Robinson Crusoe*, yet because of the minuteness of detail and absolute naturalness the story has the air of truth, and is really more plausible than are many happenings recorded in the newspapers.

STYLE

In "How *Flint and Fire* Started and Grew," Dorothy Canfield tells how she wrote one of her stories. After "the materials were ready, the characters fully alive" in her mind "and entirely visualized, even to the smoothly braided hair of Ev'leen Ann," she scribbled the story as rapidly as her pencil could go. "After this came a period of steady desk work, of rewriting, compression, more compression," rewriting of "clumsy, ungraceful phrases," and revision for correctness, suggestiveness, accuracy, movement, proportion, and sound.

In answer to the question "How can I acquire style?" Robert W. Neal says, "Don't try to . . . directly. Strive rather to report accurately what you observe and think and feel." Although struggling for a literary style is likely to lead to affectation and emptiness, by taking pains one can acquire the knack of building varied, lively, forceful, and natural sentences. Writing "A Student of Languages" in one's own words without referring to the story and then comparing one's sentences with Elsie Singmaster's simple, lucid, accurate, crisp, terse language is a good exercise.

TITLE

The title is rarely decided when one starts to write. Often it is suggested by an event in the course of the story; it may not come until after the story is complete. In a letter to Tom Taylor, Lewis Carroll describes the evolution of the title for *Alice in Wonderland*.

I first thought of "Alice's Adventures under Ground."—but that was pronounced too much like a lesson book about mines. Then I took "Alice's Golden House," but that I gave up. Here are the names I thought of: "Alice among the Elves," "Alice among the Goblins," "Alice's Hour in Elf Land," "Alice's Doings in Wonderland," "Alice's Adventures in Wonderland."

A good title should be brief, specific, colourful, and original, should be suitable for the story, and should excite curiosity. Comparatively few titles of short stories are more than five words long. The title, like the opening, should allure readers, as clover attracts bees.

Practice 17. Studying Titles

1. Which of these are good titles: "The Moon Coin," "The Commutation Chophouse," "A Thrifty Man," "The Only Child," "The Restaurant," "A Convert to Christmas," "Clothes," "A Bus Ride," "Footfalls," "Beyond the Horizon," "In the Distance," "Old Judge Priest," "One against the World," "The Striker," "All or Nothing," "A Decision," "Percival Galahad Barnose," "The Hired Baby," "Rikki-Tikki-Tavi," "Wee Willie Winkie"? Why?

2. From magazines or a book of short stories select five excellent titles.

3. Decide upon a title for your story.

SELF-CRITICISM CHART—SHORT STORY

1. *Is plot, character, theme, or atmosphere conspicuously emphasized?*
2. *Show that the story has (or has not) a single predominating incident.*
3. *Has it a single pre-eminent character? Prove.*
4. *Does the story give a unified impression. What is it?*
5. *How much time does the story cover? Does the length of time destroy the unity of the story?*
6. *What is the setting? Does the entire action happen in one place? If not, do unnecessary changes of scene destroy the unity?*
7. *In the plot what is the cause or inciting impulse, what are the incidents, and what is the effect or climax?*
8. *Show that the plot is (or is not) compressed.*
9. *What is the outstanding trait of each character?*
10. *Do the characters show their traits by their speech and acts? Does the author describe, analyze, and explain the characters?*
11. *Is each character colourful? Individual? Interesting? Do you know him intimately?*
12. *Is each character's name suitable? Suggestive?*
13. *Are there any touches of local colour? What?*
14. *Is there a struggle or conflict? What is it?*
15. *Is the plot complicated? If so, how?*
16. *If the story has suspense, show how it is secured.*
17. *Is there any variation from the chronological order 1, 2, 3, 4, 5, 6, 7, 8, 9, 10, 11, 12?*
18. *Has the story a theme? If so, what is it?*
19. *Who is the narrator?*
20. *How does the story open?*
21. *What proportion of the story is dialogue?*

22. *Show that the dialogue is (or is not) natural, interesting, and sprightly.* *What substitutes for* said *and* replied *are used?*
23. *What pictures are there?*
24. *What use is made of contrast?*
25. *Is the story plausible?*
26. *Use five adjectives to characterize the style.*
27. *Is the title brief? Vivid? Attractive? Suitable? Suggestive? Does it arouse curiosity?*

Practice 18. Writing a Short Story

1. Complete the story you have been working on. Test it by the above standards; then revise thoroughly.

2. Go to life for another plot. Start with a cause, an incident, an effect or a climax, a character, or a theme. Invent needed details. Then write the short story.

Courtesy "Saturday Evening Post"

The One-Act Play

THE one-act play is a short story in dramatic form. Instead of being read silently from a book it is intended to be presented by actors before an audience, solely by means of dialogue and action, aided by costumes, scenery, and lighting. Like the short story, the one-act play must aim for a single unified impression. "It is," says a playwright, "a story of ones—one simple setting, one continuous, unbroken scene, one main character, one main incident, and one climax. A good one-act play leaves one clean-cut impression."

WHAT MAKES A SITUATION DRAMATIC

Any situation is dramatic which can arouse the emotions of the audience. A conflict, physical or mental, between two or more characters or within the mind of one character usually arouses an emotional reaction in an onlooker. In the one-act play a conflict is revealed mainly through the actions of the characters, and partly through dialogue. The elements of conflict are identical in the play and short story.

THEME

Often, as explained in the section on the short story, an idea comes in the form of a theme—general truth which may be used as the subject of the play: Fortune is fickle; A stitch in time saves nine; Dishonesty doesn't pay. But the theme should be merely implied by the action, not drummed into the minds of the audience through constant repetition in the speeches of the characters.

The one-act play may be tragic—a character fails in what he sets out to do, or in doing it, unhappiness, ruin, or even death results. It may be comic—the hero, successful in what he sets out to do, achieves happiness. Or it may be melodramatic—an exaggerated picture of right conquering wrong.

PLOT

Theme alone is not sufficient. There must be a story or plot, presented dramatically, with beginning, middle, and end. Pantomime plays an important part. It has been said that a writer should not start to write speeches for his characters until the play is perfectly under-standable to an audience in pantomime alone.

The beginning is occupied with introducing characters and ex-plaining previous action through the speeches of characters. These preliminaries pave the way for the main action.

"The middle," as one playwright puts it, "depends for its interest on the ability of the author to swing the balance of power from one character to another." In the middle or main action the conflict takes place. The main action should reach a climax or turning point, followed swiftly but naturally by the end or result of the main action. But throughout, says George P. Baker in *Dramatic Technique*, the audi-ence must feel "a compelling desire to know what will happen next."

THE MASTER IN THE HOUSE[1]

SCENE: *The kitchen of* KATE BURKE'S *typical middle-class home. It is early evening, and the kitchen is flooded with warm light. The blinds are down, shutting out the windy dusk. There is a door* U C,[2] *elevated above the level of the floor and reached by two steps, which leads upstairs to the bedrooms. In the L wall, about centre, is a door leading outside, with a curtained window above and below it. L C is a kitchen table with kitchen chairs above and right of it. In the R wall, down stage, is a door leading to another part of the house. Above the door is the kitchen stove. U R C is the kitchen sink. Below the door D R is an old armchair. There is a clock on the wall above the sink U R C, a cupboard U L C, and a large rocking chair R C. There may, also, be innumerable objects about suggesting the atmosphere of a kitchen.*

AT RISE OF CURTAIN: KATE *is working between the stove and sink, evidently preparing dinner. She is a large, comfortable-looking woman of middle age, with dark hair and blue eyes. She is dressed neatly in a gingham house dress and has a large apron tied around her waist. As she moves around the spotless kitchen, she sings softly to herself. Her voice is filled with an undercurrent of—not exactly grief—perhaps resignation.*

KATE. But come ye back, when summer's in the meadow,
Or when the valley's hushed and white with snow,
It's I'll be here—

[*There is a knock on the door* L. KATE *breaks off with an exclamation of annoyance and then, wiping her hands on her apron, crosses to the door* L.]

KATE. Now I wonder who could that be, at this hour? [*She opens the door* L.] How do you do? [*Then she recognizes the figure.*] Denny! Oh, Mother of God, it's my boy come back! Denny, darling, come in!

[DENNY *enters* L *and stands just inside the doorway, a suitcase in his hand. He is a tall young Celt of about twenty-five, with a worn, nice grin. His suit is old and not too well pressed, and he carries a dark hat. He is followed by* ANNE. *She is a pretty, young girl of about twenty-three, with a worried look and manner. She wears a shabby suit and hat, which were originally of good cut and material, but are now plainly well worn.* ANNE *stands self-consciously in the doorway,*

[1]*Copyright, 1934, by Scholastic Corporation. Copyright, 1934, by Betty Fitzgerald. Copies of the play may be obtained for 35 cents each from the Dramatic Publishing Company, 59 East Van Buren Street, Chicago, Illinois.*
[2]*Up stage (U) means away from the footlights; down stage (D), towards the footlights. Right (R) and left (L) are used in regard to the actor as he faces the audience. (C) means centre.*

unnoticed, while DENNY *drops the suitcase above the door, sweeps* KATE *into his arms, and kisses her.*]

DENNY. Two years is a long time, isn't it, Mother?

KATE [*hugging* DENNY *roundly*]. With never a word nor a letter from you, you young scamp!

DENNY [*releasing* KATE, *holding her off, and grinning*]. But I'm back for a visit now—if you'll have me.

KATE [*indignantly*]. Have you? Don't talk so foolish, Denny!

DENNY. And, Mother—[*He turns to* ANNE.] this is Anne—[*There is pride in his voice.*] my wife.

ANNE [*putting out her hand timidly to* KATE *and stepping into the kitchen*]. How do you do, Mrs. Burke?

KATE [*startled at first, but now completely herself again, crossing warmly to* ANNE]. Come here 'til I look at you. And don't you be calling me "Mrs. Burke." Denny's wife is like one of my own. [*She kisses* ANNE *warmly and then stands back, her voice very gentle.*] You chose yourself a pretty wife, Denny, and I know I'll love her. [*Then, matter-of-factly.*] You must be tired out, the two of you, and it's that cold the wind would be to your bones. [*She puts her arm around* ANNE *and leads her to* C.]

[ANNE *and* DENNY *take off their wraps.* KATE *takes their wraps and goes out* D R, *returning immediately without them.* ANNE *sits gingerly right of the table* L C. *After a moment's hesitation,* DENNY *sits down in the rocking chair* R C. *He sighs as he relaxes,*and his face is white and drawn.*]

ANNE. It's so beautifully warm here.

KATE [*crossing from* D R *to* C.]. It is that, with the fire going all day for the washing. Well, Denny, I don't know what I'm doing, I'm that excited. [*She stands* C, *gazing proudly at* DENNY.]

DENNY. I am, myself, Mother. It's been a long time.

KATE. It seems longer, Denny, when you're old.

DENNY. Listen to her, Anne! Old, with those eyes, and her hair still black as coal!

KATE [*with a pleasant shrug*]. It's all blarney. [*She crosses to the chair above the table* L C *and sits.*] Well now, I want to hear every little thing you've been doing. It's a queer feeling to be two weary years and not knowing what your own son's doing at all!

DENNY [*gently*]. I know, Mother. You see, I wouldn't write at first, and after a while, when I tried, I couldn't.

KATE. I understand.

DENNY. Mother, I'm sorry that I had to hurt you.

KATE [*lightly*]. Well now, if you hadn't, you wouldn't have met Anne, and I'm thinking I'd look a long way before I found a daughter-in-law I'd like better. [*She lays her hand gently on* ANNE's *shoulder.*]

ANNE [*her face glowing*]. Oh, thank you!

KATE [*rises and crosses to* DENNY *and gently strokes his hair*]. Come, tell me about yourself. And don't tell me you're well. I've eyes on me, and you look peaked, Denny.

DENNY [*throwing his head back, smiling up at* KATE]. I'm all right. Just a little tired. Do you want me to begin at the very first?

KATE. Yes, Denny, I've wondered.

[KATE *remains standing behind* DENNY, *her one arm lovingly placed about his shoulders.* DENNY *looks straight ahead as he tells his story.*]

DENNY. Well, after—that night, I went to Boston as I'd intended to. The job was still open, and I took it. I liked it—every bit as much as I had known I would. I found a little boarding house where they had fairly good meals and comfortable beds, and settled down. I was a little lonely at first, of course, and then one day I met Anne.

[DENNY's *eyes meet* ANNE's *and the two young people smile bravely.*]

DENNY [*continuing*]. We saved up a little money and got married, and that's the best thing that happened to me while I was gone, for after that everything was fine. We got a little apartment and some secondhand furniture, and got along splendidly. Anne's a grand cook. And then—[*His face darkens and his voice drops low.*] that's all, I guess. [*He stares down at his feet.*

[*There is a short pause.* ANNE *looks away.* KATE *looks at* DENNY *with shrewd, pitying eyes. Then, brightly, she breaks the silence.*]

KATE [*crossing* C.] Well, now, isn't that fine? A good job and a wife at your age.

By BETTY FITZGERALD

Practice 1. Studying a Play

1. Read the selection from *The Master in the House*, a student-written one-act play.
2. How much of the story does this selection tell you? What part of your information did you receive from the speeches of Kate? Of Anne? Of Denny? From action?
3. Are the characters skilfully introduced? Prove your points.

CHARACTERS

As in the short story, the one-act play should have one principal character and a few minor ones, all true to life and individualized. Unlike the short-story writer, the playwright must make his characters reveal themselves entirely by what they say, what others say to them or about them, and how they act. Kate's kindliness to Anne, her gentleness and tact, her quick perception of Denny's true situation stamp her as a motherly, understanding woman.

DIALOGUE

Next to action, dialogue is the most important thing in the play. The speeches of the actors explain what has gone before, prepare for what is to follow, and reveal character. Make the sentences short, even clipped, like those of people in real life. Avoid cramming too much information into a speech; the audience will miss half you have to give, and your characters will seem stiff and unnatural. A fundamental rule many dramatists follow is, "One idea to the speech."

Although speeches in a one-act play cannot reproduce every word or phrase of daily life, they may be short, yet convincing, if you use specific and telling words and include only the necessary details. To avoid jerkiness, questions and comments by other characters serve as connecting links. Above all, every word that is uttered should seem so typical of the person who is speaking that no one else in the play could possibly have said it.

Beware of using dialect unless you are both thoroughly familiar with it and are also able to reproduce it so skilfully on paper that the actor will be able to interpret it convincingly. In *The Master in the House* the dialect, readily understandable, accurate, and consistently used, is a real asset.

DEVELOPMENT

As in the short story, development both of plot and character is by episode. Our selection from *The Master in the House* is the first two episodes. The first episode reveals to the audience the setting, and briefly, the character of Kate. Episode 2 is the arrival of Denny and Anne. We have a fine development of the character of Kate; we learn from the dialogue the story which has preceded the lifting of the curtain; and we have formed surmises of the future plot, rousing our interest and creating suspense.

SCENARIO

A scenario is a synopsis or outline of the play, the purpose of which is to clarify the whole play in the writer's own mind and to make the writer's wishes absolutely clear to the producer. First comes the cast of characters, each carefully described, then the time and place, the setting for the stage, the list of stage properties necessary, and finally a detailed explanation of the action by episodes, with a new episode every time a character enters or leaves. Unlike the play, the scenario may include description, narration, and characterization. A detailed plan of the action (entrances, exits, stage business) is also helpful. The completed scenario should be brief, clear, and well-proportioned, with stress on the important points of the story.

STAGE DIRECTIONS

Stage directions, as evidenced by *The Master in the House*, should be brief and concise, concerned chiefly with suggestions for the arrangement of the stage properties, the lighting, and the more important action. Properties should be simple, suggestive of time and place, and in keeping with the mood. Costumes should harmonize in style and be appropriate to the character. For the actor, the stage directions should be explicit and practical, concerned only with what cannot possibly be conveyed in the dialogue: with pantomime, tone of voice, expression, gestures.

MANUSCRIPT

In writing the final draft of your play, refer to *The Master in the House* as a guide for form. Notice that in the dialogue the names of the characters are written out, not abbreviated with initials. People are always referred to in the same way: Mrs. Burke as *Kate*, not *Mrs. Burke* at one time and *Kate* at another. Stage directions precede the speeches, are enclosed in parentheses, and are underlined to indicate italics in print.

Practice 2. Dramatizing a Story

Select from your own reading some short story which has dramatic quality and dramatize it. Be careful in your selection to choose a plot which can be presented in one place—for your scene should not shift; and at one time, for there should be only one curtain. Before starting, write a scenario. Necessary previous actions can be covered by conversation.

Practice 3. Writing a One-Act Play

1. Around an interesting incident based on personal experience, school life, a newspaper clipping, or a story you have heard, build a story suitable for a one-act play. What is the theme? Is it tragedy? Comedy? Melodrama? What is the main incident? Who is the main character? What is the conflict behind the action?

   Write a synopsis or scenario to clarify your ideas. Do you depend too much on dialogue? Are there long, awkward pauses while necessary action is going on?

   Do your characters enter naturally? Be sure that your exposition of previous action is neither long nor involved. Is there an element of suspense in the development of the action? Does the end quickly follow the climax? Make your characters real people. It is better to choose types you know (high school boys and girls, mothers, fathers, storekeepers, people of your community) than bizarre and fantastic personalities.

   Take great pains with dialogue. Study the speech of people about you as a model for the speech of your characters.

   Supply brief, pointed stage directions.

2. Write out the final draft of your play with careful attention to form.

Mastering Effective English Handbook

When in doubt consult your handbook

GRAMMAR AND USAGE
PUNCTUATION
POETRY
THE LIBRARY
PARLIAMENTARY PRACTICE

The Parts of the Sentence

Can you always recognize the subject, predicate, and other parts of the sentence? The diagnostic test will help you to answer this question.

Test 1A (*Diagnostic*). Parts of the Simple Sentence

Copy the italicized words in a column and number them 1 to 25. Then, using the abbreviations given below, indicate the use in the sentence of each word. Write the abbreviations in a column to the right of the words.

s.s. — simple subject	*o.p.* — object of preposition
v. — verb	*i.o.* — indirect object
p.a. — predicate adjective	*ap.* — appositive
p.n. — predicate nominative	*n.a.* — nominative of address
d.o. — direct object	*a.o.* — adverbial objective

1. Samuel de Champlain, *founder* of Quebec, was a *native* of France.
2. That *afternoon* the Village of the Turtle and the Shark lay very still and *clean* in the hot sun.
3. The blue *eyes* of the okapi in the zoo were mild and *content*.
4. The wife of Mr. McNamara, the cab *driver*, gave *me* a piece of griddle bread with currants in *it*.
5. In the morning the gypsies strung *beads* around the *neck* of the donkey and *tied* her tail with a bright red ribbon a *yard* long.
6. *Beatrice*, what *kind* of fruit do *you* *like* best?
7. The next *morning* the *servants* brought *Henry* a *breakfast* of goat's milk and black *bread*.
8. Viscount Alexander of Tunis, a famous soldier, was *made Governor-General* of Canada.

SUBJECT, PREDICATE, AND MODIFIER

1. A sentence is a group of words expressing a complete thought.
The Jersey cow is rated high by dairymen.

2. The predicate verb makes a statement, asks a question, or gives a command.
(Statement) A primitive type of wheat *was grown* in the Stone Age by the "Lake Dwellers" of Switzerland.
(Question) What *is* the normal temperature of the healthy human body?
(Command) *Bring* me *These Men Shall Never Die* from the library.

3. The simple subject names the person, place, or thing spoken of. The simple subject answers the question "Who?" or "What?" before the verb.

481

Where does your *community* get its water supply? (*Community* answers the question "Who does get?")

From the top of the blockhouse came a single *shot*. (*Shot* answers the question "What came?")

4. The complete subject is the simple subject with its modifiers.

A *small black turtle* clung lovingly to the lobe of Sam's left ear.

5. A modifier is a word or expression which changes the meaning of the word to which it is attached.

Lois arranges dahlias *skilfully*. (*Arranges skilfully* means something different from *arranges; skilfully* modifies *arranges*.)

He *who hesitates* is lost. (This sentence means something different from "He is lost." *Who hesitates* modifies *he*.)

6. The complete predicate is the predicate verb with its modifiers and the words that complete its meaning. Words which complete the meaning of a verb are "completers" or "complements." See rules 19–22 on pages 488–490.

A ribbon | is worn on the service uniform in place of a medal. (The vertical line separates the complete subject from the complete predicate. The simple subject is underscored once and the predicate verb, twice.)

Captain Robert S. Johnson, the famous World War II ace, | made his first solo flight at the age of fourteen.

7. When the complete predicate or part of it is before the subject, the order is inverted.

(Inverted Order) From the direction of the main highway came the sound of footsteps on crisp sycamore leaves.

(Natural Order) The sound of footsteps on crisp sycamore leaves | came from the direction of the main highway.

When *there* introduces an inverted sentence, it is called an "expletive" or "introductory adverb." It is never the subject.

There are lakes of asphalt in the West Indies. (The simple subject is *lakes*. It answers the question "What are?")

Lakes of asphalt | are in the West Indies.

8. A simple sentence has one subject and one predicate, either or both of which may be compound.

(Compound Subject) The quality and quantity of a harvested crop | depend to a large extent upon the proper timing of the harvest.

(Compound Predicate) A searchlight beam | dipped from the sky and swept across the bay.

(Compound Subject and Compound Predicate) Big three-place torpedo planes and tiny, stubby fighters | roared away from the field in groups and headed for the carrier.

Practice 1. Underlining Subjects and Verbs

Copy the following sentences, arranging inverted sentences in the natural order. Then draw one line under the simple subject and two lines under the predicate verb. With a vertical line separate the complete subject from the complete predicate.

Examples

a. Articulate every word distinctly. (The subject *you* is understood.)

(You) | Articulate every word distinctly.

b. In the days of the pioneer most industries were carried on in the home.

Most industries | were carried on in the home in the days of the pioneer.

A. 1. Josiah Wedgwood was the son of an English potter.
   2. At fourteen the boy was molding clay in his brother's workshop.
   3. In 1759 he formed a partnership with Thomas Wheildon.
   4. Before long the young man produced a beautiful cream coloured earthenware.
   5. Never before had Queen Charlotte of England seen such exquisite china.

B. 1. The fame of the young British potter spread throughout Europe.
   2. From the Empress of Russia came an offer of fifteen thousand dollars for a service of the new china.
   3. In later years Wedgwood produced matchless vases, tablets, and cameos of jasper.
   4. Have you seen in museums specimens of his art?
   5. Look for examples of Wedgwood china in the homes of your friends.

THE PARTS OF SPEECH

9. A noun is a name. Nouns name:

a. Persons, animals, places, things — *Ernie Pyle, lion, Toronto, tractor.*

b. Collections or groups of persons or things — *army, Parliament, team, club, audience, crowd, platoon, fleet.*

c. Qualities, conditions, actions, and ideas—*ambition, perseverance, happiness, beauty, wealth, mercy, time, length.*

10. A pronoun is a word used instead of a noun.

That is the girl about *whom* I wrote *you.*

11. A substantive is a noun or pronoun, or another part of speech or a word group used as a noun. The word group may be any kind of phrase or clause used in place of a noun.

Only the *brave* deserve the *fair.*

Seeing is *believing.*

As a girl Amelia Earhart liked *to play baseball.*

Captain Taylor told us *that soldiers like to receive automatic pencils, wrist watches, pocket-size books, pocket flashlights, and small toilet kits.*

12. Words which make statements about persons, places, or things, ask questions, or give commands are verbs. Three forms of the verb—the infinitive, the participle, and the verbal noun (gerund)—do not make statements, ask questions, or give commands.

(Statement) The captain *told* my brother about his promotion.
(Question) Who *told* you that ridiculous story?
(Command) *Tell* Gwen to come to the block party to-night.

An auxiliary helps a verb to make a statement, ask a question, or give a command.

For some time the *Hispaniola* had been sailing easily before the wind along the coast of Treasure Island. (*Had* and *been* are auxiliaries.)

The auxiliaries are: *is, be, am, are, was, were, been, has, have, had, do, does, did, may, can, might, could, must, shall, will, should,* and *would.*

13. An adjective is a word that modifies or describes a noun or pronoun. An adjective usually answers one of these questions: "Which?" "What kind of?" "How many?"

The narrow little streets shone with *the copper* light from *a hundred petrol* torches.

The tired young pilot was sleeping.

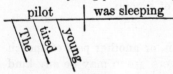

The subject and predicate, placed on a straight line, are separated by a short vertical line. Adjectives and adverbs are placed on slant lines under the words they modify.

14. An adverb is a word that modifies a verb, an adjective, or an adverb. Adverbs commonly answer the questions "When?" "Where?" "How?" and "How much?"

Speedy, carrier-based fighter planes zoomed almost continually overhead.

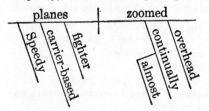

The adverbs *continually* and *overhead* modify *zoomed;* the adverb *almost* modifies the adverb *continually.*

15. A preposition is a word used to show the relation of a substantive to another word.

The wealthy planters *along* the banks *of* the river lived almost *like* feudal lords. (*Along* shows the relation between *banks* and *planters; of,* between *river* and *banks; like,* between *lords* and *lived.*)

a. The substantive following a preposition is its object.

On the *fields* of *Ecuador* in the high *mountains* the harvest season comes in *May.*

b. A preposition and its object, with or without modifiers, is called a prepositional phrase.

The first Distinguished Service Cross (of World War II) was awarded posthumously (to Captain Colin P. Kelly) (for action) (in the Philippines). (Each prepositional phrase is enclosed in parentheses.)

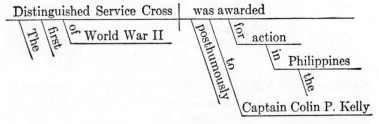

A preposition is placed on a slant line, and its object on a horizontal line joined to the slant line. The whole name is placed on one line.

Practice 2.   Recognizing Parts of Speech

Diagram the following sentences.

                    OR

Copy the following sentences, leaving a blank line after each line you write.   Underscore the simple subject once and the predicate verb twice.   Write *adj.* over every adjective and *adv.* over every adverb. Enclose prepositional phrases in parentheses

A. 1. The tiny, blue-eyed kitten mewed pitifully.
   2. The draftees were quickly assigned to barracks.
   3. The entire bow of the huge carrier was enveloped in flames.

4. The age of sheep is estimated by the appearance of their teeth.
5. For the twentieth time Lieut. Bulkeley looked anxiously at his watch.

B. 1. Planes are sometimes launched from the decks of carriers by catapults.
2. The purchase of an ice-cream machine is recorded in an expense ledger of George Washington's. (*Ice-cream* is one modifier.)
3. Rocket guns are of comparatively recent origin.
4. Helmeted soldiers careened along the beach in speedy jeeps.
5. Amid the brilliance of the field floodlights a big Douglas transport was settling down gently on the paved runway.

16. A conjunction connects words or groups of words.

After I wash *and* dry the dishes, I'll knit an inch *or* two more on my sweater.
When a succession of different crops is grown upon the same soil, it is said *that* crop rotation is being practiced.

Conjunctions used in pairs are called correlatives: *both, and; either, or; neither, nor; not only, but also.*

Neither Dr. Watson *nor* Mrs. Hudson suspected Sherlock Holmes's ruse.

1. In the armed forces medals or ribbons are worn on the left breast with the highest ranking decoration to the right.

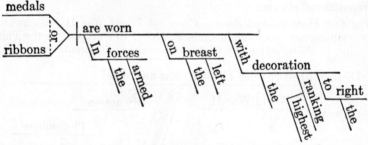

The conjunction *or* is placed on a dotted line between the words it connects.

2. Four pursuit ships attacked simultaneously but were shot down by the rear gunner and the two side gunners.

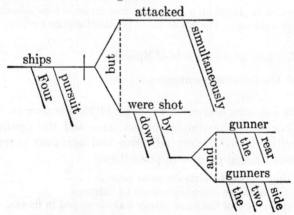

The conjunction *but* connects the verbs *attacked* and *were shot;* the conjunction *and* connects *gunner* and *gunners,* the objects of the preposition *by.*

3. Both Army and Navy training planes are vividly coloured for immediate identification in the air.

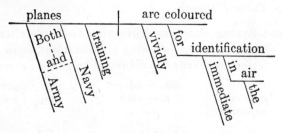

Both and *and* are correlative conjunctions and are placed between the words they connect.

17. An interjection is a word or form of speech that expresses strong or sudden feeling.

Hurrah! We've found the cave!
Oh, what a delightful spot this is!

18. To find the part of speech of a word, always ask yourself the question, "What does the word do in the sentence?" Some words may be used as a number of different parts of speech.

(Adjective) *That* package is not for you. (*That* modifies the noun *package.*)
(Pronoun) *That* won't make any difference to Sybil. (*That* is used in place of a noun.)
(Conjunction) Didn't Edward notice *that* Mother looked tired? (*That* connects *Mother looked tired* with *did notice.*)
(Adverb) *Out* flew the packages in the back of the sled. (*Out* modifies the verb *flew.*)
(Preposition) Without a word Oku Hung waddled solemnly *out* the door. (*Out* joins its object *door* to the verb *waddled.*)

Practice 3. Using a Word as Different Parts of Speech

Write sentences in which you use each of the following words as the different parts of speech named after it.

A. 1. *what* — pronoun, adjective, interjection
2. *near* — verb, preposition, adverb
3. *wrong* — noun, verb, adjective
4. *off* — adverb, preposition
5. *since* — preposition, conjunction, adverb
6. *free* — adjective, verb, noun

B. 1. *until* — preposition, conjunction
2. *patrol* — noun, verb, adjective
3. *slow* — adjective, adverb, verb

4. *after* — preposition, conjunction, adverb
5. *like* — verb, noun, preposition
6. *while* — noun, verb, conjunction

Practice 4.   Parts of Speech

Copy the following sentences, leaving a blank line after each line you write.   Then, using the following abbreviations, show what part of speech each word is.   Write the abbreviation above the word.

n. — noun	*adv.* — adverb	*prep.* — preposition
pron. — pronoun	*v.* — verb	*conj.* — conjunction
adj. — adjective		

A. 1. In population, Mexico, a land of warm colour and charm, ranks second among the Latin American countries.
   2. At the time of the Spanish conquest in the sixteenth century the Indians of Mexico had a unique civilization.
   3. They devised several kinds of calendars, studied the stars, the sun, and the moon, and produced art and architecture of high quality.
   4. On the peninsula of Yucatán a great pyramid, where religious ceremonies were performed, still stands.
   5. Near by is the Sacred Well, in which beautiful maidens were sacrificed to the angry gods.

B. 1. Under Spanish rule Mexico was exploited until Father Hidalgo a noble priest, led the people in a revolution.
   2. Although the Spaniards captured Father Hidalgo and shot him, his followers carried on the fight and won the independence of their country. (*Their* may be called an adjective or a pronoun.)
   3. After years of bitter internal strife Benito Juarez became president and worked unceasingly for education and the equitable distribution of land.
   4. Although most of the people are still quite poor, within recent years social and economic conditions have improved.
   5. Mexicans are artistic, courteous, and intelligent, with sensitive dignity and a great love for their land.

OTHER IMPORTANT PARTS OF THE SIMPLE SENTENCE

Every sentence has a subject word and a predicate verb, as a backbone to which modifiers are attached.   A sentence may have also as part of this backbone a complement or completer of the verb.   Four kinds of completers are the predicate adjective, the predicate nominative, the direct object, and the indirect object.

19. A predicate adjective completes the predicate and describes the subject.

The meadows were *gay* with buttercups and bluebells.
The forces on Corregidor were desperately weary from lack of sleep.

The predicate adjective *weary* completes the predicate and describes
the subject. The line separating the
predicate adjective from the verb,
therefore, slants toward the subject.

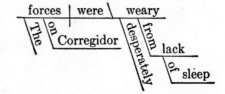

20. **A predicate nominative is a substantive that completes the
predicate and explains or renames the subject.** The predicate nominative, except with a negative, denotes the same person, place, or
thing as the subject.

> The most common trophy of the Pacific War is the Japanese personal
> battle *flag*. (trophy = flag)
> The lemming is a roly-poly little *mouse* with a furry stump of a tail. (lem-
> ming = mouse)
> The native home of Aberdeen Angus cattle is northeastern Scotland.

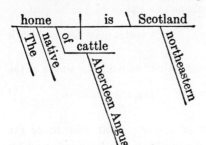

The predicate nominative *Scotland*
completes the predicate and explains
the subject. The line slants toward
the subject.

21. **A direct object is a substantive that completes the predicate
and names the receiver or the product of the action.** If the subject
acts, the noun or pronoun which answers the question "What?" or
"Whom?" after the verb is the direct object of the verb.

> On the rocks just above the line of full tide Edward found the baby *seal*
> (*Seal* answers the question "Found what?")

1. Red Cross dogs found the wounded men for the stretcher-bearers.

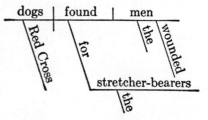

Men, the direct object of the verb,
is separated from the verb by a
short vertical line.

2. For three days each of the marooned pilots ate only half of an orange **and**
a bit of cake.

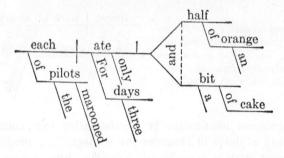

Notice the compound object on horizontal lines.

a. A verb that has a direct object is transitive active.

At 0700 on Tuesday the lookout *sighted* an enemy submarine.

b. If the subject is acted upon, the verb is transitive passive.

At 0700 on Tuesday an enemy submarine *was sighted* by the lookout.

c. All other verbs are intransitive. Many verbs may be used both transitively and intransitively.

All Tuesday night our ship *plowed* uneventfully through the waves of the Atlantic. (*Plowed* is intransitive.)

Our ship *plowed* a path through the waves. (*Plowed* is transitive.)

22. An indirect object is a noun or pronoun that tells to or for whom something is done. An indirect object is regularly followed by a direct object.

Bolton gave the little *seal* a breakfast of warm milk and bread crumbs. (*Seal* answers the question "Gave to whom?")

From Montreal an old friend of my father sent my sister and me a set of brushes and a box of paints.

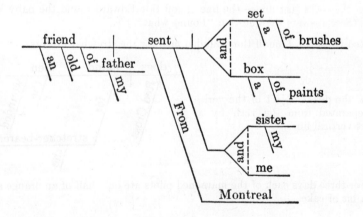

Sister and *me*, the compound indirect object of the verb *sent*, are diagrammed like the compound object of a preposition.

23. An adverbial objective is a noun used like an adverb.

The Indians of Peru generally work six *days* of the week and shop on Sunday. (*Days* answers the question "How much?")

That *night* little Daniel rolled up in a bearskin and slept by the fireplace. (*Night* answers the question "When?")

In the desert a plane on the ground is invisible thirty or forty *feet* away.

Charles Dickens often walked ten or fifteen miles at a time.

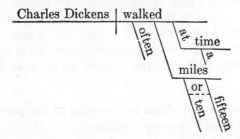

Miles, the adverbial objective, is a noun used like an adverb to modify the verb *walked*. It is diagrammed like the object of a preposition.

24. An appositive is added to a noun or pronoun to explain it and denotes the same person or thing.

Mr. Fields, a chef at the Hotel Commodore, won the tennis championship.

Jon, the cabin *boy*, was well liked by the officers, crew, and passengers of the freighter. (Jon = boy)

"Can Do!" is the motto of the Naval Construction Battalion, the famed Seabees.

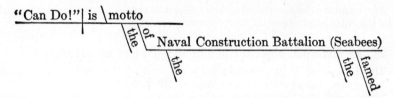

Seabees is in apposition with *Naval Construction Battalion.* An appositive is placed after the word it explains and is enclosed in parentheses.

An appositive and a predicate nominative are similar. The difference is that a verb connects the subject and the predicate nominative, while an appositive follows a word directly and is generally set off by commas. In the diagrammed sentence above, *motto* is the predicate nominative, connected with the subject by *is,* and *Seabees* is the appositive.

25. A nominative of address is the name of the person spoken to.

Ring for more speed, Lieutenant Barston.

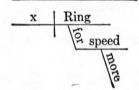

The word used in direct address is placed on a line above the rest of the sentence. The placing shows that the nominative of address has no grammatical connection with the rest of the sentence. The *x* stands for the subject *you,* which is understood.

26. A nominative absolute with a participle expressed or understood has the force of an adverb modifier, but has no grammatical connection with the rest of the sentence.

Its *head* held up like a little periscope, a water snake slipped across the creek.

The candles were scattered about the room, two tall white *ones* standing on the chimney piece.

Practice 5.   Recognizing the Parts of the Simple Sentence

Diagram the following sentences.

OR

Find the subject words, verbs, predicate adjectives, predicate nominatives, direct objects, indirect objects, adverbial objectives, appositives, and nominatives of address.

A. 1. Officer Brady, give me your report.
   2. The freshman girls on the winning team were Kathleen and I.
   3. Hydrogen is the lightest of all substances.
   4. For vitamins the soldiers in the desert drink quantities of lime juice.

5. Frank Buck, the big game hunter, is a friend of birds.
6. Carlsbad Caverns are one thousand feet deep.

B. 1. By mistake my brother sent my cousin and me two miles out of the way.
2. During the Middle Ages barley was the most important bread grain of Central Europe.
3. The Quartermaster Corps has trained thousands of carefully selected dogs for various jobs in the Army.
4. In World War I, Major General Ernest Swinton, a retired British officer, invented the tank.
5. Read me the last line of that paragraph about the use of camouflage, Alfred.
6. In airplane vernacular the ceiling is the distance between the ground and the base of a cloud layer.

Practice 6.   Recognizing the Parts of the Sentence

Diagram the following sentences.

OR

Copy the subject and the verb of each sentence. Copy also the italicized words, leaving a blank line after each line you write, and write above each word *p.a.* (predicate adjective), *p.n.* (predicate nominative), *d.o.* (direct object), *o.p.* (object of preposition), *i.o.* (indirect object), *ap.*, (appositive), or *a.o.* (adverbial objective).

A. 1. Selma Lagerlöf, the famous *author*, was the *daughter* of a Swedish *soldier.*
2. During her *childhood* she became seriously *ill* and could not walk for many *years.*
3. For consolation the little girl, an eager *student*, turned to books of poetry and *prose.*
4. Sometimes she wrote *plays* for her own *amusement.*
5. One *day* Selma made a great *decision.*
6. She would be a *teacher.*
7. With *difficulty* Lieutenant Lagerlöf and his wife scraped together the *money* for her *education.*
8. Ten *years* later Selma was a capable young *teacher* in an elementary *school.*
9. She was *happy* in her work and for a long while had written *nothing.*

B. 1. Then one day she saw the *announcement* of a contest for *writers.*
2. In her childhood Lieutenant Lagerlöf had told *Selma* weird *tales* of the deeds of Gosta Berling, a Scandinavian *hero.*
3. Now Selma wrote down the stories from *memory* and entered *them* in the *contest.*
4. To her great *amazement* the judges gave *her* the *prize.*
5. Soon Brandes, a famous Danish *scholar*, was singing the *praises* of Gosta Berling.
6. The book, in his *opinion*, was a *masterpiece.*
7. Overnight Selma Lagerlöf became *famous.*

8. People journeyed many *miles* for a glimpse of the young *author.*

9. In 1909 the Nobel prize for literature, a *gift* of $40,000, was presented to *her.*

TEST 1B *(Mastery).* Parts of the Simple Sentence

Median—16.8

Copy the italicized words in a column and number them 1 to 25 Then, using these abbreviations, indicate the use in the sentence of each word. Write the abbreviations in a column to the right of the words.

s.s. — simple subject	*o.p.* — object of preposition
v. — verb	*i.o.* — indirect object
p.a. — predicate adjective	*ap.* — appositive
p.n. — predicate nominative	*n.a.* — nominative of address
d.o. — direct object	*a.o.* — adverbial objective

1. The next *day* Sally, a little black and tan *puppy*, became a *member* of Aunt Ida's *household.*

2. Is that old *man* a *relative* of *yours, Bob?*

3. A few *hours* later Elizabeth Ann was *feeling* small and *lonely* and just a little *homesick.*

4. For Christmas, Grandmother gave *Helen* a little silk *bag* with four shiny new *quarters.*

5. The Indians adopted the *captive* as a member of their tribe and *taught him* all their customs.

6. Dash, the seasoned *actor*, took his *cue* with a friendly yip.

7. The chief *source* of radium is *pitchblende*, a shiny black *rock.*

8. Were the *children* of colonial parents *helpful* around the home?

PARTICIPLE, VERBAL NOUN, AND INFINITIVE

27. **Verbals are forms of the verb that do not make statements, ask questions, or give commands.** Verbals are used as adjectives, adverbs, and nouns. Like verbs that say, ask, and command, verbals take objects and predicate nominatives and are modified by adverbs. The three classes of verbals are participles, verbal nouns (or gerunds), and infinitives.

28. **A participle is a form of the verb that is used as an adjective.** It is *part* adjective and *part* verb. Many participles end in *ing* and *ed.*

Perched upon a high boulder at the edge of a *melting* snowbank, Oreos, the mountain goat, lazily chewed his cud. (*Melting* immediately precedes the noun modified and may be called a participle or an adjective.)

Shifting grenades from one pocket to another, the men twisted and turned in the crowded barges.

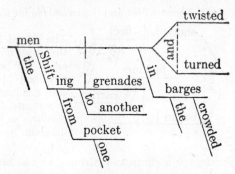

A participle is placed on a broken line. The horizontal line shows that it is a verb form; the slanting line, that it is used as an adjective. As an adjective the participle *shifting* modifies *men;* as a verb it has a direct object, *grenades.* *Crowded* is an adjective. The phrase *in the crowded barges,* which modifies both *twisted* and *turned,* is joined to the single predicate line.

Practice 7. Telling the Use of Participles

Diagram the following sentences.

OR

Copy every participle and explain its use in the sentence.

A. 1. Standing in the rear cockpit, Sandy adjusted his goggles.
   2. Planes circled the island, towing their sleeve-gunnery targets behind them.
   3. The first subway, invented by Alfred Beach, was opened in New York City in 1870.
   4. Battling past mined hill positions, the soldiers of the Fifth Army swept onto the plain of Naples.

B. 1. Led by their gallant captain, the soldiers crossed the bridge at Dieppe amid terrific enemy fire.
   2. Around the pitted beachhead were scattered the remains of German aircraft destroyed in the fierce bombing attacks. (*Pitted* is an adjective. Diagram *bombing* like an adjective.)
   3. The porcupine goes placidly through life, sometimes dawdling for a whole day in a tree with delicious-tasting bark.
   4. Quickly manning their stations, the gunners and observers searched the sky for enemy planes.

29. A verbal noun (gerund) is an *ing* form of the verb that is used as a noun.

(Object of Preposition) After *sipping* fragrant tea from little bowls, we went into a large courtyard.
(Subject) *Hunting* for butterfly and moth eggs is a fascinating pastime in spring and summer.
(Direct Object) Patricia enjoys *keeping* house.
(Predicate Nominative) An important industry of Australia is *raising* sheep.
(Appositive) My favourite exercise, *walking* through the woods, is particularly enjoyable in the autumn.

1. At 1300 we sighted the enemy fleet and began *looking* for the carrier.

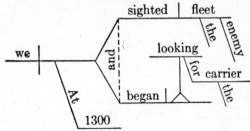

The verbal noun *looking* is the direct object of the verb *began*. When the subject, the direct object, or the predicate nominative is a phrase or a clause, it is placed on a platform as indicated in the diagram.

2. *Grazing* with livestock is a cheap and effective way of *harvesting* pasture and forage crops.

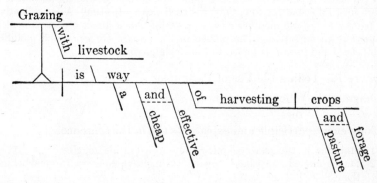

The verbal noun *grazing* is the subject of the verb *is*. As a noun the verbal noun *harvesting* is used as the object of the preposition *of;* as a verb it has a direct object, *crops*.

Practice 8. Explaining the Use of Verbal Nouns

Diagram the following sentences.

OR

Copy every verbal noun and explain its use in the sentence.

A. 1. Clyde enjoys playing golf.
   2. Fishing by torchlight was once a popular sport in Hawaii.
   3. The minimum cost of training a bomber crew is forty thousand dollars. (*Forty thousand* is one modifier.)
   4. His new hobby, building model planes, is one shared by many high school boys. (*High school* is one modifier.)

B. 1. Men in the Air Force often wear fur-lined jackets or electrically heated suits for flying at high altitudes.
   2. Part of the fun of photography is developing your own negatives.
   3. Much of the success in growing crops depends upon preparing the seed bed and planting the seed.
   4. Aerial navigation is the science of piloting a plane from one point to another and establishing its position at any time.

30. An infinitive is a verb form ordinarily introduced by *to* and used as a noun, an adjective, or an adverb.

(Adjective) The radioman, with headphones clapped to his ears, sat listening for orders *to proceed.* (*To proceed* modifies *orders.*)

(Adverb) Hamlin Garland once set out *to look* for gold in Alaska. (*To look* modifies *set.*)

(Noun) *To help* a ship in distress is the first rule of the sea. (Subject of verb.)

(Noun) Winnie-the-Pooh sat down at the foot of the tree, put his head between his paws, and began *to think.* (Direct object of verb.)

(Noun) Part of Hamlin Garland's job was *to keep* the water jug cool and well filled. (Predicate nominative.)

1. Crop rotation helps to control weeds and plant diseases.

The infinitive phrase, *to control weeds and plant diseases,* is the direct object of the verb *helps.*

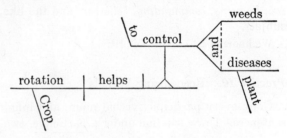

2. Planes from a near-by airfield occasionally swooped down to practise a dive against a ship.

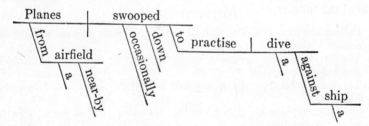

The infinitive phrase, *to practise a dive against a ship,* is used as an adverb to modify the verb *swooped.*

To, the sign of the infinitive, is commonly omitted after *bid, dare, need, see, make, let, hear, please, feel, help,* and sometimes after a few other verbs.

After a while Serge saw an old woman *stop* in front of his window.

Practice 9. Explaining the Use of Infinitives

Diagram the following sentences.

OR

Copy every infinitive and explain its use in the sentence.

A. 1. To enlist in the Cadet Nurse Corps is the main ambition of my sister.
2. The boats to carry the attacking force of marines were manned by coast guardsmen.
3. The enemy plan was to smash the airfield on Midway.
4. From the heights of Bataan the Japs began to shell Corregidor.

B. 1. Before the North African invasion several British-American units were equipped with Arctic apparel to deceive any inquisitive observer.
2. The only way to save the small force of marines was to evacuate them.
3. Edison tried to send a message by train whistle.
4. Using a parachute to screen the fire on the side toward the sea, the aviators flashed signals in Morse code.

31. After verbs of *making, telling, letting, wishing, expecting, thinking, knowing, commanding, believing,* **and the like, the infinitive has a subject.**

We know *him* to be the culprit.

Practice 10.   Recognizing Verbals

Copy every participle, verbal noun, and infinitive in the following sentences. Draw one line under a <u>participle</u>, two lines under a <u>verbal noun</u>, and a dotted line under an infinitive. Copy the whole participle or verbal noun, whether it is one, two, or three words. Include the sign *to* of the infinitive if it is expressed.

A. 1. Pulling out of a dive, the pilot of the Thunderbolt spotted a Japanese cruiser. (*Out of* is a preposition.)
2. The breakers took impudent delight in tossing us against the black rocks along the coast.
3. The British flat-top, having wrecked a German carrier, was now being bombed.
4. The soldiers, armed with grenades, braved a rain of enemy fire to reach the building.
5. The ship was travelling at full speed, making every possible manoeuvre to elude the attacking planes.
6. A profitable trade carried on in colonial times by travelling workers was making candles.

B. 1. Entertaining children by telling them stories was a favourite pastime of Lewis Carroll.
2. Horses tied at hitching posts along the street reared wildly to get free.
3. The corporal in charge came out, crouching to get through the low entrance of the pillbox.
4. Picking huckleberries was a good excuse for wearing wornout clothes.
5. In hand-to-hand fighting the marines shoved back the Japs through jungles infested with snakes and cannibals.
6. The Western cowboys show great skill in handling the lasso for roping cattle.

32. A phrase is a group of related words which does not contain a subject and a predicate. Phrases may be used as nouns, adjectives, or adverbs.

At an early age (adverb) an Indian boy learned *to follow the trails* (noun) *of men and beasts* (adjective).

a. A participial phrase consists of a participle and the words which modify it or complete its meaning.

The children watched the seals *swimming happily about*.

b. An infinitive phrase consists of an infinitive and the words which modify it or complete its meaning.

Roger was sent by the Principal *to help Arnold*.

COMPOUND AND COMPLEX SENTENCES

TEST 2A (*Diagnostic*). Kinds of Sentences

Classify the following sentences by writing *S* (simple), *Cd* (compound), or *Cx* (complex) on your paper after the number of each sentence.

1. When the passengers went on deck after dinner, they noticed that the wind had increased and that snow was falling.
2. The children sat on top of the scraggly old fence like bright-coloured snowbirds, waiting for the king to pass by.
3. Colonial churches were very cold in winter, and only by the aid of foot warmers and wood stoves could the congregation keep from freezing.
4. Jimmy lowered his voice as the big farm hand came around the corner with an armful of cornstalks.

5. The puma picked up the tawny ball of fur by the tough skin on the back of its neck and carried it to the foot of the cliff.
6. Never trouble another for what you can do yourself.
7. Thomas Edison possessed the invaluable gift of getting from a book just what he wanted and nothing else.
8. The revolving beacon on the airplane field threw its beams into the snow-filled darkness to guide the pilot bringing the holiday mail from Montreal.
9. The glow of the sun from above, its thousandfold reflection from the waves, the sea water that fell and dried upon me, caking my very lips with salt, combined to make my throat burn and my brain ache.
10. A bowl of warm barley porridge was brought to us, and with a big wooden spoon I fed my little charge his frugal supper.

33. A compound sentence is made up of two or more independent statements, questions, or commands.

Suddenly a window above the two Rangers opened, and a German soldier looked out.

The two independent statements joined are:
1. Suddenly a window above the two Rangers opened.
2. A German soldier looked out.

Each plane was assigned specific targets, and the bombardiers carried out their duties with admirable precision.

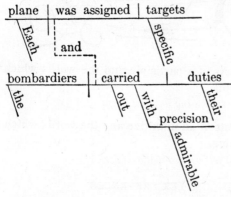

To diagram a compound sentence, (1) diagram the two independent statements, or principal clauses, (2) join the predicate verbs of the principal clauses with a dotted line, and (3) place the conjunction connecting the clauses on the dotted line.

34. The independent statements, questions, or commands joined to form a compound sentence are called principal clauses.

35. A clause is a part of a sentence that has a subject and a predicate.

When the newspapers speak of the ABC countries of South America, | they are referring to Argentina, Brazil, and Chile. (The two clauses of this sentence are separated by a vertical line.)

36. Co-ordinate conjunctions connect words, phrases, and clauses of equal rank. Principal clauses are of equal rank. Co-ordinate conjunctions used to connect the clauses of a compound sentence are *and, but, or, nor, for, so, yet,* and *while* (meaning *but*).

Not all deserts are made up entirely of sand, *nor* are they uninhabited by living creatures.

37. A subordinate clause is used as a noun, an adjective, or an adverb. Two tests of a subordinate clause are: (1) as a rule, it does not make complete sense when standing alone; (2) usually a subordinate conjunction or a relative pronoun is either expressed or can be supplied without spoiling the sense.

(Noun) Dr. Iago Galdston states *that half of all disabling diseases begin with a cold in the head.* (*That* introduces the clause.)

(Adjective) The sheep were forced to walk through a tank containing a disinfectant solution *which freed them from insect pests.* (*Which* introduces the clause.)

(Adverb) A little later in the afternoon, *when the rose of sunset lay on the snowy hills,* a stranger knocked at the door of Navelle's home. (*When* introduces the clause.)

38. A sentence with a principal clause and one or more subordinate clauses is called a complex sentence.

Although the other villagers lived in one-room huts of mud thatched with straw, Heera Singh had a two-storied house with a tile roof and a central courtyard.

39. A noun clause is used as a noun. It may be:

(Subject of Verb) *What makes the Grand Canyon a scenic feature of the first order* is its marvellously variegated volcanic colouring.

(Object of Verb) From the heights above the city the enemy could see *that everyone of their shells hit.*

(Object of Preposition) During the Renaissance, Francis Bacon laid the foundation of *what may be called the modern laboratory method of research in natural science.*

(Predicate Nominative) One of Sir Ronald Ross's greatest disappointments was *that the world did not make better use of his scientific instruction on tropical sanitation.*

(Appositive) Dr. Howard made the statement *that the medicinal properties of Hot Springs were known to the Indians long before the Spanish invasion.*

(Appositive) The discovery *that no two fingerprints in the world are exactly alike* has been of great importance in criminal investigation.

1. That we have a balanced diet is very important to our health.

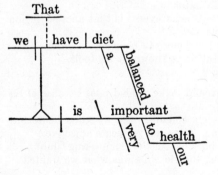

The noun clause is the subject of the verb *is* and is placed on a platform above the subject line. The conjunction *that* introduces the noun clause.

2. Is it true that successful rocket ships have been built?

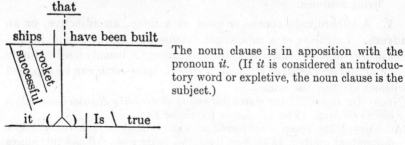

The noun clause is in apposition with the pronoun *it*. (If *it* is considered an introductory word or expletive, the noun clause is the subject.)

3. Along the shore signal lights flashed the warning of the approach of what an observation plane identified as enemy aircraft.

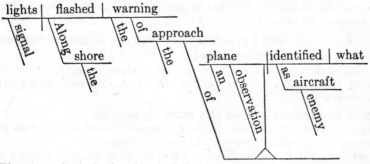

The noun clause is the object of the preposition *of*. *What* is the direct object of *identified*.

Practice 11. Recognizing Noun Clauses

Diagram the following sentences.

OR

For each sentence write the noun clause, underline the subject once and the verb twice, and explain how the noun clause is used.

A 1. Paul Eipper believes that snakes do not hypnotize their prey.
   2. What I want is to become a navigator in a D.C.4.
   3. An interesting feature of the Carlsbad Caverns is that another region to explore lies beyond each cave.
   4. Thomas Edison once said that the American people eat too much.
   5. It is an old saying that the workman is known by his tools.
   6. Do you know what blind flying is?

B. 1. Everyone thought that Curly would make a good pilot because of his initiative and coolness.
   2. That my brother was immediately commissioned a second lieutenant was due to his C.O.T.C. training. (*Due* is a predicate adjective.)
   3. Do you know who was elected president of the Engineering Club?
   4. The little cottage nestled among the old elms was what we wanted.

5. Give this package to whoever comes to the door.

6. Major Alexander de Seversky made the statement that victory can come through air power.

40. An adjective clause modifies a noun or a pronoun.

During the next week Dad insisted on running off the reels for everybody *who came into the house.* (*Who came into the house* modifies the pronoun *everybody.*)

a. An adjective clause may be attached to the word it modifies by:

(1) A relative pronoun (*who, which,* and *that*)

The battle cry of Carlson's Raiders was "Gung Ho!" *which* is Chinese for *work—harmony.*

(2) A subordinate conjunction

Fearing Indian raids, Miles Standish, the captain of the Pilgrim militia, trained his men for the time *when* battle should come.

b. The connecting word may be omitted.

The three skippers were there to give the survivors of the *Judith* a warm welcome and to marvel at the yarn (which) they spun.

1. We were greeted by heavy antiaircraft fire, which flowered around us like big black puff balls.

A dotted line connects the relative pronoun *which* with its antecedent *fire.* Since modifiers are joined by slant lines to the words they modify, the dotted line shows also that the clause modifies *fire.*

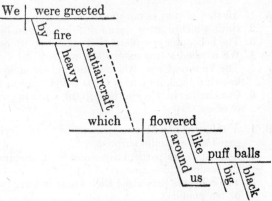

2. The enemy soldiers retreated to caves in the cliffs, where they battled to the death

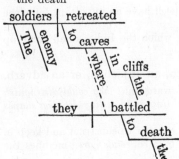

Where, a conjunction connecting the two clauses, is placed on a slanting dotted line between the adjective clause and the word the clause modifies.

3. The complicated machines of to-day require for their construction **raw** materials of which our grandfathers never heard.

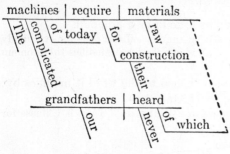

The relative pronoun *which* is connected with its antecedent *materials* by a dotted line. The adjective clause modifies *materials.*

Practice 12.   Recognizing Adjective Clauses

Diagram the following sentences.

OR

For each sentence write the adjective clause, underline the subject once and the verb twice, and explain how the clause is used.

A. 1. All that glitters is not gold.
   2. Birds which destroy harmful insects should be protected.
   3. The helicopter is a plane that is held up by horizontal propellers.
   4. We recalled a tiny café where we had had a delicious fish concoction.
   5. The Victoria Cross, which is the highest-ranking decoration, was established in 1856. (*Victoria Cross* is the name of the medal.)
   6. Our circling barges churned up the water in great swells, which splashed over us.

B. 1. A tall, red-haired young man, who was frying bacon over a stove, gazed at us in mild surprise.
   2. Lemmings are particularly common in the mountainous regions where the juniper tree grows.
   3. The colonists purchased their sugar in huge loaves which weighed nine or ten pounds.
   4. The two white-robed figures silently disappeared in the direction from which they had come.
   5. The conditions under which people dwell have an important influence upon their health and character.
   6. By the beach lay the skin canoes in which the Indians had come up the river.

41. An adverb clause modifies a verb, an adjective, or an adverb.

Cautiously Renny and his sister crept forward *until they could distinguish dim shapes in the fog.* (The clause *until they could distinguish dim shapes in the fog* modifies the verb *crept.*)

In most parts of Holland waterways are cheaper to construct and keep in operation *than railroads.* (The clause *than railroads* [*are*] modifies the adjective *cheaper.*)

George Washington's hands were so big *he had to have his gloves made to order.* (The clause *he had to have his gloves made to order* modifies the adverb *so.*)

1. Scattered rifle shots marked the advance of the marines as they crawled through the tall grass and coconut groves.

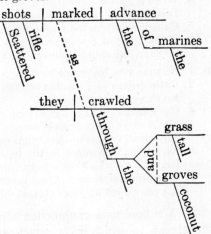

The slanting dotted line shows that the clause *as they crawled through the tall grass and coconut groves* modifies *marked.* The subordinate conjunction *as* is placed on this dotted line.

2. To attract birds to a garden, a birdbath is more important than food.

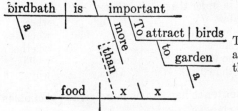

The adverb clause modifies the adverb *more.* The two *x*'s show that *is important* is understood.

3. The helicopter can hover over one spot as long as its fuel supply holds out.

The adverb clause modifies the adverb *as.*

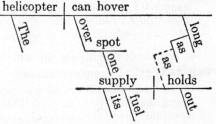

Practice 13. Recognizing Adverb Clauses

Diagram the following sentences.

OR

For each sentence write the adverb clause, underline the subject once and the verb twice, and explain how each clause is used.

A. 1. When an American sailor wins the same decoration twice, a Gold Star is given in place of the second award.
2. When the leading Mitsubishi came within range, he was a target for the concerted fire of twenty-two guns.
3. A young eel is so transparent that print can be read through its body.
4. When a pilot has twenty-five missions to his credit, he is in line for the Distinguished Service Cross and a long leave.
5. Canada produces more asbestos than any other country.
6. If the wing of a single-engine plane is located at the bottom of the fuselage, the ship is called a low-wing monoplane.

B. 1. No man ever had a harder struggle for success than Frank Woolworth.
2. Little groups of Canadian soldiers were strung out as far as we could see through the lifting fog.
3. Our soldiers held the fort as long as their food and medicine lasted.
4. The deck of the transport was so crowded with barges and gear that only small groups of men could exercise at a time.
5. As the plane plunged to the bottom of the ocean, a deflated rubber boat and a cushion came to the surface.
6. When the horseless or steam carriage was first used, drivers frequently stopped to get up more steam.

42. A subordinate conjunction connects a subordinate clause with the clause to which it is attached. Frequently used subordinate conjunctions are:

after	before	in order that	that	whenever
although	but that	lest	though	where
as	even if	provided that	till	whereas
as if	for	since	unless	whether
as though	how	so that	until	while
because	if	than	when	why

43. A compound-complex sentence has two or more principal clauses and one or more subordinate clauses.

Now and then a blue cart filled with peasants drew aside *as the tourists approached,* or a shepherd in a vividly embroidered cloak guided his flock into a huddle at the roadside and stood watching, pipe in mouth, *as they passed.* (The two subordinate clauses are in italics.)

44. A complex sentence in which a subordinate clause is itself complex is called complex-complex.

I remembered what Silver had said about the current that drifts northward along the whole west coast of Treasure Island. (*What Silver had said about the current* is a noun clause used as direct object of the verb *remembered; that drifts northward along the whole west coast of Treasure Island* is an adjective clause modifying *current.*)

Practice 14. Recognizing Clauses

Diagram the following sentences.

OR

For each sentence write the subordinate clause, underline the subject once and the verb twice, identify the clause as a noun, an adverb, or an adjective clause, and tell how it is used in the sentence.

A. 1. The leaders of the United Nations now know that the backbone of air power is the heavy bomber.
  2. Alexander Hamilton re-entered New York to the deafening shouts of a multitude that escorted him to his doorway.
  3. Juanita tickled her baby brother under the chin so that he would laugh at her.
  4. Antarctic explorers say that penguins are totally unafraid of man.
  5. Moist paper is more clearly printed from engraved plates than dry paper.
  6. In 1772 the first umbrella in the United States was shipped from India to Baltimore, where it was regarded as an item of feminine apparel.

B. 1. A high wind rattled the windows of the deserted old house until it creaked like a ship in a heavy sea.
  2. What had happened to the little mascot of Company E was a deep mystery.
  3. The stranger told the girls fascinating tales of the wandering gypsies who pitched their tents on the high steppes of eastern Hungary.
  4. The second mate made the discovery that the ship had grounded on the mud flats of Smith Bay.
  5. To the colonists starvation and disease were worse enemies than the Indians.
  6. The Louvre, in which the kings of France once lived, now contains the largest picture gallery in the world.
  7. That we had no place to land soon became evident.

Practice 15. Recognizing Subordinate Clauses

Write the subordinate clauses in the following sentences, underline a simple subject once and a predicate verb twice, label a clause *n.*, *adj.*, or *adv.*, and indicate what word or words an adjective or an adverb clause modifies and how a noun clause is used.

Examples:

  a. Benjamin Franklin gained fame among the scientists of the world by a kite-flying experiment through which he proved that lightning and electricity are one.

  through which he proved—adj., *experiment*

  that lightning and electricity are one—n., direct object of *proved*

  b. There are trees in the New England forests that are still called the King's trees, because in colonial days an officer in the British navy walked through the forest with a branding axe and marked every tree that would be suitable for a mast on one of His Majesty's vessels.

  that are still called the King's trees—adj., *trees*

because in colonial days an officer in the British navy walked through the

forest with a branding axe and marked every tree—adv., *are called*

that would be suitable for a mast on one of His Majesty's vessels—adj., *tree*

A. 1. That Louis Agassiz was one of the great naturalists of all time is the opinion of authorities.
   2. At the age of fourteen he wrote his parents that he would like to become an author on scientific subjects.
   3. Mr. Agassiz's answer was that the boy might study the natural sciences at the College of Lausanne and at the universities of Zurich, Heidelberg, and Munich.
   4. Whatever Agassiz undertook at college was well done.
   5. In his room several lively monkeys and a tub full of fish bore evidence to the fact that Agassiz had not lost his early interest in nature.
   6. About this time he wrote to his father, "I wish it may be said of Louis Agassiz that he was the first naturalist of his time, a good citizen, and a good son."

B. 1. When a well-known naturalist who had been commissioned by the king of Bavaria to edit a book on Brazilian fishes died in 1829, Agassiz took up the task and published a comprehensive volume.
   2. When his work led him to study fossil fishes preserved in rocks, Agassiz became interested in geology, in which he soon made himself an expert.
   3. Agassiz proved that most of Europe was once covered by glaciers, which had played an important role in the formation of the earth.
   4. In 1846 Agassiz, who was deeply in debt, sailed for Boston, where he had been invited to deliver a course of lectures at the Lowell Institute.
   5. Because Agassiz showed in his addresses that he was a master in his field, Harvard University offered him a position on its staff.
   6. Although many European countries extended tempting offers, Agassiz refused to leave the United States, where he worked happily until his death in 1873.

Practice 16. Building Complex and Complex-complex Sentences

Using the ideas in each of the following groups of sentences, build one forceful complex or complex-complex sentence.

Example:

(Simple Sentences) Captain Cook and his companions landed on the shores of a bay. A naturalist in the party found many different kinds of plants there. So he named the bay Botany Bay.
(Complex-Complex Sentence) Captain Cook and his companions landed on the shores of a bay which a naturalist in the party named Botany Bay because he found there many different kinds of plants.

A. 1. On the next block a hooting mob of boys and girls pursued a sprinkling truck. The truck washed the street with a strong sideward current of water.
   2. Emily and Henry knew that the salvation of their home depended on their efforts. They worked till midnight in the cornfield.

3. Young Ronald arrived in England for the first time. Then he was taken to the Isle of Wight. Here he lived with an elderly uncle and aunt.
4. In the seventeenth century the castle was purchased by a dashing French pirate. His pointed beard was a peculiar dark bluish colour. Therefore he was nicknamed Édouard de la Barbe Bleue.
5. A squirrel was leaping from tree to tree. It fell and broke its paw. Saint Florentin placed the broken paw in splints.
6. We arrived by train two days later. Rita and Horace were waiting for us at the tiny railroad station. The station is in sight of the long, white-walled house.
7. Major André boarded the *Vulture*. His youthful head carried the details of the scheme. By it he hoped to win the war practically singlehanded.
8. Mary Elizabeth waved good-bye to Nancy and the other passengers. Then she secured her portfolio from Nancy's cabin and carried it to the middle of the ship. Here a consignment of grain was stored.

B. 1. I strolled through the peaceful streets of Santa Maria del Carmine one November afternoon. A small boy told me a bloodcurdling tale. I was sharing some tangerines with him.
2. The picnic lunch was all packed. Then Sarah went out and rang the ship's bell. This hung near the kitchen door.
3. Spider monkeys often wrap their tails about themselves. They are very sensitive to cold. Their tails keep them warm.
4. Washington made Clinton think he intended to attack New York. Then he slipped away southward.
5. His leg obviously hurt him sharply when he moved. Yet it was at a good, rattling rate that he managed to trail himself across the quarter-deck.
6. The captain and the spy were in the adjoining room. They were speaking very low. Not a sound was heard. Yet Major Williams guessed the subject of the conversation.
7. Marion Tyler thought little of the manuscript of her first story. She consigned it to the wastebasket. Her mother rescued it.
8. I remember the appearance of his coat. This he himself patched up-stairs in his room. After a while it was nothing but patches.

TEST 2B (*Mystery*). Kinds of Sentences
Median—6.7

Classify the following sentences by writing *S* (simple), *Cd* (compound), or *Cx* (complex) on your paper after the number of each sentence.

1. Timothy slid down from a load of hay and came in to see if dinner was ready.
2. Crouched in a corner of the dungeon, the cat howled loudly for someone to come down and get him.
3. After deciding where you are going and making reservations, you must next consider your wardrobe.
4. The dirigible fought every yard of the way, and throughout the night an anxious world waited for a message from the airship.

5. John Ryan clattered into the city at eight o'clock on the morning of January 30 and placed the message in the hands of the governor.
6. The captain of the nearest ship shouted through his brass trumpet, but the skipper of the *Cecile* had no voice to answer back.
7. As the last rays of twilight dwindled and disappeared, absolute blackness settled down on Treasure Island.
8. Marine zoology students at the University of Miami attend class in diving helmets and take notes under water on zinc tablets with yellow wax crayon.
9. Marta and Emil were almost sorry when they saw the white gateposts before their little house, glistening with snow and moonbeams.
10. Benjamin Franklin once said, "I never sought an office, never refused one, and never resigned."

Enter your mark on your achievement graph.

Grammatical Usage

RECENTLY a radio quiz programme presented a contestant with ten dollars for knowing the answer to a grammatical puzzler. A knowledge of grammatical usage will bring you a cash bonus, too, for the better jobs go to those who express themselves correctly and forcefully.

CORRECT PRONOUNS

TEST 3A (*Diagnostic*). Pronoun

In each of the following which pronoun is correct or preferred? On your paper write the answer after the number of the sentence. (Right — Wrong = Score)

1. Ferrari offered the hand of his daughter to —— made the best violin. (whoever, whomever)
2. The church officials issued a solemn warning to Galileo, ——, they said, was printing statements contradictory to the Holy Writ. (who, whom)
3. Everyone at the minstrel show enjoyed —— immensely. (himself, themselves)
4. The ballad is passed down from generation to generation; —— usually based on a heroic deed or a terrible tragedy. (it is, they are)
5. The success of Class Night depends on —— doing his part. (everyone, everyone's)
6. To his horror Dr. Beebe found himself in the presence of a giant cobra, —— fortunately failed to notice the naturalist. (that, which, who)
7. Frantically the men on board the ship pulled in the diver, —— they feared was seriously injured. (who, whom)
8. Burton was surprised at —— offering to help him build the birdhouse. (me, my)
9. The next morning Carlton and —— set out at five o'clock for Loon Lake. (I, myself)
10. The Ancient Mariner told his terrible story to those —— he thought would profit by the tale. (who, whom)
11. The average buyer is a question asker, and a salesman must be able to answer —— questions. (his, their)
12. Joan Deary, —— I think is a senior in Alma College, has offered to tutor me in Latin this summer. (who, whom)
13. If you see a pupil throwing papers on the floor, remind —— that wastebaskets are more than mere decorations for the classroom. (him, them)
14. The persecuted and poverty-stricken —— the governor welcomed to the colony helped to build a great commonwealth. (who, whom)
15. The king promised a royal reward to —— made the most beautiful lace for the little princess Maria. (whoever, whomever)

511

16. In India lives the mongoose, the only animal —— can catch and kill the deadly cobra. (that, what, who)
17. No one can study effectively when there is noise around——. (him, them)
18. Whenever the monk found a wounded bird or a suffering animal, he did his best to nurse —— back to health and strength. (it, them)
19. Neither Harold nor Albert finished —— homework. (his, their)
20. If you neglected some of your work during the first third, you may hand ——in now but will receive reduced credit. (it, them)

Case of Pronouns

45. The subject of a verb (except of an infinitive) is in the nominative case. The case of a pronoun depends upon its use in its own clause.

He and Bob manage a small chicken farm after school.
Celia's brother Gerald is six inches taller than *she*. (*She* is the subject of the verb *is* understood.)
Those are the girls I met at the skating rink. (Not "them.")

a. An expression like *he says*, *I think*, or *I suppose* between *who* and its verb does not change the case of the pronoun. The case-form of the relative pronouns *who* and *whoever* is determined by the use of the pronoun in its own clause.

Who did she say sang the lead in *Naughty Marietta?* (*Who* is the subject of *sang*.)
The governor praised the work of the "bondadiers," *who* he said had sold or taken pledges for $250,000,000 worth of bonds. (*Who* is the subject of *had sold* and *taken; he said* is parenthetic.)
For the task of building a pontoon bridge across the swift stream, the lieutenant picked men *who* he knew were expert swimmers. (The three clauses are *for the task of building a pontoon bridge across the swift stream the lieutenant picked men; he knew;* and *who were expert swimmers. Who* is the subject of *were*.)

b. Do not let *who* or *whoever*, when the subject of a verb, be attracted into the objective case by a preceding verb or preposition.

Give the message to *whoever* answers the telephone. (*Whoever* is the subject of *answers*, not the object of *to*. The object of *to* is the noun clause *whoever answers the telephone*.)

46. The verb *to be* and other linking verbs take the same case after them as before them. *To be* never takes an object. A linking verb joins a predicate adjective or a predicate nominative to the subject.

Was it *he* who joined the Air Raid Patrol? (*He* is a predicate nominative.)
The villagers often wondered *who* Mr. Stafford's mysterious visitor really was. (*Who* is the predicate nominative after the verb *was*.)
I believed my masked visitor to be *her*. (*Visitor*, the subject of the infinitive *to be*, is in the objective case.)

47. Direct objects of verbs, indirect objects, and objects of prepositions are in the objective case.

(Direct Object) The scout *whom* Colonel Cochran *had sent* ahead to locate the enemy returned with an accurate report.

(Indirect Object) Who gave Fred and *him* that set of tools?

(Object of Preposition) That morning in front of the entire regiment Colonel Ryan presented the Distinguished Service Cross to Corporal Faust and *me*.

To determine the correct case of a pronoun in an inverted sentence, arrange the sentence in the grammatical or natural order: (1) subject and modifiers; (2) verb; (3) object, predicate adjective, or predicate nominative.

1. (Who, Whom) do you think will win the scavenger hunt?

(Natural Order) You do think (who, whom) will win the scavenger hunt? (*Who* is the subject of the verb *will win*. The noun clause *who will win the scavenger hunt* is the direct object of *do think*.)

2. (Who, Whom) do you think I met on Connor Avenue yesterday?

(Natural Order) You do think I met (who, whom) on Connor Avenue yesterday? (*Whom* is the direct object of the verb *met*.)

NOTE "Who is that package for?" "Who does the book belong to?" "Select for your captain whoever you want," and similar expressions are correct colloquial or informal English. The formal English sentences are: "For whom is that package?" "To whom does the book belong?" "Select for your captain whomever you want."

48. An appositive agrees in case with the word to which it refers.

This term our school is sending two students, Francis Lake and *me*, to the convention of the Columbia Scholastic Press Association. (*Students* is the direct object of *is sending*. The objective *me* is correct because it is in apposition with *students*.)

49. The subject of an infinitive is in the objective case. After verbs of *making, telling, letting, wishing, expecting, thinking, knowing, commanding, believing,* **and the like, the infinitive has a subject.**

I told *him* to meet me at the main entrance to the Maple Leaf Gardens. (*Him* is the subject of the infinitive *to meet*.)

50. A pronoun modifying a verbal noun is in the possessive case.

I was surprised to hear of *his* joining the Navy on his seventeenth birthday.

Kinds and Forms of Pronouns

1. Personal Pronouns

First Person

	SINGULAR	PLURAL
Nominative	I	we
Possessive	my, mine	our, ours
Objective	me	us

Second Person

SINGULAR AND PLURAL

Nominative	you
Possessive	your, yours
Objective	you

Third Person

	SINGULAR			PLURAL
	Masculine	Feminine	Neuter	
Nominative	he	she	it	they
Possessive	his	her, hers	its	their, theirs
Objective	him	her	it	them

2. Relative Pronouns

SINGULAR AND PLURAL

Nominative	who	which	what	that	whoever
Possessive	whose	whose			whose-ever
Objective	whom	which	what	that	whomever

3. Demonstrative Pronouns

SINGULAR	PLURAL
this	these
that	those

4. Compound Personal Pronouns

	SINGULAR	PLURAL
First person	myself	ourselves
Second person	yourself	yourselves
Third person	himself, herself, itself	themselves

Practice 1. Using Correct Pronouns

Supply the correct or preferred pronoun and explain its use in the sentence.

A. 1. Charlotte Brontë, ——, some critics think, was one of the most important English novelists, had a hard and lonely life. (who, whom)
2. For many years she and her sisters, Emily and Anne Brontë, were completely under the domination of their father, —— has been described as a man of cold and harsh nature. (who, whom)
3. Branwell, the only brother of the Brontë sisters, —— Emily in particular loved dearly, was an idler and a drunkard. (who, whom)
4. Always, however, his fond sisters cherished hopes of —— writing a wonderful poem or story. (him, his)
5. During the dreary years on the Yorkshire moor the three girls, ——, we know from their books, were often lonely and unhappy, turned to writing as an emotional outlet. (who, whom)
6. In 1847 Charlotte published her novel about Jane Eyre, ——, the author tells us, was created to prove that heroines may be small and plain. (who, whom)

B. 1. Charlotte did not at first admit that the author of *Jane Eyre* was ——.
(her, she)
   2. For some time the question, "—— do you suppose wrote *Jane Eyre?*"
aroused lively discussion in English literary circles. (Who, Whom)
   3. Authors and critics heaped praise on the head of —— had written the
forceful, original novel. (whoever, whomever)
   4. That same year Emily Brontë, —— most modern readers think was an
even greater writer than Charlotte, published *Wuthering Heights.*
(who, whom)
   5. Both —— and Charlotte are considered eminent British novelists.
(her, she)

Practice 2. Using Correct Pronouns

Eleven of the following sentences are wrong. Correct them, giving a
reason for each change you make.

Example:

The puppy curled up between he and I.
The puppy curled up between him and me. (*Him* and *me* are objects of
the preposition *between*.)

1. I looked around and selected a boy whom I thought would carry out my
orders intelligently.
2. Didn't you suspect that it was her?
3. Into her knitting Madame Defarge, whom everyone feared, worked the
names of people whom she considered enemies of the republic.
4. Sydney Carton, whom I think is the hero of the book, is first seen at the
trial of Charles Darnay.
5. No one in the family had heard of his sailing for Spain.
6. Distribute the rest of the posters among friends whom you know will
vote for our ticket.
7. I knew it to be he by the way he walked.
8. The men who Squire Trelawney thought were honest sailors turned out
to be bloodthirsty buccaneers.
9. Whom do you suppose dressed the kitten in baby's bonnet and sweater?
10. The time has come for we students to give our active support to the
Junior Red Cross.
11. I shall vote for whomever I think is best qualified to hold office.
12. Miss Marlowe was delighted at his offering to build a stage for the puppets.
13. Dr. Watson was surprised to see Sherlock Holmes, whom he thought was
dangerously ill with a rare tropical disease.
14. The pilot whom President Roosevelt praised in his radio address was
Captain Hewitt T. Wheless.
15. Lieutenant Pearson believes the approaching battalion to be they.
16. I recommend *Dragon Seed* to whoever wishes to read a novel about modern
China.
17. My dog enjoys me taking him for a run.

Agreement of Pronoun and Antecedent

51. A pronoun agrees with its antecedent in number, person, and

gender. Find the antecedent of the pronoun. Then decide whether the antecedent is singular or plural.

The past record of an applicant is investigated before *he* is hired.

Every pupil had an American flag in *his* right hand.

a. A collective noun takes a singular pronoun when the group is thought of and a plural pronoun when the individuals are thought of.

The crew had *its* gear in readiness for a quick take-off.

The crew discussed *their* parts in the forthcoming manoeuvres.

b. Two or more singular antecedents joined by *and* require a plural pronoun.

Correspondent Sherrod and a marine companion spent *their* first night at Tarawa in a foxhole on the beach.

c. Two or more singular antecedents joined by *or* or *nor* require singular pronouns.

Either Gary or Ray will bring *his* tennis racket to school.

d. As a rule, *each, every, either, neither, one, many a, a person,* and compounds with *body* and *one* take singular pronouns. Antecedents like *each, anyone,* and *everybody* are especially troublesome.

Each of the pilots reported that *his* mission had been successfully completed.

Every soldier and sailor in the crowd of bystanders raised *his* hand in a snappy salute as the flag passed. (Although the subject *soldier and sailor* is compound, the word *every* changes the meaning to "every one of the soldiers and sailors," treating each individually.)

e. Every pronoun should agree with its antecedent in person.

my
My mother makes *me* eat spinach, because it puts iron in ~~your~~ system.

f. *His* is generally preferable to the clumsy *his or her.*

Every pupil in Room 112 brought as *his* contribution to the scrap drive five pounds of waste paper.

g. Masculine pronouns are used in referring to most animals; neuter pronouns, in speaking of insects or small animals.

When Mrs. Kennicott entered the room, the *puppy* stood up on *his* hind legs and whined softly.

Creeping quietly up behind the *fly*, the cook demolished *it* with a vicious blow.

The *mouse* made *its* home in the granary.

h. *His* **may be used to refer to** *one.* Some authorities, however, consider *one's* better usage.

Accurate, vivid words will help one to express *his* (or *one's*) reasons for considering a particular event the biggest news of the week.

Practice 3. Using Correct Pronouns

Select the correct or preferred words. What is the antecedent of each pronoun chosen?

A. 1. Taking a picture of a person when —— not looking is often lots of fun. (he is, they are)
   2. If candidates for these scholarships are required to take an examination, when and where will —— be held? (it, they)
   3. Many a reader skips the words with which —— familiar. (he isn't, they aren't)
   4. At the first crash of thunder everyone had started for —— tent. (his, their)
   5. At the end of the summer neither of the Bennet boys had passed —— swimming test. (his, their)
   6. If Louis Pasteur or Thomas Edison had been easily discouraged, —— could never have made such great contributions to science. (he, they)
   7. It is neither polite nor fair to ridicule a loser, for —— bad enough about the defeat. (he feels, they feel)
   8. I recommend *My Friend Flicka* to anyone who wants a good book to read during —— leisure time. (his, their)

B. 1. In the Middle Ages, if one did not know Latin, —— considered uneducated. (he was, they were)
   2. When Japanese troops invaded Manchuria in 1931, the League of Nations tried to stop the aggression, but —— had no way of forcing the Japs to withdraw. (it, they)
   3. If everybody does —— share, we shall have enough gasoline, rubber, and food for the armed forces and the civilians. (his, their)
   4. Any pupil can learn to spell common words correctly if —— systematically. (he studies, they study)
   5. Everyone will do —— best to make the visitors feel at home. (his, their)
   6. A person naturally tries to secure as good clothing as possible for —— money. (his, their)
   7. If one drinks too much coffee, it speeds up —— heart, makes —— nervous, and keeps —— awake. (his, their) (him, them) (him, them)

Compound Personal Pronoun and Relative Pronoun

52. A compound personal pronoun ordinarily refers to the subject or emphasizes the noun or pronoun to which it is attached.

(Reflexive) Did Helen cut *herself* with the can opener?
(Emphatic) Joe *himself* sent to get the tickets.

53. **Most careful speakers and writers do not substitute the compound personal pronoun for the simple personal pronoun, especially in the nominative case.** "Hisself" and "theirselves" are incorrect forms.

     You   your
    ~~Yourself~~ and ‸friends are cordially invited to attend the lecture on Saturday evening.
             I
    Tomorrow Julius and ~~myself~~ are going to the aquarium to see the electric eels.

54. *Who* **refers chiefly to persons;** *which,* **to animals or things;** *that,* **to persons, animals, or things.** The relative pronoun *that* is often used in essential subordinate clauses—that is, in a clause the omission of which would change or destroy the meaning of the principal clause—but is not used in non-essential clauses.

> The Distinguished Flying Cross is awarded to any person *who* has distinguished himself by heroism or extraordinary achievement in an aerial flight.
>
> With telling precision the formation of torpedo planes launched their tin fish, *which* converged on the enemy carrier from all directions.
>
> That morning Buzz Wagner with a single P-40 had done a job *that* ordinarily would be assigned to an entire squadron. (The omission of the essential clause *that ordinarily would be assigned to an entire squadron* would change the meaning of the principal clause.)

a. *What* **never has an antecedent.** The relative pronoun *what* is equivalent to *that which.*

b. *As* **is used as a relative pronoun after** *such* **and** *same.*

My translation of the sixth sentence is the same *as* yours.

Practice 4. Choosing Correct Pronouns

Select the correct or preferred words. Give the reason for each selection. Sometimes two words are correct, but one sounds slightly better than the other.

A. 1. Such promises —— my opponent makes in his campaign speeches are difficult to fulfill. (as, that)
    2. My sister —— was married last Christmas lives in New Westminster. (which, who)
    3. In my class are sixteen boys, only five of —— were accepted by the R.C.A.F. (which, whom)
    4. This afternoon Madge, Dorothy, and —— will decorate the girls' gymnasium for the Hallowe'en dance. (I, myself)

5. Everything —— lives in the desert must learn to get along with little water. (that, which, who)
6. Mother, Dad, and —— expect to spend the Christmas vacation in Regina. (I, myself)

B. 1. France, —— happened at that time to be stronger than Spain, decided to strip the Spanish kingdom of its riches. (what, which, who)
2. How far away is the beach —— we are going? (that, to which)
3. The War Relief Committee's work is closely associated with that of the Red Cross, —— we have belonged to for a number of years. (which, who, whom)
4. The largest percentage of criminals is found among those —— have least education. (what, which, who)
5. To-morrow George and —— are going for a bicycle ride along the Belt Parkway. (I, myself)
6. Jane has a dog —— she calls Punch. (which, whom)

TEST 3B (*Mastery*). Pronoun
Median—14.2

In each of the following which pronoun is correct or preferred? On your paper write each answer after the number of the sentence. (Right—Wrong=Score)

1. Mother and Father were delighted to hear of —— winning the scholarship to Queen's. (him, his)
2. The natives, —— Emperor Jones thought were too much afraid to rebel, eventually rose against him and overthrew him. (who, whom)
3. —— do you think it was? (Who, Whom)
4. The hermit offered food and shelter to —— passed by on the lonely forest path to Eislich. (whoever, whomever)
5. Lucie Manette, —— both Charles Darnay and Sydney Carton loved, is the heroine of *A Tale of Two Cities*. (who, whom)
6. For a short time Lady Mary Carlisle was extremely gracious to Monsieur Beaucaire, —— she thought was a wealthy nobleman. (who, whom)
7. Miss Marshall was greatly surprised at —— failing the Latin test. (him, his)
8. That evening the tall man —— Sherlock Holmes thought had been the purchaser of the white goose called at the detective's lodgings in Baker Street. (who, whom)
9. Give this medal to —— wins the hundred-yard dash. (whoever, whomever)
10. If I took home a cat, a dog, or a parrot, my mother would give —— away. (it, them)
11. Labour has the right to bargain collectively with employers and choose —— own representatives for this purpose. (its, their)
12. Last Sunday my father, mother, and —— visited my brother at Camp Davis. (I, myself)
13. Dr. Stefansson set to work to collect his dogs, some of —— had gone squirrel hunting on Cooper Island. (which, whom)
14. Playing on the beach were several happy youngsters, two of —— I recognized as the children of my host. (which, whom)

15, 16. It is sometimes difficult for a boy or girl to select a vocation unless —— the advice of an older person to guide ——. (he has, they have) (him, them)

17. The title would never induce one to read this book for —— supplementary report. (his, their)

18. Neither Hilda nor Mildred has done —— share of the camp work. (her, their)

19. When in a trolley you see an old person standing, get up and give —— your seat. (him, them)

20. If lectures and programmes on the subject of education were given over the radio, —— would inspire the students to strive for higher marks in school. (it, they)

Enter your mark on your achievement graph.

CORRECT VERBS

Because about half the grammatical errors made by pupils are mistakes in the use of the verb, this section has many exercises to help you understand verbs and habitually use correct verbs.

TEST 4A (*Diagnostic*). Verb except Agreement of Verb and Subject.

Select the correct or preferred verb to complete each sentence. On your paper write each answer after the number of the sentence. (Right—Wrong = Score)

1. As the detective advanced into the room, he gazed curiously at the rose petals —— on the floor. (laying, lying)
2. After Alice had —— the little cake, she grew to a height of nine feet. (ate, eaten)
3. If Frank —— a tactful boy, he would not have criticized Beatrice's new hat. (was, were)
4. Marshall and I intended —— dinner at Murray's. (to eat, to have eaten)
5. If Nancy —— really interested in the Dramatic Club, she would attend the meetings. (was, were)
6. A large chart was —— on the table in the captain's cabin. (laying, lying)
7. If Mathilde —— known the borrowed necklace as only paste, she would not have been frantic at its loss. (had, would have)
8. When the children —— back from lunch, they found a gaily decorated Christmas tree set up in one corner of the schoolroom. (came, come)
9. This afternoon we —— probably finish our class paper. (shall, will)
10. When Mr. Holder was collecting his tools for an afternoon of gardening, he discovered that someone —— the handle of his favourite hoe. (broke, had broken)
11. No sooner had we assembled in Kathleen's room and —— our preparations for the feast than there came a stern rap at the door. (began, begun)
12. Later Paragot sent Asticot to school, where he —— educated. (is, was)
13. All this time the Great Seal of England had —— in the armpiece of the Milanese armour on the wall. (laid, lain)
14. Father strode to the foot of the stairs and —— in an outraged bellow the instant return of his white fur rug. (demanded, demands)

15. Patricia and her sister —— to leave so much work for Helen. (hadn't ought, ought not)
16. If Sam —— off the radio, he would be able to concentrate on his spelling lesson. (turned, would turn)
17. An hour later a messenger —— Major O'Neill a letter from Captain Stimson. (brought, brung)
18. After we had —— under the hickory tree for an hour, a fierce-looking bull drove us away. (laid, lain)
19. All night the prisoner —— by the barred window, staring with terrified eyes over the dark and lonely moor. (sat, set)
20. Four Maltese kittens —— on the soft padding in the basket. (laid, lay)

Principal Parts of Verbs

Practice 5. Supplying Verb Forms

Insert in each sentence the verb form named. Supply the active voice of a transitive verb unless the passive is asked for. When in doubt, consult a dictionary for the principal parts. The passive voice always includes a form of the verb *to be.*

A. 1. When the mischievous little boy stuck a pen in Arthur's balloon, it (past of *burst*) with a loud pop.
2. While touring the Middle East army camps, Nelson Eddy (past of *sing*) many times on request "Oh, What a Beautiful Morning!"
3. John (past of *do*) his homework in such a hurry that I can't read his handwriting.
4. For my birthday Aunt Gertrude (past of *give*) me a war bond.
5. The thieves killed the three priests of Klesh, who (past perfect of *come*) to find the ruby stolen from the forehead of the idol.
6. After the soldiers (past perfect of *eat*) their K rations, they stretched out on the ground to get a little sleep.
7. My brother (present perfect of *drive*) a jeep ever since he (past of *become*) attached to Message Centre.
8. Amid much excitement Gaspard (past passive of *hang*) over the fountain in the town square.
9. When the alarm bell (past of *ring*), the townspeople (past of *come*) running in frightened groups to the town hall.
10. The enemy (past of *know*) that our scouts (past perfect of *see*) the column advancing up the hill.

B. 1. On the morning of the thirteenth day the exhausted survivors of the torpedoing (past of *see*) a ship on the horizon.
2. The precious Ming vase (past perfect of *fall*) from the table and (past perfect of *break*) into a hundred fragments.
3. This morning Craig (present perfect of *swim*) the length of the pool three times.
4. The letter which (past perfect passive of *write*) by Captain Anthony so many years ago (past passive of *tear*) into several pieces.
5. The Russian guerrillas waited until the river (past passive of *freeze*) solid before carrying out their raid.

6. Every pupil in my class (present perfect of *give*) twenty-five cents to the Junior Red Cross.
7. When Dr. Jekyll (past perfect of *drink*) the drug, he changed into Mr. Hyde, an inhuman brute.
8. "A" Company's softball team (present perfect of *beat*) "E" Company's team in both games by a margin of two runs.
9. To our surprise nothing (past perfect passive of *take*) except the little sandalwood box from Ceylon.
10. If I (past subjunctive of *be*) you, I would try again.

Practice 6. Supplying Verb Forms

Insert in each numbered sentence the verb form or forms named. Supply the active voice of a transitive verb unless the passive is asked for.

1. As the white rabbit scurried past Alice, he (past of *take*) a watch from the pocket of his waistcoat and looked at it anxiously. 2. Recovering from her amazement, Alice (past of *spring*) to her feet and (past of *run*) across the field after the rabbit. 3. He (past of *dive*) into a large hole under the hedge.
4. When Alice (past of *come*) to the rabbit hole, she, too, popped into it.
5. Down, down she (past of *sink*), until she (past of *begin*) to think she would never reach the bottom.
6. After she (past perfect of *fall*) for some time, she landed with a thump on a heap of leaves and sticks. 7. First Alice made sure that she (past perfect of *break*) no bones; then she set out to explore.
8. On a crystal table she (past of *see*) a tiny gold key and a little bottle, on the label of which (past passive of *write*), "Drink me." 9. After Alice (past perfect of *drink*) the contents of the bottle, she (past of *shrink*) until she was only ten inches tall. 10. But now, alas, she was too small to reach the top of the table, where (past of *lie*) the golden key.
11. On the floor, however, Alice spied a little cake; when she (past perfect of *eat*) it, she (past of *grow*) to be nine feet tall and could easily reach the key, but now she was too big to go through the low gate. 12. In a moment she (past perfect of *burst*) out crying and before long had a deep pool of tears around her.
13. Suddenly Mr. Rabbit, elegantly dressed, (past of *become*) visible in the distance, and Alice determined to ask his help. 14. As soon as she (past perfect of *speak*), however, the rabbit hurriedly retreated, dropping his fan and white kid gloves.
Feeling a little warm, Alice picked up the fan and waved it gently back and forth. 15. Soon she (past of *see*) that she was shrinking again, and quickly dropped the rabbit's fan.

Sit, Set, Lie, Lay, Rise, Raise

The principal parts of six troublesome verbs are:

PRESENT TENSE	PRESENT PARTICIPLE	PAST TENSE	PAST PARTICIPLE
Sit (*occupy a seat*)	sitting	sat	sat
set (*place*)	setting	set	set

lie (*recline*)	lying	lay	lain
lay (*put down* or *place*)	laying	laid	laid
rise (*ascend*)	rising	rose	risen
raise (*elevate*)	raising	raised	raised

55. *Set, lay,* and *raise* are, as a rule, transitive verbs; in the active voice they require objects. *Set* is intransitive in "The sun is setting" and "He set out on a long journey." To *set* usually means *to cause to sit; to lay* means *to cause to lie; to raise* means *to cause to rise.*

56. *Sit, lie,* and *rise* are intransitive; they never take objects; they lack voice.

Mr. Meredith *laid* the new linoleum in the kitchen and then *lay* down in the hammock to read the paper.

Ray *set* the baby in her high chair, and while she *sat* there gurgling happily, Burke snapped a picture of her.

As the sun *rose* over the horizon, the German troops *raised* the white flag of surrender.

Practice 7.   Using *Sit, Set, Lie, Lay, Rise, Raise.*

Select the correct word to complete each sentence. Give the reason for each choice.

1. After eating his lunch David —— down on the grass and went to sleep. (laid, lay)
2. At the request of a soldier in the fourth row Joyce —— down and played Beethoven's "Moonlight Sonata." (sat, set)
3. Under the force of Denis' blow the masked knight fell from his horse and —— motionless on the dusty plain. (laid, lay)
4. After Robin Hood had —— for some time in dreamless slumber, he awoke, hung his broadsword at his side, and started out to seek adventure. (laid, lain)

5. As Kenneth travelled through the desert, he came upon a wounded Saracen —— on the burning sands. (laying, lying)
6. "—— down, Rover; —— down," ordered Elmer. (Lay, Lie) (lay, lie)
7. In the dirty flat Lillian Wald found a sick woman —— on the bed, (laying, lying)
8. The black-and-white pig —— in the mud puddle for several hours. (laid, lay)
9. While Professor Malzius was —— in his cell, his guard unlocked the door and told him to come out. (laying, lying)
10. All morning Audubon —— dreaming in the thick grass. (laid, lay)
11. —— on the floor was Jane's party dress. (Laying, Lying)
12. The song of the birds in Sherwood Forest awakened Robin Hood, who had —— all night under a tree. (laid, lain)
13. We made the mistake of —— the patient up in a chair instead of —— him flat on the floor. (setting, sitting) (laying, lying)
14. After marching for two hours Company D —— down to rest. (sat, set)
15. Please —— the clock back ten minutes. (set, sit)
16. —— down and tell me the whole story. (Set, Sit)
17. With unerring instinct Jerry chose the most comfortable chair in the room and —— down with a sigh of relief. (sat, set)
18. Since you forgot to put in the baking powder, you really shouldn't expect the cake to ——. (raise, rise)
19. Just then the submarine —— to the surface to recharge its batteries. (raised, rose)
20. Why doesn't this bread ——? (raise, rise)

Subjunctive Mood

57. The subjunctive mood is preferred for a wish or request and for a condition (an *if* clause) that is contrary to fact (untrue).

Right now I wish I *were* an Eskimo. (Wish.)
Heaven *help* him!
If I *were* twenty-one (but I'm not), I should join the Women's Reserve Marine Corps. (Condition contrary to fact.)
If this *were* gold, our fortune would be made.

Tense

58. Do not carelessly shift from the past tense to the present or from the present to the past.

Waving her tail furiously, the cat stalked into the room and ~~goes~~ *went* straight to Grandma's chair.

59. The past tense represents action completed in the past. The present perfect tense is used if the action began in the past and continues in the present.

I *lost* my umbrella. (The umbrella may since have been found.)
I *have lost* my umbrella. (Here the consequences extend to the present. The umbrella has not been found.)
The rosebush *bloomed* every summer for ten years. (It doesn't bloom now.)
The rosebush *has bloomed* every summer for ten years. (It still blooms.)

60. The past perfect tense is used if the action was completed before some past time.

When the Allies entered Cassino, they discovered that the city *had been* almost completely *demolished* by the fierce bombing assaults. (The discovery took place in past time, and the demolishing was completed before the discovery.)
The next day the commander received the news that the transports *had been sunk* by Japanese submarines. (*Had been sunk* is correct, because the sinking took place before the past act of receiving.)

61. To express action earlier than that expressed by the main verb, use the perfect tense of the participle or the infinitive; otherwise use the present tense.

I intended to *see* Violet before she left Pineville. (*To see* is correct, because the seeing did not occur before the intending.)
I am happy *to have been* of assistance in this matter. (The being of assistance preceded the being happy.)
Having received his Eagle Scout award, Russell became assistant scoutmaster of our troop. (The receiving preceded the becoming.)

62. The present tense may be used for the past in vivid narration.
The house lights *dim*, a soft bluish light *floods* the stage, and the audience *grows* silent.

63. *Might, could, would,* and *should,* not *may, can, will,* and *shall,* are used after a past tense.

The outlaws then *told* Gurth that he *might go* free.

Note these correct forms:

If we ~~would have~~ *had* heard about the rodeo in Cheyenne on August 21, we would have planned to be there that day.

had

I wish I ~~would have~~ known the real reason for Shirley's queer behaviour

told

If I ~~would tell~~ you what really happened, you wouldn't believe me.

had

I wish I ~~would have~~ studied art.

not

Bernice ~~hadn't~~ ought ∧ to spend so much time in the house. (*Had* is never used with *ought*.)

Practice 8. Using Correct Tense

Nineteen of the following are wrong. Correct them and give a reason for each change in sentences 1–24.

Example:

Ninety-seven enemy planes have been brought down yesterday.
Ninety-seven enemy planes were brought down yesterday. (The past tense is used for action completed in the past.)

1. I have entered Queen Elizabeth High School last September.
2. In assembly to-day two girls who are in this country only four months told us why they came to Canada.
3. Last summer and the preceding summer I have worked on a dairy farm.
4. The meteorologist pointed out that Greenland in time might have great strategic importance.
5. When I reached home, I discovered that I forgot my suitcase.
6. If Brutus had taken Cassius' advice, he would not have given Antony permission to speak.
7. Although these cases were shipped a month ago, the purchaser did not receive the goods yet.
8. The president closed his address with the hope that what has been done during his administration may benefit the people.
9. I intended to write the letter on Saturday.
10. If Squire Cass's sons loved him, they would have considered his feelings.
11. Since Shakespeare's time the stage settings became more elaborate.
12. Circe told Odysseus that he should fill the ears of his men with wax, so that they may not hear the song of the Sirens.
13. Modern history is the record of events that happened recently.
14. Enclose you will find a check for seventy-five dollars.
15. The colonists were the descendants of the English and had the English conception of liberty.
16. Sir Walter Scott wished to have repaid the total indebtedness of his publishers.
17. I intended to have gone to the museum last week.
18. You hadn't ought to go in swimming right after dinner.
19. A dividend of ten cents a share of common stock, amounting to $1,265,000, was paid on February 1.

20. During my visit to Roosevelt Field I hoped to have seen an autogyro.
21. Ernest said that he may be absent from the rehearsal.
22. Carl came into the meeting late and begins to talk to another boy.
23. The public health nurse told Mrs. Bianchi that she hadn't ought to feed the baby bacon.
24. If I had sneezed, the broadcast would have been ruined.
25. I wish I would have taken a course in typing while I was in high school.

Shall, Will, Should, Would

64. To express simple futurity (mere expectation), use _shall_ in the first person and _will_ in the second and the third.

I _shall_ probably _plant_ the marigolds and cosmos along the fence.
I _shall be delighted_ to have lunch with you next Friday.
The journalism class _will publish_ next week's edition of the _Brookdale Record._

NOTE. "I will probably enter the University of Manitoba in September," although not the best usage, is accepted colloquial English. The rule, however, indicates the practice of most writers.

65. To express the will of the speaker, use _will_ in the first person and _shall_ in the second and the third.

(Promise) You _shall_ not _be annoyed_ by these rowdies any longer.
(Willingness) We _will_ gladly _mind_ the baby this evening, Mrs. Hunt.
(Threat or Determination) I _will see_ that your father hears of this.
(Command) You _shall_ not _use_ the car again this week.

66. In first person questions use _shall._

Whom _shall_ we _invite_ to the puppet show?
How _shall_ I _return_ the book to you?

67. *Should* **is, as a rule, used like** *shall,* **and** *would* **like** *will.*

After graduation I *should like* to play on a professional basketball team.

EXCEPTIONS. *Would* is used for habitual action.

All summer I *would rush* home from business every evening to work in my garden.

Should is used (1) to express duty and (2) to express an opinion modestly.

(Duty) She *should help* her mother get dinner for all those people.
(Modest Expression of Opinion) I *should think* so.

Practice 9.

Insert the correct or preferred word. Give the reason for each choice.

A. 1. I —— like to listen carefully to both recordings before deciding which one to buy. (should, would)
2. How —— we celebrate Mother's birthday? (shall, will)
3. The work —— be completed by January 15. (A promise.) (shall, will)
4. I —— be glad to play on the baseball team you are organizing. (should, would)
5. Most of the material for my report on television I —— obtain from the *Britannica Book of the Year.* (shall, will)
6. I —— like to visit the planetarium. (should, would)
7. I —— be there on time. (Determination.) (shall, will)

B. 1. When the final examinations are over, I —— be ready for my summer job in a garage. (shall, will)
2. What belt —— I wear with this gray dress? (shall, will)
3. I —— like very much to see your collection of tropical fish. (should, would)
4. I hope I —— be able to write short stories like these some day. (shall, will)
5. I —— never give my consent to such a ridiculous request. (Determination.) (shall, will)
6. I —— be glad to teach you to knit. (shall, will)
7. I —— probably spend my vacation making a Youth Hostel bicycle trip. (shall, will)

TEST 4B (*Mastery*). Verb except Agreement of Verb and Subject
Median—14.1

Select the correct or preferred verb to complete each sentence. On your paper write each answer after the number of the sentence. (Right — Wrong = Score.

1. In an instant Edwin discovered that he had —— down on a freshly painted bench. (sat, set)
2. If Harold —— begun earlier to prepare his report, everybody would have enjoyed it more. (had, would have)
3. You —— to put that fragile goblet into boiling water. (hadn't ought, ought not)

4. For a half hour I —— on the living room floor while Jane practised for her artificial respiration test. (laid, lay)
5. Suddenly over the roar of the motors —— the dismal wail of a foghorn. (came, come)
6. After Sherlock Holmes had —— the advertisement, Dr. Watson took it to the office of the *Evening News*. (written, wrote)
7. Some of the most skillful bowmen in Lincoln and Nottinghamshire were gathered in the forest, and Little John —— tallest of the group. (is, was)
8. When I reached home, I discovered that I —— my history book in school. (had left, left)
9. What programmes —— we listen to this evening? (shall, will)
10. The letter brought the good news that on the previous Friday I —— elected a member of Senior Arista. (had been, was)
11. After Helen and I had bought our yarn and —— to take lessons, we discovered that knitting a sweater is more difficult than we had supposed. (began, begun)
12. Halfway to Chicago we ran into a storm which worried Father John because he never —— in a plane before. (had been, was)
13. If Marcus —— in his own home, he wouldn't throw paper on the floor. (was, were)
14. Last night I wanted —— *The Courage and the Glory* before going to bed. (to finish, to have finished)
15. If the weather —— warmer, we could canoe up Lake George to Fort Ticonderoga. (was, were)
16. Rogers circled over the canyon to study the white markers —— spread out on its floor. (laying, lying)
17. Tom Canty dragged himself to his wretched bed and—— down to dream of palaces, princes, and kings. (laid, lay)
18. With one mighty effort Tim and I lifted the heavy chest and —— it on the rude table in the cabin. (sat, set)
19. For two days before his rescue Carter had —— helpless on the ice pack. (laid, lain)
20. When we reached Harrisburg after a two hours' drive over icy roads, I was almost ——. (froze, frozen)

Enter your mark on your achievement graph.

Agreement of Verb and Subject

TEST 5A (*Diagnostic*). Agreement of Verb and Subject

In each of the following sentences which word or expression is correct? On your paper write each answer after the number of the sentence. (Right—Wrong=Score)

1. I think three dollars —— too much for a book on amateur photography. (are, is)
2. A hundred years ago there —— Indians all over this neighbourhood. (was, were)
3. Examinations to test scholarship —— given in medieval universities. (was, were)

4. The description of the tiny islands —— so vivid that you can almost see them as you read. (are, is)
5. *Young Americans* by Cornelia Meigs —— stories of real boys and girls. (contain, contains)
6. The churches of this community —— a great opportunity for service. (has, have)
7. Two thirds of Martha's free time —— spent in experimenting with new and unusual recipes. (are, is)
8. You, like every other candidate for graduation, —— to serve on one of the class committees. (want, wants)
9. Gradually, as your skill and courage ——, you become more and more confident of your superiority over this throbbing giant of steel and iron. (increase, increases)
10. The animals that particularly attracted my attention —— the bears. (was, were)
11. At first everyone, including Bernice and her parents, —— convinced of Kenneth's guilt. (are, is)
12. Leon is one of the boys who —— constructing a tennis court behind the high school. (are, is)
13. In the small envelope which Mr. Openshaw received in the mail —— five dried orange seeds and a mysterious message signed X.Y.Z. (was, were)
14. The number of deaths caused by traffic accidents —— decreasing. (are, is)
15. In our last municipal election all the Labour candidates but one —— elected. (was, were)
16. Many of the contributors to *Popular Science* —— how to make useful articles out of junk. (explain, explains)
17. Buckwheat cakes and maple syrup —— one of my favourite breakfast dishes. (are, is)
18. A will left by J. M. Glenarm, bequeathing his nephew a large estate under unusual conditions, —— wild adventures for Jack and his two sisters. (start, starts)
19. Where —— your committee decided to hold its final meeting? (has, have)
20. The mayor, together with the president of the Canadian Legion, and two veterans, —— dedicated the town honour roll. (has, have)

68. A verb agrees with its subject in number and person. First find the subject; then determine its number. If the subject is a pronoun, notice also the person.

They agree   They don't agree

In recent years there *have been* many changes in methods of teaching.

Allen *doesn't* know how to drive a tractor.
Why *weren't* you at the meeting of the Science Club yesterday?
✗(The subject *you* always takes a plural verb.)

Millicent, not her twin sisters, *has offered* to bake a pie for our picnic. (The verb agrees with the positive subject, not the negative.)
The Count of Monte Cristo is one of those rare books that *appeal* to almost every boy and girl. (*Books*, not *one*, is the antecedent of *that*. The relative pronoun is therefore plural.)

69. Do not be deceived by a modifier after the subject. Search out the subject and make the verb agree with it. *With, together with, as well as,* and *including* after subjects are troublemakers.

In general the procedure of our assemblies *varies* little.

Parts of *A Son of the Middle Border are* as entertaining as an adventure story.
Bob Frederickson, together with Sam Davis and Ed Morse,

↑
is building a model airplane.

One of Jane's finest characteristics *is* her composure.

70. As a rule, compound subjects connected by *and* **take plural verbs.** "Lillian and Mary were absent" means that two girls were absent.

EXCEPTION. A compound subject that names one person, thing, or idea takes a singular verb.

The secretary and treasurer of the Senior Class *writes* the minutes of the meetings, *carries* on the class correspondence, and *collects* dues. (One person is both secretary and treasurer.)
At first bread and milk *was* the baby seal's favourite breakfast dish. (Bread and milk is one breakfast dish.)

71. A verb having a compound subject connected by *or* **or** *nor* **agrees with the nearer subject.**

Either Scotty or Towser *has eaten* the chops. (Because one dog has eaten the chops, the verb is singular.)
Either Ted or the girls *have eaten* the chocolates. (The verb agrees with the nearer subject word, *girls*.)
(Right) Either you or I *am* responsible for the error.
(Better) Either you are responsible for the error, or I am.

72. A word that is plural in form but names a single object or idea takes a singular verb.

Do you think five dollars *is* too much for this hat? (Five dollars is one sum of money.)
Younger Poets is an anthology of the work of high school students.
Two thirds of a pie *is* far too much for a little boy to eat.
Mathematics *is* important to the aviator.

73. As a rule, *each, every, either, neither, one, many a, a person,* **and compounds with** *body* **and** *one* **take singular verbs.**

One of the boys *has caught* five big trout.
Every tree and every shrub *is covered* with snow.
Neither of us *was* able to finish the experiment in one period.

74. A collective noun takes a singular verb when the group is thought of and a plural verb when the individuals are thought of.

My physiography class *has decided* to visit the Hayden Planetarium.
My physiography class *are* now *discussing* plans for the visit.

75. A verb agrees with its subject, not with its predicate nominative.

To me the most fascinating collection *is* the jewels.
A gunner and a navigator *were* his crew.

Practice 10. Choosing Correct Verbs

Twenty-one of the following sentences are incorrect. Correct them and give a reason for each change you make.

1. Under the fake forecastle there was two cannons.
2. I admit that civics never were my favourite subject.
3. Many a would-be nurse has been inspired by the story of Florence Nightingale.
4. Winnie, not the committee members, were responsible for the success of Senior Day.
5. The committee are discussing plans for a masquerade party.
6. Charles, as well as his young sisters, were frightened by the piteous groans.
7. Mother is anxious to know whether Marion or June are also interested in the Cadet Nurse Corps.
8. During the next quarter the Queen's team weren't able to cross the Varsity goal line.
9. My favourite among summer sports is swimming.
10. There has been a number of robberies in my neighbourhood recently, and not one of the thieves have been caught.
11. There was several requests at the library yesterday for books about radar.
12. He don't know how to study a spelling lesson.
13. Neither of these jobs offers much scope for creative talent like yours.
14. Every stick and stone have been cleared from the west field.
15. Strangely enough, not one of the five boys has the slightest idea who batted the baseball through Mrs. Bascom's window.
16. Is it the black puppy or the white one which have just made a meal of Father's new hat?

17. Tom Eadie was one of the expert divers who was summoned by the Navy to help in the salvage of the S-4.
18. The next day Barbara and I was summoned to the principal's office.
19. Each of the stories in *Short Stories for Study and Enjoyment* are different from the others and leave a vivid impression on the reader's mind.
20. In our class fourteen dollars has been collected for the Red Cross.
21. Twenty-five years ago there was not so many large and beautiful schools as there is to-day.
22. The expression "free textbooks" means books lent to the pupils by the Board of Education.
23. Neither of us like ripe olives.
24. An alligator don't make an ideal pet.
25. Every bud and blossom are opening wide.
26. Not one of the seven passengers in the plane was injured.
27. Is it Juliet or Mary who stand first in the class?
28. It is one of the numerous books that is published by the Harvard University Press.
29. By nine o'clock James and I was ready to go home.
30. Every one of the boys is to blame for the disorder.

Practice 11. Agreement of Verb and Subject

This rapid drill is to help you form the habit of using correct verbs. First use each of the subjects listed below with *is* or *are*, then with *wasn't* or *weren't*, then with *doesn't* or *don't*. Choose quickly.

1. you	13. either the pilot or the co-pilot
2. everyone in the class	14. stamps and envelopes
3. a person	15. a bunch of radishes
4. he and his twin sister	16. one of my assignments
5. A set of encyclopaedias	17. a box of cookies
6. every pen and pencil	18. either Marie or Betty
7. ten dollars	19. students at Shaw High School
8. van Loon's *Ships*	20. three quarters of the period
9. three of the crew	21. a number of boys
10. his choice of words	22. the number of accidents
11. many an engineer	23. it
12. he	24. this kind of apples

TEST 5B (*Mastery*). Agreement of Verb and Subject
Median—14.9

In each of the following which word or expression is correct? On your paper write each answer after the number of the sentence. (Right—Wrong=Score)

1. As far as I could see, there —— only two ways to escape. (was, were)
2. Ten minutes after the end of the performance the audience —— still calling for their favourite actors. (was, were)
3. Either Bryce Canyon or Zion Canyon —— worth a trip across the continent. (are, is)
4. Captain Bligh, who had been sent to sea in a little boat with several midshipmen, —— in court to accuse the mutineers. (was, were)

5. Plenty of rest, as well as exercise and nourishing food, —— essential to the normal growth of a young puppy. (are, is)
6. The gate was open but in the yard —— two fierce-looking bulldogs. (was, were)
7. The setting of these two poems —— a farm in New England. (are, is)
8. The changes made by the new coach —— based upon his wide experience with high school baseball teams. (was, were)
9. A number of my friends —— members of the Engineering Club. (are, is)
10. In front of the parish church —— fifty or more boys and men. (was, were)
11. Apple pie and cheese —— Uncle Henry's favourite dessert. (are, is)
12. *Heroes of Progress* —— of the achievements of great scientists, inventors, naturalists, and artists. (tell, tells)
13. Two dollars —— seem an exorbitant price for that air-mail stationery. (doesn't, don't)
14. Why —— two thirds of the work always left to Margaret? (are, is)
15. Not one of us fifteen boys —— been late this term. (has, have)
16. The lines "Ten thousand saw I at a glance tossing their heads in sprightly dance" —— a thrilling scene. (picture, pictures)
17. Sherlock Holmes and Dr. Watson discover the criminals' plans and —— their scheme for robbing the bank. (upset, upsets)
18. In Pittsburgh —— located some of the largest steel mills in the world. (are, is)
19. Clyde R. Hunt, president of the Canadian Legion, together with Thomas P. Ohlert, president of the Woodhaven Lions, —— been busily working out the final details of the dedication. (has, have)
20. During recess the children at the nursery play games which —— them fairness and co-operation. (teach, teaches)

Enter your mark on your achievement graph.

CORRECT ADJECTIVES, ADVERBS, NOUNS, PREPOSITIONS, AND CONJUNCTIONS

Test 6A (*Diagnostic*). Grammar except Pronoun and Verb

In each of the following select the correct or preferred word or expression. On your paper write each answer after the number of the sentence. (Right—Wrong=Score)

1. I hope that when I return a year from now —— will be ready for college. (that you, you)
2. We could not see the lake very ——, as it was foggy. (good, well)
3. After finishing her homework Betty practised her piano lesson for a half ——. (an hour, hour)
4. I enjoy swimming more than —— sport. (any, any other)
5. When Charlie and I awoke the next morning, we were so stiff we —— hardly move a muscle. (could, couldn't)
6. Masefield's poetry is different —— Robinson's. (from, than)
7. Sherlock Holmes refused to listen to the stranger's story —— Dr. Watson was permitted to remain in the room. (unless, without)
8. Just then the puma gave an angry snarl and jumped —— the ledge. (off, off of)

9. After an early morning fishing trip broiled trout tastes ——. (delicious, deliciously)
10. —— will be many opportunities for this generation to practise the Good Neighbour policy. (Their, There)
11. In a short detective story you don't have to read three hundred pages to discover who the murderer is, —— you have to do in a full-length mystery novel. (as, like)
12. For a long time the divers couldn't find —— way to enter the sunken submarine. (any, no)
13. Why don't you like —— kind of dresses? (that, those)
14. On Christmas Eve the baby was —— excited to eat her supper. (to, too)
15. For a long time law appealed to Clifford more strongly than —— profession. (any, any other)
16. Although the commander gave the order to surface, the submarine did not rise as it should ——. (have, have risen)
17. No extensive training is needed to pilot —— kind of helicopters. (that, those)
18. Do you know the difference between a politician and ——? (a statesman, statesman)
19. Aunt Miranda's opinion of the new dress was quite different —— Rebecca's. (from, than)
20. The letters RHHS are engraved on the ring in a —— way. (most unique, unique)

Correct Adjectives and Adverbs

76. Use the comparative when comparing two.

Vivian is the *taller* and *prettier* of the two sisters.

77. When the comparative is used for more than two, exclude from the group the object compared.

other

New York has more electoral votes than any ∧ state in the Union. (The wrong sentence says that New York has more electoral votes than itself, for New York is one of the states in the group *any state in the Union*.)

78. Avoid double comparison. Double comparison ("more wiser," "most beautifulest") was correct when Shakespeare wrote but has gone out of style.

Of the two magazines, *Good Housekeeping* has a ~~more~~ wider selection of recipes and homemaking articles.

79. *This* and *that* are singular and modify singular nouns; *these* and *those* are plural.

that

I can't understand why you enjoy ~~those~~ kind of books.

Say *this boy*, not "this here boy"; *that boy*, not "that there boy."

80. Repeat the article before a second noun in a series for contrast, clearness, or emphasis.

In those days life was kind to neither the old nor *the* young.
The captain and *the* manager of the football team have agreed to address the cheering squad.

81. Say *a half hour* or *half an hour*, not "a half an hour."

By working energetically for a half~~an~~ hour, Father and I made the car shine like new

82. Omit the article after *sort* and *kind*.

(Right) The other pupils in Schuyler Academy considered Fred Laughton a likeable *kind of* boy.
(Colloquial) The other pupils in Schuyler Academy considered Fred Laughton a likable kind of a boy.

83. Use *a* before a consonant sound and *an* before a vowel sound.
Don't make the mistake of thinking of letters instead of sounds. "An hour" is right, because the *h* is silent.

Practice 12. Correct Adjectives and Adverbs

Select the correct or preferred word or expression in each sentence and give a reason for the choice.

A. 1. English is spoken by more people than —— language in the world. (any, any other)
2. —— mile farther on, the platoon came to the rifle range. (A half, A half a)
3. Which is the —— educational of these two magazines? (more, most)
4. Diamonds are the —— substance known to man. (hardest, most hardest)
5. Clarence Day's *Life with Father*, which I finished last night, is different from —— book I have ever read. (any, any other)
6. Ontario produces more winter wheat than —— province. (any, any other)
7. Go south on Park Avenue for about a half ——. (a block, block)
8. No one would order —— kind of oranges. (that, those)

B. 1. Home nursing is —— for me than first aid. (easier, more easier)
2. It is —— honour to present Major Charles P. Coates as our next speaker. (a, an)
3. Which have the —— opportunities for advancement, chemical or electrical engineers? (best, better)
4. —— kind of songs has never appealed to me. (That, Those)
5. Patsy is a peculiar sort of ——. (a dog, dog)
6. A half —— away I met Dr. Foster, who had been calling on Mr. Reisman. (a block, block)
7. The birds of Brazil are more beautiful than —— in South America. (any, any others)
8. The Navy's eyesight tests are —— than the Army's. (more stricter, stricter)

84. Avoid the double negative. Most negatives begin with *n*—*not, no, never, nothing, none, nobody.* The negative is not used with the half-negatives *hardly, scarcely, only,* and *but* when it means *only.*

> When Jane returned from Wac training camp, I couldn't hardly wait to see her
>
> *anything*
> I had to admit I didn't know ~~nothing~~ about ventriloquism.
> There isn't but one high school for the children of the three towns.

Practice 13. Avoiding Double Negatives

Seven of the following sentences are wrong. Correct them.

1. My grandfather hadn't never seen a technicolour movie.
2. The pilot searched for a landing strip, but there wasn't none.
3. Industrial engineers haven't hardly begun to find uses for plastics.
4. There was but one taxi waiting at the station.
5. In August we haven't had scarcely one rainy day.
6. By the end of the week Mr. Rogers hadn't no more gym shoes for sale.
7. Donors may give blood for plasma only five times a year.
8. The captain wouldn't take but one volunteer with him.
9. Jim Connors has said hardly a word this evening.
10. Isn't there no one here who saw the rocket flares last night?

Correct Nouns

Use these correct forms:

The high school is two miles from my home. (NOT "mile.")
Yesterday we sold ten bushels of apples. (NOT "bushel.")
My music teacher is only five feet tall. (NOT "foot.")
Last winter I lost two pairs of gloves. (NOT "pair.")

Wrong Part of Speech

85. Do not interchange conjunctions and prepositions. *As, than,* and *unless* are commonly conjunctions. Avoid the use of *like* or *without* as a conjunction. *Different from* is always correct.

The slums of a great city are far *different from* the homes of the rich.
Florence interpreted the third question *as* I did.

86. Use an adverb to modify a verb, an adjective, or an adverb.
(Right) I *surely* was frightened when I heard that noise.
(Slang) I *sure* was frightened when I heard that noise.

Slow, loud, quick, fast, smooth, cheap, right, wrong, clear, ill, well, hard, high, long, deep, and *close* are used as adjectives or as adverbs.
Drive *slow.* Come *quick.* Speaker *louder.* (Of course "Drive slowly" and "Come quickly" are also correct.)

87. After *be, become, grow, seem, appear, look, feel taste, smell,* **and** *sound,* **use a predicate adjective to describe the subject.**
Everyone thought that Louise looked beautifully.

88. Do not carelessly use *to* **and** *their* **as adverbs.**
There are *too* many adjectives in your sentences.

Practice 14.   Nouns and Parts of Speech

Eleven of the following sentences are wrong. Correct them and give a reason for each change you make.

1. How many bushel of potatoes did your father raise last year?
2. Rolly Marvin looks like he could play a great game at tackle.
3. The salutation of a friendly letter is usually different from that of a business letter.
4. Nancy wanted to talk and act as the wealthy people of Glen Shore did.
5. The first Eddystone lighthouse, which resembled a Chinese pagoda, was very different in appearance than the lighthouses of to-day.
6. No other knight in the king's court could entertain the young prince like Richard could.
7. My hobby, fashion designing, I take very serious, for I expect to make it my vocation after I graduate from high school.
8. Mother is feeling somewhat better to-day.
9. In some states, however, the candidates are chosen different.
10. Alice found that the mixture in the bottle tasted rather sweetly.
11. The voice in the next room sounded harshly.
12. Write your essay legibly on one side of the paper.
13. Constance is always to busy to have any fun.
14. Walter and George were to frightened to move from the spot.
15. There was no doubt that the letter had been read by the naval censor.
16. Other fountain pens are filled different.

SYNTACTICAL REDUNDANCE

89. A pronoun and its antecedent are not used as subject of the same verb.

The aviator who made the rescue ~~he~~ declined to consider it an unusual feat.

90. Omit every unnecessary preposition or other word.

In Rome we saw the house in which Keats died ~~in~~.

A strong gust of wind nearly blew us off ~~of~~ the observation tower.

Practice 15. Getting Rid of Unnecessary Words

Twelve of the following sentences are incorrect. Correct them and give reasons.

1. Shelley ends up "Ode to the West Wind" on the optimistic note, "If Winter comes, can Spring be far behind?"
2. The newsreel man noticed that on both trial runs when the driver brought the car to a stop, that the car swerved to the right.
3. One day a high summer flood washed the mongoose out of the burrow where he lived with his father and mother, and carried him, kicking and clucking, down a roadside ditch.
4. In this chapter we meet Charles Darnay, of whom we hear a great deal of later in the book.
5. This poem tells of a person who, although she never saw a moor or the sea, can imagine the appearance of the heather and the waves.
6. Will this extra work take the unprepared mark off of my record?
7. When Godfrey decided to claim his daughter, Silas he left the decision to Eppie.
8. It was a fresh, crystal-clear morning, with icicles hanging like dazzling pendants from the trees and a glaze of pale blue on the surface of the snow.
9. Constance is a girl of about seventeen years old, with short curly hair, dark blue eyes, and a turned-up nose.
10. When Emma Jane went home, she told her brothers of what she had done.
11. The reason for my absence yesterday was on account of illness.
12. "In Flanders Fields" by John McCrae is another poem of which I never tire of reading.
13. The first and most important step is to decide on what the biggest news of the week is.
14. Entering an arched doorway, the two found themselves in a beautiful little vaulted chapel about eighteen feet long.
15. This news dispatch tells about a young aviator who, though he had a chance to bail out, he gave his parachute to a passenger who had none.

INCORRECT OMISSION

91. Do not omit a repeated verb if it differs in form from the verb expressed.

(Right) The Western team hoped to defeat Queen's as decisively as they *had* already *defeated* McGill.

(Colloquial) The Western team hoped to defeat Queen's as decisively as they had already McGill. (*Had defeat* is not grammatical.)

92. Do not make a single form of the verb *be* serve as both a principal and an auxiliary verb.

(Wrong) Public speaking is (principal verb) valuable training and preparing (present participle) me for the employment interview.

(Right) Public speaking *is* (principal verb) valuable training and *is* (auxiliary) *preparing* (present participle) me for the employment interview.

93. Include every word needed to complete a comparison.

that of
The salary of a travelling companion is in many cases larger than ∧ a private secretary or a stenographer.

94. Do not omit a needed preposition.

(Right) Franklin D. Roosevelt *graduated from* Harvard University. (Both *graduated from* and *was graduated from* are correct.)

(Wrong) Franklin D. Roosevelt graduated Harvard University. (*Graduate* in this sense does not take an object.)

Practice 16. Adding Needed Words

Ten of the following sentences are wrong. Correct them and give reasons.

1. My sympathy has always been with the poor people and have decided that the only way I can really help them is by becoming a doctor.
2. Quinidine is a rare drug and being distributed only to the armed forces.
3. Webster told his hearers they were on the same ground their fathers stood fifty years before.
4. The ideal vocation for a person is the one for which he is best fitted and which he most enjoys.
5. Received your letter in this morning's mail and hasten to assure you that I shall be on hand on May 18.
6. Scientists say that synthetic quinine is as good, if not better than natural quinine.
7. I am hoping in your next letter to hear a great improvement in your work.
8. Richard studied Diesel engineering just as many others have and are doing.
9. More than ten thousand schools have used or are using our service.
10. Is the salary of an engineer larger than a teacher or an accountant?
11. Topography is an interesting subject and helping to prepare me for a job as surveyor.
12. Fred Waring graduated Flushing High School last June.

TEST 6B (*Mystery*). Grammar except Pronoun and Verb
Median—16.5

In each of the following select the correct or preferred word or expression. On your paper write each answer after the number of the sentence. (Right—Wrong=Score)

1. Take-offs and landings of a bus-plane would make fares —— high. (to, too)
2. Bill's courtesy, efficiency, and willingness —— have made a good impression on Mr. Burroughs. (sure, surely)
3. Thomas Edison patented more inventions than —— person who has ever lived. (any, any other)
4. Within a few months I —— hardly see the scar on my arm. (could, couldn't)
5. In our school cafeteria we never get —— kind of unbalanced meals. (that, those)
6. The secretary and —— of the Writers' Club were absent from yesterday's meeting. (the treasurer, treasurer)
7. Is an autogyro different —— a helicopter? (from, than)
8. Each year Americans consume more pounds of sugar than the people of —— nation in the world. (any, any other)
9. Your delicious hot dinner will taste —— it had been cooked aboard the plane, not at the airport hours before. (as if, like)
10. At graduation Anita Cromwell won more awards than —— member of her class. (any, any other)
11. When I visited the aquarium last week, I saw the —— fish imaginable. (most oddest, oddest)
12. —— is never any justification for discourtesy. (Their, There)
13. I don't think Miss Jordan will —— that excuse for tardiness. (accept, accept of)
14. Miss Schuyler never has forgotten and never —— that one of her distant relatives was a signer of the Declaration of Independence. (will, will forget)
15. Which of the dresses do you like better, the blue or —— one? (green, the green)
16. What is the rate for a half ——programme over a major radio network? (an hour, hour)
17. You cannot understand a difficult topic —— you give the subject your undivided attention. (unless, without)
18. This afternoon I played tennis with a boy with whom I had never —— before. (played, played with)
19. Your method of learning a poem is different —— mine. (from, than)
20. After taking one bite out of a Northern Spy, Harold said, "I like —— kind of apples." (these, this)

Enter your mark on your achievement graph.

GRAMMAR POSTERS

By drawing a grammar poster you will impress a correct form on your own mind and on the minds of other pupils who see your poster on the bulletin board.

STANDARDS FOR POSTERS

1. *Is the error real, common, and serious?*
2. *Is the correct form conspicuous and the incorrect preceded by not, crossed out, printed smaller, or otherwise subordinated?*

3. *Is the lettering easily read from all parts of the classroom?*
4. *Is the workmanship careful?*
5. *Is the picture appropriate?*
6. *Is there a touch of humour?*

Pupil Cartoon

Practice 17.   Making Grammar Posters

After studying the cartoons in this book, especially the student cartoon on this page, draw a grammar poster to help pupils eradicate a common error.

Punctuation

PUNCTUATION marks help the writer to make his ideas clear and help the reader to understand what is meant. Because punctuation marks are conventional signals, a writer needs to know what marks are ordinarily used to indicate the relationship he desires to express. Because of the tendency toward less pointing it is wise to omit punctuation marks which do not help the reader.

PERIOD

1. The period is used after imperative and declarative sentences.
Stunt flying requires altitude and speed.
Open the window.

2. The period is used after abbreviations: P.M., *Mass.* Do not use a period after *per cent* or Roman numerals in a sentence.
At 9:15 P.M. seventy-five per cent of the votes had been counted.

COMMA

3. To set off an expression requires two commas unless the words to be set off come first or last in the sentence.

4. The comma is used to set off the name of the person addressed.
Why don't you speak for yourself, John?

5. As a rule, appositives are set off by commas.
Cheerfulness is health; the opposite, melancholy, is disease.

a. Appositives preceded by *or* and titles and degrees after a name are set off.
The ounce, or snow leopard, has a tail three feet long.
Thomas Kite Brown, M.A., Ph.D., is one of the editors of the dictionary.

b. The comma is not used to set off restrictive appositives:
The poet Browning. The orator Burke. The year 1930. My friend Kirby. The word *one.*

6. Most parenthetical expressions are set off by commas—for example, *however, on the other hand, for instance, by the way, to tell the truth, to say the least, I think, I believe, I repeat.*

Lewis and Clark could not, however, have crossed the United States without the help of the Indian squaw.

The lion, like everything great, has his share of critics and detractors.

543

a. The comma, as a rule, is not used to set off *also, perhaps, indeed, therefore, at least, nevertheless, likewise,* and other parenthetical expressions that do not require a pause in reading aloud.

b. Well, why, or *now* at the beginning of a conversational sentence is commonly set off; *etc.* is always set off.

Why, I hadn't thought of that.

2, 4, 6, 8, etc., are even numbers.

7. The comma is used to separate expressions in a series. When a conjunction is used between the last two items only, it is correct to place a comma before the conjunction or to omit the comma.

There is no substitute for thorough-going, ardent, and sincere earnestness.

Verdun, Jutland Reef, the Somme, and the Marne were four important battles of the World War.

If I cannot correspond with you, if I cannot learn your mind, if I cannot co-operate with you, I cannot be your friend.

a. When all the conjunctions are used, no comma is required unless it makes the sentence clearer.

He is brave and courteous and generous.

We found very few huckleberries that were ripe, and finally decided to pick blackberries instead.

b. In the word group *two little hens,* no comma is used, because the adjectives are not co-ordinate in thought. *Little* modifies *hens,* but *two* modifies *little hens.* Likewise in *solid gold watch, gold* modifies *watch,* but *solid* modifies *gold watch.* Likewise in *puny right hand, right* modifies *hand,* and *puny* modifies *right hand.*

c. Expressions like *an honest, ambitious man* and a *ferocious, straggling mustache* require the comma. If inserting *and* between the adjectives does not change the sense, the comma is needed: *an honest and ambitious man; a ferocious and straggling mustache.*

8. In an address or date each item after the first is set off by commas.

On Congress Street, Portland, Maine, stands the home of Henry Wadsworth Longfellow.

On November 11, 1918, an armistice dictated by General Foch was signed.

9. The comma is used to set off a contrasting expression introduced by *not.*

Francis Scott Key is famous, not as a lawyer, but as the author of "The Star-Spangled Banner."

10. Use a comma after *yes* **or** *no* **at the beginning of a sentence.**

Yes, you're right.

11. The comma is used after the salutation of a friendly letter and the complimentary close of any letter.

Dear Isabel,
Yours truly,

12. Occasionally, when no other rule justifies the use of a punctuation mark, a comma is necessary to prevent misreading.

Ever since, Carter House has been deserted.
The night before, we bought a tent to take with us.
To the wise, youth is a time for training.

13. As a rule, the comma is used between the principal parts of a compound sentence if they are joined by a conjunction—*and*, *but*, *or*, *nor*, *so*, *yet*, *while* (meaning *but*). In a short sentence the comma may be omitted.

Man was made to be active, and he is never so happy as when he is doing something.
Experience keeps a dear school, but fools will learn in no other.
His country called and he went.

NOTE. Either the comma or the semicolon may be used when *so*, *yet* or *then* connects the principal clauses.

14. The comma occasionally takes the place of an omitted verb.

General Haig was the commander of the British; General Petain, of the French; and General Pershing, of the Americans.
We respect deeds; they, words.

15. The comma is used to set off a short direct quotation.

"Why, Silver," said the captain, "if you had pleased to be an honest man, you might have been sitting in your own galley."

16. Use a comma after an introductory adverb clause.

When a man is wrong and won't admit it, he always gets angry.
If you want to live and keep well, you must eat proper food.

a. The comma may be omitted after a restrictive introductory clause, especially a short one.

(Right) When he reached home he found the telegram.
(Right) When he reached home, he found the telegram.

17. Use the comma to set off non-restrictive phrases and clauses. If the omission of the subordinate clause would change the meaning of the principal clause or destroy its sense, the clause is restrictive, and no comma is required.

A restrictive adjective clause answers the question "Which one?" or the question "Which ones?"

A nonrestrictive adjective clause does not answer the question "Which one?" or the question "Which ones?" It gives additional information.

1. Peter is a boy *who watches goats.* [Answers the question "Which *boy?*"]
2. The highwayman wore boots *that reached to his knees.* [Answers the question "Which *boots?*"]
3. I was sent back to a butcher shop *which was two miles from camp* to get another pound of bacon. [Answers the question "Which *butcher shop?*"]
4. The man *who does everything for gain* does nothing for good. [Answers the question "Which *man?*"]

Nonrestrictive Clauses

1. I called to my brother Ralph, *who ran quickly for Mother.* [Does not answer the question "Which *brother Ralph?*"]
2. My father and I planned to climb Mount Washington, *which is about sixty-four hundred feet high.* [Does not answer the question "Which *Mount Washington?*"]
3. Soon we crossed Bright Angel Creek, *which comes from Bright Angel Canyon.* [Does not answer the question "Which *Bright Angel Creek?*"]
4. Tom Sawyer, *who felt like playing,* tried to get out of whitewashing the fence. [Does not answer the question "Which *Tom Sawyer?*"]
5. We flew over Brooklyn, *which from an altitude of two thousand feet appeared to be a miniature playground.* [Does not answer the question "Which *Brooklyn?*"]

a. As a rule, a participial phrase at the beginning of a sentence is nonrestrictive and is therefore set off from the rest of the sentence by a comma.

Deprived of the possibilities of importing foodstuffs, Great Britain could not sustain herself for more than six weeks without the most severe rationing.

b. Always use a comma before *as, for,* and *since* when the clause gives a reason.

I have elected advanced algebra, for I need it to enter a college of engineering.

Practice 1. Classifying Clauses

Classify the phrases and subordinate clauses as restrictive and non-restrictive, give a reason in each case, and punctuate the sentences:

1. Mrs. Akeley was received with friendliness by the Pygmies for her gifts of salt and tobacco delighted them.
2. Any boy who is intelligent can learn to punctuate correctly.
3. Mary Rafton who is in the eleventh-year English class seldom makes a mistake in punctuation.
4. Paris which is the most beautiful city in France is the world's fashion centre.
5. The Paris which is located in Kentucky is a county seat.
6. Charles Thomas running to catch a car stumbled and fell.
7. A fat man running to catch a car may injure his heart.
8. A permanent home for raccoons has been established near the southern end of the bear dens where its inmates will be near their relatives.
9. Union painters never work on a job where a spraying machine is used.
10. Be sure to visit Healthland where you will find plenty of fresh air sparkling drinking water and pure milk.
11. I lay down on the grass where for nine hours I slept soundly.
12. The next day we reached Nelson which is the natural outlet for the products of the Okanagan Valley.

Mastery Test A—The Comma

Copy the following sentences and punctuate them correctly. Over-punctuation is just as bad as underpunctuation. Therefore if you either omit a needed punctuation mark or insert a mark that is not needed, the sentence is wrong. Three of the sentences are correctly punctuated.

1. On the right the runway was blocked by two Canadian Air Line planes on which some men were loading mail and express packages.
2. The telegram said that my mother's only brother who has been travelling for years was coming the next day to visit us.
3. The woman who maketh a good pudding in silence is better than she who maketh a tart reply.
4. As there were Indian horse thieves in the neighbourhood a guard was put on duty at the corral.
5. The flaw in King Lear was that he liked to be flattered.
6. *Kim* written by Rudyard Kipling tells the life and experiences of a young boy in northern India.
7. "At present" said our guide "there are but two herds of wild bison in existence."
8. It is the guilt not the scaffold which constitutes the shame.
9. A book that is filled with good stories is what I like.
10. For two days the boys trailed the big cats through the tangled forest but in the end they failed to track them down.
11. There is however a limit at which forbearance ceases to be a virtue.
12. "About three o'clock" Big Tim recounted "we had to stop for the cattle were blind with thirst."

13. Virtue is usually though not necessarily connected with intelligence; vice with ignorance.
14. On August 30 1935 I came home from my vacation brown and strong for I spent most of the month in climbing mountains canoeing swimming playing golf and sleeping.
15. Margaret Deland has immortalized her birthplace Manchester a suburb of Allegheny Pennsylvania in *Old Chester Tales.*
16. Yes Harry I wish I had taken chemistry.
17. The night before we had stayed at the Chateau Frontenac in Quebec.
18. The girl who was called on to recite said "Uriah's hair which was red was cropped close to his head."
19. Disraeli who is responsible for all the action of the play is an old man very clever and witty.
20. Realizing that the son was not responsible for what his father had done Jim led the party and rescued the lad.

Mastery Test B—The Comma

Copy the following sentences and punctuate them correctly. Overpunctuation is just as bad as underpunctuation. Therefore if you either omit a needed punctuation mark or insert a mark that is not needed, the sentence is wrong. Three of the sentences are correctly punctuated.

1. Lincoln rewrote five times the famous speech which he delivered at Gettysburg.
2. Paul carried the blankets; Kit the folded tent; and I a frying pan a coffee pot and two tin cups.
3. Terrified by the smoke and flames the horses beautiful Kentucky throughbreds reared and plunged in their stalls.
4. Eppie quickly cut the linen strip which bound her to the loom and in a moment she had run out into the sunshine.
5. Shylock made the loan to Antonio not to make a large profit but to secure revenge.
6. While inspecting his racing stables however King George got a chill which later caused his death.
7. The knot which is most commonly used for tying two ropes together is the reef knot.
8. Toads bats and nonpoisonous snakes deserve man's protection since they are valuable in destroying harmful insects.
9. Mike's big locomotive which weighed over one hundred tons came roaring down the grade at fifty miles an hour.
10. If green plants are kept in the aquarium the fish and other animals need not be fed for long periods of time.
11. Dr. Gorgas who had already freed Havana and Cuba of yellow fever was asked to continue his work in Panama.
12. This temple which was the largest in Ceylon was the home of an ugly two-headed idol.
13. In colonial times it was impossible to foretell the length of a sea voyage for everything depended on wind and weather.
14. On September 1 1905 Saskatchewan and Alberta the two prairie provinces were admitted to the Dominion.

15. Ever since Meg has rushed to the cellar at the first sign of a storm.
16. "Well sir" demanded the colonel in a freezing tone "where have you been these past two days?"
17. Returning to England in 1801 Alexander Mackenzie published *Voyages from Montreal to the Frazer and Pacific Ocean.*
18. "Yes my lad" murmured the captain "a twelve-mile row in such a gale was hard on even the huskiest men."
19. Mr. Pickwick who had not been on the ice for thirty years slid gravely across the pond with his feet a yard and a quarter apart.
20. Our chief trouble was that we could not persuade the natives to guide us up the cliffs.

SEMICOLON

The semicolon is regularly a strong comma or a weak period.

18. (Weak period) As a rule, the semicolon is used between the clauses of a compound sentence if they are not joined by a conjunction. When the connecting word is *moreover, consequently, thus, hence, therefore, besides, also, nevertheless, still, otherwise, likewise,* or another independent adverb, the semicolon is used.

Caesar was dead; hence Rome was in confusion
The big ape beat his mighty chest with rage; his enormous hands rattled the iron bars of the cage.
Property can be paid for; the lives of peaceful and innocent people cannot be.

Exception. If three or more short clauses are similar in form and are closely connected in thought, the comma is used to separate them.

I came, I saw, I conquered.

19. (Strong comma) The semicolon is used frequently to separate co-ordinate parts of a sentence when they have commas within themselves.

For further information about my character, ability, and training you may write or telephone to Reverend H. B. Jackson, Viscount, Saskatchewan; Professor J. W. Inglis, 207 Thirty-second Street, Saskatoon; and Mr. J. W. Pichon, 131 Elm Avenue, Saskatoon.
The grazing zebra presents a picture of grace and gentleness; but if his anger is aroused, not even a lion is safe from his flying hoofs. [Either a comma or a semicolon after *gentleness* is correct.]

20. *Namely, for instance, for example, that is,* **and** *as,* **when introducing explanations, are preceded by the semicolon or the dash and followed by the comma.**

A pronoun is a word used in place of a noun; as, *he, we, who.*
A restrictive modifier limits the word modified; that is, it makes a general word more specific in its application.

COLON

21. Use the colon after the salutation of a business letter.

Dear Mr. Webster:

22. The colon is used to introduce a list of items or a long or formal quotation or statement. If such introducing word or expression as *this, thus, as follows, the following,* or *these words* is used, the colon follows it.

Christopher Morley's delightful essay, *What Men Live By*, begins as follows: "What a delicate and rare and gracious art is the art of conversation."

Each first aid kit must contain the following articles: bandage, adhesive plaster, gauze, mercurochrome, tube soap, and burn lotion.

INTERROGATION POINT

23. The interrogation point is used after a direct question, but not after an indirect question.

Why is it difficult to raise seals in captivity?

Mr. Carr asked why it is difficult to raise seals in captivity.

a. A period is used after a request courteously worded in interrogative form.

Will you please hand in the report before nine o'clock tomorrow morning.

Will you please send me your latest catalogue.

EXCLAMATION POINT

24. The exclamation point is used to mark an expression of strong or sudden emotion.

Three cheers for the Premier!

Whew! That's over!

Oh, what a wreck!

Notice the comma after the interjection *oh.* An interjection which is a real exclamation is followed by an exclamation point.

a. O is used with a noun in direct address and is never followed by an exclamation point.

O John, why did you tease your little brother?

DASH

25. The dash is used to indicate an abrupt change in the thought or grammatical construction of a sentence.

And, as for money—don't you remember the old saying, "Enough is as good as a feast"?

I mean—you know what I mean.

26. Dashes may be made to make parenthetical, appositive, or explanatory matter stand out clearly. Dashes are less formal and more common than parentheses.

There were diamonds—some of them exceedingly large and fine—a hundred and ten in all. — POE

Peters was thunderstruck—absolutely astounded—at this piece of good fortune.

27. The dash is used before a word that sums up preceding particulars.

The rolling green hills, the rocky seacoast, the prim white cottages—all were typical of New England.

Fishing, camping, touring—all kinds of outdoor activities now demand attention.

The dash is seldom used with any punctuation mark except the period.

QUOTATION MARKS

28. Quotation marks are used to enclose a direct quotation, but not to enclose an indirect quotation.

1. "Come on!" yelled Ed.
2. "Have you ever heard of Count von Luckner?" my father asked me.
3. "I found him in his cabin about twenty miles northwest of here," said Sergeant Perth.

In sentence 1 an exclamation point follows the quoted exclamation; in sentence 2 a question mark follows the quoted question; in sentence 3 a comma is placed after the quoted statement.

4. Harold said, "Now you're joking."

Here the quotation follows the introducing words. Notice the comma after *said* and the capital letter in *Now*.

5. "Well," said Ruth, "here we are."
6. "Throw these papers out of the window," said the Southerner to his servant, "and pay the boy for them."

When a quotation is broken by an expression like *said Ruth*, two pairs of quotation marks are needed. Notice that *here* in 5 and *and* in 6 begin with small letters. Note also that the quotation marks follow the commas and the periods.

Use a comma to set off a short direct quotation.

7. "No, I don't believe in luck," replied Dick. "There's really nothing to it."

What Dick said was two sentences:

No, I don't believe in luck.
There's really nothing to it.

When you enclose the two sentences in quotation marks you still have two sentences.

Put a period after introducing words placed between two sentences.

29. Single marks surround a quotation within a quotation.

Benjamin Franklin said, "It requires a good, strong man to say, 'I was mistaken, and am sorry.'"

30. A quotation mark following a period or comma always comes after it. Other punctuation marks should be placed inside the quotation marks only if part of the quotation.

The captain demanded, "Can you reef a jib sail?"
Will you say to him, "Come at once"?

31. When two or more paragraphs are quoted, place quotation marks at the beginning of each paragraph and at the end of the last paragraph.

32. Quote the titles of chapters, articles, essays, lectures, and short poems.

Have you read Keats's "Ode to Autumn"?
The subject of the lectures was "The Future of Russia".

33. In print the names of books, plays, newspapers, and magazines are usually italicized. In a composition or letter they may be enclosed in quotation marks or underscored.

I have been studying *Macbeth* this term.

PARENTHESES

34. Parentheses are used to enclose a side remark that does not affect the structure of the sentence.

I told him (and who would not?) just what I thought.

BRACKETS

35. Brackets surround words inserted in an article or speech by a reporter or editor.

Mr. Fess. The Chair rather gets me on that question. [Laughter] I did not rise—[Cries of "Vote!" "Vote!"]

APOSTROPHE

36. The apostrophe is used (1) to denote possession, (2) to take the place of an omitted letter, and (3) to form the plural of letters, figures, and signs.

John's brother makes neat *b*'s, *l*'s, ¼'s and *6*'s
He knows you're right and he doesn't care.

The Possessive

37. The possessive case of a noun always has an apostrophe;

the possessive case of a personal pronoun never has an apostrophe: *his, its, hers, theirs.*

a. To form the possessive singular of a noun, add 's to the nominative. The possessive sign is always at the end of the name.[1]

fox's, James's, enemy's, lady's, policeman's, son-in-law's

b. To form the possessive plural of nouns, first write the plural. Then add 's to the plurals that do not end in s and an apostrophe to the plurals that end in s.

SINGULAR	POSSESSIVE SINGULAR	PLURAL	POSSESSIVE PLURAL
policeman	policeman's	policemen	policemen's
Jones	Jones's	Joneses	Joneses'
mouse	mouse's	mice	mice's
enemy	enemy's	enemies	enemies'
lady	lady's	ladies	ladies'
child	child's	children	children's

For joint possession only one apostrophe is needed: *Allyn and Bacon's New York office.* If the possession is individual, the possessive sign is added to the name of each owner.

Isabel's, Mildred's, and Josephine's shares were as 1, 2, and 3.

Practice 2. Possessives

Write in four columns the singular, the possessive singular, the plural, and the possessive plural of each word:

alley	donkey	Murphy	teacher
ally	fly	Norman	trout
boy	fox	officer	week
Burns	it	one	who
child	Keats	potato	whoever
day	lady	sheep	woman
deer	man	sister	year
Dickens	manservant	spoonful	you

MISCELLANEOUS EXAMPLES

38. Notice the punctuation of the following:

1. MS.
2. 5, 647,982
3. August 3, 1914—November 11, 1918
4. Meet me at 8:15 P.M.
5. That's good advice, isn't it?
6. I have read many autobiographies, such as *Autobiography of a Super-Tramp* and *Roads of Adventure.*

---

[1]Nouns ending in s may take the apostrophe only: *Moses', James', Dickens', Burns', Jones'.* The easy way is always to add 's at the end of the word. Stabbing the name by putting the apostrophe before the s (*Dicken's*) is a serious blunder.

7. *Resolved,* That every automobile driver should be required to carry liability insurance.
8. Maitland barely made the goal, the ball teetering on the rim of the basket but finally dropping inside. [The comma sets off the absolute phrase.]

Practice 3. Review of Punctuation

Give the rule for every punctuation mark except a period at the end of a sentence:

1. *The Last of the Mohicans,* which relates the heroism of Hawkeye and Uncas, is the second of Cooper's Leatherstocking series.
2. The girth hitch, or larkshead knot, is used only for fastening a saddle to a horse.
3. Don't be satisfied with one; buy as many as you can.
4. Open your purse and your mouth cautiously; and your stock of wealth and wisdom shall, at least in repute, be great.
5. When you see a crime committed or observe a person acting very suspiciously, it is your duty to notify the police.
6. The soul of a man is a garden where, as he sows, so shall he reap. If ye would gather roses, do not sow rotten seeds.
7. True eloquence consists in saying all that should be, not all that could be said.
8. Two old men, dragging a heavy bundle of household goods between them, abandoned it in the street and fled screaming.
9. Her soul was noble—in her own opinion.
10. The word *that* may be used as follows: first, as a relative pronoun; second, as an adjective; third, as a subordinate conjunction.
11. War is the law of violence; peace, the law of love.
12. Fascinated by romantic tales of adventure, Shorty joined the Klondike gold rush.
13. Success, fame, wealth—are these all you demand of life?
14. *Julius Caesar* opens with this sentence: "Hence! home, you idle creatures, get you home."
15. "Will not someone arise," asks Mr. E. V. Lucas, "to remind young people of the fun, to say the least of it, of choosing the right word?"

Practice 4. Punctuating Correctly

Punctuate the following sentences and give a rule for each mark used. Insert needed apostrophes. Some sentences require no further punctuation.

1. On the first day one of the horses went lame on the second they lost the trail and wandered around for hours on the third a buffalo stampede destroyed the chuck wagon nevertheless they pushed on.
2. If a man has a job to which a large salary is attached he is said to be holding a lucrative position.
3. The chameleon which has naturally a bright green skin can change colour to suit its surroundings.
4. The trout which we caught in the pool were already broiling over the coals when the boys returned from their hike

5. The ungrateful King Charles however made no attempt to rescue Joan of Arc from her captors the English.
6. He uses very few words which the average educated person doesn't understand.
7. He noted the men who tried hard but were naturally slow and awkward.
8. What is becoming is honourable and what is honourable is becoming.
9. Our château lies in the valley between two hills so to obtain a clear view of the horizon I hurried to the roof with a pair of field glasses.
10. Just as we had seated ourselves comfortably in the auditorium Mr. Reynolds began a selection on the organ but soon the speaker appeared and gave us glimpses of Cairo and the Nile.
11. Hope is the mainspring of efficiency complacency is its rust.
12. Draw down the blind Jim whispered my mother they might come and watch outside.   And now said she when I had done so we have to get the key off that and whos to touch it I should like to know and she gave a kind of sob as she said the words.
13. When buying goods if you are satisfied with the price and quality make sure that you get full weight or measure.
14. As charity covers a multitude of sins before God so does politeness before men.
15. Men are born with two eyes but with one tongue in order that they should see twice as much as they say.
16. A needle made of fish bone and thread made of deer sinew were the only sewing tools the Indian squaws possessed.
17. There are more than a thousand different forms of ice crystals nevertheless each one always has either six points or six sides.
18. Dr. Frederick Grant Banting discovered insulin which is claimed to be a cure for diabetes.
19. He who works will be rewarded.
20. For information concerning my school record you may write or telephone to Mr. J. R. MacKay principal of Bedford Road Collegiate Institute Saskatoon.
21. When water power sets dynamos and turbines in action we get power to drive trains to run factory machines and to generate light and heat.
22. The boy who won the peace medal lives in Philadelphia which is often called the City of Brotherly Love.
23. The University of British Columbia which is situated on Point Grey has one of the finest sites in Canada.
24. A New York newspaper quotes John J. Pershing as follows I pray fervently that there will be no more war. With all my soul I hate it.
25. The question was thus stated Should our national defenses be increased?
26. For the old boatman the Mississippi still was something human it raged at him wept for him laughed at him and smiled for him.
27. He asked whether our national defenses should be increased.
28. A sudden and violent wind blew their tent so far away that they never found it again then torrents of rain beat down on the unprotected group.
29. The membership of the Board of Trustees was made up as follows labourers 2 lawyers 2 business men 3 doctors 2.
30. The insertion of a comma in a tariff bill about fifty years ago cost the United States government $2000000. The copying clerk by carelessly

writing *fruit, plants* instead of *fruit-plants* placed oranges bananas lemons and grapes on the free list until Congress amended the law.

Mastery Test A—Punctuation

Copy the following sentences, punctuate them, and insert needed apostrophes. Overpunctuation is just as bad as underpunctuation. Therefore if you either omit a needed mark or insert a mark that is not needed, the sentence is wrong. Do not divide one good sentence into two sentences.

1. Ships are warned off these sunken reefs by lighthouses buoys and fog-horns
2. The task of framing the constitution was performed by fifty-five of the best men that the provinces could send to the convention
3. Cuba which was thought to be a part of Asia was discovered by Columbus
4. Have you read about Marie Fish the young biologist who hatched the eels eggs
5. The terrific storm of hot air which sweeps the Arabian desert is called a simoom which in Arabian means poison
6. Next year however we shall make another attempt said Fred
7. If you and Janet can come to see us this summer for we are always delighted to have you
8. He was respectful not servile to superiors and affable not improperly familiar with equals
9. These are his exact words I rise Mr. President to ask for information
10. An adverb is a word used to modify a verb an adjective or another adverb as *rapidly often completely* and *altogether*
11. War means murder and destruction peace life and plenty
12. The food supply had to be organized and back of the various centres of organization stood the whole city glad to do whatever it was asked to do
13. Health ability education and opportunities in various fields should be considered in the choice of a vocation
14. We find the heart of the address in this sentence Our purpose is to build in this nation a human society not an economic system
15. By the way Tom did you ever get that dictionary you were saving your money for I asked
16. Many an Indian dazzled by glittering ornaments and gaudy blankets eagerly offered valuable furs in exchange a profitable transaction for the wily traders
17. Strange to say I found good air pilots hard to get
18. I was very glad to hear that you are coming to visit me soon
19. Hundreds of thousands of miles of rail must yet be laid millions of miles of hard-surfaced roads will yet be needed
20. In that moment sir continued Walker that crocodile had become a demon of fury lashing with its tail slashing at its tormentor with its huge jaws

Mastery Test B—Punctuation

Copy the following sentences, punctuate them, and insert needed apostrophes. Overpunctuation is just as bad as underpunctuation. Therefore if you either omit a needed mark or insert a mark that is not needed, the sentence is wrong. Do not divide one good sentence into two sentences.

1. The sunbonnet which every African baby wears to protect it from sunstroke is made of a hollow gourd
2. This is a trick he learned from William A. Muldoon who used to be able to run as fast backward as the average man can run forward
3. Man is a strange mixture of good and evil even the worst criminal has admirable qualities
4. All his life he had known activity people something going on here there was nothing to do but to eat drink and loaf
5. If the air about us did not move man beast and vegetation would die for the motion of the air keeps it pure and sweet
6. The Eskimo woman who allows her seal oil lamps to smoke is considered to say the least a poor housekeeper
7. The first settlers in Pennsylvania finding only snow-covered forests lived in holes in the river bank during the winter a miserable existence indeed
8. The human body it has been estimated gives off about as much heat as is produced by a candle flame
9. The next morning the sky was dark with threatening rain clouds but we determined to push on down the river until noon at least
10. Sealskin fur comes from sea bears which are not really seals at all
11. An old manuscript lists the seven wonders of the world as follows the pyramids the hanging gardens of Babylon the statue of Zeus at Olympia the temple of Diana at Ephesus the mausoleum of Halicarnassus the Colossus of Rhodes the Pharos lighthouse at Alexandria
12. The murex a shellfish like the mussel was prized by the ancients not for food but for a purple dye which it yields
13. My way of joking says George Bernard Shaw is to tell the truth
14. Since the earliest times shells have been used for all sorts of curious things for instance for money ornaments buttons dinner horns
15. Be not simply good be good for something
16. Admiral Peary was adored by Ootah and Seeglo who accompanied him on his expedition to the North Pole
17. Caroline asked Why should a lifesaver always approach the drowning person from the rear
18. Placing a knife between his teeth Chambers dived over the side of the boat into the very centre of the group of black shark fins
19. Lad never killed a sheep in his life Stan said Seward and you know it
20. Some are satisfied with their work during the past term most of us however are not

Poetry

THE MUSIC OF POETRY

RHYTHM is found everywhere about us in nature and in life: the beat of the heart, the tick of the clock, the rain pattering on the roof, the *left*-right of marching soldiers, the *one*-two or *one*-two-three of music and dancing, the ta-*rum*, ta-*rum*, ta-*rum-tum-tum* of the drum, the tolling of a church bell, the clang of a fire bell, the moaning of the wind in the trees, the alternation of the seasons and of day and night, the rise and fall of waves, the ebb and flow of the tide. Because of the rhythm children enjoy hearing poetry even when they don't understand it. Rhythm in speech and writing is a pleasing or tuneful arrangement of the accented and unaccented syllables.

Metre is a regular recurrence of accented and unaccented syllables.

FEET

A line of poetry is called a **verse**. The verse is made up of **feet**, groups of regularly recurring accented and unaccented syllables. The commonly used feet are:

NAME	ADJECTIVE FORM	ACCENT	EXAMPLE
iambus	iambic	‿ ′ (ta tum)	for**give**
anapest	anapestic	‿ ‿ ′ (ta ta tum)	una**fraid**
trochee	trochaic	′ ‿ (tum ta)	**kind**ly
dactyl	dactylic	′ ‿ ‿ (tum ta ta)	**but**tercup

Dactyl is from a Greek word meaning *finger*. A finger has three bones, one longer than either of the others.

Practice 1. Metrical Measure

List ten iambic words, ten trochaic words, five anapestic words, and ten dactylic words.

Feet used less frequently are

NAME	ACCENT	EXAMPLE
pyrrhic	‿ ‿ (ta ta)	of **the**
spondee	′ ′ (tum tum)	**white dawn**
amphibrach	‿ ′ ‿ (ta tum ta)	un**cer**tain

A verse is made up of one or more feet, and is named according to the type and number of feet. A verse having five iambic feet is called **iambic pentameter**.

$$\smile\ '\ |\ \smile\ '\ |\ \smile\ '\ |\ \smile\ '\ |\ \smile\ '$$
They al | so serve | who on | ly stand | and wait.

NAME	NUMBER OF FEET IN LINE	NAME	NUMBER OF FEET IN LINE
monometer	1	tetrameter	4
dimeter	2	pentameter	5
trimeter	3	hexameter	6

The most popular metres are tetrameter and pentameter, with trimeter and hexameter next in favour.

THE EFFECT OF EACH FOOT

Each foot has a different rhythmic effect. The iambus has been called the walking foot; the trochee, running; the anapest, galloping; and the dactyl, waltzing. The iambus is bold, masculine; the trochee is gentle, sweet, feminine.

Coleridge describes poetically the use or effect of each foot:
> Trochee trips from long to short;
> From long to long in solemn sort
> Slow Spondee stalks, strong foot, yet ill able
> Ever to come up with Dactyl trisyllable.
> Iambics march from short to long;
> With a leap and a bound the swift Anapests throng.

Notice the "leap and bound" of "swift Anapest" in Robert Browning's "How They Brought the Good News from Ghent to Aix."
> I sprang to the stirrup, and Joris, and he;
> I galloped, Dirck galloped, we galloped all three.

Robert Browning in "Boot and Saddle" makes use of quick "Dactyl trisyllable."
> Rescue my castle before the hot day
> Brightens to blue from its silvery grey.

Notice the "tripping" of Trochee.
> Then the little Hiawatha
> Learned of every bird its language.
> — LONGFELLOW

Practice 2. Metrical Measure

Discuss the metre of Browning's "My Star," Noyes's "The Barrel-Organ" or "The Highwayman," Longfellow's "Hiawatha" or "Evangeline," Byron's "The Destruction of Sennacherib," Hood's "The Bridge of Sighs," Stevenson's "Requiem," Markham's "Lincoln, the Man of the People," Moore's "A Visit from St. Nicholas," Milton's "L'Allegro," Tennyson's "Passing of Arthur" or "The Bugle Song," Gray's "Elegy," Wordsworth's "Daffodils" or "Reverie of Poor Susan," Masefield's "Cargoes" or "Sea Fever," De la Mare's "The Listeners," Thornburg's "The Cavalier's Escape," Buchanan's "The Green Gnome," or any other poem. What is the metre? Does it help to express the thought or feeling? How?

VARIATIONS

A verse lacking the last syllable is called **catalectic.**

Hate, and | pride, and | fear.

A verse with an added syllable is called **hypermetrical.** If the extra syllable is at the end of the line, the verse is **hypercatalectic.** The added syllable is a **weak** or **feminine** ending.

The down | y clouds | go soft | ly steal | ing.

These and similar variations in the metrical scheme prevent monotony, make the verse more musical, and help the poet to express his thought and feeling.

The occasional adding or omitting of an unaccented syllable does not interfere with the rhythm but may give a leap or a bound to the line. Hence feet with the accent on the first syllable or on the last syllable are interchanged freely.

SCANSION

To scan is to divide a verse into its feet. To scan a line mark first the accents of words of two or more syllables. Then mark monosyllables that are clearly emphatic. Usually these accents will give you a clue to the verse pattern or the prevailing foot.

Example:

But mercy is above this scepter'd sway.

Mer, bove, and *scep* are the accented syllables of the words of two syllables; *sway* is an important noun. The metre of the line is iambic pentameter.

RHYME

"You hunt the rhyme," says Gamaliel Bradford, "and the ideas come trooping after like quaint satyrs and nymphs after the pipe of Pan."

Rhyme is a similarity of sound, usually at the ends of lines. Words which rhyme perfectly have—
1. Accent on the rhyming syllables
2. The same vowel sounds in the accented syllables
3. The same sounds after this vowel sound
4. Different consonant sounds before this vowel sound

Rhyme is a matter of pronunciation or sound, not of spelling. *Laid, shade; hate, weight; kite, tight; pealing, reeling; nation, exclamation; gleaming, seeming; laugh, giraffe; after, laughter,* rhyme; *dough, cough;*

divine, routine; prey, key; map, hat; pain, flame, do not. Occasionally we find such imperfect rhymes as *given, heaven; shadow, meadow; earth, hearth; bare, are; move, rove; real, steal; love, move; never, river.*

Single (or masculine) rhyme consists of one rhyming syllable—*sound, found;* **double** (or feminine) rhyme, of two—*shaken, waken;* **triple** rhyme,—of three—*tenderly, slenderly.* In double or triple rhyme the rhyming syllables may be in two or three words—*brink of it, think of it.*

Blank verse is verse without rhyme. Shakespeare wrote usually in unrhymed iambic pentameter, a dignified, noble verse form, suitable for the expression of the loftiest ideas.

Alliteration is the repetition of the same initial sound in words closely following each other.

> Then star nor sun shall waken,
> Nor any change of light;
> Nor sound of water shaken
> Nor any sound or sight.
> — SWINBURNE

Here Swinburne uses the *s*-sound effectively to suggest the hushed silence of the long sleep of death.

Practice 3. Alliteration

Read these lines aloud. Is alliteration skilfully used in each? Give a reason for your answer.

1. The fair breeze blew, the white foam flew,
    The furrow followed free. — COLERIDGE
2. Bareheaded, breathless, and besprent with mire. — LONGFELLOW
3. Too English to bargain, bully, and browbeat; to wheedle, whine, or weep.
    — TRADER HORN
4. The ploughman homeward plods his weary way. — GRAY
5. A man to match the mountains and the sea. — MARKHAM

ONOMATOPOEIA

Onomatopoeia is the fitting of sound to meaning. Examples are *buzz, roar, howl, splash, cackle, whistle, whizz, rumble, clatter, clash, hiss, murmur, clang, plunge, bubble, tap, grate, drowsy, bang, gurgle.*

Some time ago in England a vote was taken on the most expressive, the most romantic, the most beautiful, the most poetic, and the most completely onomatopoetic word. The winner was *murmuring.*

Keats told how the sound of the word *forlorn* affected him:

> Forlorn! the very word is like a bell
> To toll me back from thee to my sole self.

Practice 4. Onomatopoetic Language

Is onomatopoeia used skilfully in each of the following? Prove your answer.

1. Oilily bubbled up the mere. — TENNYSON
2. When Ajax strives some rock's vast weight to throw,
   The line too labours, and the words move slow. — POPE
3. The sails did sigh like sedge. — COLERIDGE
4. Moan of doves in immemorial elms
   And murmuring of innumerable bees. — TENNYSON
5. No more! Alas, that magical sad sound
   Transferring all! — POE
6. Bang-whang-whang goes the drum, tootle-te-tootle the fife. — BROWNING
7. The ice was here, the ice was there,
      The ice was all around;
   It cracked and growled, and roared and howled,
      Like noises in a swound! — COLERIDGE
8.   Hear the loud alarum bells—
             Brazen bells!
   What a tale of terror, now, their turbulency tells!
       In the startled ear of night
     How they scream out their affright!
       Too much horrified to speak,
   They can only shriek, shriek. — POE

STANZAS

A **stanza** is a regular combination of two or more verses. A **couplet** is a stanza containing two rhyming lines.

> What wonder if Sir Launfal now
> Remembered the keeping of his vow?
>
> — LOWELL

Pope used the iambic pentameter couplet, called the **heroic couplet,** to express pointedly and tersely his ideas. Do you see why this is sometimes called the rocking-horse measure? Does the first line of each couplet seem to climb higher and higher and the second slide down?

> In words, as fashions, the same rule will hold,
> Alike fantastic, if too new or old;
> Be not the first by whom the new are tried,
> Nor yet the last to lay the old aside.
>
> — POPE

The **triplet,** a stanza of three lines rhyming together, is used by only a few poets.

> The wrinkled sea beneath him crawls;
> He watches from his mountain walls,
> And like a thunderbolt he falls.
>
> — TENNYSON

A quatrain is a stanza of four verses.

About, | about, | in reel | and rout

The death- | fires danced | at *night;*

The wa | ter, like | a witch | 's oils,

Burnt green | and blue | and *white.*

This quatrain, made up of iambic tetrameter alternating with iambic trimeter, is the typical ballad stanza. The second and fourth lines rhyme.

Practice 5. Ballad Writing

Write a ballad about a school subject, a person, or a school happening, or tell a biblical, Robin Hood, or other story in ballad form. Write, for example, the ballad of the lunchroom, the football game, the excursion, commencement, the study hall, the athletic assembly, the election, examinations, the annual play, the concert, the speaking contest, the debate, the school paper, the library, camp, a ride, a hike, or an adventure. Base your ballad, if you wish, on a newspaper article, a story, or a paragraph or chapter of a history, a novel, or a biography.

Four other quatrain rhyme schemes are favourites. Lines marked *a* or *b* or *c* rhyme. The *abab* after number 1 shows that the first line rhymes with the third, and the second with the fourth. A line which has no rhyme is called *x.*

1

Full many a gem of purest ray *serene,*	*a*
The dark unfathomed caves of ocean **bear;**	*b*
Full many a flower is born to blush un*seen,*	*a*
And waste its sweetness on the desert **air.**	*b*

(Called the *In Memoriam* stanza because used by Tennyson in *In Memoriam.* Also called the Tennysonian stanza.)

I sometimes hold it half a *sin*	*a*
To put in words the grief I **feel;**	*b*
For words, like Nature, half re**veal**	*b*
And half conceal the Soul with*in.*	*a*

— TENNYSON

3

Speed slackens now, I *float*	*a*
Awhile in my airy *boat*	*a*
Till, when the wheels scarce **crawl,**	*b*
My feet to the treadles **fall.**	*b*

4

(Called Omaric stanza because used in Fitzgerald's translation of *The Rubáiyát* of Omar Khayyám. Also called the Rubáiyát stanza.)

Yet Ah, that Spring should vanish with the *Rose!*	*a*
That Youth's sweet-scented manuscript should *close!*	*a*
The Nightingale that in the branches sang,	*x*
Ah whence, and whither flown again, who *knows!*	*a*

— FITZGERALD

The five quatrain rhyme schemes illustrated are: (1) *abab;* (2) *abba;* (3) *aabb;* (4) *aaxa;* and (ballad stanza) *xaxa.* The last line must figure in the rhyming. By varying the rhyme scheme and the metrical pattern poets construct a great variety of quatrains.

Practice 6. Stanza Forms

Using any metrical pattern (iambic trimeter, iambic pentameter, trochaic tetrameter, etc.) and one of the rhyme schemes just illustrated (*abab, abba, aabb, aaxa*), write a stanza on a topic of your own choice.

Stanzas of five, six, seven, eight, and nine lines are common. The *Spenserian stanza* consists of nine lines; the first eight are iambic pentameters, and the ninth is an iambic hexameter. The rhyme scheme is *ababbcbcc.* Spenser's *Faerie Queene* and Byron's *Childe Harold* are written in this stanza.

There is a pleasure in the pathless woods,	*a*
There is a rapture on the lonely shore,	*b*
There is society, where none intrudes,	*a*
By the deep sea, and music in its roar;	*b*
I love not man the less, but nature more,	*b*
From these our interviews, in which I steal	*c*
From all I may be, or have been before,	*b*
To mingle with the universe, and feel	*c*
What I can ne'er express, yet cannot all conceal.	*c*

— LORD BYRON's *Childe Harold*

POEM FORMS

The **limerick,** an absurd five-line poem with an unexpected snap or twist in the fifth line, is easy to write. Lines 1, 2, and 5 are anapestic trimeter and rhyme; lines 3 and 4, anapestic dimeters, also rhyme. The pattern is—

Anywhere in the pattern an iambus (‿ ′) may be substituted for an anapest (‿ ‿ ′).

1

There was a young lady of Niger
Who smiled as she rode on a Tiger;
   They came back from the ride
   With the lady inside,
And the smile on the face of the Tiger.

2

There was an Old Man with a beard,
Who said, "It is just as I feared!—
   Two Owls and a Hen,
   Four Larks and a Wren,
Have all built their nests in my beard!"
                 — EDWARD LEAR

Practice 7. Writing Limericks

Edward Lear, the author of example 2, wrote more than two hundred limericks. If you have never written a limerick, you have missed some good fun. Write, not two hundred, but two limericks about people you know, have seen, have heard of, or have read about.

A **cinquain** is a poem of five unrhymed lines, with one foot in the first line, two in the second, three in the third, four in the fourth, and one in the fifth.

Student Cinquains;

DREAMS

Lost on
A pleasant sea,
Afloat in a magic boat
Which takes him to a fairy land
Of dreams. — CATHERINE PETRILLO

TWILIGHT

At dusk
The day and night
Embrace for one light kiss;
A purple mist enfolds the two. . . .
Then dark. — DORIS M. GORDON

The **sonnet** is a poem of fourteen iambic pentameter lines. The Italian sonnet is made up of an octave rhyming *abba abba* and a sestet commonly rhyming *cdecde* or *cdcdcd*. The octave usually presents an idea, story, picture, doubt, problem, query; the sestet, a reflection, conclusion, answer, or solution. The Shakespearean sonnet is rhymed *abab cdcd efef gg.*

SONNET WRITTEN BY A LITTLE INDIAN GIRL

I own 'twas so. She said I dreamed in class—
Who would not dream? 'Twas some chance word she said;

I have forgotten what; the colour red
Perhaps, or just a prism through the glass.
Enough to free my soul and let it pass
From those four walls. Stripped of the dead,
Dull commonplace, singing through space it sped
Above cold seas of azure and topaz,
To lands whose ships lay gleaming in the sun
Laden to sail for ports of mystery;
Past gardens fair, where Dido waits for one
Who does not come, and Pan laughs secretly.
Poor, cheated class that heard but chemistry,
And missed the evening bells of Arcady.

Other examples of student verse;

THE SEA

I am in love with the purple twilight
From a dim plain,
With her star-sweet raiment blown and drifted
By the grey rain.

I am in love with silver laughter
Of a bright sea-maid,
As she binds her emerald hair with a slender ribbon
Of amber shade.

I am in love with the starlight falling
On a blue rock,
And the moon-canoe and Indian Summer in it
Drifting to dock.

I am in love with the lift and fall of the silver
Of sea-gull's wings,
Flashing above the blue wave's restless brightness
Where the sunlight swings.

I am in love with the wistful water creeping
Over the lea,
With the mystery of death and the wonder of life within it,
I am in love with the sea.

— KATHLEEN DAVIDSON.
By permission of the author

AUTUMN DUSK

Here, where the star-locked gateway of the blue sky opens
Into the infinite bosom of the purple hills
We have drunk sunlight from flasks of the golden hours
That summer fills.

Now in a tender west the fires of Autumn
Burn—a supernal rose round a core of gold—

And stray winds whisper among dead leaves and grasses
A secret old.

Up from the old gray river that winds through the silence,
Like a tarnished strand from the silver skein of the moon,
Stretches the stubble-field dark in the deepening shadows
That gather so soon.

An old witch-willow sifts through her trembling fingers
Fairy-gold bright from the moon-handled cup of night,
And whispers an ancient charm o'er her stolen treasures
That fade with the light.

Soon will the old world draw her white shawl about her,
Tenderly wrap her children under the sod,
Then, her work ended, will spend the last night keeping
A tryst with God.

— KATHLEEN DAVIDSON.
By permission of the author

WHEN I AM DEAD

When I am dead and have no longer need
Of earth-born things that once were life to me,
Take up my noblest thoughts and dreams, O Wind,
And bear them with thee to the mournful sea;
And let her tint them with her varying hues,
And fill them with her power, her depth, her strength,
And wash them with her ceaseless shadowed waves
Until, some quiet, moonlit night, at length
Some lonely, restless heart cries out, and craves
The comfort and the peace of quiet hours.
And then, O Wind, catch from the seething foam
Of some far sea my scattered salt-washed flowers
Of thought, and bear them back with thee to him
Who caused thy journey, and then softly say,
As in his groping hands thou layest them,
"Take these, the thoughts and dreams of yesterday;
Make of them what thou canst. Use but the best,
And from them gather peace and hope, and build
Upon them better, greater things." And if
He does, my greatest dream shall be fulfilled.

—M. RUTH FARNAM.
By permission of the author

The Library

PLAN OF THE LIBRARY

MANY high school pupils approach the library with timidity and awe. Too often they regard the catalogue, the files, and the arrangement of the books as unsolvable mysteries. The truth of the matter is that using the library is an enjoyable game if one knows the rules. Go to your public or school library, explore for a half hour, and test your powers of observation. Locate the card catalogue, the magazine rack, the clipping file, novels, biographies, reference books. Then wander around among the book shelves and see what you can find out for yourself about the arrangement. Notice the numbers printed on the backs of the books. Most libraries are arranged according to the Dewey Decimal Classification, which divides all books into ten groups according to subject.

DEWEY DECIMAL CLASSIFICATION

010–099 General works
010   Bibliographies
030   Encyclopedias

101–199 Philosophy
170   Conduct

200–299 Religion
220   Bible
290   Myths

300–399 Sociology
330   Economics
350   Government
394   Holidays
398   Folklore, fairy tales, legends

400–499 Language
420   English language

500–599 Natural science
500   General science
510   Mathematics
520   Astronomy
530   Physics
537   Electricity
540   Chemistry
570   Biology
580   Nature study

591   Animals
595   Insects
598   Birds

600–699 Useful arts
607   Vocational guidance
608   Inventions
613   Hygiene
620   Engineering
630   Agriculture, gardening
640   Home economics
680   Manual training, handicraft

700–799 Fine Arts
740   Drawing
770   Photography
780   Music
790   Amusements, sports
792   Theatre, movies

800–899 Literature
810   American literature
811   Poetry, American
812   Drama, American
814   Essays, American
820   English literature
821   Poetry, English
822   Drama, English

824   Essays, English   920   Biography, collective
                                          930   Ancient history
900–999 History   940   European history
910   Travel, geography   973   United States history

Practice 1.   Dewey Decimal Classification

To which of the ten groups does each of the following books belong?

1. *Creative Chemistry*   6. *Behind the Scenes at the Opera*
2. *Oxford Book of Canadian Verse*   7. *Book of the Ancient World*
3. *Appreciation of Music*   8. *As You Like It*
4. *Essays of Elia*   9. *Travels in Alaska*
5. *Trades and Professions*   10. *Story Lives of the Master Writers*

In the literature group the second figure shows the country; and the third, the kind of writing.

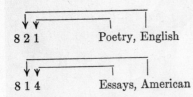

8 2 1   Poetry, English

8 1 4   Essays, American

Some libraries use 820 for both English and American literature.

If you find the 100 group and then walk around the library, you will see that the numbers are in order—200, 300, 400 etc.

Books of fiction have no call numbers but are arranged alphabetically on a separate set of shelves according to the author's name. Books by the same author are arranged alphabetically by title. On the shelf four books by Kipling will be in this order: *Kim, The Light That Failed, Plain Tales from the Hills, Under the Deodars.*

Books of individual biography, numbered *B* or *921*, are usually grouped together on a separate set of shelves and are arranged alphabetically according to the name of the person written about. Thus a biography of George Washington precedes one of Walt Whitman.

CARD CATALOGUE

The card catalogue, which indexes the library by author, by title, and by subject, will help you to find quickly any book in the library. An author card has at the top the name of an author; a title card, the name of the book; and a subject card, a topic treated. In most libraries the heading of the subject card is in red. All these cards are filed alphabetically in a cabinet of small drawers or trays. Cards are filed according to the first word or words on the first line, other than an article.

The card catalogue answers the three questions which users of a library frequently ask:

"Has the library a book with this title?"

"Are there any books in the library by this author?"

"What books on this subject are there in the library?"

Suppose you want to find a book about Theodore Roosevelt by Henry Pringle. First look under the author's last name and find—

Agfa-Ansco Film

A high school girl initiates four young readers into the secrets of the library.

Author Card

```
  B       Pringle, Henry Fowles
R781Pr      Theodore Roosevelt; a biography.   627p. por.
          New York.  Harcourt, c1931.
```

In the upper left corner is the call number: *B* for individual biography, *R* for *Roosevelt*, and *Pr* for the author, *Pringle*. The title of the book is *Theodore Roosevelt*. *627p. por.* means that the book has 627 pages and contains a portrait of Roosevelt. *New York* is the place of publication; *Harcourt* stands for Harcourt, Brace and Company, the publishers; and *c1931* gives the copyright date.

The copyright date is important in selecting material for a talk or class paper. A book on motion-picture photography published in 1920 would be of very little value in a discussion of present-day trends. If, however, you wish to trace the development of the modern motion-picture industry, you will find books copyrighted in 1900, at the birth of the industry, both interesting and valuable.

If you know the title of the book but not the author, look in the catalogue for the—

Title Card

```
B       Theodore Roosevelt; a biography
R781Pr Pringle, Henry Fowles
        Theodore Roosevelt; a biography. 627p. por.
        New York. Harcourt, c1931.
```

Under the subject *Roosevelt, Theodore,* you will probably find a—

Subject Card Referring to Whole Book

```
B       ROOSEVELT, Theodore      1858-1919
R781B   Burroughs, John
        Camping and tramping with Roosevelt. 110p.
        Boston. Houghton, c 1907.
```

Among the subject cards you may also find this one:

Subject Card Referring to Part of Book

```
920     ROOSEVELT, Theodore
W12R                        See pp. 1-65 in
        Wade, Mrs. Mary Hazelton (Blanchard)
        Real Americans, Boston, Little, Brown, 1929.
```

Practice 2. Using the Card Catalogue

Answer the following questions by using only the card catalogue:

1. List the books or parts of books in your library which contain information about short-story writing, Greek myths, the American Revolution, cartoons, world peace.
2. Find one book of collected plays by James M. Barrie, W. S. Gilbert, John Galsworthy, or Lord Dunsany. What plays are included in the volume?
3. What books by the following authors does your library contain: Wilfred T. Grenfell, Washington Irving, Eugene O'Neill, Richard Halliburton, Christopher Morley?
4. Which of the following books are in your library? Copy the name of the author of each book that has a title card in the catalogue.

Edge of the Jungle	*Adventures in Contentment*
The Winged Horse	*Self-Cultivation in English*
North of Boston	*The Life of the Spider*

Innocents Abroad   *Only Yesterday*
Lyrics of Lowly Life   *Literary Lapses*

5. Where can you find "The Luck of Roaring Camp," a short story by Bret Harte?

6. Find the call number, author, title, and date of the most recent book in the library on one of these topics: aviation, moving pictures, history of Canada, travel in Europe.

PAMPHLET AND CLIPPING FILE

Important pamphlets and clippings from newspapers, booklets, and magazines are kept in folders or large envelopes arranged alphabetically by subject in a filing cabinet. In classifying clippings librarians use such topics as—

Airplanes	Authors	Boy Scouts	College
Athletics	Birds	Camping	Cooking

A clipping file has up-to-the-minute information about prominent people and important events. If you are permitted to use it, remember that the librarian trusts you to return every clipping to its proper folder.

READERS' GUIDE

Like the index, which is a guide to a book, and the card catalogue, which is a guide to a library, the *Readers' Guide*, an index of magazine articles since 1900, is a guide to more than a hundred magazines. To search through all the magazines for recent articles on aviation or football would take hours. In the *Readers' Guide* you can find the answer to your question in a few minutes.

The Guide is published every month. Occasionally during the year a larger number covering two or more months is published. In the summer the paper-bound numbers of a year are combined into a bound volume. Every three or five years these annual numbers are combined into larger volumes.

In the alphabetical list in the Guide an article is entered under the subject and the author's last name; a story, under the author and the title; and a poem, under the author and alphabetically according to the title under *Poems*.

Here is a typical excerpt from the *Readers' Guide:*

MORLEY, Christopher Darlington

Effendi. Sat R Lit 10:471 F 10 '34

Notice the order of the items:

1. Author's full name
2. Title

3. Abbreviations for the name of the magazine. *Sat R Lit = Saturday Review of Literature.* See the key to abbreviations at the front of the Guide.
4. Volume number, before the colon.
5. Page number, after the colon.
6. Date of the magazine (February 10, 1934). If the magazine is published weekly, the day is given; if monthly, only the month.

Il, por, diag, or *bibliog* after the title shows that the article has illustrations, a portrait, a diagram, or a bibliography.

Like the encyclopaedia and the card catalogue, the *Readers' Guide* uses cross references:

RADIO plays. See Radio Broadcasting—Drama

Practice 3. Using the Readers' Guide

Using the *Readers' Guide,* answer the following questions. In your answers to questions 1, 2, 3, 4, 5, and 6, give for each article (1) the author, (2) the title, (3) the magazine, (4) the volume, (5) the pages, and (6) the date.

1. In preparation for a class discussion of leisure find references to three magazine articles.
2. To prepare for a debate on the question *"Resolved,* That high school examinations should be abolished," find references to three magazine articles.
3. Find a reference to a magazine article in which Heywood Broun discusses cowardice.
4. Find a reference to an article on white ants published in recent years. Under what heading did you find the article?
5. Find references to two recent articles on school journalism. Under what heading did you find the articles?
6. Many of Stephen Leacock's humorous articles have been published in magazines. Find references to two of them.
7. Give the titles of two of Arthur Guiterman's poems which have appeared in magazines.
8. In 1933 Mrs. Helen Wills Moody wrote a series of articles on her tennis career. In what magazine were they published?
9. In 1933 the *Saturday Evening Post* published two articles about Charles A. Lindbergh. Give the titles and authors.
10. What current magazines are in your school or town library? What bound magazines are on the shelves? How are they arranged?

Parliamentary Practice

To accomplish anything, a meeting, like a business office, must have order and system. Parliamentary law is a set of rules which provide a method of transacting business smoothly, swiftly, fairly, and, above all, courteously. A good sportsman learns the rules of the game and abides by them.

The following pages are a short handbook on parliamentary practice for a school club.

FIRST MEETING

1. A temporary chairman and a temporary secretary are elected (see page 575).

2. Someone may state the object of the meeting or move that a permanent organization be formed.

3. A motion is made to appoint a committee on constitution and by-laws. The motion may state the number to be appointed. The chairman appoints the committee at the time or at a later time. Or the motion may name the members of the committee.

SECOND MEETING

1. The meeting is called to order. The minutes are read. The chairman says, "You have heard the minutes. Are there any corrections?" After a pause he says, "If there are no corrections, the minutes stand approval as read."

2. The Committee on Constitution and By-Laws reports its work complete and hands a copy to the secretary.

3. A member moves that the constitution and by-laws be adopted.

4. The chairman asks the secretary to read the constitution and by-laws one article at a time. After each article is read, he asks whether there are any amendments. If an amendment is offered, it is discussed and voted on. After the reading he says, "The entire constitution has been read and is open to amendment."

5. The president calls for a vote on the adoption of the constitution and by-laws as amended.

6. If the constitution and by-laws are adopted, permanent officers are elected.

7. The meeting is open for the transaction of business.

CHOICE OF OFFICERS

Nominations

1. Nominations may be made from the floor or by a nominating committee. By the second method other nominations are in order after the nominating committee has reported.

2. A member says, "I nominate Clifford Watts." The chair says, "Clifford Watts has been nominated," and writes his name on the blackboard.

3. The chairman may use his judgment about accepting a declination or call for a vote of the assembly on it.

4. A nomination does not need seconding.

5. If the motion to close nominations is seconded and carried, further nominations are shut off.

6. Without a motion, if there are no further nominations, the chairman may declare the nominations closed and say, "You may prepare your ballots."

7. One who makes or seconds a nomination may at the time speak of the fitness of the candidate.

Election

1. To save time, a standing or a show-of-hands vote is sometimes permissible. The candidates by these methods are voted on in the order of nomination.

2. Commonly election by secret ballot is required by the constitution.

3. Unless the constitution or a standing rule provides otherwise, a majority is necessary to elect.

4. If no candidate receives a majority on the first ballot, the members ballot again.

5. By motion the one receiving the fewest votes may be eliminated after each ballot.

6. If there is but one candidate, a member may rise and say, "I move that the secretary cast one ballot for Marie Wilson for treasurer." If the motion is carried, the secretary writes the ballot, rises, and says, "Mr. Chairman, Marie Wilson receives one vote for the office of treasurer, and there is no vote for any other candidate." The chairman then declares Marie Wilson elected.

CONSTITUTION AND BY-LAWS

The constitution contains the most important and permanent rules of the society. The by-laws are rules somewhat less important and permanent than those included in the constitution.

The constitution commonly includes:

1. The name and purpose of the organization
2. Qualifications for membership and method of admission to the club
3. Time and manner of electing officers, and duties of each officer
4. Appointment and duties of standing committees
5. Time and place of meetings
6. Method of amending the constitution

The by-laws may include:

1. Attendance necessary for a quorum
2. The book on parliamentary practice accepted as authority
3. Fees and dues
4. Order of business
5. Method of amending the by-laws

The by-laws may contain also details about membership, officers, meetings, fines, and standing committees. There is no sharp line between the constitution matter and by-law matter.

The order of business should be somewhat like this:

1. Roll call
2. Reading and adoption of minutes
3. Reports of standing committees
4. Reports of special committees
5. Unfinished business
6. New business
7. Programme or speaker
8. Adjournment

In an English club a discussion of the programme or a criticism by the teacher or a pupil usually follows the programme.

CHAIRMAN OR PRESIDENT

1. The chairman calls the meeting to order at the appointed time, announces the business to be transacted, announces the result of a vote, decides points of order, and preserves order in the meeting.

2. When a motion is made and seconded, the chairman says, "It has been moved and seconded that this club challenge the Wilson Club to a joint debate. Are there any remarks on the motion?" or "Is there any discussion?" He should be careful to use the exact words of the maker of the motion and may ask the secretary to read the motion. The chairman may require the maker of a motion to hand it in writing to the secretary. When, after some discussion, no member rises to debate, the chairman says, "Are there any further remarks? If not, are you ready for the question?" If there is no reply or if members call out "Question!" he says, "It has been moved and seconded that this club challenge the Wilson Club to a joint debate.

Those in favour say 'Aye.' Those opposed say 'No.' The ayes have it; the motion is carried." If the chairman is in doubt, he says, "Those in favour of the motion will rise." After the count he says, "You may be seated. Those opposed will rise." After a voice vote any member may call for a standing or show-of-hands vote by saying, "Mr. Chairman, I call for a division."

3. The president sits except when stating a motion, putting a question to vote, announcing the result of a vote, and speaking upon a question of order.

4. To obtain the floor a member rises and says, "Mister Chairman" (or "Madam Chairman"). The chairman says "William." When a number wish to obtain the floor at the same time, the chairman recognizes first:

(1) The maker of the motion if he has not spoken
(2) A member on the opposite side from the one who has just spoken
(3) One who hasn't spoken on the question
(4) One who seldom rises to speak

In other cases he gives the floor to the one who first addresses the chair. If a member stands while another is speaking to make sure of obtaining the floor, raises his hand instead of addressing the chair, or otherwise makes himself objectionable, the chairman should not recognize him.

5. The chairman should always call for a second to a motion by saying, "Is the motion seconded?" or "Is there a second to the motion?" and declare the motion lost for want of a second if there is no response. A second, however, is in order even after this announcement. The seconder of a motion does not need to rise or obtain the floor.

6. The chairman should warn a member who is not speaking on the question, and if he does not then keep to the point deprive him of the floor.

7. If the chairman wishes to debate a question, he should call to the chair the vice-president, the secretary, or another member, take a seat in the assembly, and speak only when recognized by the chair. He should likewise call a member to the chair to put a motion which refers to the chairman.

8. The chairman may vote when the voting is by ballot and in other cases when his vote would defeat the motion by making a tie or carry it by breaking a tie. For example, if the vote on a motion is 8 to 7, the chairman may vote "No," thus making a tie and defeating the motion.

9. By unanimous consent the chairman may take any action that does not violate the constitution or by-laws. He says, "If there are no objections, the next meeting will be held at 3:15 instead of 3:30."

After a pause he says, "It is so ordered." If objection is raised, a motion is necessary.

10. The chairman should be prompt and decisive in his rulings, should not himself waste time, and should not permit members to delay the business to be transacted.

11. The chairman refers to himself as "the chair."

VICE-PRESIDENT

The vice-president should render valuable aid to the president and be ready to take the president's place at any time.

SECRETARY

1. The secretary should keep an accurate record of everything that is done in a meeting. The minutes should include the kind of meeting, name of body, time of meeting, name of chairman, motions lost as well as motions passed, names of members appointed to committees, important remarks, and the like.

2. He notifies members of appointment on committees and of regular or special meetings.

3. He assists the president by counting in a division, by reading the exact wording of a motion, or by giving information about unfinished business or action already taken by the meeting.

4. He is custodian of the constitution, by-laws, minutes, and correspondence.

He carries on correspondence and reports to the society, calls the roll and keeps a record of the attendance, and in the absence of the president and vice-president calls the meeting to order.

TREASURER

1. The treasurer should keep in ink a detailed record of all sums received and expended and be ready at any meeting to make a complete report. The treasurer's book should be clear to any member who may be called upon to audit it.

2. He should give receipts for dues and assessments and secure a receipt when money is paid out.

3. The by-laws or constitution should specify how bills are to be paid. In many organizations the rule is that money is to be paid out only after it has been voted by the society.

COMMITTEES

1. The constitution or by-laws may provide for the appointment of an executive committee, a programme committee, a membership com-

mittee, a publicity committee, a refreshment committee, and the like. These are standing committees with a fixed term of office. A special committee is appointed for a particular task. For example, the club may authorize the appointment of a committee to devise a plan for raising funds for the purchase of medals to be presented. Such a committee ceases to exist when it has done its work and reported to the society. The society either takes no action on a committee report or votes to adopt it. If the committee recommends a public mock trial to raise money, a vote to adopt the report means that the mock trial is to be held.

2. Committees are commonly appointed by the presiding officer. The first member named is the temporary chairman unless another is specified. If no chairman is named, the committee may select its own chairman.

3. A committee meets at the call of the chairman. A majority of a committee constitute a quorum.

RULES OF DEBATE

1. Do not refer to a member by name. Say "the preceding speaker," "the chair," "the secretary."

2. Don't rise to speak a second time unless everybody has had an opportunity to speak.

3. Address your remarks to the chairman and stick to the question.

4. A member may rise to debate up to the time that the negative vote is called for.

5. After a member has obtained the floor, he may hold it except for the question of consideration, a point of order, a call for the order of the day, a question of privilege, or a call to enter on the minutes a motion to reconsider.

PRECEDENCE OF MOTIONS

To fix time of next meeting **A, D?, R** (Symbols are explained on page 580.)
To adjourn (if next meeting time has been fixed) **r**
Question of privilege **D, A, T, P, C, R, —F?** (The first six symbols apply to a privileged motion, not to a request.)
Point of order **—F, —S**
To appeal from the decision of the chair **T, D?,R**
To suspend the rules $\frac{2}{3}$
To withdraw (or renew) a motion **R**
Objection to consideration of question $\frac{2}{3}$, **—F, —S, R**
To lay on the table **r, R?**
Previous question (closes debate) $\frac{2}{3}$, **r, R?**
To postpone to a certain time, **r, D?, A?, R**
To refer **D + , A, r, R**
To amend an amendment **D, R**

To amend **D, A, T, R.** To postpone indefinitely **D + , R**
Main question **D, A, P, C, T, R**

1. To amend and to postpone indefinitely are of the same rank.
Neither yields to the other.

2. The question mark after a symbol indicates that there are exceptions to the general statement. These exceptions are given in the discussion of the motions on pages 580–584.

3. The motions in the preceding list are arranged according to their rank, the highest first and the lowest last. Any motion takes precedence over any motion below it. For example, if a motion is before the house, an amendment is made and seconded, and a motion to adjourn is made and seconded, the motion to adjourn is acted on first. If it is lost, the amendment is discussed and voted on. If the amendment is carried, the motion as amended is discussed and voted on.

Key to Symbols

A — Amendable.
C — May be referred to a committee.
D — Debatable. Previous question applicable.
D+ — Opens whole question for debate. Previous question applicable.
–F — In order when another has the floor.
P — May be postponed definitely or indefinitely.
R — May be reconsidered.
r — Renewable after other business.
–S — Second not required.
T — May be laid on the table.
⅔ — Two-thirds vote necessary.

COMMON MOTIONS CLASSIFIED ACCORDING TO USE

To *postpone* action, move (1) to lay on the table or (2) to postpone to a certain time.

To *defeat* the question, move (1) to postpone indefinitely or (2) to lay on the table.

To *stop debate*, move the previous question.

To *change the motion*, move to amend.

MAIN MOTION

MEMBER [*rising*]. Madam President [*pausing for recognition*], I move that we hold a declamation contest.

1. A main motion is not in order if any other motion is pending.

2. If the motion is defeated, it cannot be introduced again at the same meeting.

POSTPONE INDEFINITELY

MEMBER [*rising*]. Mr. Chairman [*pausing for recognition*], I move that we postpone consideration of this motion indefinitely.

1. When a motion is postponed indefinitely, it is really defeated, because it may not be considered again during the meeting.

2. Sometimes leaders use this motion to find out how many are opposed to the original motion.

AMEND

MEMBER. I move to amend the motion by striking out *declamation* and inserting the word *speaking*.

1. To amend means to change. The wording of the motion is changed by an amendment.

2. A change in the motion may be made by adding, subtracting, substituting, or dividing.

3. By unanimous consent a maker may change his motion without moving to amend.

4. An amendment must keep to the question but may be hostile to it. An amendment to add *not* or eliminate *not* or a silly amendment should be ruled out of order.

5. When an amendment is laid on the table, it takes with it the original question.

AMEND AN AMENDMENT

MEMBER. I move to amend the amendment by inserting the word *extemporaneous* before *speaking*.

The amendment to the amendment is acted on before the amendment or original motion. To illustrate, after discussion a vote is taken on inserting *extemporaneous*. If the meeting votes to change the amendment, the amendment is amended, that the words *extemporaneous speaking* be substituted for the word *declamation*, is discussed and voted on. If the amendment as amended is lost, the original motion, that the club hold a declamation contest, is discussed and voted on.

REFER

MEMBER. I move that we refer this question to a committee of three.
MEMBER. I move to refer the question to the Executive Committee.

1. The motion is useful when further investigation is desirable.

2. Amendments may change the size or selection of the committee or instruct the committee.

3. The motion should state the size of the committee and may include a method of selection.

POSTPONE TO A CERTAIN TIME

MEMBER. I move that we postpone consideration of this question till the next meeting.

1. The motion gives time for consideration.

2. At the time set the matter comes up under old business.

3. Debate must concern the wisdom of the postponement.

4. A change in the time at which the matter is to be considered is the only amendment in order.

PREVIOUS QUESTION (CLOSE DEBATE)

MEMBER. I move the previous question.

After a second to the motion the chairman says, "The previous question has been called for. Shall debate now be closed?"

1. The motion stops debate and requires a vote on the original question.

2. If a main motion and an amendment are before the house, the previous question unlimited requires a vote on both the amendment and the main motion without further debate. To limit the closing of debate to the amendment, the motion should be, "I move the previous question on the amendment."

3. The motion to limit debate, like the previous question, requires a two-thirds vote.

LAY ON THE TABLE

MEMBER. I move that we lay the main motion on the table.

A motion laid on the table is really lost unless a majority vote to take it from the table. Hence the motion is used both to delay action and to defeat a motion.

OBJECTION TO CONSIDERATION OF QUESTION

MEMBER. I object to the consideration of this question.

1. This motion is used to dispose of improper motions without debate.

2. The objection is in order only before the question has been debated.

WITHDRAWAL OF A MOTION

MEMBER. I move that George Howard be allowed to withdraw his motion.

Before a motion has been stated by the chairman, the maker has the privilege of withdrawing it. After it has been stated by the chair, he may withdraw it only by unanimous consent or on motion to withdraw.

QUESTION OF ORDER

MEMBER. I rise to a point of order.

CHAIRMAN. State your point of order.

MEMBER. My point of order is that parliamentary rules are being violated because a majority is necessary for election.

CHAIRMAN. Your point of order is well taken. Prepare your ballots again.

1. A point of order may properly be raised if the chairman permits a violation of the constitution, by-laws, or parliamentary law.

2. If a member is disorderly or discourteous in debate, the chairman names him, gives him an opportunity to explain his actions, and then requires him to withdraw from the room. The assembly then decides to overlook the offence or to punish the member by a reprimand, fine, or expulsion.

APPEAL FROM THE DECISION OF THE CHAIR

MEMBER. I appeal from the decision of the chair.

CHAIRMAN. The decision of the chair has been appealed from. Shall the decision stand?

1. The chairman may state the reasons for his decision without leaving the chair.

2. A member may speak but once.

3. If the chair is overruled, he takes the action approved by the assembly.

QUESTION OF PRIVILEGE

MEMBER. I rise to a question of privilege.

CHAIRMAN. State your question of privilege.

MEMBER. I move that a member be appointed to stop the noise outside.

1. Privileged questions relate to the rights of the meeting and of individual members. Examples are disorder, poor ventilation, and lack of chairs, heat, or light.

2. The chairman decides (subject to appeal) whether the question is really a question of privilege.

3. If immediate action is required, the maker may interrupt a member speaking.

ADJOURN

MEMBER. I move we adjourn.

1. A quorum is not necessary for a vote on adjournment.

2. If the motion to adjourn also fixes the time of the next meeting ("I move we adjourn to meet on Thursday at three o'clock"), the rules for a main motion apply.

3. The motion is not in order while a member is speaking or while a vote is being taken.

FIX TIME OR PLACE FOR NEXT MEETING

MEMBER. I move that the next meeting be held on December 22 at 3 P.M.

1. This motion is of highest rank, because, if the constitution and by-laws do not specify the regular meeting place and time of the body, there must be every opportunity during a meeting to set the time of the next one.

2. It is debatable if no other question is before the meeting.

RECONSIDER

The details about the motions to reconsider are complicated. Only the main facts about the unprivileged form, which is in common use, are given.

1. If the motion is carried, the original question is again before the assembly for consideration.

2. The motion must be made by one who voted with the majority.

3. The motion must be made at the meeting on which the original vote was taken or at the following meeting.

USE AND ABUSE OF PARLIAMENTARY MOTIONS

In a meeting motions should never be introduced to confuse the chairman or delay business. The purpose of parliamentary law is to secure a speedy expression of the will of the majority. School practice in presiding and making motions prepares a person to take part intelligently in the transaction of business in any meeting.

Practice 1. Parliamentary Practice

1. On Parliamentary Practice Day in your English Club let A move that the class adopt a uniform for all members, B amend the motion by specifying the kind of uniform, and C amend the amendment with a change in the uniform.
2. Let D move that the class organize a literary club, E amend the motion by substituting *book* for *literary*, F move the previous question on the amendment, and G move to lay on the table.
3. Let H move that the class hold a party or a picnic, I amend by specifying the time, J move to postpone the question to the next recitation, K move to refer the matter to a committee, L rise to a question of privilege.
4. Let others make main motions and a variety of motions which take precedence over the main questions.

MANUALS

"M.P."—Canadian Young Men's Parliamentary Guide.
ROBERT—Rules of Order.
GREGG—Parliamentary Law.
GAMES—The New Cushing's Manual.
PALMER—Manual.
REED—Rules.
PARSONS, MRS.—Manual for Women's Meetings.

INDEX

Above, 253
Accent, 38
Accept, Except, 253
Acceptance, speech of, 53
Accept of, 253
Accident, reporting, 167-9
Action, describing, 325-7
Ad, 253
Addison, Joseph, 396-8
Address: of business letter, 151; envelope, 157; forms of, 173; nominative of, 492
Addressing the inanimate as if animate, 395-6
Adjectives, 233, 484, 488, 534-8; avoid unnecessary, 221; predicate, 229
Adjournment of meeting, 583
Admittance, 253
"Adventures of a Shilling, The", 396-8
Adverb, 228, 233, 484, 534-8; introductory, 228; clause, 229, 233; avoid interchange with adjective, 538
Adverbial objective, 491
Affect, 254
"Afraid", 349
After-dinner speech, 54
Aggravate, 254
Agreement of verb and subject, 529-34
Aldrich, Thomas Bailey, 140
Alice in Wonderland, 469
All of, 254
Allegory, 404
Alliteration, 234, 393, 561
All the farther, as far as, 254
"Alpha of the Plough", *see* Gardiner, A. G.
"Amazing Summerland, An", 202-3
Amendment, to motion, 581; to amendment, 581
America in the Making, 363
And, 230
Anecdote, 49-50
"Angelus, The", 353-4
Angler, The, 96
Announcement, 52, 190
Answering questions, 67, 108-17
Anti-climax, 223

Antithesis, 382
Antonyms, 248
Anxious, 254
Any place, every place, no place, some place, 254
Anywheres, everywheres, 254
Apology, letter of, 144
Apostrophe, 381, 552-3
Appeal from the decision of the chair, 583
Application, letter of, 161-6
Applying for a job, 18
Appositives, 231, 491
Appreciate, 254
Appreciations of Poetry, 358
Apt, likely, liable, 253
Arguing, (see Discussing, Arguing, Debating)
Armour Wherein He Trusted, 344-5, 392
Arnold, Matthew, 195, 357-8
As, 67, 254
As far as, all the farther, 254
At, in, 256
Athletics, 254
"At the Trial of Warren Hastings", 347
"Attitude of Young People Toward Religion", 198
Audience, spectators, 254
Autobiography, writing an, 87-90, 396-8
"Autumn Dusk", 566-7
"Autumn in the South", 337
Avocation, vocation, 254
Awful, awfully, 254

Back of, 254
Badly, 254
Baker, George P., 473
Balance, 254, 391-2
Ballads and Poems, 395
"Bank Holiday", 326-7
Barnes, Margaret Ayres, 385
"Barrage, The", 376
"Bear, A", 61
"Bear Story, A", 299
Beat, 254
Beginning: social letters, 139; public speech, 180; short story, 466

588 MASTERING EFFECTIVE ENGLISH

Connectives: words and phrases, 105-6; between paragraphs, 289

Conrad, Joseph, 369

Consonants, 31-6

Constitution and by-laws, 575-6

Consul, council, counsel, councillor, counsellor, 255

Contemptible, contemptuous, 255

Continual, continuous, 255

Contractions, 85-6

Conversation: 3-15; writing c., 85; direct, 223; in short story, 467-8

Coolidge, Calvin, 227

Cooper, Clyde, 102

Copeland, Royal S., 358

Correlatives, 77, 486

Could, might, 255

Council, consul, counsel, councillor, counsellor, 255

Couplet, 562

"Courage in Civil Life", 429

Courtesy, letters of, 143

Creative expression, mastering, 369-85: what it is, 369; finding material, 370; young writer at work, 371; choosing words, 372-5; figures of speech, 377-85

Credible, credulous, creditable, 255

Credit, giving, 290-1

Creditable, credible, credulous, 255

Cute, 255

Dash, 550-1

Date, 255

Davey, Smith and Myers, 112

David Copperfield, 341

"David's Bedroom", 341

Davidson, Kathleen, 566-7

Davies, W. H., 337, 351

Day, Clarence, 98

Dead Love, A, 236

Deadly, deathly, 255

"Death of Little Paul", 375-6

Debating (see Discussing, Arguing, Debating)

"Dedlow Marsh", 328-9

Defining, 125-6

De la Mare, Walter, 345

Description: mastering effective, 309-55; scientific versus literary, 309; observing, 309-11; word pictures, 311; describing sounds, 312; comparing, 313; sense impressions, 315; how to picture, 315-7; order and arrangement, 317; dominant impression, 317-8; fixed point of view, 318-21; changing point of view, 321-5; action, 325-7; landscape—still scenes, 328-30; nature in movement, 330-3; objects of nature, 333-6; seasons, 336-8; exteriors of buildings, 338-40; interiors of buildings, 340-1; towns and cities, 341-3; pen-portraits, 343-7; groups and assemblies, 347-8; moods and mental states, 348-52; works of art, 352-5

"Desert, The", 392

Details, in paragraph, 99-100, 269-70

Devices, effective literary, 386-409

Dewey Decimal Classification, 568-9

Diacritical marks, 37-8

Diagrams, Pictures and Charts, 123

Dialogue: radio, 421-2; in short story, 467-8; in one-act play, 475-6

Dickens, Charles, 312, 318. 338, 340-1, 342, 375-6, 380, 384, 389-90, 400-1, 402, 403-4

Different parts of speech, one word as, 487-8

Different than, 255

Diphthongs, 39

Directions, giving, 132-3

"Disaster Busters", 419-21

Discover, invent, 255

Discussing, Arguing, Debating, 194-219: thinking, 194; faulty reasoning, 196; discussion, 196; group discussion, 196-8; forum discussion, 200; symposium or panel discussion, 200; argument, 201; persuasion, 202-4; debate, 204; main issues, 205-6; introduction, 206-7, 210; body of argument, 207; brief, 207-10; clearness, 210; unity, 210; coherence, 210-1; emphasis, 211; d. custom, 211-3; first speaker, affirmative, 212; first speaker, negative, 212; rebuttal, 213-7; fallacies, 213-5

Discussion, informal, 142

Dombey and Son, 375-6

Dominant impression, 317

Dove, 255

Dramatic situation, 472

Dramatic technique, 473

Drawing conclusions, 111

"Dreams", 565

Due to, 255

Each other, one another, **255**

"Eagle, The", 335